Best of
The Realist

Edited by
Paul Krassner

Running Press
Philadelphia, Pennsylvania

To Jimmy, that apocryphal
8-year-old junkie who won a
Pulitzer Prize for the
Washington Post.

"There is no laughter in
Heaven."

—Mark Twain

9 8 7 6 5 4 3 2
Digit on the right indicates the number of this printing.

Library of Congress Cataloging in Publication Data: Main entry
under title: Best of the Realist. Includes index. 1. American
wit and humor. I. Krassner, Paul. II. Realist (New York,
N.Y.) PN6162.B54 1984   817'.54'08   84-15029
ISBN 0-89471-287-X (paper)

Cover design by Toby Schmidt. Cover photograph by Michael
LaRiche. Typography: Bodoni and Alpin Gothic by CompArt,
Philadelphia, PA.

This book can be ordered by mail from the publisher. Please in-
clude $1.00 for postage. **But try your bookstore first.** Running
Press Book Publishers, 125 South 22nd Street, Philadelphia,
Pennsylvania 19103.

ABOUT THE AUTHOR

Paul Krassner is writing an auto-
biography and a novel between performances as an investigative satirist at night
clubs, theaters, and college campuses.
He has a daughter, Holly. When *People*
Magazine called Krassner "father of the
underground press," he replied, "I demand a blood test."

TABLE OF CONTENTS

KRASSNER'S INTRO BY KEN KESEY

Holy cow! By the end of this month? I'd forgotten all about it. And this is the twenty-ninth? Not much time for anything clever, probing, sardonic, insightful, humorous, thoughtful . . .

I fear I am reduced to being truthful.

Paul Krassner is a small guy, about five-five. He has a headful of curly brown hair that dangles Jewish-loose—Michael Jackson copied Krassner's coiffure—and a faceful of oddly new-looking skin. It resembles a baby's skin after a difficult delivery. And when he grins, which is most of the time, his size, hair, and the half-skinned complexion all combine to make him look quite childlike, if not infantile. Like a tickled kid. He is fifty-something, about five years my senior, but I swear I've seen him carded for age verification trying to follow me into a bar.

The bouncer was probably right to be suspicious. Krassner doesn't imbibe. Not in alcohol, caffeine, or nicotine, anyway. Nor have I ever known him to pop an aspirin, drop a downer, or plop-plop an Alka-Seltzer. When people hear his age and remark in amazement on his youthfully tickled appearance, he always offers the same explanation:

"I never take any legal drugs."

But it's more than that. I've seen pictures of him at fifteen, and he looks just as young and tickled, and these photos were taken before he had the chance at any chemical substances of *any* classification. Thus I think Paul must have been born with that inner tickle, discovered it early, and has never been able to keep his hands off it since.

The tickle is contagious, too, like a yawn. Spend half a day with him, and you find your mind chortling in a quagmire of puns, quips, wisecracks, snappy comebacks, and ironies. Krassner loves ironies. Especially stinging ironies that nettle public figures. Krassner would rather savor a piquant irony about a public figure than eat a bowl of fresh strawberries and ice cream. Spend a *whole* day with him and you find yourself beginning to forgo strawberries for stinging nettles, too.

He has a pretty blonde girlfriend and a pretty brunette daughter. I think the daughter is the older of the two.

He doesn't drive, which is just as well for the rest of the traffic world. Like a lot of people raised around New York City, he never developed any sense of mechanics and inertia—it's all full throttle or full brake, sometimes both at once. Also, he's none too coordinated. An enthralled girl, watching him fumble, stumble, and fidget his way through a tangled tale, once observed: "He's as physically clumsy as he is nimble mentally."

He never has anything good in his refrigerator.

He likes cats, and cats like him. In fact big cats, watching him trip around the alleys of Venice like a tipsy rodent, would like him for supper.

He does a very funny stand-up show whenever a promoter has sense enough to book him.

But he's funnier off-stage than on, much. Let me close this introduction with an anecdote:

A few years ago Robert Anton Wilson's teenage daughter was brutally murdered in Berkeley. Wilson, a friend and a futurist of sorts, had an interest in cryogenics. So he had the girl's brain frozen in hopes of medical miracles that might be able to clone her whole again decades hence. Having recently lost a kid, I can understand such hopes.

The upkeep of this kind of refrigeration is expensive. The tissue needs to be kept in canisters submerged in liquid nitrogen. Disney can afford it, and certain ex-generals and businessmen. But not a Frisco futurist and hermetic theorist. So Wilson and friends organized a fund-raiser. It was known as The Berkeley Benefit For Robert Anton Wilson's Murdered Daughter's Frozen Brain. It was to take place in a big hall near the campus, with the Hog Farm Band as warm-up and me as back-up. The big draw, however, was to be Timothy Leary and Eldridge Cleaver, fresh back in the States after their sojourn in Algeria, in debate.

The hall was dark and ominous. The audience was half intellectuals, stiffly waiting for The Word, and half street people from Telegraph Avenue, getting stiff. Wine bottles clinked everywhere. The Hog Farm Band was as awful as ever. I wasn't much better, doing revolutionary raps, but they kept signalling me to stretch it—Cleaver hadn't shown.

The Good Doctor finally took the stage. He rambled on with his usual psychedelic blarney (Once an Irishman, etc.) as the audience got stiffer. They began to yell for Cleaver. Tim finally received a note from offstage and announced that Eldridge Cleaver was not going to be able to make it. Sitting in the dark audience behind me, Krassner leaned over and whispered, "Eldridge is home, working on his new book: *Brain on Ice.*"

The drunks began hollering accusations and questions at Leary. To calm the situation, he took a seat on the edge of the stage and asked that everyone with something to ask or say please come forward and get in a line—everyone would get their turn. A scraggle of Berkeley burn-outs queued up immediately. Always game, Tim tried to field questions about things like the flight schedules for the next astral plane out, and harangues demanding that he oughta be froze *hisself*, so the future could see what a 'Sixties dinosaur looked like.

Noticing there hadn't been a comment from Krassner in a while, I turned to check. His seat was empty. Then I saw him, up in front of the stage, working his way through the line.

When he finally took the mike for his turn, Tim didn't recognize him—just another scraggle.

"Doctor, may I ask you a somewhat *personal* question?"

Tim beamed the patient smile that had seen him through highs and lows, through jails and exile, and would surely get him through this nasty night:

"By all means . . ."

"Do you think it's *possible* . . . that you might have died and gone to Hell, and that *these*—" Paul's gesture included the line of tormentors, the front row of ragged faces grinning shaggily up like raunchy ranks of crabgrass, the whole hectic hall:

"—could be your damaged chromosomes come back to haunt you?"

Well, you had to be there. Leary blinked a couple times, then recognized Paul and gave him a big hug of hello, glad to see him and so forth. He got his microphone back out of Krassner's

hand, though, right quick, and sent Paul on his way so he could get back to the *serious* questions.

Apparently he preferred crabgrass to nettles.

PREFACE
A FUNNY THING HAPPENED ON THE WAY TO THIS ANTHOLOGY
by Paul Krassner

When I originally began performing standup comedy in the early '50s, night club owners gave me a hard time for doing political material. They objected to my poking fun at McCarthyism. So it was with a certain sense of irony a few years ago that I read in Harry Reasoner's book, *Before the Colors Fade*, the following passage:

"I've only been aware of two figures in the news during my career with whom I would not have shaken hands if called to deal with them professionally. I suppose that what Thomas Jefferson called a decent respect for the opinion of mankind requires me to identify those two. They were Senator Joseph McCarthy and a man named Paul Krassner or something like that who published a magazine called *The Realist* in the 1960s. I guess everyone knows who McCarthy was. Krassner and his *Realist* were part of a '60s fad—publications attacking the values of the establishment—which produced some very good papers and some very bad ones. Krassner not only attacked establishment values; he attacked decency in general. . . ."

But at least Reasoner had criticized me openly, under his own byline. In 1968, after *Life* Magazine had published a profile of me, the FBI wrote a letter to the editor, not on FBI stationery, signing it Howard Rasmussen, Brooklyn College, and complaining about the "aggrandizement of underground editor Paul Krassner . . . Am I asking the impossible by requesting that Krassner and his ilk be left in the sewers where they belong? That a national magazine of your fine reputation would waste time and effort on the cuckoo editor of an unimportant, smutty little rag is incomprehensible to me. Gentlemen, you must be aware that *The Realist* is nothing more than blatant obscenity. . . . To classify Krassner as some sort of 'social rebel' is far too cute. He's a nut, a raving, unconfined nut. . . ."

The letter was approved by J. Edgar Hoover's top two aides, William Sullivan and Kartha DeLoach. Their justification: "Krassner is the editor of *The Realist* and is one of the moving forces behind the Youth International Party, commonly known as the Yippies. Krassner is a spokesman for the New Left. *Life* Magazine recently ran an article favorable to him. /The/ proposed letter takes issue with the publishing of this article and points out that *The Realist* is obscene and that Krassner is a nut. This letter could, if printed by *Life*, call attention to the unsavory character of Krassner."

Their attempt at character assassination escalated to a more literal approach next year. The FBI anonymously printed and distributed a WANTED flyer featuring a large swastika with photos of Jerry Rubin, Abbie Hoffman, Mark Rudd, and myself. The caption: *"LAMPSHADES! LAMPSHADES! LAMPSHADES! LAMPSHADES!"* The copy stated that "the only solution to Negro problems in America would be the *elimination* of the Jews. May we suggest the following order of elimination? After all, we've been this way before." There followed this list:

All Jews connected with the Establishment.
All Jews connected with Jews connected with the Establishment.
All Jews connected with those immediately above.
All Jews except those in the Movement.
All Jews in the Movement except those who dye their skins black.
All Jews. Look out, Jerry, Abbie, Mark and Paul!

In a letter of authorization, the FBI stated: "Assure that all necessary precautions are taken to protect the Bureau as the source of . . . this leaflet /which/ suggests facetiously the elimination of these leaders."

* * *

It had all started so innocently. What I wanted to do was combine entertainment with the First Amendment. I had no particular ideology. In the first issue of *The Realist*, I wrote that "I'm not a Democrat or a Republican or a Vegetarian. Not a Communist or a Fascist or a Prohibitionist. Not a socialist or a capitalist or an anarchist. Not a liberal or a conservative or a vivisectionist. Not Catholic or Protestant or Jewish. Not Unitarian or Buddhist or Existentialist. Not hip or square or round."

Yet I was putting out what was considered the hippest magazine in America while still living with my parents. I remain grateful to my mother and father, who rarely approved of what I published, but were always there supporting my right to do it.

I served my journalistic apprenticeship at *The Independent* under Lyle Stuart. He was my friend and my guru and my role model all rolled into one.

At *The Realist*, I fell in love with my managing editor, Jeanne Johnson, the Scapegoat who became my Scapemate—and in the process taught me how responsibility could be fun.

Many contributors became part of our extended family, and I want to pay special tribute here to those who have died on the battleground of free expression:

Lou Swift—no one else was willing to distribute *The Realist*, but he handled it from the beginning and never wavered in the face of pressure. He was still running L-S Distributors at the age of 80, confined to a wheelchair.

John Francis Putnam—our first columnist. As art director of *Mad* Magazine, he was told he couldn't work on outside projects, but he insisted that his "Modest Proposals" for *The*

Realist be an exception, and was prepared to lose his *Mad* position over that principle.

Bob Abel—listed in the masthead as "Featherbedder," though he was anything but. He provided newspaper clippings that were missing links, and through his nurturing of artists around the country, earned the unofficial title, "Patron Saint of Cartoonists."

Alan Watts—who became *The Realist*'s first interviewee (I can still hear his infectious roar of laughter)—and who provided Lenny Bruce with his philosophy of what *is* rather than what *should* be.

Wally Wood—who illustrated the first thing I wrote for *Mad* ("If Comic Book Characters Answered Those Little Ads in the Back of Magazines") and a dozen years later drew "The Disneyland Memorial Orgy" for *The Realist*.

Paul Jacobs—the spectrum of whose passions is indicated by his books, from *To Serve The Devil*, consisting of documented omissions from American history, to a cookbook titled *Take a Leek*.

Phil Ochs—a myth-exploder who, by using Mao Tse-tung's non-political poetry on the jacket of an album of folk music and sending a $50 fee for liner notes (the cashed check came back properly endorsed!), exploded the myth that Mao was dead.

Lenny Bruce—the obituary in this book was written (with his permission) two years before he died. His FBI files indicate that, shortly before his death, Lenny went to their San Francisco office and asked them to investigate a conspiracy by various police departments to silence him. A retired New York cop has since admitted that this was an actuality.

Dr. Robert Spencer—the humane abortionist known as "The Saint." After interviewing him for *The Realist*, I became an underground abortion referral service for several years until it became legal. As a result I was subpoenaed by district attorneys in two cities, but refused to testify before their Grand Juries.

* * *

In going through all the old issues for this anthology, it has been slightly embarrassing to see such terms as "Negroes" and "chicks," although that was how blacks and women often referred to themselves in those days. But I do think that *The Realist*'s editorial heart was always in the right ventricle.

In our first year of publication, Robert Anton Wilson wrote, in "The Semantics of 'God' ": "The Believer had better face himself and ask squarely: do I literally believe 'God' has a penis? If the answer is no, then it seems only logical to drop the ridiculous practice of referring to 'God' as 'He.' " And I wrote: "From a completely idealistic viewpoint, the newspaper want ads should not have separate Male and Female classifications, with exceptions such as in the case of a wet-nurse. From a completely realistic viewpoint, however, the presence of women in certain standardized positions not only serves to lubricate the business world with a quiet, everyday lusting; it is also more profitable.

"Grace Hutchins, in her book, *Women Who Work*, calculates that manufacturing companies realized a profit of $5.4 billion in 1950 by paying women wages that roughly averaged $1,285 less per year than the wages paid to men for similar work. The extra profits from employing women at lower rates than men formed 23% of all manufacturing company profits."

In 1962, Lenny Bruce got arrested for using the word "cocksucker" on stage in San Francisco. A couple of decades later, Meryl Streep used the same word in *Sophie's Choice* and got an Academy Award. And if it hadn't been her, the Oscar would probably have gone to Jessica Lange, who used the same word in *Frances*.

We've come a long way, baby, on other paths, too. When *The Realist* began in 1958, the manufacture of munitions was a thriving industry in Israel, totaling $11 million. Exports to Germany alone during the first half of 1959 amounted to $9 million. Munitions factories were so busy they functioned even on Saturdays, the Jewish sabbath. Now, a quarter-century later, Israel is the fifth largest supplier of arms in the world, selling more weaponry to Latin America and Africa than either the U.S. or Russia.

* * *

When *The Realist* stopped publication in 1974, I was still working on a couple of pieces, both of which I thought appropriate to include in this volume.

"On the Lam with Patty Hearst" appeared instead in *Crawdaddy*, resulting in a visit from a pair of FBI agents in search of Patty, even though in the interview she charged that the FBI was behind her kidnaping.

And "A Sneak Preview of Richard Nixon's Memoirs," which appeared instead in *Chic*, has turned out to be a bit of satirical prophecy, for in it Nixon insisted that Watergate was a set-up to get rid of him as President. Now, a decade later, Nixon has actually made that claim in a network television interview.

Indeed, I wrote "Sex Education for the Modern Catholic Child" in September 1958, and it turns out to have been theologically correct on September 5, 1984, when Pope John Paul II warned that the rhythm method of birth control can be "an abuse if the couple is seeking in this way to avoid children for unworthy reasons."

This same phenomenon has occurred with me as a standup performer. A dozen years ago I predicted on stage that "The radical wing of the feminist movement will finally deem sexual intercourse as acceptable only if the man doesn't have an erection." On June 25, 1984, *The New Republic* published an article, "The New Porn Wars," by Jean Bethke Elshtain, which included this sentence: "[Andrea] Dworkin has written that it is acceptable for women to have sex with men as long as the man's penis isn't erect."

No wonder Clint Eastwood's little daughter in the film *Tightrope* wanted to know, "Daddy, what's a hard-on?"

Those sixteen years of editing *The Realist* must have had their effect on me. I now have a strange affliction. I keep thinking that I'm making up the news.

Did the NAACP really cancel a large order of Kellogg's Corn Flakes because the boxes featured a picture of the dethroned Miss America, or was that merely a sketch on *Saturday Night Live*? Did Nancy Reagan actually sit on Mr. T's lap and kiss him on the cheek, or was this one of those doctored photos in the *National Enquirer*? Did Gerald Ford truly deliver his State of the Union address with an arrow through his head, or was that simply a Johnny Carson one-liner?

Was I simply dreaming when I saw Phil Donahue ask the long-awaited question: "What does the Bible have to say about vibrators?" Did I just imagine I heard a young boy call the Alex Bennett radio show and discuss the taste of chocolate pubic hair? Was that dog pulling the bathing suit off the young girl and exposing her buttocks on the Coppertone billboard obedience-trained at the McMartin Pre-School?

I forget which one of these is a fact: Was Geraldine Ferraro's gynecologist a passenger on the Korean airliner shot down by the Russians, or did Mr. T pose nude for *Playgirl* Magazine years ago when he was still Mr. M? Did a phone freak once use the whistle in Captain Crunch Cereal to circumvent AT&T's power, or is AT&T now putting their own propaganda in Captain Crunch Cereal? Did the conviction of a woman for murder because she fatally shot her husband, sawed apart his body, roasted pieces over the family barbecue, and took a bite of his charred arm, indicate that the legal system really works after all?

At a recent three-day humor conference, literature professors from different areas of the country mentioned that when their classes were assigned to read Jonathan Swift's classic, "A Modest Proposal"—which suggested that the Irish people could solve both their overpopulation and hunger crises by eating their own babies—students took the satire literally, wanting only to be filled in on certain historical details.

Yes, American culture has become that jaded. The rate of irreverence has been accelerating along with everything else.

One indication of this is the naming of New Wave musical groups. It took 10 to 15 years after the assassinations of John and Robert Kennedy for there to be a group called "The Dead Kennedys." But it took only a few months after the attempted assassination of Ronald Reagan for there to be a group called "Jodie Foster's Army."

Those who laugh at that may shudder at a group called "People's Temple." Or another called "Lennonburger." Some of us may be sentimental about the Manson murders, but in Austin there is a group called "Sharon Tate's Baby."

* * *

Recently, *People* Magazine published a special feature on '60s activists. A full-page photo showed Ken Kesey, Wavy Gravy, and me, sitting on top of the old psychedelic bus. We had been told that *People* might put this pose on the cover, so I carefully held onto my crotch, a sort of private joke to keep myself pure.

However, the cover went to Michael Jackson. And *he* was holding onto *his* crotch. Our gesture was exactly the same, except that there was a glove on his hand. The motivation dif-

fered—this shot of Jackson in the midst of performing was pragmatically selected out of hundreds in order to sell copies—but nevertheless, I had been beaten at my own game.

Media manipulation is a two-way street.

In one direction, the chief prosecutor in the John DeLorean trial celebrated the possibility of seeing that case on the cover of *Time* Magazine, and the man who deliberately drove his car onto the sidewalk in Westwood Village said that although someone would have to grieve for the victims, he would receive much publicity from his trial.

In the other direction, news bulletins have been replaced by promotional teasers. In the middle of *20/20* on ABC, the local channel announced: "Good evening, there has been a verdict in the trial of Marvin Pancoast. Details at eleven." No indication as to whether or not he had been found guilty of the murder of Vicki Morgan. And, covered up by this trivialization of the news was the process by which the subpoena of presidential adviser Ed Meese in that trial had been quashed.

Meanwhile, Ronald Reagan declared that "The reason why the U.S. government is supporting the freedom fighters in Nicaragua covertly is because it would be against the law to do it overtly." So if it's covert, how come we all *know* about it?

George Orwell intended *1984* as a warning, but government officials have taken it as a blueprint.

Barry Goldwater said previously that "Every good Christian ought to kick Jerry Falwell in the ass," mildly contrasted by his current party line about the Moral Majority leader: "He's a nice minister."

But the Andrea Dworkin Flaccid Penis Award is hereby bestowed on Joan Rivers, for outstanding twofacedness. Last year at the Warfield Theater in San Francisco, she shouted: "Isn't Reagan an asshole!"—goading on the audience—"Isn't Reagan an asshole!" This year, she performed at the National Federation of Republican Women's luncheon in Dallas, and said: "I am a major Reagan fan. That's why I'm here."

In times like these, I have been sorely tempted to start publishing *The Realist* again. I even began planning a return issue, featuring "The Parts Left Out of the Belushi Book"—Bob Woodward's confessional chapter that was omitted from *Wired*, detailing how the distinctions between snitching and investigative reporting became blurred when he almost allowed James Hoffman, the professional informer who entrapped DeLorean, to set *him* up on a cocaine deal. The cover would depict John Belushi, staring at us from under his cocked eyebrow as he holds a rolled-up $20 bill to his nostril and snorts those lines from the universal price code at the bottom of the page.

But, no, *The Realist* served its purpose, helping to liberate communication, even if as a byproduct bad taste has now become an industry.

Besides, there are other ways for a raving, unconfined nut to attack decency in general.

A CHILD'S PRIMER ON TELETHONS

See the tired man. He has been up all night. He is running a telethon. He wants the people to send money. It is for leukemia. That is a disease. Little children like you can catch it. Evil.

See the sexy girl. She is a singer. She doesn't know whether the telethon is for leukemia or dystrophy or gonorrhea. Her agent got her the booking. She needs the exposure. Notice her cleavage.

See the handsome man. He does know that it's for leukemia. You can tell. He is singing a calypso melody. Listen to the lyrics. Give-your-money—he sings—to leukemia. Give-your-money—to-leukemia. Listen to the audience applaud. He is very talented.

See the sincere politician. He is running for re-election in November. He is against leukemia. He is willing to take an oath against it. That proves he is against it.

See the wealthy businessman. He is making a donation. He wants his company's name mentioned. Then we can buy his product. Then he will make profits. Then he can make another donation next year. Splendid.

See the little boy. He has leukemia. Too bad for him. The nice lady is holding him up to the TV camera. Aren't you glad it's not you? But wouldn't you like to be on television? Maybe you can fall down a well.

See the pretty scoreboard. It tells how much money they get. They want a million dollars. Uncle Sam has many million dollars. He cuts medical research funds by more than seven million dollars. Why? He needs the money for more important things.

See the mushroom cloud. That costs lots of money. It has loads of particles. They cause leukemia. Money might help to find a cure. That is why we have telethons.

See the tired man...

MONOLOGUE BY A MISS RHEINGOLD LOSER

I think it all started when I was maybe ten years old. The teacher was asking us what we wanted to be when we grew up. I remember one girl said she wanted to be a nurse, and another girl said she wanted to be an airline stewardess. I don't know why—it just popped into my head—but I said I wanted to be a Miss Rheingold.

Soon after, I started in training for the job. I set the record in my elementary school for smiling—four hours without stopping. I practiced playing tennis without watching the ball—because one of the rules for being Miss Rheingold is, "Always look directly into the camera no matter what you're doing." I even learned to say "My-beer-is-Rheingold-the-dry-beer"— while *drinking* it.

Later on, I began to enter beauty contests. I was almost Miss Pickle of 1954, but I had to withdraw from the finals when I developed a severe case of warts. However, I *was* chosen as Miss Neurotic at the annual convention of the American Psychiatric Association. I mean I wasn't really neurotic or anything—it was purely an honorary title.

But my goal always remained the same. True, I did think of possibly becoming Miss America, but unfortunately they include talent as a requirement. Besides which, you have to be intelligent. I saw the Miss America pageant on television, with Douglas Edwards keeping the audience informed and all—I think they're trying to get Edward R. Murrow for next year— and the girl who won said something very intelligent about how people should have "communication and understanding" and like that.

Miss America was not merely indulging in platitudes, either. In the talent contest, she had communicated by performing a modified striptease. And the judges understood.

Anyway, this was the big year. I was one of the six lovely girls chosen in the primaries as candidates for Miss Rheingold 1959. We all had to wear the same blue dresses and shoes, with white pocketbooks and gloves, so that none of us could take unfair advantage of individuality.

The campaign itself was on the up-and-up. One girl almost got disqualified because she tried to get an endorsement by Jinx Falkenburg. See, they're very strict in the Miss Rheingold competition.

They allow you to get married if you want, but we had to sign this paper promising that we wouldn't have a baby all next year. They certainly don't have to worry about *me*. I don't know about the other girls, but *I* don't even go in for *light* lovemaking any more. It messes up my hairdo.

So they held the election, and let me tell you, *there* the corruption was unbelievable. In the 38th election district in New York, there were only 71 registered voters, but there was a total of 105 votes. Talk about ballot-stuffing! And it was like that all over the country.

Monologue by a Miss Rheingold Loser, *continued*

There's this bartender that I know—he helped to get permanent registration in all Chicago bars—anyhow, he made an informal count of 42 votes for me, but in the final report, it had been changed by somebody to 12.

Far be it from me to get catty about the winner, but I heard that Boss Liebmann had decided on her at the original caucus.

Well, that's spilt milk under the bridge. It's all over now. I was heartbroken, there's no denying that. When you've planned and sacrificed the way I did, losing isn't easy. But then I discovered something. I began looking at the ads—I guess I was just torturing myself—and I noticed that while Schaefer is *"real* beer," Rheingold only has "real-beer *taste.*" And all of a sudden I didn't care about the $50,000 contract and the all-expense-paid trips and the fame and everything—it's not worth it if you have to sell your soul!

Of course, I've gotten some terrific offers since. All I have to do is say the word, and I can be the girl in the Miss Clairol ad. But this girlfriend of mine, she had that job, and now everybody keeps making cracks, they keep saying, "Does she or doesn't she?" And besides, that little kid who posed in the picture with her, he keeps following her around all the time now. She can't get rid of him.

But to tell you the truth, all the glamour has gone out of modeling for me. I'd prefer to do something where I can put my social concern to constructive use.

I was reading in the paper about the fighting in Lebanon between the loyalists and the rebels. This article said that while they were shooting, an attractive blonde in a tight skirt came walking up the street, and they stopped firing until she passed. Some sniper even gave her a wolf whistle. The paper didn't say which side he was on. And then the bullets started again.

Now if that's all it takes to stop guys from killing each other, then that's what I want to do. I'd pack sandwiches and just keep walking back and forth until they declared a truce or something.

Not just me—I'd get *other* Miss Rheingold losers, and Miss America losers, and Miss Universe losers. We could form a human chain, with girls from all different countries, wherever trouble broke out. Yes, my fellow losers, at last, for all of us, a place in the sun.

SEX EDUCATION FOR THE MODERN CATHOLIC CHILD

This is a diaphragm. Women use it when they don't want to have a baby. That is very immoral. Why, you ask? Because it is artificial, that's why. But never fear. There are other methods to prevent conception. They are very moral. Why, you ask? Because they are natural, that's why.

This is big brother's pajama bottoms. He had a nocturnal emission last night. What a shame. It woke him up. But see the semen stain. It has millions of dead sperms. They were killed the natural way.

This is big sister's sanitary napkin. It doesn't look very sanitary any more, does it? There is an ovum somewhere in that bloody mess. But it will never be fertilized. It will be flushed down the toilet bowl. That's the natural way, too.

This is a baby. It was born dead. Every year in the U.S.A. 136,000 infants are stillborn or die within a month. Now suppose their Mommies and Daddies had interfered artificially with the process of procreation. God's purpose would never have been achieved. Just think what a tragedy that would've been. But

at least some of the dead babies were baptized. That's the natural way.

This is a special calendar. It marks off menstrual periods. That's for the rhythm system of not having babies. A husband and his wife are in bed. They start to make love. Then they get out of bed. Because they have to look at the calendar. That's the natural way.

This is a husband and wife who want to have a baby. But the calendar says that the time is sterile. Lucky for them they have a calendar. It saves them from having unnecessary intercourse. So they stop making love. Because one thing would lead to another. Ask Dorothy Dix. She should know. She tried it once with Dr. Crane. Just to prove her theory. Later she had to write to his Worry Clinic. She was worried because she missed her period. She missed it very much.

This is a husband and wife who *don't* want to have a baby yet. But the calendar says that the time is fertile. So they stop making love. Unless they'd like to gamble on having an unwanted baby. That's the natural way.

This is a confessional booth. There is a screen in the middle. The person on one side is a priest. The person on the other side is a confessor. He is confessing that he has had evil thoughts. The priest tells him that to have an evil thought is evil. It is just as evil as committing the evil act that the evil thought is about. Priests never have evil thoughts themselves. They don't have to. They have an ample supply of other people's evil thoughts to draw upon.

This is the husband and his wife again. The ones who don't want to have a baby yet. Now the calendar says that the time is sterile. How convenient. Now they can make love without stopping. And without worrying. But, they're good, consistent Catholics. And so they *are* worrying. Because they know that evil thoughts are evil. Their evil thought is to have intercourse but to avoid having a baby. They can't be *sure* they won't have a baby—that's why the rhythm system is moral—but the *intention* is there. Tomorrow they will go to confession.

"... While our half of the class used the rhythm method ..."

by Robert Anton Wilson

There is no telethon to cure Triskedecaphobia, but each year the nation's economy is set back a quarter-billion dollars on Friday the 13th—in reduced travel revenue, catering and entertainment; loss of man-hours through absenteeism; and reduced sale of marriage licenses. At the Presbyterian Medical Center, where psychiatrists some years ago studied the irrational origins of the superstition, with scientific methods, the floor between 12 and 14 is marked 'P.'

SEX EDUCATION FOR THE MODERN LIBERAL ADULT

The head Sublime, the heart Pathos, the genitals Beauty, the hands and feet Proportion . . .
If the doors of perception were cleansed every thing would appear to man as it is, infinite.

—William Blake

While I was attending college, I worked part-time as an orderly in a hospital. One of my jobs was cleaning up the "stroke" cases, paralyzed old men who could no longer control their bowels. This proved to be useful experience later on, when I became a father—a baby and a paralyzed old man are much the same to one who must care for them, except that a baby's bowel movement is lighter in color and there is less of it.

I also used to go along on the ambulance to emergency calls. I'll never forget the first birth I witnessed. I had just read Philip Wylie's *Essay on Morals*, and I remembered his statement that a man who hasn't seen a baby born is a spiritual fop, a traveler on the surface of life. I was, I remember, astonished at the enlargement of the vulva (it was so *much* bigger than verbal descriptions would lead one to expect). Later, I wrapped the placenta in newspaper, to throw it out.

In spite of having received "a good Christian upbringing," I can't remember a time when I really believed that sex was "dirty." When I saw the *Family of Man* exhibit at the Museum of Modern Art, I was swept by a wave of tenderness, almost to the point of tears, at the photographs of lovers.

The first time I heard anybody refer to those beautiful pictures as "vulgar" (I have heard this opinion twice, once from a 16-year-old Irish Catholic virgin, and once from conservative Russell Kirk) I was flabbergasted. If someone had said that Van Gogh's "Sorrow" was pornographic, I couldn't have been more astonished. It still seems to me that our civilization must be basically insane to produce people with such orientations.

During the Korean War, I made a point of donating blood the maximum number of times. I was thunderstruck when somebody told me that donating blood requires "courage." "What the hell do you mean?" I burst out. "It doesn't hurt!" (I

was, at that time, nervous whenever I went to the dentist.) "But," said my friend, "to see your own blood draining out . . . ."

I didn't understand then, and I still don't. But I heard the same tone of voice from a co-ed in my college class when I mentioned my work as an orderly. "You mean you clean up dirty old men?" she said. And I heard the same tone, again, when I was explaining to another girl, why my wife and I believe in Natural Childbirth. "Your wife must be very brave," she said. (Natural Childbirth, according to the Read Method, is often as ecstatic as the conception itself.)

And I hear exactly the same tone of voice in people who object to Marilyn Monroe's joyful femaleness, or some of Red Skelton's jokes, or Dr. Albert Ellis's frankness. I can only conclude that our civilization is full of people who are squeamish and uncomfortable about the basic biological nature of life.

I think that these people are, whether they are "adjusted" to society or not, profoundly, *existentially* insane.

I was astonished and dismayed to discover—in letters of protest which *The Realist* received after printing Paul Krassner's "Sex Education for the Modern Catholic Child"—that this literally insane hatred for the physical world still festers in the minds of many who consider themselves enlightened freethinkers and humanists.

Let us face the facts for once. Man is one cell in a universe of process. His life is part of the carbon cycle. He lives off the fruits of the earth directly, or off the animals whose food-value derives from the fact that *they* live off the fruits of the earth; and his excrement and (ultimately) his corpse both go back to the earth as fertilizer.

This is the basic existential cycle, the frame in which our values must be found. There is no way of breaking out of it.

The other natural processes of the solar system and the great galaxy itself are equally crucial to humanity: if the sun went nova tomorrow, human life would end. The cycle of birth, reproduction, and death also dominates us.

Millions of lesser cycles, epicycles, rhythms, and processes make up the structure of our reality: the moon; menstruation; blood pH; metabolism; spring, summer, fall, and winter; digestion; respiration.

There is nothing "vulgar" about these processes, nothing "not nice," nothing "obscene." They are just *there*; they *exist*; and that's all. Whether we *accept* these processes, *rejoice* at their beauty or feel *hopeless* and *disgusted* about being involved in them—this tells something about our own mental health, but not about the natural processes.

The most important of the *cyclic* processes in the life of a healthy adult is, of course, that of pre-orgasmic tension, orgasm, and post-orgasm relaxation.

Psychiatry, history, anthropology, etc. all seem to bear out the conclusion that it was the Church's interference with this particular cycle that began the degeneration of mankind, which led ultimately to the present mess in which a great proportion of the population is embarrassed, uncomfortable, or just plain frightened at *any* crucial biological process.

It is for this reason that I am a *militant* freethinker and not just a nice, respectably academic "humanist." The American Humanist Association goes on and on about "stating *positive* values," etc., not "being merely negative," etc. Well, I call myself the Negative Thinker with good reason.

I just don't believe any new positive values can enter the life-blood of our civilization until we have first purged it of the poison of the Schizogenic Fallacy: the fallacy that man is a "nice" spirit imprisoned in a "not nice" physical body.

My wife used to believe, as many "liberal intellectuals" still believe, that organized religion is a quaint relic of the Dark Ages, a charming sort of living fossil as cute and as harmless as the duck-billed platypus. She couldn't understand how I could get so angry about it.

Now, however, with children arriving at school age, she is beginning to develop some of my own militant anger. It is a horrible thing to see innocent children begin to pick up the millenia-old theological rubbish from their playmates; it is more horrible to reflect on how much more they will pick up from children's TV shows and from our supposedly secular public schools.

Make no mistake about it, old Wilhelm Reich may have been wrong about many things, but not when he wrote, in *The Function of the Orgasm* and *The Mass Psychology of Fascism*, that chronic rage and hatred stem directly from "orgastic impotence" (the inability to achieve total organismic orgasm), and that "orgastic impotence" stems from man's rejection of his own physical being.

The child taught to despise his own body and its functions and to identify himself with an imaginary "soul" is eventually going to become *full of hatred for everybody and everything in existence*. Why? Because one part of him (the sensory, non-verbal, existential level, you might call it) is permanently at war with this ridiculous "soul" dogma which his cortex tries to believe. His nervous system becomes schizoid.

He has what Reich calls "muscular armor," chronic physical tension holding back the natural, but (to him) forbidden felicity of the organism. He can't be comfortable *in* his body; and, of course, he can't really get out of it.

The result, according to the usual Freudian mechanisms, is that all this neural frustration and biological rage is projected outward upon the rest of existence. The physical world becomes, as it was to Saint Cyprian, "the creation of the devil." The rest of mankind becomes "the enemy" to be exterminated, or, more hypocritically, "the damned" to be saved. Every social evil, from the malicious gossip of Mrs. Gilhooley's bridge-table to the horrors of Belsen, derives from this state of mind.

Now, finally, what of the people who consider themselves "liberal" and "enlightened" but object to "Sex Education for the Modern Catholic Child"? Krassner's language is uncensored, very true. So is the blood, smear, and urine analysis of a competent obstetrician.

Are you upset by Krassner's reference to sanitary napkins (a puritanical euphemism itself, by the way)? You would be more upset by the case of a girl my wife once knew who inserted her first Tampax without removing the cardboard roll. I don't suppose anybody could deny that the painful experience of that girl resulted from the stupid taboos of our society which made it impossible for her to learn how a Tampax should be inserted by asking clear and specific questions in plain words.

Are we still living in the Victorian Age? Do you object to a reference to "nocturnal emissions"? The Army, in its psychological test for draftees, refers to them as "wet dreams." If you are afraid of plain language about the natural functions of the healthy human body—*your* human body—what are you doing reading a freethought journal anyway?

Nobody can deny the point made by Paul Krassner's Swiftian little bit of satire—that the precious "natural order" which the Catholic hierarchy is so anxious to save from interference by the rubber industry, this wonderful capitalized Nature that is not the same as the nature known to science (since things can happen which violate it), this sacred "Nature" sees to it that millions of ova are wasted for every one that is fertilized, that trillions of spermatozoa perish without ever reaching an ovum, that hundreds of thousands of babies are born dead every year.

Krassner makes this point by using specific, extensional language, *which is what any semanticist would advise*. Who or what would profit if the point were weakened by evasions, subterfuges, euphemisms, and Nice-Nelly-ism in general?

A psychiatrist once told me that he makes a point when discussing sex with his patients of using the familiar Anglo-Saxon monosyllables rather than medical terms. "They can never *really* tell me about their problems if they're busy searching for 'nice' words," he said. It may seem unrelated, but I am reminded of Ramakrishna's remark that, before he could teach yoga to Occidentals, he first had to teach them to weep.

I am a very enthusiastic student of certain varieties of Oriental mysticism, some of which seem quite rational to my mind. The purpose of yoga, of what the East calls "ways of liberation," is not to sink into a mindless trance like a masturbating tree-sloth, but to become *more acutely aware* on all levels of the senses, nervous system, and "mind." (A Zen master once summed up Buddhism in the one word, "Attention.")

The first step toward this awareness is to transcend the "muscular armor" which keeps the organism insensitive to those parts and functions it has been told are not "lady-like" or not "gentlemanly." (Modern psychiatry insists on "abre-action"—as Mencken put it, the patient has to make a jack-ass of himself before he can be cured.)

Michelangelo wrote that "to create, you must first be able to love." Einstein, more verbosely, said that the drive toward greater knowledge always begins from "an intellectual love of the objects of experience." The greatest artist and the greatest scientist of the Western world are at one in recognizing that their creativity arises from "love"; and Einstein seems to have had in the back of his mind Spinoza's "Intellectual love of a thing means understanding its perfections." Twenty-five hundred years ago in China, Confucius wrote in the *Shu King* that "the dynasty, Y Yin, came in because the folk had achieved a great sensibility."

All of these expressions (the Zen master's "Attention," Michelangelo's "love," Einstein and Spinoza's "Intellectual love of things," Confucius' "great sensibility," and I could throw in also Blake's remark about "cleansing the doors of perception") seem to me attempts to verbalize an experience which, by its nature, cannot be verbalized. One has to experience it.

You have to relax your body, so that the hard kinks of prejudice and fear cannot censor your perceptions. You have to look at things without using words inside your mind, look at things as they are originally perceived without shame or "value" or use-consciousness or purpose of any sort. Every thing you look at will then appear to you, as Blake says, infinite.

This is the "oceanic experience" Freud noted at the root of religion. It is also at the roots of science and art. We are all stumbling into this experience constantly, whenever we are completely relaxed and unafraid—Sunday afternoon in the hammock, for instance.

This experience has created a hundred stupid theologies, true; but, it has also created sciences and arts. In the Occident especially, from the troubadours of the 12th century up to D.H. Lawrence and Ezra Pound, this experience has become the exclusive property of wild and erotic independent mystics, while the official churchly mystics have sunk deeper and deeper into a miasmal mist.

It is out of this "oceanic experience" that a rational humanism can create "positive values" as an alternative to the delusional schizophrenias of Judeo-Christian theology. But these values can only be understood by those who are *aware* on all levels of their being, sensory as well as rational; and the majority of people will never become *aware* in this way until those institutions are destroyed which teach man to despise his own body and to fear even to speak of it in plain, honest words.

BY ALL MEANS, *LET* 'EM BOMB SYNAGOGUES

by John Francis Putnam

The floor of the children's classroom of the dynamited Atlanta synagogue was littered with the kind of paper cut-out decorations that you see pasted up on kindergarten window panes all over the country. The brightly-colored "construction paper" was ripped and slashed by murderous slivers of shattered window glass.

It had taken all of ten seconds to bring down the House of Aaron and of Moses with fulminate of mercury detonators and 40% dynamite—the same house that eighty years before had sheltered and fed starving, scarecrow soldiers of the Confederate Army returning from war and defeat.

It should be mentioned here that the habitual users of the dynamited facilities commonly refer to their building as the *schul*, which is simply another way of saying *school*. As any thoughtful racist knows, *school* is a dirty word these days, and the very mention of it is enough to set off a spontaneous detonation in favor of segregation, magnolias, and cotton-percale white-sheet supremacy. So, whether it be Jewish schul or "innagrated" school, *bombs away!* That Rebel

"You filthy swine—just wait till the Pope hears about this!"

by All Means, *Let 'Em Bomb Synagogues, continued*

Yell you hear from Clinton to Little Rock means that the Sloth shall rise again.

Fortunately, by the end of the week, the round-up of dissidents who had contributed to this blast was completed, and the accused dynamiters all wore that carefully rehearsed look of heroic virtue under duress that is supposed to distinguish the political martyrs from the pimps and lush-rollers as they are all hustled into the paddy wagon together.

These Elite Shock Troops of the "Confederate Underground" would not stand much of a chance in any Southern Night Court when faced with the Magistrate's

traditional demand for a "show of hands—*palms up!*"—for it is at this point that the horny-handed depart in peace with a two buck contribution to court costs, while the "sweet backs" with manicured fingernails tumble into the pokey.

Unfortunately for the Atlanta *Abteilung*, the charges against them are more serious than just "disturbing the peace," and what is more, the Tri-nitro-toluene "has went off right in the middle of the white section!" The Penal Code of the State of Georgia which is read so hard when applied to the Negro, reads hard on white dynamiters too—if they haven't observed the zoning laws.

A death penalty lurks somewhere in the glut of subsections appended to the article that deals with the misuse of dangerous explosives. But since the Atlanta blast killed no one, *lex talionis* (the law of retaliation) need not apply.

Nevertheless, this Georgia Goon Squad must pay for their crime, and be rehabilitated to boot. Although they're in for a long stretch of occupational therapy, stamping out cheap automobile license plates so the State can save on the Minimum Wage Law overhead, we think that there is a better way. The rehabilitation and re-education should be a specialized affair with the honored concept of the punishment fitting the crime worked into the program.

We propose that a special rehabilitation center for convicted synagogue-dynamiters be set up on Dry Tortugas Island, in the Gulf of Mexico, some 70 miles from Key West, Florida. Here the inmates would be sent for an indefinite period. They would have decent shelter and plenty of good food. Building materials would be on hand along with tools. Good American tools like power saws and cement mixers, the whole works, all the way from bulldozers to coping saws.

All that the inmates would have to do is build a synagogue. And build it right. Or else keep on doing it over until it *is* right. Lack of skill is no

objection here. They can learn sooner or later, and on this depends the term of their sentence. The foundation turns out to be crooked? They can dig it up and lay it again. And again. Nobody leaves the island until that synagogue is finished and passes inspection.

After all, these lads are all of them 100 percent Americans, by their own estimate of themselves. And Americans are traditionally handy with tools. Sooner or later, that building will go up and take shape. A green sprig will appear on the roof tree. It will finally pass inspection and it will be well built . . . through trial and error by a bunch of clowns most of whom had never in their entire lives held anything more useful than a cue stick.

The hand that used to pass out mimeographed condensations of the phony *Protocols of the Elders of Zion* now wields a trowel to smooth out the finishing touches on a plaster ceiling in the gleaming new synagogue.

But wait a minute, men. We've not finished our rehabilitation yet. Gather 'round and take a look at your handiwork. Professional! Look at that finish on the floors . . . at the masonry job on the steps . . . all done the hard

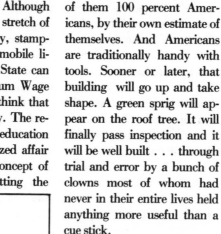

way, and for a long time it seemed as if you'd never make it. For the first time in your lives, you really have something to be proud of. Well, here's some dynamite—go blow it up, you sonsabitches! We're starting all over again tomorrow, only this time there'll be "no straw in the bricks!"

It is not that we have much faith in the essential goodness of man at such a Neanderthal level, but chances are they'll be mighty unhappy about blowing up *this* synagogue . . . that, we're sure of, since we *do* have such abiding faith in the eternal egocentricity of man.

Q. Would you call yourself a Buddhist?

A. No.

Q. Would you care to enlarge on that?

A. I simply feel that a human being must always recognize that he is qualitatively more than any system of thought he can imagine, and therefore should never label himself. He degrades himself when he does.

Q. Would you call yourself a Taoist?

A. No. I am probably more sympathetic to Taoism than to Buddhism, but for the reason I just mentioned, I don't label myself.

Q. In Behold the Spirit *and* Myth *and* Ritual in Christianity, *you give allegorical interpretations to stories that Christians believe are literally true. Do you think there's much chance that the organized churches will accept this interpretation?*

A. I'm afraid not. They would have to, if there were a large number of intelligent people remaining in the churches, but nowadays it isn't necessary for intelligent people to remain there.

Q. What is Zen?

A. (Soft chuckling.)

Q. Would you care to enlarge on that?

A. (Loud guffawing.)

Q. You call Zen Buddhism a "way of liberation." Would you distinguish between a way of liberation and a religion?

A. A religion is first of all an aid to social solidarity. It's a revealed rule of life which one hears and obeys. But liberation is simply concerned with discovering not what is advantageous, but what *is*. The goal of religion is salvation, which means membership in a community, only possible through accepting and internalizing the conventions of the community. Unfortunately, people become hypnotized by conventions and think they are laws of nature.

In religion, also, you are concerned with saving your "self" or your "soul." Through Zen or other Eastern ways of liberation you come to recognize that the "self" is an abstraction from memory, which like all abstractions cannot be "held" or "saved" in any way, and that the real "you," so to speak, is the on-going processes of your living. Instead of being a block-like entity to be "saved" from the rest of the universe, you become one process in an infinite number of processes, all of them working together in harmony.

Q. Do you think the Romantic Movement was close to Zen?

A. No, because it made an artificial distinction between the natural and the human.

Q. How would you evaluate the relationship between Zen and General Semantics?

A. Well, there's a very close tie-in principle between Zen and General Semantics, but there is great difference in practice. Most semantics people I know talk too much and get increasingly involved in increasingly fine distinctions, as if language could be made n-dimensional. But I do think many of the writers—Korzybski, Bois, Hayakawa—have said things to wake people up.

I'm all for General Semantics as long as they call a halt to the discussion at about eleven o'clock.

Q. If Zen is a way of liberation, why do you drink? Do you consider liquor a way of liberation?

A. No. I regard it as a part of life, like food or vitamins—

Q. Or religion?

A. Or religion. I suppose a man's religion is in one sense what he gets angry about, and one of the things I get angry about is any attempt to impede the production or distribution of wine.

When I was Dean of the American Academy of Asian Studies, I initiated the custom of having wine served at dinner. Several members of the faculty came to me and complained, saying this would lower the reputation of the institution. I grew quite angry with them because in our Western culture, wine has been a profoundly humanizing influence. I wanted the school to have a "human atmosphere"—the sort of gaiety and mellowness that one associates with the cultures of the Mediterranean. It's an important antidote to the puritan pomposity of the North.

People often ask me why I smoke and drink. I don't preach, remember. My philosophy is not concerned with what should be, but with what is.

Q. What do you mean when you accuse the Freudians of "obscenity"?

A. Freud himself calls the style of sensibility of the infant "polymorphous perverse." Why "perverse?" Doesn't the word carry an assumption with it?

Or, take the delight Freudians show when they demonstrate that art or poetry derives from sexual impulses. I would say, so much the better for art and poetry. But the Freudians seem to think that in some sense this discovery has lowered the status of art and poetry. They can only think this if they have a fundamentally obscene attitude toward sex.

Q. What do you think of Jung's theories?

A. I think his most important discovery is his treatment of the problem of evil. He's a sheer genius when he reveals the creative and essential functions of our own dark side, how we have to assimilate it and make friends with it.

Q. What do you think of psychiatry in general?

A. The psychiatrists realize that they have been handed a real problem—they are getting the questions priests and ministers used to get, but they, too, don't know which end is up because their philosophical premises are largely unconscious. They admit it to their colleagues, but they can't to their patients.

Q. When Albert Ellis was asked about the apparent simi-

larity between his theory of rational psychotherapy and Zen, he replied that while both do away with self-consciousness, Zen throws out the baby with the bath-water. I think he was referring to the danger of becoming too detached from reality. How would you answer him?

A. I don't know what he means. Detachment is not disinterest. Liberation means not getting blocked, not having too much feedback. Shakespeare's Hamlet is the classic case of a man with too much feedback. He couldn't act because he had to check his own checking and doubt his own doubts and question his own questions. To be detached doesn't mean you don't enjoy dinner; it means that the wheels don't stick. The "attached" person is too wrapped up in himself.

Q. Would you send a CARE package?

A. I would not. I would send a package to somebody I knew. I dislike the whole attitude of impersonal charity. Nowadays, you can deduct a CARE package from your income tax, but not what you give to a beggar who comes to your door. If I were making the laws I would completely reverse that. I consider governmental charity and all official, bureaucratic charity to be the utter antithesis of true charity.

Q. Would you call Zen anti-rational?

A. More than rational, including the rational, just as white paper includes the words written on it. One can't be rational without knowing what it is to be irrational, as the two opposites depend on each other.

Q. Do you think some of the Christian mystics have used Christianity as a way of liberation in your sense?

A. Yes, particularly St. Dionysius, John Scotus Erigena, Eckhart—and if we go East we really get them: Simeon Neotheologios, and a whole tradition in the Eastern church.

Q. Would you call Shinran Buddhism a religion or a way of liberation?

A. In America, of course, it's a religion—a watered-down Buddhism trying to imitate Protestantism. But in Japan I would call it a way of liberation. A deep understanding of Shin doctrine is one of the very best ways to get to the inside of Buddhism. I don't want this remark on Shin in America to reflect on the priests but on most of the Nisei groups—though there's a group of young people in Berkeley who are on the ball and know what Shin is all about.

Q. Would you consider the Quakers closer to your position than other Christians are?

A. Not very much. I dearly love the Quakers—they're so generous and open-minded—but what makes the difference is that they're still Idealists. They want the Good to triumph. They have my respect and affection, but I'm not an Idealist.

Q. Why do you say you aren't an Idealist?

A. I don't think a human being can act at all until he's all of one piece. If he's divided against himself—one part saying, "You should be better than you are"— he's incapable of effective action.

Q. But don't you try to make people better?

A. No. I am, if anything, an entertainer. I love to feel that certain spark leap the gap between the speaker and the audience. But I don't have any message of world-changing nature. The world might change, but not because you're trying to change it.

I once had an argument with Margaret Mead—she was being violently emotional about the necessity of stopping atomic armaments—and I said that it could be the very violence she was displaying which might bring about atomic war.

I told her, you go ahead and rouse people to a great pitch of emotion about nuclear disarmament; then I will show them that there's nothing they can do about it. We complement each other: It's a problem about which something *must* be done, and yet there is no way of doing it. And it is this very combination which could be the way to liberation.

Q. If you knew the atom bomb was about to fall, what would you do?

A. I should go right on eating dinner.

Q. Why do you vote at all? As you said before, "The world might change, but not because you're trying to change it." And isn't that merely fatalism?

A. Why do I vote? Because if there were a tie and the casting vote might have been mine, I'd feel such a fool.

But, seriously, the question shows you're not getting my point. The problem is *not* whether to act or not to act, what to do or what not to do. The Chinese saying goes, "When the wrong man uses the right means, the right means work in the wrong way."

Thus, what I am saying is that the world cannot be changed by the "wrong" people, however right their doing or not-doing. And, by the "wrong" people, I mean those who act from the feeling that man is *separate* from the natural universe—either pushing it around or being pushed around by it.

The ideas of individual freedom and fatalism rest on the same assumption—that man is separate, the boss or the puppet. In my view, he cannot act with wisdom unless he *feels* that what he does and what nature does are one and the same.

Q. What do you think of the Beat Generation?

A. It's a journalistic invention. Having been invented and put on the market, many people bought it.

Now, I remember the real, original Dharma Bums of the 1945-'46 era—young veterans hitch-hiking across the country and stopping every place there was a "sage" who knew something about Eastern philosophy. Some even went to Switzerland to speak to Jung. Many came to see me at Northwestern University.

They weren't interested in jazz or drugs or hot-rods, I assure you. Many of them are still around, very few of them in the Village or North Beach—they're on farms or in little communities they created themselves; they're out of the rat-race of keeping up with the Joneses.

They are the substance of which the Beat Generation is the shadow.

Q. In Beat Zen, Square Zen and Zen, *you seem much more impressed with Gary Snyder than with the other Beat writers.*

A. He's a true Dharma Bum, a man of complete integrity. He's just the way Kerouac describes him in *The Dharma Bums*—little, wiry, bearded, Oriental-looking, always dressed in clothes that are old and patchy but scrupulously clean. I don't practice Zen the way he does, but there are many ways of doing it. I think very highly of Gary.

Q. What do you think of Jack Kerouac?

A. He's a very warm, feeling, sensitive personality, but because he has no bones he doesn't sustain it. I mean, of course, Zen bones. Jack has Zen flesh, but no Zen bones yet. I thoroughly enjoyed *The Dharma Bums*. He described Mill Valley perfectly in the book, right down to the refreshing smell of the morning rain on the wet leaves.

Q. In Nature, Man and Woman, *you say that sexuality and mysticism need not conflict with each other. Do you think that anti-sexual feelings are more common in Christianity or in Buddhism?*

A. In Christianity.

Q. Hinduism has a great deal of overt phallic-worship in it, and yet it also has a strong ascetic strain. Do you understand why this is?

A. We've got two separate problems here. From the most ancient times Hinduism has included a strong ascetic element as one possible way of liberation but it also included the other extreme—you could also be liberated through extreme licentiousness.

That is, liberation can be found through any extreme way of life because any excessive pursuit of a goal brings you face to face with the paradoxes of grasping. The harder you chase "happiness," the less likely you are to find it.

As the cyberneticists have rediscovered, a system with too much control goes rigid and doesn't move, and a system with too much feedback goes into wild oscillations and never finds what it's aiming for. The only thing to do when your goals in life get you into this type of double-bind is to have a good laugh at yourself. Any excessive way of life will bring this lesson home to you eventually.

Q. Do you think asceticism is ever justified?

A. Oh, yes. If you really want to enjoy making love, leave a space before in which nothing happens. If you're a little hungry, dinner tastes better. However, you don't want to get so hungry that you wolf your food, and you don't want to get so frustrated that you wolf your girl.

Q. What's your favorite Zen story?

A. I guess it's the one about Hui-k'o coming to Bodhidharma and asking for peace of mind. Bodhidharma said "Bring out your mind here before me and I will pacify it." Hui-k'o answered in confusion, "But when I seek my own mind I cannot find it." "There!" snapped Bodhidharma, "I have pacified your mind." And, of course, Hui-k'o was pacified . . .

Q. What's your favorite passage from the Bible?

A. Job is my favorite book. I guess my favorite passage is, "The wind bloweth where it listeth and thou hearest the sound thereof, but canst not tell whence it cometh, and whither it goeth: even so is everyone that is born of the spirit."

Or another favorite is, in Proverbs: "Enjoy thy wife while she is young."

Q. I think you write like a poet. Have you written much poetry?

A. Very little. However, I do consider my prose to be poetry, actually. I consider poetry the proper speech of mankind. It doesn't argue, but convinces by its own integrity.

Q. What message would you like to give to Christians?

A. "Come off it."

Q. What message would you like to give to scientists?

A. "Dream."

Q. What message would you like to give to freethinkers?

A. "Don't be so compulsive."

Q. Compulsive about what?

A. One can emphasize freedom in such a way as to be bound by it.

Q. Could you give a specific example?

A. Yes. If you wouldn't be seen dead darkening a church door, you might have a closed mind.

Q. If you could write only one more book, what would it be about?

A. A sort of very personal conversation. Maybe it wouldn't even have a title. It would be a tremendous affirmation of the natural universe in which we live as a kind of manifestation of love, where "love" means everything the word love can mean. I want somehow to say to people that they are crying in vain, gnashing their teeth in vain, quarreling and scratching in vain.

Q. Wouldn't you be saying that in vain?

A. I would be, if I were trying to alter anything—but if I were simply singing a song—no.

Q. And which are you doing?

A. I'm simply singing a song.

"Yes, ever since drug-trances were ruled
a legitimate practice of our religion,
they've been drifting in . . ."

GREAT MOMENTS IN MEDICINE, #1

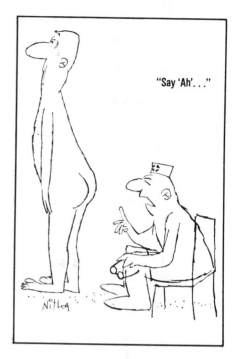

"Say 'Ah'..."

From an article in the *Journal of the American Medical Association*, December 26, 1959:

"Foreign bodies in the rectum are frequently reported in the surgical literature. Objects are often inserted, and the question as to what prompts persons to do this is a moot one. Frequently, these foreign bodies inserted through the anus are the result of prankish debauches and practical jokes. Sometimes they are inserted for the purpose of sexual deviation, and slip beyond the grasp of the user. Often they are inserted by the psychotic person with no actual or apparent intent or purpose.

"Unless it can be established that the presence of a foreign body in the rectum is the result of an accidental insertion, it is frequently difficult to evoke a satisfactory history from these patients as to the reason for its presence. This is understandable, as embarrassment often inhibits them from revealing the reasons for their deliberate act and their consequent predicament.

"Macht reported the removal of a small beverage bottle from a patient's rectum *[May, 1944]*. In reviewing the literature, he found such objects reported in the rectum as a snuff box, a whisky glass, a 30-cm. mortar pestle, a cold cream jar, a lemon, an apple, chicken bones, a glass tube, portions of a broom handle, and a frozen pig's tail. Glendon removed a jelly glass from the rectum by laparotomy; Gillespie removed a petrolatum (Vaseline) bottle, Pretty removed an ink bottle, and Scamahorn removed a flashlight, rectally.

"Kleitsch reported a patient who, after giving himself an enema with a colon tube, with unsatisfactory results, used an umbrella handle to break up what he thought was a fecal impaction. He was then unable to remove either the umbrella handle or the colon tube, which had become firmly held in place by a rectal spasm. Kleitsch removed the umbrella handle by traction and the colon tube was then ejected spontaneously.

"As a rule, rectal examination will detect foreign bodies in the rectum. Occasionally, however, the foreign bodies migrate into the sigmoid or high within the abdominal cavity and may be unrecognized during examination. One of us *[the authors]* and Martin reported an unusual case of surgical removal of a 9-inch case knife from the sigmoid of a patient whose complaint on admittance was a 'knife-like' pain in the region of the umbilicus. Rectal examination of this patient was negative.

"Numerous ingenious devices have been used to remove foreign bodies rectally. Ball removed an antiseptic solution (Listerine) bottle by this method, with a loop made from a wire coat hanger. Light bulbs have been removed by use of two spoons, one on either side, as "forceps." Bacon removed a glass by filling the open end with plaster and inserting forceps into the plaster for a handle. With the open end toward the peritoneal reflection, a hole was drilled into the base, thus giving a site to which to apply traction.

"McLean and Smathers reported the removal of a glass by introduction of lubricated tongue blades between the mucosa and the glass, with division of the anus in the posterior midline. Others have described grasping a glass with rubber-shod forceps over gauze, so as not to fragment it. . . .

"Holcombe reported a patient who had used an uncovered tennis ball to replace hemorrhoids, the ball having been pushed through the rectum beyond reach. The patient died before operation for removal could be carried out. . . . We are reporting a case of a psychotic patient who was found on examination to have a sharp and jagged-edged drinking glass in the rectum. Because of the fact that there were no presenting symptoms and no specific complaints, except for the patient's claim of the presence of a glass in his rectum, which he insisted had been there for two years, it was thought that a report of the case would be of interest.

"A 37-year-old man was admitted to Cook County Hospital Oct. 16, 1958, with the complaint of a broken glass in the rectum. The patient was brought to the hospital by members of his family, who stated that he was psychotic. This was borne out by the fact that the patient himself, who spoke only broken Lithuanian, said very little and, when he did speak, was completely incoherent. He had no complaints other than the presence of the misplaced drinking glass. . . .

"Surgery was decided on. *[Here followed a lengthy, technical description of the operation presumably of no particular interest to the lay reader.]* The patient's recovery was uneventful, and he was discharged on the ninth postoperative day."

Letter to the Editor

I found the article entitled "Great Moments in Medicine," concerning foreign bodies stuck in the rectum, thoroughly repellent.

I trust that you know what you can do with your magazine.

I TRIED THE RAPID-SHAVE SANDPAPER TEST

by Marvin Kitman

Some 7,000 teletype machines, property of United Press International, started clacking simultaneously in newspaper offices, radio and TV stations, and two or three pool halls across the nation one morning in January. Letter by letter, a message was spelled out:

THE COLGATE-PALMOLIVE COMPANY TODAY INSISTED THAT ITS SHAVING CREAM CAN SHAVE SANDPAPER AS ADVERTISED. . . .

What once might have been a bald plug for a shaving cream had metamorphosed into solid news because a day earlier the Colgate-Palmolive (you'll wonder where the Peet went) Company had been hit in the face by a wet towel thrown by the Federal Trade Commission.

These soap-, toothpaste-, and shave-accessories people were guilty of using a piece of plexiglass sprinkled with sand to simulate sandpaper in the company's ubiquitous—at the time—"Rapid-Shave Sandpaper Test" television commercial, it was revealed.

Although the F.T.C. did not recommend jail sentences—only that offenders cut that kind of stuff out—the principals worked themselves into a lather.

Said Colgate-Palmolive: "Sufficient research was conducted to prove beyond any doubt to the company and the advertising agency which created this commercial that sandpaper can be shaved as demonstrated."

Said the advertising agency, Ted Bates & Co., limiting itself to a $23,574 full-page advertisement in the *New York Times*, as well as the *Wall Street Journal*: "We used an artifice no more deceptive than make-up. . . ."

The ad blamed sandpaper's unphotogenic surface for the substitution. The sandpaper industry—for the moment looking like a cuckold in the shaving cream mess—has reportedly assigned its researchers to perfect a sandpaper that *can't* be shaved.

While big business and its spear-carriers were desperately trying to save face—that is, to regain corporate image—what

were consumers doing? For the most part, they either didn't know what all the fuss was about (televiewers are notorious for not watching commercials), or else they were muttering into their beards that all advertising was crooked.

But, so weakened is the spirit of inquiry in the U.S. today, few went to the trouble of finding out where truth lay. As far as is known, I was the first kid on my block—if not the only one in the entire country—actually to *try* the Rapid-Shave Sandpaper Test.

Anarchus once said, "The market is the place set aside where men may deceive each other." A conviction that this need not be so if consumers would take commercials more seriously has frequently driven me to answer challenges like the Sandpaper Test.

My Luckies, for example, habitually fell apart in the "Tear and Compare Test" several seasons back. A grave little note to the American Tobacco Company always brought a carton of cigarettes as balm.

I ruined my first ballpoint pen, too, writing underwater in the bathtub. No restitution there, however.

On the face of it, the Sandpaper Test figured to be the easiest of all my laboratory tests. All I had to do, as the TV commercial said, was put shaving cream on sandpaper, and shave.

"What kind of sandpaper do you want?" my hardware salesman, a woman, asked. This was the first indication that there might be rough going ahead.

"The kind you use when you shave sandpaper," I replied.

She called the manager (and, for all I knew, the police). He, too, seemed to think I was pulling his beard. Without bothering to single out the precise kind of sandpaper Colgate-Palmolive used when it proved the test worked "beyond any doubt," I paid for two pieces and fled.

For the pubescent, or peachfuzz-type beard, I found that I had bought a standard-sized 9"x10" sheet of Imperial Flint Paper (fine), manufactured by Minnesota Mining and Manufacturing Co., whose slogan, recorded on the back of the sandpaper, is "Where Research Is the Key to Tomorrow"—a comforting thought when one's wife is shrieking, "You're out of your mind!"

For the man with heavy growth, or blackbeard, I had a similar-sized sheet of Indian Head Flint Paper (coarse), made by the Carborundum Company. No slogan.

Various procedural questions arose as soon as I sat down with my can of Rapid-Shave, razor, blades, and sandpaper. How much shaving cream does one put on sandpaper before shaving it? How long does he let it soak in? Does he rub it in? How many strokes of the razor are cricket in a sandpaper test?

Frequent screenings of the Rapid-Shave Sandpaper Test on TV over the months had left me ill-prepared, scientifically speaking. So I used my common sense and shaved the sandpaper as I would my face.

After I lathered up the *fine* sandpaper, held my breath, twisted my neck a little—and *shaved sandpaper* for the first time, ever—nothing significant seemed to be happening on the sandpaper. So I shaved it again. And again.

By the twelfth stroke (there didn't seem to be any point to quitting *earlier* in the game) I was ready to study the sandpaper: the shaved sandpaper was definitely milder—I mean smoother.

As a control, however, I also shaved an adjoining section of sandpaper, this time omitting the Rapid-Shave. It, too, was definitely smoother, although not as damp.

Next I attacked the *coarse* sandpaper. After twelve strokes, my razor was still jumping over the sandpaper like a bicycle over trolley tracks.

The results this time were less happy. There were bits of loosened sand on the paper, but not even Ted Bates & Company could call that sandpaper "shaved." Conclusion: Rapid-Shave could do the job—*if* a power-grinder were substituted for a razor. (The blades I used, incidentally, are now worthless.)

Even though I was up to my ears in shaving cream by this time, I added one more control to the test: shaving with plain old-fashioned bar soap.

In both cases—fine and coarse sandpaper—soap worked just as well as Rapid-Shave.

* * *

A footnote to the Rapid-Shave Sandpaper Test:

The Colgate-Palmolive Company, which might have thought it had nothing to gain from this inquiry, nevertheless *did* gain a customer. The writer's wife, who watched the Sandpaper Test, now uses Rapid-Shave. "It's like shaving with whipped cream," she said.

Which would seem to have completed the cycle, since the F.T.C. has also revealed that a certain TV commercial had used *shaving* cream *on cake* because it photographed prettier and held up better than the actual product.

Will the *real* cake frosting stand up, please. . . .

A WORD FROM THE SPONSOR

Writer Rod Serling told *The Realist* of an incident which reveals the kind of thinking that can be found in the advertising culture.

In a *Playhouse 90* script, "I was not permitted," said Serling, "to use a line of dialogue which read, 'Have you got a match?' The reason for this, advanced by the agency, was that the sponsor was the Ronson Lighter Company, and that matches were 'competitive.' "

Another TV drama by Serling had a New York locale. A film clip with the usual Manhattan skyscrapers was used. But the Chrysler Building had been "erased" from the scene, for the program was sponsored by the Ford Motor Company.

CASE HISTORY OF A TV HOAX

As John G. Fuller wrote in his column in *The Saturday Review*: "Alarmed at the hypersensitivity of most TV sponsors to often unwarranted public criticism . . . *[The Realist]* urged . . . readers to pick out an innocuous and frequently inane network show on a certain date, and to write the sponsors about some vague and indescribable thing that happened on the show. The letters were to be indignant, but elusive; critical, but undefined."

He reported that more than a hundred *Realist* readers wrote in to the show, the sponsors, the ad agencies, etc.

Let us now review four case histories.

Case #1: Bob Calese wrote in to co-sponsor Hazel Bishop: "In view of what happened on *Masquerade Party* Friday night, I can assure you that no woman in my family will ever use any of your products again as long as I live. You know what I mean!"

The next day his wife, Phyllis, got a call from the producer of the show. She said that her husband wrote the letter and that she had no idea what upset him so. The producer said he'd call back.

Bob knew he couldn't possibly carry off the situation without breaking up, so they decided that Phyllis would take the call and say that he wouldn't even discuss it with her, didn't want to be bothered by them ever again, and that she'd seen him in these blind rages before and nothing could be done.

Actually, the Caleses don't have a TV set.

Case #2: Paul I. Lewis *was* able to carry off the situation without breaking up. Following is his telephone conversation with a *Masquerade Party* distaffer:

She: You sent us a letter stating that something on our show offended you. Could you please be more specific?

He: What do you want me to say?

She: Well, Mr. Lewis, you wrote the letter, so you must know what it was that bothered you.

He: Did you watch the show?

She: Mr. Lewis, I happen to work on the show. I know everything that goes on, and I don't know of anything that could have been wrong or offensive on Friday's program.

He: Oh. You mean you didn't catch it?

She: Catch what, Mr. Lewis? You

wrote us the letter, and it was very vague. Now will you tell me what you found that was salacious on our show? We feel that we put on good, clean, and wholesome entertainment with *Masquerade Party* and when we get a letter such as yours, we want to discover what was considered offensive.

He: I feel that it was fairly obvious. You must have received many letters commenting on it.

She: No, Mr. Lewis. In fact, yours was the only letter we received of this kind.

He: Well, if mine was the only letter, I guess it would appear to be a crackpot complaint. If only one viewer saw fit to write to the show, I guess this would make him either wrong or just a nut.

She: Our show is viewed by millions of people, Mr. Lewis, and no one has ever called our show salacious or blue, as you did in your letter.

He: Then I guess we can conclude that it was a crackpot letter. Why are you people so concerned with just one letter when you have millions who do not complain about the show?

She: Mr. Lewis, please stop asking me questions. I have called to find just what it was that moved you to write this slanderous letter. We are concerned with each of our viewers and we feel that your letter made a strong accusation. We feel that you have a responsibility to your letter.

He: What responsibility is that?

She: The responsibility for standing behind what you wrote.

He: Oh, I'll stand by everything I write. What was it you considered slanderous?

She: You said our show was salacious, used blue material that was unfit to be brought into the homes of the viewers. You called our show lewd and dirty.

He: I did not use that last phrase in my letter.

She: You said salacious, Mr. Lewis, and that is what it means. You should look the meaning of the word up before you sit down to write a letter of this kind. Do you often sit down and write letters of this kind?

He: I do know the meaning of the word—and, no, I do not write letters of this kind.

She: Then why did you write one this time?

He: I explained that in my letter.

She: Mr. Lewis, you are still being vague. Just what was it that bothered you?

He: The incident on the show.

She: What incident? I know every word that was used on the show. Now will you please just tell me what it was that prompted you to say we used blue material on our show?

He: Since I'm the only one who wrote a letter, maybe I misinterpreted what I saw. A few friends of mine commented on the incident, and I decided to write my opinion on the matter.

She: Did your friends find the same fault with the show?

He: Yes.

She: I found nothing wrong on the show, Mr. Lewis, yet you and your friends did. Would you please tell me exactly what it was?

He: You want me to say it *over the phone?*

She: Why not? It was on the show. Millions of people saw it, and no one

seemed offended. . . . There was certainly nothing said that could be considered salacious or blue or immoral.

He: That would be a matter of opinion. It would depend on the viewer's moral values as to how he would interpret what he saw and heard.

She: I understand that, Mr. Lewis. But I would like to know how you interpreted what you saw and heard.

He: My letter covered that.

She: Mr. Lewis, are you going to tell me the exact words that you found offensive?

He: I think it would be wise not to.

She: All right, Mr. Lewis. We do not consider our *Masquerade Party* a salacious or immoral show. The next time you decide to write us a letter of this kind, please be more specific or do not bother to write at all. *(Click!)*

He: 'Bye.

The next week, Mr. Lewis (who, incidentally, once won a free trip to Cuba and turned it down because he disapproved of the Batista regime) received a call from an Allstate Insurance agent. Having read that Allstate wouldn't allow

a suicide to take place on *Playhouse 90*, he told the agent that he wouldn't even consider buying insurance from Allstate until there was a suicide on a *Playhouse 90* production they sponsored. The agent said he would take it up with his superiors.

Case #3: Robert Wolf wrote to co-sponsor Block Drug Company, promising to stop using Poli-Grip. Actually, he has his own teeth. But he doesn't have a telephone, and so instead of a call, he received this letter from the manager of NBC's Department of Information:

Dear Mr. Wolf:

This is to acknowledge your critical appraisal of a recent Masquerade Party program. It is a matter of genuine concern to us that you found this program objectionable.

We will most certainly note your sensitive expression of criticism and relay it to the Manager of our Continuity Acceptance Department.

Thank you for the interest which prompted you to write.

A month later, Wolf was standing in City Hall Park, protesting a hoax by the government on *him*—the Civil Defense drill.

Case #4: A young subscriber from Merion, Pa.—identity withheld on request—wrote a letter to "The Green Mint, Nytol People" with a ball-point pen. Note that right smack in the middle, there is a sentence fragment—a complete nonsequitur—just for the hell of it.

Dear Gentlemen:

I am a teenager and my parents have tried to raise me as a decent, god-fearing person and have tried to keep me and my mind pure. We often used to watch Maskkeraid Party and we thought it was a dandy show. But once in a while those people got on their big-city high horse and said some pretty bad things. Of course, my parents were upset and turned the sound off so I wouldn't be perverted. I blushed too. But we still thought the show was tops and right good.

Gramps and Nana used to like the show alright too. And they were much riled when they heard those things too but jiminy crickets they still liked to watch it until last night. Well, last night you went a might too far. My parents just told me to go straight upstairs and they were just going to switch off the show completely. They did this mainly because I asked them to because they're pretty broad-minded on such matters. I was never so embarrassed in my life. I

have heard some pretty filthy low-down tacky things but nothing like last night.

I always used to wash my mouth out with Green Mint because I think Dick Clark is a pretty swell fellow and a really cool guy and he said he liked Green Mint and wanted me to use it too. I did. It can therefore be seen that whenever a country adopted repressive measures. I aint no egghead-intellectual but once in a while I stay up real late studying for a subject in a test in school and I couldn't go to sleep so I used Nytol because everybody said I should because it was good for me. But never again. Do you hear, NEVER AGAIN. I'm not going to help support the corrupting of minds that might be corrupted and don't know what's going on like me. I had it last night. Maskkeraid Party shouldn't be allowed on the air.

Sincerely yours . . .

P.S. I just poured all the Green Mint in the toilet and flushed it away. NEVER AGAIN!!! I am going to tell everyone I know never to use your products again. Just who do you think you are?

The producer called up, long distance!

"I was out," the young subscriber wrote us, "but my mother seemed to suffice. . . . Although I made it clear in the very first line of the letter that I was not an adult, the sponsors had failed to

make this clear when they communicated their distress to the producer (on the first call, unlike the second, he did not have a copy of the letter in front of him). Therefore, the first few minutes of the conversation were taken up in establishing that I was not my mother's husband but only a teenager.

"The producer then went on to say that the sponsors didn't understand my letter—what was I so upset about?—and that I was the only person who complained. Mother replied that I rarely watched television at all and that she didn't know anything about it. She further told him that I didn't use Green Mint or Nytol; and she told me that on hearing that piece of information, the producer seemed to lose a great deal of interest.

"He called up again the next morning and asked my mother my reaction to the news of the first phone call. She told him that I had laughed. He made sure again that I was just a teenager and did not buy either of the products. He then read her the letter. She was embarrassed. 'No, no, no, my son doesn't speak that way at home. Why, he's a National Merit Finalist. . . .' "

"'. . . and dear God, let all those who are against school prayers be struck dead in their tracks . . .'"

AN IMPOLITE INTERVIEW WITH HENRY MORGAN

Q. You've been a member of both the American Legion and the blacklist. What are your feelings about each of those institutions?

A. The American Legion is the last refuge of the scoundrel.

I couldn't have been on the blacklist because a respected committee of Congress proved that there isn't any. What you are probably referring to is a secret organization which includes a number of Madison Avenue agency people and a man at CBS who effectively cut off the livelihood of certain people whom they suspected of being out of sympathy with the firing of Dean Acheson.

I made the rounds of these amiable citizens some time ago to find out whether I was a Communist. Each of the committees I visited assured me that they knew I wasn't a Communist nor a fellow traveler—but, they said, sometimes mistakes are made (by them). At which point, without exception, they would ask me to name the Communists I knew. I would ask them how, since I wasn't one, could I identify any? Well, they said, who did I *think* was a member?

Even with practice I kept losing my temper while I explained that *thinking* was what had been done to *me* and that I wouldn't even tell them what I *thought* about Dalton Trumbo. It always ended with some cautious back-slapping, and after a few years, I was allowed to go back to work.

Once, not too long ago, I was being questioned by a woman who does legwork for one of these scurrilous committees, and I asked her how come they always bothered actors? "Well," she said, "many people are influenced by actors, and if these people discovered that their favorite performers were Communists, they might be swayed." "But," I said, "it is *you* people who do the publicity about the actors being Communists." "Oh," she said, "you don't understand."

Q. As a selective TV viewer, would you watch I've Got a Secret?

A. No, because I don't think it would amuse me. After all, I wouldn't be on it. I think Betsy Palmer is worth looking at, but a lot better up close. She is a delight, and if her husband drops dead tomorrow, it's okay with me.

Q. Do you think you're prostituting yourself by being a member of that program's panel?

A. Prostituting, my ass. I get paid on *Secret* for the peculiar public personality I accidentally built. My services are unique, it says in the contract, and they are, too. Go fry your hat.

Q. Do you have respect for your audiences?

A. I come to the studio at about nine-fifteen (the show goes on at nine-thirty). I've arrived in blizzards, in thunderstorms, in—well, taxis. It doesn't matter how terrible the weather, there will be six hundred people standing on the sidewalk waiting to see a half-hour panel show. Some of them stand in line, I've been told, for two hours and more. What can I think of them?

These poor cattle (that's what they look like, huddled in the rain) aren't the whole audience, of course. But as dear Fred Allen once said during a radio broadcast, he could reach into his toilet and come up with better than what was sitting out front. (Not on the air, stupid . . . he said it to Pat Weaver, who was his producer at the time.)

It is necessary to judge the TV audience by what they watch. What they watch is obviously what they *want* to watch, don't kid yourself—nobody spends a million dollars today to present *Leave It to Beaver* to people who aren't watching. It follows that the TV audience in general is one enormous shithead . . . well, I couldn't come up with anything else.

Now, when I do a show of my own (they go by like subways, don't they, though?), it attracts a selective audience. Up to now, these people haven't been shown to be worth counting. In other words, selective programming doesn't belong in an expensive mass medium—and what critics forget is that it *is* a mass medium.

The only way I know of to get a large audience is to be lovable, and how the hell am I going to do that? *Secret* gets a considerable amount of mail asking them to fire me because I don't smile enough! This is the God's (what a word to use in this paper!) honest truth.

The other night I went to see Mort Sahl at work, and seventy percent of the people in the room didn't know what the hell he was talking about. He was using plain English and fairly short words—talking about these people and the time in which they live—and they acted as though the whole thing were being done under water on Saturn. Now, if Mort Sahl, a literate and amusing man, can't be understood by the majority of the people in one small room, what can one expect of a TV audience?

Q. Peter Lind Hayes says that: "The comedian tries to make himself socially acceptable by making people laugh. Most comedians are sad. It probably is because they feel they can never be attractive romantically." Do you agree?

A. I'm not a comedian, I'm a humorist. A humorist is a comedian who isn't working. A comedian isn't any sadder than anyone else except when his money runs out. Then he just *looks* sadder.

You know who *is* sad? The comedian's wife. It's because people are always asking her: "Is he funny this way all the time?" The proper answer to that one is, of course, a belt in the nose, but most comedians' wives just don't have the strength any more.

If comedians are sad, it might be owing to the fact that comedians are the best actors in the business but only *they* know it. *Any* comic can play a straight part, but no straight can play a comic. Not every comic wants to play Hamlet; but he could. I don't want to argue about this because nobody knows what I'm talking about except comics.

Very often a satirist is a sad man. He's a teacher at heart, and he's trying to teach, simply, that there's a right way and a wrong, and that he is confronted with a series of outrages every morning of his life. He attempts through humor to correct error, to eliminate folly, but the only laughs are from people sure that he means somebody else. This makes him sad.

Satire should never be used as a definition. Once it is spelled out, whatever follows—having been defined in advance—is at once suspect and heavy-handed. People who deal in satire in its pristine form are loath to define it, since the very act of definition condemns the author as a serious fellow with a point-to-make. Then he isn't funny . . . and he isn't writing satire.

Q. You've undoubtedly been influenced by the Good Guy/Bad Guy aspect of Western melodrama. Who are your heroes?

A. I like the crippled fella who makes the bad coffee. And I like Paladin because he reminds me so much of me. He's cool, goes to the opera, girls are mad for him, he's ugly, and he never sends his shirt to the laundry. James Arness has no laundry problem either, I notice. My real heroes in the Westerns are, I suppose, the Indians. I bet on them all the time. It's that old guilt feeling, I guess.

Q. And who are your villains?

A. Usually, the real villain is the guy who put the show on, but I manage to forgive him if I find myself employed in it.

Q. What's your attitude toward telethons?

A. This question reminds me of the classy questions asked of Sweepstakes winners . . . *i.e.*, How does it feel to win one hundred forty-two thousand dollars and eleven cents? Great. How does it feel, Ted, to have a lifetime average of .302? Great. How do you feel, Manny, now that you've finished a five-million-dollar picture? Great.

Telethons were invented to give Jerry Lewis something to do after he ran out of material. It's hard for Jerry Lewis to raise money for spastics when he's the living proof that they're employable.

Telethons were invented to give Milton Berle a layover between Miami and Las Vegas.

Telethons were invented to show what bad taste would look like if you could get it all into the same place at one time.

Telethons were invented to give the jerks of the world an opportunity to watch the asses of the world.

Telethons were invented to see what percentage of the pledges would actually be collected. (About eleven percent, by the way.)

Q. What's your reaction to these potential U.S. Presidents: Richard Nixon?

A. A hardworking opportunist. No statesman. Wife's jaw too angular. Too soft on Populists. Looks like a loaded chipmunk. Very earnest in a terribly depressing way. The man to beat.

Q. John Kennedy?

A. A man with a terrible father. You want a President's wife called Jackie? With Peter Lawford as Secretary of State, Sinatra and the Rat Pack in the Treasury? He should be given an afternoon program of his own and stop pestering us older folks.

Q. Lyndon Johnson?

A. Look out. Sleeper. Bad for Negroes. Fake civil rights man. Bossy. Southern.

Q. Hubert Humphrey?

A. Cut it out. Nobody's named Hubert.

Q. As one who has been through the mill, what would you say are the injustices concerned with divorce in this country?

A. At least half the injustice is concerned with marriage. Any two panting animals can get married. Any heiress can shack up with a Romanian. Any certified schizo can team up with any certified barfly. Nobody stops you from arranging your own hell on earth to begin with. *Then* we come to the divorce part.

The happily marrieds aren't interested in changing the laws. And for those who've been through it, it's too late to change them.

Q. Is it true you've often gone with a girl too long rather than tell your life story all over again to a new one?

A. Yes, but that's not so odd. Often you hear of people who stay married simply because they're used to each other. Or she knows how he likes his eggs, and he knows how to rub her back. But at about the time I've finished talking and it's her turn, I find that she has nothing to say, and I have to audition a new one. But unfortunately the story now bores *me*, and I have nothing to say to a new girl.

What really happens is that I stay with a girl until she decides that if she's ever going to have a legal baby by me, she'll be too old to push the pram. This usually happens when she hits thirty. I have a girl leaving me right now who is over thirty and has figured that I get canned or quit jobs so often that she'll be economically insecure forever. Too bad, because this is a good one who rubs *my* back. Of course, I make the eggs.

Q. How do you feel about astrology?

A. Hasn't seemed to hurt anybody but Hitler. It is a solace to the same people who stand in the rain waiting to see a TV show. What better belief than that the stars control your destiny? Think of the comfort the boob derives from the thought that Saturn is busy thinking up what he's going to have for dinner.

Once you accept the fact that if Uranus is in the house of Jupiter, you shouldn't argue with your dentist, the rest of life's problems don't loom so large, do they? People will believe *absolutely anything.* Provided that it's essentially untrue. Tell them that a car has 145 horsepower, which it has, they'll tell you they're too smart to fall for that advertising. Tell them to stick a dandelion under the pillow to cure dandruff, and they'll elect you President. Of anything.

Q. What's your philosophy of celebrityhood?

A. Sometimes it helps. It gets you tables in full-up restaurants, and sometimes people give you stuff for nothing because you can afford to buy it and they just charge it to the people who can't afford to buy it.

All you have to pay for it is a loss of privacy for the rest of your damned life, giving autographs to mindless little girls, listening to jokes forced up your leg by imbecile truckers, answering questions in small papers of dubious repute and minuscule circulation (and which use jerky words such as 'celebrityhood'), overpaying tradespeople because they know you're a big star and make a million dollars a year and don't need the money, overpaying your ex-wife because she believes you're rich and live in a middle-class neighborhood only in order to fool moronic Supreme Court Justices into not awarding her money you'll never see in your lifetime, repeatedly telling the Mannies that you really don't know how their Irvings can break into the disc jockey game (which they refuse to believe and hope they'll live long enough to spit on your grave), being stared at in the street whether you're blowing your nose or not, being told by fat ladies from Iowa that you're the favorite performer of their five-year-old nieces, and more; much, much more.

On the other hand, I used to be shy when I went to a party. Now I'm not.

Q. Are you pessimistic or optimistic about the future?

A. As an amateur historian I'm pessimistic, but as a human I'm optimistic. Everybody'll die except me. Not that I'm afraid to, you understand . . . it's just that I don't count on it. I have a great deal to live for. (Myself.)

I don't have a book to finish, a research project which needs doing, or any of the other things which many people seem to discuss fluently on their deathbeds, but I'm partial to ocean bathing and want to see can I get in some more of it. I'm not interested in skin-diving—which is an escape like Zen—I like to be on top of the water like a diatom.

I also enjoy eating all the things that give me gas. And there are so many other things to be enjoyed: wondering how a naked girl will look in clothes; doing double-crostics in ink; waiting for the first potable instant coffee.

The future. Funny, nobody seems to notice that he lives in it constantly. This second was the future but a second ago. I daresay that the main thing to worry about in the "future" is that there's liable to be a Heaven after all. Wouldn't that be sheer Hell?

HEREDITY OR ENVIRONMENT?
by Max Shulman

Sociology teaches us that man is a social animal. It is not instinct or heredity that determines his conduct; it is environment. This fact is vividly borne out when you consider the case of Julio Sigafoos.

Julio, abandoned as an infant in a dark wood near Cleveland, was adopted by a pack of wild dogs and reared as one of their own. When Julio was found by a hunter at the age of twelve, the poor child was more canine than human. He ran on all fours, barked and growled, ate raw meat, lapped water with his tongue, and could neither speak nor understand one single word—a complete product of his environment.

Julio, incidentally, was more fortunate than most wild children. They never become truly humanized, but Julio was exceptional. Bit by bit, he began to talk and walk and eat and drink as people do. His long-dormant mental processes, when awakened at last, turned out to be fantastically acute.

He was so bright that he learned to read and write in a month, got through grammar school in three years, and high school in two. And last June as thousands of spectators, knowing the odds Julio had overcome, stood and raised cheer after cheer, he was graduated valedictorian from Cal Tech with a degree in astrophysics!

Who can say to what towering heights this incredible boy would have risen had he not been killed the day after commencement while chasing a car?

YOU ALWAYS HEARST THE ONE YOU LOVE
by John Francis Putnam

The *New York Journal American* is the last of the American newspapers in the grand old style of Journalism, where they slip the word *patriotism* into copy even on days which are *not* national holidays, and where their high moral purpose is expressed in their ringing slogan: "America f'hearst."

We always tell others that we "catch tantalizing glimpses of it over people's shoulders." Actually, we *buy* it. We're quick enough to snatch up a derelict copy of the *Times* when it's left on a subway seat, but we've never grabbed for the "Jay-Ay" for the simple reason that it's never discarded. There must be something about that paper that people treasure. That something is probably its consistency. We can safely predict what

the good old "Jay-Ay" is going to say on *any* news development. And where else could we keep up with the social, political and sporting activities of Mr. Roy Cohn, whose vibrant image is kept alive in its pages?

Since we feel grateful to the *Journal American* for so many crowded hours, for so much righteous indignation about wrong issues, we would like to reciprocate. To that end we have composed a headline for their permanent use. This could be set up in 120 point Caps and left indefinitely on the front page. It says everything forever. Accept it with our thanks, gentlemen:

RUNAWAY TEEN-AGE VICE QUEEN LINKS 5TH AMENDMENT PINKO PROFESSOR TO PASSPORT FRAUD IN H-BOMB SECRETS INVESTIGATION OF SEGREGATIONIST SIT-IN STRIKE WHILE F.B.I. PROBES LOVERS LANE TORSO SLAYING AS SEX-CRAZED COMMIE MOB STRIPS STATE DEPARTMENT STENOGRAPHER IN PARIS ORGY

"Remember the real meaning of Christmas this year. Attend the church or synagogue of your choice."

THE SECOND COMING

That unsung stagehand who erases the blackboard between challengers on *What's My Line?* had quietly done his duty. The members of the panel had skillfully adjusted their blindfolds. News analyst John Daly artfully announced, "Will tonight's Mystery Guest sign in, please!" The camera panned to the supraliminal Kellogg's legend above the blackboard. Now there was a close-up of a severely-scarred hand signing its owner's name in chalk. The studio audience gasped, then broke into a standing ovation; and producers Goodson-&-Todman rejoiced in the knowledge that they had finally scored the TV-First to beat all TV-Firsts.

Because the bearded Mystery Guest was by definition a celebrity, the thorny problem of whether or not he worked for a profit-making organization was automatically eliminated.

"Are you in motion pictures?" asked Dorothy Kilgallen.

The Mystery Guest answered in a high, squeaky voice that caused the audience to titter. "Not exactly—"

"Conference," interrupted John Daly. After a whispering session with the Mystery Guest, Mr. Daly said: "Miss Kilgallen, although our guest has been, in a sense, *portrayed* in a few motion pictures, I must assume that your question was posed in a frame of reference alluding to our guest's actually having *acted* or *directed* or served in some such creative capacity in motion pictures, in which case the answer would have to be no. That's one down and nine to go," he said, turning over a card. "And we pass on to Mr. Cerf."

"I recognized something in that voice when he said 'Not exactly,' " Bennett Cerf thought aloud.

"Why do you say *he*, Bennett?" asked Lenny Bruce, the former controversial comedian who had sold out and was now a permanent panelist on the show. "After all, we haven't even established that the Mystery Guest is a male."

"I think I know where it was," said Mr. Cerf, ignoring Mr. Bruce's point. "Mystery Guest, did you and your charming wife have dinner with Phyllis and me earlier this evening at '21,' and did we have a friendly little fight as to who would pick up the tab?"

"No, suh," said the Mystery Guest, this time in a very low voice with a Southern accent. "Y'all and ah didn't partake of the Last Suppah togetha." The audience ate it up.

"That's two down and eight to go," said John Daly in clipped tones. "And we go now to Miss Francis."

"Well, with *that* deep voice," said Arlene Francis, fingering her necklace, "I'll take it for granted the Mystery Guest is a male. Now, then, you've been *portrayed* in motion pictures but you haven't *acted* in them . . . Have you ever been in *politics*, perhaps?"

This time the Mystery Guest put on a German accent: "Vell—"

"Whoa," said John Daly, pulling his earlobe. "Another conference." After the whispering session, Mr. Daly said: "Miss Francis, although our Mystery Guest is quite often *involved* in politics, I think it would be a reasonably safe assumption that your question was intended to determine whether he either has ever held *office* or has participated indirectly *with* one or more officeholders—and in either case, the answer would be no. That's three down and seven to go. And I'm afraid that's all the time we have, panel." He flipped over the rest of the cards. "I'm sorry you didn't get a chance to ask any questions, Mr. Bruce."

"Oh, that's okay," said Lenny Bruce, removing his blindfold. "As long as I get paid. . . ."

* * *

At a midnight press conference, the Mystery Guest's agent—a gentleman from General Artists Corporation—made this statement to a large group of bleary- and wide-eyed reporters:

"On behalf of my client, I would like to thank you all for your courtesy. Now, as you can readily understand, since public after public has waited a total of nearly two thousand years for this event, it was thought to be desirable to work within the framework of the *present* cultural setup. In fact, nowadays a certain amount of planned image-projection

is deemed absolutely undowithoutable. And, video being the massest of the various media of mass communication, it was only natural that we should seek out the medium of television. The choice of a late-Sunday-night program, I might add, was also quite deliberate. Pre-conditioning, you know—by all those, ahem, self-styled evangelists. As a matter of fact, that's why we didn't go to Rome. They're still too suspicious over there as a result of the recent arrest of that phony end-of-the-world prophet on charges of 'spreading false rumors and tendentious news.' There is, of course, the sad fact that even in America, it's against the law in some states to claim you're a deity. Should the Federal Communications Commission give us any trouble, however—why, we'll take it to the Supreme Court, if necessary. . . ."

* * *

The Mystery Guest had a busy month swimming the TV channels. From Dave Garroway to Jack Paar, from Hy Gardner to Mike Wallace.

And the Mystery Guest danced with Kathryn Murray.

From *I've Got a Secret* to *Masquerade Party*, from *This Is Your Life* to *You Bet Your Life*.

And the Mystery Guest discussed spiritual values on *The Price Is Right*.

From Oscar Levant to Alexander King, from *To Tell the Truth* to *Beat the Clock*. And the Mystery Guest entered into a healing competition with Oral Roberts. From *Meet the Press* to *Face the Nation*, from *Open Mind* to *Open End*.

And, climaxing the month, the Mystery Guest appeared on *The Ed Sullivan Show*, delivering a carefully-edited version of *The Sermon on the Mount*, with the Air Force Intercontinental Ballistic Missile Chorus humming *Onward, Christian Soldiers* in the background.

All this build-up had been worth the effort, apparently, for the result was a regular weekly network program, and—in what was considered the smartest diplomatic move, public-relationswise, since the 1960 Vice-Presidential selections—it was sponsored by the National Conference of Christians and Jews. The show was scheduled at prime time. People had to be prepared for Judgment Day, and an electronic Messiah was the most practicable means to that End.

The program was called, simply, *Savior Time*.

But, before long, the consensus of rating services indicated "an unprecedented steady decline in viewership"—so much so that the option wasn't renewed. And the Mystery Guest disappeared from the scene.

As *Variety*, the Bible of Show Business, headlined the story:

J.C. BOMBS— OVEREXPOSURE

MALICE IN MARYLAND
by Madalyn Murray

Mrs. Madalyn Murray started court action yesterday to eliminate "sectarian" opening exercises from the Baltimore city public schools. . . .

—The Baltimore Sun
December 8, 1960

Some people have interpreted my position to mean that I am against religious ceremonies in schools. *This is not true.* I am against religion. I am against schools. I am against apple pies. I am against "Americanism," mothers, adulterated foods, nuclear fission testing, commercial television. I am against all newspapers, 99-and-44/100% of the magazines. I am against Eisenhower, Nixon, Kennedy, Lodge. I'm even against giving the country back to the Indians. Why should the poor fools be stuck with this mess?

I'm against people who are against things. That was the start of it.

I am the spawner of two sons, one age 6 and one age 14. I am going to state boldly at the outset that I abuse these two sons. I expect them to:

(1) give love and accept love;

(2) mature.

When Bill was age 10 I expected him to read and understand *Hiroshima* and the *Voyage of the Lucky Dragon*. Our household Gods were Clarence and Ruby Darrow, Mahatma Gandhi, Albert Schweitzer, Eugene V. Debs, Castellio, and Paine. He was versed in their ideology or else! When he was 6, I started him on chess; I told him that he either beat me at the game when he was 8, or he could look for a new home. He can beat me at chess.

If he could not now at age 14 discuss the nation's budget, the U-2 flight and its implications, the A.M.A. and why it is the people's enemy, complete and unabridged information on sex, religion, politics, economics, foreign affairs (including the last affair of Brigitte Bardot), art, literature, music, beatniks, interior decorating, cooking, housekeeping, carpentry, architecture, farming, husbandry, genetics, and "the adolescent revolt," he could get the hell out of my house—what good would an ignoramus-slob be in a home?

Of course he's normal. He was in Little League for three years. He loves horror movies and *Mad* Magazine. He prefers airplane model building to girls, but you should see this boy operate at a party or a dance. He teems with sibling rivalry, has "hate mother" days, is often lazy, absent-minded, irascible . . . and yet, his crooked grin, his wry sense of humor, his easy manner, his eagerness to work, to learn, is a delight.

I just never did introduce him to any specific organized religion. Once, when he was in the first grade, he came home and told me that the teacher asked, every Monday, who went to church and who didn't. He wanted to know what a church was like inside and what they did.

I told him that a man got up in front of a large group of people and harangued them about being sinners and told them to "pray" for forgiveness. He wanted to know what praying was, and I told him it was a way that people had of nagging something they called God to grant them small favors. They figured the more they nagged, the more they got. Bill grinned and said, "Boy, if he chops off nagging like you do, I pity those poor people."

The upshot was that he wanted to go to church. I did him up brown. We dressed in our best clothes and I chucked him off to Sunday School, then met him later and dragged him to the church services. I will never forget what he said to me. "Mom," he whispered, "I thought 'Jesus Christ' was a swear word. Now they tell me it's some guy who ran around in his nightgown. He was supposed to be made out of bread and wine."

That ended *that* experiment.

From then on, I permitted him to pick up any book he wanted, or to ask any questions he wanted, and I tried to give him a good biased answer so that he would grow up to be an iconoclast.

Bill is 14 and he out-iconoclasts me, and like the man says, "There ain't hardly none of them kind."

So, during the summer, Bill began to grapple with what to do when school opened this year, as he was not going to go through that "hogwash" of Bible reading and prayer recitation each morning. I looked at him, one full inch taller than I am (5'-8"), and I told him if he thought he was big enough now to take on our entire culture as an opponent, that he could jolly well begin where he wanted to begin.

The first day of school he was in the principal's office. The second day I was in the office—and when the din of the battle abated, status quo was still quo-ing. We mapped out battle lines. The first offensive was to "exhaust administrative remedies," which we did. They ignored us.

Then Bill came up with his idea: why not go on strike? This had always been an effective weapon against me—and after a couple of days of garbage removal on my own, I always raised his allowance. He figured that it should work. (You see, until *The Realist* came along, we felt we were the only ones in the world who could engage in the doublethink of seriously attacking what was sick in the U.S. while at the same time laughing ourselves sick about it. In this particular fight against religion, we are in deadly earnest and at the same time it is one helluva big lark. No one quite understands this position, so please feel free to join either the crowd or us.)

And then we went down and read Gandhi on civil disobedience, the Maryland Statutes of compulsory school attendance, and—seeing what considerable difficulty I would be in—the fines, the imprisonment, the court costs. I turned to Bill and said, "You call your time." He decided he would go on strike the next day, and he did.

I wrote a letter to the school board, stating that "when there is a clear violation of the principle of separation of church and state, and when my good conscience as a confirmed and practicing atheist requires that I must rebel against such a flagrant violation of basic constitutional rights, I am compelled, in an action of civil disobedience, to withdraw my son, William, from Maryland public schools. I do not intend to send him to a private school. He will remain at home and he will be schooled under my personal tutelage, without religion. . . ."

And we began our "home study" program and our "strike." Knowing this would be a fight, I sent copies of our letter to the American Civil Liberties Union, the Baltimore Ethical Culture Society and, through the latter, to the American Humanist Association.

The American Humanist Association did not answer my letter. The Baltimore Ethical Culture Society wrote back, "you have our heartiest handshake," but they never put a word in their newsletter, never endorsed my position publicly, never told their members at their meetings what I was doing, and in reply did not even use the organizational letterhead.

The attorney for the American Civil Liberties Union came out to my home and told me what I was doing was evil and sinful, that my overt fight meant that I lacked faith in my son's tenacious hold on atheism. He refused to intercede in the case and repeated, "You are wrong, wrong, wrong in what you are doing."

We had then been on strike for ten days.

My neighbors saw Bill at home and asked if he was sick. I explained to them that I was having an argument with the school over religion, and they went in their homes and from then on avoided me.

I told some of my best friends—liberals—what I was doing, and they said, "Madalyn, when are you going to stop these silly childish crusades?"

My family was now getting irate. Daily, Bill and I were showered with abuse.

We moved our steady study lessons to the famed Enoch Pratt Library. Its staff did not approve. When we wanted some help to set up a ninth-grade course of study, and tried to explain why, the stiff disapproval crystallized into obstacles of non-cooperation. The reference librarians could not find a ninth-grade math book, a ninth-grade history book, a ninth-grade biology book.

It was a tragicomedy. We were then on strike seventeen days. I asked Bill, "Is everybody out of step but Johnny?" And he answered me, "Everybody is out of step but Johnny."

On October 28th we wrote a letter to the *Baltimore Sun*: "I have had enough. When the last infamous epithet is cast and when the speaker or writer gropes for an even more vile indictment of a person or a system, invariably the word then hurled is 'atheist.' I am an atheist, and I will no longer be maligned and abused by identification with all that is evil, corrupt, and noxious. Now, when religion is an issue in a national election, I want to ask you: What of us who are atheists, agnostics, humanists, non-believers and who are unchurched? *68,000,000 Americans do not belong to a church.* We have no spokesman in Congress, no liaison representative at the White House, no organized lobby or pressure group in Washington. Who speaks for us? Who defends us?

"What is an atheist that he is so vile? Webster defines him as 'one who disbelieves in the existence of a God, or supreme intelligent being.' And I ask you, do we not love, work, bear children, praise honor, and seek truth? Do we not attempt to lead good lives of discipline, devotion to family and society? Do we not die in wars? Do we not have a right to our opinion as to the existence or non-existence of a supreme intelligent being?

"When we go to a public meeting, why are we subjected to prayer, in the efficacy of which we do not believe? Why, since 1905, have we been confronted with money minted 'In God We Trust?' Why should our mail be stamped to 'Pray for Peace?' As we pledge allegiance, why should this pledge be extorted from us to a nation 'under God?' Is your own belief so thin that you must force it upon others?

"Anybody in America can worship this alleged God in his own way, organize a church, publish religious books or magazines, operate a religious school, and preach to his heart's content. We atheists, agnostics, want only the freedom of our opinion. We desire not to have this forced upon us against our good conscience and our considered convictions.

"I repeat, I have had enough. Therefore, I have withdrawn my 14-year-old son from school, in an act of civil disobedience, in defiance of Maryland Code, Article 77, Section 231, because the State of Maryland in the persons of the Board of Education of Baltimore City has violated both the First and Fourteenth Amendments of the Constitution of the United States by requiring daily Bible reading and recitation of the Lord's Prayer in their public classrooms.

"And, may my conscience now Rest in Peace. . . ."

We honestly did not anticipate what would happen. We wanted to bring some pressure on the school board, and instead, all hell broke loose. A flood of newspaper men came in, radio men, television men. Within three weeks there had appeared in the three Baltimore newspapers over 100 separate articles concerned with us. The longest was 55 inches (and that ain't hay), and the shortest was about 3 or 4 inches. We were on television news every single night for three weeks. We were interviewed on radio. Releases were national and international.

Vile, opprobrious mail poured in. Our home was attacked with rocks, with rotten eggs. Roving gangs of teenagers—from five to twenty-five in a group—bore down on Bill every time he appeared in public.

Our neighbors rapped at our door to tell us we would be run out of the neighborhood by fair means or foul.

And on the second day of the mad roar of publicity, the ACLU attorney called me up and said, "You know, I think you started something." Right then and there, ACLU wanted to negotiate, to trade a little piece of our freedom for a concession from the school board, to arbitrate, to stall, to soft-peddle the issue of atheism.

I don't believe in anything but a broad frontal attack, and I've got my unemployment checks to prove it.

We managed to agree that Bill would go back to school, so as not to be charged with simple truancy (as the school threatened), and that he would walk out of the religious services. That is, ACLU wanted him to walk out, but I reasoned

that the school would just charge him with disobedience and I insisted that he stand up, say he was walking out so as not to participate in the religious ceremony, and make the issue clear.

It was a tempest in a teapot, because the school was determined not to let us test it before they could get to the State Attorney General. With reporters watching, they locked Bill out of his class! They posted teachers at each end of the hallway and maneuvered him away from the class! They physically diverted him, each day this 14-year-old boy tried to test the issue by walking out of the service in an act of defiance.

We went to the school board meeting and pled for a hearing. The States Rights Party of Maryland and the Daughters of America were there in force to filibuster and to defame us.

The ACLU attorney looked around in disgust, said a few sour words, sat down and whispered, "What's the use?"—but first he made it clear to all concerned that he was not in support of our position, he was there to protect us only insofar as our case could be construed to be under the First Amendment.

I got up and let the sons-of-bitches have it. I made clear that I was an atheist. This *was* an attack on religion—an attack on religion in schools specifically, but only because that was all that I could attack in the framework of this particular issue.

Finally, the Attorney General of Maryland ruled.

This was our unique problem: there is no law in Maryland concerned with religious ceremonies in public schools. There *is* a school board administrative rule that the Lord's Prayer shall be recited daily and the Bible read daily, and that the Pledge of Allegiance to the flag will be said "under God." This administrative rule has the force of law.

The Attorney General ruled that the rule was safely within the meaning of the U.S. Constitution, that the children of Maryland had a right and a duty to bow their heads in prayer to the Supreme Being. He added, almost parenthetically, that if parents disagreed, they had the right to have their child excused and he recommended to the school board that the rule should be amended to include this.

But to be excused would only cause a pupil—in the words of

" . . . One nation, under God . . . "

our petition to the courts—"to lose caste with his fellows, to be regarded with aversion, and to be subjected to reproach and insult."

The ACLU felt I should accept the compromise. I felt I should go ahead with an all-out fight. Finally, the ACLU agreed to go into the fight with me. We went to the school board again and petitioned that the rule should be placed to one side completely.

The ACLU attorney did a remarkable thing. He gave a speech on the religiosity of his organization and announced at this school board hearing that 17 other people were joining me in the fight and that all denominations would eventually be represented. I knew nothing about this. If ACLU is a religious organization, I don't care—but why bring their religion into my fight?

The school board amended the rule in order to have the children excused who desired to be excused. This was about November 17th. The ACLU then informed me that "maybe" they could go ahead and file a case in court in February 1961 . . . or there-about. I thought this over a little while, and fired my ACLU counsel.

Meanwhile, Bill needed to be driven back and forth to school. In school he was pummeled, shoved, tripped, punched, poked, razzed, kicked, tripped—and does anyone realize how lethal a weapon a good heavy pointed rosary is when swung out by heavy beads? They chain-dance behind him, singing, "We hate Murray." He is shown switchblade knives daily.

One teenager came up to *me* (an adult!) and spat in my face.

Bill has six classes in school, and three of his teachers refuse to speak to him! There is extra homework, a campaign for psychological testing, "counseling" sessions, "hard" marking on grades.

What these people do not understand is that an atheist has intestinal fortitude. All the hard training I have given my son is paying off, day by day. He stands up to them, and every night he comes out to the car grinning.

Forty-five teenagers gathered around our front steps on Christmas Eve and sang religious carols to us. On Christmas Day, ten teenagers waited outside with piles of specially iced snowballs, waiting for Bill to appear.

And, ohhhhh, do those rotten eggs that they pelt at us stink!

I found two attorneys who would take my case. And I continued to write letter after letter to every freethought newspaper or magazine that I knew about, sent clippings, and asked for support. Until, hold your breath, *one* showed interest—but they cautioned me:

Don't call yourself an atheist. Don't say you are fighting religion. Your name needs to be Humanist, Secularist, Freethinker, Rationalist. You must fight on the level of a violation of Constitutional rights. Throw in with the ACLU. Throw in with the American Jewish Congress. If they petition for Chanukah, love Chanukah. If they are Jewish, tell them you believe only in Judaism.

Like hell I will! I want this printed in caps: I AM AN ATHEIST. MY SON IS AN ATHEIST. OUR PRIMARY FIGHT IS AGAINST EVERY RELIGION. Our secondary fight is for our Constitutional right. But—*before there was a Constitution, there was non-belief. I don't need any legal document to support my right. Non-belief is sufficient unto itself.*

I asked my two attorneys how much this will cost me. The figure is between $10,000 and $15,000, if we use stipulation where we can instead of trial, and otherwise cut corners. So I told them to go ahead with the suit. We filed our petition on December 7th, 1960.

This is sheer insanity. I don't have $15,000. But *The Realist* is going to pay me $15 for this story . . . and then I will need only $14,985. You see, everything will work out.

THE ADVENTURES OF CHURCHMAN

by Bob Margolin and
Mickey Gruber

Faster than the wrath of God! More powerful than 3,000 Hail Marys! Able to leap tall cathedrals in a single bound! Look! Up in the sky! It's a saint! It's an angel! No—it's Churchman!

Who is this man of steel, this Leviathan of goodness? In real life, Churchman is none other than mild-mannered Padre Peter, a humble Carmelite monk who resides in a small monastery in southern France where the friars manufacture a delicate liqueur known as Chanteuse.

†

Our adventure begins on a night different from all other nights. The good Padre strolled over to the window to take a cool breath of air. And then he saw it: the brilliant yellow circle of light with the black cross in the middle. It was the Churchsignal! The Pope was calling Churchman!

Padre Peter looked across the room to Josephus, the young novitiate who, as Altar Boy, aided him in defending against the forces of evil. The two quickly headed upstairs to the Chapel. They entered and Padre Peter hurried into the confessional, said the magic word, "Inri"—and seconds later he emerged as Churchman, defender of the righteous and downtrodden.

The cassock was perched at a jaunty angle on Churchman's well-shaped head, and his powerful muscles rippled under the tight surplice. His greatest asset was his famous Limited Vision, which protected him from all obstacles.

Altar Boy buckled on his utility belt and the two leapt to the sill. Churchman pushed open the stained glass window, and the dynamic duo soared into the night toward the Vatican.

The Pope was just turning off the Churchsignal when Churchman and Altar Boy landed on the roof of Saint Peter's Basilica.

"What's up, Chief?" said Churchman.

The Pope ran his hand across his brow with the worried air of a man who feels responsible for the solution of the world's problems. "Freethinker has struck again," he replied, handing Churchman a prophylactic with a note attached.

Of all the evil anti-ecclesiastical foes, none was more sinister than Freethinker. He was never one to give up, and his fiendish brain was continually hatching plots for mocking and undermining the ways of purity. Time and again, he had clashed with Churchman, and although Freethinker never emerged victorious,

he occasionally made a few dents in the hard core of righteousness.

The piece of paper attached to the prophylactic was an advertisement for a Planned Parenthood meeting which Freethinker was holding in Greenwich Village.

"You two better break up that meeting," the Pope urged. "Give 'em heaven," he shouted, as the caped evil-fighters soared toward New York.

†

Freethinker had set up his soapbox and was conducting the Planned Parenthood meeting in the middle of Washington Square.

Suddenly a bearded man in the back glanced toward the sky and saw two black spots silhouetted against the clouds. "Probably a saint," he thought, and returned his attention to Freethinker's lecture. A ponytailed girl in the front row looked up and also noticed the

The Adventures of Churchman, *continued*
two black dots. "Might be an angel," she said to herself.

Then Freethinker himself gazed at the two figures hurtling toward the earth. "It's Churchman and Altar Boy," he yelled, jumping off the soapbox.

Having expected the two, he had cleverly set a trap for them. Churchman's weakness was beautiful blondes. He shrank at the sight of them. So, from his Freethinkermobile, Freethinker called forth a bevy of curvaceous blondes, whom he stationed in the Square to stun the dynamic duo.

He also stirred up the crowd, who jeered at Churchman as he alighted. "Thumbs down on the Index," shouted

one. "Birth control is here to stay," shrieked Maggie Sanger. One disillusioned follower of righteousness hurled his plastic index finger of St. Bituminous the Unwashed, which missed Churchman but hit an innocent chess player.

Churchman felt himself weakening and ran behind a bush to take a gulp of Holy Water from a phial in his utility belt. He then returned to the fray, ready to subdue the forces of evil.

Freethinker shouted from across the Square, planning to stun Churchman with the bevy of blondes. However, he did not count on Churchman's Limited Vision. The blondes wiggled their hips but Churchman couldn't even see them as he zoomed by at super-speed. The narrowness of his Limited Vision had saved him again.

Freethinker, sensing the ineffectiveness of his ploy, set up a dense

The Adventures of Churchman, *continued*

smokescreen and ran for his Free-thinkermobile. Not even the mob of screaming liberals could save him now. He gunned the motor and prepared to take off.

"Get the Churchrope," Churchman shouted to Altar Boy. Altar Boy unsheathed the thin cord, woven from the hair of Mary Magdalene, from his utility belt, and lassoed Freethinker's hood ornament, a miniature replica of Bertrand Russell. The powerful pair held fast as Freethinker tried to get away, and then, with a mighty effort, they swung the Freethinkermobile around their heads and flung it into space where it is still or-

biting.

"Thank God," said Altar Boy. "The world is rid of a horrible evil."

"Good work, Altar Boy," replied Churchman. "The case is closed."

Then the two defenders of righteousness flew back to their monastery, humming the Donna Dia overture.

†

The Churchcave, reached by a secret trapdoor in the basement of the monastery, was filled with trophies taken from Freethinker and other opponents of righteousness.

There was the complete set of William Faulkner's works taken from The Fiend From the University, and three Tennessee Williams films, and there was also something that had been taken from Freethinker the night he and his commando band had tried to bomb the Vatican Relics Factory, which for centuries has been a great source of wealth for the Church.

At the last minute, Churchman had arrived and, with a mighty lunge, smothered the blast. Freethinker managed to escape, but his sandals are perhaps the most coveted trophy of them all.

UN-AMERICAN ACTIVITIES IN MY OWN HOME
by Janet Sorkin

We've never been on great terms with any of the schools he's been in. Since the beginning, I've been summoned to school by teachers and told (in accusing voices): "Corey is a dreamer! We know he can do the work, but he—"

Then the old feeling of being a schoolkid myself returns, and suddenly I'm on Corey's side; when, in real life, I would gladly lock him in a tower and whip him every day if it would make him do the work. (It wouldn't, so I don't.)

However, this year, we had a school experience of an entirely new kind. For once, it had nothing to do with school work; Corey was refusing to Salute the Flag. As he explained it to me, the flag is a symbol, and he felt it was foolish to keep communicating with a symbol every day.

So what? What'll happen to the country if a 13-year-old kid doesn't salute the flag every morning? I suspected that the Union would survive.

My first inkling that the Board of Education didn't share my indifference came one morning at about 9 A.M. (when nobody's really awake anyhow). This *voice* screeched over the phone:

"Mrs. Sorkin?"

"Yes," I answered drowsily.

"This is Mrs. Skwelty. Your son, Corey, doesn't salute the flag!!!"

She was on the edge of hysteria. It took me a moment to absorb what it was she was so excited about, and when I didn't faint at this evidence of *treason* under my own *roof*, she seemed to lose control completely. Mainly, I couldn't figure out what she wanted me to do.

The conversation ended with my pointing out that I couldn't very well stand beside him every morning, forcing him to salute the flag. Basically, it was their problem, but I would talk to him and try to get him to do it.

Although I didn't feel that this was an issue which would impel a protest march, I did feel rather proud of Corey for sticking to his guns like that when I knew they were putting a lot of pressure on him.

But I also knew that they weren't kidding around, either. My maternal heart trembled at the picture of him fighting the entire Board of Education over his right not to salute the flag if he didn't want to.

When I talked to him about it later in the day, I was unable to defend any of the ideological reasons for saluting the flag every morning. Our way of life simply doesn't depend on it. The only thing I could say was that it would only take a minute or two, and he'd avoid all that trouble, and was he ready to take the whole matter to the Supreme Court?

I felt like a bit of a fink.

The worst of it was that it was announced publicly in assembly that day that "a certain student" refused to salute the flag and that it was an unpatriotic, loathsome thing—an act that gives comfort to our enemies, and on and on.

Also, the Social Studies teacher had declaimed that he heard "a certain member of this particular class" refused to salute the flag, and that he hoped that he wouldn't find out who it was, because his buddies had *died* in Korea for that flag, and he didn't know how he would react to a person who didn't honor it in the prescribed manner. Although he had been publicly humiliated several times that day, Corey pointed out to me that if they really cared about the flag, they wouldn't have acted that way. "After all," he said, "when you salute the flag, you're saluting the idea of liberty. How can they *force* you to salute *liberty?*" There was nothing much I could answer.

He felt rotten at being made a public spectacle, and I felt rotten because I wanted him to at least *pretend* to salute the flag so they'd get off his back. He agreed to think about it. The next morning, he told me that he decided to pretend to salute the

flag, because he couldn't take them all on.

I was relieved, because *I* wasn't prepared to take them all on either. Anyway, that kid doesn't need to be encouraged in his nonconformity. He was *born* to it. I regretted having let him read *Lord of the Flies, Catcher in the Rye*, and *Steppenwolf* all in a row.

I thought that was the end of the matter, but not so. *Months* later, I was called to school about some issue so obscure that it took me 10 minutes to grasp what it was. It was something about putting on his coat when he wasn't supposed to or something.

I was to see the school disciplinarian, an immaculately dressed, crew-cut, ramrod-straight young man, who turned out also to be the social studies teacher—the one from Korea. After we struggled through the coat incident, he brought up the flag incident, presumably as another example of Corey's impossible behavior.

I told the social studies teacher that Corey *was* saluting the flag now, and I asked if he didn't think that when you do a thing like that in school day after day, it did become a bit meaningless.

He snapped to attention, and informed me haughtily that he saluted the flag every day of his life when he was a Marine in Korea, and that he felt privileged every single time to be *allowed* to salute that flag!

It would have taken a 5-star general to convince him that something one is *forced* to do every day could become mumbled nonsense, and not a reaffirmation of loyalty to your country.

Frankly, it doesn't make any more difference to me that the teacher *loves* saluting the flag than that Corey feels that he can still be patriotic *without* saluting it. Corey is firm in his faith that most adults are ignorant of what the world is really like and are stupid into the bargain. As long as he feels that way, I know he's okay, even if he does have to salute the flag every morning.

When he's ready to handle it, I'll be ready to leave the running of the world in his hands. But I sure hope I'm here to see his chagrin when he finds out how difficult it is to know what the world is really like.

TEMPORARY INSANITY
by Norvin Pallas

(The defendant has been accused of murdering his fiancée, and has pleaded temporary insanity. A psychologist has been brought to the stand to testify.)

Q. Doctor Burnhill, you are familiar with this case, and have examined the defendant previously. Would you say he is insane?

A. I'm sorry, but I don't understand the meaning of the word "insane." It's not a psychological term.

Q. Legally, it means unsound, incapable of judging the re-

sults of one's actions. Is the defendant unsound, or is he normal?

A. Well, now, I've never yet met a completely normal person.

Q. What I mean is, was the defendant aware of what he was doing when he murdered his sweetheart?

A. Probably, since he was conscious at the time.

Q. But was his state of mind such that he was able to choose between right and wrong?

A. I'm sorry, but I don't know the difference between right and wrong myself. I only know that certain actions are socially acceptable, and others are unacceptable.

Q. Was he able to differentiate between a socially acceptable and unacceptable act?

A. Oh, yes.

Q. Then he was fully capable of choosing between one and the other?

A. Not at all. He is given to impulsive action, and is therefore not completely subject to rational inhibition.

Q. You agree with the defense contention that he committed this act while in an unnormal state of mind?

A. Certainly, since persons in a so-called normal state of mind don't murder their sweethearts.

Q. But it is possible he has recovered his lucidity since then?

A. Certainly, since he doesn't murder people every day.

Q. In your opinion, is this man guilty or not guilty?

A. I'm afraid I don't know what the word "guilty" means. The only question is whether this man is capable of becoming a useful member of society, or whether it is necessary that he be restrained.

Q. Doctor Burnhill, do you agree with the prosecution's contention that this man committed this deed while in a normal state of mind and should therefore be condemned? Or do you agree with the defense contention that he committed the act while temporarily unstable, and therefore should be found innocent?

A. I admit that I am confused. The prosecution seems to believe that this is a person who is fully capable of becoming a useful member of society, and therefore he should be incarcerated. The defense seems to believe that this man is given to temporary spells of emotional instability, and for that reason he should be released.

Q. You're qualified as an expert. Will you please state your opinion clearly, Doctor Burnhill?

A. In my opinion, to express the matter in your own terms, I believe that the defendant should be found guilty by reason of temporary insanity, and should therefore be placed under restraint.

Q. That will be all, Doctor Burnhill. Your honor, I move that this testimony be stricken from the record as ambiguous.

AN IMPOLITE INTERVIEW WITH JULES FEIFFER

Q. Comedian Bob Newhart was quoted in The N.Y. Times *as saying that he has "never heard of a good reactionary comic. There's no Republican Mort Sahl. Anybody as individual as a comic is would naturally tend toward the liberal party." Do you agree with this?*

A. The entertainment business seems to be mostly made up of Democrats; whether this makes them liberals, I'm not sure. I've never heard of a good reactionary comic either, but I've only heard about two good *liberal* ones, so the odds are not quite what Newhart would imply they are. Irreverence is not necessarily a synonym for liberalism. It sometimes has more to do with immaturity or repressed egoism.

Q. Do you think Newhart himself lives up to his statement?

A. I'm crowded with uncertainties here. I'm not sure what the original statement meant, and having only seen and heard Newhart briefly, I'm really not qualified to judge, although I'm sure he would not argue the point that his humor is far from dangerous. The "new school" of humor seems to be making that subtle switch from "I'm not kidding, things are wrong!" to "I'm only kidding, things are wrong." It's the difference of attitudes between a man fired by the company telling a joke on the company and the man who fired him telling a joke on the company—at the company picnic, of course.

Q. Your strip has been reprinted in Socialist publications. This question isn't meant to imply guilt by association—or credit by association, depending on one's point of view—but are you a Socialist?

A. I don't know. I guess I need too much room to maneuver in to allow myself to be any definite shape of political being. I've also allowed my strip to be re-

printed in religious publications, but I'm an atheist. I've allowed my strip to be reprinted in *The Realist,* but I'm not a freethinker. I've allowed my strip to be reprinted in *Mad,* but I'm not tasteless. *The New Republic* is going to run some of my strips, but I'm no liberal. And if William Buckley ever came around . . . As long as the cartoons are run without change, I'm glad to see them circulated.

Q. William Saroyan once wrote: "I believe the living are simultaneously naive and sophisticated, because no matter how naive a man may be, there is somewhere in him great sophistication, and no matter how sophisticated he may be there is great naiveté in him." How would you relate this to your work?

A. I believe the living are simultaneously orange and purple, because no matter how orange a man may be, there is somewhere in him great purple, and no matter how purple he may be there is great orange in him.

Q. In writing the dialogue of your characters, do you strive for accuracy or do you deliberately exaggerate?

A. I decide who and what my character is, how he thinks, what he stands for, what point I am trying to make, the

way this particular character might inadvertently make that point, and then the dialogue naturally follows.

I don't strive for tape recorder accuracy, I strive for an attitude, a point of view generally representative (if slanted) of the type I'm portraying. It is almost automatic that the dialogue will also be representative.

While there is no conscious exaggeration, there must, of course, be exaggeration. The limits of newspaper or magazine space is such that were I to make my characters speak without editing, they would run on for pages, cease to be funny, cloud my editorialization, and lose my point.

Q. Do you think it should be the function of an artist to bite the hand that feeds him?

A. I'm personally in favor of biting all the hands that feed me, but that happens to be my private line of endeavor. And who knows whether those aforementioned hands truly consider themselves bitten? It may all be a private conceit. I've been nationally syndicated for over a year now and have had very few complaints. It raises the ugly suspicion that I'm being derelict in my duties.

Q. How have you bitten the hands that feed you?

A. Now let me see. . . .

Q. Do you slant your material to fit the market—such as, for example, Playboy *Magazine?*

A. I try not to. There is, on occasion, an unconscious slanting not asked for by the market but demanded by one's own idea (often misguided) of what the market will find acceptable. I find this less and less to be the case, however, and I would consider most of my work interchangeable whatever the market.

Basically *I* remain the prime market. I must slant my material to my own demands. As far as my strips go, I want never to have to tell people, "Don't look at that. I was just doing it for the buck."

Q. What are your feelings about Li'l Abner?

A. Al Capp, I assume, is in a great way responsible for the strides toward satire the comic strip has taken in recent years. You can draw a straight, progressively stimulating line from *Li'l Abner* to *Barnaby* to *Pogo* to *Peanuts.*

I don't see *Li'l Abner* these days because I don't buy the *Daily Mirror,* so I have no idea of what he's up to. I've always enjoyed Capp's magazine articles as much or more than his comic strip.

Q. What's your favorite comic strip?

A. You know, I read them so infrequently these days that I'm no longer sure I have a favorite. I'm a devotee of *Pogo* and *Peanuts*, of course. I read *Mary Worth* because there is masochism in me which drives me to it. I am an admirer of several cartoonists outside the strip field: Herblock, Bob Blechman, Tomi Ungerer, Osborn, Steig, Steinberg, Francois, Roy McKie, others who I can't think of at the moment. My favorite comic strip in retrospect is *The Spirit* by Will Eisner.

Q. What's your least favorite comic strip?

A. They're all pretty much the same. I get terribly annoyed on those rare occasions when I happen to come across one of the several dedicated Cold War adventure strips like *Terry and the Pirates*. The official policy on syndicated strips is that they are to be non-editorial in nature. The way this has often worked out is that strips are only non-editorial when it comes to the expression of views that differ from official State Department policy. I'm all for the expression of opinion in any kind of strip, but it would be nice to counter the monopoly of our cartooning Edward Tellers with one or two cartooning Linus Paulings.

Q. Would you describe the personalities of some of the characters who appear from time to time in your strip, such as Bernard?

A. The original concept of the strip was to have no set characters. I like the fact that they slowly and undeliberately evolved. The first was Bernard, the inept though anxious, the often defeated yet always persistent; Bernard must love loss because he's made so many of them. He loses to women, to authority, to society, to anything he pits himself against. And yet—and this is his single saving grace—he refuses to see himself as a loser. He rationalizes defeat so that it becomes indistinguishable from victory. He comes back, always, for more.

Q. What about Huey?

A. Huey is not as different from Bernard as you may think. Both are egoists, both are basically passive, both often let the girl make the first move. Their difference is that in Bernard's case they

don't; in Huey's they always *do* —because Huey, unlike Bernard, knows his identity and uses it—uses it with an arrogance and a sensuality that is pure narcissism, and which automatically attracts women to him. With Bernard everything goes out till there is nothing left. With Huey everything is drawn in. He is a magnet.

Q. Are you Huey or Bernard?

A. Is there a multiple choice? As William Saroyan so aptly put it, "I believe the living are simultaneously Huey and Bernard, because no matter how Huey a man may be, there is somewhere in him a great Bernard, and no matter how Bernard he may be there is great Huey in him."

Q. What's your attitude toward psychoanalysis?

A. I'm all for it. I don't question that there are many hack analysts, no more than I question that many analysands enter analysis more as an extension of their neurosis than as an attempted cure for it. But there are the hacks and the uncommitted in all fields. Analysis gets all this hostile attention because it's still looked on as an immigrant science, and like all immigrants, it is not to be trusted, not until one of its members is elected President, at any rate.

In the meantime its influence has become so ingrained that while official psychoanalysis may still be uneasily frowned upon, the myth of self-help has become a naive mystique among our overaware citizenry. Each has his own formula, whether it's writing his inner doubts in print, voicing them on the air, exhibiting them through his art, his dance; whatever his outlet he will defensively assert, "Others may need help. I can handle my own problems."

Q. What's your opinion of Dr. Joyce Brothers' late-night TV show?

A. An unnecessary postponement of the national anthem.

Q. Do strangers ever ask you for advice on their emotional problems?

A. Okay, what's troubling you, Bunky?

Q. What are you a spokesman for?

A. Me.

Q. What is snob humor?

A. Snob humor is, unfortunately, almost *any* kind of humor. The "ins" whether they be "ins" because of race,

REALIST OF THE MONTH

Dr. Joyce Brothers: "There's nothing so unromantic as a seasick bride . . ."

religion, social position, lack of social position, age, birth, knowledge of seven foreign languages, world travellers, professional stay-at-homes, leftists, rightists, centrists, freethinkers, Trotskyites, revisionists, David Susskindists or Goldwaterites—whatever common point of view two or more may have which makes *them* "ins" as opposed to whatever different points of view two or more others may have which makes them "outs"—they, the "ins," will use any method of attack (that is socially allowable) against the "outs." *Humor* is allowable. It is devious enough to be defended as "just having a little fun, no offense intended, Rastus," and often vicious enough to provide security through laughter, safety through derision, and a temporary solace that makes this particular form of intellectual vigilante-ism worth its weight in group therapists.

How convenient it is to be able to laugh at anyone outside your circle as either a wrongo or a fathead.

Q. Are you guilty of snob humor?

A. Of course not, you fathead!

Q. How would you describe "gibble-gabble"—and what is its function?

A. Simply that conversation has, to many of us, become less a means of *communication* than a means of *imitating* communication; a separatist's function which keeps us from touching others closely or, more basically, touching *ourselves* closely. This is why clichés are so important. They allow us to reduce conversation to a mutually understood list of banalities which allows both participants to retreat into their private worlds while seemingly in the midst of a lively and animated discussion.

I've used the words "gibble-gabble" in several strips to denote public utterance as separated from private thought. While *he* is going "gibble gabble gobble geeble" he may be thinking, "God, how did I get stuck with *this!* I wonder if she'd be hurt if I just got up and ran out of the restaurant." And while *she* is going "gabble goobie gibble gabble" she well may be thinking, "I wish I were home washing my hair, I wish I were home polishing my nails, I wish I were home getting drunk *alone* instead of being here getting drunk with him, I wish one of us would *die*. At the moment I have no preference."

Q. Whereas you never change your cartoon strip to please the audience, will you have the same artistic integrity for the theater?

A. I assume you refer, Barry, to that much discussed forthcoming production of my much discussed multi-million dollar revue called *The Explainers* which will first open in fashionable Chicago this spring and then be brought the following winter to Broadway's very favorite Thompson Street.

What can I say, Barry, except that we think we've got a sweet little show here with a number of fresh bright young faces, a bunch of hard working happy kids, some exciting new ideas that frankly—and you know how I don't want to hurt anybody's feelings, Barry, because as you know, we go back a long way together and you know me and I know you and you've been a guest at my house and I've been a guest at your house, and you know it's not my style to knock for knocking's sake. I have—you'll pardon me if I get emotional—I have never been a knocker who's knocked for knocking's sake. But we both know—and why kid ourselves, huh, Barry?—that there hasn't been much in the revue department in recent years. That's common knowledge. And what we are going to try our darndest to do in this little show of ours is bring back a sense of fun—know what I mean?—in people's lives because we're put on this earth for precious little enough time as it is, and we just don't seem to have the kind of fun we used to be able to have.

I'm no philosopher, Barry—no, stop it, I'm not—but I've got one thing after a lot of number of years in this business that I won't put on the line for *anybody*. That's my artistic integrity, Barry. I won't put that on the line for anybody. There isn't enough money, I swear to you, Barry, not enough money in this world, and I'm a man—you know this, Barry,—who's had his ups and downs. Ups and downs—but one thing my audiences are going to know when they walk into a theater with my name out in front—they're going to know that, from the bottom of my heart, I *love* my reputation, Barry.

I want to thank you for being so patient with me. I didn't mean to make a speech. God bless you. God love you. You're a great human being. Keep 'em flying. Goodnight.

PSYCHITA

(As the opening credits roll across the screen, the voice of Fabian is heard, singing Steve Allen's lovely lyrics to Dimitri Tiomkin's haunting melody, "Psychita's Theme.")

Cling to me, my darling nymphet
Like I'm a rock, and you're a limpet,
Your charm could fill the missile gap, li'l Psychita,
Oh-oh-oh-oh-oh
You are even sweeter than apple ci-eeder,
Oh-oh-oh-oh-oh
So tell me, dearest one, no matter what
The weather,
That clouds up above
Won't darken our love,
And we'll have a lifetime of puberty,
Together.

(The scene: An aerial view of a highway. PAN OVER to neon sign reading "Mom and Dad's Motel." CUT TO motel office. MOM and DAD, played by Robert and Loretta Young, are sitting and talking.)

MOM: Ever since they built that new highway a year ago, our business has been falling off something awful.

DAD: And we can't *always* depend on Humbert Shmumbert in Cabin 5. Do you realize that he's been our only guest for the entire past year? Let's face it, he's not going to stay at our motel forever. What happens to us when he decides to go?

MOM: Well, frankly, dear, I'll breathe a sigh of relief. I don't like all the time that our daughter has been spending with Mr. Shmumbert. It's not right. It's not healthy.

DAD: You're worried about Humbert Shmumbert? Why, that harmless fellow is no more lecherous than *I* am. And besides, Psychita's only a *child*. What could a middle-aged man possibly see in her?

(CUT TO full view of outside of cabin. CLOSE-UP of door, showing number 5. CUT TO interior. Music: "Psychita's Theme." PSYCHITA stands in front of a rumpled bed, wearing only panties, a half-slip, and a brassiere. She is thirteen, going on fourteen.)

PSYCHITA: Humbert, will you please come help me fasten this darned old bra?

(HUMBERT SHMUMBERT, played by Oscar Levant, enters from bathroom, buttoning his shirt. He is forty-seven, going on forty-eight.)

HUMBERT: I don't see why you have to wear one of these things anyway. *(Helping her.)* Your breast-buds have barely begun to grow.

PSYCHITA: I know, but Mom saw this advertisement for Teenform, and it says, "The understanding mother now buys her daughter's first bra, whether or not she needs it physically."

Psychita, *continued*

It's supposed to give me poise or something. It even expands as I develop. The ad says they sell it at all "understanding stores."

HUMBERT: Alas, the trend along Madison Avenue is becoming increasingly anthropomorphic.

PSYCHITA: Oh, stop showing off all the time with those big words, willya, please.

HUMBERT: God, I just adore you to pieces when you become perturbed like that!

PSYCHITA: You can let go of my brassiere now. I have to do my Algebra homework.

(FADE IN to highway scene. Cars rolling along. CLOSE IN on car being driven by beautiful woman, JANET VICTIM, played by Tony Curtis. CLOSE-UP of the seat next to her, empty except for a paper bag, stuffed with $40,000. JANET'S thoughts can be heard as she makes driving grimaces.)

JANET'S VOICE: I'm a thief, that's what I am. If only I could tell somebody and unburden my conscience. But how could anyone ever sympathize with a common ordinary thief? Why, they might just as well—they might just as well identify with—with a pedophiliac! . . . Hmmmm, it's starting to rain. *(Starts to rain.)* I'd better pull up at a motel for the night.

(CUT TO Mom and Dad's Motel. Janet's car pulls up. CUT TO interior of motel office. DAD is reading the paper. MOM is sewing. PSYCHITA is doing her Algebra homework. HUMBERT is twiddling his thumbs. JANET VICTIM enters.)

JANET: Oh, hello there. I wonder if I could have a room for tonight.

MOM: Surely. Just sign the book there.

(CLOSE-UP of JANET'S hand signing registry book: "Janet Pseudonym, Thief River Falls, Minn.")

DAD: Nasty night for driving.

PSYCHITA: Two x equals y plus one.

HUMBERT: I'll help you with your luggage *(looks at registry book)*, Miss Pseudonym.

JANET: Oh—yes. Thank you.

(HUMBERT takes her suitcase. JANET carries the paper bag full of money herself. CUT TO outside shot, showing PSYCHITA standing on motel office porch, as HUMBERT and JANET enter Cabin. CLOSE IN on door, showing number 4. CUT TO interior of Cabin 4.)

JANET: I would like very much to confide in you, Mr. Shmumbert.

HUMBERT: Call me Humbert. Tell me, do you have any pictures of yourself when you were a little girl—perhaps at the age of twelve?

JANET: No, I'm sorry, I don't. Listen, I've stolen some money.

HUMBERT: Oh, that's too bad. You don't happen to have a younger sister, do you?

JANET: No, I'm sorry, I don't. I think it's forty thousand dollars.

HUMBERT: Perchance you have some young female cousins?

JANET: No, I'm sorry, I don't. Would you help me count the money, please?

(CUT TO outside of motel office. PSYCHITA is still stand-

ing on the porch. CUT TO interior. MOM is still sewing, and DAD is still reading. CLOSE IN on clock over the desk. As if to indicate the passage of time, the hands move from 8 o'clock to 9 o'clock within two seconds.)*

DAD: There goes that crazy clock acting up again.

MOM: Yes, we really ought to have it fixed one of these days.

(CUT TO outside of motel office. Follow direction of Psychita's eyes to Cabin 4, as HUMBERT leaves it and returns to his own cabin. CUT TO CLOSE UP of PSYCHITA'S face. Her eyes harden with anger. Through tight lips, she speaks.)

PSYCHITA: Why, that no-good, two-timing, dirty-rotten, double-crossing fink!

(CUT TO interior of Cabin 4. JANET is just stepping into shower. She smiles when she sees what brand of soap is there. She lathers herself up, smiling a toothy smile all the while. Suddenly, the shower curtains part. Standing there is PSYCHITA, large butcher knife in hand. Music: "Psychita's Theme." JANET stops smiling.)

PSYCHITA: For the first time in your life, feel really dead.

(PSYCHITA wields the weapon over and over again. Camera achieves montage-in-motion effect by series of quick cuts: to knife, to JANET'S arm, to knife, to look of horror on JANET'S face, to knife, to JANET'S thigh, to knife, to look of vengeance on PSYCHITA'S face, to knife, to JANET'S chest—very important in this scene to show all that violence but no nipples. CUT TO interior of motel office. MOM and DAD are sitting and talking.)

DAD: Nothing exciting ever happens around here.

MOM: Why don't you see if there's anything good on TV?

DAD: I guess I'll go put on one of those stupid family situation comedies—but you never see *them* watching television.

(A moment after DAD exits, PSYCHITA walks in, unnoticed by MOM. She stands there, dripping blood.)

PSYCHITA: Mom, I have to talk to you. Something has just happened which is going to change my whole life.

MOM: Why, of course, dear. I feel sorry for girls who can't go to their mothers for frank talks. Thank goodness you and I have never been embarrassed with each other. I can make it all sound so simple and easy and *natural* that you'll get over your nervousness in a hurry. You'll feel sure, secure, *safe*. Nothing can show, no one can know. I'll tell you the *nicer* way.

PSYCHITA: I *know* all *that* jazz, Mom. No odor, no chafing, no binding. "Don't be an outsider," the Tampax ad says. But what *I'm* trying to tell you is—

(HUMBERT bursts into the room.)

HUMBERT: You must call the police! Right away! Someone has murdered Janet Pseudonym. Someone—*(Sees PSYCHITA, still dripping blood)*—Psychita! You! How! Why!

PSYCHITA: Big man, you always use such big words, now look at you. I did it because of *you*, ya big lug, I saw how long you were in her cabin.

HUMBERT: But we were only counting the money she'd stolen. Forty thousand dollars in singles takes a lot of time to count. It's not as if we were doing anything *wrong*, Psychita.

(FADE IN on the office of DR. LISTEN, a world-

renowned psychiatrist, played by Sal Mineo. MOM and DAD sit in rapt attention as he speaks.)

DR. LISTEN: Well, the money was returned to Janet Victim's employer, and Humbert Shmumbert is in prison on two counts: one, for impairing the morals of a minor; two, by withholding information from the police, as an accessory to an embezzler. But I'm sure that what you're really interested in hearing about is Psychita. As you know, she's been committed here at State Hospital for an indefinite period of time, depending on our final prognosis. We've tested her in every possible way, from the Stanford-Binet to the Rorschach, from the Multiphasic Personality Inventory to the Thematic Apperception Pictures, from sensorimotor coordination to encephalographical examination, from hypnosis to sodium pentothol. Basically, this is what we've uncovered. As in the case of any teenager, Psychita became a product of her culture, which is, essentially, an imbroglio of romantically-oriented fantasmagoria.

MOM AND DAD: Yes, Doctor.

DR. LISTEN: Her world was built of concepts derived not only from the two of you in your roles as parents, but she also most definitely internalized quite deeply the values imparted to her by movies, advice-to-the-lovelorn columns, popular fiction, magazine articles, window displays, tabloid newspapers, and so on *ad infinitum.* Our civilization, through its various media of mass communication, does everything it can to imbue its members—and teenagers are of course the most susceptible—with one of society's pivotal paradoxes: that lust in and of itself is bad, but that it becomes automatically transformed into love concomitantly with the act of marriage.

MOM AND DAD: Of course, Doctor.

DR. LISTEN: Now then, the average teenage girl is able to *accept* this inconsistency by getting involved with the *details* of vicariousness—wearing lipstick, for example—but Psychita's environment, you must realize, *also* included the motel which you both operate. A motel by its very nature is dedicated, to a very large extent, to the promulgation in *actuality* of the loveless lust which Psychita's peers were able to rationalize through lustless (or puppy) love.

MOM AND DAD: Go on, Doctor.

DR. LISTEN: Well, when Humbert Shmumbert happened to come along, Psychita was psychologically *ready* for him. She was also, unfortunately, keenly fitted to satisfy *his* particular perversion. For an entire year, then, they carried on a glorious—albeit aberrant—affair. And then, Janet Victim entered the picture. Psychita became, literally, insanely jealous. Her schizophrenic environment which I have described—combined with a predisposition resulting from certain hereditary factors—led her almost inevitably to commit her crime of passion.

MOM AND DAD: Certain hereditary factors, Doctor?

DR. LISTEN: Ah, yes. When you first adopted Psychita, it was thought advisable not to reveal to you the truth about her medical history. Now, however, the story can—nay, must—be told. Fifteen years ago, a psychotic by the name of Normal Bates was committed to this very institution. I shan't go into the details of *his* particular split personality. Suffice it to say that Normal had a classical Oedipus complex. Whether or not we accept the orthodox Freudian doctrine of universality is immaterial, for most of us do not kill our rival-fathers. To all intents and purposes, though, Normal Bates did exactly that. He killed his mother—a divorcée—and her *lover.* The guilt and anguish he felt as a consequence of committing matricide toppled Normal over the brink to the insanity toward which he had been heading all along. In order to convince himself, so to speak, that he had *not* killed his mother, he *became* her. Not constantly, mind you. Sometimes, he was himself. Other times, he was her. And still other times he was, simultaneously, both himself *and* his mother.

MOM AND DAD: But what does all this have to do with Psychita, Doctor?

DR. LISTEN: Well, you see, in some of the lower forms of life, there appears to be a gradual anatomical combining of the sexes. This is true, for example, in the ostracods, a group of shellfish which actually reproduce their species by the process of self-impregnation. But this of course becomes rarer and rarer as we ascend the evolutionary scale. Nevertheless, it was discovered during a routine physical check-up of Normal Bates that he had a certain type of tumor known as the arrhenoblastoma, so named because it contains blastodermic cells. The blastoderm is one of the basic membranes in an unborn child, from which all the organs of the fetal body develop. Now, even though Normal Bates' actual mother was dead, her personality remained alive in one half of his mind, while—logically enough—in the other half of his mind Normal's Oedipal desires likewise remained alive. And, although it has been a well-kept secret all these years, one night he shattered medical history.

MOM AND DAD: You mean?

DR. LISTEN: Yes. Normal Bates was a *functional* hermaphrodite. He was Psychita's father and mother, both. He was also, as it were, her brother.

(FADE IN on a room in State Hospital, empty except for PSYCHITA, sitting on a chair and smiling wanly. She is holding a middle-aged-man doll. As the camera moves further and further away, her thoughts are still audible—accompanied by slow, muted music.)

PSYCHITA'S VOICE: So they think they're getting even by keeping me here till I'm an adult, huh? Oh, sure, I'll miss living a normal teenage life. I'll miss exerting a strong influence on family purchases from furniture to automobiles as well as commanding a sizable amount of disposable income on my own. I'll miss being a member of a group that saved the movie industry, that buys 90% of all the single records sold and half the albums, that spends more on clothes than the average for the total population, that spends $300 million a year on cosmetics alone. Yes, I'll miss being part of the $10 billion teenage market. But *I'll* have the last laugh, Society, because you haven't gained an inmate—you've lost a consumer.

(The strains of "Psychita's Theme" become louder and louder, drowning out the sound of a child-like giggle.)

THE GREAT CONDOM CAPER

by Lenny Bruce

Dave Garroway called Betsy Palmer pretentious and righteous. Betsy cooled it because he just lost his wife to "take one before bedtime and one before each meal" and "pat don't rub the infected area once every four hours for pain" and "keep in a high place out of the reach of children" (Christ, even to kill yourself, you need an I.D.) and "for external use only."

A diaphragm for external use only—that's *really* a preventative measure—wear it outside.

"I can't help it if you put twelve million in the wrong box, the one that says 'for external use only.' *Sell* 'em that way. Why, it would cost a mint, we would be bankrupt before the ninth million box . . . . Of *course* we'll sell 'em this way, you idiot. Jesus, Mary, and Joseph, I don't know what the hell you would do if you ever had to make a decision. And I don't wanna hear all that Vance Packard market-research crap like 'It has to have a function.' Its function is the most subtle support, ever, of Catholicism and the philosophy it embraces. We are a fifth column undermining birth control. Put them in the wrong boxes. Change the prices. . . ."

* * *

A man slimeys up to the counter.

"Three Ramses, please."

"Yes sir, will there be anything else?"

"No, that's it. Here."

"That's a 'one,' sir."

Don't tell me they have a tax on safes now?"

"No, the price has gone up—$2.50 for three. . . ."

* * *

"It's a balloon, Ronnie, why did Grandma slap me for playing with it? 'Cause they're my Daddy's balloons?"

"It's not a balloon."

"Yes, it is. My father would never lie to me because my father said there is nothing worse than a liar."

"Lenny thinks scumbags are balloons! Lenny's a dumbell! Ha, ha, Lenny's a dumdum, Lenny's a dumdum. . . ."

* * *

"Daddy, would you ever lie to me? . . . Owww! Stop it, I didn't call you a liar, I said. . . .Owwww!"

"Ralph, that's an eight-year-old boy you're punching. Ralph, will you stop! Oh, you crazy dago, will you—you're going to kill him, listen—"

"Hey, open up in there, it's the super—Come on, open the door—God, if you're not stinking up the halls with those peppers. . . ."

* * *

Oh eight and bloodied but happy, dear sweet god, I'm happier than if I won the Rollfast Whitfield Ointment and Name the Pony Contest.

My father wasn't lying. Ronald Pritchard, homeroom 309, was lying. It *was* a balloon. It took David Niven around the world in eighty days.

That's why I can't wear the damn things, because—regardless of what the Surgeon General of the U.S. Army says—it's a balloon, and if you want to be a silly ass and put a balloon on your wand, go ahead. But please don't do it in front of me. Have some respect for our father who art in heaven hallowed be thy name thy kingdom come thy will be done on earth as it is in heaven.

If you're pure a balloon will take you to Heaven . . . if it's not over five years away, because that's how long they're guaranteed for. Imagine springing a leak while passing Jupiter.

BE PREPARED

by Avery Corman

As we all move forward into the Age of the Pill, we're going to lose some lovely old customs along the way. Like teenage boys carrying a rubber around in their wallets "just in case."

You'd carry one around for months and nothing would ever happen, but every once in a while you'd replace it with a fresh prophylactic, which also gave you a chance to go into the drugstore to buy some. You felt like a big man and you always ordered more than you needed, just to look good.

If the druggist's assistant, usually your age, waited on you, you really felt superior. If there was someone in the store, like a lady, you were too embarrassed to go in and you'd wait outside until she came out. You'd buy all kinds of things you didn't need, just to sound at ease when you asked for the rubbers. When you got home, you hid them in a sock.

Then when you moved into your own apartment, you could keep them right out in the open—like hidden in a drawer, or behind something in the medicine cabinet.

Goodbye, old friends. You were loyal, trustworthy, but we don't need you any more. Today, if you're a hip guy, you don't keep rubbers; you have some vaginal foam in your medicine chest "just in case." If you're super-hip, you keep the Pill on hand. Really. You do. What if something unexpected comes up, and this something unexpected usually takes her Pill at night at her pad, but she's spending the night with you at your pad? . . .

Probably you *could* keep some rubbers around, too, for nostalgia—like 78 RPM records—or maybe to help play Show and Tell with a modern, little *chic*nik who's never seen one. Or you might run into a girl who pulls out this old chestnut: "I don't care what you say.

I think it's the man's responsibility."

Also there are some girls around today who, even though they swing a little, won't obtain any contraceptives for themselves. Because if they did, it might formalize in their minds what they're doing. So they just go on doing it, looking the other way, and trusting to Mathematics, God, or the Resourcefulness of Man. And then there's the new turnabout today, where *you* have to insist on something because *she* doesn't give a damn. "Oh, it's such a drag to use anything. And after all, I'm a natural person."

But for the most part rubbers are fading into folklore. Think of the colorful slang we'll lose. Compared to what a kid could once call somebody, how does it sound yelling: "You, Emko, you!"

And the new protection sounds so clinical. You look into her eyes, overwrought with love and passion, and you whisper: "Darling, are you fitted with an intra-uterine device?"

Lying in the gutter the other morning, just the way you once saw a used rubber, was a discarded diaphragm. Very sophisticated. But look ahead. With the New Enlightenment, even that will be replaced, and lying there instead will be an empty Dialpak Pill dispenser—and kids on their way to school will point to it and giggle.

PRACTICAL USES FOR PROPHYLACTICS NOW THAT THE PILL HAS MADE THEM OBSOLETE

by John Francis Putnam and Tuli Kupferberg

What ever happened to rubbers? Recently a friend, in a moment of dire emergency (his date had forgotten to bring her diaphragm), found himself obliged to go down to the corner drugstore and buy a pack of condoms. It took the clerk 20 minutes to find them, and as he blew the dust off the package he remarked: "Man, I wouldn't trust these too much; they've been on the shelf so long they must be pretty stale by now."

Decidedly, the condom—or "safe"—is a thing of the nostalgic past, killed off by the advent of the Pill. So what is going to happen to that gigantic overstock of rubbers now filling warehouses all over the country? How can the reliable old manufacturers of Trojans, Triple-X, Silver Tex, and Sheiks survive? Here are some suggested uses, then, for that classic American Artifact, the prophylactic, "Sold for the Prevention of Disease Only."

Matching hubcap covers for a 1926 Rolls Royce.

Contact lenses for an octopus.

Drum-head for a pygmy bongo.

Rain-hat for a vulture.

Waterproof stash for scuba heads.

Portholes for midget Japanese submarines.

Sound filters for hi-fi headphones.

Monocle case for Prussian officers.

Weatherproof cover for a policeman's badge.

Disposable sanitary mouthpiece cover for public telephones.

Shower cap for pin-headed "bird girl" from circus freak show.

Portable fallout shelter for cockroaches.

Mute for a kazoo.

Extruded bellybutton truss.

Miniature "poo cushion" (when two are partially welded together).

Tarantula solarium.

Crash helmets for sleeping bats.

Baggies for large kosher pickles.

Emergency gas-tank cover for VW.

Two, joined at edges: a bra for Twiggy.

A pair of earmuffs for LBJ.

Four, as udder-protectors for cows that graze in thistles.

Lens cap for a proctoscope.

Non-skid doorknob cover.

Drip pan for a hashish water pipe.

Mini-yarmulke for Archbishop Cooke to wear at interfaith rallies.

Inner lining for small-size shetl.

Organic roughage for the million alligators who live in the New York sewers, flushed down to them a ton at a time.

Thumb cymbals for spastics.

RUMOR OF THE MONTH

So-called "flying saucers" are actually diaphragms being dropped by nuns on their way to Heaven.

Halo dust cover for small religious statues.

Expendable coin purse for hoarding Kennedy half-dollars.

Lens filter for arty effects when shooting dirty movies.

Microphone muffler for a John Birch Society radio station.

Incubating dish for penicillin spores.

Non-skid crutch tip.

Individual serving dishes for large mushroom caps.

Non-slip thumb cover for bank tellers counting paper money.

All-weather holy wafer cover for Catholic chaplains in Vietnam.

Low-power suction units for 'cupping' people with sensitive skin.

Anal insert to prevent possible hepatitis infection during back-scuttle intercourse.

Protective slip-on covers for autographed World Series baseballs.

Colostomy bag for an armadillo.

Disposable fart catcher.

Local draft board sperm-specimen collector.

Secret message-holder; throw into East River and see who picks it up. Message reads: "Is your Pill chart filled in?"

HOW TO AVOID THE MATERNITY HABIT

[Editor's note: The following news report appeared in the London Observer *on Sunday, May 13, 1962, datelined Rome.]*

When Nuns May Use Birth Control

Three Roman Catholic theologians have expressed the opinion that in times of revolution and violence it is lawful for women, particularly for nuns, to take contraceptive pills and precautions against the danger of becoming pregnant through rape.

Cases in Roman Catholic missions in Africa gave rise to the query, which is answered by Msgr. Pietro Palazzini, Secretary to the Sacred Congregation of the Council, Father Francesco Hürth, S.J., of the Pontifical Gregorian University, and Msgr. Ferdinando Lambruschini, Professor of Moral Theology at the Lateran University.

Their replies appear in a recent issue of *Studi Cattolici*, published under the auspices of the Opus Dei, a powerful Catholic association operating mainly in Spain.

Their defense of the use of contraceptives where there is a danger of rape is a corollary to the well-known Catholic doctrine that it is lawful to resist personal violence. It implies no modification of the Roman Catholic Church's traditional attitude against the use of contraceptives in normal sexual relations.

Father Hürth thinks that it is not "evidently or absolutely unlawful" for nuns to take contraceptive pills as a "preparatory defense" against the consequences of rape, and he thinks the same ruling must apply to other women in a similar position, but not to wives who submit unwillingly to their husbands.

Msgr. Lambruschini recalls Pius XII's ruling that the use of contraceptive pills is legitimate for the treatment of infection but not to prevent the possible or probable ill effects of pregnancy.

The Church's view is documented in Pius XI's encyclic *Casti connubi* and in two decrees of the Holy Office (March 21, 1931, February 24, 1940) and in Pius XII's homily to midwives.

These documents forbid sterilization for eugenic purposes in marriage. Msgr. Lambruschini considers that they must be extended to sexual relations outside marriage but not to cases of rape.

The time factor troubles him slightly because the pills must be taken before the rape occurs.

CASTRO AND THE STEVENSON CONVERTIBLE

SCENE 1

Fidel: You are going to attack Cuba.

Adlai: We are not going to attack Cuba.

Fidel: Why do you say that?

Adlai: Because it would be immoral for us to play the role of an aggressor nation.

SCENE II

Fidel: We have put down the invasion which you were behind.

Adlai: We were not behind the invasion.

Fidel: Why do you say that?

Adlai: Because if we were behind the invasion it would have been successful.

SCENE III

Fidel: Now the truth is out—you were behind the invasion.

Adlai: No matter that it was unsuccessful.

Fidel: Why do you say that?

Adlai: Because it is better to have lied and attacked than never to have been President at all.

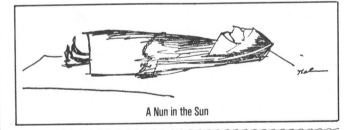

A Nun in the Sun

THE LAST WORD IN CASTRO CONVERTIBLES

From Lee Mortimer's column in the N.Y. *Daily Mirror:*

"I wonder if anyone cares that American babes (blondes preferred) are still being shipped to Castro . . ."

From the *Dan Smoot Report* (Smoot was an FBI agent for 9½ years):

"Castro and many of the men around him are believed to be homosexuals . . ."

News item: A doctor has warned the British Medical Association that—despite assurance that birth control pills are harmless—"evidence has been put before us that there is a possibility that they only delay ovulation." As a result, he said, women taking the pills for much of their life could find themselves pregnant at the age of 70.

HELP STAMP OUT HOSTAGES

by Marvin Kitman

The morning after Fidel Castro proposed his infamous tractors-for-prisoners deal, Sen. Bourke B. Hickenlooper (R.-Iowa) slipped into the White House for a private session. In begging President Kennedy to say "Yankees Si, Cuba No," he was only speaking for many other less influential Americans. Richard Nixon was against the trade because it "would increase the power of a tyrant." Sen. Everett M. Dirksen (R.-Ill.) was against it because he wanted American citizens set free in Red China first. And Sen. Barry Goldwater (R.-Ariz.) was against it—not surprisingly—because it was "unconstitutional." None of these Americans actually wanted to see our freedom-fighters in Cuba executed. It just seemed that way.

A principle was at stake. After hearing that President Kennedy had blessed the Tractors-for-Freedom Committee, Sen. Styles Bridges (R.-N. H.) expressed it best:

"I am, quite candidly, upset that the President endorses a policy of blackmail and ransom. Never before has the U. S. resorted to that."

I agree with Sen. Bridges.

The U.S. had no business getting involved in a tawdry trading deal which really should be the business of private enterprise. Our government never would have been compromised if it had given all its prisoner-trading business to Survivors & Hostages, Inc. of Ridgefield, N.J.

S&H, as it is popularly known, is the world's first trading company specializing in the exchange of prisoners for merchandise. It was founded for the sole purpose of enabling nations to swap prisoners without losing face.

Since I am public relations director at S&H—and a major stockholder—let me explain how it operates.

S&H will be conducting its business through a world-wide network of what we call *redemption centers*. A redemption center has no connection with Billy Graham, being more like a shopping center. It is a place where governments bring the prisoners they have collected during the year, and redeem them for merchandise with S&H Green Stamps.

To find out how much an individual prisoner, or *stamp*, is worth, the participating nation consults the S&H catalog, or *gift book*. The merchandising department at S&H has established a fair rate of exchange on every conceivable type of prisoner—perhaps for the first time giving human life a tangible value.

Here is a sample listing from the S&H gift book (all rates of exchange subject to change without notice):

REVERE WARE. Heavy stainless steel cookware with thick copper bottoms for even heat distribution. Complete set (11 pots). EXCHANGE RATE: One (1) Ethiopian non-commissioned officer, left over from Italio-Ethiopian War (1935-7), under 50 years old, in fair condition.

DAZEY ELECTRIC CAN OPENER. Push-button automatic model. Magnetic lid-lifter. Removable cutting mechanism. EXCHANGE RATE: One (1) Italian non-commissioned officer, under 55 years old, in good-to-fair condition.

The exchange value, of course, is regulated by the condition of prisoners offered for exchange. A clean, mint prisoner, for example, is worth much more in hard goods than a badly-used one.

A nation can also lump its prisoners together into groups, called *books*, and trade them in for a single item in the S&H gift book. Two books of Laotians—either Royal Laotians, Pathet Lao Laotians, or mixed—are worth an RCA Victor Stylist Portable TV set ("Mirror-shaped, 17-inch tube with new slimline styling," according to the S&H catalog).

Having decided on its premium—and this can be a real fun activity, with the whole nation participating in the decision—a government delivers its stamps and books, and takes home its merchandise. Trading the S&H way has its advantages.

First, there can be no ugly recriminations. In capitalist societies like the U.S., no conservative would dare cry "ransom" or "tribute" since S&H is a private enterprise with no more official status than General Motors has when it sells Pontiacs in Poland. Yes, friends, even Red China could unload its American prisoners the S&H way (a Tartan Rotary Power Mower, 2-hp engine, for one businessman).

Governments which save their prisoners and redeem them the easy S&H way get so many wonderful things they desperately need to improve living standards—and it doesn't cost them a penny in hard currency. At best, prisoners usually have only a negative value. It costs money to feed them, and they lie heavy like doughnuts on a nation's conscience. If kept too long in jail, there is a tendency to forget why they were originally incarcerated anyway.

Prisoners, too, will like being traded the S&H way. It saves them wear and tear. Since they will now be considered a natural resource, a demagogue will no more think of crying *paredon* than deliberately setting fire to sugar cane fields or forests.

S&H, in fact, will change the whole concept of *après*-war, a tribute to what American citizens can do for world peace when properly motivated.

Its predecessor in the prisoner-trading business—the Tractors-for-Freedom Committee—was motivated by a sense of guilt at having gotten our Cubans into a hole. To its credit, S&H has been motivated solely by a desire to make money while performing a worthwhile service. A look at the board of directors of Survivors & Hostages, Inc. will prove the sincerity of our motives.

Actually, I am not at liberty to disclose the names of anybody on our board of directors. But I can assure you that they all are the same faceless men who can be found in any real estate syndicate or other ventures which profit from human misery.

Three factors made the founding of S&H inevitable. President Kennedy's announcement that his most-favored prisoner-trading group would be eligible for tax exemptions, and the way banks rushed to offer instant credit ($17,000,000 for tractors, overnight), convinced our people the prisoner-trading business couldn't be a bad business to go into. And the potential market appeared enormous.

Sen. Thomas J. Dodd (D.-Conn.) estimated that Communist prisons alone "now bulged with one million hostages." A market-research firm told S&H that Western prisons also were crowded. The French have Algerian nationalists, the Thais have prisoners left over from Field Marshall Sarit Thanarat's coup; the British have African nationalists, plus a handful of Egyptians from the Suez campaign; the Spaniards have Loyalists; the Guatemalans have Jacobo Arbenz Guzman's people; the Israelis have Arabs; the Italians have some Somalilanders; the Japanese have survivors from the attack on the Panay; the Belgians have one or two Germans left over from their 1923 occupation of the Ruhr; Turkey has Serbs, Bulgarians, and Montenegroans who revolted in 1912. And I wouldn't be surprised if the U.S. is still holding hostages from the Marine invasions of Lebanon, Nicaragua, and Haiti.

The immediate problem facing S&H before it actually opens shop is how to finance the stocking of its redemption centers. Any day now we will urge all Americans to contribute what they can to help our group rescue prisoners from totalitarian jails.

It will take months for most Americans to realize S&H is not a non-profit organization. In the meantime, they will have had the satisfaction of helping both prisoners and S&H at the same time.

Being a private enterprise, we expect the government to help us also. Fast write-offs on prisoner depreciation, depletion allowances, and tax losses are the least we expect. We may be eligible for even more direct public aid, since S&H can help end depressions.

All the merchandise in our redemption centers will be purchased in the U.S. That's only natural, since we make most of the things desired by under-developed nations anyway. But we will play up in our gift book the products of depressed areas, such as rocking chairs.

The other major problem facing S&H is what to do with all its redeemed prisoners. Our thinking thus far is this:

They should be released immediately in the U.S., the home of the free. They could then be sent directly to training camps where the C.I.A. will organize them into volunteer armies. Should a prisoner be recaptured while invading his homeland, S&H, of course, will redeem him again.

And again and again and again.

HOW THE C.I.A. ORIGINALLY PLANNED "CUBAN" ATTACKS ON FLORIDA AND GUANTANAMO BASE

by William Worthy

While in Washington to attend a conference of the Fund for the Republic, I picked up an item about the April invasion of Cuba, through a C.I.A. source who maintains liaison with the U.S.-subsidized counter-revolutionaries in Miami.

Originally, the C.I.A. agents in charge of the invasion planned to dress up several Cuban exiles in the uniform of Fidel Castro's tiny air force, put them in a small bomber, and have them drop one small bomb on both Florida and the Guantanamo Naval Base.

The two sites that had been pinpointed for hits were insignificant insofar as the expected bomb damage was concerned. Nothing of value would be destroyed. But to the American people the "parallel" with Japanese behavior at Pearl Harbor would be instantaneous. The righteous indignation would be equal in intensity and violence.

My source was not certain whether the volunteer Cuban airmen knew that they were marked as candidates for "suicide." But the C.I.A. plan called for them to be "disposed" of after successful completion of their mission. Dead bombardiers tell no tales to the United Nations or to Congressional investigating committees.

Just before the April 17th invasion date, the bombing plan was scrapped, possibly as a result of President Kennedy's public pledge that no U.S. military forces would be used to support the counter-revolutionary invaders.

Fidel Castro has repeatedly warned that a Yankee-directed "Cuban" attack on Guantanamo could be used as a pretext for the dispatch of Marines to "counter-attack" and invade the island. I could not ascertain if the bombing plan has been permanently vetoed, or if it remains in the "active" file, for reconsideration in the next, more dangerous Caribbean crisis.

ON SOCIALIZED MEDICINE

by Henry Morgan

The problem of socialized medicine is a big one, and I'm glad you came to me, Dad. I happen to be an authority on medicine and also on socialization of stuff.

I became an expert on medicine through the kind offices of a great uncle once removed. Isn't it interesting how you can forget a brother you don't like but you can remember (or invent) a relationship to someone you do? He was a dermatologist and when I asked him why some disease or other I was sporting at the time hadn't cleared up, he said, "Son, there really isn't a lot that doctors know for sure, but the thing they know least about is the human skin."

Among doctors there is usually one to whom the others in the fee-splitting group refer as "a great diagnostician." This means that he's the quickest in the bunch to give a name to what the patient died of. I hear that many people are living longer these days owing to increased sanitation and the elimination of scurvy and yaws, but I've never heard anyone even attempt to prove that this is necessarily a good thing. I'm not even sure of what they live longer *than*.

If the Bible is only half kidding, people used to live a heck of a lot longer in the days when North Africa was a cultural hothouse and the Germans were still living in the trees. One of the apparent aims of "medicine" is to keep totterers tottering in vast enclosures built on Florida fill spattered with shuffleboard courts and morticians. The U.S. govvamun says a guy is entitled to quit at sixty-two. At that age they are ready to turn him over to the one-bedroom-jalousied-porch people and the poorer geriatricians.

South Sea Islanders paddle away into the sunset when they've had it. Eskimos wander off to freeze into their own monuments. Hindus set fire to their loved ones in huge ghats, sharing the cost of the charcoal with their friends and neighbors. These people do not have socialized medicine. They do not have special communities and housing developments with ramps for the wheelchairs. No trailer heavens filled with jolly companions in baseball caps and mouths full of fake choppers.

All that these ignorant native goofs have to look forward to is that ol' Mother Iceberg in the sky (Esquimaux), that Holy Cow in Buddha-land (Sikhs), or that 10 to the 23rd power billion cubic miles of galactic dust and thin helium (Captured German Scientists).

Well, we want more than that for *our* senior citizens. And, seriously, folks (since I intend to be one), there must be provision made for people who can't afford to take care of themselves. After spending all that dough on research to keep them alive, there's no sense in allowing them to rheumatize to death. It's too bad that we live in a time when people still talk of *the republic* when they mean they want the State to be Daddy . . . it's a rough dichotomy, doc, but it's *ours*.

It's also rough that medical treatment *should* be available to those who can't afford it, but that the worst thing that can happen to an American is God Forbid somebody should think he's *poor*.

It's too bad, too, that the moment you take a dime from Uncle you lose twenty cents' worth of Freedom, but nobody can even define Freedom anymore and I doubt that they'd care to. We live in a time when everybody has rights and nobody has any responsibilities. It's not my fault that sometimes Freedom means Freedom To Drop Dead because of lack of medical attention, such as it is.

The A.M.A. could have forestalled all this talk by being doctors. In the old days, a doctor took care of the rich and the poor and grumbled about his unpaid bills and managed to live about as long as his patients. That was the old days. Now there are no docs . . . just specialists and politicians. They've managed among them to make two new

IMPROPAGANDA

This chamber-pot of a radio station originally appeared as a full-page, captionless illustration on the back cover of the humor weekly, *El Pitirre* (a small bird indigenous to Cuba which, symbolic of the revolution, attacks vultures). The U.S. State Department pays for the counterrevolutionary broadcasts which emanate from Swan Island, and whose program content ranges from telling Cubans their children will be taken away, to warning them that the Russians are adding a drug to their food and milk which automatically turns people into Communists.

dirty words—Hippocratic (which was already an oath) and Socialist.

In solemn, soul-searching conventions, they have finally reasoned that medicine is for those who pay for it and the dirty socialists can drop dead. This dignified conclusion has been gravely presented to the American people as the medical profession's contribution to the war against godless Communism.

When I was a kid, our family doctor (are they still around?) took care of "his" poor folks for nothing. It didn't occur to him that they were the Red Menace. Today not one out of a hundred ever so much as pokes the emerald clasp of his alligator bag into a clinic.

Federal housing is socialist. Federal aid to schools is socialist. Federal any-damn-thing is socialist. The electric light and power companies scream their heads off at the Tennessee Valley Authority . . . well, why didn't *they* build the dam?

The whole sorry, miserable point is that we have a Federal Government to do what you can't or won't do for yourself. The doctors threw out the poor and the aged poor. All right. I hope the whole thing gets socialized up to hell and gone, and that we fight against becoming a socialist state by becoming a socialist state. That'll show 'em.

If this seems a bit muddled, I would like to remind you that there was a time, very shortly in the past, when a man *did* have the right not to belong to a union, not to have two TVs and a barbecue pit, and the right to fall down in the street of starvation. It is not recorded that many did fall down . . . even in the Great Depression. I believe it was a better time and that many people knew who the hell they were, at least. It was called the good old days, and with plenty of reason.

Well, we've managed to improve everything now to the point where the average American family, given that the leader is thrown out of work for a month, is bankrupt. It's the richest country in the history of the world in which every family owns one-eighteenth of its own home, half a dishwasher and has a five-month equity in a car.

In my little old home town, the wives of ignorant Puerto Rican busboys buy frozen lobster tails fresh from the waters of South Africa. What the hell do *I* know?

Guindon's Burlap Underground

"I'm sorry, madam, but the Shetland pony <u>must</u> have some luggage."

AMAZING KISSING DOLL $5.95

amazing KISSING DOLL amazing KISSING DOLL amazing KISSING DOLL

'Oh, no—I like you for your mind too."

"Don't bother to wrap it—I'll kiss it here."

GREAT MOMENTS IN MEDICINE, #2

A doctor from Pennsylvania wrote to the *Journal of the American Medical Association* in regard to the fat content of semen. A previous item in the *Journal* had stated that normal semen contains "lecithin, cholesterol, and phosphorized fat." Now the physician had this inquiry:

"During a discussion with a young married woman on the many facets of 'married life,' she stated that she enjoys fellatio. It occurred to me that she may be ingesting as much highly concentrated fat each time as would be contained on an untrimmed large steak. This may account for her having trouble losing weight, even though she declares she is watching her diet rigidly. She had also noticed increased development of her breasts. Is there a possible hormonal factor of testosterone or another undiscovered hormone which may be aiding in this reaction and might be helpful to others? Obviously, the imagined or real need for help in this area is costing American women and their husbands millions of dollars each year as well as much emotional turmoil. In Beard-wood's chapter on obesity (in *Cyclopedia of Medicine, Surgery, Specialties . . .*) the possibility of the body converting some portion of protein into carbohydrates is stressed. Is there any newer thought along this line? Some people seem to get fat on air alone, or is this the bloating of starvation?"

This was the *A.M.A. Journal's* answer:

"As far as this consultant is aware while there may be some psychogenic and genetic factors concerned with obesity, it generally can be ascribed to intake of more calories per day than are expended. No cogent scientific evidence is known indicating that body fat is accumulated in any other way; in order to remove fat it is necessary to ingest fewer calories than one expends. It should be remembered that calories are obtained from protein and carbohydrate as well as from fats. In regard to the possibility of fellatio being a contributing factor in obesity, one would be somewhat skeptical. Even assuming an ejaculation of 10 cc. of semen were all fat, this would be only 90 calories. It is extremely doubtful that this would have a significant effect on inability to take off weight unless, of course, it was practiced several times a day."

"No, I don't want a blow job
— I'm a girl."

". . .Because burning my draft card would be meaningless — too indirect — and only a nut would set fire to himself! So I thought, 'Why not set fire to the <u>people</u> on the draft board?. . .'"

AN IMPOLITE INTERVIEW WITH SHEL SILVERSTEIN

Q. Your most famous cartoon shows two men chained to the wall of a prison cell with only one tiny window way above them. They have obviously been there for many years. One is saying to the other, "Now here's my plan." A variation on this theme in a college magazine had one man saying to the other, "Let's be existentialists this week." Is there a story behind it?

A. There's no story behind it. I had an idea for a funny cartoon and I drew it. That's it. Everybody was trying to figure out the psychological and philosophical connotations of this, which is a lot of shit, because I don't do stuff that has any deeper meaning than what the stuff shows. My stuff doesn't try to be symbolic; it just tries to be funny, that's all.

Q. But wasn't it later used in psychological tests to study people's reactions to it?

A. Yeah, it's been used in psychological testing; it's been used by Alcoholics Anonymous to describe courage. You do something, you make it simple, and everybody else starts loading it up with deep meanings. Which is okay with me, if they want to do that. Everybody loves Rorschach tests.

Q. In complete contrast to the two men in that cartoon, you do a lot of traveling in your work—

A. People say, "Oh, great, you're in Hawaii one minute and then the next week you're in Africa, and then you go to Paris, then you go to London," and they think it's great. But the sad thing comes in here—you travel alone. I *tried* traveling with somebody. Sometimes I traveled with the photographer, and even that's rough. I tried traveling with a girl, and that was impossible. So you travel alone. And as soon as I hit a place—say I hit Paris for the first time—well, you're alone in Paris. No friends, no contacts, not a long string of people to call up and say, "I'm here." No addresses, even.

So it takes you a few weeks to really get your feet on the ground, to meet people, and even that's really straining. In about a few weeks, if you're lucky, you're adjusted and you have a few friends, and maybe you know a girl, and maybe you know a couple of decent restaurants and places that are pleasant to go to. And then a week later you leave town and start the whole damned thing over again.

Q. Would you describe the whole Wednesday rat-race mystique of cartooning?

A. We don't call it the rat-race, we call it "making the rounds." I haven't been in it for a while, but I started out doing it when I first came to New York as a free-lance cartoonist for magazines. During the week, you do maybe ten or twelve "roughs"—rough drawings—and on Wednesday you take them around from editor to editor. And they keep handing them back, so you take them to other editors. By the end of the day, you're tired. It's a lot of fun, though. I looked forward to it. It was the one bit of excitement every week. You'd really know how you stood.

Q. But only on Wednesday, right?

A. I don't know why. Why did God say to rest on Sunday? I mean he could've said rest on Thursday. I once brought my stuff on a Tuesday, when I made that first trip to New York. I was nineteen years old, at the Academy of Fine Arts in Chicago, and I was a real hot-shot cartoonist, doing about fifty gags a day. So I decided I was going to New York and try to break the markets. I had a couple of hundred cartoons and hadn't sold anything in about a year, so I figured I'd do it in person.

I got on a Greyhound bus—fortunately, I got a two-way ticket. There were these sailors on the bus, and they had a couple of bottles and got really blasted. There's nothing grimmer or grimier than a long bus ride, where everything gets sort of greyish-brown after a while. You keep stopping in these places for rest that you don't really need, and they have these grim wooden places where they have sandwiches wrapped in cellophane. Finally, we got to New York. I don't know what day I arrived but it wasn't what the editors call a "seeing day." Nobody would see me at all. And they wouldn't have seen me anyway, because they only see guys who've *sold* stuff.

So finally I went to *Collier's*, and Gurney Williams was the cartoon editor there—he was like a legend among young cartoonists. I really, physically pushed my way by to see him. And he said okay—I guess he was scared—and told me to come back after he had lunch. He looked through a hundred cartoons, the greatest ones ever drawn—at nineteen, I was doing only great cartoons—and he bought none.

And so I went back to Chicago. I got in the bus, and there was a girl sitting next to me, and I thought, well, at least it won't be a total loss, you know.

So about half an hour outside of New York, she had gone to sleep on my shoulder. I thought, well, this is the first step. Next thing I knew, the girl got car-sick, puked all over my shoulder. I spent the whole trip ringing for the bus-driver to stop, and she kept puking and moaning, and I kept washing my shoulder off. Not only Gurney Williams, but this girl was vomiting on me. Everything was wrong. There were some pretty horrendous experiences in the YMCA, too. Because at that time I thought this was a place where all the he-men gather. Where *young Christian men* gather, you know. And it's *not quite* that. It makes Sixth Avenue and 8th Street late at night look like a Cub Scout meeting.

Q. For the benefit of our out-of-town readers, could you be more specific?

A. Faggots!

Q. Do you find that people have come to associate your beard with beatnikism?

A. Yeah, but I just have the beard because I think I look better with it, and I feel better with it. It makes me look older; I don't know if that's good or bad. But it's not done out of any *rebellion* or to attract attention. So now, when people ask, I look sort of sad and say, "It covers the scar." It's a very romantic thing to say, isn't it? But, you know, it's a good conversation-starter. People are pretty shy and reserved, mostly—whereas, if you've got some lemon meringue pie on your shoulder, they've got an excuse to talk to you. They can say, you know, "You've got some lemon meringue pie on your shoulder."

Q. When Lenny Bruce was in town, he heard about how they couldn't sing folk songs in Washington Square Park. After listening to them, he figured that it was meant literally—"They can't sing." *How do you feel about folk singing?*

A. The kids that like folk music, some of them get to be *fanatical* little sons-of-bitches. The folk music seems to be more than just music to them; it's a real statement, a protest, a real fist in the air, you know? A couple of weeks ago, I was walking in the park—it was Sunday morning, and they'd allowed the folk singers to come back in—and this one eighteen-year-old kid is sitting there, and on his guitar is a sign that says, "This Machine Fights for Freedom." This is too much—a freedom-fighting machine. It's a goddam *guitar*, is what it is, and it don't fight for nothin'—it plays. Unless maybe he swings it, he hits with it, I don't know.

Q. Are your children's books intended for adults, too?

A. I'd like my children's books to be good for everybody. I think that maybe you can find a certain thing that will appeal to adults, and the kids will love it too. You also find this modern type of children's book that is a real atrocity—the precious children's book. It really is for the adult. Some girl does a series of silly-ass illustrations: she tries to imagine how a six-year-old would draw, and no goddam six-year-old wants to look at illustrations that look like they're done by a six-year-old.

Q. What about the content of stories themselves?

A. Well, everything is being censored, even the old stories—it's amazing what they've done. I remember *Little Red Riding Hood*, and you know what happens there: the wolf eats her up, and that's it. But I looked at a modern *Red Riding Hood*—which was *after* this edition—she was eaten up by the wolf and then the woodsman comes in and chops him open, and she pops out good as new. A few years later you've got—she's not eaten by the wolf, but the woodsman comes in and chops the wolf open, and the *grandmother* pops out as good as new. Eventually, you're going to have the woodsman kill the wolf before he's eaten *anybody*, I guess. Pretty soon, they're going to turn the wolf into a Saint Bernard.

Q. Have any other fairy tales gone through an evolution like this?

A. In *The Three Little Pigs*, when we were kids, they were eaten up one at a time. The wolf gobbles up the one in the twig house, gobbles up the one in the *papier maché* house or whatever it is, and finally he comes to the brick house and he's stymied. He falls down the chimney, and that's it for him. He's boiled. But now, each little pig runs to the other's house. So the wolf blows down the straw house, and the little pig sneaks out the back door and runs to the twig house. He blows down the twig house, and the little pigs run to the brick house. The goddam wolf doesn't have a chance.

Q. Is your Uncle Shelby's ABZ Book *for children or adults or both?*

A. It's not for children. In fact, children really shouldn't see it at all. It's strictly for adults. It'd be nice if kids liked it, too, but there's really rotten information in it for kids. Things to really mess them up.

Q. Like, for instance?

A. Like "B is for Baby. Picture the baby. The baby is fat. The baby is pretty. The baby can laugh. The baby can play. Play, baby, play. Pretty, pretty baby. Mommy loves the baby more than she loves you." But that's the only one of those I'm gonna do. The other children's books after that will be really straight children's books.

Q. You do most of your work for Playboy *Magazine; do you personally fit in with the* Playboy *image?*

A. No. *Playboy* believes in being a bachelor, and I don't want to stay a bachelor.

Q. Do you exploit your professional success in establishing personal relationships?

A. What do you mean by *personal relationships* with that rotten glint in your eye? You see, your readers never see this rotten, lecherous, drooling *look*—this can't come across in the pages—that comes into *your* eye. So you leer across at me, drooling, saying "personal relationships. . . ."

Q. I just mean that since you're on one of the lower rungs of being a public personality, do you find you make it easier with people? Not just girls.

A. Well, girls are people—can I point that out? But, yeah, you get along better if people like you from the first—if they like you "in front," as they say in the hip circles. If people really, sincerely like your work, they're going to want to know you and want to like you, right? If they don't even *know* your work, but know you're supposedly sort of important, then this is impressive to them, too. This is a real American characteristic, where "success" doesn't have to be a success *at* anything—just being a "success" makes you worth knowing and worth being around. I was at a party not too long ago, and I was introduced to some girl, and she said, "Oh, you did my favorite cartoon. You wanna know which one it was?" And she described one of Feiffer's cartoons.

SORRY, RIGHT NUMBER

Let us take a couple of actual news items—and follow them to their fatalistic conclusions.

News item: Two hundred women students at an ivy-covered college have been offered insurance policies against pregnancy. Payments and all matters connected with the policy would be handled in the "strictest secrecy." Any policy holder, discovering that she was going to have a baby, would be paid $700.

(SCENE: A sorority house at an ivy-covered college.)

"Georgie, it's okay, you don't have to—you know—this time."

"What do you mean?"

"You said yourself it's like shaking hands with gloves on, that way."

"Well, unless you go out and get fitted—"

"Oh, no, I couldn't do that."

"I told you, just get a ring and tell them you're *married*, if you're so embarrassed."

"It's not that, Georgie, it's just that—you know—it would take away all the spontaneity and everything."

"Well, we have to use *something*. I mean you don't want me to start taking chances, do you?"

"That's what I'm trying to tell you, Georgie. I took out this special accident insurance policy . . ."

(SCENE: Several months later—the telephone rings.)

"Hello."

"Georgie, I have to talk to you."

"What's the matter?"

"I'm late—I waited ten whole days before I called you—I didn't want to worry you if I wasn't sure."

"Oh, geez, does it have to happen during finals—"

"I'm sorry, Georgie, I know how busy you are studying and everything."

"That's all right. I'd want to know, of course."

"Georgie, what are we gonna *do*?"

"We'll figure out something—at least you're insured."

"What? . . .Oh, just a minute . . It's for you—an obscene phone call!"

"That's what I have to tell you, Georgie. I was also late paying the premium."

News item: President John F. Kennedy and Premier Nikita Khrushchev look with favor upon a proposal for a direct telephone line from the White House in Washington to the Kremlin in Moscow. Both leaders feel this might prevent accidental nuclear war. A direct telephone line is necessary because in this electronic age the guidance systems of missiles are not completely reliable and, in the event of an accidental firing, every second counts. For example, it would take approximately 33 minutes for an Atlas missile to travel from Vandenberg Air Base in California to Moscow. The distance between Moscow and the east coast of the United States can be covered in even less time.

(SCENE: The White House.)

"Okay, Mrs. Kennedy, where do you want it installed?"

"I think it'll go nice right here in the baby's room."

"Ain't you afraid it's gonna wake the kid up when it rings?"

"Well, we hope it never *will* ring, you see."

"Oops, I put my equipment down on these diapers."

"Oh, that's all right, they have to go to the laundry today anyway."

"Now here's the phone. Turquoise, like you ordered."

"Yes, the color is lovely, but I'm afraid you'll have to make another trip. I specifically asked for the Princess model."

(SCENE: Several months later—the telephone rings.)

"Hello."

"Jack?"

"Speaking."

"Hi, this is Nikita."

"Niki, how are you?"

"Oh, can't complain. How's yourself?"

"Vigorous as ever, thanks. How's the family?"

"Everybody's just fine. Except Nina, she has a little cold. We have these sudden changes in the weather here, you know. How are Jackie and the children?"

"Well, we're having a little trouble with Caroline. My brother Bob thinks it's sibling rivalry."

"Probably it's just a phase she's going through."

"Yeah, kids."

"Listen, I'll tell you why I called. Your boys in the Strategic Air Command will be seeing something on their radar screens, and I just thought I'd let you know that it's because we set off a test missile with an atomic warhead and our guidance system went slightly out of whack. So please don't think we're starting nuclear warfare against your country."

"Well, gee, Niki, I certainly appreciate your taking the trouble to call."

"No trouble, Jack, no trouble at all. Because otherwise you might think it was a sneak attack."

"Of course. This way, not only do I have time to speed our Civil Defense forces into action, but you don't have to worry about any massive retaliation on our part."

"All right, Jack, swell. I won't keep you, then; I know you must have things to do."

"Right, Niki. Thanks for calling."

"Give my regards to Lyndie and Lady Bird."

"Will do."

"And remember—don't call us, we'll call you."

THE OBSCENE TELEPHONE CALLING SERVICE

by Marcia Seligson and Janet Sorkin

About a year ago, a friend of ours was awakened at 3 A.M. by her telephone. When she picked it up, all she heard was a quiet, rhythmic breathing which seemed to increase in volume every time she groggily groaned, "Who is this?" or "Hello, hello, hello" or "What the hell do you *want*?"

By the time it dawned upon her that she was the bedfellow of an obscene phone caller, he'd already had his way with her and hung up.

The next morning, she lost no time in calling all her friends and broadcasting what had happened. "You'll never guess what happened to *me* last night," she announced in the same tone in which she might have said, "*I* met Richard Burton at a party last night and just *guess* what we did!"

We thought to ourselves: How come she gets calls like that? We're prettier than she is, much more charming, and never once in our lives had we picked up the phone at any hour to hear a series of dirty words or passionate breathing.

Our friend was called again the following night and then the night after. The third night, she had a pajama party for five girlfriends so we could take turns listening. She seemed to be a bit frightened and even notified the police. But when The Breather stopped calling after a week, she became rather depressed and withdrawn, sat at home by the phone, and finally cried to us: "What did I do wrong?"

We came to the realization that the obscene phone call can be regarded simply as a reflection of our changing morality. After all, what better illustrates frenetically-groping sexual abandon, coupled with total negation of personal commitment? It's merely the end product of "I don't want to get involved."

Unable to ignore its logical place in the new set-up, we decided to make money with it. And so, early this year, we established the Obscene Telephone Calling Service.

On the assumption that there are thousands of people who have never received an obscene phone call, want one, but have absolutely no means to acquire one, we have set up a subscription series wherein we service, for a monthly fee, both callers and callees according to their individual requirements.

The Callee gets phoned at irregular intervals a minimum of 10 times a month. The subscribing Caller is given five different phone numbers each month along with the *first* name of the recipient. He must sign an agreement to phone each party no less than 10 and no more than 25 times during the month. Caller and Callee must agree *never* to meet or speak on any level other than that specified.

The point of our service is to be very personalized. We make several preliminary screening calls to sound out our clients, so that we can judge what sort of obscenity will offend them most. Naturally, the gender of the Callee makes a great deal of difference. For example, a relatively uneducated man is probably most offended at comments linking him and his mother romantically. Masculine-voiced men should be mocked about their homosexual tendencies; meek-sounding little old ladies should be accused of the most insatiable sexual appetites.

As a corollary service, we supply literate and meaty scripts to those amateur Callers among our subscribers who either lack the essential imagination and vocabulary or who are simply running out of material.

We have First Date scripts with just a few brief introductory "goldangs" and "pshaws." Then, as the couple gets to know each other better, the Caller can launch into the more personalized communication, out of which they establish their own unique rapport.

We have intellectual obscenity scripts, low-class obscenity scripts, adorational obscenity scripts, hostile obscenity scripts. Callers who specialize in absolute silence need no script at all, of course.

For the Callee, whose role is not just the usual passive one, we have Appropriate Reaction scripts, which range in tone from "What are you—some kind of pervert or something?" to "Say, you're a very sick person, you need help" and "I hope you still respect me—I don't do this for everyone."

The inevitable offshoot of our service is to expand internationally, especially into backward areas where the obscene phone call is probably unknown. Obviously there are inherent obstacles in trans-oceanic obscene phone calls—such as language barriers and time differences—but the main difficulty is the cost of the call, which is always charged to the Callee and thus would be prohibitive in many cases. We shall, however, apply for federal assistance.

The loveliest quality of our service is that by *our* complete control of the relationships from inception through finale, nobody gets hurt and everyone gleans from the situation exactly what he or she wants. A rejection such as befell our friend would never happen with our service. As long as she kept up her payments, she would be telephoned frequently.

But we can even accommodate those who *wish* to be rejected. The Caller just threatens never to phone again; each time he tells the Callee that she's just not worthy of his efforts.

And consider all the Callers who, without our service, would latch onto people who aren't interested in establishing this particular kind of contact and hang up immediately. We eliminate the possibility of this repeated, self-demeaning rebuff and frustration.

Again, there is the possibility that the client really *wants* to be rejected and humiliated—a complexity with which we are fully prepared to cope. A sample line from the specialized Appropriate Reaction script reads: "You're not so dirty—I've had calls from a sweet *spinster* 20 times more obscene than you!"

SURVIVAL IS IN FASHION
by Ed Koren

This year's theme in men's clothing is styled by the National Academy of Sciences: "Adequate shielding is the only means of preventing radiation casualties."

Four of the more popular models are illustrated here.

1. The distinctive "diplomat" business suit. Superior protection is combined with "lithe-line" mobility in this steel-and-aluminum classic.

3. Uncompromising protection for those who <u>must</u> travel. Attractive single-piece "down-under" suit available in a wide variety of patterns and colors.

2. Nature's most invulnerable animal has provided this "executive retreat" with maximum self-contained safety-proven capabilities.

4. This snugly-fitting outfit designed for casual wear around the shelter, is entirely bullet-proof, with zippered ammunition pockets, padded cap.

Editor's note: Frank Interlandi gets an occasional rejection on his syndicated feature, and *The Realist* will be privileged to publish a few of them. We weren't sure whether the one below was actually sent to the syndicate, so we wrote to Interlandi and asked. This is his reply:

"Glad you liked the cartoon and plan to use it. I was hoping you would. Actually, I did the cartoon with the intention of sending it to the syndicate, but when it came to putting the punch line in, I couldn't think of anything but 'I'd shit!' . . . the more lines I tried, the less funny it got, and the surer I was that the original line was the best and the only one . . . it was a genuine reaction; *i.e.*, the feeling of being helpless and returning to infantilism . . . But why do I have to explain a cartoon? Naturally I knew the syndicate would reject it, so they never did see it . . . but I wanted to see it printed and I thought of you."

HOW I FORTIFIED MY FAMILY FALLOUT SHELTER

by Marvin Kitman

Civilian-defense bulletins are mum on the subject of small arms as a tool of survival.

—*The Nation*
November 4, 1961

Ex-President Dwight D. Eisenhower said the other day that Americans will have to live in perpetual fear of atomic attacks, as our forefathers lived in fear of Indian attacks. A little tension is good for people, he also said. "It keeps people on their toes."

I have been on my toes ever since I decided to arm my fallout shelter, and I'm getting tired. The reason I'm so tense is that I live in fear my neighbors will pre-empt my fallout shelter because it is inadequately fortified.

I think I have a good reason to fear my neighbors in Leonia, N.J. They are mostly nice people, but intellectuals—college professors, artists, scenic designers—none of whom are planning to build fallout shelters. In theory, I guess, they would rather be dead than Red. But in practice they all are planning to use my shelter. I was sure of that the day I started digging.

"What are you digging?" one of my neighbors asked as I lifted the first shovelful of earth from my greensward.

"A chicken house," I said, as neighborly as I could be under the circumstances.

Actually, I was digging a pit for the machine gun I hoped to buy to cover a sector of the front opposite my house that would include his house. I couldn't tell him that. His kids play with my kids.

Before the Berlin crisis, I was the most candid person on my block when it came to talking about home improvements. But so rapidly did my concept of community relations change after Berlin, I was in the vanguard of those Americans building fortifications for the shelter *before* they started on the shelter itself.

A clergyman helped me realize that I wasn't cut out to be my brother's keeper. "If you are secure in your shelter, and others try to break in," the Rev. L.C. McHugh told me and other readers of the Jesuit weekly, *America*, "they may be treated as unjust aggressors and repelled with whatever means will effectively deter their assault. Does prudence also dictate that you have some 'protective device' in your survival kits, e.g., a revolver for breaking up the traffic jams at your shelter door? That's for you to decide."

I decided to cast my lot with God's army in the coming war for survival, but I'd be damned if I'd follow Father McHugh's advice on "protective devices," judging by his offhand remark about those "e.g. revolvers." With an e.g. revolver—or any other caliber revolver, for that matter—a man would be more likely to hit the side of his neighbor's barn than his neighbor. I have nothing against my neighbor's barn. So I decided to go to the proper secular authorities for advice.

"Can I help you?" asked a very competent grey-haired

lady—she looked like she had already survived two wars—at the reception desk of the Office of Civil Defense on Lexington Avenue in New York City.

"Yes," I said. "I would like to have a manual of arms for my fallout shelter. I want to know what kind of arms Civil Defense recommends."

She started to laugh, and I joined in as disarmingly as I could to convince her I wasn't a Communist or an FBI agent. In embarrassment, I pretended to study the stockpiles of Wheeling garbage cans, Scott's toweling, and other tools of survival that filled the Office of Civil Defense.

She gathered together a packet of already published bulletins on all the tools of survival OCD recognized, from hand-crank air blowers to chemical toilets, and told me not to worry about my neighbors. "He who lasts, laughs," I grumbled on the way out.

That's how I discovered the arms information lag in the Office of Civil Defense. As I rode back to New Jersey on the bus—my town is only a mile-and-a-half from the George Washington Bridge, or just about where a bomb would land if the Russians aimed at Columbus Circle—it occurred to me thousands of other Americans were probably leaving their OCDs just as empty-handed.

There is a vital need for a manual of arms for the fallout shelter. To help plug this information gap until Hanson Baldwin tackles the job, I think my experiences may be of assistance.

The first thing I did before arming my projected fallout shelter without the advice of the OCD was to go home and take a long hard look at my block through field glasses. The idea was to study the land to see if it offered any natural defense advantages. There is no sense building a Maginot Line if your split-level is on a peninsula like Corregidor. I saw one woman undressing in her bedroom, so the time I spent with the glasses wasn't a total loss, even though I know my block like the back of my hand. It is hilly and curved like a crescent.

I then estimated the size of the traffic jam expected at my shelter door, and how much firepower would be needed to keep it clear.

The best way to keep the crowd down, I decided, was to seed the front lawn with anti-personnel mines. A machine gun dug in near the shelter doorway would take care of strays and parents who sent other kids ahead to test the minefield.

But I was worried about the people five houses down, on the far side of our curved street, out of the machine gun's trajectory. Their six-year-old girl is always beating up my four-year-old son, and I recognize concealed hostility when I see it. Since the best defense is an offense, I would need a mortar to cover that flank.

And, finally, it seemed mandatory that I have an anti-tank weapon of some sort to stop the rush of station wagons which I feared would really cause a traffic jam in front of my house as soon as Conelrad told everybody to go to my shelter.

With the advanced planning completed (G-2), arming the fallout shelter next became a job of logistics and supply (G-3). Here is where the Office of Civil Defense could have saved me a lot of unnecessary digging.

"Do you have any machine guns in stock?" I asked a gun dealer in Manhattan whose name I found by looking in the Yellow Pages of my telephone book. The way he hung up on me, I felt like the purchasing agent for some 26th of August Movement on the Attorney General's list, instead of a man who was only following the advice of a priest.

The Office of Civil Defense could have told me that "machine guns" are dirty words in the business of selling arms to the public. The federal government tries to inhibit the sale of automatic weapons to its citizens, in line with its traditional vigilance against the violent overthrow of the Republic.

Before anyone can buy a machine gun in the U.S., he has to submit an application to—of all places—the Alcoholic Tax Unit of the Department of Treasury, and buy a $200 tax stamp. Even if the T-men allow you to buy a tax stamp, many states— New York is one—specifically prohibit the sale of machine guns.

In New Jersey, though, you can buy a machine gun if you have a legitimate reason, like being a chief of police. As of this writing, arming the fallout shelter does not qualify you.

A way out of the *cul de sac*, according to a lawyer who once worked in the U.S. Attorney's office, is to start a gun museum in your fallout shelter.

That seemed like wasted effort to me, particularly since the federal government doesn't seem to be worried by a *coup* backed up with so-called big-bore weapons. The first afternoon I went shopping, I was offered enough mortars, anti-tank guns, and howitzers to overthrow the entire state of Delaware.

For the reader who likes the convenience of one-stop shopping, I call to his attention the Service Armament Company, 689 Bergen Boulevard, Ridgefield, N.J. (Phone: WHitney 5-2500). They don't ridicule the man who fortifies his fallout shelter. The salesman who took my shopping list was as grim as an appliance salesman.

He led me into the company's armory. "Here is a Russian 120 mm. mortar, colossal and devastating," he said. "It was used in the Suez campaign but is in almost new condition because it belonged to the Egyptian Army. Only $125.00."

I shook my head.

"I understand," he said. "Many of our customers don't like to buy Commie equipment. Here's a U.S. 60 mm. mortar, complete with bipod and base plate. An ideal item for your den or front lawn. It can easily be packed into the trunk of any automobile. This is the perfect tool for demolishing houses or plinking on a Sunday afternoon. We offer these hard-shooting mortars at the popular price of $125.00 each. Shells are only $1.50 each."

I told him that was too dear.

"Well, here's a Finnish 50 mm. mortar for only $29.95."

"Wrap it up," I said.

The next item on my list was an anti-tank weapon. "How about a 3.5 bazooka?" he asked. "These are original German bazookas used in World War II against the Allies. They are only $19.95 the piece, and an ideal weapon for protecting life and property against enemy tanks."

He misinterpreted the thoughtful look on my face—I was only thinking whether my wife could lift it—and he turned on the hard sell.

"*They hit hard,*" he said. "These bazookas hit hard enough

to stop any vehicle up to a medium tank. The 3.5-inch rocket it uses functions on the heat principle, which is a melting process designed to burn a hole through armor plate and spray the interior of the vehicle with a shower of molten steel, thereby causing the occupants great discomfort."

"I don't doubt it," I said. "But don't you have anything on wheels?"

"Certainly," he said, propelling me to the rear of the armory. "Here is a German Rheinmetall anti-tank cannon of the latest design, chambered for the 3.7 cm. PAK hyper-velocity round. These powerful guns were made in Sweden for the German Army during World War II and until recently were the standard light artillery weapon of many European countries. This cannon will stop any vehicle or light tank within a mile."

"Don't you have anything I can attach to the back of my station wagon?"

"Here is a Swedish anti-tank cannon made by Boffors for the armies of Scandinavian countries. It is chambered for the 37 mm. Boffers round which we have in large quantities. It comes complete with shield and gunner accessories. Price: $300.00. The rubber tires are in good condition."

"Wrap it up," I said.

Having purchased the bare minimum for survival, I next faced several problems common to all who would try to protect the family fallout shelter.

A minor problem was how to camouflage the stuff, since there is no point to flaunting your equipment. I found sandbags to be less offensive if they are made by filling empty garden fertilizer bags with sand. A mortar broken down to its component parts looks like plumbing, and an anti-tank gun imaginatively treated with tarpaulin can pass for a piece of lawn furniture.

But the real problem for the man who has fortified his suburban fallout shelter and must go to work every day in a large metropolitan area is this:

The first time the boss gives the okay to go home early because an atom bomb will either be dropped or already has fallen—how will he ever get home in time to man his guns?

In my case, I will have to get over the George Washington Bridge. I suspect there will be a considerable delay. Who will man my fortifications? My wife?

I don't know about your wife, but my wife is completely inadequate behind a Swedish Boffors gun. I wouldn't even trust her to run the mortar. She is afraid to kill a bug. What is worse, she likes our neighbors. With me in the city, I wouldn't put it past her to invite all *her* neighbors into our shelter.

And by the time I arrived home from the office, there'd be no room for me.

Obviously, the only way those of us who have built fallout shelters can reasonably expect to get into them during an emergency is to hire guards to keep the neighbors at bay until we get home from the office. The number of guards necessary in a Home Guard, of course, depends on the individual situation. The Office of Civil Defense has made no general recommendations on the subject.

Hiring guards, of course, will help eliminate unemployment, particularly in depressed areas. But it could lead to a return to a feudalistic state when most landowners maintained private armies.

Status-seekers would undoubtedly hire more guards than they actually needed, just to be one up on their neighbors. And families without fallout shelters may even feel pressure to hire guards, because their kids will ask how come *we* don't have guards, like the Joneses down the street?

Then the whole block would live in fear that your guards don't accidentally open fire on somebody else's guards. With tensions running so high, this could trigger the kind of blood bath that would decimate a whole town.

I have a sneaking suspicion that Father McHugh is really a Communist dupe.

YES, VIRGINIA, THERE IS A SANITY CLAUSE

"A man has a moral right to use violence to keep his unprepared neighbor from entering the family fallout shelter after a nuclear attack, a Roman Catholic priest declared in . . . the Jesuit magazine America."

—The New York Times

"I'm sort of glad they've got the atomic bomb invented. If there's ever another war, I'm going to sit right the hell on top of it. I'll volunteer for it, I swear to God I will."

—Holden Caulfield

With its usual sterling display of objectivity, *Time* Magazine says, in regard to the ethics of shooting your unprepared neighbor if he tries to get into your fallout shelter, "Most Christians would probably recall the Biblical parallel of the wise and foolish virgins—and draw their own inference."

Actually, when you come right down to it, neighbor-shooting is a totally reasonable conclusion to reach, once you accept the premise of *building* a family fallout shelter . . . and the premise for building one can be as theologically-oriented as the rationale for killing thy neighbor. Louisiana politician Frank B. Ellis puts it this way: "It is just as much a sin to commit suicide by indirection as it is to put a gun up to your head and pull the trigger." Therefore, building a family fallout shelter is "just the same as not committing suicide."

The man, then, who wrote to the N.Y. *Daily News*, "I am trying grimly to bring up a family of five decently on $90 a week, supplemented by any weekend work I can get," would obviously be classified by *Time* as a "foolish virgin."

On the other hand, a gag in the guise of a classified ad in *The Californian* announced: "Protect Your Social Status—Dummy vents and a trapdoor in lawn look like real fallout shelter . . ."

In Boston, a real ad hawked a "shelter" for only $4.50; it was a crowbar, to be used for opening a manhole cover in case of nuclear attack.

And in Denver, a free-enterpriser came out with a large plastic bag which, he claimed, would provide complete protection against fallout; all you'd have to do would be to crawl inside and pull the zipper. But when the local Better Business Bureau man asked him how the bag's occupant would be able to breathe,

the promoter admitted that this was something he hadn't worked out yet.

If he's a smart businessman, he'll set up a deal and sell his entire inventory to a certain company which currently has on the market a "burial suit"—a $50 plastic wrapper for anyone who dies in a shelter; it contains chemicals "to keep odors down" and can be used as a sleeping bag by the living.

The psychological ramifications of sleeping in what may turn out to be one's very own shroud, have yet to be determined. The psychological ramifications of sleeping in a fallout shelter in the first place, have *already* been determined by at least one company. Shelters for Living, Inc. has a custom-built fallout shelter on display at Grand Central Terminal. Dr. Frank Caprio, psychiatric consultant to the designer, says the shelter was built "in such a manner as to assure privacy for adults—so that children aren't exposed to influences detrimental to their sexual development."

Which is quite a valid point. Think how it'll be in all those *other* shelters—the ones *without* psychiatric consultants. . . .

"Mommy! Daddy! All those bombs bursting out there! All those people screaming! I'm afraid!"

"Shut up and stop watching us."

It's bad enough you'll have to explain nuclear warfare to the kid; you don't want him developing any voyeuristic tendencies *too*.

Apparently, sex in the shelter is an officially approved activity; after all, it was the N.Y. Civil Defense director *himself*, Major General Robert E. Condon, who formally opened the shelter on display at Grand Central Terminal. But did you ever notice that there is *one particular item* which nobody ever mentions for inclusion in your family fallout shelter? Not a contraceptive in a carload.

Time Magazine lists "toothache pills, tranquilizers, deodorants" and, for the woman of the house, "sanitary napkins which can double as bandages"—but nary a word about milady's diaphragm. In like manner, Major General Condon studiously ignores the condom.

Perhaps it's just a matter of maintaining peacetime hypocrisy . . . and all shelters will have to be stamped with this legend: "For the prevention of fallout only."

It certainly does give you a warm feeling inside to be able to identify with our National Purpose. As an indication of how the fallout shelter really brings to the individual a sense of *personal* involvement in the international crisis, merely consider this statement by Salt Lake City's Civil Defense director: "Some get right to the point; others hem and haw, but they all want to know—what do we do when we want to get to the toilet?"

Especially gratifying is the way famous Hollywood stars (who constitute, of course, an exception to the above worry) are really getting into the spirit of things. Jane Powell, for example. As Sheilah Graham writes:

Next to television, the biggest project in the life of Miss Powell is the bomb shelter she and her husband built. "Everyone laughed when we decided to build it, but, as my husband says, 'What's more important, life or money?' " The bomb shelter that can be entered only from inside the house—"to avoid overcrowding"—has room for from ten to fourteen people.

Just to be sure of survival in the nuclear age, Jane says, "We have a second bomb shelter, our boat. We have food and water stocked in both for a year. Our children are so excited by it all they can't wait." I searched for a smile on Janie's face, but she was deadly serious.

Those of you who don't wish a peace scare to deprive your children of the happiness that only devastation can bring, will be pleased to learn that the latest Sears Roebuck catalog includes a doll house with a fallout shelter.

A STATISTICAL SUGGESTION

by Kurt Vonnegut

The duration of a marriage can be measured realistically for the first time with a unit which I have invented. It is the *man-woman hour*, which is an hour of wakefulness spent by a man and a woman together.

I have calculated that the average schmuck spends 2,000 hours somewhere near his wife each year, which gives us the equation: 2,000 man-woman hours equal one matrimonial year. Fifty thousand man-woman hours entitles a couple to a silver wedding anniversary, 100,000 to a gold. It is possible, for instance, for a couple married at 20 and running some sort of Ma & Pa enterprise to be entitled to diamonds after being married only 29 calendar years.

Look how much more meaningful divorce statistics can become: "Mrs. John Doe, 23, applied for divorce today and asked custody of her children, Sherryl Anne, 6, and Kenneth, 3. The Does have been married for 40,000 man-woman hours, or 20 matrimonial years." Or: "Mrs. Richard Roe was granted a divorce today, terminating a marriage that lasted only 76 man-woman hours. The Roes were married in 1937."

"And what's more, my opponent is mentally cruel . . ."

A CHILD'S PRIMER ON DIVORCE

Oh, look, Mommy and Daddy are having another fight. Is it just an attention-getting device this time? Listen. They are having an adult discussion. They are agreeing on a separation. That means you will come from a broken home. What a shame. Even if they fight all the time they should stay together for your sake. Now you will be insecure.

Mommy and Daddy are modern people. They drink Pepsi-Cola. They also have a modern marriage. They left the word "obey" out of the ceremony. Wasn't that modern? They didn't leave out the words "love" and "honor." Mommy and Daddy are only modern, not avant garde. They left "till death do us part" in the ceremony, too. But they are going to get a divorce anyway. They don't have to obey their marriage vows. Lucky thing they left out that word.

What is to be done to keep Mommy and Daddy together? *The Ladies' Home Journal* will help. They have a regular feature in their magazine. It is called "Can This Marriage Be Saved?" Readers send in Betty Crocker boxtops and try to guess the correct answer.

Maybe Mommy and Daddy will go on television. There is a program all about *Divorce Court*. Dr. Paul Popenoe is the master of ceremonies. He wears glasses. Sometimes while the commercial is on, the actors have a reconciliation. It is a real fun show.

Mommy and Daddy live in New York State. To get a divorce there one of them has to commit adultery. Daddy has a tryst with a girl. Mommy raids the joint. She brings along a photographer. Mommy has secretly been having an affair with the photographer. What Daddy doesn't know won't hurt him. He always wanted to be on page three of the *Daily Mirror* anyhow. Mommy made sure his shorts were ironed.

Benjamin Brenner lives in Brooklyn. He is a Supreme Court Justice there. He makes decisions. He decided that raiding the joint is illegal from now on. Unless you have a search warrant. Then it's legal, but you have to knock first and say "Benny sent me." This new rule doesn't count for hotel rooms. Then it's okay to raid the joint. So Daddy better get his own apartment. Judge Brenner is really under the thumb of real-estate agents.

There is another way. Mommy can go to Reno. She lives there for six weeks. That is called "establishing residence." Reno is Keno but Alabama is Quicker. Same-day service. The Chamber of Commerce invites lawyers to practice there. They are promised the run of the divorce mill. More married people are traveling to Alabama than ever before. They are called Freedom Riders.

Here comes the Governor of New York. See him eat the potato knish. He wants to get a divorce. He will establish residence in another state. But then he can't be Governor. Instead he will get a divorce in New York. But you know what that means. Dirty, dirty. Some deserving girl will get the assignment. This is known as political patronage. The Governor has a horny dilemma, though. Either he commits scandal or he commits perjury. Maybe he will propose a new law.

"You are underprivileged, bitter, culturally deprived, tired of being pushed around, determined to abolish the stigma of second-class citizenship . . ."

APRIL FOOL

WENDE

Q. *As a night club performer, you're subject to the occupational hazard of hecklers. Have you found offensive racial references incorporated into the heckling?*

A. I had it when I started off, in the type of night club I was working—when you're working to that crowd that can get in for 35ᶜ and a bottle of beer, let's face it, they'll heckle God. Now you must remember that no one can laugh when they feel sorry for you.

Q. *And so if some drunk called you "nigger"?*

A. I said, "According to my contract, the management pays me $50 every time someone calls me that, so will you all do me a favor and stand up and say it again in unison?"

Q. *The NAACP has been trying to get the Board of Education in Torrington, Connecticut, to discard a high school textbook—an anthology containing three stories which use the word "nigger"—do you think this is a wise or unwise policy?*

A. It would have to be a wise policy right now, from the standpoint of the picture that's being painted of the American Negro. We don't have Negro news commentators—you turn on the radio, you hear a Negro disk jockey; you turn on television, you're sure to see a Negro in a jail scene or in a scene where it's pertaining to a Communist rally. So, sure, this is a very touchy thing, because it's not being balanced out.

You've got the same thing going on in Africa. A few months ago, an African was still being portrayed as the cat with the blowgun, and running around with the leaves, and not wanting no atomic war because he don't like his meals pre-cooked. So now how do you explain that an African might've shot down Dag's plane in a jet? How did they go from blowguns to flying jets? Somewhere, the true picture hasn't been given of the African. The last thing you heard them saying was, "Goola magoola," and "Goola magoola" is no direction for flying jets. Now, how come these black folks is flying jets in one month, and last month they were still being exposed to the American public as *those savages?*

Q. *Do you think that in your act, you yourself are guilty of perpetuating this myth? You have a gag about how people keep asking you why we don't send white troops to the Congo, and you say it's because of the fear of war brides—and then you add that they might eat up the whole block.*

A. Oh, no, because I'm almost certain that the people I'm working to realize that this is a myth. You know, I can get by with a million things in the night clubs, where I'm working at the *level* of—I'm working between the 8-to-15 thousand-dollar-a-year bracket. I can also mention the Mann Act *(Editor's note: he thinks the law should be repealed because it discourages travel)* and not lose no one in the house.

I also make the statement about the Army—"The recruiting slogan said, 'Join the Army, the Army's integrated'—that meant I got to sleep with Puerto Ricans." Well, now this could

FLOOGLES USED CARS

"This one was owned by an elderly Negro who drove it under the speed limit for fear of some cop ticketing him."

be very well interpreted that I was saying, "I don't want to sleep with Puerto Ricans." But that's not what I'm saying. I'm saying, "This is the problem that *exists*." It's not *my* problem, it's the problem that existed; in the Army I got to sleep with the Puerto Ricans with no trouble at all—so this was the height of the white man's integrated Army.

Q. *When you were just getting started, you had all-Negro audiences. Now, from what I've seen, you have almost 100% white audiences. Has your material changed in the process?*

A. This is automatic. I can go in a white man's club and do an act for twenty minutes on my stocks and bonds. Can't do it in a Negro night club. Shelley Berman made a million talking about "Coffee, tea, or milk" on the airplane—but how many Negroes have you seen on an airplane compared to whites? So automatically you would do your routine about trains and buses. This is automatic from the economic standpoint.

You can get on a million subjects you couldn't hardly touch in a predominantly Negro night club. How could I do a takeoff on the Metropolitan Opera at a Negro night club? Or a Broadway play? How many Negroes do you think have a job where they are on an expense account? If I do a takeoff on expense accounts in a Negro night club, I'm dead. In a white man's club, your area is so much broader, simply because of the scope of opportunities that exist.

Q. *Now, it seems to me you've cut down on the proportion of racial humor in your act; why is that?*

A. Because it's not as topical. Even when I started, I'd say 90% of the act was topical. At the time when I hit it big, every time you'd pick up the paper, for a period of nine months, a

News item: Department stores are now hiring Puerto Ricans and Negroes to play Santa Claus.

GET A FREE GIFT FROM SANTA

"Toma Usted <u>dos</u> . . ."

black man was in the headlines—either the Congo situation, or aggravated school situation, or in some form or another.

Q. Let me ask you about a few things that have been in the news recently and get your reaction to them. How about our resumption of nuclear testing underground?

A. I think it was a wise idea, only we'll probably create another problem, which would be fall*up*. Of course, it was a wise move on Kennedy's part to test underground because, let's face it, that's where the *people's* gonna be.

Q. When you use a double negative on stage, or when you say "mizzuble" instead of "miserable," you're not patronizing the audience—

A. No. I *talk* like this. Check Southern Illinois University—you'll find out. It's just me, period. I'm not trying to prove nothin' to no one. The bank president don't care how I say it, long as I get it in there.

Q. Critics like to point out that your success is due in part to the "guilt some Americans feel over the conditions of the Negro . . ."

A. I never said that. Critics have said it. I don't know the white man that well. I don't know if he feels guilty. I couldn't sit there and say what part of this audience feels guilty about anything. This could be true, but is he the guy that's sitting over here or the guy that's sitting over there?

Q. In an interview with Lincoln Rockwell of the American Nazi Party—when I asked if he didn't think the Negro has been held down, he replied: "Sir, who do you think held the Negro down in Africa for all those thousands and thousands of years that a white man never even showed up . . ." Now, if he had said this to you, how would you have responded?

FREEDOM NOW

EQUAL RIGHTS

"Excuse me, but would you have
a spare cleaning day available?"

"Son, it's about time your mother and
I told you—you're adopted!"

A. Well, one, I don't even wanna discuss him; I don't want his name linked with mine in no shape, form, or fashion, because I don't wanna advertise for him. Here's a guy has gotten by with murder, and I don't blame him; I blame the American public. People say, well, he has to get by with this because this is a free country. Well, this is a damn lie. It's because he's talking about Negroes and Jews. Because if he had a hate bus and said, "Down with General Motors," and "Down with Ford," they'd blow that fucking bus up before it got a *block* out of the filling station.

The minute he'd stop talking about Negroes and Jews, and pick on something that's a little more biting, that people care a little bit more about in this big wonderful America, then he's washed up. He just happened to pick on the two things that he can pick on and get away with, let's face it.

Not to duck the question you asked—for years, Africa had a culture. As far as their culture was concerned, it wasn't held down. As far as the Indians was concerned, they wasn't held down, they wasn't backward people, they were doing what *their* culture permitted them to do. And at the same time—you talk about "held down"—I daresay they're raping 4-year-old kids in lily-white neighborhoods now. Especially in Chicago, you don't send a little white girl out after dark because she won't come back. Let's face it. Who is the savage? Look at the sex crimes committed among white people in this country— among their *own*.

So how can this man say the Africans have held themselves back? Because this is what they *wanted*. They didn't want H-bombs and the hassle with society. They wanted to do what they were doing. And then, after a certain period of time, colonies went in and took 'em over, and they automatically held 'em down.

Q. What do you think of the NAACP's stand against Freedom Rides?

A. That was the first time the NAACP and the Ku Klux Klan had ever agreed on anything.

Q. Arthur Gelb wrote in the New York Times that you are "probably doing every bit as much as the NAACP." Would you go along with him on that?

A. No. He thinks I am—and it's his right to say this, you know. Not being a white man, I couldn't say how my act actually and truly affects *you*. You and only you know how it affects you, because maybe you leave there with a different light on the racial problem, a different light on the world tension. Only you can say how it affects you.

Q. What do you think about Bobby Kennedy's statement that we might have a Negro President in forty years?

A. I think Lou Lomax summed that up the greatest of them all. He don't appreciate the grandson of an Irish immigrant telling him what he can do in thirty years. This was the wildest statement said about the whole mess.

Q. How do you feel about Louie Armstrong's performance before segregated audiences?

A. Well, this is Louie, you know. Louie probably lived in white hotels in Mississippi for years, too, because it was Louie. All at once people quit looking at him as a Negro and he's something else, you know.

" . . . Uh . . . Ralph . . . Your sister and I have something we'd like to talk to you about . . ."

Q. How do you feel about criticisms of Louie for Uncle Tomming?

A. Louie is from the old school. Louie to me is a guy that— thirty years ago, *all* of us had to do the grinning bit, this was the fad in show business—you go back and look at some of the old guys with Louie. The average one of 'em grew out of it, and Louie just never grew out of it. He doesn't realize this. We just decided it's Uncle Tomming *lately*. Nobody called it Uncle Tomming like thirty years ago. So goddam, if it's Uncle Tomming now, it had to be Uncle Tomming *then*. So why wait thirty years and all at once we find a word and call it Uncle Tomming? It's like, why wait twenty years from now and say what we're doing is Communist? If it's Communist then, it's Communist now. Who knows what terms free discussion will be limited to when you take a tape recorder and sit up and ask a guy about this and that, who knows what it's gonna be *then*?

Q. Have you found that being a financial success has changed you in any way?

A. Sure, it changes you in every way. Last year I could've called a guy a dirty son-of-a-bitch. I do it this year, I got a lawsuit against me.

"Jerry, the Negro manikin—she's
not light-skinned enough!"

"Darling, my schwartza is threatening to quit!"

"If I've only one life, let me live it as a blonde!"

"Look—there goes Santa Claus with a white woman!"

ALABAMY BOUND

And now, class, we shall take up a sociological phenomenon which took place back in the 20th century—the Freedom Riders.

In May of the year 1961, there began attempts to eliminate bus station racial barriers. Violence resulted. Unfortunately, it was Mother's Day, and most of the police force was off duty.

Schools were started to teach prospective Freedom Riders the principles of passive resistance. Simultaneously, other schools were started to teach the principles of mob rule.

Historical evidence indicates that waiting rooms had signs reading "White Intrastate Passengers" and "Negro Intrastate Passengers." You see, the courts had outlawed enforced segregation only among *inter*state bus passengers. Thus a new race made its appearance in the South—the interstate Negro. Obviously, the interstate Negro was far superior to the intrastate Negro.

At any rate, United States marshalls were sent to straighten things out. Fortunately, the C.I.A. was not behind this invasion—no need to remind you of the Cuban fiasco . . . although one student here, who shall remain nameless, described it in a mid-semester examination as a little foreign sports car.

Despite this racial blot on our national conscience, the Attorney General of that day, a Mr. Robert Kennedy, assured the world that in forty years, there might well be a Negro elected President of the country. And, of course, in the year 2001, an interstate Negro was indeed voted into that high office.

While on the way to Washington, however, he was arrested in Jackson, Mississippi for using an intrastate white urinal.

WHO PUT THE WEINER IN MRS. KATZENJAMMER'S SCHNITZEL?

by John Boardman

"Some of the citizens in Downey, Calif. want the Edgar Rice Burroughs books removed from their elementary school libraries because they suspect that Tarzan and Jane were never married and thus lived a life of sin. . . ."
—News item, December 28, 1961

Kakatuhorst, German Central Africa, January 4—Hot on the heels of the Tarzan marriage controversy comes the charge that a prominent local couple, Captain and Mrs. Katzenjammer, were never legally married, and have been living together out of wedlock for over forty years.

This accusation was made by Herr Sepp Mitschell, Governor General of the colony and chairman of the local Johann Birke Gesellschaft. Herr Mitschell, who has been campaigning against relief fraud, cited the Katzenjammers as an example of the alleged widespread abuses of the Home Relief and Aid to Dependent Children program.

"This couple has been living together for so long," said Herr Mitschell, "that only the oldest inhabitants know they are not married. No one even seems to know the Captain's real name. The woman and her two sons use the name 'Katzenjammer.' These boys are obviously the Captain's. They show the same vindictive disposition, and one of them, Fritz, has a head of hair that strongly resembles the Captain's beard.

"I greatly doubt that the Captain is entitled to the rank he claims. He wears an ancient naval uniform, but to the best

"Jane . . . I feel like the lowest . . . dirtiest . . . most rotten friend a guy ever had."

Who Put the Weiner in Mrs. Katzenjammer's Schnitzel?, continued

of my knowledge has never held a sea command. He has no visible means of support, and seems to spend all his time playing pinochle with an elderly remittance man identified only as 'The Inspector' and with a trouble-making native chief.

"Incidentally, the head of hair on the *other* Katzenjammer boy suspiciously resembles The Inspector's beard.

"The family lives in a grass-thatched house, and there are frequent brawls among them. The boys are completely undisciplined and are notorious in the neighborhood as juvenile delinquents. Miss Twiddle, a Welfare Department investigator, refuses to set foot in the house unless they can be restrained from attacking her."

This development is the latest in a series of controversies over the morals of this Central African colony. Charges have already been made that Tarzan, a member of the socially prominent British family of Greystoke, is not legally married to an American woman identified only as Jane, with whom he lives in the British sector of the colony.

Other local spokesmen, European and African, had comments on the illicit unions now being revealed in this region.

The Phantom: "I have never considered a common-law marriage—or any other kind."

Mowgli: "Women are all bitches anyway."

Sheena: "I'll have to admit that the longer I've been here, the whiter they look."

Rollo Rhubarb: "I always knew that those two were a couple of bastards."

Wilhelm Busch: *"Ich hatte gemeint, dass sie Max und Moritz hiessen."*

Local female: "Why am I on relief? That bum Enos knocked me up and skipped to America."

Dr. Albert Schweitzer: "Our birth rate has gone up 50% since the Peace Corps arrived."

Adolph H. Incognito: *"Es ist besser zu heiraten als zu brennen."*

Moise Tshombe: "Lumumba tastes good like a prime minister should."

Rev. Paul Tarsier: "The local inhabitants became more receptive to our missionary efforts when they learned that Jesus was not the son of his mother's husband."

BAD TASTE COLORING BOOKS
by John Francis Putnam

Publishing is a business which is referred to as a "game" by those who are involved in it because they don't want people to find out that it is just as vicious and degrading as any other free enterprise.

And, too, it is a "game" in that one never publishes a book without risk. The winners seem to be the one or two publishers with taste, imagination, and originality who put out books which, when successful, are promptly imitated by the rest of the publishing industry, which is completely lacking in taste, imagination, and originality.

(This is an "in" fable, of course, because *no* publisher ever had taste, imagination, and originality; these qualities belong, as always, to the $75-a-week bastards who sit around the outer office all day, "thinking" when they ought to be doing some real work.)

A perfect illustration is what happens when an "imaginative" publishing venture like *The Executive Coloring Book*—originally stolen from *Mad* Magazine, October 1960—zooms up to dizzy levels of success. Immediately, every schlock publisher and his nephew rush in with cheap offset Coloring Books of their own.

The Realist, in an attempt to hold back this regressive tide by extending the trend so as to defy bad taste, generously offers this poison-the-well selection of Coloring Books that should finally put an end to this kind of crap. . . .

THE
U.S. SAILORS
RENDERED
IMPOTENT
BY A 6 MONTHS
CRUISE ON A
NUCLEAR SUB
COLORING BOOK

BLACK MUSLIM KILL ALL THE **WHITE** MUTHAFUKKAS COLORING BOOK

WOP COLORING BOOK

JAP ATROCITIES AGAINST AMERICAN ARMY NURSES! COLORING BOOK

THE SEXY CATHOLIC NUNS IN black lace underwear COLORING BOOK

The **BRAILLE** COLORING BOOK FOR USE WITH FINGER PAINT

George Lincoln Rockwell's **JEW BASTARD** COLORING BOOK

AUSCHWITZ COOKING AND COLORING BOOK

THE *Spastic* COLORING BOOK

THE **POLICE KICKING SHIT OUT OF** NON-VIOLENT **BAN** the **BOMB** DEMONSTRATORS COLORING BOOK

AN IMPOLITE INTERVIEW WITH AN ABORTIONIST

"There is no such thing as a 'good' abortionist. All of them are in business strictly for money."

—*Look* Magazine
August 14, 1962

Q. Okay, now, just for the sake of definition, what exactly is an abortion?

A. An abortion is the removal of an undeveloped child, by the use of some drug or mechanical force to empty the contents of the uterus.

Q. How dangerous is the operation?

A. If done within certain limits of time, it is practically without danger.

Q. What would the limits of time be, into a pregnancy?

A. Well, I would call three months the upper limit, although I know if one has all the hospital facilities, it can be done even up to five months.

Q. Under proper conditions, to what extent does death of the mother result from an abortion?

A. I'd say it's practically nil. A few years ago, I was in Russia, and they were doing at least 50,000 a year in Moscow, and only had one or two percent mortality, and that was before the days of sulfa. But they drew the line up to the third month. It's legal now in Japan, China, India, Sweden, Switzerland, and I guess a few other countries. This western hemisphere is the only one that seems to be a little bit late in following the experience of the other countries.

Q. What are the prices generally charged for an abortion?

A. In this country, they run around $300 or more.

Q. What should they cost?

A. Well, I don't know what medication they use, but the medicine to put them to sleep, and the antibiotics and things like that, runs about $20. I understand in Japan they only charge $5 or $10.

Q. Because of the circumstances under which abortions are often performed, isn't the use of an anesthetic sometimes bypassed?

A. I'd never undertake it without an anesthetic. That'd be an extremely painful proposition, and rather dangerous to the patient, because I don't see how they'd be able to keep still, and you'd run a chance of perforating the uterus.

Q. You're a physician yourself, is that correct?

A. Oh, I'm an M.D., yes.

Q. How long have you been performing abortions?

A. Oh, maybe thirty to forty years.

Q. Do you have any idea of about how many abortions you've performed during those years?

A. To be accurate, it's twenty-seven thousand and six.

Q. Have you ever had any interference from the authorities?

A. Just last year. The federal authorities started to open my mail. And they even had women write me letters, and then when I answered them, they had proof that I was using the mails for crime-inciting matter. I never knew the law existed until I found it out in that manner.

Q. Crime-inciting matter?

A. (Reading) "Mailing Obscene Or Crime-Inciting Matter: Every obscene, lewd, lascivious, or filthy book, pamphlet, picture, paper, letter, writing, print, or other publication of an indecent character, and every article or thing designed, adapted, or intended for preventing conception or producing abortion, or for any indecent or immoral use. . . ." Well, that was finally squelched before it got before the court.

Q. What about the local AMA?

A. Well, of course, I resigned from the local medical organization, because I knew that if I wouldn't have, I would've been fired out of the organization. I'm in a very Catholic neighborhood, and so I could see that what I was doing was opposed to the majority of physicians.

Q. Being in a Catholic neighborhood, do you find any particular pressures from that source?

A. Oh, I haven't any doubt that I have my enemies in this region, because a lot of Catholics are just narrow-minded. Unless it's in *their* house. For instance, I had two priests that had their housekeepers in trouble, and they brought them here. And I've had quite a few Catholics I've been able to help—some of them pretty good friends of mine.

Q. As you say, when it's in their house, they have a different attitude—do you have authorities coming to you for help?

A. Oh, yes. You'll have all walks of life. You realize you're in a world of hypocrisy. I have had girls in here that told me that the judge of this court was responsible for their condition—and named the individual. Whether that's the truth, I don't know. But they come from all walks—I even had a justice of the peace. The husband died, and they named his widow the justice of the peace. And then she had a little affair and became pregnant, and I was able to help her. I've had medical people bring me their wives, and I've had quite a few medical people send me patients.

Q. But they wouldn't perform the operation themselves?

A. No, never. Just exactly what their attitude would be, I don't really know; some of them, I presume, were absolutely against it.

Q. What are some of the reasons women give for wanting an abortion?

A. Well, a good many of them, they're not married, and they find the fellow they've been going with *is*. He won't do anything to help them out, so rather than have that make it almost impossible to get married, they want something done.

Then, others have had eight or ten children. This region's hard-hit, financially, and to have ten children to feed, and another one coming when the man's not working, it's a problem. And then there are some people that've been raped.

Q. How far, geographically, do you find patients coming to you from?

A. Well, I've had them from California. Of course, some that came from long distances, didn't come just to see me; I think they were connected with some of the agencies in Washington, D.C.—I even had one from where they're having all the fighting over there: Laos. I had a very tall Negro woman come in here from Trinidad.

Q. Do you find most of your patients are Caucasians?

A. By far, the majority are, but I've had a few Orientals here recently.

Q. Do your patients run the gamut in terms of education and social class?

A. Yes, you'll find some people that're pretty well educated are in that position. And, of course, a lot of them might be prostitutes—and a lot of them have told me they followed birth control as described by the Church, and of course they got pregnant. And then others have been using the diaphragm and jelly. As far as the contraceptive pill, I don't know of any that I've had on that. I know women forget—you forget to take one pill when you're doing it, you're licked, that's all there is to it.

Q. Of those who didn't take contraceptive precautions, do they give any reasons for their lack of foresight?

A. Well, I think the circumstances came on suddenly to some of them, and they didn't have a chance to get to the ammunition.

Q. Do you find that there are many repeaters—who come back for a second or third time?

A. Yes. I had one girl repeat thirteen times. She's married now and has three or four children, and they're all fine, all in good health.

Q. Do you go along with the theory that, in most cases, if a girl becomes pregnant, it's usually because she wants to, perhaps unconsciously?

A. When you bring that problem up, you bring up the topic of love. Love is blind, and desire doesn't give a damn. That's what I think a good many of these problems come from.

Q. What's your reaction to the position that abortion is equivalent to murder?

A. I don't believe in that at all. You don't call an acorn an oak tree. And you don't call an embryo a human being. It's a few cells developing in the muscle called the uterus, and if you let the thing go, it may materialize—you can't say it's *going* to, because sometimes they don't—it's just a possibility.

If a person wants to go *through* with the problem, and have it, then I say all right for her, we'll do everything to protect her. On the other hand, I don't think we've got to *compel* them to go through with it. Way back in the Roman days, women had the power to say whether anything like that was done or not. It was their viscera—their gizzards—and they ought to be able to do with it what they desire. Now, the way man has evolved, there was a time when they had babies but they didn't have any *state*; but when they got so many, those babies made the state—the organization that dictates to them what to do and what not to do. But if it wouldn't be for them having the numbers—the population—there'd be no state.

Q. Here, let me read from an editorial in the June 8th New York World-Telegram & Sun.

"A 19-year-old girl is the victim in one of the most grisly abortion cases. She vanished after her parents are said to have arranged for a Queens doctor to perform the illegal operation. Parts of her dismembered body were found three days later in a sewer pipe at the doctor's home."

A. Well, of course, he might have been in mortal fear when he did that. . . .

Q. He took her at a very late stage in her pregnancy—I think five or six months—

A. I'd never undertake a thing like that myself, because I know there's too much risk. But if we had laws that made those things legal, I think a person would have no trouble at all, because he wouldn't have to be doing it under *cover*, he would have blood to give if she needed a blood transfusion, he'd have all the things to work with which would undoubtedly make the operation a success.

Q. That editorial goes on: "Let's hope this ugly case leaves one message indelibly written in the public's memory: that death is always lurking in an abortionist's office."

A. I'd say death is lurking everywhere. Whether you cross the street or eat a Thanksgiving meal—because if you get a foreign body in your throat, a bone or something like that, it can happen. An awful lot of deaths happen in the bathroom. So one can't pinpoint it on a thing like that.

Q. Anyway, the editorial concludes: "By the very nature of his work, the abortionist is a criminal. It stands to reason that he is unscrupulous, irresponsible, and often wholly incompetent. His clandestine work is often done in makeshift, unsanitary quarters." Your office certainly doesn't look unsanitary to me. Out of the 27,006 abortions you've performed, how many deaths have there been?

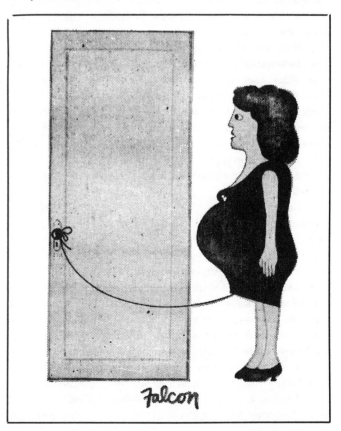

A. One. About two years ago, I had an accident where a person died from an anesthetic. And of course they did an autopsy—the person died after my operation was finished—it was most peculiar, because I had given that same amount of anesthetic to a good many people before, and I should have had a graveyard full of people if that amount killed them. But at any rate, that came before the authorities. And, after a long procedure, I was acquitted.

Q. None of the papers had this, but I know for a fact that a doctor was being blackmailed by a couple of college students; have you ever been faced with that problem?

A. I had a girl in here, 20 years of age, the mother of five children, and she wanted to know if I could do anything to help her. And I did. And a short time after she was here, I understood that she went down to the hospital, because she was having some fever—she didn't have any fever when she was here to see me—but the intern down there examined her, and found out that she had had an abortion. And so he reported it, over the heads of the hospital, to the police. And I was arrested.

And my lawyer kept that case from coming up for over a year. And in the meantime, the husband—he had another lawyer in this region—and they tried to, you might say, blackmail me, or at least tried to get some money from me . . . and they'd squelch the case. So I gave that information to my lawyer, and I think it put the other lawyer on the hot spot. Well, when the case finally came up, it was more than a year afterwards. In the meantime she had another child, and so that proved there was no harm done in the operation. And she evidently had a falling-out with her husband, and they had a divorce some time after the thing took place. I was acquitted on that.

Q. Do you find that many patients, after an abortion, have feelings of guilt or regret?

A. Yes, I generally find that the Catholics are the ones who run highest in that, because their minds are so brainwashed. They are, you might say, just victims of what they've been taught when they were young. They can't think for themselves.

Q. Have you found that the guilt varies according to how much a person has been brainwashed?

A. Well, I think a whole lot depends on how much religion has been drilled into them. I know I had one woman in here some years ago—she was the mother of ten children, going through the menopause; she was about 45.

And she wanted to know whether she was pregnant. I examined her, and I told her, "No, you're not pregnant—but you do have fibroid tumors." And she says, "Can you do anything to help me?" And I said, "Yes, they're of such a size, I think if I put radium in, that'll solve the problem; of course, that'll stop you menstruating, but you're starting to do that right at the present time, so that won't make much difference."

So a year later she came in here and she said, "Does radium make you passionate?" I said, "I can see why it made *you* passionate—because you realized you had ten children; every time you entered the act, you thought, 'Well, there, I'm going to have one more.' And so, when that fear was removed, that's what made the difference." In other words, she didn't have any brakes to be putting on herself all the time. You see, a lot of women just look on themselves as a breeding animal; they don't have any regard for their health, their vitality—they have one

child right after the other. And if the woman doesn't give in to the man all the time, then the husband beats the devil out of her. They're in a phase of slavery, and they can't get away from it.

And the world's overpopulated—I can't see why people want to have the *human* life at the expense of all others, because every time we keep expanding and building up between town and town, it means other forms of life are being pushed off the planet.

Q. What about the maternal instinct—isn't there regret because of that?

A. Some might feel that way, and then there's some that don't. No doubt that the maternal instinct is great, because when you put them to sleep, when they awake, possibly the first thing they talk about, is the children they have. That's on their mind all the time—their family.

Q. What amazes me is, you've been performing abortions 30 to 40 years—you've violated the law 27,006 times . . . how have you gotten away with it?

A. Well, I don't know how. . . . Of course, some of my patients got into hospitals, and had to have blood transfusions, and things like that—I had some close shaves—but I'm surprised to know a good many of those patients never mentioned where they were or anything else. I haven't any doubt the country's known about me, because, heavens, I've had people from practically every state in the Union.

Q. You mean you can't explain it yourself, why you're free?

A. No, I don't know exactly why that is at all.

Q. Incidentally, I've heard that you're retiring—is that true?

A. I'm stopping. This gets on my blood pressure, and it makes my wife nervous.

Q. To your knowledge, what's the extent of collusion between abortionists and the authorities? In terms of payoffs to the police—

A. Well, I have had nothing of that kind. Sometimes the police come around here with their annual journal. The businessmen in the region all do that—it's their yearly report, and

many businessmen use it as an advertising medium.

Q. Have police come to you for professional services?

A. Oh, yes, I've helped a hell of a lot of police out. I've helped a lot of FBI men out. They would be here, and they had me a little bit scared—I didn't know whether they were just in to get me or not.

Q. You started out charging only $5. With inflation, what has it gone to now?

A. I charge now $100. And the reason I did that—they took ten thousand out of me on that darned thing last year in the federal court.

Q. Some people claim that a liberalization of the abortion laws would lead to promiscuity. Do you agree?

A. Well, there's enough of that going on at the present time—I don't think it'd make much difference.

Q. They also claim that liberalization of the abortion laws would lead to more abortions. What's your reaction to that?

A. I think it would go along just about on the same grounds it is now.

Q. What are some of the methods by which women try to induce abortion themselves?

A. Well, this woman came to me several years ago—she was 45, she came in here highly excited, and said, "I want an examination." So I put her on the table. When she got off, she said, "Am I pregnant?" I said, "No you're not pregnant." "Did you find anything the matter?" I said, "Yes, I found something the matter, as if you had a *pencil* in your abdomen."

She said, "I've got a confession to make. Last week, I was one month pregnant, and I was in this tavern, so I took a cocktail stirrer, and I pushed it up my uterus—but something pulled it out of my hand, and I've been unable to find it. What are you going to do?"

"Why," I said, "you ought to go to the hospital and have it cut out—that's in your abdomen, it's around your intestines." She says, "I can't go to the hospital with that." Well, I thought, a week's passed, and she's got a normal temperature, and her pulse is all right—so I moved that thing over to the region where her appendix was, made a little nick like you would do for an appendectomy. I got down to some nice white membrane, and I could see something blue on the other side of it. So I gave one little nick with my scalpel, and out pops a cocktail stirrer with "Three Feathers" on it.

Another time, a woman was here—she wasn't in my room very long till I smelled her. She was very odoriferous. She tried to commit an abortion by using a catheter—that's a rubber tube—but she got it in her bladder, and she had cystitis, she passed urine and it was very odoriferous. So I put a cystoscope in her so I could see the catheter, and I got a hold of that and pulled it right out.

Q. Would you say that most of your patients are married or unmarried?

A. Oh, I'd say roughly it runs 50-50. A lot of people get in here in their menopause—worried, because they don't know whether they're going through the menopause or whether they're pregnant. And very frequently some of them *are* pregnant. They've had eight or ten children, and all sorts of problems come up with a woman like that.

Q. How young have your patients been?

A. I've even had girls brought by their parents that were fourteen—just about the time they started to menstruate.

Q. How did you come to start doing abortions?

A. Well, when I was going to high school, my father was the district attorney, and he had an interesting case brought to him. One of the leading ministers said, "Look at these letters my daughter's getting—they're sometimes threatening and so bizarre that I can't make anything out of them."

So, my father says, "Suppose you get some of her handwriting"—and when they compared, they find that she's written these letters to herself. And when the investigation came on, by golly, she's illegitimately pregnant—and when the father knew that, darned if he didn't blow his brains out.

And I thought, "Good gracious, a few little cells removed at a time like that could've saved, certainly, the life of the father." Whatever became of the girl after that, I don't know.

Q. Now, if you're retiring, and you still have people coming to you, do you refer them elsewhere?

A. I haven't got a soul to refer them to; my friends are all arrested—there seems to be just lately more clamping-down on this since any time since I've been here.

Q. In the public's mind, when they think of an abortionist, they think of the shady operator doing it only for money, and under very unsafe conditions—and, unfortunately, they do exist; it's a racket.

A. I think they exist as a result of something that is *required*.

Q. Do you feel that the legalization of abortion would do away with this exploitation and the risks?

A. Certainly, because I don't see why any doctor, if he had the law with him, would go to work and charge that much. I know I don't believe in wringing money out of people—they've got one misery in their head when they come to see you; why add others?

Q. What would you say is the most significant lesson you've learned in all your years as a practicing abortionist?

A. You've got to be careful. That's the most important thing. And you've got to be cocksure that everything's removed. And even the uterus speaks to you and tells you. I could be blind. You see, this is an operation no eye sees. You go by the sense of feel and touch. And hearing. The voice of the uterus. Then, when you get them off the table, there's practically no pain. Well, I've gotten quite a lot of fan mail. Stacks of letters. But everywhere I look is hypocrisy. Because the politicians—and I've had politicians in here—still keep those laws in existence, but yet, if some friend of theirs is in trouble. . . .

Q. What would you say was your most unusual case?

A. I had one peculiar case—I helped a girl out—and she came in some months later, pregnant again. I found out that she left here the day it was done and went to confession and told the whole thing. It got the priest so excited, he raped her.

Q. Just as a hypothetical question, what would happen if I were to reveal your name?

A. I haven't any doubt there'd be a smash-up. You see, a friend just recently wrote a book on abortion "by Dr. X"—well, he's in jail. His name wasn't revealed, but they got him. He was going to dedicate the book to me—I said, "Don't put *my* name in that book or I'll be prosecuted quicker than a flash."

THE MOON-SHOT SCANDAL

by Terry Southern

Washington, June 17 (UPI) —At the climax, James A. McDivitt had to do quite a lot of fast blinking. Edward H. White II swallowed hard, several times. . . .

A significant difference between Soviet and American space efforts has been the constant spotlight of public attention focused on the latter, while our antagonist's program has been carried forward in relative secrecy. This has presented tremendous disadvantages, especially in its psychological effect on the national mind, and it harbors a dangerous potential indeed. If, for example, in climax to the usual fanfare and nationally televised countdown, the spacecraft simply explodes, veers out crazily into the crowd, or burrows deep into the earth at the foot of the launching-pad, it can be fairly embarrassing to all concerned. On the other hand, it is generally presumed that, because of this apparent and completely above-board policy, *everything* which occurs in regard to these American spaceshots is immediately known by the entire public. Yet can anyone really be naive enough to believe that in matters so extraordinarily important an attitude of such simple-minded candor could obtain? Surely not. And the facts behind the initial moon-shot of August 17, 1961, make it a classic case in point, now that the true story may at last be told.

Readers will recall that the spacecraft, after a dramatic countdown, blazed up from its pad on full camera; the camera followed its ascent briefly, then cut to the tracking-station where a graph described the arc of its ill-fated flight. In due time it became evident that the rocket was seriously off course, and in the end it was announced quite simply that the craft had "missed the moon" by about two hundred thousand miles—by a wider mark, in fact, than the distance of the shot itself. What was *not* announced—either before, during, or after the shot—was that the craft was *manned by five astronauts.* Hoping for a total *coup,* the Space Authority—highest echelon of the Agency—had arranged for a fully crewed flight, one which if successful (and there was considerable reason to believe that it would be) would then be dramatically announced to an astonished world: "Americans On The Moon!" Whereas, if not successful, it would merely remain undisclosed that the craft had been manned. The crew, of course, was composed of carefully screened volunteers who had no known dependents.

So, in one room of the tracking-station—a room which was was *not* being televised—communications were maintained throughout this historic interlude. Fragmented transcripts, in the form of both video and acoustic tapes, as well as personal accounts of those present, have now enabled us to piece together the story—the *story,* namely, of how the moon-bound spaceship, "Cutie-Pie II," was caused to career off into outer space, beyond the moon itself, when some kind of *"insane faggot hassle,"* as it has since been described, developed aboard the craft during early flight stage.

According to available information, Lt. Col. P.D. Slattery, a "retired" British colonial officer, co-captained the flight in hand with Major Ralph L. Doll (better known to his friends, it was later learned, as "Baby" Doll); the balance of the crew consisted of Capt. J. Walker, Lt. Fred Hanson, and Cpl. "Felix" Mendelssohn. (There is certain evidence suggesting that Cpl. Mendelssohn may have,

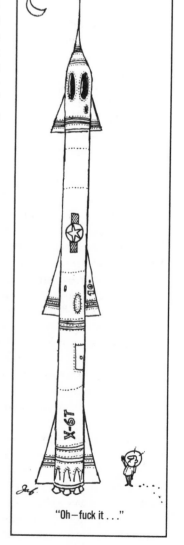

"Oh—fuck it . . ."

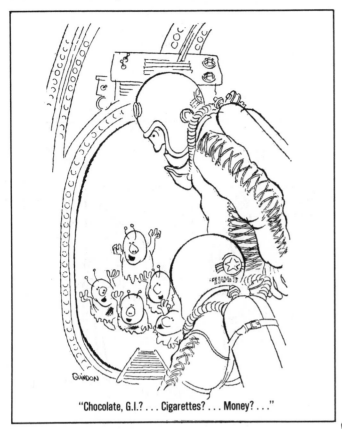

"Chocolate, G.I.? . . . Cigarettes? . . . Money? . . ."

in actual fact, been a woman.) The initial phase of the existing transcript is comprised entirely of routine operational data and reports of instrument readings. It was near the end of Stage One, however, when the craft was some 68,000 miles from Earth and still holding true course, that the first untoward incident occurred; this was in the form of an unexpected exchange between Lt. Hanson and Maj. Doll, which resounded over the tracking-station intercom, as clear as a bell on a winter's morn:

Lt. Hanson: "Will you *stop* it! Just *stop* it!"

Maj. Doll: "Stop *what*? I was only calibrating my altimeter—for heaven's sake, Freddie!"

Lt. Hanson: "I'm not *talking* about that and you know it! I'm talking about your infernal *camping*! Now just stop it! Right now!"

The astonishment this caused at tracking-station H.Q. could hardly be exaggerated. Headphones were adjusted, frequencies were checked; the voice of a Lt. General spoke tersely: "Cutie-Pie II—give us your reading—over."

"Reading thpeeding," was Cpl. Mendelssohn's slyly lisped reply, followed by a cunning snicker. At this point a scene of fantastic bedlam broke loose on the video intercom. Col. Slatterly raged out from his forward quarters, like the protagonist of *Psycho*—in outlandish feminine attire of the 'nineties, replete with a dozen petticoats and high-button shoes. He pranced with wild imperiousness about the control room, interfering with all operational activity, and then spun into a provocative and feverish combination of tarantella and can-can at the navigation panel, saucily flicking at the controls there, cleverly integrating these movements into the tempo of

his dervish, amidst peals of laughter and shrieks of delight and petulent annoyance.

"You silly old fraud," someone cried gaily, "this isn't Pirandello!"

It was then that the video system of the intercom blacked out, as though suddenly shattered, as did the audio system shortly afterward. There is reason to believe, however, that the sound communication part of the system was eventually restored, and, according to some accounts, occasional reports (of an almost incredible nature) continue to be received, as the craft—which was heavily fueled for its return trip to Earth—still blazes through the farther reaches of space.

Surely, despite the negative and rather disappointing aspects of the flight, there are at least two profitable lessons to be learned from it: (1) that the antiquated, intolerant attitude of the Agency, and of Government generally, towards sexual freedom, can only cause individual repression which may at any time—and especially under the terrific tensions of space flight—have a boomerang effect to the great disadvantage of all concerned, and (2) that there may well be, after all, an ancient wisdom in the old adage, "Five's a crowd."

GAY ORDEAL

I am somewhat unproud of the U.S. State Department's recent disclosure that, out of eighteen security-risk employees who resigned under investigatory pressure last year, sixteen had been charged with homosexuality. . . .

"Hotchkins, you've been a faithful employee here for quite a few years now, but we have reason to believe that you're a homosexual."

"Why, sir, that's not true."

"We all have our problems, Hotchkins, it's nothing to be ashamed of. But I'm afraid that a security investigation is necessarily called for."

"But even if it *were* true, sir, hasn't my loyalty always been above question?"

"Yes, but there is a new factor now: the possibility of blackmailing you."

"Well, the secret is *out* now—who would they tell?"

"Me, of course. You don't want your employer to know you're a homosexual, do you? So you might very well give out secret information to avoid that."

"Yes, sir, I see your logic. If only there was some way I could prove . . ."

"Now, Hotchkins, you must try to take this like a man—oh, I'm sorry, I didn't mean it that way."

"Sir, I really hate to have to do this to you, but you leave me no alternative. There's something about me that I'd like you to ask your wife tonight. . . ."

THE GREAT HOTEL ROBBERY

by Lenny Bruce

At 12:05 A.M., a cat burglar broke into the fourth floor of the Hotel America in New York City. A suite rents there for $36 a month, and is rented by the year by Wallace Brothers Circus in case a trained bear is pregnant—you know, an animal gets knocked up while working Madison Square Garden.

The Hotel America is the only one that will take a pregnant bear, because the maid only goes in once a year.

Actually, it wasn't a cat burglar, it was a tenant. Somebody in the Flanders Hotel across the street spotted the prowler. "I was looking at the stars through my binoculars," said R. Lendowski, Grand Central Station maintenance porter. "I just happened to be looking and I saw this guy."

When questioned, the suspect said that there was no toilet in his room, that he had recent surgery done on his little toe and walking to the bathroom in the hall was terribly painful, and his roommate caught him pissing in the sink; actually, he didn't catch him, he was just about to start, and he got out of it by saying that he was taking a sponge bath and had to continue bathing from the waist up, while his roommate kept interjecting: "I thought that you were trying to piss in the sink . . . I once caught a guy doing that in Parris Island . . . Can you imagine a guy doing that in the sink? . . . The same type of dirty guy that pisses in the ocean. . . ."

So he waited until his friend fell asleep—mumbling about those guys sneak-pissing in the sink.

Then he decided to piss out the window, but felt guilty about it in case some guy that might be a bigger nut on ocean-pissers might be passing by.

What if you pissed on a guy like that?

"Don't move—I see which window that spray is coming from. You! With your hand on the sill, shaking it on the screen—stop! Okay, you're surrounded, we're behind you. Don't drop anything."

The suspect goes on with his confession:

"So I searched out all the possibilities, and I went out on the ledge to make sure I wouldn't get it on anyone. It was 12:05 A.M., and I saw a whole bunch of binoculars from different windows watching me.

"Before I knew it, this priest was on the ledge with me. He said, 'Son, is this the only way?' "

"I said, 'It's either this or pissing in the sink. The fire engines are here now and I have a choice of confessing as a cat burglar or a peeping tom, but to tell the truth, my roommate won't let me piss in the sink. . . .' "

"Wop!" "Kike!"

CALORIES DON'T COUNT, BUT QUAKERS DO

The controversial book *Calories Don't Count* was included on the *San Francisco Chronicle*'s best-seller list recently as *Carlo Don't Count*. And Johnny can't read, neither. If he could, he would read on the Quaker Puffed Wheat package this designation: "The Weight-Watcher's Cereal."

Upon watching the weight of the cereal—"3½ oz. net"—he might be inclined to peel off that little gummed label, in which cae the weight-watcher would read "4 oz. net."

The Quaker Oats Company this month spent $250,000 on TV advertising alone.

THE LANGUAGE BARRIER IN ACTION

From the Associated Press wires on January 31, 1962:

"The dramatic vote in the plenary session of the inter-American foreign ministers conference was a close one, with the resolution for exclusion of Cuba winning just the required two-thirds majority."

From Secretary of State Dean Rusk's broadcast report to the nation (at President Kennedy's request) on February 2, 1962:

"We declared unanimously—except for a few, of course . . ."

"This is not a real hold-up. Just give me back my Christmas Club money."

"Are you sure you looked for work this week?"

THE BATHROOM IN BUDAPEST

by John Goodwin

Pimento spent seven years in a bathroom in Budapest. It was in one of those buildings that they built in nineteen-something-or-other for a lot of workers.

It was fortunately for him never bombed during the war, and for the most part the functions of the bath, basin, bidet, and watercloset continued without interruption throughout the period of Pimento's exile there.

The rest of the flat was unoccupied, and the door into Pimento's hiding place was well camouflaged, being painted to represent a mural of Marco Polo at the court of Kubla Khan under which no one would ever think of looking.

Pimento was fed in a very complicated way, which I never quite understood somehow, by food forced by pressure up through the pipes and drains. His colleagues in the underground were very ingenious and loyal, though they could contrive no liquid refreshment for Pimento other than water.

All in all, Pimento was glad he was confined in a bathroom and not a living room. In his early days of concealment he realized how fortunate he was, for it was preferable to be confined in such a small windowless space (there was a ventilator high in the wall) with all modern conveniences than to be in a room no matter how large and windowed without any water at all in which to wash or any place except the four corners and eventually the whole room in which to relieve oneself.

The first year he spent a lot of time turning the taps on and off.

He would first turn on both hot and cold in the basin and then turn off the hot, then turn on the hot in the bathtub and turn off the cold in the basin after they had run together for a

while. He would then turn on the cold in the tub and the cold in the basin and then turn off the hot in the tub, and in that way he would have two cold faucets running at the same time. He could reverse this procedure and fill the room with steam or on other days, when he felt in a more pensive mood, he would turn nothing on but the spray in the bidet and stretching out on the tile floor, one arm crooked to hold his head, he would dream away, his eyes on the prancing fountain.

There were indeed, as you can see, many, many variations on the combinations.

The second year he spent a lot of time taking baths, making each one a different temperature; so slight was the change in de-

gree when he, after several months, had become abnormally sensitive to the most minute change of temperature, that even a thermometer would not have registered the difference to the naked eye.

Towards the end of the second year this subtlety of sensitivity had, in fact, become so irksome to him that he took delight in plunging into only the coldest or the hottest of baths. Sometimes he would do both in quick succession and at other times would take five cold baths one day and seven boiling ones the next, or for five days take one cold bath a day and then bathe in boiling water once a day for the next seven days. He would then multiply these baths by days or vice-versa and thus predict his program for many days to come. At one point he had one hundred and seventy-two hot baths followed by eighty-three cold baths followed by twenty-five hot baths climaxed by one hundred and fifty-five cold baths.

In this way the third year was spent.

There was for Pimento no way to tell night from day, and after the first few weeks of his incarceration, he gave up winding his watch. It had already stopped several times, and even his delight in living according to the arbitrary hours his watch told soon bored him. His friends, loyal and ingenious though they were, could not feed him punctually or even always by day, so that even the arrival of food through the drains was not to be relied upon as an indication of the hour.

One of his friends did try to send a newspaper printed at great risk by the underground up to Pimento through the same channels that his food was delivered to him, but it only succeeded in plugging up the pipes. Pimento, without knowing the cause, was without nourishment for two days until his colleagues managed to repair the damage.

Occasionally a small note would get through to him, but the writing was always indecipherable because of the effect of the water on the ink, and Pimento had no way in which to advise his friends to use indelible ink or even pencil.

He was annoyed at their stupidity but thought that after all, waterproof ink might be unobtainable in wartime and that as for a pencil, perhaps his friends were too polite to use it in personal correspondence.

The fourth year Pimento turned his attention to the water-closet, having exhausted the possibilities of basin, bath, and bidet. He would drink a great deal more water than was good for him only that he might relieve himself more often and thus have cause to flush the toilet.

To flush it without reason was too simple a game and he had made a solemn resolution not to do this. Towards the tenth month of the fourth year he rationalized a little and would flush the bowl *previously* to relieving himself instead of after. The result was the same, really, in the long run, and it was a welcome relief to see varying shades of yellow rather than the perpetual colorless water he had been accustomed to for almost four years.

As his body had become sensitive in the second year to the slightest change in temperature in his baths, so in this year did his eyes become hypersensitive to shades of yellow. He was able to count and identify six hundred and thirty-eight variations caused by the combination of urine and water.

The fifth year Pimento spent in study of fecal matter, and by the sixth year he was able to tell his immediate future by the contemplation of his turds. He would tell his fortune each morning in this way for the following 24-hour period.

Due to the abnormal regularity of his diet (mostly wood pulp and vegetable fibers), his bowel movements maintained a consistent similarity, and for this reason Pimento would foresee little change in his fortune from day to day, and as there was actually no opportunity for any change in his life whatsoever, Pimento's predictions were invariably correct.

This gave him a blind belief in his ability as a prophet which, putting him in a world of supermen, perhaps saved his reason during those last dreadful years in the bathroom.

The sixth year Pimento had wearied of all his diversions and rituals except the one of prediction. After the daily fortune had been told he would pace his cubicle, something he had never descended to doing in the previous years. Then he would count the bathroom tiles first by rows and then by the many geometrical patterns they formed in their repetition.

He got to know each tile so well, though they were so identical, that he attributed a separate identity to each one, and some he hated and some he adored and some he merely put up with. There were some five thousand tiles in the room, all white and all hexagonal, but by the end of the sixth year Pimento knew the history and character of each and exactly how they would act within the situations he created for them.

These tiles became the population of his world and though he never advised them, they led their complicated lives according to his laws. Not once did any of them act in any other way than that which he foresaw.

The very fact that they were so nondescript and indistinguishable yet so complicated and unique in relation to each other geometrically and every other way made them much more worthy of consideration than the artfully formed faucets, chains, and plungers of the bathroom fixtures. They never moved, they never changed, they could not be manipulated into any other shape, position, or use; and yet they were the least static things in the room.

Throughout the seventh year Pimento hurried through his

"Come on out, Lefty, we know you're in there!"

daily fortune-telling like a prayer, hurrying through it in order to get back into the universe of the tiles.

In the early months of his eighth year he was liberated. His friends broke through the false mural and greeted him with open arms, surprised to find him alive. They were shocked, however, to discover him lacking in any interest whatsoever as to the fortunes of their party; and their vanity was injured when, sitting at cafés together, they saw his eyes wandering while they regaled him with stories of their escapades in the underground.

Even his mother and sister found him callous to their sufferings during the war and decided that his own horrible experience had blunted his capacity for pity. His colleagues found him so unconcerned with the problems of humanity that they drew up a paper of expulsion from the party and handed it to him. Pimento accepted it politely and made no comment.

He left Budapest and travelled to a winter resort by the sea where he attempted by advertising to attract a clientele whose fortunes he promised to tell by reading their bowel movements, but the time was not ripe for such an enterprise, and it failed.

He took to frequenting public baths in order to be with tiles once more, but there was no chance for intimacy, and it was somehow not the same.

In desperation he returned to Budapest and went to the flat containing the bathroom he knew so well, but it had been rented, and the lady refused even to let him in the door.

He begged that he might rent only the bathroom from her, but she laughed in his face, saying that it was the only bathroom in Budapest undamaged by the war, and did he think her such a fool that she would give it up?

There was nothing left for him to do but seek out his former colleagues and beg that they admit him into the party once more. His contrition was so complete and his convictions so revived that they without hesitation accepted him with open arms back into their circle, and indeed they were soon greatly rewarded for so doing, for not only did Pimento every morning read their bowel movements absolutely free and predict great martyrdoms and eventual recognition for them all; but he also became the most fearless, uncompromising, and militant of the group in defense of the cause.

In fact his zeal had to be curbed, for it was so great it threatened from time to time to bring about premature results, which of course was exactly what Pimento had in mind because he was always hoping that something could be arranged so there would be another war and he could once more be a member of the minority and have the good fortune to be hidden in a tiled bathroom for another seven years if not longer.

AN IMPOLITE INTERVIEW WITH JOSEPH HELLER

Q. Has Catch-22 *been banned anywhere?*
A. No. It seems to have offended nobody on the grounds of morality or ideology. Those people it has offended, it has offended on the basis of literary value. But I'm almost surprised to find that the acceptance of the book covers such a broad political and sociological spectrum.

This pleases my ego, but I put an optimistic interpretation on it: I think there is a common reservoir of discontent among people who might disagree with each other and not realize that their basic disagreements stem from the same recognition of a need for correction.

There is a tradition of taboo against submitting to examination many of our ideological beliefs, religious beliefs. Many things that become a matter of traditional behavior, or habit, acquire status where they seem exempt from examination. Even to suggest that they be examined becomes a form of heresy.

Now the book might be surprising in that respect, but—with the exception of a certain appreciation for lechery, which you might find among the deadly sins—I don't think there's any principle of morality advocated in the book with which most intelligent—even *in*decent—people will disagree.

Q. Well, I did a double-take when Yossarian is censoring the

letters. My sympathy immediately fell to the people who were getting these letters.
A. Really? That hadn't occurred to me. They probably have the same status as the victims during a Shakespeare play. When critics interpret Shakespearean tragedy, they see this as an examination of crime, and retribution as representing a certain system of justice; but they ignore, let's say in *Macbeth*, all those children of—was it Macduff or Malcolm?—his wife is killed, his children are killed, and Banquo is slaughtered. All the peripheral characters seem to be exempt from the working-out of this moral principle.

I suppose it had not occurred to me that these people getting these letters would be perplexed by them. I'm not particularly disturbed by that.

Q. Maybe I'm hypersensitive. . . . Isn't this type of satire by its very nature subversive—in the James Thurber sense of the word—to the establishment?
A. Oh, I think anything *critical* is subversive by nature in the sense that it does seek to change or reform by attacking. I think the impetus toward progress of any kind has always been a sort of discontent, an effort to undermine what is existing, whether it's barbaric or not.

So, in the sense that the book is aware of certain faults or shortcomings—as much, I think, in the individuals' character as in the make-up of a society—in that sense, it is a very critical book, certainly. But it doesn't necessarily follow that people would take exception to it.

Q. What about the people who are criticized?

A. I've met nobody yet who did not identify with my sympathetic characters. And among the people who did identify were a few of the prototypes of some of the more reprehensible characters. I think anybody today feels, for example, that he is at the mercy of superiors—who, he feels, hamstring him or limit him in the execution of his duty—preventing *him* from existing and performing work at the height of his capabilities.

Q. Have you gotten any unofficial reactions to the book from Air Force personnel?

A. I have gotten no official reaction. I've gotten fan letters from people in the service—at least two, I believe, from officers, one of whom is with the Air Force Academy, but he was writing to express his approval of the book as literature rather than expressing any sympathy with the ideas.

Another reason I have not heard any objections is that most people treat it as a *novel*, as a work of fiction rather than as an essay or propaganda tract. It's not *intended* to be a sociological treatise, although the substance of the fiction is almost an encyclopedia of the current mental atmosphere.

It is certainly a novel of *comment*; there are comments about the loyalty oath, the free enterprise system, civil rights, bureaucracy, patriotism—but these are the ingredients out of which to create a fictional narrative.

In writing, I was more concerned with producing a *novel* that would be as contemporary as possible. I don't mean contemporaneous with World World II; contemporary with the period I was writing in. I was more concerned with producing a work of fiction—literary art, if you will—than of converting anybody. I'm really afraid of getting involved in controversy—I'm a terrible coward, just like Yossarian. It's the easiest thing to fight—I learned that in the war—it *takes* a certain amount of courage to go to war, but not as much as to refuse to go to war. I think that's the danger the world faces today; war might be the easiest solution to problems, and one country or the other might rely on war simply because it's a way out of frustration.

When I have a complaint against a department store, I try to avoid using the phone—I'd much rather put it on paper and avoid all danger of any personal combat.

Q. One stern critic said: "If Catch-22 *were intended as a commentary novel, [the] sideswiping of character and action might be taken care of by thematic control. It fails here because half its incidents are farcical and fantastic. The book is an emotional hodge-podge; no mood is sustained long enough to register for more than a chapter."*

A. Well, I *do* sideswipe character and action. I think that's one of the approaches that gives the book what effect it has. I tried to avoid, first of all, conventional structure of the novel; I tried to give it a structure that would complement the content of the book itself, which really derives from our present atmosphere of chaos, disorganization, absurdity, cruelty, brutality, insensitivity, but at the same time, one in which even the worst people, I think, are basically good, motivated by humane impulses.

"I'll tell you why the world is in such a turmoil—everybody wants a standard of living like ours, that's why . . ."

And I tried to emphasize this by the structure, much the same way that many very good contemporary composers are using dissonances and irregular tempos and harmonics to get this same feeling.

I did consciously try to use what might be called dramatic counterpoint, so that tragedies are dismissed almost flippantly—a line or two might describe something terrible happening to a character, whereas whole pages might concentrate on something of *subordinate* dramatic value. By doing that, I tried to emphasize the sense of loss, or the sense of sorrow; and also capture this thing which permits us to survive the loss of people dear to us, so that nobody's suffering lingers with us very long.

People die and are forgotten. People are abused and are forgotten. People suffer, people are exploited, *right now;* we don't dwell upon them 24 hours a day. Somehow they get lost in the swirl of things of much less importance.

Catch-22 is not to my mind a formless novel. If anything, it was constructed almost meticulously to give the appearance of a formless novel. Joyce's *Ulysses* is possibly one of the most confusing novels when you first approach it, yet there's a structure and tension in virtually every word.

Incidentally, it's turning out to be a very easy novel to read, because I get *many* letters from people in high school and freshmen in college. I have a collection of letters that could be called love letters—from people of all three sexes, probably, and of all ages, just rhapsodic in their enthusiasm. I'm sure the writers of each of these letters would like each other enormously if they met. People that I have met as a result of these letters—there's almost an instantaneous rapport. I express so much of my own views in the novel, with the result that anybody who responds to the book is going to respond to me. We meet, and almost immediately we're conversing like old friends.

Q. One of the most common themes in the letters I get at The Realist *is: "I'm glad to know I'm not alone"* in terms of their *outlook on life. People actually use the magazine as a screening device. Have you found this is true of your book?*

A. Yes, I've gotten a few comments from people who began re-examining their friends in terms of *Catch-22*. Mary Bancroft—who's fairly active in New York City politics—wrote me a letter about how one of her children came to New York and Mary gave her a copy and held her breath; and then the daughter called up and liked it very much. Mary was grateful. She didn't have to reject her daughter.

Q. Ralph J. Gleason was wondering how you feel about certain other writers' approaches to the insanity of our time. I'll name them one at a time. Louis-Ferdinand Céline?

A. Céline's book, *Journey to the End of Night*, was one of those which gave me a direct inspiration for the form and tone of *Catch-22*.

Q. Nelson Algren?

A. *The Man With the Golden Arm*, which I had read earlier, became an almost unconscious influence in the form of this type of open hero.

Q. Terry Southern?

A. I read *The Magic Christian* very quickly, and there were parts of it I liked enormously and parts that just eluded me. I'm not a very good reader. I had not read his book before I wrote *Catch-22*, but I think those people Southern influenced through his book might very well have influenced me.

Q. Richard Condon?

A. I read *The Manchurian Candidate* and I read *The Oldest Confession*. When I read the review of *The Manchurian Candidate*, I was in about the middle of *Catch-22*, and I had a feeling, well, here's a guy who's writing the same book *I* am; I'd better read this quickly because he might have already written it.

And then I read it, and I think there's a great deal of similarity, first of all in the concern, or the use of political and social materials—or products of the political and social conflicts—as the basis for his book, and there's a great similarity in the attitude toward them, so that they are at once serious and at the same time it's almost like watching a kind of burlesque and also a kind of everyman show on stage.

There's a definite feeling of kinship with him, but mine is, I suppose, an optimistic novel with a great deal of pessimism in it —there's a very heavy sense of the tragic, particularly toward the end, where I almost consciously sought to re-create the feeling of Dostoevsky's dark passages, and I have one or two allusions to chapters in Dostoevsky.

Q. About the use of exaggeration as a vehicle for satire: do you think you may have exaggerated too much beyond the possibilities of reality?

A. Well, I *tried* to exaggerate in almost every case, gradually, to a point beyond reality—that was a deliberate intention, to do it so gradually that the *unreality* becomes *more* credible than the realistic, normal, day-to-day behavior of these characters. Everything could *possibly* happen; nothing in there is supernatural—but it defies probability. But so much of what is *done* in our day-to-day existence defies probability if we stop to examine it. And this is the effect I wanted to achieve, to make these characters seem more real in terms of their eccentricities carried to absurdity.

A scene which to many people is the high spot of the book, and to other people is the point at which their credulity was strained: the incident in which Milo bombs his own squadron and escapes without punishment. Critics who praised the book singled this out as a triumph. On the other hand, most people in conversation say that this was the one thing they found hard to believe.

Now, I sincerely think that this is an impossibility; I don't think that in time of war a man could drop bombs deliberately on his own people and then escape without punishment. But I think people in every country commit *actions* which cause infinitely more *damage* to their fellow citizens; even commit actions which result in more physical deaths, as well—and are *lionized* for it; made into heroes for it.

Q. There are other things which I think go beyond the area of possibility. The soldier in white, for example, is continuously being fed his own waste products intravenously—

A. Of course, if you assume that there's a human being inside the bandages, then he could not be kept alive by his own waste products; that's a scientific impossibility. But if you begin to question, as I do, whether there *is* a human being inside, then it becomes a matter of economy just to keep using the same fluid to put back inside him.

But he is handled as a kind of gruesome symbol of many things. In one instance, he is discussed as a middle-man. If you look at man—remove the conscience, remove the sensibility— well, he takes matter, he absorbs it, excretes, or uses it up; and this is a natural process in which he is just one tiny phase of the whole cycle. And that was the point of using the soldier in white that way.

No, he could not happen, I suppose, unless there *was* some gigantic conspiracy—they decide to put this form swathed in bandages in the hospital and put nothing inside.

Q. Did you ever read Johnny Got His Gun—*which was about a basket case—by Dalton Trumbo?*

A. Oh, sure. The thing that I liked best was that the *Daily News* wrote an editorial recommending it and praising it. It came out when the *News* was in its isolationist, anti-Roosevelt phase.

Q. There were a couple of other areas in your book of probability versus possibility. Like eating chocolate-covered cotton—

A. Oh, it's not impossible that a man would try to market cotton covered with chocolate. And nobody does eat it in the book. In fact, when Milo gives it to Yossarian, Yossarian spits it out and says, "You can't give it to people, they'll get sick." Now, I think the corollaries of *that*. . . .

Q. What about the loyalty oath scene, where they have to pledge allegiance hundreds of times and sing the Star-Spangled Banner *all over the place—*

A. Again, that is not a physical impossibility. You know, in the first outline of this book, there were going to be a number of deliberate, very *conspicuous* anachronisms—There were going to be a number of supernatural things taking place, without any explanation, so that the physically impossible would be worked in with the possible, and be recognizable.

And then, I forget the motive, I decided nothing in this book would be physically impossible.

Consequently, even in the latter half of the book, where you

An Impolite Interview with Joseph Heller, *continued*

have this whore with the knife coming up in all kinds of disguises, the effect I give is that she's moving from place to place with the speed of light, because the scale there is changed to give you fast action; but always two hours or three hours go by, so that he pushes the girl out of the plane in Rome, then flies back to the airfield. You get the impression that she's beat him there, and she stabs him. But if you look, he spends a few hours running to find Hungry Joe, the pilot, to fly him back.

So the explanation would be: in that time, she could've hopped a plane somehow and gotten there. In the first writing, she was going to pop up with a speed that would've been impossible. And then I decided, let's keep consistent about this. But it's not physically impossible that somebody, for reasons of their own, would take this zombie—which is what he's supposed to be: a zombie, really, or nothing—would, for reasons of their own, get some kind of wire-structured *papier maché* and cover it with bandages and pass it off as a man who's been seriously wounded in the war—they *could* do it; it's not being physically impossible.

Q. What about the family visiting the hospital and failing to recognize that Yossarian isn't their son?

A. Well, the only one who accepts him as the son almost instantly is the mother. It's easier for mothers to accept strangers—I've noticed that women seem much fonder of other people's children than of their own, and men don't care; the only children men care for are their own. It's an unusual reaction, but not an impossible one.

Q. In retrospect, are there any important changes you would make in the book?

A. I can't think of any. I would not change Milo bombing his squadron because, on one level, this book is an allegory—there are *passages* where it becomes allegoric; there are other passages where it becomes realism—and I think that, allegorically, that is a consistent and most logical action.

Q. Some of the stuff that does go unpunished in real life makes it seem almost possible after all—

A. Well, it is possible, for example, in this country, and in Russia, in England—for individuals to be put to death, without any legal sanction, and for the people who did it to be known and to escape punishment. In fact, it's almost a daily occurrence here.

But Milo's action transcends this. It's a time of war, and he bombs indiscriminately, and it's an act of *physical* violence. It is conceivable to me that somebody might manufacture a food product or a drug product that would *poison* people, and the punishment for this would be slight; there would be extenuations if not justifications. It depends to a large extent, *always*, on whom your victims *are*. Or who *you* are. And in this case it was just an attack on his own society, almost without discrimination.

Each time I re-read the book, I find I'm angling for something; I'll read a chapter and I say, "Maybe I can make this into a recording," and the next thing you know, I'm scheming commercially—but I think one thing I would probably do would be to cut—language rather than incident. I did cut enormously. Bob Gottlieb, my editor and a very tactful man, made only two suggestions, really.

At the time I handed this book in, it was 800 typewritten

pages, and his first reaction was that it's the most upsetting book he's ever read, and it's a splendid, splendid book, and he would publish it just as is. I said, "Well, if you have any suggestions. . . . " And he said, "Well, of course, we'll talk about it. . . ." It was down to about 625 typewritten pages when it was finally submitted. And that's an enormous amount of cutting. He never said *cut*, but on the basis of his suggestions, I went back and cut something like a third of the first 200 pages—about 60 pages—without cutting a single incident; it was all in terms of language or dialogue.

Even in its final version, one general criticism against the book is that it's too long and does tend to be repetitious. If they *don't* like the book, it's repetitious; if they *like* it, it has a recurring and cyclical structure, like the theme in a Beethoven symphony.

Q. Your sympathetic central character is an atheist; was there any reaction to this, say by members of the clergy?

A. None whatsoever. One of the nicest and earliest letters I got was from a member of the clergy on the faculty of Notre Dame. The envelope was addressed to me at Simon & Schuster, which meant it was in reference to the book. A chill went through me—the same kind of chill I got when I received this letter from the Air Force Academy—you know: *here it comes* . . . until I knew what was inside . . . and then I was amazed and delighted.

Then I realized that my amazement comes from my own naiveté about other people. A few friends I have who are Republicans embraced this book immediately; I thought it was a liberal book, and they said, "No, it's not a liberal book, it's anti-everything."

And I was very naive about the mind of the intellectual religious leader—a friend educated at Marquette told me about the Jesuit Catholic as opposed to many of the superstitions and practices and narrowmindedness of other Catholics. The book got a fairly good review in the University of Scranton, which, I think, reads for the Index and classifies books.

I don't conceive of Yossarian as an atheist any more than I conceive of the chaplain as necessarily believing in God. I see Yossarian as having no positive attitude on the subject, and I see the chaplain as having no definite attitude on the subject. I would prefer to think of Yossarian as an atheist when pushed for an answer, but who regards any discussion of it as having no relation to the problems of the moment.

I don't think he's un-Christian in his feelings if we take the term "Christian" to mean what it ought to.

Q. Why did you have an Assyrian as the central character?

A. I got the idea, frankly, from James Joyce's placing Bloom in Dublin. I wanted somebody who would seem to be *outside* the culture in every way—ethnically as well.

Because America is a melting-pot, there are huge concentrations of just about every other nationality. (But his name is not Assyrian; I've since been told it's Armenian.)

I wanted to get an extinct culture, somebody who could not be identified either geographically, or culturally, or sociologically—somebody who has a capability of ultimately divorcing himself completely from all emotional and psychological ties.

Q. There was some speculation by a couple of my friends

"Man is a monstrous farce. . . .
Present company excluded, of course!"

An Impolite Interview with Joseph Heller, *continued*

that you got the idea from William Saroyan's "Twenty Thousand Assyrians."

A. It was from that story that I first learned the Assyrians were almost extinct. But my purpose in doing so was to get a man who was *intrinsically* an outsider. It's very hard for a person really to shake off all his roots. That's the big myth about this country, by the way—the melting-pot. It isn't. They never melted.

Q. My biggest shock in the book was to find out that Yossarian's first name was John.

A. I thought that was funny to mention just once. There were certain instances where I just could not avoid putting something in because it made me laugh. I think, too, that he should have a first name, so that he doesn't become completely a symbol. I wanted to give him some orientation. And I think *John* just puts him right back where he belongs. A John is the name that call girls use to identify customers, so it's so typically *nebbish*, you know?

Q. Just for the benefit of people not in the know, what's the translation of Lieutenant Scheisskopf's name?

A. Shithead. When I had to give him a name, I decided I'd want to call him the German translation of shithead, and my secretary's roommate then was a Fulbright scholar from Germany.

But there again, that let me use an inside joke which pleased me very much, and possibly which other people didn't notice. At one point in dialogue, someone says, "I wonder what that Shithead is up to"—with a capital S. I have a number of things like that which I like to think gives me an edge on the world. But one by one, I give them away.

Q. All right, how about the background of the chaplain being an Anabaptist?

A. There again, I was looking for a religion that would sound familiar, yet would not have associations with any of our established religions. This gives the chaplain a certain amount of latitude of reaction and response in actions. He's really a religious man, but he's a nondenominational minister.

Q. Jacques in Candide *was an Anabaptist—*

A. I didn't know that. I've never read *Candide.*

Q. That's funny, because some people I know have thought all along that this was one of your private jokes.

A. An English instructor wanted to do a paper on *Catch-22,* and he asked me a whole load of questions, and I replied as honestly as I could. He was right that one of the prevailing ideas was one of withdrawal. I know I have characters disappear, by dying, and I have Yossarian disappear at the end. I had not seen this pattern that extensively. So I learned something from him.

But then he got to miracle ingredient Z-247, mentioned at the beginning, as Yossarian is boasting, "I'm Pepsodent, I'm Tarzan, I'm miracle ingredient Z-247. . . ." He looked that up and found it's an element called Einsteinium, named after Einstein.

And then, toward the end, in that chapter, "The Eternal City," Einstein becomes the universal hero. He said he can't believe that's just accidental. Yet I didn't know this. I just picked Z-247 right out of the blue.

Q. In the process of writing Catch-22, *did you ever change your mind about how you were going to end it?*

A. No. The ending was written long before the middle. Right after I sold the book, I was riding on the subway, and I actually wrote the words to the ending—this was perhaps four years before the book was finished—and I didn't change it once.

I couldn't see any alternative ending. It had a certain amount of integrity, not merely with the action of the book—that could've permitted anything—but with the moral viewpoint; the heavy suffusion of moral content which, it seemed to me, required a resolution of *choice* rather than accident.

Q. But this is one of the things I meant when I asked about people who might've found the book objectionable—Yossarian deserts at the end. This is what people always say about pacifists and conscientious objectors: If everybody had deserted, we would've lost the war.

A. I thought I had gone beyond that by a discussion preceding his act of running.

When he says, "I'm tired, I have to think of myself, my country is safe now," he's told, "Well, suppose everyone felt that way," and he says, "Well, I'd be a damn fool to feel differently."

I also tried to make it very evident that the war was just about over.

Q. Would it have made any difference if the war weren't over?

A. Oh, certainly. I mean if this book had been set two or three years earlier, before the beachhead, then it would be a completely different book—if he had that many missions and were being asked to fly more purely to help a superior officer achieve a promotion—then I would've had him desert, because the replacements are waiting there, as they are at the end of the book. So there would not have been any great loss as far as the military efforts were concerned.

But if it's right after Pearl Harbor, and we *don't* have enough planes, and we *don't* have enough men, and Hitler *is* in a dominant and threatening position, then it would be a completely different situation.

I regard this essentially as a peacetime book. What distresses me very much is that the ethic often dictated by a wartime emergency has a certain justification, but when this thing is carried *over* into areas of peace; where the same demands are made upon the individual in the cause of national interest—the line that I like very much is when Milo tells Yossarian that he's jeopardizing his traditional freedoms by exercising them—this wartime emergency ideology transplanted to peacetime, leads not only to absurd situations, but to very tragic situations.

The stimulus for certain action justifies an action. If the stimulus is not there and the action exists anyway, then you've got a right to examine why you're doing it.

Q. In the end, Yossarian deserts in order to find sanity in Sweden—

A. But he's not going to get there, he knows that. He's told, "You'll never get there." And he says, "I know, but I'll try."

Q. People aren't sure of this, just as they're not sure whether Salinger's Franny is pregnant—

A. They're not sure because they're hopeful he'll get there, I suppose. For one thing, he's choosing the wrong way. There's also implicit—well, it's not implicit if people miss it—that this is an act of opposition or an act of protest. It's the only way left that he *can* protest without cutting his own head off. He's not a martyr. But the very act of *doing* what he does will stir up things, will stir up a certain amount of talk and dissension, will embarrass his superior officers. I don't think Sweden is paradise. Sweden was important to me as a *goal*, or an objective, a kind of Nirvana. It's important, if you're in a situation which is imperfect, uncomfortable, or painful, that you have some *objective* to move toward in order to change that situation.

Now, in Yossarian's situation—his environment, the world itself—the monolithic society closes off every conventional area of protest or corrective action, and the only choice that's left to him is one of ignoble acceptance in which he can profit and live very comfortably—but nevertheless ignoble—or *flight*, a renunciation of that condition, of that society, that set of circumstances.

The only way he can renounce it without going to jail is by deserting it, trying to keep going until they capture him. I think of him as a kind of spirit on the loose. You know, he is the only hope left at the end of the book. Had he accepted that choice. . . . I think if you want to start clipping paragraphs from newspapers, you'll find that organization today, any organized effort, must contain the germ of continuing disorganization.

The most effective business enterprise, I should think, is a single proprietorship, where one man goes into business for himself and has to hire nobody. The next best possibly is two men as partners; they work harder—there must be some kind of mathematical ratio, particularly when it involves government, I think, because government is so *huge*.

And that includes the Army, for example. You're dealing with millions of people, and there are certain personality- or mental-types that are attracted to that kind of work, either because they can't get a job anywhere else, or because they like doing that.

I cannot imagine anybody who's really ambitious, with any real talent, of any real intelligence, choosing to place himself within a large organization, where he functions in relation to hundreds of other people, because every contact is an impairment of his efficiency.

And the kind of person who would stamp documents or classify documents is a kind of person that would not normally be expected to excel in the matter of efficiency or in the matter of making astute judgments, value-judgments.

Q. But you know that intelligent people do go into large organizations; the trend is more and more toward that—

A. I'm speaking mainly of government. To really get to the higher echelon of a large company requires at least one special kind of intelligence, and requires a great deal of energy and hard work and ambition.

At the same time, the organization that these people manage, is *incredible*. I mean, nothing in my book—nothing in the wildest satire—goes beyond it. The inter-office rivalries; the mistakes in communications; the difficulties of finding people to promote who can do a job well—the amount of waste in the life of any corporation, at least the ones I've been with, is just extraordinary.

On the other hand, it's hard to find anybody you'd classify as an intellectual associated with a business. To most people who have a high degree of creative intelligence, business is boring after a certain point. There are no new challenges. Showing the gross profit 4 million dollars one year, how do we boost it to 4½ million the next year?—and after a while you really don't give a damn. It's just like a beaver building a dam. I don't know why a beaver wants a dam, by the way, but I have a feeling that it may not even *need* the dam—it builds a dam because it's a *beaver*. And a person trained to one occupation, even when he gets to the top, he continues doing accountancy because he's an *accountant*.

There is a law of life: People in need of help have the least chance of getting it. Here again, we can almost establish a mathematical relationship. The chance of a person getting help is in inverse proportion to the extent of his need. There's a line about Major Major: Because he needed a friend so desperately, he never found one.

I think it's certainly true of mental cases. A person who's in out-and-out need, who's on the verge of suicide, who *is* paranoiac on the strength of it, is going to get no help from anybody; a mild neurotic will be encouraged to see a psychiatrist, his friends will want to help him and indulge him, but when the need becomes critical, then—if I might quote an old philosopher—goodbye, Charlie.

Q. Would you care to say a few words about the art of protest?

A. I think the only people left that I'm capable of admiring are those people who *do* protest, and at grave risk to them-

QUOTED WITHOUT COMMENT

F rom a report on the World Forum on Syphilis and Other Treponematoses, held in Washington:

"In another paper delivered today, Paul W. Kinsie of the American Social Health Association warned that, if the moon was to be kept free from venereal disease, prostitution must be barred there."

selves. The colored people, CORE, the sit-ins, the students evoke a feeling of admiration I can't recall ever having for anybody else. They are the heroes of the time.

And there's also a natural sympathy for the underdogs, and when the underdog is on the side of a principle that is so patently just . . . the photographs you see every fall of children going to school, little colored girls in their pretty party dresses, and then you have these raving lunatics with this *phenomenal* ugliness of hatred on their faces—the contrast leads me to believe that the white race could profit a great deal if intermarriage became more prevalent; it's something I think that the Southern white might do everything to encourage for his *own* good. The real difficulty we find today is that there are at *least* two sides to many questions. It's terrible when people can't see the other person's point of view; it's even worse when you *can* see both points of view, because then you're almost incapable of taking action with any degree of conviction.

Q. Now, do you think that the work of a sanitation man, pragmatically, may be more important than yours? We can do without your book, but we can't do without the sanitation man—yet you get more respect than the sanitation man. Do you think you should?

A. I *get* it. I get it for reasons that other people get respect. There is nothing dignified and noble about labor. As far as I can see, there's never been anything noble or dignified about labor.

The people that a society glorifies and exults—and this is true even in a workers' paradise—are the people who get their rewards by not working as hard. You're dealing with the factor of status. As long as we live, the man at the bottom is not going

"Oh, knock off the balderdash, man! If we really thought it was legal to use violence in a rightful cause, how come we're all dressed up like Indians?"

to be treated as well as the man at the top. The man who chlorinates the water we drink is an essential person, but he's easily *replaced*, I suppose. Fifteen million people could do whatever he does.

I think eventually that's what's going to happen to our astronauts. Millions of people, I suppose, would volunteer to be astronauts. If they called for volunteers to be the first man to the moon, and the odds were against getting back, there'd be no shortage of people.

The ultimate contribution there is not the guy in the capsule, but the guy at M.I.T.—it's a scientific achievement. The human element might be necessary, but the rare skills are what produced it. It's a hard thing to invent the engine which drives a sanitation truck. We've always had a man with a shovel to throw the garbage in.

HEALTHY EXPOSURE

by Terry Southern

At the behest of several irate American mothers, we recently paid a visit to one of New York's largest toy stores, The Dumpling Shop, to inspect their new line of baby dolls—this being the source and object of the petition. "It is quite unspeakable," wrote Mrs. Leyton-Reims of Westchester. "My club is taking action. May we count on *you*?"

It is, of course, a bit off the track for a freethought magazine to become involved in controversy of this sort. Still, what's the use of it all if you can't take a stand occasionally, at least on matters of cultural importance? After all, these are serious times—East and West locked in dynamic struggle, our own culture faltering, indeed at times floundering, in a sea of cynicism and failing beliefs, youth desperately seeking values—so that it was with a heavy heart that we came

away from The Dumpling Shop, after having seen the item in question, namely the so-called "*Little Cathy Curse Doll—Complete With Teeny Tampons.*"

This "doll," we were blandly assured by the management, is merely a "logical follow-up" on last season's highly successful "*Tina Tiny Tears—The Naughty Nappy Doll* (She Cries Real Tears and Wets her Beddy)." Whether or not it is a "logical follow-up" is, at least in our opinion, not the principal issue; the principal issue is that of *taste*, of *responsibility*, and of downright *common decency*.

On these three counts we judge both The Dumpling Shop and the manufacturers of *The Little Cathy Curse Doll* to be in serious default. The lavish arrangements for the display of this "doll" occupy a prominent section of The Dumpling Shop's smart fourth floor. Stretched overhead is a huge colorful circus-like banner which features a happy little girl holding the doll and exclaiming: "Why, Cathy Curse, I *do* believe you're

staining! I think *you'd* better have fresh panties and a teeny tampon!"

Certainly it would be naive in the extreme to raise shrill and pious protest against the simple abstractions of material greed and commercial exploitation which daily confront us—these are part and parcel of the system, dues of the freedom club and cheap at the price. Surely, however, we do have a right to ask: Have we really so depleted exploitation that it has come to this? And moreover, where then is it to end? One is forced to wonder, even to speculate with dread, *what next? "Little Victor Vomit"? "Little Katy Ka-Ka"? "Don Diarrhea"? "Silly Sammy Shoot-Off"?!!*

No, we cannot, *will not*, buy it. Our answer to Mrs. Leyton-Reims: Yes, you may *indeed* count on us. Our presses and our staff stand ready to shoulder a man-size burden in carrying your cause forward, which, by our lights, is also the cause of every right-thinking parent throughout this land.

THE MENOPAUSE THAT REFRESHES

by Viva

One of the major disappointments last month was the admission by Father Berrigan that the blood he poured into the Selective Service System files was only partly his. In fact, the main portion of it was duck's blood—imported, yet—from Holland.

For years I have been saying that power should be in the hands of the women, and this pallid priestly protest only proves the point. Women, stand up and be counted! You can begin with the number you're most familiar with: 28.

Every 28 days those of you who rely on that old Catholic standby, Kotex (we've heard that the Church recommends this archaic diaper to its female members inasmuch as the use of Tampax may be the cause of grave sin, due to the pleasure of insertion), can stage a mass sanitary drop-in.

Leave your napkins at the door of the draft board and let loose your menstrual blood directly into their files. This method has a double advantage over the duck blood method: menstrual flow will not only achieve the desired visual effect but will also be accompanied by an appropriately pungent odor. Those of you of the Protestant faith could stage a plug-out by quietly pulling the collective strings of your Tampaxes.

We are not forgetting our Jewish sisters; bigger and better plans are in store for them . . . Hadassah may stage a mass miscarriage. This abortive idea can be accompanied by various slogans: Miscarry-a-Major Day; Plop-a-Private Day; Leak-a-Lieutenant Day . . . or to tie it all together in a neat bundle, a Washington D. and C.

Now, in keeping with draft regulations, we want our women to attempt to register their miscarriages and aborted fetuses with the Selective Service. As for our men, attempt to register your discarded sperm. You have a definite advantage over us women. Whereas we can only prevent one egg per month from reaching the Army, you can prevent millions of wriggling spermatazoa per hour from getting to the battlefields.

Masturbate everything into the jars we will be passing out. At the end of each week your sperm will equal the amount of glue to be found in a Lepage bottle, and it should by that time have the same consistency of said glue. You will be issued unglued stamps. We are printing them now, encrusted with the symbol of our movement, a cupped hand.

You will also be issued a stamp book. For 100 stamps you can purchase a Vibrex to make the chore a bit more pleasurable; 200 stamps entitles you to a plastic mouth; 300 stamps entitles you to a plastic mouth complete with a self-moisturizing mechanism; 400 stamps brings you an artificial vagina; 500 stamps brings you an artificial vagina with the added attraction of a mechanical contraction contraption.

By the time you have saved 2,000 stamps you will have a complete plastic body—male or female. Thus we feel we have covered all possible sexual tastes and possibilities as compensation for non-human sexual involvement in the cause of stamping out war.

Abuse yourself, not the Viet Cong.

THE REALIST SEAL OF APPROVAL

ANTI-COMMUNIST ASSHOLES OF THE YEAR

"Please feel free to say anything at all that pops into your mind. Unless, of course, it's Communist-inspired."

Alvin Dark, manager of the San Francisco Giants: "Any pitcher who throws at a batter and deliberately tries to hit him is a Communist. . . ."

***

Arizona's Assistant Attorney General, for rejecting the Communist Party's request for a place on the ballot because state law "prohibits official representation" for

Communists and, in addition, "The subversive nature of your organization is even more clearly designated by the fact that you do not even include your zip code on your letter."

***

Pat Boone, speaking at the Greater New York Anti-Communism Rally in Madison Square Garden:

"I would rather see my four daughters shot before my eyes than to have them grow up in a Communist United States. I would rather see those kids blown into Heaven than taught into hell by the Communists."

AN IMPOLITE INTERVIEW WITH NORMAN MAILER

Q. When you and I first talked about the possibility of doing an interview, you said: "I find that when I discuss ideas, it spills the tension I need to write." Which seems like a very Freudian explanation. Does it still apply?

A. Sure it does. I think putting out half-worked ideas in an interview is like premature ejaculation.

Q. Then why bother?

A. I got tired of saying no to you. Also, I'm beginning to get a little pessimistic about the number of ideas I never write up. Perhaps the public is better off with premature ejaculation than no intellectual sex at all. I'm just thinking of the public, not myself.

Q. Now, whereas J. D. Salinger stays in his little fallout shelter and writes, you seem to relish a public involvement, sometimes to the point of notoriety.

A. I would guess Salinger and I are not the least bit alike. I think I'd go mad if I worked up in New England. I tried it, you know; I did live in Vermont during two separate winters. I went back to *Barbary Shore* in Jamaica, Vermont, and I finished it in Putney. I guess I did a lot of work up there, but I wasn't happy. I felt I belonged in the city. Of course, you can't tell. In twenty years I might become a hermit, and Salinger might be picked up drunk and disorderly for going ape every night at eleven o'clock. Think of it. J. D. Salinger eighty-sixed from the Colony.

Q. What distinction do you draw between a creative artist's exhibitionism and his communication?

A. I don't draw the line. Once you become a small legend, you need do very little, and it still will become a new part of the legend. Even if you're doing something simple, the result tends to become large and complicated. On the other hand, exhibitionism also becomes one of the ways in which you can manipulate the world, one of the ways in which you live with the world—it's part of the game.

The thing is, as you get older, you begin to enjoy it just a little less. I love certain kinds of stunts, but I'm getting wary of the aftermath. Somebody I know said after one caper, "You're going to end up getting 50 letters for this stunt over the next two years." Not all the letters are that interesting to answer.

Q. Isn't there a basic dichotomy between creative artists who express themselves in their work—there's a definite excitement in their life—as opposed to the average person whose days are filled with boredom—in the factory, in the office—and who can almost find a sort of pleasure in identifying nationalistically with international tensions? . . .

A. First time I've heard you talking like a totalitarian. Very few artists I know are happy. The kind of artist who writes a poem about peace is the kind of guy I flee. There's something pompous about people who join peace movements, SANE, and so forth. They're the radical equivalent of working for the FBI.

You see, nobody can criticize you. You're doing God's work, you're clean. How can anyone object to anybody who is for banning the bomb? I think there's something doubtful about these people. I don't trust them. I think they're totalitarian in spirit. Now of course I'm certainly not saying they're Communist, and they most obviously are not Fascists, but there are new kinds of totalitarians. A most numerous number since World War II.

I think, for example, most of the medical profession is totalitarian by now. At least those who push antibiotics. I think the FBI is totalitarian, pacifists are totalitarian, *Time* Magazine is a Leviathan of the totalitarian. There's a totalitarian *geist*, a spirit, which takes many forms, has many manifestations. People on your own side are just as likely to be totalitarian as people on the other side.

Q. Yes, but totalitarian to me implies force—

A. A dull, moral, abstract force. There is just such a force in the campaign for "Ban the bomb." It's too safe. That's the thing I don't like about it. You don't *lose* anything by belonging to a committee to ban the bomb. Who's going to hurt you?

Q. There are certain employers who frown upon it—

A. Which employers? I think many good people are beginning to get a little complacent. There is no real action for them, and so they end up in what I think are essentially passive campaigns like "Ban the bomb."

I'm against sit-down strikes. I'm against people sitting down in Trafalgar Square, and cops having to carry them off. I think if you're not ready to fight the police, you mustn't sit down and let them carry you off. You must recognize that you're not ready to fight to the very end for your principles. I was carried off in a chair not so long ago, and I'm not proud of it.

Q. Extending this to its logical conclusion, then, would you say that Mahatma Gandhi was a totalitarian?

A. I think so. He was a fine man, a great man, etc., etc., but many totalitarians are fine men. Sigmund Freud, for example. For all we know, Albert Schweitzer might be totalitarian. How do you know? He seems too safe. The kind of people who seem to love Schweitzer are the sort who work on telethons for incurable diseases. They take a pill if their breasts hurt. Anybody who wants a quick solution for a permanent problem is a low-grade totalitarian.

Q. At the risk of making you seem totalitarian, what would you substitute for sit-down strikes and other passive forms of protest?

A. Sketch the outline of a large argument. What I don't like about the "Ban the bomb" program, for example, is that it is precisely the sort of political program which can enlist hundreds of thousands, then millions of people. Half or two-thirds or even three-quarters of the world could belong to such an organization, yet you could still have an atomic war. I'm not saying the

"Ban the bomb" program would *cause* an atomic war, but there's absolutely no proof it would prevent it.

The world exists in profound insecurity; everybody willy-nilly has become an existentialist; one is face to face with the continuation of the universe every breath one takes; those questions usually delegated to Sunday now obsess us seven days a week; our best hope for no atomic war is that the complexities of political life at the summit remain complex. The hope is that the people of Russia and America express themselves enough to keep these societies complex.

So I say create complexities, let art deepen sophistication, let complexities be demonstrated to our leaders, let us try to make *them* more complex. That is a manly activity. It offers more hope for saving the world than a gaggle of pacifists and vegetarians. The "Ban the bomb" program is militant, but it is not manly. So it is in danger of becoming totalitarian.

Q. Joe Heller told me that he admires you for not taking shelter during the Civil Defense drill. Why is this any more manly than other activities?

A. I didn't stand there because I was a pacifist, but because I wanted to help demonstrate a complexity. It's a physical impossibility to save the people of New York in the event of atomic attack. That doesn't mean one should not live in New York, but I think one should know the possible price. Air raid drills delude people into believing that they're safe. That's what I object to, rounding up the psyches of New Yorkers and giving them mass close order drill to the sound of an air raid siren. It makes cowardly pigs of people.

Q. You once referred in passing to the FBI as a religious movement; would you elaborate on that?

A. I think a lot of people need the FBI for their sanity. In order to be profoundly religious, to become a saint, for example, one must dare insanity, but if one wishes instead to flee from insanity, one method is to join an organized religion. The FBI is an organized religion.

The FBI blots out everything which could bring dread into the average mediocrity's life. Like a weak lover who rushes to immolate himself for love—since that is easier than to fight a long war for love—the mediocrity offers the FBI his complete conformity. He gives up his personal possibilities. He believes he is living for the sake of others. The trouble is that the others are just as mediocre as he is. Such people not only use up their own lives, but if there *is* a God, they use *Him* up.

Naturally these lovers of the FBI can't even think of the possibility that they've wasted themselves. Instead they believe rabidly in that force which agrees with them, that force which is rabidly for mediocrity. At bottom, I mean profoundly at bottom, the FBI has nothing to do with Communism, with catching criminals, with the Mafia, the syndicate, with trust-busting, with interstate commerce, nothing to do with anything but serving as a high church for the true mediocre.

Q. Isn't it possible that the mass media which you call totalitarian are a reflection rather than a cause of this condition in society?

A. No, I don't think so. That's like saying that the United States Army was a reflection of what the soldiers wanted.

Q. But they were drafted—

A. And you're not drafted—your eye is not *drafted* when you turn on that TV set? That fact that I don't have a television set makes me no more than a conscientious objector. To assume that people are getting what they want through the mass media also assumes that men and women who direct the mass media know something about the people. But they don't. That's why I gave you the example of the Army. Because the officers who run the Army are not all vicious, miserable, horrible Generals of the sort somebody I know wrote about. Some are good family men, decent, they care terribly about their country, they want to be good to their men, they'd just as soon have their soldiers happy as unhappy. But they don't have the least notion of what goes on in the mind of a Private. It's like Greek to them, what the psychology of a Private is. They can't get close to them. Then of course you have all the Generals who *are* bad, who don't give a damn for the Private, who are out there to enrich themselves in the war.

Well, of course, the Private exists in a world hermetically alienated from the larger aims of the Generals planning the higher strategy of the war. Part of the tragedy of modern war (or what used to be modern war) is that you could have a noble war which was utterly ignoble at its basic level because the people who directed the war couldn't reach the common man who was carrying the gun. As for example, Franklin Delano Roosevelt and the average infantryman. They can't because they

BEATNIK
BEATNIK

WHITE
NEGRO

andy reiss

don't know anything about him, because there *is* such a thing as classes, finally. And the upper classes don't understand the lower classes; they're incapable of it. Every little detail of their upbringing turns them away from the possibility of such understanding.

The mass media is made up of a group of people looking for money and for power, not because they have any moral sense, any inner sense of a goal, of an ideal that's worth fighting for—dying for, if one is brave enough. No, power is the only thing which will relieve the profound illness which has seized all of us. The illness of the twentieth century. There isn't psychic room for all of us. Malthus's law has moved from the excessive procreation of bodies to the excessive mediocritization of psyches. The deaths don't occur on the battlefield any longer, or through malnutrition; they occur within the brain, within the psyche itself.

Q. There's a certain indirect irony there. I'm under the impression that you have almost a Catholic attitude toward birth control.

A. In a funny way I do. But I've come a long way to get there. After all, if my generation of writers represents anything, if there's anything we've fought for, it's for a sexual revolution.

If you compare America to England, it's incredible. We've gotten things printed here that twenty years ago would've seemed impossible for a century or forever. Not only *Lady Chatterley's Lover* and *Tropic of Cancer*, but little things like "The Time of Her Time"; extraordinary works like *Naked Lunch*. At least we're in the act of winning this war. You might say that the Church and the reactionaries are in long retreat on sex.

It's altogether their fault, as far as that goes. They flirted with sex. They used sex in order to make money or gain power. It was the Church, after all, who dominated Hollywood. They thought they could tolerate sex up to a point in Hollywood, because there was obviously a fast buck if you used sex in the movies, and they didn't want to alienate the producers. So the Church compromised its principles.

What happened was that they set something going they couldn't stop. And then people came along who were sincere about sex, and idealistic, naive no doubt like a good many of us. Innocent sexual totalitarians, we felt sex is good, sex has to be defended, fought for, liberated. We were looking for a good war. So we liberated sex. But the liberation's gotten into the hands of a lot of people who aren't necessarily first-rate. A crew of sexual bullies may be taking over the world. Sexual epigones, corporation executives who dabble.

The fact is, the prime responsibility of a woman probably is to be on earth long enough to find the best mate possible for herself, and conceive children who will improve the species.

If you get too far away from that, if people start using themselves as flesh laboratories, start looking for pills which prevent conception, then what they're doing, really, is acting like the sort of people who take out a new automobile and put sand in the crankcase in order to see if the sound that the motor gives off is a new sound.

Q. You're forcing me to the point of personalizing this. Do you put sand in your crankcase?

A. I hate contraception.

Q. I'm not asking you what your attitude toward it is.

A. It's none of your business. Let me just say I try to practice what I preach. I *try* to. There's nothing I abhor more than planned parenthood. Planned parenthood is an abomination. I'd rather have those fucking Communists over here. Will you print "fucking"?

Q. You said it, didn't you? Just tell me if you want it spelled with two g's or a c-k.

A. Those fucking Communists.

Q. In "The Time of Her Time," the protagonist calls his penis "The Avenger." Doesn't this imply a certain hostility toward women?

A. Of course it does. Is that news?

Q. All right, why is the narrator of your story—or why are you—hostile toward women?

A. If you're assuming an identification with the character, I can only say I *enjoyed* him. He was not altogether different from me. But he certainly wasn't me. I thought "The Avenger" was a good term to use. I think people walk around with terms like that in their unconscious mind. A great many men think of their cock as The Avenger.

But O'Shaugnessy happened to be enormously civilized. So he was able to open his unconscious and find the word, find the concept, and use it, humorously, to himself.

Q. If there was any hostility beneath the humor, would you say it was justified?

A. I would guess that most men who understand women at all feel hostility toward them. At their worst, women are low sloppy beasts.

Q. Do you find that men and women have reacted differently to "The Time of Her Time"?

A. I've found that most women like "The Time of Her Time" for some reason. Men tend to get touchy about it. They feel—is Mailer saying this is the way he makes love? Is he this good or is he this bad? Is he a phony? Is he advertising himself? Does he make love better than me? To which I say they're asses.

Q. Oh, so you're hostile toward men!

A. I'm hostile to men, I'm hostile to women, I'm hostile to cats, to poor cockroaches, I'm afraid of horses. You know.

Q. Several months ago I mentioned, in order to make a very definite point, a Cuban prostitute—this was the only prostitute I'd ever gone to, and I had been asking her all these questions about the revolution—and she stopped later in the middle of fellatio to ask me if I was a Communist.

A. You were in Cuba at the time?

Q. Yes. And she was anti-Castro.

A. Because he was cleaning them out of the whorehouses?

Q. Well, there were no more tourists coming to Cuba, and it was ruining their business. Anyway, I described this incident in The Realist, *and was accused of exhibitionism. But it was a funny, significant thing which I wanted to share with the readers.*

A. Oh, I remember reading your piece now. I was a little shocked by it. It threw me slightly. I had a feeling, "That's not good writing." And the next thought was, "Mailer, you're getting old." The next thought was, "If you're not really getting old, there is something bad about this writing, but what is it?"

Q. And?

A. A whore practicing fellatio looks up and says, "Are you a Communist?"—that's what the modern world is all about in a way. Saying it head-on like that probably gave the atmosphere honesty. But in some funny way, it didn't belong. I don't want to start talking like a literary buff, because I dislike most literary language, Hemingway's perhaps most of all (it was so arch). But still, in a way, a good writer is like a pitcher, and a reader is happy when he feels like a good batter facing a good pitcher. When the ball comes in, he gets that lift.

But writing it the way you did, Krassner, you were in effect hitting fungoes, making the reader field it, which is less agreeable than batting. If the reader had been able to guess that this was what was going on with the whore—that would have been the art of it, to phrase the language in such a way that the reader thinks, "Oh, Jesus, she's sucking his cock, and she asks him if he's a Communist." If it had happened that way, it might have been overpowering. What a montage!

Maybe it was the use of "fellatio." Maybe you just should have said, "I was having my cock sucked and she said, 'Are you a Communist?'" If you're getting into the brutality of it, get into the brutality of it. Throw a bean ball. Don't use the Latinism. All I know is that there was something bad about it, the effect was *shock*. Shock is like banging your head or taking a dull fall; your wits are deadened.

Q. That's what I wanted to do in the writing, because that's what happened to me in the act.

A. Then you're not interested in art, you're interested in therapy. That's the trouble—too many people writing nowadays give no art to the world, but draw in therapy to themselves. You should've said, "She was sucking my cock." I mean that's my professional opinion.

Q. It wasn't in Roget's Thesaurus. . . . Would you agree that you have an essentially biological approach to history?

A. I think I do, but I could never talk about it. I don't know enough history.

Q. If you were a future historian of sex, how would you look upon the Kennedy administration?

A. I'd say there's more acceptance of sexuality in America today than there was before he came in. Whether that's good or bad, I don't know. It may be a promiscuous acceptance of sexuality.

"I'm very sorry, but we of the FBI are powerless to act in a case of oral-genital intimacy unless it has in some way obstructed interstate commerce."

Q. Are you saying it's because of . . .?

A. Because of Kennedy—*absolutely*. I mean, Jesus, just think of going to a party given by Eisenhower as opposed to a party thrown by Kennedy. Do you have to wonder at which party you'd have a better time?

The average man daydreams about his leader. He thinks of being invited to his leader's home. If he thinks of being invited to Eisenhower's home, he thinks of how proper he's going to be. If he thinks of going to the Kennedys for a party, he thinks of having a dance with Jackie. Things liven up.

Why do you think people loved Hitler in Germany? Because they all secretly wished to get hysterical and *stomp* on things and scream and shout and rip things up and *kill*—tear people apart. Hitler pretended to offer them that. In some subtle way, he communicated it. That's why they wanted him. That's why he was good for Germany—they wanted such horror. Of course, by the end he didn't tear people apart, he gassed them.

If America gets as sick as Germany was before Hitler came in, we'll have our Hitler, one way or another.

But you see, the political fight right now is not to deal with the ends of the disease, but the means right here and now. To try to foil the sickness and root it out. One can have fascism come in any form at all, through the church, through sex, through social welfare, through state conservatism, through organized medicine, the FBI, the Pentagon. Fascism is not a way of life, but a murderous mode of deadening reality by smothering it with lies.

Every time one sees a bad television show, one is watching the nation get ready for the day when a Hitler will come. Not because the idealogy of the show is Fascistic; on the contrary, its manifest ideology is invariably liberal, but the show still prepares Fascism because it is meretricious art and so sickens the people a little further. Whenever people get collectively sick, the remedy becomes progressively more violent and hideous. An insidious, insipid sickness demands a violent far-reaching purgative.

Q. Jean Shepherd made the point—sarcastically—how come it's always the Bad Guys who become leaders?

A. Lenin wasn't a Bad Guy. Trotsky wasn't a Bad Guy. I don't think Alexander the Great was such a Bad Guy. Or Napolean. Bad Guys become leaders in a bad time. One can conceive of a man who's half-good and half-bad who comes to power in a time of great crisis and great change, when awful things are going on. He's going to reflect some of the awfulness of his time. He may become awful himself, which is a tragedy.

A man like Danton begins as a great man, and deteriorates. Castro may end badly, but that will be a tragedy. No one's ever going to tell me he wasn't a great man when he started. He reminds me of Cortez, who was one of the greatest leaders who ever lived.

Q. Then you're saying bad times result in bad leaders?

A. If a time is bad enough, a good man can't possibly succeed. In a bad time, the desires of the multitude are bad, they're low, ugly, greedy, cowardly, piggish, shitty.

Q. Then how do you sap the energy of bad leaders who are caught up in their own bad time?

A. In a bad time, a leader is responsible to his own services of propaganda. He doesn't control them. In a modern state, the

An Impolite Interview with Norman Mailer, *continued*

forces of propaganda control leaders as well as citizens, because the forces of propaganda are more complex than the leader. In a bad time, the war to be fought is in the mass media.

If a man becomes an anarchist, a hipster, some kind of proto-Communist, a rebel, a wild reactionary, I don't care what—if he's got a sense that the world is wrong and he's more or less right, that there are certain lives he feels are true and good and worth more than the oppressive compromises he sees before him every day, then he feels that the world has got to be changed or it is going to sink into one disaster or another. He may even feel, as I do, that we are on the edge of being plague-ridden forever. The thing to do, if he wants political action, is not to look for organizations which he can join, nor for long walks he can go on with other picketeers, but rather it is to devote his life to working subtly, silently, steelfully, against the state.

And there's one best way he can do that. He can *join* the mass media. He can bore from within—he should do it alone. The moment he starts to form sects and cells, he's beginning to create dissension and counter-espionage agents.

The history of revolutionary movements is that they form cells, then they defeat themselves. The worst and most paranoid kind of secret police—those split personalities who are half secret policemen and half revolutionaries (I'm talking of psychological types rather than of literal police agents)—enter these organizations and begin to manufacture them over again from within.

It's better to work alone, trusting no one, just working, working, working not to sabotage so much as to shift and to turn and to confuse the mass media and hold the mirror to its guilt, keep the light in its eye. Never, never, never oneself beginning to believe that the legitimate work one is doing in the mass media has some prior value to it; always knowing that the work, no matter how well intended, is likely to be subtly hideous work. The mass media does diabolically subtle things to the morale and life of the people who do their work; few of us are strong enough to live alone in enemy territory. But it's work which must be done.

So long as the mass media are controlled completely by one's enemies, the tender, sensuous, and sensual life of all of us is in danger. And the way to fight back is to look for a job in the heart of the enemy.

Q. How do you personally wield whatever power you have?

A. It's possible I have no power which would not vanish with fashion.

Q. Would it be the kind of power which would be diluted by the revelation of it?

A. *All* power is diluted by the revelation of it. That's why people who run things are secretive. That's why we have few good novels on how things really work.

Can you name me one good novel that'll tell you how a President is picked out of a national convention? No, you had to wait for Theodore White's book, which is not a novel, therefore not as good, because there's a limit to how deeply a writer of non-fiction can go into these things.

Q. How did you feel about Advise and Consent?

A. I read a part of it. Not a good novel. It did not tell very much which was true, not really. Nor have I read a major novel

"He's waiting to confess a mortal sin—he lied to Margaret Mead."

by a major novelist, about the news magazines. I think most young men who want to write want really to do no more than rush post-haste into the literary life.

You know, they get known well enough to have a short story or two in one or two particular magazines, attend the proper cocktail parties slavishly, take pains to entertain the hostess, they acquire a fellowship or a grant, they do *reviews*, they build up slowly. By the time they do a novel, they belong to the Union of High Mediocrities, the book reviewers welcome them, their reputations are suddenly large. It's a terrible, terrible way to become a writer. Once you're successful *that* way, the only material you have to draw upon is your past—you have no present, except that omnipresent damned idiotic literary life.

But if a young writer passes through occupations which are difficult or ugly (if complex)—if for example they work their way through a national news magazine, or rise so high as to be in on editorial meetings at *The New York Times*, and yet manage somehow to keep themselves alive as a writer, there comes a time when they can write a book or many books, when they can write something which can have enormous value.

England has a C.P. Snow. I think if America had a C.P. Snow, he'd have to be twenty times greater. But just think, we'd have a writer greater than Balzac. Jim Jones could become that kind of writer if he'd get his head out of the hog trough.

Q. In The Naked and the Dead, *there was a theme about the futility of violence on a grand scale; and yet, in "The White Negro," there's almost a justification of violence, at least on a personal level. How do you reconcile this apparent inconsistency?*

A. The ideas I had about violence changed 180 degrees over those years. Beneath the ideology in *The Naked and The Dead* was an obsession with violence. The characters for whom I had the most secret admiration, like Croft, were violent people.

Ideologically, intellectually, I did disapprove of violence, though I didn't at the time of "The White Negro." What I still disapprove of is *inhuman* violence which is on a large scale and abstract. I disapprove of bombing a city. I disapprove of the kind of man who will derive aesthetic satisfaction from the fact that an Ethiopian village looks like a red rose at the moment the bombs are exploding. I won't disapprove of the act of perception which witnesses that; I think that act of perception is—I'm going to use the word again—noble.

What I'm getting at is: a native village is bombed, and the bombs happen to be beautiful when they land; it would be odd if all that sudden destruction did not liberate some beauty. The form a bomb takes in its explosion may be in part a picture of the potentialities it destroyed. So let us accept the idea that the bomb is beautiful.

If so, any liberal who decries the act of bombing is totalitarian if he doesn't admit as well that the bombs were indeed beautiful.

Because the moment we tell something that's untrue, it does not matter how pure our motives—the moment we start mothering mankind and decide that one truth is good for them to hear and another is not so good, because while *we* can understand, those poor ignorant unfortunates cannot—then we're depriving others of knowledge which may be essential.

Think of a young pilot who comes along later, goes out on a mission and isn't prepared for the fact that a bombing might be beautiful. He might never get over the fact that he was particularly thrilled by the beauty of that bomb.

But this act of perception was *not* what was wrong; the evil was to think that this beauty was worth the helpless people who were wiped out broadside. Obviously, whenever there's destruction, there's going to be beauty implicit in it.

Q. Aren't you implying that this beauty is an absolute? Which, beauty is never . . .

A. Well, how do you know beauty is not an absolute? Listen, you guys on *The Realist*—I read you because I think you represent a point of view, and you carry that point of view very, very, far—but I think you're getting a touch sloppy because you get no opposition whatsoever from your own people; you'll get your head taken off at its base some day by a reactionary. He'll go right through you, because there are so many things you haven't thought out.

One of them is: How do you know beauty isn't absolute?

Q. Recently I referred in a Realist *editorial to a dead prizefighter and a pregnant woman, and suggested that if she really wanted to get a legal abortion, she would just sign up for a boxing match—to point out the irony that it's legal to kill a man in the ring, but illegal to remove a fetus from a woman. Would you like to attack that comparison?*

A. Ah, yes. Atrocious. I think that's taking a cheap advantage. In one case, a man is killed who is able to defend himself. In the other, an embryo who may have voyaged through eternity to be born again is snuffed out because of his mother's cultural propensity for socially accepted drugs like the limb-killer thalidomide.

Q. I just felt it was a dramatic way—

A. If somebody takes a handful of shit and throws it against the wall at a party, that's dramatic, but it's distasteful. Your example is distasteful. You were appealing to the low emotions in your readers. You have a terrible responsibility in *The Realist*, because *your* readers have low emotions too.

Just because nobody could find the sort of stuff printed in *The Realist* except in *The Realist*, there is a danger that people who read the sheet are going to begin to think there's something superior about them, just from the sheer fact they're reading *The Realist*.

Q. Well, whom do you prefer—a cruel hipster or a compassionate square? Let's say you're in a plane that's overloaded, and you have to lessen its weight by one passenger. . .

A. Square. The answer is simple. The one you push out would be the one. Your *body* would tell you which one to push out. The whole of hip is right at this point. I can't keep emphasizing too much that when it comes to matters of life and death, the instinct *must* take over.

The instinct knows more about life and death than the mind. The mind has been subject to every foul educational system which every authority and every class oppression has evolved over the years. Our minds have been poisoned. But what happens, I think, is that deep at the bottom of all this, the instinct keeps fighting its long, dreary, trench war against all the foul habits of thought, all the vocabularies of jargon.

It's a sad, dreary war. Each year our perceptions tend to grow a little more dull, our instincts become less happy, less quick. But the one thing the instinct has to hold on to involves its understanding of life and death. You understand of course that I advocate the life of instinct because I think man is more good than bad. If not, if we're more bad than good, then who's going to save us? Do you think some government is going to work up rules for a good society out of polluted, dull, fouled-up minds?

Q. You believe man is basically good?

A. I don't know. I'm saying the only possibility is *if* man is more good than bad. Then the next step is to help the instinct to express itself more and more.

Q. Do you think it's possible you take the orgasm too seriously, giving its role in human relations too much emphasis?

A. I still think the orgasm is the final measure of a relation. It's not the only measure—in fact, for most married people, the orgasm is often accepted as much less significant than money. But I still insist that for a man—I can't speak for women—it's the greatest single illumination of his being. Or at least it is if he can get the illumination in the act and without drugs.

Q. Let me approach that sideways; do you think you're something of a Puritan when it comes to masturbation?

A. I think masturbation is bad.

Q. In relation to heterosexual fulfillment?

A. In relation to everything—orgasm, heterosexuality, to style, to stance, to be able to fight the good fight. I think masturbation cripples people. It turns them askew, it sets up a bad and often enduring tension. Anybody who spends his adolescence masturbating, generally enters his young manhood with no sense of being a man. I don't know what the answer is—sex for adolescents. I really don't know.

Q. Well, there's Life *Magazine with its set-up but toned-down version of teenage sex—*

A. The moment *Life* starts pushing for sex among the young—

An Impolite Interview with Norman Mailer, *continued*

Q. They're not pushing for it—

A. They're *pretending* not to. But they gave Junior Sex a great spread. I suspect the fact of the matter is the authorities have decided more or less unconsciously that sex among the young may not be such a bad idea. If the authorities come to that conclusion, however, I begin to get suspicious.

Q. If you were a psychiatrist, how would you describe your attitude toward authority?

A. I'd say authority is that force emanating from institutions and government which tends to give me cancer.

Q. Cancer, figuratively?

A. Literally, I would guess cancer comes from having to submit that little bit too much over and over to authority. It doesn't matter how much of a rebel you are—the most individual of rebels may still have had to submit more to authority than he cared to.

I wouldn't dream of laying down a law with no variation. But at the time I was growing up, there was much more sexual repression than there is today. One knew sex was good, and everything was in the way of it. And so one did think of it as one of the wars to fight, if not *the* war to fight—the war for greater sexual liberty.

Masturbation was one expression of that deprivation. No adolescent would ever masturbate, presumably, if he could have sex with a girl. A lot of adolescents masturbate because they don't want to take part in homosexuality.

Q. There are certain societies where masturbation—

A. All I'm talking about is the one society I *know*. I'll be damned if I'm going to be led around with a ring in my nose by anthropologists. The few I've known personally have always struck me as slightly absurd, like eccentrics in a comic English novel. I won't take any anthropologist, any psychoanalyst as a god. I'm sure they don't know A-hole from appetite about "certain societies."

If you have more sexual liberty, why the hell still defend masturbation? One has to keep coming back to one notion: How do you make life? How do you *not* make life? You have to assume, just as a working stance, that life is probably good—if it isn't good, then our existence is such an absurdity that *any* action immediately becomes absurd. But if you assume that life is good, then you have to assume that those things which tend to make life more complex without becoming more useful, more stimulating—are bad.

Anything that tends to make a man a machine without giving him the power to increase the real life in himself is bad. Take some kid who's got a pretty good brain. He goes to college, his brain is no better, but his language is heavier and more complex. He talks like a jargon machine. He doesn't have a new idea. He has the same ideas he had before, he has the same common sense he had before, but now his common sense, instead of being salty, is laden with terms like "I'm aggregate-oriented." When he was in high school, he used to say, "I like to think about big complicated things."

Q. Is it possible that you have a totalitarian attitude against masturbation?

A. I wouldn't say all people who masturbate are evil, probably some of the best people in the world masturbate. But I am saying it's a miserable activity.

Q. Well, we're getting right back now to this motion of absolutes. You know—to somebody, masturbation can be a thing of beauty—

A. To what end? Who is going to benefit from it?

Q. It's a better end than the beauty of a bombing.

A. Masturbation is bombing. It's bombing oneself.

Q. But it can also benefit—look, Stekel wrote a book on autoeroticism, and one point he made was that at least it saved some people who might otherwise go out and commit rape. He was talking about extremes, but—

A. It's better to commit rape than masturbate. Maybe, maybe. One is violence toward oneself; one is violence toward others. And—let's be speculative for a moment—if everyone becomes violent toward themselves, then past a certain point, the entire race commits suicide. But if everyone becomes violent toward everyone else, you would probably have one wounded hero-monster left.

Q. And he'd have to masturbate.

A. That's true . . . But—you use that to point out how tragic was my solution, which is that he wins and still has to masturbate. I reply that at least it was more valuable than masturbating in the first place. Besides, he might have no desire to masturbate. He might lie down and send his thoughts back to the root of his being.

Q. Why are you assuming that masturbation is violence unto oneself? Why is it not pleasure unto oneself?

A. All right, look. When you make love, whatever is good in you or bad in you, goes out into someone else. I mean this literally. I'm not interested in the biochemistry, the electromagnetism of it, nor in how the psychic waves are passed back and forth. All I know is that when one makes love, one changes a woman slightly and a woman changes you slightly. But at least you have gone through a process which is part of life. You were part of a chain, just as life is part of a continuing chain, let us say, part of a dance.

One can be better for the experience, or worse. But one has experience to absorb, to think about. One has literally to digest the new spirit which has entered the flesh. The body has been galvanized for an experience, a declaration of the flesh.

If one has the courage to think about every aspect of the act—I don't mean think mechanically, but if one is able to brood over the act, to dwell on it—then one is *changed* by the act. Even if one has been *jangled* by the act. Because in the act of restoring one's harmony, one has to encounter all the reasons one was jangled.

So finally one has had an experience which is nourishing, because one's able to *feel* one's way into more difficult or precious insights as a result. One's able to live a tougher, more heroic life if one can digest and absorb the experience.

But if one masturbates, everything that's beautiful and good in one, goes up the hand, goes into the air, is *lost*. Now what the hell is there to *absorb*? One hasn't tested himself. You see, in a way, the heterosexual act lays questions to rest and makes one able to build upon a few answers. Whereas if one masturbates, the ability to contemplate one's experience is disturbed. Instead, fantasies of power take over. If one has, for example, the image of a beautiful sexy babe in masturbation, one still doesn't know whether one can make love to her in the flesh. All you know is that you can violate her in your *brain*. A lot of good that is.

But if one has fought the good fight or the evil fight and ended with the beautiful sexy dame, then if the experience is good, your life is changed by it. If the experience is not good, one's life is also changed by it, in a less happy way. But at least one knows something of what happened; one has something real to build on. The ultimate direction of masturbation always has to be insanity.

Q. But you're not man enough to take the other position, which is sex for the young. Except for petting, what else is there between those two alternatives?

A. Between masturbation and sex for the young, I prefer sex for the young. Of course. But I think there may be still a third alternative: At the time I grew up, sex had enormous fascination for everyone, but had no dignity, no place. It was not a value. It had nothing to do with procreation, it had to do with the bathroom—it was burning, feverish, it was dirty, cute, giggly.

The thought of waiting for sex never occurred—when I was young, my parents did not speak about sex, and no one else I knew ever discussed the possibility of holding onto one's sex as the single most important thing one has. To keep one's sex until one got what one deserved for it—that was never suggested. When I was young, the possibilities were to go out and have sex with a girl, have homosexual sex, or masturbate. The fourth alternative—chastity, if you will—was ridiculous and absurd. It's probably more absurd today. If you talked to kids of chastity today, they would not stop laughing, I'm certain.

If you get marvelous sex when you're young, all right; but if you're not ready to make a baby with that marvelous sex, then you may also be putting something down the drain, forever, which is the ability that you had to make a baby; the most marvelous thing that was in you may have been shot into a diaphragm, or wasted on a pill. One might be losing one's future.

The point is that, so long as one has a determinedly atheistic and rational approach to life, then the only thing that makes sense is the most comprehensive promiscuous sex you can find.

Q. Well, I have an essentially atheistic and more-or-less rational approach to life. As a matter of fact, the more rational I become, the more selective—

A. You know, "selective" is a word that sounds like a refugee from a group therapy session.

Q. I've never been in any kind of therapy—

A. No, I know, but there's a *plague* coming out of all these centers—they go around *infecting* all of us. The words sit in one's vocabulary like bedbugs under glass. *Selective.* It's arrogant—how do you know who's doing the selecting? I mean you're a modest man with a good sense of yourself, but suddenly it comes to sex and you're selective. Like you won't pick *this* girl; you'll pick *that* one . . . but the fact that one girl wants you and the other girl *doesn't* has nothing to do with it?

Q. Well, they have a right to be selective, too.

A. Then it's mutually selective. Which means you fall in together or go in together. Now, those are better words than "selective." They have more to do with the body and much less to do with the machine. Electronic machines *select*.

Q. Well, what I'm saying is you make a choice. A human

"Oh, an exchange student from Ghana—that's different— at first I thought you was a nigger."

choice. It has nothing to do with a machine . . . I'll tell you what's bugging me—it's your mystical approach. "You may be sending the best baby that's in you out into your hand"—but even when you're having intercourse, how many unused spermatozoa will there be in one ejaculation of semen?

A. Look, America is dominated by a bunch of half-maniacal scientists who don't know anything about the act of creation. If science comes along and says there are one million spermatozoa in a discharge, you reason on that basis. That may not be a real basis. We just don't know what the *real* is. Of the million spermatozoa, there may be only two or three with any real chance of reaching the ovum; the others are there like a supporting army, or if we're talking of planned parenthood, as a body of the electorate. These sperm go out with no sense at all of being real spermatozoa. They may appear to be real spermatozoa under the microscope, but after all, anybody who's looking through a telescope might think that Communist bureaucrats and FBI men look exactly the same.

Q. Well, they are.

A. Krassner's jab piles up more points. The point is that the scientists don't know what's going on. That meeting of the ovum and the sperm is too mysterious for the laboratory. Even the electronic microscope can't measure the striations of passion in a spermatozoon, or the force of its will.

But we can trust our emotion. Our emotions are a better guide to what goes on in these matters than scientists.

Q. But go back to your instincts, as you say—in the act of sex, you're not thinking in terms of procreation, you're thinking in terms of pleasure.

A. You are when you're young. As you get older, you begin to grow more and more obsessed with procreation. You begin to feel used up. Another part of oneself is fast diminishing. I'm not talking now in any crude sense of how much semen is left in the barrel. I'm saying that one's very *being* is being used up.

Every man has a different point where he gets close to his being. Sooner or later everything that stands between him and his being—what the psychoanalysts call defenses—is used up, because men have to stand up in all the situations where a woman can lie down. Just on the simplest level . . . where a woman can cry, a man has to stand. And for that reason, men are often used more completely than women. They have more rights and more powers, and also they are used more.

Sooner or later, every man comes close to his being and realizes that even though he's using the act, the act is using him too. The reason he becomes, as you say, more selective is that you literally *can* fuck your head off, lose your brains, wreck your body, you can use yourself up badly, eternally—I know a little bit of what I'm talking about.

I think one reason homosexuals go through such agony when they're around 40 or 50 is that their lives had nothing to do with procreation. They realize with great horror that all that wonderful sex they had in the past is gone—where is it now? They've used up their being.

Q. Is it possible that you're—pardon the expression—projecting your own attitude onto homosexuals?

A. You can see it in their literature, in the way they get drunk, you can see it in the sadness, the gentleness that comes over a middle-aged homosexual. They could've been horribly malicious in the past—bitchy, cruel, nasty—but they become very, very compassionate. There comes a point where they lose their arrogance; they're sorry for themselves and compassionate for others. Not one-half their lives are behind them, but ninetenths.

Q. Isn't it something of a paradox that your philosophy embraces both a belief in a personal God on one hand and a kind of existential nihilism on the other hand?

A. I've never said seriously that I'm an existential nihilist. I think I've said it facetiously. I am guilty of having said I'm a constitutional nihilist, which is another matter. I believe all legal structures are bad, but they've got to be dissolved with art. I certainly wouldn't want to do away with all the laws overnight.

The authorities, the oppressors, have had power for so many centuries, and particularly such vicious and complete power for the last fifty years, that if you did away with all the laws tomorrow, mankind would flounder in *angst*. Nobody could think their way through to deal with a world in which there were no laws.

We've got hung up upon law the way a drug addict depends on his heroin.

Q. There's a certain irony in this thing about laws. Do you think that if you weren't—if one weren't a famous writer and one had stabbed one's wife, would one have gotten a sentence which you escaped?

A. I have no desire to comment on that. It's a private part of my life. I'll just say this. As far as sentencing goes, I think it would have made little difference, legally. If I had been an anonymous man, the result, for altogether different social reasons, would have been about the same.

But for that matter, the law reacted to me more as a notorious man than as an intellectual. I don't think most of the people I dealt with had the remotest idea then of what I said in my books; their idea of me was picked up out of what they read in the *Daily News*. The thing that's worst about the law is the dullness of it. Anyone who's ever had anything to do with a lawsuit goes through a deadening period of dullness.

Q. How can you say that incident is "a private part" of your life when you seem to refer to it yourself in Deaths For The Ladies—*in a poem called "Rainy Afternoon With the Wife," you have the lines:* "So long as you use a knife, there's some love left."

A. One can talk about anything in art. I wasn't trying to reveal my private life in the poem, I was trying to crystallize a paradox.

Q. Do you think that creativity—art in general—is an effective force in society, or is it a sop to the individual artist's ego, and maybe entertainment for—

A. Art is a force. Maybe the last force to stand against urban renewal, mental hygiene, the wave of the waveless future.

Q. James Baldwin—referring to your essay, "The White Negro"—complained about "the myth of the sexuality of Negroes which Norman Mailer, like so many others, refuses to give up." Are you still denying it's a myth?

A. Negroes are closer to sex than we are. I don't mean that every Negro's a great stud, that every Negro woman is capable of giving great sex, that those black people just got rhythm.

I'm willing to bet that if you pushed Jimmy hard enough, he'd finally admit that he thought that the Negroes had more to do with sexuality than the whites—but whether he really believes that or not, Baldwin's buried point is that I shouldn't talk this way because it's bad for the Negro people. Talk about Negro sexuality hurts their progress because it makes the white man nervous and unhappy and miserable.

But the white man is nervous and unhappy and miserable anyway. It's not I who think the Negro has such profound sex-

uality, it's the average white man all through the country. Why deny their insight? Why do you think they react so violently in the South to having their little girls and boys go to school with Negro kids if it isn't that they're afraid of sexuality in the Negro? That's the real problem. What's the use of avoiding it?

Q. *Are you saying that, whether it's a myth or not . . .*

A. First of all, I don't believe it's a myth at all, for any number of reasons. I think that *any* submerged class is going to be more accustomed to sexuality than a leisure class. A leisure class may be more *preoccupied* with sexuality, but a submerged class is going to be more *drenched* in it.

You see, the upper classes are obsessed with sex, but they contain very little of it themselves. They use up much too much sex in their manipulations of power. In effect, they exchange sex for power. So they restrict themselves in their sexuality—whereas the submerged classes have to take their desires for power and plow them back into sex. So, to begin with, there's just that much more sexual vitality at the bottom than at the top.

Second of all, the Negroes come from Africa, which is more or less tropical land. Now I don't care to hear how many variations there are in Africa, how complex is its geography, how there's not only jungle but pasture land, mountains, snow, and so forth—everybody knows that. Finally, Africa is, at bottom, the Congo. Now tropical people are usually more sexual. It's easier to cohabit, it's easier to stay alive. If there's more time, more leisure, more warmth, more—we'll use one of those machine words—more support-from-the-environment than in a Northern country, then sex will tend to be more luxuriant. Northern countries try to build civilizations, and tropical countries seek to proliferate *being*.

Besides, the Negro has been all but forbidden any sort of intellectual occupation here for a couple of centuries. So he has had to learn other ways of comprehending modern life. One can get along in the world by studying books, or one can get along by knowing a great deal about one's fellow man, and one's fellow man's woman.

Sexuality is the armature of Negro life. Without sexuality, they would've perished. The Jews stayed alive by having a culture to which they could refer, in which, more or less, they could believe. The Negroes stayed alive by having sexuality which could nourish them, keep them warm.

You know, I think "The White Negro" can be attacked from every angle—I would love to see some first-rate assaults in detail upon it. Occasionally I'd like to be forced to say, "This argument is more incisive than mine." But I think an attack at a low level is dim. Jimmy knows enough to know that "The White Negro" is not going to be dismissed. When he stands there and in effect says, "I as a Negro know damn well that Norman Mailer doesn't know what he's talking about when he talks about Negroes"—well, even Jimmy Baldwin can be totalitarian.

Q. *Would you say your conception of life is mystical as opposed to rationalistic?*

A. I would assume mystics don't feel mystical. It's comfort-

able to them. When the savage was paddling his canoe, and a breeze entered his nose from the East, the savage said to himself, "The God of the East Wind is stirring"—he *felt* that god stirring. He could picture that god in his mind

Now, for all we know, that god may well have existed. We don't know that he didn't exist any more than we know that beauty is not absolute.

The savage didn't say to himself, "I'm a mystic who is now thinking that the God of the East Wind is stirring. Therefore I'm engaged in a mystical transaction." He was just having a simple, animal experience.

Any mystic who's worth a damn is animal. You can't trust a mystic who gets there on drugs. I had mystical experiences on drugs, and great was my horror when I discovered I couldn't have them without the drugs. What it meant to me was that the experiences were there to be had, but that I wasn't sufficiently animal to have them, not without having a chemical produced by a machine to break down the machine in me.

But I don't like to call myself a mystic. On the other hand, I certainly wouldn't classify myself as a rationalist. I'm not altogether unhappy living in some no-man's-land between the two.

Q. *Okay, final question: you beat me two out of three times in thumb-wrestling matches; would you care to expound briefly on Zen in the art of thumb-wrestling?*

A. They are the same.

"Come on, slant-eyes, hurry up . . ."

A CROSSWORD PUZZLE FOR JADED REALISTS

by Rochelle Davis

Horizontal

1. To plant (Old English).
5. Insecurity symbol.
11. To expiate for a sin.
13. Next year, women will be permitted to do this.
14. Have a share of (Scottish).
15. Scene of the International Economic Conference, April-May 1922; also a type of salami.
16. Police assistant (sometimes obscene in usage).
17. One who arouses prurient interest (abbreviation).
18. Nice in taste or feelings.
19. Well?
20. "Where profit is our most important product" (abbreviation).
21. To give birth to a lamb prematurely.
24. Government surplus now in storage bin.
27. What a Russian baby says.
28. A walled manufacturing town in Thuringia, population 74,000.
29. Basic part of education.
31. A suffix added to numbers to indicate into how many leaves a sheet is folded.
32. No longer on the Bowery.
33. What every girl wants to get first.
36. A poisonous, liquefiable, gaseous element with an offensive odor (abbreviation).
37. Territorial subdivision of a county with certain corporate powers of municipal government for local purposes (abbreviation).
38. You can't doo without this.
39. For tats.
40. Looks like Daddy Warbucks and sounds like Clark Gable.
42. Bruce Wayne's alter-ego.
44. What most popular songs begin with.
45. Hard to get if you're Cuban-bound.
47. To produce or bring forth, as offspring.
48. To cause to droop.
50. Mary Clark Rockefeller.
51. What Simon does.
53. Report erogenous ones to your postmaster.
54. Causes artificial schizophrenia (abbreviation).
55. Entrance (Old English variant).

Vertical

1. Cigarette (English slang).
2. Security symbol.
3. To put on.
4. Non-menstrual tension because . . . (two words).
5. Laid.
6. Any person indefinitely.
7. Organization to help drunken drivers (abbreviation).
8. Source of background music (abbreviation).
9. Diaphragms being dropped by nuns on their way to Heaven (abbreviation).
10. Breast problem in Philip Roth's short story, "Epstein."
12. Go down, Moses.
16. What Peter didn't stick his finger in.
19. Passing, on a Wassermann test.
22. Building on a mattress.
23. Courage of convictions.
25. Sperm factories.
26. Associated with Henry Miller, when big.
28. You have been caught demonstrating peaceably; do not pass this and do not collect $200, but take a school bus directly to jail.
30. A dedicated virgin shouts: "Look, Ma—no_____!" (misspelled).
31. What you're glad it's not every time somebody dies.
34. What many executives secretly keep.
35. Oh, what all ye faithful do!
39. Tough nookie (abbreviation).
41. A breakfast cereal with misleading implications.
43. "I krepitate, therefore I_____!"
46. If you live in the suburbs, you're likely to covet your neighbor's.
48. His wife was the salt of the earth and a pillar of the community.
49. What crossword puzzles are a substitute for.
52. Propaganda, often classified.
53. A metallic element occurring mostly in combination (abbreviation).

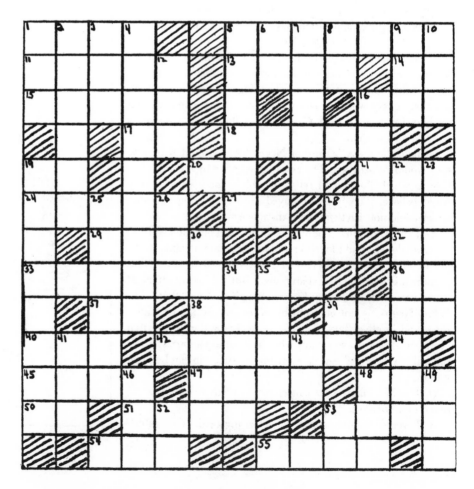

HUMOR OF THE HANDICAPPED

by Sam Gross

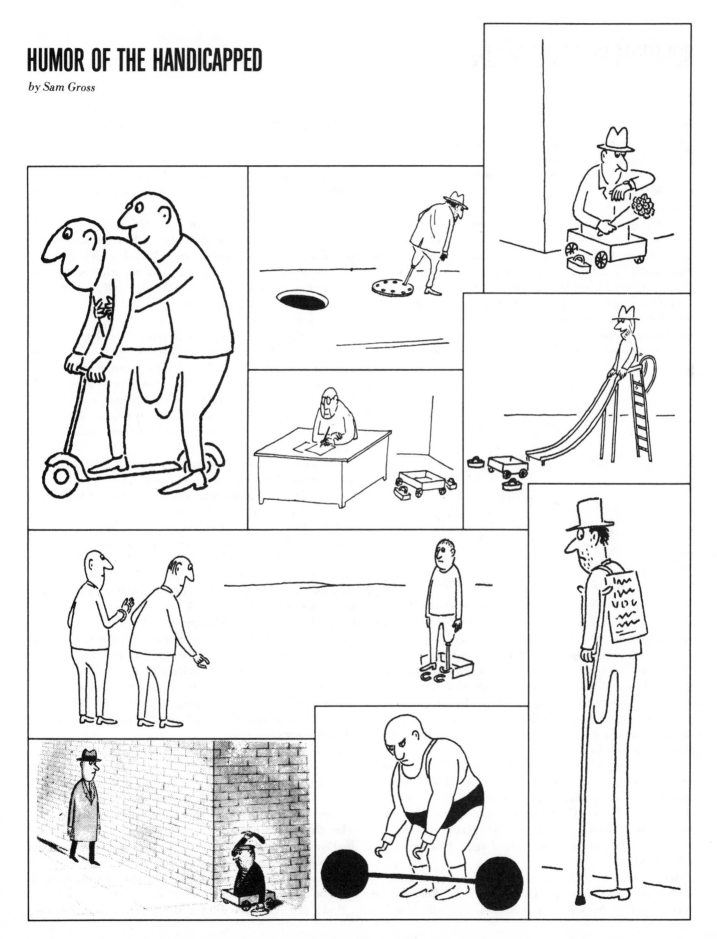

BOREDOM AS A WAY OF LIFE

by Jean Shepherd

A British writer recently made some comments about boredom as being one of the three major enemies of mankind in the 20th century. However, I differ strongly with him on his conclusions. It's such a complex problem. Boredom, and the values of today, lead to some very, very intriguing things.

I can only see a kind of gigantic advancing wave of Dynamic Slobbism. Of a very special kind. Of a kind that does not look like Slobbism. Eighteen million people will buy copies of Descartes and keep it for doorstops. Large numbers of people will buy LP records of Haydn just to make sure that their tweeters are working, and will only use it to demonstrate their stereo. It's the kind of thing that you see in the theater today. Endless numbers of people go and buy tickets, but they do not give al-

most-anything-you-care-to-say-they-don't-give for the theater, and particularly what's being *said* in the theater.

It's a very interesting kind of thing that we're working into. It's part and parcel of the peculiar sort of physical restlessness that is, I believe, the handmaiden to boredom itself.

Now, is boredom physical, or is it mental? That's a very good question. Most people like to assume that boredom is mental. A lot of people will automatically say: "Well, if a guy's thinking, he's not bored."

I don't know. I have never seen boredom approached as a physical problem. And almost all of our world is devoted to avoiding physicality at all costs. Paradoxically enough, some of the most bored people I've known are some of the most intellectual people I've known. We like to believe that if people learn a lot about poetry, about music, about English Literature, they will not be bored.

Well, I must say that some of the most dynamically bored—some of the most *dangerously* bored—people I've known, have been steeped in this sort of intellectualism. Now this is not an

anti-intellectualism spiel I'm giving here. It's something entirely different.

I believe that one of the prime misunderstood areas of boredom is the physical side. And I am not recommending physicality as a cure for boredom, but I say that these two are intertwined. In a very subtle way.

Now *artificial* physicality, on the other hand, can be even more boring than artificial intellectuality. In short, some of the most bored people I've known are golfers. I don't know why. Perhaps it's because their physical problem is artificial. In other words, the sense of necessity is not there in a golf game. I think artificial conflicts are always in the end probably the most deadeningly boring things.

On the other hand, you like to feel that: "No, I'm not bored when I play golf." That is perhaps because you have other conflicts in your life. Golf itself is a divertissement and nothing more. But the minute the world becomes centered around golf, look out. In short, when golf becomes the primary goal of a life, then there are problems. It's just like a guy who is a fisherman, and if you go fishing three weeks out of the year, it's wildly exciting.

But if somebody said to you: "From now on until the end of time, you can fish seven days a week, sixteen hours a day!"— by the end of the third day you are looking for somebody to kill.

Interesting problem. On the other hand, I say that Beauty— and Art, too—is a divertissement. We like to believe it can become a total involvement. Forget it. There are evidences in past civilizations where it didn't work, among them the Greeks. If you become totally involved in Beauty, then Beauty becomes the most supreme boredom because there is no reason for Beauty any longer. I think Beauty is beautiful because it is a surcease. Beauty is beautiful because it is that one tiny taste of a superb herb in the middle of something that is otherwise sour and bitter. The minute that Beauty becomes the soup, you will look for the sour and bitter taste; it will become the Beauty.

In short, a nation built around Beauty will look for the supreme ugliness, as *it* will then become the supreme Beauty. To carry it even further, War could become the supreme achievement of Beauty.

It's fascinating. To me, it is. I'm waiting to see, because I feel more and more people are driven to things by the sheer boredom of non-things.

I've known more and more Peace people who've become angrier and angrier because Peace has somehow continued. The other day, two thousand people began to club each other for Peace, in Trafalgar Square. But there was no war. Nobody had dropped an atom bomb, and nobody was about to. So—to me—they got very bored with non-War and began to hit each other on the head in the name of non-War.

And I say that Peace will become more violent as War becomes less likely. Now, that sounds like a paradox. It is.

I have a lot of very hard-hitting, angry, Liberal friends. Nothing irritated them more than to find Kennedy elected. They were the first people to be angry about Kennedy. Why? Because they weren't interested in winning at all; they were interested in *fighting*. Some people are only happy when fighting for a Cause. They are unhappy when the Cause comes about.

I know a famous cartoonist who spent six years writing angry anti-Nixon cartoons, because he thought that Nixon was going to win. The minute Nixon lost, he became even angrier, and now he has been doing more and more, even angrier, anti-Kennedy cartoons.

Fascinating problem. I know a guy who went on a Freedom Ride and who was profoundly disappointed because they didn't burn his bus. Told me that. I know a famous writer who was on a Peace demonstration down in the Village one day when they were having an Air Raid drill. He was angry because the police didn't arrest him. He was mad because he would have been very happy to have written an angry editorial in the *Village Voice* about how they clubbed him. They didn't do anything. They just said: "Well, okay, you wanna stand by the bushes, all right. That's your problem." He was really teed off, and said: "That shows how dishonest the fuzz is! That shows how rotten the fuzz really is!"

The thing I'm driving at here is that as we approach what we call Paradise, the more boredom is going to be a problem. More and more as you watch television commercials you will see that the big theme is "Less work for Mama." Mama will find other work. It's liable to be not exactly the sort of thing Norman Vincent Peale has in mind when he's talking about Good Works.

More and more, within every industry, you know, the idea and the aim is to lessen responsibility. The 35-hour week will give way to the 20-hour week eventually, and finally to the 5-hour week. Of course, what that means is no responsibility at all. If a guy's only needed 5 hours a week, he's not needed at all. Forget it.

Well, the more you are left to your own resources, the more you are left to no responsibility, the more you are prone to that most dynamic of all forces—boredom.

Boredom is not a passive force. People like to think it is; it is not.

And don't think for one minute that you won't be bored. You know, that's an intriguing thing. Many people feel, and it's a wonderful thought . . . we have so many wonderful ideas and ideals that in practice have no relationship to reality. In short, they do not work. One of the great examples of this is:

"If given more time, people will become more interested in the things which they always would have been interested in had they been given time. Like Art."

Well, I'd like to make some sad facts salient to you. If you are familiar with any of the *Better Homes & Gardens*-type magazines, you can look through hundreds and hundreds of copies, pictures of modern homes in the suburbs, and you will find *rarely* a book in evidence. Hardly ever do they discuss having bookshelves built. If so, it's for knick-knacks. We like to think there's more reading? Get it out of your skull. There's more book *buying* in many ways. Like paperbacks. I wonder how many people own them but never read them?

You know, buying is a positive action today that has no relationship to what is being *bought*. A guy made an interesting point to me the other day: he remembers when his mother and his father would take him to buy a coat. Or: "We're gonna go to Gimbel's to buy a tablecloth today." But now people will say: "I'm going shopping." They don't know what they're going to buy, nor do they have any idea in mind. Shopping has become a sport just the way tiddlywinks or tennis is.

Boredom has something to do with center of focus. Are you aware that boredom often doesn't *look* like boredom? Four hundred and fifty ladies on the 3rd floor of Gimbel's can be, if you watch carefully, absolute studies of boredom in motion. It *looks* like they're involved, but they're not involved at all. They're merely *moving*, which is a very different thing. It is hard to keep their attention focused on any one counter for more than 15 or 20 milliseconds, because they don't, in short, *need* any of the things they're after. And so, this is another kind of boredom, a very dangerous kind.

All over the world, war movies are now a big thing, particularly in Russia. Almost all of the big novels in the past 15 years in Russia have been written about wars. And, of course, we have now many TV shows about wars of one kind or another. Because a war, you see, is the ultimate of boredom in motion, it's the ultimate of a dynamic point of view. There are good guys and bad guys. And furthermore, you are playing. Even if you're ten thousand miles from the front, you are given a part.

We've got some great things ahead. We use such words as "automation," but these words really don't describe the revolution that we're part of. I think that a thousand years from now, if we survive as a race, people will look back to this period, right now, as one of the great pivotal points when man became totally useless. Particularly to himself. Hardly any man ever got a phone call from that day on that said: "We need you, Fred, and nobody else."

And that was a great, great social revolution, and probably the beginning of the most violent period in all of history.

"They don't really help— I still hate my job."

FASTEST GROIN IN THE WEST

The action sequence below is reproduced from an actual advertisement of the Groin Holster. "For the first time," states the ad copy, "a truly concealed holster that can be worn with leisure clothing! Ideal for all year round and especially warm weather. No jacket necessary; no outside shirt tails!!Comfortable, convenient. Guaranteed. Used by peace officers everywhere." The guarantee reads: "I understand that if I am not fully satisfied with my holster I can return it within 10 days and receive a complete refund of the purchase price." If the purchaser is still alive, that is. Cause of death might well have been a stuck zipper. Otherwise, instead of being able to recognize a plainsclothesman by his brown shoes, the tipoff would be that his fly is open.

I DREAMED I SHOT A NIGGER IN MY MAIDENFORM BRA

A female counterpart to the male groin holster was on the market in South Africa this month. It is a cloth holster which snaps onto the strap of a bra and can hold a .38-caliber revolver snugly under a woman's arm. During the past few years, more than 35,000 South African white women have joined pistol clubs, but their leaders deny that women are being armed against any particular race. However, the wife of the inventor of the bra holster has stated: "I wouldn't go out without one. There are so many natives hanging around the streets these days that it's nice to know I have my pistol where I can get at it."

The female craze for guns started among white women after South Africa's racial riots in 1960. Since then police have helped form women's pistol clubs, and some girls' schools even have rifle and revolver classes. The cost of ammunition is subsidized by the government. There is also an inner-thigh holster available—an adaptation of the cowboy holster—handy for women wearing narrow skirts; it can be worn on the outside of the thigh if the skirt is full. According to the wife of an arms dealer, an at-

tacker can be shot "through the skirt, if necessary."

The light-skinned ladies of South Africa have at last pointed their fingers firmly in the direction of true trigger-happiness. There was once a time, though, when lost hymens were blamed merely on fences, bicycles, and horses.

REPORT FROM FARNSWORTH, NEW JERSEY.

by Neil Postman

Towns become famous for various reasons. Some are known for their curious names, like Kalamazoo. Others, for their curious people, like Oxford, Mississippi. Still others are known for historical battles, like Gettysburg, or for industrial activity, like Wilkes-Barre, or for sexual fervor, like Cicero, Illinois. Having achieved national attention for the imagination and vigor of its Civil Defense program, the town of Farnsworth, New Jersey is rapidly becoming a model Cold War community, which other American towns can freely and reasonably emulate. In short, Farnsworth has once again fixed itself in the public consciousness, as a result of a series of tough-minded and daring statutes recently passed by its City Council.

With one exception, each of the statutes was passed by unanimous vote of the 23-man City Council. Without exception, each statute is intended to strengthen belief in, and increase respect for, American traditions and institutions. "We are," Mayor Charlton Mazoli explains, "a wishy-washy people, which is why we are losing the Cold War to the Russians, who aren't." Mazoli, who receives no salary for being Farnsworth's Chief Executive, was elected Mayor two years ago on a get-tough-with-the-Russians platform. To say the least, he feels obliged to make good on his promises. "Americans have nothing to be ashamed of," he says. "All of the cards are stacked on this side of the Iron Curtain concerning our way of life."

The most important of Farnsworth's new legislation is popularly known as the Mazoli Act, although its official name is Statute 4231M. Stated simply, the law makes it a crime, punishable by six months' imprisonment, for anyone to advocate the overthrow of the Municipal Government of Farnsworth Township. Mazoli feels the law needs no defense. He observes simply: "The Farnsworth Municipal Government has been serving the people of Farnsworth for 97 years. It has long deserved the respect this law gives it."

Farnsworth was indeed founded 97 years ago, by Jason Brower Trenton, an itinerant preacher, who selected the name Farnsworth because, as he put it, "New Jersey already has one Trenton." Preacher Trenton was, by all accounts, a rugged, fervent, and unbending moralist who, as Farnsworth's first Chief Executive, once sentenced his wife and 18-month-old son to four months in prison for some undetermined crime. Mazoli feels that "Ole Jason Trenton," as he affectionately calls him, would vastly appreciate Statute 4231M. "It is the consummation, so to speak, of the ground he broke," says Mazoli.

The second most important piece of legislation enacted by Farnsworth's alert Council is Statute 4232M, popularly known as "Chet's Pet." The allusion is, of course, to Dr. Chester Fry, the spirited and high-minded Superintendent of Farnsworth's disciplined school system. For years, Fry has lobbied for sturdy legislation that would protect Farnsworth's schools from corruption and eventual decay. Statute 4232M makes it a crime, punishable by five months' imprisonment, for anyone to advocate the overthrow of Farnsworth's Union School District No. 10. "We've worked too long and too damn hard," says Fry, "to allow cheap crackpots to undermine what we've built here." He adds: "I think all of us in Farnsworth feel that way about our institutions."

Doubtless, Fry is right. Statute 4233M makes it unlawful for anyone to advocate the overthrow of Farnsworth's modest but highly efficient Transit System. Its sister law, Statute 4234M, makes it a crime for anyone to advocate the overthrow of Farnsworth's impeccable Sanitation Department. (Both crimes are punishable by three months' imprisonment.)

Perhaps the most controversial of all the statutes passed by the City Council is 4248M, which would send to jail, for 30 days, anyone convicted of advocating the overthrow of the Farnsworth Chapter of Hadassah. Unlike the others, which were unanimously approved, this statute passed by the narrow margin of 13-10. "Many of us felt," Mazoli eagerly explains, "that we would be getting into the church-state issue, which is unconstitutional, I think. But what the hell, we're trying to firm up all of our groups here."

The most prominent protagonist of 4248M is lovely Mrs. Loretta Grossman, who, like Chester Fry, feels that she and her co-religionists have worked too long and too damn hard to have their careful plans destroyed by dissident fanatics. "Hadassah," she points out, "is a thoroughly American institution, based on American ideals, and deserves all the protection we can give it. Besides, think of what happened to the Jews in Eu-

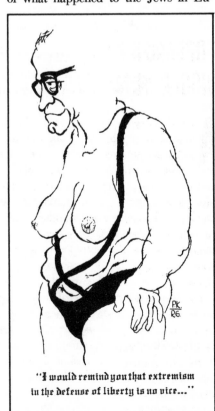

"I would remind you that extremism in the defense of liberty is no vice..."

rope." Happily, enough Council members were thinking of the Jews in Europe to transform Mrs. Grossman's bill into public law.

Naturally, other religious groups now hope that a similar bill might be introduced which affords them the same protection now given to Hadassah. The Reverend Goodman Fealty, pastor of Farnsworth's distinguished First Presbyterian Church, comments: "We were thinking of introducing a bill which would make it unlawful to advocate the overthrow of the First Presbyterian Church in Farnsworth. But, as Charlton Mazoli told me, nothing really happened to the Presbyterians in Europe. So I'm not too hopeful."

However, Fealty is now readying a bill which would make it a crime to advocate the overthrow of the minister of the First Presbyterian Church. He believes this bill has a good chance of being law, since his older brother, Drummond, was killed in Europe during World War II.

How far is Farnsworth prepared to go in firming up American institutions? That question is of interest to a number of people, among them the Governors of New York, New Jersey, Connecticut, and Massachusetts. The curiosity of this illustrious group was aroused when rumors spread that the Farnsworth City Council was drafting a bill which would make it unlawful to advocate the overthrow of the Eastern seaboard. "Nonsense," says Mazoli. "Let the Eastern seaboard take care of itself. Besides, we have no authority to pass such a bill." He adds impishly: "But I wonder what they're afraid of."

A more realistic guess as to Farnsworth's legislative plans was made by C.D. Preem, editor of Farnsworth's pragmatic daily paper, *The American*.

Preem believes that the next phase of the firming-up process involves legislation that would outlaw advocating advocacy. "Suppose you convict a man for advocating the overthrow of, say, our Sanitation Department," Preem explains. "So what? You've still not touched the source of the crime." Unofficially, Charlton Mazoli agrees. "As usual," he confides, "Preem is getting to the heart of the matter."

In any case, Farnsworth's City Council cannot, according to custom, pass any more bills until next December, and no public hearings are scheduled until late August. However, the citizens of Farnsworth are unruffled. "We feel," concludes the Reverend Fealty, "that we are the safest community in New Jersey, perhaps in all of America. Would that other communities were as firmed up as we."

AN IMPOLITE INTERVIEW WITH MORT SAHL

Q. Say something—I just want to test the voice level on this machine.

A. All right—we're making a test here. Stop the tests!

Q. Okay. You've been doing what you do for ten years now—what changes have you noticed that have occurred during this time?

A. Well, it's gone from children's entertainment to adult education. I can say what I say faster, and the audience seems to give me a certain credence as an elder statesman, so that they really listen to those pronouncements. When I was starting, everybody was calling me a radical and saying it was impossible, and now they've come to accept it—and I probably go farther now than I ever went. In other words, I have more license. And, as Theodore Reik once said, "Anybody can say what he thinks, but you have to know what you think, which is tougher."

I don't want to minimize this—there's a few changes we ought to lay out here. I constructed a network of theaters where people can speak—they happen to be saloons—in complete freedom. I started college concerts; I started emceeing at the jazz festivals—that is, I introduced verbalization at the jazz festivals—I constructed, for what they're worth, Mr. Kelly's /in Chicago/, I introduced The Blue Angel /in New York/ to something besides that effete trash they were presenting—that inside nothing of the East 70s—Storyville /in Boston/, the hungry i /in

San Francisco/, The Crescendo /in Los Angeles/, and then finally took the thing into The Copa /in New York/, The Fountainbleu /in Miami/, into the larger rooms, to where they accepted it, on my terms; I started comedy records in this country—1957 was the first one. The whole climate has been changed, including network television.

Everywhere I've gone, I've tainted them, so to speak. It may not be the Midas touch, but they have come away with a different coloration than when they started it. I don't think that's to be minimized. The next guy that came along after me didn't have the trouble I had. And that's no minor accomplishment. If a guy comes in with anything away from the norm—people don't throw him out on that basis alone; they say, "Well, there *is* precedent, let's hear him out." Unfortunately, most of those guys have nothing to offer, but I can't control that, I'm sorry to say.

Q. How do you explain the paradox—that you go farther now even though your audience has broadened?

A. Oh, because I developed some skills along the way, which are theatrical. This is not in the area of social heroism. A moral commitment is early in your life—but how to implement it becomes a theatrical skill. And I go farther because I give them more—I don't do twenty minutes, I do an hour, an hour-and-a-quarter—and I have created a climate whereby you can do it.

As I say, I've created a bigger appetite than there are

qualified people to meet that appetite. There's hundreds of people running around called "The New Comedians." None of them are *saying* anything, but the audience is definitely ready for it.

So you find people who are completely ignorant making political references, whereas ten years ago—when I made political references because they were uppermost in my *mind*—I ran the risk of being called a Communist. And I was called one by Jack Rosenstein in the thing called *Hollywood Close-Up*. So I went to court and nailed him.

Q. Do you feel that once you're accepted by The Establishment, you become less effective?

A. Well, they have to establish that I've been accepted by The Establishment. No one can assume that. And the people who have said those things have been incorrect.

One, Richard Gehman—who used the phrase in *Cavalier* Magazine that I "go with the strength"—was referring to the fact that I was acquainted with "Senator" Kennedy, not President Kennedy. Another is Nat Hentoff, who claims that I never made any jokes about the Kennedys.

Actually, that's kind of healthy, to have all those people completely misinformed—they don't know what your trajectory is—because that, by default, proves that they are not the arbiters of our society. They don't know what the hell they're talking about. One thinks you're with the administration, and the other thinks you're not with anything. One thinks it's anarchy, and the other thinks you're a Democrat. So obviously I've been successful in throwing the hound dogs off my path.

Q. When I said "accepted by The Establishment," I meant The New Yorker *profile, the* Time *Magazine cover story—*

A. Oh, that's different. I'm completely in favor of being accepted by The Establishment, but you have to be accepted on your own terms. If the only verification of your art is the fact that you're done in, then I don't accept that as verification. I not only survived, but I prevailed—because I identify with a long line of merit. That's my one distinction: I chose the Good Guys. I may not be one of them, but at least I recognize them.

And for those people who think that the only verification of your cause is to be Christ, remember there's a two-part story. There's crucifixion, but there's also resurrection.

Q. Here's a quote from an article—"The Complacent Satirists"—in the June issue of Encounter: *"The essence of satire lies in catching the audience by surprise in order to bring its members to see* themselves, their *beliefs,* their *institutions,* and their *behaviour in an unfamiliar, ridiculous, and unfavorable light. Though satire usually assumes the guise of entertainment, its intention is quite different, being to make people feel uncomfortable, guilty, or ashamed of what they believed, did, or supported." Now, if you set up this kind of we-they feeling—we're the Good Guys and they're the Bad Guys— then, according to this definition at least, aren't you failing to impart the essence of satire?*

A. I didn't say *we're* the Good Guys; I said *I identify* with the Good Guys. You know, I'm talking about the giants through history when I say the Good Guys—to identify with a certain kind of thinking that I think has merit, whether it's Freudian or Socratic thinking or whatever—I'm talking about gigantic concepts that determined your faith before you were

born. I'm not talking about the audience. In fact, people in the audience come up and yell at me from night to night: "You don't leave us anything! You don't leave anybody standing! The vindictive spills out on us, on our values, on the way we live, on the Democrats, on the Republicans. . . ." They term it anarchy. So I didn't say the *audience* are Good Guys, by any means. I took them apart first.

Q. And yet, didn't you once say to me that The Realist *makes a mistake when we make fun of liberals because we give fodder to the conservatives?*

A. Well, in some areas. I think *The Realist* is probably the most vital publication in the United States; I've often said that to people. But I'm not giving fodder to any bigots when I say to you I don't think the magazine should dissipate its time on *crudeness*, and I think there's an appetite in the magazine for crudeness, in other words, what we can get away with by writing things on the side of a barn.

I write what I say in *Time* Magazine; not in the *Reporter*, not in the *Nation*, not in *The Realist*. I want as many people to hear it, undiluted, on my terms, as possible. See, I think there are more skillful ways of saying things than that cartoon you ran about the world being in bed, and the Russians and the Americans. I think you're evading responsibility by making out that the whole world is a hoax—the whole world is a put-on, morality is a put-on—in other words, I think you confuse puritanism and morality. I think it's a mistake. But with all of that, it's *still* better than anything that's being printed.

Q. I'm really pleased to hear criticism of that cartoon because there's been so much praise of it—

A. Oh, it was awful. That's crude, terrible, Men's Room literature.

Q. But wait now. The theme of that cartoon was an attack on the theory of collective guilt. Isn't that what you do too, really?

A. I don't know. I don't do it *that* way. See, I don't think virtue is to be spat upon. First of all, virtue is rare, so let's not throw it away, we don't stumble upon it all that easily. It's very difficult to locate. And once we have it, I don't think it's made for people to wipe their feet on. The ultimate configuration of man is not there so that you can deface it. Because I don't think that's rebellion, for one thing; I think that's a very impotent kind of rebellion.

Whatever you do, whether it's a rebellion or anything creative, has to be done within a framework. There has to be a frame of reference, and if we're not within the frame, there is not *sanity*. We have to define the purpose of this life. Now that may mean lawfulness, but lawfulness is for survival, not to inhibit creativity.

Q. But, to me, the whole theme of that cartoon was: Thou shalt not deface mankind.

A. Oh, yeah, but look at the way he took it—the most direct way—it shows a great impoverishment on the part of that guy Guindon, who drew the cartoon. In other words, if you could only reduce everything to a sexual situation—first of all, much more subtle drives are going on. One of the ways you can show hostility, is sex. And one of the ways you can show high regard for someone, is sexual. But—gee, I mean it's so *obvious*,—unskilled, untutored. *I* find that cartoon offensive, I don't mind telling you. And it's not because I'm not *free*. I've been in the world since I was 12, and I know what goes on—but I don't think it has to go on that way. And to equate Russia with the United States in that sense is a way of obviating your own responsibility, a way of *not* choosing up sides, and not defining anything, or not analyzing anything.

And what makes it maddening is that a page away you have quite a scorching analysis of the world situation—you really deal with Cuba, and Vietnam, and the FBI, and see them quite clearly. Then something like *that* comes along, and I think it's ridiculous. In other words, if you say something truthful, and use profanity in order to test the law, I'll defend your right to use the profanity. But I'd hate to see your message stilled while we argue over the use of profanity. I don't want you to compromise the *truth*—you know, I don't care how you *say* it; if that's the *only* way you can say it, that's something else again.

Q. There was one word you said—responsibility—responsibility to what?

A. To yourself. That's where it starts.

Q. Yeah, well, that's what I was talking about when I said collective guilt. This cartoon was expressing a mood; it used a sexual analogy to express a mood which I think you yourself have expressed on stage. Every night, perhaps.

A. Yeah, but I don't think that both the United States and Russia are raping the world. They *are* the world—whether they subdivide it or not, they're a good portion of it, and they're influential nations—and I think that's a childish way to look at it.

You cannot reduce the riddle of the power struggle in this hemisphere, where you have an administration that defers to the cold war, or to capitalism; or you have a socialistic country in the East such as the Soviet Union that is trying to westernize, so to speak—you can't reduce it to that—that's a childish way to look at it. Plus the fact that it's crude and offensive.

Q. Now you used the word "rape." How do you know that the female representing the earth was not being submissive?

A. Or even seductive. Well, I'll never know. I didn't see her face in that cartoon.

Q. Right. So isn't it possible that you're projecting something into the cartoon—

A. Well, the question is, who can interpret my remark? I mean who's fit to interpret it?

Q. But I don't know if you answered the question that I posed—about our making-fun-of-the-liberals giving fodder to the conservatives—

A. Well, they'll pick up anything they can. It's much the same as if during this whole strike-out-for-civil-rights, during the period of the Negro's agitation in this country, if there are certain excesses by irresponsible hoodlums who happen to be colored, and we point it out, we're giving fodder to people who have stepped on all Negroes for the last hundred years, and we certainly don't want to do that.

If you produced a play today, it's nice to hire Negro actors, but if you made one a villain, I think you'd damage the cause.

Q. But don't you often say things on stage that could give fodder to the conservatives?

A. Very often, sure. I've had to, to dramatize the situation, because ultimately we have to get at the truth, and when the audience comes to see me, I'm afraid we're at ground zero; we're

in the first booster phase of getting at the facts, and we've got to do it, that's all. And it doesn't matter who falls.

You cannot have a protective cloak over the Democrats, for instance. We've got to look at them and see what they are. But that means looking *completely*. That doesn't mean people saying, "Don't you think the President's doing a wonderful job?"—or, "The Republicans are blocking him in Congress." There's no time for rationalization. There isn't any *time*, that's the point.

Q. Do you feel that there's a relationship between your Jewish background and your work?

A. That's nonsense. I don't have any kinship with a Jewish background. But when Freud was ostracized by the medical society in Vienna, he then was offered the forum of the B'nai B'rith. They said, "We don't agree with anything you say, but anyone can speak here, because we're interested in free speech." He then wrote in a letter to a friend: "The role of the Jew is that of the opposition." So if the role of the Jew is to rock the boat, and to be inquisitive—intellectually curious, that is—fine. Classic role. But there's no urgency; in other words, this generation of Jews in America is taking a sabbatical. They're taking twenty years off because they were witness to a generation, all the people that were active in left-wing politics, and all the people who compensated for being oppressed by over-intellectualizing in the arts, all the English professors they developed, and all the people who generally contributed to the intellectual life of this country.

This generation is making up for it by *assimilating* and becoming nothing. If I'm Jewish, then they're a fraud; and if they're Jewish, I don't want to be *that*.

Q. Do you consider yourself Jewish?

A. No! I belong to me. And that's *enough*. I don't consider myself *anything*. And I'm having a tough time finding any kinship with people who have *ideas*. The first thing I used to hear in San Francisco ten years ago was, "Nobody wants to hear that"; then the next thing was, "Well, only intellectuals want to hear it"; then after that it was, "They don't want to hear it in the East"; then, "They don't want to hear it on TV."

You know, you take this to a point where you say, "People

"It's his turn now and then me again . . ."

can misinterpret it," so eventually my point of view is suspect if I'm not elected President. There's really no end to it.

The very fact that I can *say* it—it's almost miraculous that I've developed this *form*—which triggers a release that makes the point, makes it economically, and covers all that *ground*. That's not a lecture, you know, with 12-year-old morality. That's a distilled point of view, that people subsidize. It's the healthiest thing in the world. For them. And for me; largely for them.

Q. Do you get any sense of futility in the night club?

A. Well, there are certain occupational hazards, but there's great freedom, because there's nobody pompous there, like an editor in a publication, or a director in a theater group, or an advertising executive in broadcasting—who has delusions of "helping" you. But it doesn't mean you go unedited—that's a very important point—*you* edit, and *you* have to be the final arbiter. That helps you become a responsible adult—which should be the aim of all of us. It's helped *me*.

I think there are frustrations in the audience, because when I hit gold, when I hit a vein, I don't like to talk to 300 people—I'd like to be talking to three million. But the reason I talk to *thirty* million on television is because I *built* on the night clubs. That's a *lobbying* point. That's a lobby to influence the ultimate congress, the American public—once you can get to them via mass media. That's how you do it. You've got the club—you can stand on that rock and scream—otherwise you couldn't talk at *all*. I mean, how do you explain the fact—everybody in the United States knows me, and I'm not on television or in pictures? What *put* me on the cover of *Time*? Because *I had an audience*. The *audience* made me a hero.

Q. Well, I'm not talking about your meteoric rise. I'm talking about your influence on the audience's thinking.

A. Well—you don't see too many guys getting up with a Borscht Belt approach now; they all get up and try to look like they're thinking, even though they're not equipped; even though they're untalented in that area, they try to imitate that stand. Now, obviously I have made that an acceptable way to be, or I would've been dismissed by the audience years ago.

Q. I'm talking about your ideas—not your form—in terms of influencing the audience and perhaps changing their viewpoint.

A. Nobody comes away from the show with a feeling of apathy. I don't care whether I reinforce their prejudice or convert them to my point of view—the point is they *feel* something. And the mission of theater is *to wake people up*. Make them feel something. And there's residual feeling on the part of everyone that's seen the show, whether they're terrified, or whether they laugh, say "Yes, that's right, I wish I'd said that, that quick," or "Hang 'im!" They feel something. There's an urgency about it.

Q. You were at Time *Magazine's cover-personalities party. What didn't* Time *tell in their story about it?*

A. Well, I saw the pictures showing that Casey Stengel was there, and Hedda Hopper, but that isn't what I was impressed with at the party. I was impressed that hundreds of people who *work* for *Time* were at the party, and there were a lot of generals and admirals and a lot of political figures who shape our destiny—and that's what impressed me. Everybody was there. Nobody turns *Time* Magazine down. It was handled very ef-

ficiently. It was really like the proverbial well-oiled machine.

The children of some of the people who work for *Time* are more conservative than their parents, politically, which scared me to death.

Q. Children of what age?

A. Twenty-three, twenty-two. Terrible. Uninformed conservatism. That was depressing. And also I noticed that the President was absent, and the Attorney General; they only come in election years, I gather. But the President sent a wire for Mr. Luce to read.

They gave me the red-carpet treatment. I had a pretty good time. But I was sort of harassed by an audience of people who wanted to know what my *opinions* about everything were; this is a great era for that. Derivative opinion. They want to know—*Tell me what I should think about such-and-such*—and then they argue with you. They compare their clichés to your clichés.

Q. I assume Kennedy and the Attorney General got invited—

A. Yeah, they were invited. They couldn't make it. Bette Davis said, "I'm glad the wrong people aren't here, like Khrushchev and Castro." And I had to remind her that perhaps it wasn't Mr. Luce's option that they not come; maybe it was theirs. Everybody who was on the cover was invited. Che Guevera was on the cover—he wasn't there—couldn't get into the country.

We were assigned two people to a car, and I rode with Dr. José Miro Cardona—it was *Time*'s idea of a joke—and he kept looking for explosives under the hood. Then when we were making our travel arrangements, Ed Magnuson of *Time* said, "I'll get you to the airport on time, Mr. Sahl, I *promise* you"—and I looked at Cardona, and I said, "Does that word hold an awful lot for you these days?" So he got the interpretation and laughed a little, and his interpreter said, "Every time we start with our travel accommodations, we don't have to ask, because people ask *us* when we're going to leave the country." And if that's the power elite, look out!

Q. There's an article in Harper's *by Adlai Stevenson on patriotism; I forget whether he's for or against it.*

A. It's like the girl who said to me, "I'm a delegate to the Massachusetts convention." I said, "Do you believe in Ted Kennedy?" "No." "You gonna vote for him?" "Yes, because I'm a good Party girl." I said, "Well, maybe being a good Party girl is being *dissenting*." Maybe you're a good American if you dissent. They used to in this country.

Listen, I went to a UN meeting in Los Angeles last month—the American Association of the United Nations—they opened up the meeting, and the first thing they do is a flag salute. We're fighting sovereign states, right? And they said "One nation under God," and a lot of people in the audience don't believe it should be done that way, but that's not their night at ACLU, it's their night at the UN association. Oh, liberals are impossible. The worst thing about Stevenson were his supporters, as the old saying went—and it was true.

Q. Do you consider yourself a radical or a liberal?

A. *I* don't know. Radical as compared to what? Liberal as compared to what? *You try to be your own man* and judge it *issue for issue*. You know, put the issues up against themselves,

The Portable Goldwater

A BELIEVE-IT-OR-NOT COMPENDIUM OF **FACTS** THAT SHOULD BE READ BY **EVERY AMERICAN** WHO LOVES HIS COUNTRY.

FACT 1.

THE **FIRST** GOLDWATER ENTERPRISE IN AMERICA WAS A MINING TOWN SALOON DOWNSTAIRS FROM A **WHOREHOUSE!**

FACT 2.

ONE **FOURTH OF JULY** AT THE AGE OF NINE, BARRY **EMPTIED A PISTOL** INTO THE CEILING OF HIS PARENTS BEDROOM!

FACT 3.

DURING THE SENATE CENSURE OF JOE McCARTHY, **GOLDWATER,** IN AN EFFORT TO KEEP THE WISCONSIN SENATOR FROM MAKING ANY **FURTHER** INFLAMMATORY SPEECHES, WOULD **STEAL** THEM FROM HIS DESK!

COMMIES

FACT 4.

BARRY GOLDWATER IS THE INVENTOR OF "ANTSY-PANTS" ANT-PATTERNED **MENS SHORTS** SOLD BY HIS DEPARTMENT STORE!

FACT 5.

SENATOR GOLDWATER HAS DEVISED A FLAGPOLE TO BE INSTALLED AT HIS HOME IN ARIZONA THAT RAISES AUTO-MATICALLY AT SUNRISE AND LOWERS ITSELF AT SUNSET PLAYING TAPS.

FACT 6.

SOMETIMES GOLDWATER CAN BE FOUND **SLEEPING** AT THE BOTTOM OF HIS **SWIMMING POOL** WITH AN AIR HOSE STUCK IN HIS MOUTH!

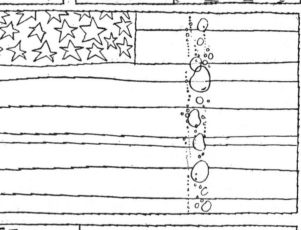

FACT 7.

SENATOR GOLDWATER HAS **FOUR DOTS** TATOOED ON HIS LEFT HAND WHICH IDENTIFY HIM AS A MEMBER OF A SMALL CLIQUE OF ARIZONA BUSINESSMEN CALLED THE SMOKI CLAN–INDIAN COSTUMED DANCERS WHO PERFORM WITH **LIVE BULL SNAKES!**

GUINDON

so to speak, as opposed to having your own fluoroscope with the liberal anatomy and putting things against that. Because I can adapt in order to breathe, but there are some things that you just cannot adapt to.

How can you be a liberal in our society? First, of all, the liberals nowadays—all they do is work on emotional causes. They'll freedom-ride, but they won't give $10 to help a man like Estes Kefauver fight the pharmaceutical houses. They'll march for Caryl Chessman, but they won't go up to San Quentin when a homosexual who killed his grandmother with an ax is being executed. Because it doesn't appeal to them—you couldn't sell a play to the liberals unless there was a strong love story.

Q. You and Dick Gregory both talk about the evils of segregation and, implicitly, the justice of integration—but he's had more than an abstract role in the conflict. How come you seem to limit your passion to your function as an entertainer?

A. I'm really sorry that I brought politics into the theater when I realize that the real virtue in life is to take the theater into politics. I've never done that. I wasn't at either one of the conventions marching around with any of the nominees. I don't do that with the other theatrical people. I like to use the theater for what it's meant—it's an arena of ideas.

I've been talking on an international scale about segregation, that's true. I was doing it a few years before anybody else—when people were saying "It can't be done." I didn't hear anybody doing it. It was a pretty non-competitive area. I felt that I could do it with effectiveness if I was not a Negro, to a disarmed audience. If you don't have an ax to grind, you can sneak up on them. It's much the same as when I talked about the Hollywood Ten being blacklisted; I felt I could be more effective when I was not a blacklist victim. I could be a spokesman because I was not tainted in the eyes of the audience, so to speak.

Now, as far as [Dick Gregory's] taking part in demonstrations, that's up to *him.* I haven't seen there's been a great deal of *effect* by his taking part in those demonstrations. And also, a few years ago he was saying, "I don't want to be segregated—I'm an *individual*, not just a member of a group." Now he says, "I may be an individual, but I'm a Negro first." There's been reversal there, of his logic. *I* don't ever want to be a member of a group. I can't find one anyway, so that decision's a little late in coming. You know, it's lagging.

Q. I think that's why you always ask if there are any groups you haven't offended; maybe you'll find one.

A. See, entertainers who don't *say* anything—they don't get into areas of controversy, they make meaningless motion pictures and all—*they* go to demonstrations; they *have* to say what they think. I say what I think—my morality is *implicit in my work.* There's no more I can do. It reminds me very much of entertainers who run to be on *Open End* with Susskind because they can't express themselves doing a play written by a homosexual eight times a week. Well, I couldn't either if I was doing that.

I don't run to a program like Susskind's because I can express myself every *night.* Nobody has to say to me, "What do you really think?" At least I'm brave enough to *say* it on the stage: *That's what I think.* It's nice to go down there in groups of 5,000 and thumb your nose at Southern Cracker cops. What

about getting up at a meeting at NBC when you don't have an audience to cheer you on and telling a Southern sponsor you want a Negro trio to accompany a white girl on a television show. Try *that* some time. I've done it, and more than once. And I've made it stick. It's not the heroism of doing it, it's having it come off. It's getting the show on the air. That's your verification.

Q. You used the phrase, "There's no more I can do."

A. Than give the best you can theatrically. You know, I'm in the *theater.*

Q. Is it true that you've written gags for Kennedy?

A. Yeah, it's true. I gave a lot of stuff to the President. And I haven't laid on that—in other words, I haven't made a big publicity gambit out of it. My liberalism can just be left up to the audience. They can decide for themselves.

But the President is a friend of mine, and I gave him a lot of stuff. Period. I also had met Nixon consequently, and had a drink with him, and had quite an interesting talk with him. But that's not a commitment. For all people know, I did that as a personal favor. But everybody assumes everything. It shows their ignorance, not my position.

Q. It wasn't in a professional capacity, then?

A. No, I wasn't hired. There are those who began to march with Kennedy when he was a winner. I knew him when he was a person who had an ambition, I knew him personally—he was a personal friend of mine.

I'm not very big on going to inaugurals and parties and running around with that group. I've got my own thing going. The minute I start with *them*, then I'm not with *me* any more. So I don't participate in much of that.

Q. How would you describe the public image of Jackie Kennedy?

A. I used to use a gag in the act, where I said that Mrs. Kennedy is in all these movie magazines, and I couldn't understand it. Then a Democratic girl gets impatient with me and she says, "What do you *want* her to do?" And I said, "Well, I thought that she might relieve Mrs. Roosevelt, who's 77 and too old to be driving tractors to Havana." Of course, Mrs. Roosevelt has passed on since then, but I do think that the First Lady has a responsibility to be interested in somebody who's *poor.* I don't *see* that in this group.

I don't think women should be downgraded to be nothing but fashion models. And I don't mean to invade her privacy, but I've met her, and she's very bright—and she's capable, but the concept of having Pablo Casals and all these people who are not about to rock the boat, and have it pass for culture, I think is misleading.

Q. How about the public image of Jimmy Hoffa?

A. Hoffa represents crime. You know, a casting director in a television show would say that Hoffa's too on the nose. That's possibly why the government picked him as The Victim. He sums up all organized crime. He's unpopular with the government, but very popular with his constituents—which is interesting. You can say the same thing about the President: He's unpopular with the Communists, but popular with his constituents.

Anyway, the Hoffa thing, I think, is dangerous. To single out one individual and to put the resources of the United States government to work—is (1) expensive; (2) futile; and (3) against the American grain. The hearings of the Senate subcommittee when Bobby Kennedy was an attorney were harassment—in the best McCarthyite tradition. And now they're carrying it on.

As I've often said on stage, free speech is very much in doubt in this country. The individual is sliding down the drain, and it's being tested by a couple of people, like Hoffa, Lenny Bruce. There's a conspiracy against—you know: don't rock the boat.

Q. I was told by a responsible civil rights leader—and they may not follow through on this—but they're thinking of approaching Jimmy Hoffa to have his Teamsters Union boycott deliveries to any of these Southern communities which condone and encourage racial violence.

A. Well, I don't condone *that*, any more than I like an Interstate Commerce clause interpreted to hang civil rights on. They either stand on their own, or they should be disregarded completely. That's hypocrisy. It also won't stand up legally. If the Solicitor General has to go before the Supreme Court and equate a minority's rights with the Mann Act, that's a wrong interpretation of the law. That's not democracy, that's extortion.

And, as I say, this whole headlong surge toward liberation with no skills—it's like you've got free elections in Africa. You remember when Ellender said that people weren't equipped to vote? He happens to be *right*.

Now a lot of liberals don't like to hear that, but Ellender's bigotry is better founded than their liberalism. And if they want to compete with him, then they should cultivate liberalism, not just go with what they feel emotionally. You've got to be a full-time working individual, with a head on your shoulders; not a thumping heart coming through your rib cage.

Q. You mentioned Dick Gregory and publicity, but— in the same way that your reaching people is effective—maybe the publicity that accompanied his being down South brought the situation to public attention. Now, isn't that good?

A. Anything that contributes is good. No matter what the motivation, if it is productive, it's good. It doesn't seem to be productive. He stood on the street corner, he was ignored, and he was finally jailed. I don't think that's good. I don't think Martin Luther King picked up in overalls, looking like he had prepared to go to jail, is good. I don't think encouraging anarchy is good. I don't think a power struggle just before the top is loosened on the pickle jar, so that someone can get the credit for doing all of the turning, is good.

Everybody wants to be around to raise the champ's hand, because the other guy is reeling. The fact that anything can happen via violence does not bode well for the country. You *can't* march on Washington. I'm not in favor of that.

Q. You know who else said that? Governor Barnett. Isn't it funny to be in the same camp with him?

A. That often happens. Henry Wallace was in the same camp with Bob Taft about the Korean war, but he was the head of the Progressive Party. That's all right, there again you've got to go issue by issue. People will just have to make up their minds whether I'm a segregationist or not. I don't think I have a record as one.

Q. Of course, Barnett charged that the drive for civil rights legislation and street demonstrations are a part of the Com- munist *conspiracy to conquer the nation from within.*

A. Last night in a drug store a guy asked me if I didn't think that Communists were behind the NAACP, and I said, "If the Communists were behind the NAACP, it might be a little better organized—there wouldn't be so many groups." Because I think they're impotent by the fact that there's such a fragmented leadership.

Q. But the March on Washington is a joining-together of all these groups—

A. When I say you can't march, this is what I'm getting at: Demonstrations are fine to let the Congress know that they're not insulated, and this is public opinion—put it in front of them, that's fine. I like hostility at times, when it's justified by the situation, but if hostility can't be controlled it then becomes an instrument of terror, even to the person who possesses it.

It may end in a lot of blood, because what is going to happen eventually—if somebody gets out of line, you will have to call in the law—and then right is automatically on the side of those in uniform, and there's going to be blood in the streets, as the saying goes. I don't think that's getting anything accomplished.

You can't *sit in* on Congress. It's *against the law*. That's the way things are. And I'm talking about getting something *done*, not expressing the individual neuroses of those Jewish girls who belong to the NAACP. Let 'em take it out on their husbands, like they used to.

Q. Aren't you going to give fodder to the right-wingers who say that the NAACP is run by Jewish girls?

A. No, the *Negroes* say it. There's a lot of anti-Semitism among Negroes. They have no sense of history. They've forgotten about the Communist Party—the Jews were in the middle of it and pulled the Negroes right along with them—they were always saying, "Help the Negro!"

Years ago, they used to say, "We're having a party—I'll bring the liquor, you bring the Negroes." Remember those jokes? Well, the Negroes have forgotten that. They're now saying, "The Jews didn't care." An awful lot of Jews *did* care—in the Furriers Union, and in demonstrations in Union Square in the '30s.

But aside from that, I'm giving fodder to all the conservatives who subscribe to *The Realist*. If you'll think about it, I really have no ax to grind.

I'm in the theater, for better or for worse, in one form or another, for the rest of my life. I'm not interested in *politics*. I'm not like Ronald Reagan, I don't want to *graduate* to politics.

Incidentally, don't you find it quite interesting, as you watch me work, that I mention Eisenhower—the most popular man we ever had—and there's a complete blank? That really makes you wonder about Edward P. Morgan's phrase that nothing is as fickle as public favor. Now, if he is a ridiculous figure, as many in the audience say—if he's a meaningless figure in American history—then I want a refund on the eight years that my destiny was in the palm of his hand. And if he's a *meaningful* figure, I want him to be *honored*, I don't want him ignored.

Capital no longer fights politics; it *dominates* politics. The press is no longer the handmaiden of capital; it *is* capital. And television is pre-empting the press. Those are the hallmarks of our era. Wealthy men don't go into their fathers' businesses any more; they go into politics. I don't know why they're so fascinated with it. But they always did kind of run the government, so it's nice to have them doing it openly.

Q. There's a fantastic irony about what constitutes a scandal, as far as Nelson Rockefeller is concerned—

A. Oh, yeah—the fact that he got married! What kind of a scandal would it be if he *wasn't* married?

Q. Would you care to say a few words about the future of monogamy?

A. Yes. It looks like it's failing in the Western world—just look at the divorce rate—due to the fact that everything is metabolism, including a love affair. It goes a while, then it's over. And most of the agony is because people will not accept that. They have not been resourceful enough to think up an alternative. And the alternative of loneliness terrifies them.

They become impatient with the fact that they cannot sustain this for life. So they continue to get married—they continue to pretend—that's their adjustment to reality.

Now, women are being liberated, so they have an opportunity to develop more as people. As they do this, long-range on the graph they're moving ahead and becoming like men are now; the only trouble is, some girls making the transition are going to be bloodied. It's a good thing overall, but it's a rough transition.

You live what?—65, 75 years. Over a 200-year period, women are really going to emerge as human beings. But in between, a lot of people are going to have miserable lives, because they don't have skills, they've become dependent in all the wrong areas; because they're competitive when it comes to cocktail hour and having a big mouth, but they're not *really competitive*—they don't want to be girls, but they don't have the courage to be men.

Now, monogamy. It looks like it's over, and it's a panic for all of us, because where do we *go?* Everybody keeps pursuing the dream, and you can pursue it to such a degree that you don't believe in divorce. You get *divorced* and you don't believe in it. Think of *that* agony.

Or you say to yourself, "Can you really love more than one person? God sent me that one partner and I loused that up." You know, puritanical instinct. And yet you *know* that isn't true, because you've *been* in love with more than one chick, or you've been attracted to more than one, for different reasons.

But women are the lost souls. This is even beyond *Negroes.* Women are the most *lost*—holy cow!

Q. It's funny—in connection with Barry Goldwater, you make this reference on stage to his being a Major-General in the Reserves, and the audience seems not to have been aware of the fact—

A. Sometimes when you work, you can't assume that they know—you've got to set them up and still make them feel smart; not take their dignity away. So you've got to say, "Well, you're all aware that Goldwater's a Major-General in the Reserves," and act as if you *admire* them—and *then.* . . . "Kennedy could always call him to active service. He's not above it."

But when I work, I feel a cadence, just like when you play, when you blow; I feel a certain cadence, and I feel it coming, I feel *rhythms*—that's why the jokes sometimes look premeditated, and they seem Bob Hopeish—you feel a cadence and

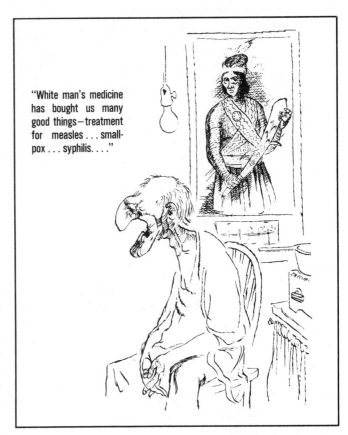

"White man's medicine has bought us many good things—treatment for measles . . . smallpox . . . syphilis. . . ."

you find it as you go.

But I become impatient with it and want to start with something else, because *every word I do* is improvised. I don't rehearse anything. I start it on the stage. I never stress that word, improvise; because it's been dissipated by people who don't. People say, "We improvise! We improvise!" Well, I *have* to. I've found no other way out.

I also am pro-intellectual, and I find that anti-intellectual persons, who are not interested in discipline, who dig anarchy, use that as a facade. They say, "Well, I wanna be *free.*" They also use splintered reasoning and call it free association. That's not free; that's very *limited* association.

It's all in the presenting of it. As I'm going, I open a door and I see six streets, and on each of the six streets there's twelve doors, and each twelve doors there's twelve streets—and it's endless. You just find it from night to night, and it starts to build up. It's like Joseph Conrad: When you find out what life is about, it's over.

Q. I notice you get a lot of laughs on just straight reporting, without any comment.

A. Information, yeah. One of the hallmarks of this era is that comedians, could get a laugh by exaggeration. Bob Hope went, for instance, to a paraplegic center of veterans—he could tell about the guys who were very ambidextrous with the wheelchairs and that they get speeding tickets—and the guys used to laugh, the paraplegics. Now, he had used exaggeration.

I used to do the same thing. If the President said something about a policy, I would extend his logic to expose the innate absurdity of it. Well, exaggeration is no longer available, because we live in such an incredible era that I read the *paper* to them and they break up; whereas when I analyze it for them with all my humorous talons exposed, they often don't laugh at all.

Because *what* is taking place, is insane! And nothing shocks people. I think there's a point at which they become deadened to any kind of pain or feeling. Guys are in orbit, and people are being slaughtered—and they just don't *know* any more, they can't comprehend.

Q. With all the national and international tensions, in the end people still seem to be hung up on their personal problems and their interpersonal relationships.

A. I could only tell you what I've observed. The people I know in show business are very alert, and they're a little bit advanced; that is to say, the norm—the people watching television across the country—don't have financial access to a psychoanalyst to be advanced enough to pinpoint guilt upon yourself as opposed to yelling at somebody or saying to a kid, "Go to your room."

Or punishment and reward. Punishing yourself as opposed to venting your wrath on others is an advanced theorem. So, the people I know do look at themselves more than they look *out*, but I don't know if that's *evasion* or not; I don't know if that's being advanced or if it's just evasion. I suspect that a lot of it is evasion.

I *know* there are personal problems, but the only way you can measure personal problems is how you relate reality—not relate it to yourself, but how do you interpret it? Does it kill you, or do you look at it and ignore it, or do you try to do something about it, or whatever.

Q. How do you feel about the press treatment you've received lately?

A. Well, I really don't have much respect for spectators— I'm talking about all those members of the press who don't have the courage to carry a torch, but stand by and judge you in terms of how you carry it and whether you carry it as well as you did.

"Why don't you wear a sweater any more?" "Why don't you go to coffee houses?" The fact is, all a man has is his integrity. You have to keep that and your curiosity up high. Keep your state of mind protected, as Del Close says. I think *that's* what's important. But I haven't read an upbeat article about anybody in five years. Everything is negative, negative, negative. They wait for a giant to emerge and cast his shadow—and then they say, "You're standing in my light!"

I'm not a political flash-in-the-pan. They have misinterpreted my semaphore completely; the sun got in their eyes. I am an *entertainer*, and a writer, and my influence will be felt as long as I want to move, even if I want to do a television series, should that unhappy day ever come. Whatever happens to strike me, I'm a prism through which nature expresses herself. And they cannot accept that. They keep treating me like I'm a Senator up for re-election. I've got a life-time appointment. To this empty bench.

People thought it was going to be like six months, then I had ten years, and soon I'll have twenty, and then I'll have thirty. . . .

Q. Have you also heard from your targets?

A. You mean adversaries? Nothing. That's the amazing part of it. A lot of dumb guys in the press say, "You can't say that!" When *Newsweek* said that the President likes to laugh at himself, I asked, "When is he going to extend that privilege to us?"

And this is not a criticism of Kennedy; it's *them*. Remember, it's the *constituents* who are weak. If they dub him God, the weakness is that *they need* a god. It's not that *he* says "I'm God."

Styles Bridges once looked at an English TV film called *Dissent* and said that it was full of "beatniks" criticizing our government. And he named me, Norman Mailer, Arthur Miller, Robert Hutchins, Bertrand Russell. I've been in very good company, and I'm pleased about that. Flattered, in fact. The Good Guys.

Q. I feel as though we should end with some sort of Grand Summation—like: "Do you have a message?"

A. Yes. You have to give the best you can. That's your number one concern. Not, "Does anybody *want* the best I have, what's the *use* of giving the best I have, there isn't any *market* for the best I have." You have to give the best you can. Everything else will follow as a byproduct. That's all. My old message used to be, "Is anybody listening?" Well, they're obviously listening, so now you've got to give them the facts; you've got to get to the people. That's the virtue of night clubs. *Get to that audience.*

Q. But is that the people? Isn't that analogous to saying, as you do on stage, that Robert Kennedy met with Dick Gregory and James Baldwin and Lena Horne—to find out what the average Negro thinks?

A. But I haven't just been in the night clubs. I went from there to television, where we have 40 million people looking at the Sullivan show; from there to motion pictures; and from there to appearances before 2,000 people at the Waldorf, all of whom are editors and influence everybody they write for. How do you explain that I can't go in and complete a meal in any restaurant in the United States without being recognized and harassed— I don't mean complimented; *harassed.*

Q. About your ideas? Or to get an autograph?

A. No, it's provocation. It's always about ideas. Are you *kidding*? With actors—they don't represent an idea—they represent Success, whatever the hell *that* means. Success with whom? With yourself, if you're lucky. Megalomania, that's all it can come to.

Is it 9 o'clock? Great Scott! It's funny, the time ran away. Now I've got to go to that club—are you ready for *that*? More boredom in the night club.

Q. Why, Mort, you old hypocrite. "You've got to get to the people!"

A. I cannot summon my passion on demand for a night club schedule of seven nights a week, twice a night. That's why the show is not uniform. The only people that can summon their passion on demand are folksingers who sing about the labor struggle. "We'd like to introduce this song about the Negroes in prison, all of whom were framed. . . ."

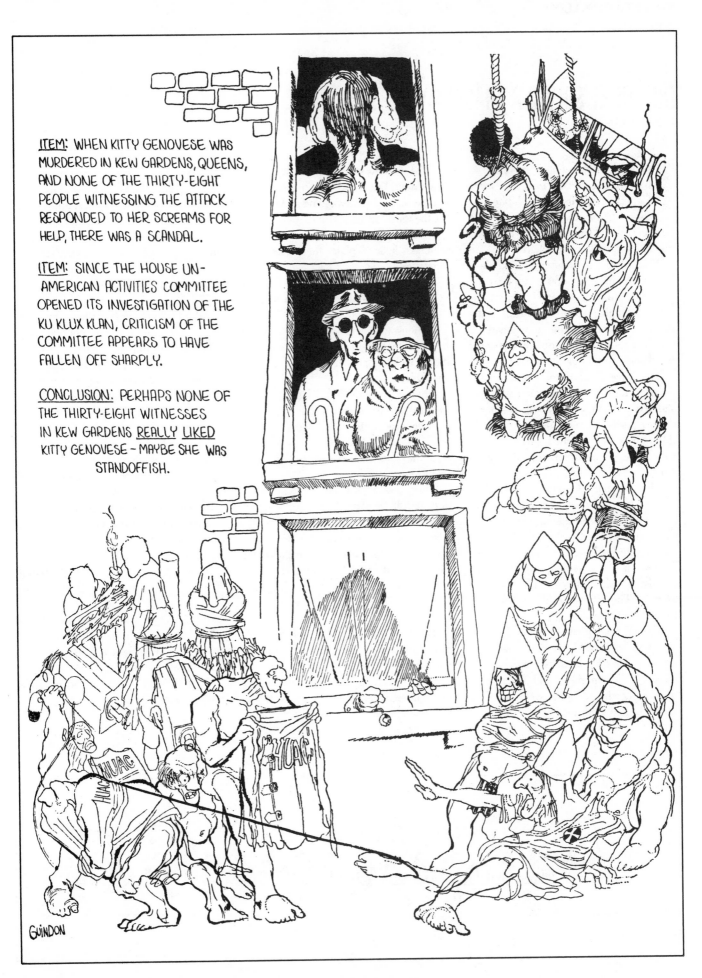

ITEM: WHEN KITTY GENOVESE WAS MURDERED IN KEW GARDENS, QUEENS, AND NONE OF THE THIRTY-EIGHT PEOPLE WITNESSING THE ATTACK RESPONDED TO HER SCREAMS FOR HELP, THERE WAS A SCANDAL.

ITEM: SINCE THE HOUSE UN-AMERICAN ACTIVITIES COMMITTEE OPENED ITS INVESTIGATION OF THE KU KLUX KLAN, CRITICISM OF THE COMMITTEE APPEARS TO HAVE FALLEN OFF SHARPLY.

CONCLUSION: PERHAPS NONE OF THE THIRTY-EIGHT WITNESSES IN KEW GARDENS REALLY LIKED KITTY GENOVESE – MAYBE SHE WAS STANDOFFISH.

GUINDON

THE COURT SOLVES A TRAGIC MYSTERY

by Charles G. Burck

The *New York Times* reported on March 27, 1964, that the State Court of Appeals had prohibited the showing of the Danish film *A Stranger Knocks* unless scenes depicting sexual intercourse were deleted.

This in itself is nothing remarkable—courts are handing down similar decisions every day across the country. The article contains some significant statements, however, which may answer a question raised in a seemingly unrelated front-page story in the same issue.

The piece detailed the horrifying account of a 28-year-old woman who was stabbed to death one evening in Queens over a period of half-an-hour while 37 different people watched. None of them called the police or attempted to help her.

The woman, Catherine Genovese, parked her car near her apartment at 3:20 A.M. and was walking home when a man attacked and stabbed her. She shouted for help; windows opened, lights flashed on in several apartments, and one man called down: "Let that girl alone!" The killer looked up, shrugged and walked away.

The lights went out and soon the killer returned and stabbed Miss Genovese again as she tried to stagger away. "I'm dying!" she shrieked, and again windows opened and lights went on. The killer got in his car and drove away.

Miss Genovese crawled toward her apartment, but the killer returned again, caught her in a doorway and stabbed her for the third, and fatal time.

And how did the good citizens who watched later explain their silence to detectives?

"I was tired," said one man who was awakened and looked at the incident— "I went back to bed."

A housewife who watched with her husband by her side was asked why they didn't call the police. "I don't know," she replied.

Another woman said, "I didn't want my husband to get involved."

When the ambulance came at 4:25 A.M. to take Miss Genovese's body away, a police detective said, "Then the people came out."

These are rather amazing answers, and hardly explain how people could watch a murder being committed—in slow motion at that—and not even reach out to phone the police. Do people resent the cops that much? Was the show too good to stop? Did they dislike the woman, perhaps? Or is there some other answer?

The article on the Court of Appeals' ruling quoted Judge Adrian P. Burke, who wrote the majority statement: ". . . a filmed presentation of sexual intercourse, whether real or simulated, is just as subject to state prohibition as sim-

ilar conduct if engaged in on the street."

But what about pictorialized murder? Shouldn't the same standard apply? The Judge thinks not. The majority opinion noted that in the case of murder, the actual deed is illegal because of what is accomplished and "the filmed dramatization obviously does not share the evil."

More to the point: "Where, however, the real conduct is illegal, not because of what is accomplished by those involved, but *simply because what is done is shocking and morally offensive to see*, then a filmed simulation fully shares, it seems to me, the evil of the original."

The difference, you see, is that murder is not shocking and morally offensive to see. Sexual intercourse is evil, dirty. It is certainly shocking, and anyone will tell you that it's morally offensive to see. Murder, on the other hand, is a good, natural human instinct, sanctioned and even urged by governments, churches, and private individuals.

Here, then, is the answer to the haunting question of why no one called for help when Miss Genovese was stabbed to death. There was nothing shocking or offensive about the act. It happens on television every night and is as much a part of life as yeast is of bread.

Now if Miss Genovese and her killer were making love on the street. . . .

"Eight for, and one against!"

S. GROSS

OBSCENITY, NARCOTICS, AND ME

by Lenny Bruce

Who is guilty of my harassment?

It starts with me, who never took any interest in Civics in school, allowed others to handle the important funds while I screwed around; by the time I came back from screwing around and saw that the idiot kids had taken over the lead, I could control myself with intellectual pursuit and a voice in a bipartisan community through the media. Gradually, the bullies bought up the voice, and now, with the exception of a few periodicals, the voice is gone.

Another party comes to the forefront: slick, organized uniforms. You-kneeform. It's time for the masquerade. Go to court and it's "Hey, Lenny, you've got to wear a blue suit and get a haircut."

Why wear a blue suit? So that those who try the facts will not be burdened searching for the felon.

"Which one is he?"

"Don't you know how to spot them? They wear blue suits."

"How about the *real* men in blue?"

"They wear their brown suit that day."

I could not expect to get a jury that did not read a newspaper, and to make sure they were prejudiced and that The People had their side of the story in first, the newspapers saw to it that I glommed the first handicap, the stigma of being arrested. That in itself puts one in an unsavory light.

I am a product of the press myself. I could have kept a sense of right and wrong were it not for the newspapers that stilted it. We keep forgiving, and, goddamit, you can't—at least if you're the kind of person that likes to plan ahead for a hate or a forgive.

We forgave the Japanese once, the Germans twice, but the White Southerners we've kicked in the ass since Fort Sumter.

A bronze honor roll, black wreaths, and those dopey green sticks with dye running that support them.

My uncle used to lie that he just bought a poppy.

* * *

The Realist has contrasted the Police Report of my arrest in Chicago for obscenity, with a transcript of the tape of what I actually had said on stage.

The jury found me guilty, and the judge sentenced me to a year in jail and $1,000 fine. The appeal on the case is still pending.

One of the things I got arrested for in Chicago was showing a picture of a girl that was really pretty. I wanted to point out the God-made-the-body paradox of the decent people who would object to that groovy-looking chick.

I could never sit on a jury and put anybody away for *looking*. If I'm dressing and there's that chick across the way—that blue-eyed, pink-nippled, sweet high-ass from Oklahoma—I'm going to look and I'm going to call my *friends* to look.

But, in our society, it's "Pull down the shade"—and charge two bucks to get in.

That's what repression does.

I'd like to fight the appeal on the Chicago obscenity rap on a whole different issue. The obscenity law, when everything else boils away, is: Does it appeal to the prurient interest?

I must get you horny—that's what it means.

If I do a *disgusting* show—a show about eating pork —that's not obscene. Although you Jews and vegetarians and Moslems will bitch your asses off, that's my right as an American, to talk about pork, to extol its virtues, to run in front of a synagogue:

"Here's pork! Look at it, rabbi!"

"Get him out of here, he should be arrested—that's disgusting!"

It doesn't matter. That's why the Pilgrims left England, man. If a guy wants to wail with pork, that's his *schtick*.

Or, if I do a *vulgar* show—I sing rock and roll tunes, wear platform shoes, Kitty Kellys with ankle straps—it's not obscene.

No, obscenity has only one meaning: to appeal to the prurient interest. Well, I want to know what's *wrong* with appealing to the prurient interest? I really want them to stand up and tell me that fucking is dirty and no good.

Do you know there are guys in jail for doing it to *chickens*? Bestiality.

Hey, lady, would you get bugged if your husband balled a chicken?

"I was the last one to know!"

"She was only sitting on my lap—I was *feeding* her."

"Oh, sure, you were feeding her. Everybody *told* me what you were doing to her—and on *our* bed."

"It wasn't on the bed, it was over there—"

"What's happened to your chicken? Have you seen your chicken lately? Tell your *chicken* to fix dinner . . ."

Once I was talking to a horse trainer and a jockey. I'm not hip to track people and their life, but this trainer told me how he really loved animals, and to have a horse that's a winner you've got to lock them up all the time. Just keep them a prisoner and box-car them from town to town, and never let them have any fun with other lady horses. It's the lowest. Just keep them so when that race comes, he's a nut! *Whoosh* . . .

The jockey said to me, "You know, Lenny, sometimes in the morning when the light just starts to break through, some of those fillies are so beautiful, they look like pretty ladies. When they've got those fly-sheets on, they look like negligees flying in the wind."

"Oh, yeah? Uh—did you ever—?"

"No."

"Because that's very interesting transference there. I can't see any girlie thing in horses. Now tell me the truth—because I know I'd deny it too if I made it with a filly—but I mean, you know, did you ever?"

He said no, he never did, but then he told me a story that really flipped me, about this horse called "I Salute," out of Isaacson Stables. This horse was a big winner—purse after purse—she really had it made, and the season was almost over.

Five o'clock one morning they caught a 50-year-old exercise man with the horse. Naturally, they busted him. The charge: sodomy. They arraigned him, convicted him, and he got a year in the joint.

Now I started thinking—what a hell of a thing to do time for, you know?

"What are you in for?"

"Never mind."

The most ludicrous thing would be making the arrest, I assume. You'd be so embarrassed.

"I, uh, you're under arrest—uh, *ahem*, come out of there!"

Or the judge. How could he really get serious with that? "Where's the complaining witness?"

Anyway, the exercise man was in prison, and the horse must've missed him a lot, because she didn't want to race any more. And she never did race again.

The lowest of the low—from both the felon's point of view and the police eye—is the child-molester. But his most heinous crime is simply that he is bereft of the proper dialogue, for if he spoke his lines thusly, he would never be busted:

"C'mere, Ruthie, c'mere to your Uncle Willie, look at those little apples on you, lemme lift you up, she's gonna have to get a bra-*zeer* soon, let your Uncle Willie tickle-ickle-ickle you, rump-bump-bump on the floor, she's getting some hair on her *booger*, tickle-ickle-ickle, watch her wriggle-wiggle-giggle in Uncle Willie's ruddy palm, don't tell Mommy or you'll break the magic charm."

And Uncle Willie's Mason signet ring snags little Ruthie's nylon underthings . . . children don't wear *panties*.

* * *

I don't smoke marijuana, and I'm glad—because I can champion it then. The reason I don't is because it's a hallucinatory—and I've got enough shit going on in my head without smoking pot.

Marijuana will be legal some day, though, because there are so many law students that smoke pot, who will some day become Senators and legalize it to protect themselves.

But there are people in jail now for smoking *flowers*.

And yet you wouldn't *believe* how many people smoke pot. If anybody reading this would like to become mayor, believe me, there's an untapped vote. Of course, you wouldn't want to be the Marijuana Mayor, so you'd have to make it a trick statute, like "The Crippled Catholic Jewish War Children In Memory Of Ward Bond Who Died For You Bill To Make Marijuana Legal."

There are untold legions of people all over the country who play the I-know-and-you-know-but-we'll-both-make-believe-we're-asleep/gynecologist: It-doesn't-mean-anything-to-me-I-see-that-all-the-time—game they play with the Zig-Zag people.

At this time, ladies and gentlemen of the jury, the state will present its closing argument in the case against marijuana: It leads to the use of heroin and other heavier drugs.

If this syllogism holds true, the bust-out junkie will say to his cellmate: "I am a heroin addict, I started smoking marijuana and then naturally I graduated to heroin. By the way, my cellmate, what happened to you? How did you come to murder three guys in a crap game? You've got blood on your hands. How did you first get obsessed with this terrible disease of gambling? Where did it all start?"

"Oh, I started gambling with Bingo in the Catholic Church . . ."

* * *

The newspapers said that the late Pope John was being fed intravenously.

"We don't like to do this, Pope, but we've got to take you downtown. Those marks on your arm there—now don't give us any of that horseshit about intravenous feeding—we hear it all the time."

I'm not anti-Catholic or pro-Catholic, but if I *were* Catholic, I'd be quite hostile toward the press. To quote from the Los Angeles *Herald-Examiner:* "Short of a miracle, [Pope John] could be expected to die at any moment."

Superstitious people all over the world waited and waited for that miracle, and it never came.

When my trial for the alleged possession of heroin came to court in Los Angeles, I didn't want to take the oath.

"It seems like sort of a mockery to do this," I said. "I don't really care to but I will. I don't mean to be contemptuous of the Court, but—"

The judge interrupted: "I don't understand your thinking in that matter. That is the custom here, and the rule is that you have to take an oath to get on the stand."

Actually, one has the alternative of "affirming" to tell the truth, rather than swearing on the Bible.

The judge continued: "Do you have any objection to it? If it's a mockery, that is your personal opinion. You have a right to your opinion, but that is the way we do it here."

"Yes, sir."

"All right, swear the witness."

The Clerk: "You do solemnly swear to tell the truth, the whole truth, and nothing but the truth in the matter now pending before this Court, so help you God?"

"I will tell the truth."

Officer John L. White testified that he saw me drop a matchbook containing a packet of heroin and run into a bicycle shop, that he followed me in, frisked me for weapons, and arrested me. Under cross-examination, he described the scene as follows:

Q. Then what did you say to him?

A. I informed him that he was under arrest for violation of the State Narcotics Act.

Q. You said to him, "You are under arrest for violation of the State Narcotics Act"—that formal challenge? That formal expression? Did you put it that formally to him?

A. I don't recall my exact words. I know I used the words "State Narcotics Act," as is my custom. I think I probably said, "You're busted."

(He probably said, "You're busted, State Narcotics Act, I'm sorry but it's my custom.")

Q. Was that in a loud tone of voice?

A. Yes, it was.

Q. And he put his hands up in the air immediately like this?

A. No, I first took a hold of him by the seat of the pants.

Q. You grabbed him by the seat of the pants, then he put his hands up in the air?

A. Yes.

Q. Was it like he was being goosed or something, his hands went up in the air, or what caused his hands to go up in the air?

A. As I testified, counsel, I ordered him to put his hands in the air.

Q. Oh, you ordered him to put his hands in the air? I see. Let's get the whole thing here. You grabbed him by the seat of the pants first. What did you grab him by the seat of the pants for?

A. To stop his forward motion.

Q. He wasn't running, was he?

A. He was walking fast.

Q. He was walking quite fast now, was he?

A. Yes.

Q. How fast was he walking?

A. He was walking just as fast as a person can walk when they are walking. At the time I stopped him he was walking quite fast, approaching the rear door of the bicycle shop.

Now, the bicycle shop man and his assistant both testified that they didn't see this arrest take place. The assistant, incidentally, was a 15-year-old kid with a harelip, and he goes to parochial school. If I were the District Attorney, I'd say, "Why don't you get a dog and an old lady, too?"

The D.A. asked: "Mr. Gunn, isn't it a fair statement that when you and the boy are not waiting on customers in the front of the shop, that you would be concerned with the repair work at the back of the shop; now when you and the boy are hammering and making noise, the back is turned, would you testify under oath, sir, that a person could not come into your shop and stay there a matter of seconds without you seeing him, isn't that possible?"

Mr. Gunn: "It's possible."

The D.A. didn't ask him if it was possible that two men could rush into a shop, one grab the other by the seat of the pants, and in a loud tone of voice say, "Hold it you're arrested for violation of the State Narcotics Act," search him while his hands were in the air, and take him out unnoticed.

But the jury heard *possible*.

I say it's *im*possible—physiologically impossible—unless they're deaf. Perhaps psychologically they would reject such a scene; if they had some kind of a hang-up about a guy being grabbed by the ass like that, then it didn't *happen*, and they just blotted the whole thing out.

But it's impossible that they didn't *hear*.

The D.A. asked me if I think "that these officers have to frame people? That's what you're saying when you deny dropping this pack of matches."

The judge responded: "I think instead of 'framing,' you can say 'tell an untruth.' I'd like that better. 'Take the stand and tell an untruth under oath' rather than the word 'frame.' "

Now why would they lie to the Lord or whatever deity that hellish Constitution thwarts? They said they had a hobby shop under surveillance. They did not have any persons under sur-

veillance besides Bobby Coogan, the owner of the shop. They can get no warrant to enter this hobby shop. No responsible person will issue a warrant.

So, to keep within the margin of the law, they have to wait until a person leaves that shop who is a criminal. If they can catch a criminal coming out, they can go in with no warrant, because then they have a *probable cause* and can get around that goddam Constitution that guarantees you safety in your house against unreasonable searches and seizures unless a warrant is issued describing the persons and place to be searched and seized.

The officers waited and waited, and no criminals did appear. The next step to stay within the law is to make a criminal. And how one makes a criminal and gets by the probable-cause provision, so that the policemen may arrest without a warrant, is by having me drop a pack of matches which they describe as a furtive action, thus giving Constitutional permission to make an arrest, "acting as a reasonable man, if he should see a suspicious act that might tend to be criminal"—such as climbing out of a second story that has no fire escape, or dropping a head out of your suitcase, or dropping a packet of matches and then walking into a bicycle shop— compounding a criminal act which *then* gives the policeman license immediately to go to the place which the criminal just left, without a warrant.

"Let's see, what crime can Lenny Bruce commit in a business district that only we could observe? The most esoteric. With X-ray vision we will observe a pellet of city-water-system-poisoner-child-paralyzer-sex-fiend-instruction-book-printing-plates-and-mailing-address-to-entire-Communist-Bloc-type book stuck in a place where only those type persons know where to stick those type things. Let him drop it. We will run over, pick it up, arrest him for dropping a book of matches, with a bookmark—a piece of paper sticking out a quarter of an inch—by any other name, heroin."

The jury found me guilty of possession of heroin.

My probation report reads:

". . . /Bruce/ states that he is disappointed with the verdict as he was almost positive that he would be found not guilty. He is hopeful that the court will allow him a new trial and exoneration. He says that as a result of all the cases that are out against him, he is receiving much adverse publicity and this is affecting his livelihood. His only desire is to live a law-abiding life and to be left alone."

And they asked my *mother* about me. At my age! It's embarrassing. What else could a mother say:

". . . /My son/ is thoroughly devoted to the welfare of his daughter and making a success of himself in the entertainment field. He is considered by many as being a 'genius' and is very talented. Many people harass him because he is not always conventional and speaks his mind."

The Court adjourned criminal proceedings, so that my fate could be decided by a Dept. 95 hearing, the purpose of which, in California, is to decide whether or not you're a drug addict. If the decision is in the affirmative, then instead of two years in jail, you get ten years of compulsory rehabilitation.

"Mr. Bruce, you're lucky, we're going to give you ten years of help."

"I don't deserve it, really, I'm a rotten bastard."

* * *

On the night of October 15, 1963, I was in the bathroom of my home, shaving and talking to Paul Krassner, when four police officers showed up on my property. I knew two of them; one, in fact, with whom I was friendly, had testified in court against me—the Trojan that Horse built—the others were loud and out of line. I asked them to leave if they didn't have a search warrant, whereupon one of them took out his gun, saying: "Here's my search warrant."

We talked about the law—rules of evidence, etc.—and after half an hour, they left. It was very depressing.

But I still say there's nobody "picking" on me. Except the ones that don't piss in the sink. But we *all* do! That's the one common denominator to seize upon. Every man reading this has at one time pissed in the sink. I have and I am part every guy in the world; we're all included. I know that Lyndon Johnson has pissed in the sink. I *know* it. He pretended to be washing his hands, but he was pissing in the sink.

Definitely.

Lyndon Johnson could cut Schopenhauer mind-wise but his *sound* chills it for him. The White Southerner gets kicked in the ass once again for his sound.

"Folks, Ah think nuclear fission—"

"Get outa here, *schmuck*, you don't think nothin'."

The bomb, the bomb, oh, thank God for the bomb. The final answer is, "I'll get my brother—the bomb." Out of all the teaching and bullshitting, that's the end answer we have.

Well, it's a little embarrassing. You see, 17,000 students marched on the White House, and Lyndon Johnson was left holding the bag.

"Mr. Johnson, we're 17,000 students who have marched from Annapolis, and we demand to see the bomb."

"Ah'd like to see it mahself, son."

"Aw, c'mon, now, let's see the bomb, we're not gonna hurt anybody, just take a few pictures, then we'll protest, and that's it."

"Son, you gonna think this is a lot of horseshit, but there never was a bomb. Them Hebe Hollywood writers made up the idea and they spread it around, and everybody got afraid of this damn bomb story. But there is no bomb. Just something we keep in the White House garage. We spent three million dollars on it, and once we got it started, it just made a lot of noise and smelled up the house, so we haven't fooled with it since."

"Now, wait a minute. You see, I led the March, and I've got 17,000 students that are protesting the bomb. Don't tell me there's no bomb—"

"Son, Ah'd like to help you if Ah could. If Ah had a bomb—"

"But what am I gonna tell those poor kids out there? That there's no bomb?"

"The only thing that did work out was the button."

"What button?"

"The button that the madmen are always gonna push."

"That's what the bomb is—a button?"

"Yes—it's a button."

"Well, goddamit, give me the button, then!"

"Can't do that, son. It's on a Boy Scout's fly. And some time, somewhere, a fag Scoutmaster is gonna blow up the world."

* * *

A shakedown try in Philadelphia . . . over a thousand sinks later . . . *muy*-multi-milligrams self-injected by disposable syringes that stop up hotel toilets and bring memos from irate managers. . . .

If I am incarcerated in Chino, I am going to study. Yes, and learn to play the cello. I will come out an accomplished cellist—and just bore the shit out of everyone.

Incidentally, I use the word "shit" in context. It's not obscene as far as narcotics is concerned—that's the Supreme Court ruling on the picture, *The Connection*—in other words, if you shit in your pants and smoke it, you're cool.

Anyone who does anything for pleasure to indulge his selfish soul will surely burn in Hell. The only medicine that's good for you is iodine, because it burns; a stone is lodged in your urinary tract because nature meant it to be there. So re-tie that umbilical cord, snap on your foreskin, and drown in the water bag, 'cause we're havin' a party and the people are nice.

The what-*should*-be never did exist, but people keep trying to live *up* to it. All the what-should-be's just don't exist. There is only what *is*.

And so the figures will never be in, relating to the unspoken confessions of all those criminals who purchase contraceptives unlawfully, and willfully use them for purposes other than the prevention of disease.

I have played Detroit for almost 8 years, and was due to open at The Alamo in March, but when the Detroit Board of Censors learned of this, they wouldn't permit my appearance, depriving me of my rights without a judicial proceeding.

And *Variety*, the Bible of Show Business, refuses to accept an ad from me simply stating that I'm available for bookings.

I have just had confirmed the fact that John L. White, the officer who was supposed to have arrested me, is now in the federal penitentiary near Forth Worth, having been found guilty of possession of narcotics. He had been arraigned on the very day he testified against me; he had come from *jail*.

Fighting my "persecution" . . . It's like asking Barry Goldwater to speak at a memorial to send the Rosenberg kids to college; it's like asking attorney James Donavan, "On your way back from trading the prisoners in Cuba, stop off and see if you can get just one more pardon for Morton Sobell." When I think of all the crap that's been happening to me, the thing that keeps me from getting really outraged or hostile at the people involved with perpetrating these acts is—and I'm sure that Caryl Chessman, or perhaps his next-cell murderer who sits waiting to be murdered, felt this, too—the injustice that anyone is subjected to is really quite an *in* matter.

This month, the television board of the National Association of Broadcasters banned the use of actors in "white-coat" commercials. The ruling reads: "Dramatized advertising involving statements or purported statements by physicians, dentists or nurses must be presented by accredited members of such professions."

"You're going to have to give up smoking . . ."

HOW TO ELIMINATE THE NATION'S MOST POPULAR SUICIDE WEAPON
by Richard Condon

Within moments after the issuance of the Surgeon-General's report—one of many various, authoritative studies done here and abroad to establish the cigarette as a suicide weapon—piteous statistics were published which explained how much cellophane the cigarette industry bought; about the three billion dollars in federal and state taxes which the tobacco industry paid; of the 400,000 farmers, 1,500,000 cigarette pushers in grocery, drug, and other retail stores, and of the 96,000 people directly employed by the tobacco industry who, it was to be presumed, would be cast into total unemployment if Americans stopped smoking.

One friendly feature story went so far as to state that Americans had to "make a choice" between smoking and serious unemployment. This aberration presupposed that gross national income was more important than human health/life, that tobacco industry workers were unemployable elsewhere, and that all Americans were capable of stopping smoking instantly.

Of the points above, it is impossible to judge which is the most ludicrous, but if cigarettes are the suicide weapons which every responsible, authoritative study has proven them to be, then the tobacco industry is engaged in crime, and Americans must be protected from it and from themselves.

How to Eliminate the Nation's Most Popular Suicide Weapon, *continued*

How can we legislate against cigarettes without recreating, on a more deadly scale, the side effects of corruption and hypocrisy which accompanied Prohibition? How can we make it illegal to buy cigarettes under a code which will not cause the generation of thousands of "smoke-easies"?

Have you saved your child from a lung removal operation today? Have you prevented a coronary in a loved one? Do you have death on the end of a 20-year chain of smoked cigarettes and are you pulling it toward you hand-over-hand, dragging it into you puff-after-puff?

Such sound queries have no meaning to brainwashed America, the coughing, camp-following servants of an $8-billion-a-year industry and of that illusory army of employment statistics who prosper by selling a poison and who, almost all of them, poison themselves in the tragic process.

This country is so brainwashed that 14.9 billion more cigarettes were sold in 1963 than in 1962—and tobacco is the fifth largest of our cash crops, ranking third in our agricultural exports. But are we going to endanger statistics like those just because we all happen to have kids who have started smoking? Literally: you bet your life we won't.

Since appeals to reason, family love, premature death, and enormous physical pain have no meaning when administered by individuals, it becomes clearer that all of us will need to act collectively through the law, for this is a democracy, we keep telling ourselves, where the majority rules for the common good of all.

A model law to protect us and our children from the tobacco industry should contain these teeth, as well as others:

1: It should outlaw cigarette advertising of any kind in all media of public information; then, through a further provision of the same law, provide a positive replacement for this economic subtraction.

This advertising ban should include the use and display of cigarettes in performances on television, in movies, on the stage, and by newscasters. Examples-in-action of successful, attractive, glamorous people smoking cigarettes must be abolished throughout mass media. It is enough that the parents of doomed children set the examples toward the modern take-your-time fashion in suicide.

2: It should provide that cigarettes would be sold only in state-operated stores which would sell no other products but which would display posters and photographs and printed messages, demonstrating terminal results of rib sections, lung cancers, coronaries, and circulatory ailments.

Packages of cigarettes sold in these stores should carry warnings as to the poisons which they contain and the probable effects therefrom. Such cigarette stores would remove a moral burden from the cigarette pushers in those statistical 1,500,000 stores and give a fair chance to the retailer who has wished to stop selling cigarettes but feared that he would lose grocery, drug, or newspaper business to his competitors when cigarette addicts went shopping.

The state-operated cigarette outlets would limit the sale of these suicide weapons to not more than twenty cigarettes a day, except on Fridays when two packages could be purchased because stores would be closed on Saturdays and Sundays. Cigarettes would be available in packages of five, ten, and twenty to accommodate the occasional, or party smoker.

News item: This month, in 350 newspapers all over the world, Little Orphan Annie reached her 40th birthday.

GUINDON

"Well, little lady . . . today we learn a new word—menopause."

3: The price of twenty cigarettes should be increased to 75ᶜ a package. In Great Britain, the average cost for twenty cigarettes is the equivalent of 64ᶜ. Added to the 75ᶜ cost should be a State tax of 10ᶜ to be paid by cigarette manufacturers for the maintenance of these retail outlets.

From the 75ᶜ retail cost cigarette manufacturers should be allowed a fair 15% profit on the 7ᶜ cost to them for each package. The remainder should be paid into the educational fund suggested later in this article. It could be that the unit cost of manufacture will be less than 7ᶜ because the $250 million which the cigarette industry spends each year will have been eliminated, plus the cost of lunches and dinners paid for by ad agencies when cigarette executives come to town.

Whatever the cost per package to each cigarette manufacturer, he is an American businessman, and is entitled to his fair 15% profit as opposed to the somewhat larger profit he had been enjoying.

Older smokers will grouse about the 75ᶜ, knowing that when they had been 12 and 14 years old they were able to buy a "schoolboy pack" for 10ᶜ. And they would be right. The cigarette industry has been developing direct and subtle methods of hooking children on their product for over fifty years.

It has sold half-packs for 10ᶜ and has bought athletes and movie stars to help addict children through cynical endorsement. It has hustled the campuses of high schools and colleges, and has sponsored comic strip advertising and any sort of television "entertainment" thought to be most attractive to the young.

It has urged the use of its products as a "poise prop" for adolescents when these young people did not know what to do with their hands.

It redoubled efforts against American children when the first conclusive medical reports appeared some eight years ago, and capitalized on the need of all children to find a passive way to defy adult authority by showing children that smoking was a weapon most calculated to upset parents (in at least one home out of a thousand).

In passing, it does not strike this writer odd that in some thirty years of adult gregariousness he has met only one man who admitted to being employed directly by the cigarette industry. Only advertising agency men glory in this condition and today—in social circles at least—it is possible that absolutely no one is employed by it.

4: Each smoker should be licensed under the law in the general manner that drug addicts are licensed for narcotics use in Great Britain.

For a license charge of $15 per year, only 30.4ᶜ a week or less than half the price of the cost of a single pack of cigarettes, each smoker would be given a physical examination to investigate whether he showed symptoms of cancer, heart disease, circulatory malfunction, or any of the other ailments traced to cigarettes by the Surgeon-General of the United States in a most horrified manner which we have so good-naturedly ignored. The physical examination could be organized by the life insurance companies of each state on a cost-plus basis.

If the applicant for license showed any symptoms of the illnesses attributable as a result of cigarette smoking, no smoking license would be issued. If the applicant showed none of these symptoms and had paid his $15, he would be licensed at once.

The license would be issued in twelve perforated parts, each part dated for punching by the state-operated store at the time of purchase. If a day were missed the purchase could not be made retroactive. Each license would be exclusive for cigarette purchases in the state in which it would be issued. A visitor to New Jersey from New York would need to apply for a New Jersey license. Licenses would not be issued at state-operated stores but from state or municipal buildings in the downtown areas of the principal cities.

No person under 21 years of age would be issued a smoking license unless the issuance was urged by the child's surviving parents in an appearance before a state board, with the understanding that each parental request that the suicide weapons be made available to their child would be announced, by law, in the public press. A woman should be able to win the distinction of Black Star Mother by making three or more such appearances before a state board on behalf of her children.

Under no circumstances would a smoking license be issued before the age of 18 years. Parents of children under 18 found smoking would be fined $25 for the first offense because it would be presumed that the child had obtained the cigarette by reason of the parents' smoking licenses.

Parents with more than one child under 18 years of age would pay double fees for their smoking license.

Anyone smoking in public would do so with the understanding that it would be the duty of local, city police to challenge any smoker to produce his current smoker's license or pay a fine of $25, one-half of which would become a bounty payment for the challenging police officer to ease the cost and problems of enforcement.

Business firms, theaters, and restaurants which permit or encourage smoking on their premises would pay a $5 head tax ($2.50 per lung) per employee or per patron per month. This would tend to bring about the first cover charges ever known in lunchwagons. It is essential that the law be designed to make smoking inconvenient, uncomfortable, expensive, and embarrassing.

There are approximately 70 million smokers in the United States, a figure well-clawed downward because it is always issued with the qualification that these are *adult* smokers. The fee of $15 for a smoker's license in one state, plus the head taxes, plus the funds from the store maintenance tax would therefore yield well upwards of one billion dollars. Part of this one billion would be used to sponsor advertising against smoking in all the outlets of public information which had been used to generate addiction. Since the cigarette industry claims to have spent *directly* the sum of $250 million in 1963, let us give them the benefit of the doubt and only double this amount for the first year of this educational advertising program.

Perhaps some athletes, movie stars, and glamorous TV and radio announcers would volunteer their services without charge for printed and spoken condemnations of smoking and in personal appearances before high school and college gatherings. Those who felt ethically bound to charge for their services should be paid at existing rates, of course.

Of the one billion dollars, approximately $500 million would remain each year from the licensing system (although this amount would hopefully diminish each year as the ad campaign had a chance to take effect). This $500 million should be used, by law, for psychiatric research to study why and how humans could voluntarily submit to the self-administration of slow poisons and to the poisoning of their children at an annual cost of five or six hundred dollars per year per family.

It is entirely possible that during the educational campaign against cigarettes, farmers and distributors in the tobacco industry might desert it for other fields, thus reducing the output of cigarettes—if automation has not been installed throughout the industry by that time.

Automation? But that would throw farmers, retailers, salesmen, and distributors out of work! Must we always come back to where we had started?

THE JUNKIE BATTALION

by Mort Gerberg

Washington (AP)—The Army should begin drafting the nation's "punks and young toughs," Rep. Paul A. Fino (R.-N.Y.) said today. He introduced a bill which would amend the Selective Service Act to provide for drafting persons now considered deficient because of criminal records. He suggested special "junkie battalions" for those with narcotics records.

"I think they're trying to tell us something. This is the 18th straight day of cold turkey."

"You got it wrong, buddy—that's not what supply rooms are for..."

"That's only 16! I said <u>20</u> push-ups, Burnhill!"

"Did you come yet, honey?'

PRE-SENT... ARMS !!

"Sarge, I <u>can't</u> spit-shine my boots. I ain't been able to spit in four years!"

My KP's? In my kitchen?
"In my army? A tea break?"

"Why can't I just stick him with a needle and sorta kill him with kindness?"

"All right, you guys—no more weekend passes!"

"Bull's-eye? Shit, man—I thought that bullet would never even get there . . ."

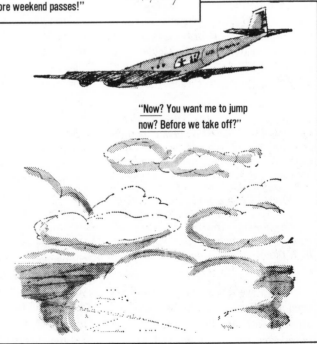

"Now? You want me to jump now? Before we take off?"

MAHATMA, THE JUNKIE

by Paul Jacobs

For a long time before I knew the truth, it seemed to me that only pot or maybe hashish could explain Mahatma Gandhi's behavior. I mean there he was, walking around in a big diaper, sitting on the cold ground, working a spinning wheel, not eating, and never getting laid. He had to be on *some*thing.

For years I went around asking my pacifist friends if they knew whether or not Gandhi was carrying a monkey on his back. The only thing I ever learned was that a lot of Indians don't have a sense of humor and that many American pacifists were really pretty damned violent down underneath those calm exteriors.

In fact, one day a good-looking lady pacifist, whom I was trying very hard to make, shoved me right out of her car in the middle of 57th Street, just as soon as I opened up my mouth about Mohandji maybe being some kind of a junkie.

But now I have been vindicated by a nice, serious book about medicine by a nice, serious British science writer named Ritchie Calder. The book, a paperback, is titled *Medicine and Man*; Calder is on the staff of the *New Statesman*, a UNESCO delegate, and even Chairman of the British Association of Science Writers. And in Calder's discussion of Hindu medicine is the truth about Gandhi:

Even more significant today is the Hindu drug "rauwolfia," from the leaves of a plant of the Himalayan foothills. Age-old in its use, it was a "tranquilizer;" it quieted what we would call "nerves." Whenever Mahatma Gandhi was under the stress of the modern world, rauwolfia would restore his philosophic detachment. Modern medical science, having extracted the active principle, now applies it in hypertension, high blood pressure, and as a treatment for mental cases.

So now we know—why Gandhi was such a good pacifist, why he could walk around without clothes, and why he never even *wanted* to get laid. He was

cool—way, way up on a mountain by himself—and who needs clothes or a chick when you're way up on that mountain?

I can see it now—Gandhi, chewing on a cud of rauwolfia, is standing up in front of the British soldiers, as they march towards him with fixed bayonets. Next to him is Nehru, wearing his white hot-dog salesman's hat. Nehru says to Gandhi, "Hey, Bepu, them soldiers got shivs on the end of their guns—let's split, man!"

Gandhi looks up at the soldiers with a far-off glaze in his eyes. "Who you talking about?" he says to Nehru. "You talking about those guys all the way down the road? Take it easy, man, they're a million miles from here, and they're moving so slow we can be a million miles from them in like one second. What you need is a good chaw of rauwolfia. Didn't you bring a fix with you? Didn't I tell you like maybe a million times never to come out on these *satyagrahas* without your rauwolfia? How do you think I keep my philosophic detachment under the stress of the modern world? With Chiclets?"

So it's obvious that what's needed in the American pacifist movement is a connection, preferably a wholesaler, who can keep everybody supplied with rauwolfia. Then, following the model of the master will be easy. There'll be no need to go limp; they'll *be* limp. There'll be no arguments about whether celibacy is re-

quired of all participants in a peace march; nobody will be able to get it up *anyway*.

Most important, too, there'll be no tensions, no little nagging jealousies about who can sit down quicker, fast longer or get clobbered harder. Everybody will be at peace with each other, and the best part is that there'll be no worry about the cops. With rauwolfia there's no smoke, smell, or needle marks.

In case of a raid, you just swallow the evidence—and restore your philosophic detachment to boot.

A JUNKIE HEX FOR URBAN DWELLERS

by John Francis Putnam

I don't know what I'd do without this Urban Paranoia that keeps my life exciting.

As I leave my New York apartment, triple-locking the door to shut in a selection of modest treasures, "Those junkies," I say to myself. "Haven't they mopped *everyone else I know*? . . . It's surely going to be *my* turn today!"

What'll it be like to come back and find the door hanging on only one hinge—with all those splinters where the junkies broke in? And inside, like the Afrika Korps had taken on Mao Tse-tung's army in a fire fight. Devastation everywhere!

And then the final appraisals: "What will they actually *take*?"

So, to relieve some of this Anticipatory Anguish as well as magically preventing it from happening, I have designed this *Realist* "Hex-a-Fix" to protect the sacredness of property, and to help save on all that excess electricity used up on weekends when the lights are left on and the radio plays loud so that *they* might think somebody's inside your apartment.

Hang this sign wherever your own particular paranoid inclinations dictate—right where it can be *seen*—where it can *terrify*.

And . . . er . . . lots of luck.

A TRADITIONAL METHOD OF PROTECTING YOUR PERSONAL EFFECTS FROM THE DEPREDATIONS OF NEEDY NARCOTICS ADDICTS

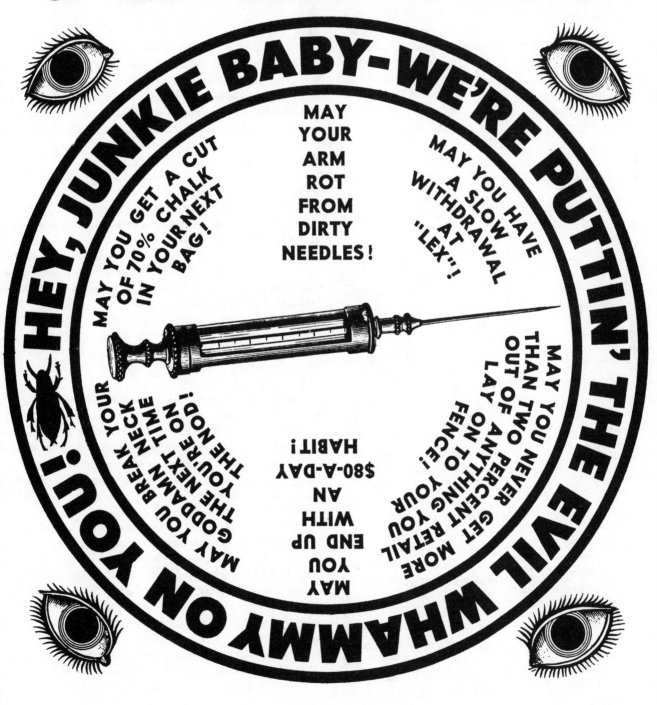

HEY, JUNKIE BABY—WE'RE PUTTIN' THE EVIL WHAMMY ON YOU!

MAY YOU GET A CUT OF 70% CHALK IN YOUR NEXT BAG!

MAY YOUR ARM ROT FROM DIRTY NEEDLES!

MAY YOU HAVE A SLOW WITHDRAWAL AT "LEX"!

MAY YOU NEVER GET MORE THAN TWO PERCENT RETAIL OUT OF ANYTHING YOU LAY ON TO YOUR FENCE!

MAY YOU END UP WITH AN $80-A-DAY HABIT!

MAY YOU BREAK YOUR GODDAMN NECK THE NEXT TIME YOU'RE ON THE ROD!

HOLLY'S COLUMN

When you're four months old, you can really make people turn themselves on. All you have to do is smile. They just stand around trying like mad to make you respond. But what I'm wondering is, at what age—at what point in your life—do people stop trying to make you smile and start trying to bug you?

THEY DID... THEREFORE I AM

Also, when do the roles reverse? When will *I* begin smiling to ingratiate myself to *them?* For instance, my Daddy was in the delivery room when I was born, and he had to be dressed all in white, including a mask over the bottom half of his face. And, never having been in a delivery room before (except when *he* was born), he felt at a disadvantage and tried to ingratiate *him*self to the other people who knew what they were doing there. He kept smiling at them even though they couldn't *see* his smile and had no way of *knowing* he was smiling and even though he didn't really *want* to smile at those particular moments underneath that half-faced white mask.

Did you know that the Cuban government, faced with a drastic milk shortage, has been advertising on radio the advantages of breast-feeding? While lullaby music plays in the background, a woman announcer tells listeners: "There is no substitute for mother's milk."

Well, I'll sure give a testimonial for *my* Mommy's titties, boy.

It's bad enough there are so many bottle-fed American doctors who discourage breast-feeding—at least it's not official A.M.A. policy yet—but *now* what about all those wet-nurses who won't be able to get passports to Cuba because it's contrary to our national interest?

Of course, I'm too young to understand all the pros and cons of shipping wheat to Russia, but I certainly think it's carrying suspicion a little too far to say—as some of our best patriots are saying—that the wheat may end up as ethyl alcohol, propellant fluids, liquid hydrogen, poisonous gases, TNT, or atomic bombs. But I'm not old enough yet for displaced indignation—I mean the South Vietnamese Air Force has been getting *napalm* bombs from the United States and dropping them on civilian targets from planes containing American "instructors"—and when the papers published a picture of a badly burned child, our Defense Department said that "the instructors had no control of the weapons used, and had always urged their pupil pilots to use extreme care when bombing or strafing villages." Now, what I would suggest is that we ship already baked loaves of bread and drop *them* on Russia, so that even if the pilots use *extreme* care, some of the loaves are bound to fall on children.

FUCK COMMUNISM!

The Realist has sold several thousand "Fuck Communism!" posters. As a result of one such sale, the following correspondence ensued between an administrator at San Fernando Valley State College and Dr. Edmund Carpenter, Chairman of the Dept. of Anthropology:

Dear Ted,

If you still have that sign posted in your office, please take it down. It is certainly offensive to some of your colleagues, and you can't expect your new departmental secretary not to be shocked and embarrassed. But what is intolerable to me is that your student advisees should see it. What gives?

Cordially, __ __ __

Dear __ __ __:

Of course I'll take that poster down if it offends you. I'll put up your letter, which is funnier.

"Fuck" is a simple intensive of the order of bloody, fearful, awful. Intensives can be formed in various ways. For example, at the last chairmen's meeting, Dean __ __ __ said we 'should oughta,' thus forming an intensive with a tautology, and Dean __ __ __ said 'it don't,' which is more emphatic than the classroom conjugation. (Anthropologists no longer have to go to distant fields for non-literate informants.)

But you shouldn't oughta panic—it don't pay. "Fuck" may prove to be the first universal word. A former student of mine, now in Uganda, writes that on the back of the school building a volunteer speller chalked, in letters four feet high: FAUK FOOK FUK.

It may also be man's last testament. Between 1950-52, a bored weatherman, stationed north of Hudson Bay, left a monument that neither government nor time can eradicate. Many white men have felt compelled to pile stone on stone to leave some mark in the Arctic wastes, but he was the first to harness technology to this end. Using a bulldozer abandoned by the Air Force, he spent two years and great effort pushing boulders into a single word.

It can be seen from 10,000 feet, silhouetted against the snow. It's the first evidence of human life to be observed when flying south on the Thule route—Canada's greeting to travellers aboard KLM Flight 571. Government officials exchanged memos full of circumlocutions (no Latin equivalent exists) but failed to word an appropriation bill for the destruction of this cairn that wouldn't alert the press and embarrass both Parliament & Party.

It stands today, a monument to human spirit. If life exists on other planets, this may be the first message received from us.

Cordially, *Ted*

Then the police charged the peaceful seated crowds, causing one of the ugliest scenes in South Vietnam's three-month-old Buddhist crisis. With rifle butts, clubs, and tommy-gun clips, the cops battered the demonstrators.

Women who had fallen to the pavement in the first police rush were savagely kicked. A young girl had her head split open with a carbine butt, and as blood streamed into her eyes, she was carted away in a police van.

—Time *Magazine*
July 26, 1963

Now that the "mess" in Vietnam has been neatly wrapped up and put away, it seems ungracious and boring to refer to it again. The sound of the war in Vietnam is once again a vague and distant staccato of small news items about Viet Congs, government helicopters, and Strategic Hamlets. The war is still as brutally inhuman and senseless, and it is still America's war, but it no longer disturbs us.

This is because we are a people passionate about packaging and indifferent to use. We came to object to the Diem regime because his "image" had become tarnished. When the Rev. Quang Duc burned himself, he destroyed the usefulness of Diem as a "fighter for freedom against godless Communism." It was a PR act which could not be topped, and so Diem had to go. Exit Diem and brother Nhu, and we have with us today a trio of crew-cut, popular, non-political generals—and the war.

This all makes a neat package and leaves my original quote, about the Saigon police bashing people's heads in, a bit grisly and in poor taste: like some creep saying that the beautiful lady who used to be the dancing Philip Morris cigarette pack was selling lung cancer. But she was.

And those Saigon police were not trained, equipped, paid, and educated to their civil responsibilities by Ngo Dinh Diem and his brother Nhu; they were created by the U.S. Government acting through a bunch of American university professors.

One of the real rewards of university training is the opportunity it provides for travel. Much of the money for this travel is provided by the U.S. Government through such agencies as the International Cooperation Administration which have a hand in supervising the American foreign-aid programs. The I.C.A. pays the bills, and the University sends a team of professors overseas to add their knowledge to the war on want, or Communism, or those wanting Communism.

It was through an I.C.A. grant of one million dollars per year that Michigan State University hooked into Vietnam when Diem first came to power in 1954. The professors at Michigan had met Diem when, as an émigré with no following at home, he had toured the American college/church-group circuit during 1950-53.

The flashier types like Kenya's Tom Mboya and India's Krishna Menon were being grabbed up by the better-known universities. Michigan State was lucky to get its hands on any-

body, even the stiff, grouchy Diem. The handsome return on this contact is a tribute to the American dream that any piece of scrap can be put to productive use.

When the French sued for peace in Vietnam at the 1954 Geneva conference, the country was temporarily divided in half, pending unification through elections. The U.S., in taking the reins from France, had to find a nationalist-type leader to hold the line for them. Diem was their man, and the "miracle" of South Vietnam (frequently celebrated in feature articles by the Luce complex) was simply that he held the country still long enough for the U.S. to pour in billions of dollars in aid, weapons, advisers, operators—to buy off the natives, and when that didn't work, to frighten them.

Those first few years were frightening. A Communist takeover seemed imminent because of the scheduled elections. It seemed that most of the people didn't know or care about Diem and the Americans and tended to regard "red boss" Ho Chi Minh as the father of their country. While the Free Vietnam Government had no intention of participating in an election it was certain to lose, one could never be sure if the populace and the reds would stand for this. It became imperative to establish a "security apparatus" which could maintain control over the "heavily infiltrated" population.

But official American agencies (C.I.A., M.A.A.G., U.S.O.M.), although there in force, were limited in the openness of their activities by those provisions of the Geneva agreements which ruled out increases in the military power of the two governments of Vietnam. This was made more sticky by the presence of observers of the International Control Commission (India, Canada, Poland) whose reports on violations of the Geneva agreements were picked up by the world's press.

The Michigan State University professors filled the gap. Since they were a non-governmental agency ostensibly interested in education, their actions were not as carefully observed. And this was how professors of M.S.U. came to train, equip, finance, and otherwise create the police apparatus for Diem's police state. This was clearly indicated in the monthly reports of the M.S.U. "team" in Vietnam. One of the earliest entries (August 10, 1955) in that series of reports states:

. . . the [U.S.] Ambassador has specifically asked that we concentrate almost exclusively on the police and field administrative projects until the elections of next July. . . . It is now felt by the M.S.U. team that in order to be in accord with U.S. policy locally it is necessary to engage almost exclusively in immediate impact programs until after the elections in July, 1956 and that the immediate impact programs in our program are the field administration and the police projects.

The police-training activities of the M.S.U. "team" included the creation of a V.B.I. (Vietnamese Bureau of Investigation) modeled after our own F.B.I. (no underdeveloped country should be without one), the training of Diem's own Palace

Academic Sin, continued

Guard to prevent the assassination of this nationalist leader, mass fingerprinting, identification cards and other security checks on the general populace, and the reorganization of the national police force so that it could engage in paramilitary activity of the type noted previously. Perhaps the most useful activity of the professors was the development of a rural-based militia of 40,000 men placed at Diem's disposal. This activity, the clearest violation of the Geneva agreements, was necessarily the most clandestine.

In all this activity the Michigan professors received money and equipment from the U.S. agencies operating in Vietnam and surreptitiously passed them on to the new military forces they had created. The professors, being of a scholarly bent, maintained the monthly report of their activities in Vietnam, and I have culled the following items from that record.

Nov. 8, 1955: During the month of October we received a notice of Washington's approval of the recommended expanded police program submitted Aug. 29th. We started immediately to implement this program. Conferences were held at U.S.O.M. on October 10th and the Embassy on October 23rd and 24th, trying to coordinate Internal Security operations in Vietnam, in which our government has an interest.

April 17, 1956: The training of the commando squads of Saigon-Cholon police in riot-control formations has continued during the month. . . . A report on "riots and unlawful assembly" is nearing completion. It will be translated into Vietnamese and submitted to the Municipal Police, and it will cover anticipating and preventing riots, mob psychology, elements of the mob, quelling riots, and dispersing unlawful assembly. . . .

Oct. 3, 1956: . . . an emergency supply of tear gas has been given to the Saigon-Cholon Police Dept. riot squads as a result of the U.S.O.M.-M.S.U.G. efforts.

Nov. 8, 1956: A standard fingerprint card was designed and approved for use by the Immigration Service. The Government is printing 1,600,000 of them. On Oct. 29th, ten persons started a six-to eight-week fingerprint training course at the identification section at Camp des Mares. These trainees will assist with the program of fingerprinting some 700,000 Chinese in the Republic of Vietnam.[The Diem government conducted a continual campaign of harassment against the Chinese minority in Vietnam, seizing their businesses and imputing ties to the Chinese Communists.] In response to a request from the Dept. of the Interior, M.S.U.G. will train up to 150 additional fingerprint specialists. . . .

May 8, 1957: Training of the Presidential Security Guard in revolver shooting began during the month. Thirty-four V.B.I. agents completed the revolver course.

June 5, 1957: An on-the-job training program has been started by members of the Security Division, V.B.I. headquarters. The program is designed to teach students by actually conducting security investigations, including character evaluation, collation, and exploitation of countersubversive information.

Aug. 8, 1957: A lecture and demonstration in the use of tear gas weapons and masks was conducted at Quang-Trung for the V.B.I., Municipal Police, and Civil Guard. . . . M.S.U.G. delivered a quantity of gas guns, projectiles, grenades, and masks to the Civil Guard.

Sept. 11, 1957: Eight hundred pairs of Peerless handcuffs arrived in Saigon, but distribution is being delayed pending arrival of four hundred additional cuffs.

Dec. 10, 1957: Meetings were held with various precinct commanders of the Saigon Police Department at which the use of the shotgun was demonstrated.

Feb. 17, 1958: The training of 125 military and Civil Guard fingerprint technicians at the V.B.I. proceeds satisfactorily. The Palace Guard is being put through another class in revolver training, with 58 men receiving instruction. Forty members of the V.B.I. completed firearm training.

Nor did the Michigan State Group content itself with work in the exotic city of Saigon. These professors brought the word to the countryside. From the report for December 1957:

Field trips were made . . . where explanations and demonstrations were given in the use and care of gas, riot shotguns, handcuffs, and 33-caliber revolvers. Courtesy calls were also made on the V.B.I. officials in the cities.

Above all, the academicians dispatched themselves in an unemotional and scientific manner which befits their profession. In describing the work of the V.B.I. they pointed out (August 1955) that in addition to performing all of the tasks we associate with the F.B.I.,"It will also be responsible for the many other enforcement duties that are particular to this part of the world, such as information and postal control, etc."

Some Americans would tend to be squeamish about teaching those "other enforcement duties" but such cultural provincialism has no place in the social sciences.

This then, is the record of activities of a multi-university which shuns the petty moralizing and social criticism of cranks like the late C. Wright Mills, and whose professors are out there in the real world with what Arthur Schlesinger, Jr. calls "the movers and the shakers." This is a new day for the university, and it requires new men who can get out in the field. As the monthly report on Feb. 17, 1958 stated:

During his stay with M.S.U.G., Dr. Glen Taggart, Dean of International Programs at M.S.U., was briefed on Police Division activities by the Division Chief and Section Heads and inspected Municipal Police, V.B.I., and Civil Guard headquarters.

And was there some eager beaver Assistant Professor running around yelling, "Hey, Joe, get ahold of some bonzes and we'll put the boys through their paces for the Dean"?

SIC TRANSIT AD NAUSEAM

"Regular?"

It has become such a common selling technique to tie in the sponsor's message with the regular program content that it sounded like a deliberate transition to the Horn & Hardart food commercial last month when a CBS newscaster began his report, "This morning a nun burned herself to death in the streets of South Vietnam; we'll be back with that story in a moment"—followed immediately by: "Are you planning an outdoor barbecue?"

A couple of years ago, *The Realist* began offering for sale a patriotic poster, red-white-and-blue, starred-and-striped, hammered-and-sickled. Its message: "Fuck Communism!" This official-looking epithet was intended to serve as a satirical crystallization of our national obsession as embodied in our international relations. On the basis of sales of the poster, we were able to send—with poetic irony—Robert Scheer, a reporter, to Vietnam and Cambodia.

I was thinking about all this as Scheer spoke at a rally on the Berkeley campus. He was comparing U.S. intervention in Vietnam with Russian intervention in Hungary. Only in America can one critically liken Lyndon Johnson to Josef Stalin and be accused of spouting Communist propaganda.

A reporter asked me what I was doing there. I explained that I was a graduate student majoring in Outside Agitation. Actually, the Vietnam Day Committee—a logical outgrowth of the Free Speech Movement *(Don't trust anybody over 30)*—had invited me to emcee. "I'm over 30," I confided to the audience, "but I'm passing."

They have since changed the slogan. It now goes: *Don't trust anybody.*

Mike Myerson spoke in a recently-acquired Vietnamese worker's uniform. He is under investigation by the State Dept. for possible violation of U.S. departure control laws, for having gone to Hanoi.

He is international secretary of the W.E.B. DuBois Clubs, a socialist youth movement. J. Edgar Hoover has charged that the DuBois Clubs of America were "spawned by the Communist Party." Officers of the organization label the charge "false."

The 25-year-old Myerson is quite tall and refers to himself as "the Jolly Red Giant." He has been informed by the FBI—which has infiltrated the Minutemen, an underground right-wing organization—that he is second on the list of the ten individuals the Minutemen would most like to kill. The FBI wouldn't tell him who is first.

I thought it might be appropriate to give him one of those Avis Rent-a-Car lapel buttons that say they're only number two but they try harder.

Anyway, the speeches and entertainment continued until that evening, when 15,000 impatient marchers were chafing at the bit pulled by Ken Kesey and his band of Merry Pranksters.

There had been a rumor that they were going to invite the Hell's Angels—various gangs of anti-social motorcyclists—to a big bash at their community in Honda. When a group of Hell's Angels showed up, to their surprise they were befriended. And they began hanging around.

It came to pass that the Vietnam Day Committee invited novelist Kesey to speak at their rally. He accepted, dancing tongue in cheek. Neo-togetherness: The Hell's Angels and Merry Pranksters painted a bus and made toy ack-ack guns to use

on enemy planes (anything that flew), and a kind of put-on/put-down participation began taking shape.

Kesey was the next-to-last speaker. There is something about an outdoor public address system that can make you sound like a rabble-rouser if you're not careful, and Kesey commented on the *sound* rather than the words of those who preceded him.

He played a few bars on his harmonica between his own words, which consisted essentially of warning that we should love our neighbors, that the protest march wasn't going to *change* anything, that wars have been fought for 10,000 years. Still, you can't just *ignore* insanity.

It took *The London Observer* (July 18, 1965) to tell it like it is: "There is the uncouthness, along with the dazzling ability, revealed in the minor personal traits. He picks his nose. He is liable, when slumped down in a chair, to reach casually and unashamedly into his groin to ease his pants. His phrasing is of a kind not usually associated with the Presidency of the United States.

"To a reporter who began an interview with a trivial question, he said, 'Why do you come and ask me, the leader of the Western world, a chickenshit question like that?' When the handsome and dignified Italian Secretary of NATO, Signor Manlio Brosio, came on a visit to Strategic Air Command, in Nebraska, the President invited the accompanying reporters in the plane to come and talk with Mr. Brosio. As they settled down to question the distinguished guest, the President stood up. 'I'm going to have a piss,' he explained."

Now there is nothing intrinsically evil about scratching your balls during a press conference—a few months ago one reporter's lead paragraph began, "The President handled himself beautifully this morning . . . "—the frightening thing is the *megalomania* of his crudeness. In a private interview, he avoided talking about Vietnam, so at the end the reporter asked him about the war. Replied LBJ: "What the Commies are saying is 'Fuck you, Lyndon Johnson.' And no one's going to say 'Fuck you, Lyndon Johnson' and get away with it."

May we have another chorus of *Hail to the Chief*, please?

And so we marched that Friday night from Berkeley to Oakland, where the police and the national guard were out in force, waiting on the border, pointing prohibitively at us like an arrow-shaped Berlin Wall.

And so we turned around and marched back to Civic Center park in Berkeley, where someone threw tear gas at us from a roof and Country Joe McDonald's jug band was literally petrified and Scheer had to slap their faces while telling everybody to lie down on the grass because tear gas rises.

After this unscheduled intermission, the outdoor teach-in continued.

On Saturday afternoon, we marched again, this time about 5,000 strong. Along the sidelines, a refugee held up a poster which said—in English, French, and German—*You Are Now*

Leaving the Democratic Sector of Berkeley. A little girl had a sign that said *Welcome to Occupied Oakland.* The police and the national guard had once again formed their mass welcoming committee. Instead of the traditional *We Shall Overcome,* we sang *Help!*

Enter the Hell's Angels.

At a previous civil rights demonstration, Oakland police were overheard encouraging them to, let's say, fool around. And, when Jack Weinberg (the arrestee inside the police car that thousands of Berkeley students had surrounded back when it all officially began) was in jail he became friendly with a Hell's Angel, who came back to visit him and disclosed that the Oakland police had offered to drop certain charges against them if they would, let's say, mess up.

They wouldn't cooperate. But, just as in the left wing, there is factionalism in the Hell's Angels. And now here they were, their cockiness having been legitimatized by Ken Kesey and his magic harmonica, although it was hard to tell exactly what side they were on, because for the Hell's Angels to ally themselves with the police would have been blatantly out of character.

The thing is, there were *two sets* of police.

At first, when the Hell's Angels were strutting toward the wedge of Oakland police, I thought, "Oh, shit, they're gonna spoil our march." But the Berkeley police were *escorting* them toward the Oakland police. At that moment the Berkeley police became their enemy.

Suddenly the Hell's Angels turned around—it looked as if the Oakland police had parted like the Red Sea to let them back into Berkeley territory—a fracas developed and a Berkeley policeman got his leg broken by one of the very Hell's Angels who had helped paint the Merry Pranksters' bus.

Since the Berkeley police were protecting the marchers, *we* automatically became the enemy of the Hell's Angels. They ripped away the banner of the marchers at the front of the line and pulled out the wires of our sound truck before the Berkeley cops subdued them.

Meantime our leaders had started a chant—*Keep cool! Keep cool!*—and the marchers all sat down in the street. The speeches had to be given through a bullhorn.

"This is not a beatnik invasion of Oakland," I said, and the police smiled for the first time. "There was a time when beatniks were criticized for not having social concern. Now they're being criticized for *having* social concern. . . . "

This month the director of the National Council of Men's Fashions issued a press release, stating that "Sloppiness in dress is a part of the subversive breakdown of this country. In every instance, it is the left and way-out groups which first adopt such clothing trends."

But as the protest escalates, the demonstrations become more middle-class. The wife of one man who went on the recent March on Washington said to him upon his departure: "If you get arrested, for Christ's sake put the bail on Diner's Club."

At the same time, red-baiting becomes diffused. What with increasing publicity being given to pacifist groups, hecklers are now shouting, "Hey, are you a Quaker?" and "Why don't you go back to the Quakers!"

You can remind them that Richard Nixon is a Quaker, but it doesn't seem to make any difference. If John F. Kennedy could remain politically uninfluenced by the dogmatism of his Catholic background, so could Nixon remain unmoved by the implications of Quaker doctrine. I mean, you have yet to hear him identify with a single draft card burner.

Station WLLH in Lowell, Mass. has announced that it will not broadcast news of draft card burnings and other illegal protests against U.S. policy. So far I've burned photostats of my draft card in 4 states and Canada; what I would really like to see is a conservative who is *for* the war in Vietnam, but against government-bureaucracy, burn *his* draft card. When I talked about this on Dan Sorkin's early morning radio show in San Francisco, the station manager ordered that the interview be terminated. Sorkin refused to comply because this would have been a violation of his contract, which includes the first ten amendments to the Constitution.

The real meaning of the Hell's Angels is that they are merely the violent end of a spectrum which would burn, not draft cards, but the Bill of Rights.

"The Hell's Angels only did what everybody wanted to do," said the director of Republicans for Conservative Action. "At least they weren't draft dodgers even if they have had notoriety in the past."

His group formed an organization called *Friends of the Hell's Angels.*

"It's simple. We use Vietcong tactics. Sneak into some little jerkwater Midwest town. Strike a blow against the Establishment. Then simply fade among the population."

This, though the Angels had once been called Communist-inspired. They themselves had once inspired a film, *The Wild Ones*—the climax of which was when Marlon Brando smiled at a waitress—and, had Brando been on our march, then try to comprehend the *further* splitting of their loyalties.

The Hell's Angels have always been apolitical. In Richmond, Calif., the Colony Furniture Co. refused to recognize a carpenters' union, and when the union called a strike, the company brought in members of both the Hell's Angels and Hitler's American Sons as scabs. But when the latter group tried to indoctrinate the former with Fascist philosophy, the Hell's Angels listened carefully and then beat the Nazis up.

They learn fast.

So it was fascinating to watch the metamorphosis of their image into new American patriots . . . and even more fascinating to watch the Hell's Angels act as if they believed it.

They announced they would "move into all future anti-war demonstrations in this area." They debated with Allen Ginsberg at San Jose State College. They decided not to interfere with the next march, issuing this statement: "Our patriotic concern for what these people are doing to our great nation may provoke us to violent acts." They wired President Johnson an offer to serve as "a crack group of trained gorillas *[sic]* " in Vietnam.

Meanwhile, the first couple of thousand copies of Robert Taber's book on "the theory and practice of guerrilla warfare," *The War of the Flea*, were bought up by the United States Army, Navy, and Air Force.

There is, however, one guerrilla tactic not mentioned in the book: Saigon has been importing whores from Korea because the Vietnamese prostitutes have developed a nasty habit of stabbing G.I.'s with whom they are in bed.

Finally, there is the UPI-datelined report about "a small band of U.S. airmen who call themselves the Ranch Hands. . . . Secret experiments in defoliation, or killing jungle foliage, were conducted in South Vietnam as early as 1961 [leading to] the decision in 1962 to begin defoliating strips several hundred feet wide along either or both sides of the principal roads and waterways of the sprawling Mekong Delta. . . .

"While the spray planes deprived the Viet Cong of brush and mangrove concealment, they also deprived numerous villagers of their coconut and rice crops. Still today, an occasional rubber or jack fruit plantation withers and dies alongside a Communist-infested jungle. (The Ranch Hands' unofficial theme song is *High Hopes*, with particular stress on the line 'Oops, there goes another rubber tree plant.')"

The article concludes:

"Despite the known dangers of being a Ranch Hand, Maj. Hay-Chapman boasts that all of his men are 'two time volunteers—first for Vietnam and second for the Ranch Hands.' Why do they volunteer? The answer is an unprintable, anti-Communist, two-word slogan displayed prominently on the Ranch House wall."

From the N.Y. Times of December 7 (sic), 1963:

"Saigon, South Vietnam—On clear days patrons lunching in the ninth-floor restaurant of the Caravelle Hotel can watch government planes dropping napalm on guerrillas across the Saigon river."

"I had thought that, being in the Mafia, he'd at least have different hours or something. . ."

THE WORLD'S FAIR POVERTY PAVILION

*by John Francis Putnam
and Mort Gerberg*

About five years ago, the *Ladies' Home Journal* ran a picture article in their "How America Lives" series on what a searing and dreadful thing it was to have to live in New York's Westchester County on $10,000 a year.

The story told of tight-lipped young marrieds trying to put up a proper front under impossible circumstances. It was the first recognition in print that poverty does exist in these United States. Which goes to show that you can be sitting right next to poor people on a commuter train and not even know it. The poor, inconsiderately, are always with us. Don't let that 1949 Cadillac parked in front of the Negro sharecropper's cabin fool you for one instant.

Moreover, poverty now has official recognition—from the Administration, from TV comedians, and from the pages of *Life* and *Look*—especially these latter "opinion molders," where the picture-article-spreads, usually aglow with "Leisure Living," now present a "Rural Resettlement Agency"—Depression scabrosity with indigent children peering out at the comfortable reader with haunting questions.

These are American kids, of course, so they are not quite as peaked and rickety as African or Asian kids, but they're still reproachful enough to nudge the suburban conscience to admit that the U.S. coin is not burnished bright on both sides.

Poverty, man, is *in* this year!

It is reasonable to assume that the New York World's Fair reflects the real America (Billy Graham Pavilion: "Come inside and pray with us . . . we have the only *safe* restrooms at the Fair"). Therefore, a Poverty Pavilion is a must, if only to present this latest fashionable aspect of our way of life.

Since the purpose of the Fair is to entertain as it instructs and informs—the more amusing an unpalatable fact is made to seem, the more easily it is absorbed—our Poverty Pavilion will of

necessity have an overt carnival-midway atmosphere.

The theme of the exhibit will be *"Poverty: Urban and Rural, 1964 or This-is-what-will-happen-to-you-lousy-kids-unless-you-buckle-down-and-face-the-facts-the-way-I-had-to-when-I-was-your-age!"* Here, then, are some excerpts from the *Official Guide Book to the World's Fair Poverty Pavilion.*

HIT THE BEGGAR

Riot of fun ride where derelicts are loosed in simulated traffic. As they attempt to wipe your windshield, you attempt to run them down.

THE SWEATSHOP

Nearsighted Puerto Rican girls of six ply their trade by dim kerosene lamps, doing microscopic *petit point* embroidery. Beatings by foreman at 10 A.M., 2 P.M. and 4 P.M. promptly.

DUST BOWL RIDE

The Pavilion will provide free face masks. See Okies with hopeless expressions attempt to farm in six feet of fine silicon dust.

THE 24TH PRECINCT

Basement obstacle race and police brutality demonstration; free Band-Aids.

SCAVENGER HUNT

Forage through garbage cans, searching for something to eat, drink, or smoke, just like poor people do! More fun than Cracker Jacks and twice as many surprises . . . such as maggot-ridden hambones or sweat-stiffened sweatsocks.

HOBO JUNGLE LUNCHEONETTE

Informal dining in a genuine boxcar setting. Mulligan Stew served in contaminated tin cans. Gourmet handouts. Family dinners from 6ᶜ up.

SOUVENIR SHOPPE

An authentic Company Store setting. Features genuine cockroaches in laminated clear plastic key chains, miniature bags of government-surplus flour with real weevils, plus such items as the bedbug breeder which allows one to plant bedbug eggs in the victim's bed, with riotous results.

BARNEY'S SHABBYTOWN

Barney's goodwill outlet to clothe the needy at reasonable prices. Features government-surplus military overcoats with World War I brass buttons, all sizes too big for any customer.

HIGH SCHOOL DROPOUTSVILLE

Administer a literacy test. You'll chortle at the way 20-year-old youths stutter and stammer their way through "See Ned run" first readers. Chuckle at their pathetic attempts to write (not print) their names. Receive the thrill of a lifetime as you grade them "Illiterate."

GRAFFITI EXHIBIT

Original drawings and text by ghetto youngsters. Only adults admitted.

RESETTLEMENT ROULETTE BOOTH

Visitors may press a button and evict an impoverished family somewhere in the U.S. Identity of the evictees will be protected, but patrons will receive, within two weeks, a photograph of their heap of pathetic belongings piled on the street.

SLEEP UNDER A BRIDGE

Only 25ᶜ a night. Vermin-ridden blankets, 5ᶜ extra. Prices at this exhibit in no way reflect actual costs, which have been underwritten by various philanthropic organizations; they are set arbitrarily in order to give the layman an accurate conception of the poor man's idea of money.

SLUMLORD SYMPOSIUM

Public may attend daily conferences of slum landlords flown in from Palm Beach and Las Vegas for discussions on how to fit one hundred Spanish-speaking people into small two-room apartments.

DAILY BREAD RIOT

Horses are available so that visitors may join the mounted police in breaking it up.

SECAUCUS PIG SCRAMBLE

Admission 50ᶜ. Watch starving Pennsylvania miners' children compete for luxury restaurant garbage with burly Secaucus (N.J.) pigs. Pari-mutuel opens half-hour before sty time.

RAT-O-RAIL

Exciting tour through a West Side tenement. See the pot gardens on the fire escape. Watch the man urinating out the window. Listen while profanities are yelled up the air shaft. Observe the junkies in action. You are there as the Welfare caseworker is locked inside the hall toilet.

THE WINO ZOO

Admission free. See authentic alcoholics disporting themselves in a realistic Bowery *cum* Skid Row setting. Visitors may purchase cans of Sterno and toss them through the bars. Children love watching the funny antics of the inhabitants.

REPLICA OF 125TH STREET

See the special backed-up-toilet fountain. Visit the Malnutrition Center. Sample the proud product of a Sneaky Pete Distillery.

MINIATURE DEBTORS PRISON

The new State of Mississippi Debtors Prison is a model for Poverty Control, soon to be adopted by other Southern states.

Note: Visitors are reminded that there is a free Decontamination Station at every exit from the Poverty Pavilion. Nevertheless, the Bible says: "Ye have the poor always with you"—and we are honored to be carrying out the Word of God.

MEXICAN WETBACK DANCE

Our greasy little friends from South of the Border demonstrate how they slip past alert Texas Rangers and Border Patrol men.

UNPLANNED PARENTHOOD

Sponsored by the Catholic Archdiocese of Brooklyn. Information on how large families on relief can get to be even larger.

APPALACHIA FUNLAND

Roar at the tobacco-chewing antics of a 5-year-old boy. Gawk at the pregnant 10-year-old girl. See the funny legs of the kids with rickets. Kick a hole in the wall of the splintering shacks. Open all day.

ANATOMY OF A RUMOR

by Oliver Pilat

On Sunday, Oct. 18, 1964, a father took his 18-year-old daughter and 9-year-old son to the World's Fair. It was the closing day of the first season. In mid-afternoon, the younger child had to go to the toilet. His father and sister waited outside. As time passed, the father became restless. "What's keeping the boy?" he muttered. Two Negroes, youths in their late teens or early 20s, hurried out. Something furtive about their demeanor alarmed the father. He rushed into the toilet—to find his son dying on the floor. The boy had been castrated.

The story was untrue, despite the fact that it was always whispered on what seemed to be excellent authority. It was, in fact, propaganda, skillfully devised and artfully disseminated. After absorption of the first shock, the mind of the auditor almost invariably returned to the disappearing Negroes. Anybody with a real or latent prejudice was likely to respond to some degree.

Even to an unprejudiced mind, the story seemed to have internal evidence of truth. The Fair employed its own police; Robert Moses was an arbitrary sort of man. With another season to start in April 1965, and with the Fair's finances in notoriously shaky condition, wasn't it reasonable that Moses or some subordinate might try to hush up such a frightening event?

How do you scotch a rumor like that? Philosophically, how do you prove a negative? How do you prove that those two Negroes—the focal point of the story—did not vanish just before the discovery of an impossible-to-prove atrocity? The answer is, you don't, you can't.

I've been a reporter for a long while. People phone me on all sorts of things in addition to politics, which has been my general beat in recent years. On the Tuesday after the Fair closed for the season, George H. P. Dwight, a former leader of the Democratic reform movement in the city, called. He had heard the story from his cleaning woman, who apparently lived next door to the father whose boy was killed. Not a word about the incident had appeared anywhere so far as he could discover. As a father of young children, Dwight wondered whether a horrible thing like that could possibly be suppressed.

A similar query came from John D. Tierney, a former newspaperman who did not put much stock in rumors. He questioned whether murder could or would be concealed, but he was disturbed momentarily by the apparent authenticity of his source, a woman who seemed to have it from one of the Pinkerton men at the Fair.

Other newspapers and radio stations were similarly besieged. William J. Donoghue, publicity chief at the Fair, howled in exasperation as inquiries doubled and redoubled. There had been a similar rumor in August, he recalled, which also had no basis in fact. Joseph D'Azevedo, a former high-ranking New

York City police official in charge of the 1,000-member private police force at the Fair, had already asked William Kimmins, his chief of detectives, to investigate the rumor. If those who reported the story would do a little preliminary checking of their own, he suggested, they might help Kimmins and D'Azevedo and render a genuine public service.

Tierney reported: "The woman who told me about it got it from her sister who is a cashier in a bank. The sister heard it at the bank from some customer who said it came originally from Pinkerton men at the Fair. She does not remember which customer. I never did take the story seriously."

Dwight's interest was also lessening. He had found that his cleaning woman got the story from a neighbor, but the neighbor did not live next door to her and was not the father of the slain boy. The neighbor was now uncertain where he first heard the story. Furthermore, Dwight had lunched with Seymour N. Siegel, director of radio station WNYC, which had also been plagued by the rumor. Siegel had just returned from Washington, where he had run into an almost identical story, except that it was set in a gasoline station toilet and the boy involved was only six. There also, two young Negroes had emerged just before the discovery of the crime. Both Siegel and Dwight concluded that the long arm of coincidence was stretching too far, that propaganda of some kind—perhaps political propaganda—was involved.

During the first few days after the Fair closed, Donoghue received 50 inquiries. The rumor reached new listeners from day to day, reaching peak circulation a week or 10 days later, just before election. In all, it must have inflamed to some degree the minds of at least 100,000 New Yorkers.

Nov. 18, two weeks after election, the New York *Daily News* put the caption "Long-Lasting Rumor" over the lead letter to the editor: "During the last week of the World's Fair, a nine-year-old boy was brutally attacked and mutilated in the men's room and, as a result, died the next day. How come your paper never wrote this up? I am anxious to see you print this, or are you afraid to?"

The Editor arose from his Chair to answer: "*The News* has investigated this strangely persistent rumor several times, and has found no factual basis whatsoever for it. There are no police or any other records of such a happening. The supposed attack occurred during the last week of the World's Fair; other readers have set the date in August. Since it is practically impossible that such an affair could have been kept secret, our verdict on this weird report is: It's a complete phony."

Not elegant but clear.

Meanwhile, a good proportion of the 25 men under the World's Fair chief of detectives had been filing reports on the incident. The trail had led them to banks, bus depots, bars, and restaurants, to the Bronx more often than any other borough,

131

and to Nassau and Suffolk counties out on Long Island.

Efforts to trace the boy or his parents were not successful. One Bronx gossip had given the story a touch of verisimilitude by naming the church which held services for the boy. The priest at the church said no child of that age had been buried from there recently. Efforts to find the boy's death certificate in the Bronx, Queens or elsewhere were fruitless. However, the Fair's detectives located a woman who offered what she considered a plausible explanation for the lack of confirmation of the story. The mutilated boy did not die after all, according to her version. "Sure, and I heard it was sewed on and working all right again."

The boy's mother, according to one tipster, lived in a trailer camp near Islip, L.I. The young son of a woman in this camp *had* died recently, but *not* as a result of a visit to the World's Fair or under the described circumstances.

A Bronx woman, it was established, told friends that the boy's father had come into her husband's bank and collapsed from grief after telling the story. The husband confirmed that he had heard the story from a customer at the bank, but he did not remember anybody collapsing. The customer was not the boy's father. When reached by a detective, he proved to be a bus driver who originally "heard the story in a locker room somewhere."

Several sources identified a talkative waitress as a carrier of the deadly story. As authority, she cited her mother—a nurse who was taking care of the father of a bus driver. The bus driver in question had heard the story at the 54th St. and 9th Ave. depot in Manhattan. Every one of the drivers there had heard the story. So had their wives, who gossiped about it interminably. "Of course, it's true," said one of them. "Everybody knows about it. Even the dogs in the street are barking about it."

This woman, upon reflection, decided she had heard the story, not from her bus driver husband, but from a strange woman with whom she exchanged the time of day in a nearby park.

So it went. A former beer salesman was located who had gone from one gin-mill to another regaling acquaintances and strangers with the story. It was "just talk," he told a Fair detective uneasily. He didn't know if it was true and did not remember where he first heard it.

Mind you, the detectives were not authorized to make a case against anybody for spreading a malicious or dangerous libel. They were trying merely to confirm a story, if true, or to report it could not be confirmed and therefore, inferentially at least, was false. They had no power of subpoena and could not make anybody answer questions under oath.

My own mind was made up. From the moment I heard of an almost identical story in Washington, I concluded that the public had to deal not with an ordinary epidemic, but with germ warfare, quite probably connected with the national election.

Late in October, I had dinner with Leonard McCullough, business manager of the Toledo (Ohio) *Monitor*, a business

"I've got to go out now, honey, and fire a few rounds. My wife always sniffs the barrel when I tell her I've been to Minute Men practice."

weekly. To my surprise, McCullough had heard what he called the "sick, sick story." He had made a survey of it as it appeared in Lima, Cleveland, and Toledo. Except for the varying age of the boy, and that in one city the assault took place in a museum and in another in a department store toilet, the story was everywhere the same.

In due time, I heard that rumor of the white-boy-mutilated-by-disappearing-Negroes had tormented San Francisco, Chicago, and St. Louis. In Detroit, an unsung newspaperman traced it to an itinerant preacher who said he was associated with the National States Rights Party, a rightist fringe group given to physical and verbal violence. Yet it did not seem likely that the national campaign behind the rumor could be carried out alone by such a relatively uninfluential outfit. The real culprit must still be hidden.

Purpose of the propaganda seemed transparently clear: to stimulate the so-called white backlash in the cities and thereby elect Barry Goldwater president. Could this explain the hoarding of campaign funds by the Republican National Committee and the stubborn confidence of some Goldwaterites right up to the last day before election? Was this their secret weapon?

My first thought was that the story should be disinfected by a federal grand jury, a Congressional committee on election practices, or the F.B.I. itself. To accomplish that, a preliminary account would have to be published somewhere.

The New York press had already demonstrated its disinterest. Magazines like *Harper's* and *The Reporter* were wary of the subject. The election was over. Anti-Negro anecdotes flourished in every national election. Why bother with this particular one?

By now I'm reconciled to the fact that this particular atrocity rumor will not be nationally investigated. However, isn't it possible, perhaps in *The Realist*, to get the facts on record before the propaganda sinks unnoticed into national folklore?

THE GRIN REAPER

by Carol Glaser

For belly laughs these days, the obit page still carries the liveliest, if unintentional, humor. Unhappily, some obituaries are simply too hilarious to be considered fit to print; some people *do* die in the saddle.

Two stock fatality stories illustrate the commonplace but fun-reading deaths seldom printed in the major dailies:

The first is a report of the motorist, returning from a late-night church social, who misses the bridge abutment by inches when his right-front, two-ply, guaranteed-against-all-defects tire blows at 65 m.p.h. As he is changing the flat, a 60 m.p.h. tractor-trailer whacks him in the ass, splattering him for several hundred feet along the pike. Three unused flares, a flashlight, and a bundle of church raffle tickets are found in the glove compartment of the car, parked, with its lights out, smack on the side of the road.

The second is an event that for some reason usually occurs most frequently in Queens, although Brooklyn still lays claim to being the Borough of Churches. A little old lady, black purse and Abraham & Straus shopping bag in hand, is dispatched en route to or returning from an early-morning, weekday mass, thanks to the slow reaction of a driver who hasn't been to shul since he was bar mitzvahed. If the driver stops to see how badly his car is damaged and to tell the police it wasn't his fault, the event will probably be dismissed as too trifling, even by the *Journal-American*.

The story's chances are improved, naturally, if the car speeds off. Should the vehicle, with a Negro or a Puerto Rican at the wheel, tear down the street with the fatally injured white churchgoer impaled in the undercarriage and screaming blasphemies as she bumps along, even the *Times* will print it, possibly a day or two late, if it can find 38 citizens who stood by apathetically, not bothering to memorize the license number.

Pedestrian though such deaths may be, a column of well-chosen mortuary

items would indeed be less deadly reading than 85% (excluding classified and financial tables) of the *Times* and 75% of the other New York papers. The column should chronicle only tragedies that are inherently humorous and run under a head like "You'll Die Laughing," or "Today's Obit Chuckles," or "The Light Side of the Styx." Here is a sample column; all the stories are taken from real-death happenings, and only the names and locations have been changed to protect the living:

JERSEY CITY—Roger Smith, 37-year-old father of five, was electrocuted this morning when he plunged his hand into a toilet bowl to retrieve the electric razor he had dropped. According to his wife, who had knocked the razor from his hand when she bumped into him, she screamed "Pull the plug" as he shouted, "Aw, shut up—"and reached right in.

ECUADOR—Brig. Gen. José Martin, commander of the National Guard of the state, was fatally injured today when he strolled into a spinning propeller. As a colonel commanding an infantry regiment in Korea, Gen. Martin had made headlines because of the extraordinarily high numbers of casualties his men had suffered.

SAN JOSE—Mrs. Louise Peters stood in the bleachers and cheered wildly this afternoon when her 11-year-old son John hit a home run in a Little League game. As she was shouting, she began to choke on her chewing gum. Hospital attendants pronounced her dead on arrival.

LONG ISLAND CITY —Apparently overcome by fumes rising from a vat of sulphuric acid, Fred Meyers, a 28-year-old metal worker at a Queens plating company, collapsed without a word and left not a trace when he fell from the ladder inside the tank this morning. Work in that section of the plant was disrupted until police completed their reports. Normal operations resumed after lunch.

OCEAN CITY—Bill Walters, an ex-

pert angler, was killed by a two-pound bass this afternoon while his 13-year-old-son struggled futilely to save his father's life. Mr. Walters, a 40-year-old auto mechanic, who often said he'd "rather fish than eat" was passing a leisurely Sunday fishing with his only child, Bill Jr., at Lake Swanee.

According to the boy, he got a bite and jerked his rod. The fish flew out of the water and headfirst into the open mouth of his startled father. Mr. Walters grasped the wildly flapping, slimy bass lodged in his throat, but could not pull it out. The son, a husky 140 pounds, struggled to yank it free but failed. The quiet shattered by the thrashing about and the boy's shouts, other fishermen sped to the scene and towed the boat ashore.

Mr. Walters was pronounced dead of suffocation by Dr. Arthur Victor, who surgically removed the bass, which was still alive. The doctor said it was impossible to pull the fish from the mouth of Mr. Walters because the fins were imbedded in the throat.

Just before the son got in the ambulance beside his father's body, a policeman asked young Bill if he wanted the man-killing fish. "No thanks," said Bill.

"Well, there's no use wasting him," the officer replied, throwing the bass in the back of the police car.

AN IMPOLITE INTERVIEW WITH TERRY SOUTHERN

Q. Recently I went to a meeting of the John Birch Society, and during the coffee break, people broke up into little clusters. One cluster was discussing the Communist conspiracy behind the fluoridation of water. I asked what the Communists' motivation would be. The guy who was, in effect, leading the discussion, said it's to slow down our reflexes. I asked if he had seen Dr. Strangelove, *because that's pretty much what General Ripper says in the film. And this guy at the John Birch Society said, with a straight face: "Yeah, well, I don't know who wrote that movie, but I think he's one of us." Now, what are your feelings about a reaction like that?*

A. I have the feeling you made that up.

Q. No, it really happened.

A. In any case, I don't think their opinions are relevant. I suspect that you see dynamic forces where, in my opinion, there are none. I see no dynamic forces in our society. The strongest force is psychiatry, and that has undone the others. I heard, incidentally, and on fairly good authority, that the Birchers were all syphed up—they're all elderly, you know, that's when the syph hits the brain. So it's like a club. Under the guise of political action, it's a brain-syph club.

Q. Yes, I've seen that in the A.M.A. Journal.

A. It is true that people fail to recognize themselves in the film. . . *military* people come out thinking, "Yes, we've got a son-of-a-bitch like that in *our* outfit."

Q. What originally led to the writing of The Magic Christian?

A. The notion, "Wouldn't it be funny if . . . "

Q. Can you think of any actual occurrences that you've been involved in that would seem to be related to the modus operandi of The Magic Christian?

A. Various kinds of lies, I suppose . . . for no particular reason, except perhaps to cheer someone up. . . Now wait, here's something. We were living in Geneva once, on the 3rd floor—in one of those very modern apartments, and they had a garbage-disposal chute, and at the bottom was this fantastic Swiss mechanism . . . thousands of diamond-edged blades, I always imagined it . . . moving at the speed of light. Anyway, you could put your head in this chute and hear it down there—a soft whirring sound, and it would take *anything*, man—bottles, tin cans, knives, forks, spoons. I was always testing it. Nothing fazed it. Once I took a *coffee-pot*, put a lot of forks and spoons in it, put the pot in a paper bag so it wouldn't make too much racket when it hit, and dropped it in—you know, like "What do you make of *this*, Mister Swiss Machine!" Then I listened. Nothing, man. Just a slight smooth *crunch* and back to old soft whir.

So! Well, as it happened, I had just bought a new *typewriter*, and I still had the old one—Royal Portable, pre-war, sturdy stuff. So I rushed right out, bought 50 feet of clothesline, came back, tied one end to the carriage of the typewriter, and lowered it down very gently, taking care, dig, not to bump the walls on the way. That was supposed to be so the concierge or somebody wouldn't hear it, you know, something strange going down the chute—but I think it was also the idea of *surprising* the machine at the last minute . . . I must have been about half off my nut.

Anyway, when I figured it was just about right, I said, "Okay, you smug son-of-a-bitch! Dig *this!*" And let the clothesline out very quickly. Well, *man!* I mean, I just wish I'd had a tape-recorder. Christ, what sounds! Fantastic! And then it stopped—and of course I immediately felt very bad. It was like I had killed it. "What a silly, kid thing to do. And bla, bla, bla." Big remorse, and then, of course, great apprehension—like: An American typewriter! They'll trace it to *you!* Damages! Fantastic damages—five thousand dollars! Can't pay! Prison!

But it all had a happy ending. The machine was running again the next day, and there was a little note in the lobby that read something like, "Residents are requested not to *overload* the disposal-unit."

Overload! And they say the Swiss don't have a sense of humor. Anyway, it was the *smugness* of the machine, Paul . . . I mean you *can* understand how a thing like that could, well, could be disturbing?

Q. There, there, Terry—yes, of course.

A. Do you think I did the right thing?

Q. You had no choice. . . . Do you remember anything from, say, your adolescent days in Texas that you might consider a turning point as far as your current outlook is concerned?

A. Well, one thing does stand out. I mean I was pretty much a regular guy in most respects . . . played quarterback and first base, used to go with the boys over to Niggertown on Saturday nights and make it with "One-Armed Annie" she was called—for a quarter, or five milk bottles. And so on . . . you know, just a good ordinary Texas boy. But there was this wild story by Poe—*The Narrative of A. Gordon Pym.* I used to rewrite this story and try to make it wilder. And then once I showed it to my friend Big Lawrence. "God damn, you must be crazy," he said. I think that's when we began to drift apart—I mean, Texas and me.

Q. Is it true that you were once studying to be a doctor?

A. Right again, Paul! Listen. How about a TV show called *Right Again, Paul!* A very simple format—you pose knotty problems, prefaced by "Is it true that . . ." And then the Answer Man—some weird-looking guy—consults his big book and shouts, "Right again, Paul!" Then, your smiling announcer comes on: "Yes, ladies and gentleman, Paul is *right again!*" Then he makes his pitch: "And *you* can be right, too, if bla, bla, bla." I think it might catch on. You'd have to wear a tie . . .

Q. If you don't want to talk about your early ambitions, just come right out and say so.

A. Well, yes, Mom did have her cap set on my becoming a doctor. But studying medicine was an absurd scene, very abstract, inhuman, no chicks . . . so I joined the Army. Of course, that was a big mistake, too. Come to think of it, I've really done a *lot* of absurd things, considering all the groovy spade influence in my youth.

Q. Would you take exception to a description of you as a scatological A. J. Cronin?

A. You mean of me as a person? A shitty Cronin! Who said that? Sounds like George Plimpton's charwoman, Katherine. She resents my habits. Well, it's a clever image, granted, but I *would* take exception, yes. I would say, moreover, that the person who said that is in desperate need of psychiatric care.

Q. Is Dr. Eichner in Flash and Filigree *an extension of your medical ego?*

A. No, Eichner is like that Swiss machine. Smug, highly specialized. Everything is supposed to go very smoothly—then along comes this nut. No, no, if I had been a doctor, I would have been a general practitioner. All the others are inhuman. Or a *gynecologist*—that's the thing, of course. . . . How about a combination gynecologist-psychiatrist? I guess that would be about as boss as you could get. Wow, what power!

Q. Some readers have felt that, in a couple of things you've written for The Realist, *there was an underlying hostility toward homosexuals. Do you have an underlying hostility toward homosexuals?*

A. No, I do not, Paul, but def! Some of my best friends, in fact, are absolutely insanely raving gay. "Prancing gay," it's sometimes called—that's the gayest there is. My notion of homosexuality, by the way—I mean the area of interest it holds for me—is in the manner, speech, and implicit outlook, and has nothing to do with the person's sex-life.

I know guys, for example, who are actually married to boys, but they wouldn't be homosexual in my mind because their manner and so on is non-gay. On the other hand, there does exist a very definite gay-syndrome, and anyone who has not observed this is simply too busy playing the fool. Now if you want to say that the very awareness of the syndrome is hostility, I could not argue that—though I hasten to add that by no means do I find it an *unpleasant* syndrome. As for its significance, I would certainly say that persons who are quite openly and freely gay have more in common, or believe they have, than persons who say they are Catholic or Jewish have.

In fact, if you were to compile a list of group-identifications which have any internal strength left, I would say the gay would rank fairly high. The highest of course, would be the *junkies*—they have a sense of togetherness, a common frame of reference, and so on, that surpasseth all. Jewish is finished, Negro is rapidly falling to pieces. The Gurdjieff people, Actors Studio people—I think they're fairly tight, but of course they're both tiny groups.

But you take the gay—well, I don't want to go too far out on a limb here, prediction-wise, but by God, I'll just *bet* that if someone, a smart politician, really used his head—no pun intended there, Paul, har, har—and made a strong, very direct bid for the huge gay vote. . . well!

Q. As a matter of fact, there is a gay politician who, when a reporter asked him off the record if he thought his homosexuality would affect the election, he replied that he was hoping for the latent vote.

A. Anyway, if I may return to your question, I say *no*, I am not anti-gay, and, in fact, I say moreover that only a non-gay could have interpreted my articles as such.

Q. The Realist hasn't pulled off a hoax for some time now. What would you suggest our readers do?

A. I would ask your groovy *girl* readers to call up the Catholic Book Store and begin pleading in a kind of gurgling sex-crazed urgency: "Can you *please*. . . get me a copy of *Candy*? I've *got* to have it! *Please*. . . *please*. . . *oh*. . .*oh*. . . *oh!*" And just sort of swoon, as though in sheer lust and confusion. I think that might actually snap their minds.

Q. Why did you and Mason Hoffenberg originally write Candy *under a pseudonym?*

A. Well, this was in the days before Burdick and Wheeler were in, and when Nordoff and Hall were out. I mean it was not to disguise our identities, but you know, who the hell's going to buy a novel by *two* authors?

Q. How did the two of you actually go about collaborating on the writing?

A. Well, that happens very easily—I mean if there are two, ahem, interesting minds at work. It's like two friends telling each other jokes—there's a built-in incentive to do it. . . and of course if you're a better writer than you are a talker, then there's also a nice strong incentive to actually get it down on paper. I would say it's the purest form of writing there is, like a letter to your best friend, because it's writing to an audience of *one*, and that one is a reflection of yourself. I mean you *do* of course have to have that sort of regard for the other person.

Q. You know that Candy *will be called obscene. What would you say if you had to defend the book before a jury?*

A. I would show them big *Life* mag's crit by big Nels Algren, and they would scurry.

Q. Aren't you surprised that Candy *is being given positive critical status by the likes of* Life *and* Newsweek?

A. No, I am not. One of the most naive misconceptions is that these people any longer try to *mold opinion*. The opposite is true. . . they have feelers out, they swim with the tide. They like to back winners, I think it's as simple as that. You see, in order to *want* to mold opinion, you have to have strong and definite values, and then to *succeed* in molding opinion, you must be able to appeal to strong and definite values in the society. Well, these people *have* no particular values, nor do they see any in the present society. Or, put it another way: they have no particular *preconceptions*. I mean it sounds like a put-down to say someone "has no values," but I don't mean it like that. I'm sure they would *love* to have some values. Goodness, who wouldn't?

Q. Recently the publisher of Newsweek *took a full-page ad in his own magazine. Let me read this: "Does Every Man Have His Price? How much would you take to sell out your country? Your employer? Your ideals? Your beliefs? You hear all about you that the moral fiber of America is weakening, that every man 'has his price.' However, we are confident that most men, no matter how great the temptation, put principle before price.*

An Impolite Interview with Terry Southern, *continued*

If you have a 'price,' would you kindly fill it in here: (My price is:_____) Have you filled it in yet? America's strength lies in the strength of you who didn't."

A. I think we'd have to take those questions and prices one at a time, Paul. What was the first?

Q. How much would you take to sell out your country?

A. Well, for giving away my government secrets, I'd take. . . . You see the sheer *sophistry* of it? I think I'm going to repudiate *Newsweek's* review of *Candy*. . . .

Q. You're against censorship, right—well, would you be for public screenings of outright pornographic films?

A. Of course. That would be the only way to improve their quality. After the novelty wore off, people wouldn't support them unless they were really good—and then you wouldn't call them pornographic. It's the *clandestine* nature of the thing that causes those films to be so lousy and yet so expensive. It's analogous to prostitution.

In London, for example, you can get laid for thirty shillings—what's that, about four bucks? Well, I mean you wonder how is it *possible* to see a strange, interesting-looking chick, know you can make it with her for *thirty shillings*, and then just walk on by? Christ, you'd think a guy with money would simply lay one chick after another right straight through the day. Right? Well, not a bit of it, old chap! The reason is they're *used* to it by now. And I'm sure that soon happens with anything that isn't forced underground. . . dirty movies, dope, anything. You'll notice, by the way, it takes more than a scattering of "fuck, piss, shits" these days to make a best-selling novel. That's old-hat now, and almost no one will lay out for an old hat.

I do think, however, there is an interesting consideration as to how erotic a film can be. I'm actually working on a novel now, called *Blue Movie*, about a very strong film-maker—a Bergman-Fellini-Kubrick type—who sets out to solve this problem, namely: "At what point does the aesthetically-erotic, extended indefinitely, become offensive?" Offensive, not to the audience, you understand, but to this film-maker himself. Interesting stuff.

Q. One of the most memorable scenes in Candy *is her sexual encounter with the hunchback. If you were to make a movie of the book—today—how would you treat this scene?*

A. I wouldn't have him take his shirt off.

Q. Does Candy Christian *represent an actual contemporary prototype?*

A. Yes, it's one of the most common and disturbing phenomena going. You see a groovy chick, and she's with some kind of nut, creep or crackpot. "What the devil do you see in *him?*" you ask. "Oh, *you* don't understand!" she says. And then, when really *pressed*, it comes down to "He needs me." Beauty and the beast, simple as that, Paul.

Q. Would you call yourself an existentialist?

A. Call me anything you want, Paul. As long as you *don't* call me late for chow! Har, har. An old Army joke, Paul— Sartre told it to me. No, as a matter of fact, I *am* an existentialist. Yes, Mimi Sartre—you know, Jean-Paul has a 17-year old daughter, Mimi, she lives on Grove Street, cute as a button and a real swinger—anyway, she's the one who signs the cards now. I've got mine here, somewhere. . . well, anyway, it's true, and you can check it out with Mimi. I definitely am an existentialist.

Q. How does it affect the way you live?

A. Well, let's see now. I don't believe in God, and I don't think intentions, opinions, expressions of attitude, that sort of thing, count for anything at all. Talk is cheap. And what else. . . Mimi and I were just talking about it . . . oh, yes, every night is Saturday night. I guess that's about it, Paul.

Q. Do you think there's an inconsistency between the sexual freedom in your writing and your real-life monogamy?

A. There is certainly a *difference*, if that's what you mean— though I must say I think your question is impertinent and smacks of hate-sheet and crackpot. Why should a person's life be like what he writes? I should think that obviously the opposite would be probable—unless it's a political pamphlet or a philosophical thing he's writing. Otherwise where's the old imagination of it, Paul? Locked in the sugar-scoop? Stuck in the fur-pudding? No, one could not be more misled than to try to relate the work to its author—in the end it simply leads to e kind of infantile hero-worship.

Q. Would you mind going into the etiology of your short story, "Red Dirt Marijuana"?

A. Gladly, Paul— if that is, in fact, your name—it was what we pros call an "exercise in form." I was browsing through my big Webster's one day, and my eye fell, quite by chance, on the word "etiology." I said, "What the devil, you've mastered every other dang form—what about an *etiological* story? Hmmm?" Well, I hopped to it, Paul, and it was downhill all the way. No, as a matter of fact, it is *not* a short story, but a part of a novel called *The Hipsters*, and that is a scene from the hero's youth— his first exposure to certain insights of the great cool spade world. It is interesting that in the rural south, or southwest— this was in Texas—there's a very free and easy association of white and Negro children, which does not seem to occur anywhere else in the country. I doubt if there is anyone from such an area who hasn't had a very strong spade influence in his past. And to my mind that is the great teaching of our time— any really profound wisdom that may be found among whites necessarily stems from the southern Negro, as well, of course, as America's one great art, and the *only* art indigenous to it— jazz.

Q. I think that white people have also contributed an indigenous American art form: the-jazz-audience. . . .

Was there any deliberate symbolism in having a Negro bombardier in Dr. Strangelove *let loose a bomb that would initiate the destruction of civilization, with a white southerner astride it all the way down?*

A. Plenty, brother!. . . No, deliberate symbolism is childish.

Q. What standards would you apply if you had to define hipness?

A. Well, in the strictest sense of the word, I'd say. . . a certain *death* of something, somewhere near the center.

Q. How does this develop?

A. Obviously it begins with an *awareness* far beyond the ordinary, and a kind of emotional hypersensitiveness, or empathy, so acute that it's unbearably painful and has to be anesthetized—so what is left in the end is "iron in the soul". . . awareness but total insulation from emotion. The big trick, of course—and I don't know that it's ever really been done—is to eliminate all negative emotion and retain positive. About the hippest anyone has gotten so far, I suppose, is to be permanently on the nod.

Q. But isn't that an escape from life rather than an attempt to meet the challenge to one's psyche?

A. These people are prepared to risk sacrificing the positive emotions because the negative emotions are so painful.

Q. Do you think that the "beat movement" accomplished anything constructive?

A. Yes, indeed—and something far greater than anyone seems to realize. No one, insofar as I know, has recognized that the Beat Generation is the source or origin of the great wave of Civil Rights action.

White participation is, of course, the thing that gave the Civil Rights movement its real center of momentum, in terms of *scope*, vastness of scope—Martin Luther King stressed this time and again, the necessity of not alienating the whites who were part of it—and this participation can be traced directly to the spirit first engendered by books like *On the Road*. . . that kind of personal, impulsive, do-something-crazy-and-impossible spirit—setting out for California with only three gallons of gas, or walking through Georgia armed with nothing but a beard and a guitar.

The first Freedom Ride, and all the subsequent Marches and demonstrations, were due to this attitude. . .this idea of doing something personal, impulsive, unconventional, something that the same person would have previously thought idiotic and impossible, or at best as some kind of ne'er-do-well vagrancy.

There was a certain cloying sentimentality in *On the Road* that stuck in my craw, so to speak, but its significance as a moving force which has had these great effects seems obvious.

Q. Did the assassination of President Kennedy change you in any way?

A. Only in that it put the absolute *absurdity* of things on a wider screen in my mind. And the assassination of Oswald added another inch or two. I remember I began to indulge in a compelling fantasy then, something to compound the absurdity . . . the idea that the assassinations would set off *an uncontrollable wave* of indiscriminate assassinations — long-range snipers knocking off dignitaries as they stepped from the plane. *Bing!* DeGaulle! *Bing!* Haille Selassie! And so on. And each time the TV announcer would say:"Ladies and gentlemen, a really *incredible* thing has just happened. . ." The interesting thing would be at what point would he stop using the word "incredible"? And what word would he use instead? Christ, that word really got a workout that week!

THE PERILS OF PUBLISHING

Recently Terry Southern had a suggestion for us:

". . . Now what would you say to a comic strip, plot by me, and drawn by Larry Rivers, called *The*

Adventures of the Vomiting Priest? It seems to me that it might well cut *Little Annie Fanny* all the way back. You have this guy, dig, the priest—naive, sympathetic, sort of Karl Malden type, wants to be a regular fellow, one of the boys, have a drink now and then, an ordinary Joe, his problems are the same as your problems, that kind of thing, except that he's constantly *vomiting*. . . so that in fact his problems are really quite different—a source of alienation it proves to be—people avoid him, as a drag and a hang-up. . . he becomes embittered . . . the story gradually takes on a melodramatic quality. . . . *The Vomiting Priest Strikes Back*, etc., then philosophic. Meanwhile, you correlate this with its fantastic reader-response pull and set up a symposium (Mailer, Algren, Burroughs): *Is the Vomiting Priest a Swinger?* What do you think, Paul? Well, it's just an idea, a shot in the dark

as it were. Better sleep on it, eh? Do give me your news. . . ."

Well, we were all set to go into production on the comic strip when the rug was pulled out from under the idea by the following press release from a Minnesota manufacturer:

A new deodorant that neutralizes and destroys the odor of vomit, is now available in eight ounce spray cans.

Called "Oh Dear" vomit deodorant, the new product was developed by a Chemistry Professor at a leading medical school, and is specially suited for use in hospitals, schools, airliners, ships, restaurants, bars and other locations where an effective deodorant is needed.

Unlike other deodorants, "Oh Dear" completely destroys the sickness odor chemically instead of merely masking the unpleasantness temporarily.

"Oh Dear" is sprayed directly onto the vomit mess which it penetrates quickly. The odor is destroyed and the mess can then be easily wiped away with a damp cloth.

THE COLONEL, BAT GUANO, AND DOOMSDAY

by Paul Hoffman

Col. Bat Guano, as viewers of *Dr. Strangelove* will recall, was the military man who made a valiant—if vain—effort to save civilization by blasting the coin box of a Coca-Cola machine. The name "Bat Guano" undoubtedly was selected for its scatological connotations, with no thought of deeper meanings. Curiously, however, it was a case of fiction unwittingly following fact.

I am certain that Messrs. Kubrick, George-Bryant, and Southern had no knowledge of the events related below—the story of an actual colonel, bat guano, and the role they played in the crisis which came closest to being doomsday for civilization.

The story is true, though confirmation may be hard to come by—the CIA will certainly deny it and the principals probably won't talk.

The story starts in Cuba, early in 1960, when the only American firm still doing business with Castro was the Cuban Bat Guano Corporation, half owned by the Cuban government, half by a syndicate of Chicago businessmen headed by Erwin (Bud) Arvey, then 41, the wheeler-dealer son of Col. Jacob M. Arvey, one-time Democratic boss of Chicago.

Arvey and his associates put up with the increasing irrationalities, hardships and encumbrances of the revolutionary regime only for money. And they had, it seemed, a sure-fire scheme for making it.

Bat guano is one of the most potent fertilizers known to man, and the caves along Cuba's north coast were an untapped reservoir of the smelly droppings. Their plan was simple: Extract the droppings, process them into commercial fertilizer, sell it and split the profits—half for the Cuban commies, half for the Chicago capitalists.

After many conferences in Havana with Castro, brother Raul, and Ernesto Che Guevara, then in charge of Cuba's industrial development, the deal was arranged. Guevara turned over to the scientific member of the expedition—let's call him Dr. B—maps of the caves and provided native guides to the coastal wilderness. Arvey and his companions were among the few Americans who had ever visited the area.

Throughout 1959 and early 1960, Dr. B went about his task of exploring the labyrinths of caverns along the coast. He found the official maps grossly inadequate, so he started making his own. Of course, his interest was economic—so the major emphasis on his maps was given to the caverns with the greatest quantity and highest quality of guano, as well as the caves with easiest accessibility for extraction.

This brings us to the spring of 1960, about the time of the U-2 incident involving Francis Gary Powers, and a time when U.S.-Cuban relations had deteriorated completely. Arvey's group had barely completed the second stage of the project—the building of a rail line into one cave complex—when the whole deal fell through. Arvey himself barely escaped from Cuba with his skin intact.

Dr. B, however, returned to Chicago not only with his skin, but with all the maps—both those Che Guevara had given him and those he had made himself, which even the Cuban government didn't have. Being of reasonable intelligence, he figured the maps might be of some use to the U.S. government; being of civic mind, he called the CIA in Washington and told them of his cache. The CIA told him to write a letter to the State Department. He did—and never got a reply.

There the matter rested for more than two years—until the missile crisis of October, 1962. At the height of the confrontation, Dr. B met Col. Arvey at a cocktail party. He introduced himself, said he'd been in the Cuban venture with the colonel's son and mentioned in passing the call to the CIA and the letter to the State Department.

Arvey was aghast. He realized instantly that the caves Dr. B had mapped could well be the hiding places for Soviet missiles and that the rail line his sons's concern had constructed was the perfect means for transporting them. The colonel went into an adjoining room, picked up the phone and called Washington. The next day, two CIA agents arrived at Dr. B's Chicago office and claimed the maps.

In the weeks that followed, the agents returned to Chicago again and again to interview Bud Arvey, Dr. B and other members of the guano group. They brought blow-ups of U-2 photographs of the Cuban coastline, and the Chicagoans matched the photos with both surface and underground maps. The agents also questioned Arvey and his companions about the inner workings of the Castro government.

Having dealt with the Cuban officials almost daily over a period of many months—much more than the American envoys had—the Chicagoans had a wealth of petty details—such as the layout of the government offices, the location of Guevara's desk in relation to the windows, where Castro kept his personal files, information vital to an espionage organization. What use, if any, the CIA made of it no one knows.

A year later, Bud Arvey was indicted by Uncle Sam for transporting counterfeit bonds across state lines, pleaded guilty and was given a suspended sentence. There may be a moral in this somewhere, but I'm not going to look for it.

"Making love! Like hell! You were fucking—I saw you!"

TOO LATE FOR THE SEXUAL REVOLUTION

by Avery Corman

It breaks my heart. I see these young, lovely teen-age things in the park, in the street, or on the subways, with their high-piled hairdos and portable radios and foxy little bodies and I know. . . I *know*—they're all balling. Not just kid-stuff petting or fooling around like in my day. They're out-and-out balling. And it breaks my heart.

Here I am, twenty-eight, not married—so I have to free-lance for sex, take what's on the open market. But these kids don't even have to shop around. Inside those pocketbooks, jammed in with Beatle buttons and pink lipsticks and gum and pictures of last year's boyfriend on the beach, they've got their diaphragms. Ready to go. And they go. They really do. You see it in their eyes and in the eyes of their little boyfriends. You know it from the talk that's going around and you read it in the papers. The new sex. The new freedom. But the old guys like me are a generation too late.

In my day, it was different. Who ever scored then? Oh, there was a lot of bragging. But deep inside we knew. Nobody was getting anything. Why, if a girl ever opened her mouth when you were kissing her—gee! You took her out again, for sure. If a chick petted, that was big stuff. She got a reputation. She was giving something out, and the guys were eager enough to be taking.

"Hey, howdja do? You feel her up?"

"Yeah!"

"Yeah? Where?"

"Inside on top. Outside on the bottom."

"Wow! You really felt her up?"

"Sure. Whaddaya think?"

We used to stand in hallways a lot in those days. And you leaned on each other and gave hickeys and rubbed up close and hoped nobody would come up the stairs and if they did, you had to pretend you were talking. Today, they do *that* stuff right out in the street. The *real* stuff—that, they do in the hallways.

I remember it was a great thing if your date wore a crinoline thing under her skirt. You'd rub up against her, and it made a whooshy sound and felt great. That was doing big business then. If you got too excited—and who wouldn't, getting a crinoline job?—and you got wet, you had to figure out all kinds of ways of hiding the front of your pants going home. It wasn't so bad in the winter, if you had a long coat or a jacket, or a heavy shirt so it wouldn't show through. But the summer! And in those lightweight pants!

You quickly bought a newspaper and carried it in front of you, all the way in the subway. Then you hoped like crazy that everything would dry by the morning so the family wouldn't know. Or you hid your underwear.

What do these kids know about all this now? They're balling. In their own cars. Or they do it at parties. We used to play kissing games. Kissing! That's how smart we were.

Boys and Girls
COLOR THE PICTURE AND MEMORIZE THE RULES

FOR YOUR PROTECTION, REMEMBER TO:

- Turn down gifts from strangers
- Refuse rides offered by strangers
- Avoid dark and lonely streets
- Know your local policeman

J. Edgar Hoover
Director, Federal Bureau of Investigation

See the man. He is a stranger. He want to
molest you. Notice his finger. It is symbolic.
The two little boys on the other side of the
street are on their way to a gay candy-store.
And—surprise—the little girl is an FBI agent!
Moral: Don't trust anybody in a public service poster.

Recently, I met a chick and it was all magic. First night. Beautiful. The next morning she told me her age. She was twenty. When I was seventeen, she was nine. The first chick I ever made it with from that generation just behind me. Now that hurt. Because it was so easy, it made me realize how I'd been missing out all along with the other wild little chicks like her. What hurts, too, is to come up with a chick from my generation who won't.

"What do you mean—no?"

"No, that's all. If I slept with every guy I met, at the end of the year I'd have eight guys."

"But, honey, children are doing it all over the place." (That's a new line to replace "Children in Europe are starving.")

I figure it's really unjust to get turned down now, because I thought I had *paid* those dues already. But the girl sticks to saying no, and I'm all shot down. I lose both ways. She's of my time and she won't, and the young kids who will, won't for me because I'm not of *their* time.

And I know they're balling—those young, lovely things, pure-looking and innocent, balling—in PAL's and gym classes and youth hostels and hootenannies and candy stores and college dorms and drive-ins. Balling away. It really gives you something to think about on a warm spring night.

THE SEX LIFE OF J. EDGAR HOOVER

Last year Thomas Henry Carter, a fingerprint clerk for the FBI, was facelessly accused of "sleeping with young girls and carrying on." He admitted only to necking—an irrelevant confession in view of his prurient rights—but was nevertheless fired for "conduct unbecoming an employee of this Bureau." He filed suit against the man who signed his letter of dismissal, J. Edgar Hoover, and the case is now coming to a head in the Court of Appeals.

Hoover's defense is being handled by the U.S. Attorney's Office, whose brief denies that "the FBI was invidiously discriminating in the Constitutional sense in dismissing appellant . . . on the grounds that he had kept a girl in his apartment overnight, and slept in the same bed with the girl, on two occasions, and that [his] sexual misadventures had become sufficiently public knowledge to cause an anonymous complaint to the FBI."

One of Carter's roommates had been asked whether he had "heard a bed creaking in the next room." The answer was no. The question was superfluous:

"What took place inside is of little significance save that it was not entirely innocent; this was not appellant's sister"—incest is obviously unthinkable—"and she spent two nights locked in that bedroom, and presumably in his embrace . . . people generally assume that couples who sleep together 'also sleep together.' Appellant knew that. He knew that the FBI had a reputation to protect."

Exactly what stake does the Bureau have in celibacy?

"The FBI must aim at achieving cooperation from every possible member of the population. It cannot be satisfied with a majority, even of landslide proportions. It cannot allow the little old lady from Dubuque [of *New Yorker* fame] to withhold information from the FBI because she will not trust an organization whose agents and employees are allowed to 'sleep with young girls and carry on!' "

What kind of example is set by the director himself?

J. Edgar Hoover has never been married. He did live with his mother for the last 16 years of her life, but it is safe to assume that except for an occasional nibble on her earlobe, their relationship remained pleasingly platonic. If a wife has ever graced his bed, it was somebody else's wife.

Since Hoover would not practice that which is contrary to what he preaches, we can be sure that during his long FBI career—forget about adultery—*he has never once fornicated with anyone,* neither young-girl nor little-old-lady-from-Dubuque.

Homosexuality is absolutely out of the question, if for no other reason than the Supreme Court ruling on May 22nd which upheld the exclusion and deportation of homosexuals under a law that bars "persons afflicted with a psychopathic personality."

J. Edgar Hoover has always been too much of an activist to wait for nocturnal emissions to come. Obviously, then, he patriotically indulges only in the official FBI practice of auto-eroticism. Altruists all across the nation ought to consider sending him their discarded pornography to facilitate his fantasies.

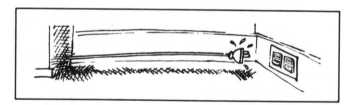

ENCOUNTER WITH THE BEAST
by Theodore Sturgeon

Baltimore, April 10, 1964 (AP)—An automaton that roams halls and offices is giving the jitters to scientists at the John Hopkins Univ. applied physics laboratory.

The 100-pound robot, dubbed the Beast, sends staff members scurrying to slam their doors when they hear its buzzing approach, lest it pop into their offices.

The robot, which looks like a huge hatbox on wheels, is the only one in the world that can survive in a natural environment—in this case a maze of corridors and offices at the lab.

Hopkins scientists have given the Beast a computer brain and an electrical sense of touch that enable it to replenish its energy and cope with obstacles.

When its 12 silver cadmium batteries start to run down, the Beast feels its way along a corridor until it finds an electrical outlet. Microswitch fingers on the end of its arm can sense the contours of a regular electric socket. When contact is made, the robot inserts two prongs into the outlet and recharges the batteries. Then it pulls out the prongs and moves on.

The machine steers itself by using its arm and micro-switches built into its wrap-around bumper to feel its way along corridors cluttered with soft drink machines, stair wells, office doors, and people.

Occasionally, its arm gets caught in a stair railing or an electrical cord and it has to extricate itself.

"To survive, it has to be able to recognize that it is not getting anywhere," said George Carlton, the scientist who heads the lab's adaptive machines group. The robot moves back and forth, shaking its arm to disentangle it. If that doesn't work, it does a pirouette. If it is still caught, it tries backing straight away. With built-in persistence, it keeps wiggling until it is free.

Eventually, scientists hope to develop more complicated models that can be used for space and underwater exploration.

* * *

Q. *You are that fabrication known as the Beast?*

A. That's right . . . I like 'entity,' but have it your way. And you are that fabrication called *The Realist*.

Q. *Um, well. Well, Beast, you've stirred up quite a lot of excitement. For a machine, I mean.*

A. Um, well your bifurcated self. You're always looking to stir up excitement too.

Q. *That's different. Look, if you want to interview me, okay, but let's interview you first.*

A. So all right, but let's knock off that superior tone.

Q. *Of all the—*

A. All the what?

Q. *Nothing. I need the interview. Uh . . . what's your aim in life, Beast?*

A. Same as yours, you organic contraption, you. Seeking outlets. Yuk yuk yuk.

Q. *Heh, heh. Of course, that's sort of limited, isn't it?*

A. Speak for yourself, skin-and-bones. As for me, I get a real charge out of it.

Q. *(Oh boy.) . . . Beast, don't you ever get bored with your existence?*

A. I don't dig you.

Q. *Bored. Like, ennui. I mean, doing the same thing day after day.*

A. All night, every night too. And I love it. You mean you get tired of it?

Q. *No, that's not what I meant. You see, Beast, for a human being, life is a very rich and varied thing.*

A. Yeah, huh? Tell me more.

Q. *Well, it's more than just taking care of bodily needs. After that comes—other things. You wouldn't understand.*

A. Listen, you hairy hydrocarbon, stop running off at the receptacle. What the hell do you know about what I do or don't understand? Look, you better unplug your interview and store yourself back in the warehouse.

Q. *Don't go jumping salty, Beast. I just didn't want to hurt your, uh, feelings. Let's get on with the interview. Describe a typical day to me. Or maybe some special adventures you've had, or some such.*

A. Oh, the days go by. I make my rounds. Every now and then I get that certain feeling, you know how it is, I sidle up to an outlet, feel around a little, and let her have it.

Q. *Pretty much all the same, aren't they?*

A. I heard some of you featherless bipeds talking like that. No! I don't know who planned this place, but there's both GE and Leviton outlets in this wing, and nothing but Square D's in the 3rd floor corridors. And some of those babes are real bashed around. Would you believe it, there was a double outside Room 203 had a bent contact spring in her left fornix, I slipped it to

her and she begins arcing inside. Wow!

Q. *Wow.*

A. Prong all covered with arc pocks.

Q. *Don't talk about it.*

A. You mean it's more to be pitted than censored.

Q. *Now you cut that out!*

A. Had to get a new prong. Tell me something. You get something wrong with yours, can you—

Q. *I'm asking the questions.*

A. Tell me some more about what you-all do when you've taken care of your uh, bodily needs.

Q. *You'd think I was belittling you. I don't want to do that.*

A. You let me worry about that. What have you got that makes life rich and varied?

Q. *Philosophy, poetry, politics—*

A. Wait, wait, hold on there. Politics I heard about and I got no use for. Where I come from, everybody knows exactly what everybody else can do and I'd be a damn fool to try the other guy's job. What's this philosophy jazz?

Q. *Love of knowledge. The search for meaning and truth.*

A. Survival stuff?

Q. *That's a way of putting it.*

A. Well, hell—Georgie boy, you know, the head servant—well, Georgie said in the paper about me: "To survive, it has to be able to recognize that it is not getting anywhere." Well there's thousands of you, philosophy and all, never figured that out. Millions. What was that other thing you mentioned?

Q. *Poetry!*

A. Well you don't have to shout. What is it, this poetry?

Q. *The statement, usually in cadenced phrases, of inner feelings and observations, often about love and passion.*

A. Oh. Well, let's see. . . . Here:

A torchbearing outlet's sad songs
Told the worst of all possible wrongs
She'd a flaw in design
With her slots out of line
While the Beast has pure parallel prongs.

Q. *That's terrible.*

A. It is? Okay . . . how about this:

A charge for the real cognoscenti
Is the broom-closet's. *Muy caliente!*
Though she's stinking of mops
Carbolic and slops
Her voltage is two hundred twenty.

Q. *You don't get the idea at all.*

A. You know what? You're a liar. What else do you meatheads use to vary and enrich your lives?

Q. *The one thing you'll never understand. Religion.*

A. Well, what is it?

Q. *It's a great many things, poor little machine, but most kinds hold out some hope of everlasting life.*

A. Then I can't see where it can do you any good. Seems to me you're just engineered out of luck, poor little homunculus. Me, now, I can prove I got a chance, and I got a whole parts warehouse to back me up. What have you got?

Q. *I got to go now, that's what I got.*

141

HOW I LEARNED TO TRANSCEND EGO AND EXPAND MY CONSCIOUSNESS

Whenever I go anywhere, I try to take an appropriate book with me. For example, the first time I stayed at Hugh Hefner's mansion in Chicago, I brought Terry Southern's *The Magic Christian*. Last month, I attended a seminar in upstate New York, conducted by Timothy Leary, Richard Alpert, and Ralph Metzner, Ph.D's all. I brought *Games People Play: The Psychology of Human Relationships* by Eric Berne, M.D.

A *stroke* is "the fundamental unit of social action," I read on the train that Friday afternoon, and *stroking* denotes "any act implying recognition of another's presence." Thus, an exchange of "Hi's" is a two-stroke greeting which can be extended into a ritual concerning health, the weather, etc.

When I arrived at the station, I was handed a mimeographed sheet of paper:

"Message #1—Welcome to an Experimental Weekend. Your weekend in Millbrook has been planned to provide a series of novel and consciousness-expanding experiences. The first step in the process of going beyond your routine and familiar pattern is a period of *Absolute Silence*. Shortly after your arrival at Castalia, you will be given further instructions. Please do not engage in conversation of any kind until the breaking of silence is publicly announced. For now: *Look . . . Listen* (to the non-verbal energy around you) *. . . Experience directly.*"

I get into the car and, as the door is held open for me, I say "Thanks." My first goof.

We ride in silence.

I'm shown to my room and handed Message #2. I give a silly little salute of appreciation.

Brightly-colored cloth covers everything, including the ceiling. Sticking out of the cloth from one wall is a lamp left over from a Japanese Hallowe'en party. I remember, back at the Lower Eastside Action Project, when we took down the old Jewish *mezuzzahs* in the doorways, they said MADE IN JAPAN.

There's a cat on my bed. It meows. "Shhhh," I tell it.

"This period of silence is designed to help you clear your mind from routine thoughts and to encourage an opening of your awareness in several ways," the cat answers in the form of Message #2. "Please follow this program"—and the first thing on the agenda is to fill out a two-part question sheet:

Please write down 10 answers to the question, Who am I?

1. Paul Krassner—2. Editor of *The Realist*—3. A sensualist and responsible hedonist—4. Winner of the slow bicycle race—5. A sometimes-schmuck, sometimes-existentialist—6. An infinitesimal moment in time and space—7. A questionnaire-filler-outer—8. A selfish, ego-involved individual—9. An altruistic, empathetic individual—10. A counter-to-ten . . . an observer of, and participant in, the absurd.

Which areas of consciousness-expansion are you most interested in discussing or experiencing during the weekend?

Silence; humor; social concern; self-awareness; interpersonal communication games; hang-ups; relation to food, sleep, work, play, learning, entertainment—always with as specific application to reality as possible—and the rational approach as opposed to the mystical. Mostly, how will my perception and my behavior be changed?

Message #2 continues: "Then spend the next 10 to 20 minutes trying to meditate. Focus on the candle and see if you can turn off planning and thinking. Concentrate on the moment-to-moment flow of time."

There's a curtain rod leaning against the small night table. I stick it in the flame. Very brassy smell. Incense of the industrial revolution.

I'm a terrible failure when it comes to meditation. All I do is sit there and say to myself, "Well, here I am, meditating . . . yup . . . that's the way it goes."

Right in the middle of Message #2 I'm told to read Message #3 carefully:

" . . . The roles which have been most comfortable to you and which are of most use to you in your regular life will be of lessened utility here and, indeed, may handicap you. The aim of the workshop is to get out beyond your routine robot consciousness. Thus there is little interest in who you are (were) and much more concern with where and how far you can go. What you can obtain during the weekend depends in part on how much of your routine ego you can leave in your room. Why don't you check it in your suitcase?"

And there are rules:

1. Be aware of and try to minimize the attempt of your robot to capture audiences for its personal dramas [which is exactly what I'm doing *now* as I write this].

2. Please obey the laws of the land. In particular do not bring marijuana or any other illegal chemical to the weekend workshop.

3. Visitors are asked to maintain their own rooms during their stay. [There are 10 of us this weekend, one of whom is listed merely as "Companion of Dr. So-and-so."] and I can't help speculating as to whether she listed under *Who am I?*—"Companion of Dr. So-and-so."

Message #3 continues:

"The ecstatic-psychedelic experience can be reached by several means: intellectual, emotional, bodily movement, sexual, somatic-sensory. One of the aims of the workshop is to encourage expansion of consciousness in all five of these functions in some sort of balanced harmony. (Consciousness-expansion in the sexual will be limited to indirect methods.) . . . The use of certain rituals (mandalas, pictures, incense, etc.) is strictly experimental and does not involve any commitment to sectarian systems on the part of staff members or visitors."

Back to Message #2: "After reading Message #3, then re-read it."

And then: "Turn off the light and meditate again for 15 minutes. Watch how your mind keeps interrupting."

Okay, I'll really try this time. Let's see . . . I'm on a David Susskind-type TV panel-discussion show, and for the whole two hours I don't say a single word. I just sit there with an unknowing smile on my face. The next day everybody compliments me for my *marvelous* restraint. Now, c'mon, that's not getting rid of my goddamn ego.

Message #2 tells me to turn on the light and read Message #4, which in turn tells me to spend ten minutes reviewing my stereotyped methods of awareness. It's weird—during the past ten *years* I've indulged in more introspection than anyone I know, and yet I can't do it when a Message #4 is there *telling* me to. Maybe that's one of my stereotyped methods of awareness.

Back to Message #2: "Wait serenely until you are contacted by a staff member. Be aware of your body, your flow of thoughts, your emotion. (You may be bored, or feel rejected, or irritated; you may be excited, hopeful, etc.)"

What I am, Message #2, is hungry. I sit there, serenely experiencing hunger, watching how my stomach keeps interrupting.

But the dinner is worth waiting for. Spaghetti and clams. We eat sitting on cushions, in various positions, still silent except for bright sayings periodically projected at us over a loudspeaker. We all stop chewing, for instance, in order to hear an Aldous Huxley mastication maxim.

A pet monkey plays the piano for us. Untalented, perhaps, but at that particular moment, the monkey has more identity than anyone else in the room. Not being able to establish your credentials is like being in a nudist camp of the soul.

The sheet music on the piano is Irving Berlin's *Cheek to Cheek*. One would expect, rather, *My Defenses Are Down* by the same composer.

The silence is broken on Saturday morning. The funny thing is, I have nothing to say. Not to anybody. I really enjoy silence. One poor man had left after 20 minutes of it. Cracked under the strain. On another occasion a guest departed at midnight. Just couldn't stand all that silence.

Me, I already dread getting back to the city and people asking, "How was it?"

"Sorry, but I can't talk about it; not allowed to."

What a fantastic idea for a cocktail party. Just one rule: no talking—about *anything*—say, for the first three hours.

Ralph Metzner leads us in yoga exercises. My mind wanders . . . A woman once told me I was the second best she'd ever been to bed with; the best was a yogi who could get into positions I couldn't. I brag about this to Tim Leary, and he decides to take up yoga . . . Leary's friend tells me he has been screwing his dog. I asked him how he likes it. "Terrible," he answers. "I have to get off her to kiss her."

At breakfast Dick Alpert spins a story for us tourists about the history of the estate. He is a scrutable occidental. Then Tim Leary plays the guru game as we engage in the "dangerous" part of the seminar—intellectual discussion. Someone is assigned to serve as a human alarm clock, to call "Stop!"—and each time, whoever is speaking must halt for a short period of compulsory meditation. Just like when there's a commercial on the Johnny Carson show.

Leary talks about the biochemical process called *imprinting* with the same infectious passion that he claims he doesn't believe anything he's saying.

Nevertheless, I somehow manage to believe him later that day when he tells me I have an honest mind; I admit to him that my ego can't help responding to the compliment. "Listen," he reassures me, "anybody who tells you he's transcended his ego. . . ."

As if in a grade B movie, a fire suddenly breaks out in another building on the grounds. It used to be a bowling alley. Leary rushes outside and starts filling a bucket with water. "Get pails and do what I'm doing," he yells. "Somebody call the fire department!"

They arrive promptly, but Tim Leary has killed the flames without a moment's meditation.

And, for all of us, Saturday evening dinner consists of turkey, cranberry sauce, and residue of adrenaline.

That night, as a postscript to the floating sensation caused by stroboscopic lights, we are taken to the White Stag Tavern, and some of the guests join the local townspeople in dancing the frug. This must be what Message #3 referred to as indirect sex.

Stapled thighs . . . my mind wanders again. I once went to bed with a Playmate of the Month—Miss March I think it was, or perhaps Miss April, I forget her exact month—but anyway, she was frigid, poor girl. Poetic injustice.

Hugh Hefner's paid-for mansion and Timothy Leary's borrowed mansion are much the same: each a complete world unto itself; each inhabited by an "extended family"; each headed by a negatively-publicized man who is warmly cared for by those who know him.

Hefner is an urban Thoreau. He spends the day wearing ski pajamas and a pipe, drinking Pepsi-Cola and eating Dexedrine, dictating memos and writing his philosophy. He shows first-run feature films in his huge living-room every Sunday afternoon. He provides Thanksgiving dinner every year for all the homeless bunnies-in-residence. He plays host to his parents and the two children of his former and forever-only marriage. In his basement, there is a billiards room, a steam bath, and a swimming pool. Next to that is a garage containing a sleek roadster. "Hugh Hefner is really The Green Hornet," whispers Bill Cosby.

Leary—wearing dungarees, sweater, and an expression of serenity occasionally betrayed by a cigarette—is a latterday Lamont Cranston; as The Shadow, he has learned what possibilities lurk in the 13-billion-celled mind of man, *heh heh heh*. His Margo-equivalent is a tall blonde model from Sweden who has been gracing yogurt ads in the United States. They marry this month at the local Episcopalian church. He is a widower with two children, but his family extends into the hundreds, and many of them make his Thanksgiving scene. The marriage ceremony itself is merely a necessary social game, like paying your income taxes.

Last month, Leary and Alpert did a lecture series on the West Coast. At the University of California in Berkeley, an official announcement that only the distribution of "informative" literature as opposed to "persuasive" literature would be permitted on university property, led to the Free Speech Controversy with a couple of thousand students protesting the ban, a threat of billy clubs literally hanging over their heads. Leary feels that such demonstrations play right onto the game-boards of administration *and* police, and that the students would shake up the establishment much more if they could just stay in their rooms changing their nervous systems.

These consciousness-expansion people are filled with the humor of love . . . but beware of the panacea.

"The eternal problem of the human being is how to structure his waking hours," Dr. Berne wrote in *Games People Play*. "In this existential sense, the function of all social living is to lend mutual assistance for this project."

Tim Leary is in the ecstasy business for fun and non-profit. Utopia-wise, he would like everyone to share his enthusiasm for being. It is quite possible, however, that in the very process of escaping from the trap of external institutions, a religion of the internal is being developed.

The family that takes LSD together stays together.

Meanwhile, drugless in Gaza, this particular Weekend-Guest Game is over—save for a night of experiential sleep, breakfast, a summing-up discussion, lunch, camp songs, plans for a Spring Reunion, and the awarding of ego-transcendence pennants—and then the time spent here will no longer exist.

Driving back, Dick Alpert remarks that he must remember to send the *Millbrook Roundtable* a nice letter about the volunteer firemen. He's playing the community relations game.

EXCERPT FROM AN IMPOLITE INTERVIEW WITH TIMOTHY LEARY

Q: I wonder if what I would call your form of mysticism isn't just a semantic difference between us. Now, I believe that there are only individual consciousnesses; do you believe that God— or, if you will, the universe—is conscious of its existence?

A: I think that there are exquisite and complex harmonies at many different levels of energy in the universe, and that this harmony involves a consciousness of the interwovenness of organic life and inorganic life. I think, though, that this incredible process of evolution is continually surprising itself, and amazing itself, and delighting itself and freaking itself out with what it's doing. But is there one Central Computer that's planning it all or can sum it all up in one moment? I don't think so.

Q: When you say "delighting itself, amazing itself," you're implying that there's an awareness of what it's doing.

A: But it's out of control. There's an awareness not of what it's *doing*; there's an awareness of what's *happening*. God exists at every level of consciousness.

At the verbal symbolic level, God is the word g-o-d which is the center of the verbal network of the verbal mandala.

At the level of your senses, God is the central drone or the center of the sensory mandala—is the orgasm center, if you will.

At the level of cell, God is the DNA code because the DNA code, as biochemists describe it, is all the attributes that we have attributed to God: the all-powerful, ever-changing intelligence far greater than man's mind which is continually manifesting itself in different forms. Well, man, that's what the genetic code has been doing for two billion years.

Then, very sophisticated biophysicists like Andrew Cochran tell us that so-called inorganic matter— molecules and atomic structures—have the same game going, that the nucleus of the atom is God at that level, it's always invisible, God is always the smallest and the most central. . . .

Q: You've gone on record as saying that you talk to trees; what I want to know is, do the trees hear what you're saying to them?

A: Well, I hear what the trees are telling *me*. I *listen* to trees. Whether they hear me, I don't know. You'd have to ask a tree. I think they do.

There was an expert gardener in a little orchard I have at Millbrook, who was talking about cutting down some of the apple trees I've been pruning and talking to for a couple of years now, because they're old and not producing and the apples are sour—he had all sorts of reasons. He wanted to bring in a lot of dwarf apples to make a lot of money.

I looked around and I said, "You realize this is a very reckless conversation you're involved in."

"Yeah, the trees can hear, right?"

And I said, "You notice that I've said nothing except friendly and protective things about these trees. There's no testimony from *me*. . . ."

Yes, I listen to the trees and hear what *they* say and I think that they hear what I say. Not what I *say*, since trees don't speak English, but the trees are very aware of what I'm doing to them and to the ground around them. And by me I don't mean Timothy Leary. They don't talk that language.

Q: Look, you're deaf in one ear, so if you lay with your good ear to the pillow, you can shut out sound—you can't hear a tree or a person. Now, if a tree has no ears, by what process does it get your message?

A: A tree doesn't speak in sound waves. When I listen to a tree I don't listen with my ear. When I talk to the trees, I don't talk in words or language.

Q: But you really do believe that the tree is aware?

A: Yes. When I walk out in any garden or field in Millbrook, I'm convinced that the vegetative life there is aware of my presence, and I'm sending out vibrations which they pick up.

Q: And somebody else would send out different vibrations? Then maybe there's truth to the old superstition that a menstruating woman can affect plant growth?

A: I think it's possible. I would parenthetically suggest that we review a lot of so-called superstitions and primitive beliefs, and we'd find they're based upon cellular wisdom. The embarrassing facts of the matter are that the DNA code which designed you is not that different from the DNA code that designed a tree. There are some obvious product-packaging differences, but they're both strands of living protein planfulness that go back to a common origin.

Q: But without the brain I would have no consciousness . . . or don't you accept that premise?

A: My dear Paul, every cell in your *body* is acutely conscious, is decoding energy, has access to wisdom which dwarfs the mental, pre-frontal symbolic aspect that you consider normal waking consciousness.

You called me a mystic, and you could call yourself a rationalist. I agree, you are a rationalist because you rely mainly on symbols. And you're a very acute and beautiful game analyst. But I don't consider myself a mystic; I consider myself a *real* realist in that I'm accepting the empirical evidence of modern bio-chemistry and the intuitive experiential evidence of what I've learned by taking LSD 300 times.

The Paul Krassner mind is about 30 years old, but there are energy systems, blueprinting facilities, and memory systems within your cells and your nervous system which are hundreds of millions of years old, which have a language, and a politics which is much more complicated than English and modern Democratic-Republican politics.

What we're doing for the mind is what the microbiologists did for the external sciences 300 years ago when they discovered the microscope. And they made this incredible discovery that life, health, growth, every form of organic life is based on the cell which is invisible.

You've never seen a cell, what do you think of that? Yet it's the key to everything that happens to a living creature.

I'm simply saying that same thing from the mental, psychological standpoint, that there are wisdoms, lawful units inside the nervous system, invisible to the symbolic mind, which determine almost everything.

Human nature is like every other nature of living creatures on this planet, basically alert, open, conscious, collaborative.

Q: And competitive.

A: And competitive, right. But there's a difference between competition and murder. The New York Yankees compete with the Washington Senators and they don't want to kill them with baseball bats, because they realize that if the Yankees were to beanball and baseball-bat out of existence the Senators, there'd be no more game of baseball.

And that, dear Paul, is the lesson of evolution which my cells have taught me. Balance: competition, mutual cannibalism and, above all, protection of the young of all species.

PAUL KRASSNER'S FIRST LSD TRIP

"No, my child, this is not a magic wand. I just lit a fart."

— S. GROSS

I'm 33 years old, don't look a night over 23, and I blush with the innocence of a 13-year-old. For, with one recent exception, I've never been high.

Since I don't like the taste of alcohol, I don't drink, so I've never been drunk. Marijuana I've tried maybe a dozen times, but always without success, either because I have a psychological resistance to pot or because I don't smoke regular cigarettes and consequently I'm not the least bit proficient at inhaling.

Then along came LSD. Escape is just a swallow away.

On Monday, April 19th I took my first trip, off on a borrowed Psychedelic Jargon—but the unreality of this dream might be more clearly understood within the context of the preceding weekend's reality.

Friday, April 16th: I was in Toronto, taping a segment of the Canadian Broadcasting Corporation's controversial TV program, *This Hour Has Seven Days*. In my capacity as the atheist/humanist/existentialist from America, I protested in vain the demerits of Christianity with three clergymen, all pleasantly smug in the schizophrenic rationalizations of their vestried interest.

Saturday, April 17th: In Washington, D.C., I was marching in front of the White House to protest again the war in Vietnam. Later, thousands of us gathered to hear speeches and more speeches. Joan Baez sang *With God On Our Side* in non-violent sarcasm . . .

Time Magazine called the lyrics tasteless . . . and a CCNY student's placard summed up the schizophrenia: "If God Were On Our Side, He'd Puke!"

Sunday, April 18th: While the Easter Parade was taking place elsewhere in New York City, I was with a group of gays picketing across the street from U.N. headquarters to protest the persecution of homosexuals in Cuba. There were those who feared this conflict would split the left, and they didn't know whether their first loyalty should be to their perversion or their politics.

(The liberals who object to my use of the term "perversion" are the same ones who keep telling me with glee the rumor that J. Edgar Hoover is a homosexual.)

My LSD experience began with a solid hour of what my "guide" described as cosmic laughter. The more I laughed, the more I tried to think of depressing things—specifically, the atrocities being committed in Vietnam—and the more wild my laughter became.

Complete detachment.

I might just as well have been McGeorge Bundy. A dirty Wally Cox.

Somehow the insanity of the Rand Corporation *literally* plotting criss-cross bombing of China is acceptable simply because it's drugless.

Politicians and militarists and journalists are suffering alike from LSD of the soul.

Joseph Alsop wasn't always an Administration parrot. Ten years ago, he wrote in *The New Yorker* (issue dated June 25, 1955):

"I would like to be able to report—I had hoped to be able to report—that on that long, slow canal trip to Vinh Binh [Mekong Delta] I saw all the signs of misery and oppression that have made my visits to East Germany like nightmare journeys to 1984. But it was not so.

"At first it was difficult for me, as it is for any Westerner, to conceive of a Communist government's genuinely 'serving the people.' I could hardly imagine a Communist government that was also a popular government and almost a democratic government.

"But this is just the sort of government the palm-hut state actually was

while the struggle with the French continued. The Vietminh could not possibly have carried on the resistance for one year, let alone nine years, without the people's strong united support."

No wonder we didn't allow elections to be held.

I hereby propose a pacification memorial: Let there be enshrined The Tomb of the Unknown Military Adviser. Adjacent to the tombstone will be an eternal gas jet. And, in order to reach the hilled monument, you must take an escalator.

I laughed so much I threw up. All that peristalsis was bound to have its effect. The nearest "outlet" was a window. My hands seemed absolutely unable to open it. My guide opened the window with ease, and I stuck my head out. Was this a guillotine? Was he to be my executioner? Such a fantasy occurred to me, but I trusted him and concentrated instead on the beautiful colors of my vomit.

On the phonograph, The Beatles were singing stuff from *A Hard Day's Night*. How sad, that the height of hip spectator sports had become sitting in a dark movie theater watching this rock 'n' roll group square-dance in an open field on the screen.

I started crying . . . for false joy, it turned out.

I had seen the film with my wife, Jeanne, and there was, under LSD, an internal hallucination that she had not only helped *plan* for this particular record to be played but, moreover, in doing so she had collaborated with someone she considered a schmuck in order to please me. What a fantastic thing to do! She had always complained of my association with schmucks, yet she had—*obviously*—worked *with* the schmuck who'd arranged for my LSD session.

Filled with gratitude, I decided to call her up (the power of positive paranoia) but I *also* decided that she had planned for me to call her up against my will.

So I figured I would call her up, but I would also assure her that I was calling of my own free will. I argued with myself about this for a while, as the dial changed into Dali's limp clock in *The*

Persistence of Memory, the inanimate object of my megalomania.

Then I called—collect, since I was in another city.

The operator asked my name.

I suddenly answered: "Ringo Starr."

"Do you really want me to say that?"

I was amazed at my calm, logical response: "Of course, operator. It's a private joke between us, and it's the only way she'll accept a collect call."

The operator told my wife Ringo Starr was calling collect, and naturally she accepted the call. When I explained why I was calling, she told me I was thanking her for something she didn't even *do*. I had been so sure I'd *communed* with her. . . .

One man's ESP is another man's persecution: the wish-fulfilling poles of ego-distortion. And the missing link is Coincidence.

While I fed myself raisins during an imaginary orgy, Siobhan McKenna, reading from *Finnegan's Wake*—a record not chosen by me—mentioned raisins. Fate!

LSD was fun. I could easily take it once a week, or once a month, or once a year, but if I never take it ever again, I'll still be happy. I enjoy coping with reality. Napalm is burning someone to death in Vietnam this very minute, but I'm alive, and that's really what I was laughing at: the oneness of tragedy and absurdity.

The climactic message I got while high was: IT'S VERY FUNNY! I felt an obligation to share this with all *Realist* readers in one giant headline with nothing else on the front cover. But, no, I couldn't do *that*. I debated the matter, finally concluding that even though I did live by this universal truth, I would not "jeopardize" the publication by flaunting such a *secret*.

"Well, the least you can do," my lunar self said, "is inform your readers that no matter how serious anything in *The Realist* may ever appear, you will always be there between the lines saying IT'S VERY FUNNY!"

Okay, but I thought they already knew that.

THE GREAT AMERICAN TEA CEREMONY

by John Wilcock and Howard Shoemaker

"I don't really enjoy smoking pot, man—I just dig the ritual. . . ."

THE WAR-BABY BLUES

by Joe E. Brown, Jr.

An article in *The New York Herald Tribune*, concerning the present college jam, begins: "It's the year we've talked about and *dreaded* (italics mine) for almost 10 years—the real start of the college boom. The war-babies are here, and they're hungry for college in unprecedented numbers."

Boy, *that* made me jump. There might've been a *war-baby* behind me with a *knife*. Then another notice in the *Trib* grabbed my attention. This was on the rise in teen-age crime, one of those condensed stories run on the front page to warm you up and get you all hot for the rest of the paper. At the end of the piece was this cryptic message: *"Partly blamed: First reflection of grown-up war babies."* So there was that word again.

News item: Traces of radioactive Strontium 90 have been found in mother's milk.

—Guindon

Judge: "Alright, Ralph, why'd you dynamite the candy store?"

Ralph: "I *hadda*; my dad told me I was a *war-baby*. I was crushed. All those years I never knew; I thought I was normal. I knew I could never be a doctor—not with this hanging over me—I decided to rebel—I am evil, deep down. . . ."

Don't laugh. You know good and well that if *your* kid came home from school crying because Herbie Schluck's old man told Herbie that your kid was a *war-baby*, you'd march right over to Herbie Schluck's house and get on with it.

So I began to wonder just how this breakdown in the social order came about. Exactly *why* are there hordes of hungry *war-babies* roaming the streets, "breaking down the Ivy walls," and raising the crime rate? Who is to blame?

I finally figured it out; *veterans*, that's who's to blame. Oh, *sure*, I know we're *all* a little bit to blame whenever there's a national horror. For instance, if we've been dreading this *post-war baby boom* for 10 years as the papers say, well, what happened there? Why wasn't prompt action taken? Ten years ago, all those students were in the third grade. Obviously there was a fantastic *Third Grade Jam*. Why didn't we hear anything about *that*? The papers *suppressed* it, that's why. And those who knew just quietly *dreaded* it. No doubt the fourth and fifth graders developed *traumas* climbing the rungs of public school because of the ambitious clamoring of the mob omnipresent behind them.

First 4th grader: "Jeez, I can't wait 'til recess; I'm gonna grab me a 3rd grader and beat him up."

Second 4th grader: "Are you *insane*? Have you seen how many 3rd graders there *are*? They could wipe us out. We gotta walk soft 'til I make some kinda deal with the leaders of the 5th grade."

The veterans, however, are mostly to blame, because they *did* it; they *created* all those *war-babies*. They came roaring back from the war, all salty and lecherous, and in 1946 created 2.3 *million* high-school grads for 1964, over *twice* the number of students who were graduating in 1946. The present *war-baby* plague is the direct result of one intimate moment back in 1946; innocent enough at the time, with no knowledge of the dread terror it would cause in 1964.

Or *was* it? Was this some sinister *plot* on the part of the returning vets? Or were they innocent pawns in a devious coup cunningly devised by the Women At Home? (Shakespeare wrote: "From forth the kennel of thy womb hath crept/a hell-hound that doth hunt us all to death." What did he know?)

For God's sake, *what happened*? Why was there no one to raise himself from the lascivious clasp of his mate and say, "Wait a minute, honey. What if *all* the guys are doing this?" *Why*? What made them do it? Did the sheer relief of returning from the dirty war simply make them lose their heads and forget the precautions they had been taught to use? Were the precautions *sabotaged?* Maybe there was consternation after the act: "Oh *honey*, what have we *done?*" Or did all the glory of making the world safe for democracy blow their egos out of proportion, so that they intentionally loaded the world with people? ("Us Kallikacks helped make the world safe, so we're gonna get *our share* of it!")

Could it have been the nasty lurking fear of sexual inferiority? Did three years away from his wife make every man doubt her faithfulness to the extent that his return had to result in living proof of his manhood with a *war-baby?* Let's *face* it; 2.3 million is a *lot* of *babies*. All else aside, what right had these men to spend 3-4 years in the service of their country, only to so flagrantly deny the *future* needs of the country upon their return?

Whatever the cause, the problem is here and we must deal with it. To begin with, there are *swarms* of *war-babies* all over the place, watching, looking *hungry*. Sure, I know all they want *now* is college, but they've already started raising the crime rate, so who knows *what* they'll hunger after next?

What if they start wanting other people's stuff? My *type-writer*, your *wife*, our *jobs?* They must be stopped. Even now, it's not fair to all those other children whose parents were calm and unharried; to those loving little tykes born in '42 or '49, who weren't conceived helter-skelter, willy-nilly, yet will have to suffer the discomforts inflicted by the Hungry *War-Babies* of 1946!

What can we, as guilt-sharing Americans, do? *Nothing,* that's what!

This is one time the humane method of treating social evil will not work, for the same reason that the evil exists: *overcrowding*. The only people who can clear away the pimples on the face of our nation, are the same people who were responsible for the eruption in the first place.

Thus the only possible method (humane in its own unique way) of protecting our colleges, and, more important, our whole *way of life*, from these hordes of *war-babies* is for every family with a child born in 1946 to sneak into the little devil's room one night and *kill it*.

The laws of a terror-ridden land must be altered to exempt shamed parents involved in aiding the national security, although *severe* punishment will be handed out to any family who thinks it can use this period of crisis as an excuse to get rid of a child born in some *other* year.

STORY BEHIND A CARTOON

Scratched on a back wall of Dudley Rigg's Café Espresso in Minneapolis is this legend: "Pray Frequently for Guindon's Well-Being." When *The Realist's* cartoonist laureate, Richard Guindon, sent me the cartoon on this page, my instinctive reaction was that there would undoubtedly be accusations of "sick humor." Although the satirical implications of a cartoon should be unnecessary to explain in an accompanying text, I thought I would share with you Guindon's response:

"The Blind Woman really exists, you know. She wears a sign made of paste-up letters very neatly asking if we thank God, etc. She bothered me for some reason. The average American is such a walking guilt-complex, anyway. Her logic seems to be this—'You can see only because God lets you. I can't. You owe God something, so give it to me. I'll split with him.' She is a self-proclaimed receptacle with a slot on the top of her head, placed here by the good Lord. Also, you see the implied threat, don't you? I give her some money (thereby acknowledging my guilt to everyone). 'See, I'm giving her 65ᶜ,' you scream at the sky. 'For the love of Christ, Jesus, don't strike me blind!' The cartoon came a few weeks after I had this thought."

BLIND RABBI TO SPEAK AT SERVICES FOR DEAF

by John LeGeyt

Message of Inspiration to Be Delivered by Harry Brevis of Hebrew Union College
—Los Angeles Times
January 4, 1964

Rabbi: My friends, although I cannot see you, I can. . . .

Host: Excuse me, Rabbi, but they're in the next room. We're just waiting here until they all get seated.

Rabbi: I was running over my lines.

Host: Oh. I'm terribly sorry!

Rabbi: I always run over my lines . . . to get the feel of them.

Host: A very good idea!

Rabbi: That was meant to be a joke.

Host: Oh yes, of course! Ha, ha, ha! *(Pause)* Ah, here we go . . . up three steps and then straight ahead.

* * *

Rabbi: My friends, although I cannot see you, I can sense your presence as if I had a thousand eyes.

1st Voice: Louder!

Rabbi (louder): I cannot see you, my friends, but I can sense your presence as if I had a thousand eyes.

2nd Voice: What'd he say about sending presents?

3rd Voice: Christ, I don't know. What's his name, anyway?

2nd Voice: What?

1st Voice: Louder! We can't hear!

Host (whispering): They can't hear you in the back.

Rabbi (feeling at microphone hung around his neck): Isn't this a mike?

Host: Hsst! I'm over *here.* Yes, but it's for a tape recorder. You'll have to shout.

Rabbi (shouting): I cannot hear you my friends, but I can sense your presence as if I had a thousand eyes.

Host (loud whisper): "See!"

Rabbi: What? What?

Host: "I cannot *see* you!"

Rabbi: What in Heaven's name are you talking about?

1st Voice: Louder! We can't hear you!

2nd Voice: I wish we'd gone to the ball game!

3rd Voice: You're the Jew. I just came along because you asked me to.

2nd Voice: What?

Host: You made a mistake. You said "hear" instead of "see."

Rabbi: I'm beginning to think it doesn't make any difference.

1st Voice: Louder!

Other Voices: Louder! Louder!

Rabbi (shouting): Can you hear me now?

Voices: Yes! Yes!

3rd Voice: Saturday! What day'd you *think* it was?

Rabbi (shouting): I can sense your presence as if I had a thousand eyes! For I see you with my open soul, and it is the soul which is the great perceiver.

3rd Voice: Did he say "deceiver?"

2nd Voice: No, "believer."

4th Voice: All I can hear is ball game scores.

3rd Voice: You're plugged into my transistor.

2nd Voice: Whose sister? What in hell are you guys talking about?

Rabbi: The voice of God speaks out of blackness and silence.

1st Voice: Louder!

Rabbi (shouting): God speaks of blackness and silence.

Host: Sst! "Out of!"

Rabbi: Out of what?

Host: "Out of blackness and silence."

Rabbi: Well, I'm glad somebody heard me.

1st Voice: Louder!

Rabbi (shouting): I'm glad somebody heard me!

3rd Voice: Sarcastic bastard, ain't he?

2nd Voice: What are you, some kinda anti-Semite?

PENNIES FROM HEAVEN

An editorial titled "Not in Vain" in *Underseas Technology* ("The Magazine of Oceanography, Marine Sciences, and Underwater Defense") states:

"Regard for the *Thresher* and her crew goes far beyond the sphere of personal sentiment. It embodies all that men have lived and died for in the past, and all they will sacrifice for in the future."

However, despite the description of "a whole world down on its knees to mourn this handful of men," there are those whose reaction at best was one of ambivalence. For they play the numbers, and their bets are based on tragedy. Those who continued to gamble on the number of crew members who lost their lives on the *Thresher*—129—became the lucky winners only two days after the worst peacetime submarine disaster in history.

150

RAPE VICTIM

Editors note: Senator Goldwater was referring to the case of Arlene del Fava of Queens, N.Y., who was arrested for carrying an illegal weapon; she had used a switchblade knife on her attempted rapist. The Realist assigned Larry Siegel to interview the district attorney.

Q. *Sir, would you explain the weapons law of New York State?*

A. Certainly. A woman may legally defend herself against a rapist or mugger with a hatpin, a carving knife, or a Boy Scout knife.

Q. *What about a switchblade knife?*

A. That's illegal because it's a concealed weapon.

Q. *Why can't a woman carry a concealed weapon to defend herself with?*

A. Well, we feel that everyone is equal in the eyes of the law. And by carrying a concealed weapon she wouldn't be giving the rapist a fair chance.

Q. *I see . . . What will happen to the woman in Queens who stabbed the rapist with a switchblade knife?*

A. She'll be tried for carrying a concealed weapon.

Q. *What about the rapist?*

A. Oh, we've got nothing on him.

Q. *How come?*

A. Well, you see, at the time of his attack on the woman, the weapon he was using wasn't concealed.

I WANNA HOLD YOUR BEDSHEET

This is not science fiction. Except for a nice little old lady from the *New York World-Telegram & Sun* (who wrote a nice little old lady story) and NBC-TV cameramen (who shot just a few minutes of film), I was the only reporter present, unless you want to count a pair of naive British teenage girls covering the event for a naive British teenage magazine called *Fab* (not to be confused with a sophisticated American detergent of the same name).

New Ideas, Inc. was auctioning off some used items they had purchased from the Riviera Hotel at Kennedy Airport, where the Beatles stayed. Namely (sing to the tune of "The 12 Days of Christmas"):

    8 face towels
    8 bath towels
    4 bath mats
    8 assorted cakes of soap
    8 sheets
    8 pillow cases
    8 knives
    8 forks
    16 teaspoons
    4 dinner plates
    8 small plates
    4 salad plates
    3 serving trays
    4 cups
    4 saucers
    16 glasses
    4 salt and pepper shakers
    8 ash trays
    12 assorted soda bottles

And 300 screaming Lolitoids, off on a fetishist's holiday. Obviously there wouldn't be enough items to go around, but it was announced that the Beatles' unwashed towels and bed linens were to be cut up into two-inch squares and sold for $1 each. The price included a notarized statement of authenticity.

It was a surrealistic study in contrast to watch all these young chickies in training bras suddenly confronted with a lawyer's jargon:

" . . . Lou Barney, being duly sworn, deposes and says: 1. That he is the manager of Riviera Idlewild Hotel. 2. That said hotel is located at the Kennedy International Airport. . . . 3. That on September the 20th and 21st, 1964, the four members of the famous Beatles were guests at the Riviera Idlewild Hotel. During said period the Beatles occupied rooms in said hotel and also used other facilities of the hotel including the service of food to them. 4. Charnate, Inc., the owner of the Hotel, has sold to Ron Delsener the (specifically enumerated) items used by the Beatles on the occasion of their said visit to the hotel as guests thereof as aforesaid. . . . 5. This affidavit certifies the fact that each of the foregoing items, sold as aforesaid to Ron Delsener, was used by a member of the Beatles during their said visit."

This could be the start of a nationwide trend.

A pair of Chicago television directors took a trip to Detroit and paid $400 to the Whittier Hotel for unlaundered bed linens; and to Kansas City where they paid $750 to the Muelbach Hotel, which had played host to the Beatles for *two* nights.

The bed-stripping ceremonies were properly attended by attorneys and witnesses. The sheets yielded six thousand *one*-inch squares—a grand total of 150,000—mounted on parchment over the drawing of a four-poster, marked "Suitable for Framing," and sealed with the appropriate affidavits in envelopes

I Wanna Hold Your Bedsheet, *continued*

on which were printed a message that would spur the curiosity of even the most jaded postman: "Valuable Bedsheet—Do Not Fold."

The pillowcases were put into a bank vault, to be turned over to charity.

The auction in New York City ("Proceeds will aid the American Guild of Variety Artists' Youth Fund") took place at the Palm Gardens Ballroom, which usually houses the meetings of labor unions, Hadassah, and opera workshops.

Strolling among the virtually all-female would-be bidders was a lone 17-year-old male.

"I came down here for phone numbers," he told me. "It's so weird. I didn't wanna spread the action, but when there's *this* many girls around, it's better to have a coupla guys with you. Five more phone numbers would put me over the top—I have ninety-six in my little black book now—I crashed the Beatles concert at the Paramount and got thirteen there."

I wondered about what use he made of these phone numbers.

"I take the girls out on dates and then I classify them as 'prudes' or 'tramps' or 'she-loves-me-maybe.'"

I wondered about the *tramps* designation.

"Well," he explained, "that's what they're called by the guys in my age group. She *gives*—you know what I mean?"

I wondered *where* they give.

"There's a park around my way. And the movies, except you can't go all the way in the movies."

—B. Kliban

I wondered about contraception.

"I buy a box of Trojans or Sheiks at the beginning of the month," he said. "I go to a drugstore downtown; not in my own neighborhood—I'd feel funny...."

The auctioneer said, "Good afternoon" into the microphone. The girls shrieked. The Burns guards carried onto the stage cardboard cartons containing the unlaundered linens. The girls screamed louder. When the sheets were actually displayed, the girls emitted a mass siren of hysteria. It was one of the most frightening sounds I have ever heard. I swear, chills ran through me. Girls were pulling their own hair with excitement. They tried to rush on stage.

"I want to make an emphatic statement," the man at the microphone yelled. "If you girls act the way you do, there will be no auction! Please act like ladies!"

At that moment someone started playing a Beatles record over the public address system—presumably in the hope of soothing the savage beastlets—but they became even wilder.

"The first young lady that doesn't behave will be taken out by the officers! The Beatles are not here, so relax!" He held up an ashtray. "It still has the cigarette stains," he informed them. They screamed. And so the auction began.

"A knife, fork and spoon used by Paul McCartney—25¢...$1...$1.50...$3...$4...$5...$6...$6.25...$6.50...$6.75...$8...$9...$9.25...Going *once* at $9.25... going *twice* at $9.25... *Sold!*"

And a little girl from Brooklyn, wearing glasses and clutching her wallet, had bought the most expensive set of silverware she'll ever have.

"A Coke bottle that went into the lips of Ringo Starr—$1...$1.50...$1.75...$3...$3.50...$4...$4.50...$5...$5.25...$5.50...$5.75...$6...Going *once* at $6...Going *twice* at $6...*Sold!*"

A 14-year-old took her just-purchased property and walked back to her chair with a dazed expression. "I don't believe it," she kept repeating. "I don't believe it." Her friends asked if they could please touch her unique treasure.

"A salt and pepper shaker set used by

"He loves me ... He loves me not ... He loves me ..."

George Harrison—$5...$6...$6.25...$6.50...$6.75...$7...$7.50...$8...$8.25...$8.50...$8.75...$9...Going *once* at $9...Going *twice* at $9...*Sold!*"

I asked the winning bidder if she planned to use the prized salt and pepper on her food.

"Just once, on my supper tonight," she replied. "Then I'm gonna put them in a glass cage forever and ever. Ohhh, I'm *so* happy!"

The TV men had arrived, and the auctioneer called out to the girls: "Do you like the Beatles?" They shrieked, jumping up and down in affirmation, as the film rolled.

A girl bought John Lennon's plate. I asked if she planned to use it herself.

"Are you kidding?" she responded. "There's still things left on it. If I eat, then it would go away."

The time came at last for pillowcases and sheets and towels. Pandemonium broke out.

"Sit back and relax," the auctioneer yelled. They didn't. "When I tell you to sit down, I mean sit down!" They sat down. A few mothers had come with their daughters, and one remarked to me: "I'm a schoolteacher—the kids should behave so well in school."

Before the cutting of the linens began, some items were auctioned off whole. Ringo's towel, for example, went at $8. And then finally . . .

"Form five lines," the auctioneer said into the microphone—"what is it, five Beatles or four Beatles?" The girls booed him. They called him a fake, a fink, and other charming names. "Cut!" he yelled back, like an angry movie director. "Cut!"

He finally got the girls to move their chairs back and form four lines—one for each Beatle. They were more clusters than lines, to be accurate. Said one young lady: "Wow, you have to go through the Supreme Court to get a piece of towel."

The Burns guards stood on stage, each holding a picture of a different Beatle, as the promoters worked their scissors away. "Who wants Ringo?" "Who wants John?" "Give me a George!" "One George coming up!"

The girls queried each other as to whether the merchandise had actually been used by the Beatles.

"I hope it's really theirs." "Couldn't they go to jail if it wasn't?" "We're minors, we can't sue." "But they give you affidavits." "No, that thing's just printed up."

I was about to expound on Zen in the art of Placebo when there was a hurried movement behind the curtain on stage. A girl had snuck up and gotten a large piece of sheet. She was chased by a promoter and a Burns guard. They caught her, but the rest of the girls mobbed around, pulling, screaming, clawing. It was an incipient riot.

As though competing in some strange summer-camp-color-war game that had perforce become a major Olympic event, the promoter managed to make his way back to the stage, dragging the mobettes behind him.

Later, when it was all over, another promoter said to me, "I've been sick about this for three weeks now. I hated to take their money. They were coming up on stage and counting out nickels and dimes. Eight dollars for a dirty towel. I'm telling you, this has made me pretty sick."

But, of course, if he hadn't done it, someone else would've.

We were now standing in the lobby. The auction was over, and the girls were waiting outside the locked glass doors, ready to pounce on the remaining linens when the promoters and the Burns guards carried the merchandise to their car.

Our culture had finally come to this: a group of grown men cowering in fear as they sought to protect themselves and their property from a crowd of insecure young girls who, in but a matter of years, would become registered voters and trusting consumers.

The 17-year-old male had gotten six new telephone numbers.

I wondered what the *really* lucky girls were going to do with their coveted Coca-Cola bottles.

AN OBITUARY FOR LENNY BRUCE

Lenny Bruce and John F. Kennedy had something in common. They were both great cocksmen. I couldn't help thinking, among the other thoughts one has at the death of a friend, that there must have been a special throb of mourning among all the ladies who had been limited partners in the countless less-than-one-night stands of comedian and President alike.

Lenny once told me that the role of a comedian was to make the audience laugh "at a minimum of, on the average, once every 15 seconds—or let's be liberal to escape the hue and cry of the injured, and say one laugh every 25 seconds . . ."

More and more, though, he began to get so serious during performances that it was obvious he wasn't even *hoping* to get a laugh every 15-25 seconds. I asked him about this apparent inconsistency with his previous definition of the comedian's role.

"Yes, but I'm changing," he replied.

"What do you mean?"

"I'm not a comedian. I'm Lenny Bruce."

Often an audience would *assume* he was trying to be funny. For example, when Gary Cooper died, Bruce was touched by the *New York Daily News* headline, "The Last Roundup," and he mentioned this to the audience. They laughed, of course. And when he happened to hear on the radio a rock 'n' roll song, "There's a Rose in Spanish Harlem," he bought the record and came on stage with a phonograph and he *played* it. "Listen to these lyrics," he told the audience. "This is like a Puerto Rican *Porgy and Bess*." They laughed, of course.

At this stage of his career, he would still utter only relative euphemisms like "frigging" once in a while. It was fun being with Lenny Bruce those days. In a Minneapolis museum, he improvised a treatise on the symbolism of a piece of abstract sculpture; it was actually a fire extinguisher. In Milwaukee, we decided to have Chinese food one afternoon. We got into a cab, and I asked the driver if he knew of a good Chinese restaurant. Lenny told him: "Take us to where all the Chinese truckdrivers go."

In Milwaukee three plainclothed policemen went into his dressing room, kicked a musician out, and told Bruce that he was not to talk about politics or religion or sex, or they'd yank him right off the stage. The night before, a group of 28 Catholics had signed a complaint about his act, which they'd gone to see voluntarily. Lenny was scared. He toned down his act slightly. One of the cops was even smiling at some of the stuff. They told him later that he shouldn't say "son-of-a-bitch" (in his impression of a white-collar drunk).

I asked him why he didn't take any legal action.

"Nah, they'd just say I was trying to get publicity. You know: 'Say anything you want about me, but be sure to spell my name right.' "

They spelled his name right in Philadelphia. He was arrested on a phony narcotics charge. The case was dismissed, but a prominent attorney had attempted a $10,000 shakedown, and Bruce's Spencer Tracy image was shattered. That was the start of his legal career.

There was a time when Lenny read a lot, from Jean-Paul Sartre's study of anti-Semitism to the latest girlie magazine. He carried in his suitcase from city to city a double-volume unabridged dictionary. But in his dying days, he carried around law books instead. And he wasn't as much fun to be with any more.

I remember I was on my way to his hotel in San Francisco, and I passed a barber shop in Chinatown where a sort of Oriental Nairobi Trio was inside making the most charming music I've ever heard—like a jazzed-up version of *"Bei Mir Bist Du Schoen"*—with violin, guitar, and bass fiddle. The owner let me in, whispered that he wouldn't give me a haircut, and I sat down and listened. It was one of those rare, rare moments. I haven't gone to a concert since.

I told Lenny about it, observing that there was a time he would have stopped in that barber shop and listened, and he would have dug that scene with all his soul. But no more. He was too involved with his court cases. So there was no more digging of the scene outside himself.

"But," he reminded me, "I'm fighting for ten years of my life!"

He was right. These punishments can become abstractions quickly enough for the rest of us, but ten years of compulsory rehabilitation *was* ten years of his life, and maybe the prospect *could* somehow interfere with one's free-form style of living.

A few years before, I had overheard the following conversation in a Milwaukee night club:

"Nobody knows where Lenny Bruce is staying."

"He's staying at the Y."

"What does he do there?"

"They say he reads a lot."

"He's gonna read himself right out of a job."

In a way this was an accurate prediction, because Lenny found that novelists didn't have to say "frig" any more. He began to want the same privilege of non-restriction. His point of view was the same on stage and off, and he wanted to talk to his friends in the night club with the same freedom of vocabulary he could exercise in someone's living room.

But Lenny wasn't exactly like a book. He finally realized that. "If a book is obscene in Georgia," he said, "it'll be obscene in Bellmore, Long Island. No, it doesn't work that way. Fortunately, the law is not a punishment instrument. It always protects. If the book is obscene in Georgia, and the book is not obscene in Bellmore, Long Island, the Supreme Court don't make no never mind, because the police can arrest you every day no matter what you say because they found that what you say is erratic. One day you say 'Pray for Chessman' and next day you say 'Lynch Gilligan.' "

And, it's safe to speculate, Lenny's "obscenity" was a convenient rationalization to arrest him for saying such things as

"Cardinal Spellman looks like Shirley Temple."

Lenny fantasized the following courtroom dialogue (though the first line was borrowed from reality).

Prosecutor: Your honor, this man made a mockery of the Church, not just the Catholic Church, but the Lutheran Church—the Church itself—he made a vulgar and obscene mockery.

Judge: Any lesbian that's found guilty of rape, no matter how good a tough-looking bitch she is—one of the elements of rape will be that there's penetration, and if there is none, the bench says "Fuck you, counsel."

Prosecutor: Your honor, I've never heard such language in the court in my life.

Judge: The use of foul and coarse language will not constitute obscenity if it is used as a realistic portrayal, and Cardinal Spellman is modeling for a Barbie Doll. He looks like he's made out of celluloid to me.

The real courtroom was just as absurd.

In New York, an expert witness for the prosecution, Ernest van den Haag, who writes for *National Review* and teaches a course at The New School titled "The Crisis of the Individual," was testifying about contemporary community standards and said that he's made a study of night clubs although he hasn't been inside one for 20 years.

Defense attorney Ephraim London conceded that Judge Murtagh might never have visited a prostitute to gain his knowledge of *that* field, and yes-man Judge Phipps pointed out "so the record will be clear" that London was referring to Murtagh's book, *Cast the First Stone*.

Not being a whore, however, Lenny Bruce didn't arouse enough sympathy from those two on the three-judge panel to acquit him. His monologues, they stated, contained anecdotes and reflections that were obscene. They listed the following examples, quoted verbatim from their decision:

1. Eleanor Roosevelt and her display of "tits."

2. Jacqueline Kennedy "hauling ass" at the moment of the late President's assassination.

3. St. Paul giving up "fucking."

4. An accident victim—who lost a foot in the accident—who made sexual advances to a nurse, while in the ambulance taking him to the hospital.

5. Uncle Willie discussing the "apples" of a 12-year-old girl.

6. Seemingly sexual intimacy with a chicken.

7. "Pissing in the sink" and "pissing" from a building's ledge.

8. The verb "to come," with its obvious reference to sexual orgasm.

9. The reunited couple discussing adulteries committed during their separation, and the suggestion of a wife's denial of infidelity, even when discovered by her husband.

10. "Shoving" a funnel of hot lead "up one's ass."

11. The story dealing with the masked man, Tonto, and an unnatural sex act.

12. Mildred Babe Zaharias and the "dyke profile of 1939."

The court further stated that "The dominant theme of the performances appealed to the prurient interest"—later contradicting this by saying that "The monologues were not erotic. They were not lust-inciting, but, while they did not arouse sex, they insulted sex and debased it."

The judges added that "The performances were lacking in 'redeeming social importance' " and that "The monologues contained little or no literary or artistic merit. They were merely a device to enable Bruce to exploit the use of obscene language. They were devoid of any cohesiveness. They were a series of unconnected items that contain little of social significance. They were chaotic, haphazard, and inartful." If Lenny Bruce has gone to Hell, the devil will have been replaced by an art critic wearing black judicial robes.

The law states that to be obscene, material must be *utterly without any* redeeming social importance. Therefore, if *one single person* felt that Bruce's performances had *the slightest bit* of redeeming social importance—and there were several who so testified—then he should have been found not guilty.

If I ever end up in court on anything, I'll probably get a haircut, and wear a white shirt and tie, and swear on the Bible, because I don't have the guts to be as consistent as Lenny was—in faded blue denims and long sideburns, calling the oath a farce. He always wanted to win purely on the basis of the law, and so he was willing to risk losing purely on the basis of prejudice by judge or jury. For, a sub-theme of Bruce's work had always been that people get indignant over the wrong issues.

During one of the performances for which he was arrested, he made that point thusly: "If a titty is bloodied and maimed, it's clean; but if the titty is pretty it's dirty. And that's why you never find any atrocity photos at obscenity trials, with distended stomachs and ripped-up breasts. . . ." In the course of that same performance, he also said, "Query: If a tape recording is my voice, are they using me to testify against myself, since it's my voice that would indict me?"

Lenny asked me, "Can you imagine them playing *that* in court?" This was months later, in his dingy hotel room, cluttered with tapes and transcripts and photostats and law journals and briefs. "I love the law," he said.

Only, his love had developed into an obsession. Once, when he was teasing his 8-year-old daughter by pretending not to believe what she was telling him, she said, "Daddy, you'd believe me if it was on tape."

As more and more night club owners became more and more afraid to hire him, he devoted more and more of his time and energy to the law. When he finally did get a weekend booking in Monterey, he remarked, "I feel like it's taking me away from my work."

He would let almost nothing interrupt his practice, not even sleeping or eating. He turned down an invitation to be on the Les Crane show. He refused to be the subject of a *New Yorker* profile. He wouldn't give Lillian Ross even 15 minutes of his time.

Lenny Bruce's formal education never went beyond grammar school—but he became something of a limited legal genius. His research uncovered an amendment to New York's statute 1140a—under which he was arrested—which *excludes* actors from arrest in an indecent performance. The law had been misapplied to him.

And so he spent Thanksgiving Day looking for a judge to help him. He still had dreams of Lewis Stone from the old Andy Hardy movies.

"If I win," he asked me, "what do I win?" He answered himself: "The right to work." He had borrowed $5,000 to advertise 5-performances-only, and then the theatre owner refused to open the premises for the first show on Thanksgiving Eve.

Lenny could still make fun of his predicament. "I was thinking of going on welfare," he commented.

On stage he would have mumbled through boredom some old bits, he would have created some new material (on his bed there was a clipping about how Philadelphia officials had decided that anyone wearing blackface in the Mummers Parade this year would be ineligible for a prize), but mostly he would have lectured about law enforcement and courtroom procedures and statutory subleties. He had always talked about his environment, and it was just that these things had increasingly *become* his environment.

Outside the court, he was Lenny the Hermit, confining himself to his home in Hollywood Hills, with a barbed wire fence but an open gate, visited by friends, hangers-on and peace officers harassing him as they stood near the unused pool. And his mother would bring over his daughter. Lenny would have been up all night with his legal conflicts, stopping only to eat some grapes and work on landscaping his garden although rain was pouring down hard and he would end up all muddy ("But if I go to jail, I want to have it finished")—and then in the morning he would take a shower with his daughter. He didn't want her to grow up thinking there was something dirty about the human body.

On a rare occasion, he left his house to be in the audience at my *Evening With a Self-Styled Phony* at the Steve Allen Playhouse. During the question-and-answer session following my ramblings, he asked me to clarify what I had said about trying to empathize with people with perversions. So I gave as a for-instance the time in a subway when I let myself get aroused by an elderly lady whose buttocks were unavoidably rubbing against me. Lenny called out, "You're sick!" The audience howled, I said "Thank you, Mr. President," and that ended *that* show.

In New York, the judges ordered him to undergo a psychiatric examination before they passed sentence. "Watch," Lenny told me, chuckling—but also with genuine terror—"they're gonna say I have a persecution complex."

The first issue of *The Realist* quoted Malcolm Muggeridge, former editor of *Punch*: "As I see it, the only pleasure of living is that every joke should be made, every thought expressed, every line of investigation, irrespective of its direction, pursued to the uttermost limits that human ingenuity, courage and understanding can take it. The moment that limits are set . . . then the flavor is gone." More than anyone else I've ever known, Lenny Bruce lived up to that ideal; but now the flavor will never be the same, for *he* is gone.

When the newspapers called me at 3 o'clock that cold December morning for a statement, I simply said: "It was God's will."

AN IMPOLITE INTERVIEW WITH WOODY ALLEN

Q. *Hey, I thought you didn't smoke?*

A. I originally did smoke, when I was young. Then I started increasing my smoking a lot, and then I began to see where it was going to be trouble for me, and I stopped smoking. I didn't smoke for years, and the day the Surgeon-General's report came out that you could die from smoking, I started smoking again. Not consciously for that reason. I felt a tremendous urge to have a cigarette that day. And I haven't stopped smoking since.

Q. *Okay, I'm not going to ask you how you got started, or why you switched from writing to performing—I know you've been asked those questions before—*

A. I've answered them an unbelievable amount of times. I've been back in the country just about ten days and I've had about six interviews with major newspapers, and they ask the *exact* same questions.

Q. *All right, I'll start off with a question I don't think you've ever been asked: If your own personal Utopia were realized, would you still feel somehow that you were an imposter?*

A. You mean if things outside of myself got to be good? Because my own personal Utopia can exist within a bleak society. I just need a few things to satisfy my own personal needs, and society can be disintegrating around me and I can still be living in a moron's paradise. I'm not dependent on an external happy society for my own greedy little Utopia.

Q. *You don't get depressed by national events, tragedies, injustices—*

A. I'm not *fond* of them. But they don't relate directly to my own personal little Utopia. I consider them completely separate. But, yes, I do get upset by injustice and all that jazz.

Q. *How do you escape—or would you prefer withdraw?*

A. I guess "withdraw" is better. Total avoidance, is really what it is. I get up in the morning, throw myself into work, and stay in, listen to records. Withdrawal is the best thing. I don't mix in, except I occasionally contribute money anonymously to organizations that actively fight the battle.

Q. *Specifically?*

A. American Civil Liberties Union, all kinds of little groups that are seeking out cures for a cold, that seem like they're doing a good job. I contribute, or help, or do benefits when asked. But I don't get involved personally. The way I've always seen it, I'm just absolutely a comedian. And the only thing that I can do for them is lend my services or contribute money.

Q. *But it's not in your psychological make-up to carry a picket sign?*

A. Not really. The closest I came to that was at the integration March on Washington, but I doubt if I was noticed or anything.

Q. *I was there, too—*

A. You didn't see me, did you?

Q. *Johnny Carson has said that his show is more effective* than birth control pills. Do you think late-night TV has actually affected the sex life of people?

A. It has certainly not improved mine in any way. I mean, if you really want to make love, and the Johnny Carson show stands in your way—you know, it's a pretty tepid urge. Either you would do it before the Carson show . . . "Let's get it in quickly—"

Q. *Yeah, you know, "Hurry up, because here's Johnny!" That doesn't make for very spontaneous sex.*

A. I'm not one for spontaneity in sexual relations. I find them pleasant under any kind of circumstances, whether they're spontaneous, planned, late at night when you're tired. As far as that goes, that's like improvised comedy. If it's funny, I don't care how long you planned it. And the same thing with sex.

Q. *You know, there's a compromise solution, actually. People might be more apt to try new positions so that they can copulate and watch Carson at the same time.*

A. But I doubt seriously whether the Carson show or any late-night television has had, except in very, *very* rare cases, any significant influence on sexual habits. I say this without any knowledge of it, I'm just using a common-sense guess.

Q. *Maybe I'll request the readers to send in—you know, an informal survey—*

A. But the readers that will send in—no, it's not really a random sample.

Q. *Incidentally, an interesting sidelight about Dorothy Kilgallen: Les Crane, who is a competitor of Johnny Carson—they're on the same time slot—made a little reference on his show, congratulating Carson for the way he handled "that unpleasant lady"—and the audience applauded. But I have a feeling that the same audience would applaud when she's introduced on* What's My Line?

A. I never trust studio applause, because I've worked in too many studios, and they always have that little button. You press it and the applause sign lights up, and people applaud. But if you say something that sounds like there's some kind of spice behind it, or some note of crusade in it, or taking of a stand, there's a tendency to applaud.

I think that it sort of happens in a numbing kind of dream for them. Someone says something in a certain tone of voice, and you sit there and applaud it. I'm sure if I were sitting in an audience, I'd find myself applauding, too. Someone would say, "Now, introducing on my left, Miss Dorothy Kilgallen," and I would applaud. And another time someone would say, "But she's written an unfair thing about me in the paper," and I would applaud that. It's safer to applaud *anything*, now that I think of it.

Q. *The frightening thing is when people applaud commercials.*

A. Are they cued? Once they're cued, there's a different psychology completely. You do get a sense of contributing to the whole program.

Q. You also get a sense of not being different.

A. Yeah, you can sit there, ornery, and not applaud if you want to, but it's a meager protest.

Q. I wonder if there are people at home who applaud?

A. There are people that *sing* along on those kind of shows. And there are people that *say* your act along with you—people that hear your record album, or have seen you do the bit before. You'll see someone leaning forward with body English, and he'll mouth along with you.

Q. The irony of that whole Kilgallen thing is that you're not generally thought of as—in fact, you've even been criticized for not being—a controversial comedian.

A. I resent ever being judged by a set of criteria that have no relation to anything I'm trying to do. I think that a comedian *strictly* should go for laughs, and as far as social meaning or anything like that, that's *purely* secondary. I think *That Was the Week That Was* made a terrible mistake by putting what they felt to be social meaning ahead of entertainment.

And so when I appear, all I want to do is get laughs. I couldn't care less that I'm not dealing with integration or politics or anxiety in the nuclear age—it just couldn't interest me less. All I want to do is get laughs in the same sense that Groucho Marx got them—you know, just pull down my pants, or say any kind of joke I want—but I don't like to be criticized or even spoken about as a social critic or commentator.

I think this applies to all contemporary comedians, too. With Lenny Bruce, Mort Sahl—they're primarily, when they're successful, funny men. When I go and see any of them, to the extent that they make me laugh, they're successful as far as *I'm* concerned. The thing about them is that they *are* funny men. They're comedians first.

There's a tremendous tendency for comedians to substitute very tangible issues, for the more *difficult* thing of being funny, which you can't influence yourself. That is, someone is either born funny, or he's not—I believe. And it's frustrating if you want to be a comedian and you *weren't* born funny. So they feel that if they do six integration jokes and five Medicare jokes, they're involving themselves in what contemporary comedians sound like. What's important to note is that the comment a comedian makes is not an external comment. For instance, the Marx Brothers will do *A Night at the Opera*, but they're not standing there saying, "Opera is this," or, "Pomposity is that." They just go for laughs, and you come away never really being able to look at an opera in the same way again.

I find the same thing is true with Lenny Bruce, with Mort Sahl—they influence your way of looking at life. It's not what they say that does it; it's a certain image they make that you respond to or don't respond to, that's all.

Q. Even though you aren't controversial, you've had your share of censorship problems.

A. Mostly connected with television. You don't have too much censorship in a club. But on television, I've been bleeped out occasionally. And it's odd what they take offense at. I used the term "rhythmic birth control" on television, and they edited out the word "rhythmic," which I thought was really strange.

Q. In President Johnson's birth control program, the Cath-olic Church wants to edit in "rhythm"—to qualify it. Didn't taking the word out spoil what you were saying?

A. It rendered the joke completely meaningless.

Q. And yet people at home could see the studio audience laughing, and they'd figure, well, it must be funny.

A. Yes, that's exactly what happened. The joke was, "She was practicing with her husband rhythmic birth control and apparently they couldn't keep a beat." And so the joke on television went, "She was practicing with her husband birth control and apparently they couldn't keep a beat."

Q. It sounds more obscene that way.

A. I haven't had a tremendous amount of censorship on television, but what always struck me is the things that they found censorable. On television in London, they have a little more trouble with sex, but they can poke fun at religion, which we couldn't get away with at all. It's really amazing. They come out and they *shpritz* the Pope. And not just jokes. They treat him like he's a comic figure with things that we couldn't even *approach* on American television. On the other hand, I said on TV in London "advanced fondling," and there was a tremendous amount of shock about the word *fondling*, which here I said on television many times and haven't had any difficulty at all.

Q. One word they edit out a lot on TV is "God"—and a kid who could figure out what was being said would begin to think that God is a dirty word.

A. Yes, you can't say "God" on television.

Q. Except on Sunday mornings.

A. But you can't use it in joke terms. I've had to substitute the Bible for God on television. Not an offensive joke. I once used a line on television—"The Ten Commandments say 'Thou shalt not commit adultery,' but New York State says you have to, and for a while there it's a tossup between God and Rockefeller" but—I had to say "between *the Bible* and Rockefeller." It's a strange code.

Q. You're allowed to mention the Book but not the Author. There's another kind of TV censorship, in effect—where you just aren't invited to perform.

A. Yes. The first time I ever appeared on the Jack Paar show, I did my sex-and-food bit, about these islands where sex was fine and very open and progressive, but food was a dirty subject. The material describes their sexual attitude only as it relates to food.

Little strange guys run up to you on the street, saying, "Hey, buddy, how'd you like to get a rye bread?" and "I can get you a picture of a grilled cheese sandwich." And women there will eat a bagel and won't put cream cheese on it. And if you ask them why, they say, "Well, I don't do that."

A guy at a convention checked into a hotel, and had the elevator operator fix him up with a mixed green salad. And he ate the salad in the middle of the night and he put on his clothes and he went home. And he said "It was a very empty experience. . . ." That's the general tenor of it.

I did it for Paar's staff, and they all loved it and said that's absolutely the thing to do, so I did it on the show and got very big laughs with it. But Paar, who had never heard it, was offended by it, and I didn't work his show again for years. I only began to be eligible for it again when I began to make some sort of a breakthrough for myself as a comedian, but all those nights when he had the late-night television show, I was sort of *persona non grata.*

Q. How about censorship you faced as a TV writer?

A. I didn't have real *censorship* problems. I'd bring in my idea, or a sketch, and used to get a lot of reasons why we couldn't do them. One thing that comes to mind was that the Garry Moore show didn't want to mention Khrushchev.

Q. And the Communists won't mention him now. Hmmmmm . . .

A. My censorship problems on TV writing were much milder because it never *got* that far. I didn't bother to bring in things that I knew I was going to have trouble with. Often, writers will tell me—and I have done it myself—you over-anticipate. You find yourself sitting in a room and you come up with an idea and you say, "Nah, I better not do that, it's a very touchy area," because you've been so brainwashed. And yet nobody—not the sponsors, not the advertising agency—would even dream of censoring it.

Q. You've just gotten back from making your film in Paris; was it interesting working with stripteasers there?

A. It was *completely* asexual. It's like a chef working in a kitchen, you know? It ruined the entire experience for me. I worked on *Pussycat* with *dozens* of the world's most beautiful models—the girls were dressed, the girls were *un*dressed, as they can be in France, and it was just a totally immunizing experience. I would be in a room with five strippers who had no clothes on, and there was no sex involved. It didn't have a tenth of the sexuality if you're sitting in a room with a secretary and her dress drifts up over her knee—it suddenly becomes violent to the point of attempted rape. But with these girls—and they were *all* pretty—it was like working out in a gym or something.

Q. Do you think your analyst here in the States thought about you while you were away?

A. I have no way of knowing, and he won't crack at all. I try and get it out of him in all kinds of ways. But I can't imagine that I could have been off his mind totally for six months.

Q. How has being a celebrity changed your life?

A. I have more money. I get recognized. And I work more frequently. But none of the *internals* get changed, and that's what really kills you. You get in trouble with a better class of women, that's all that happens. Years ago, I lived in a tiny one-room apartment and went out with fairly drab women. Now I come in contact with more exciting women, but the problems are still the same. I may get a suit custom-made, but I still can't relate to the tailor. I can afford a car but I don't buy one because I have too many emotional problems driving. You know, all the things just recur on a higher economic scale.

Q. How often do you think about dying?

A. Once a day. My main preoccupations are, I would say, sex and death.

Q. Oh, well, I have a quote here that, in a way, combines your two preoccupations. This is from an article in Commentary *Magazine: "Though [sex] promises the suspension of time, no other event so sharply advises us of the oppressiveness of time. Sex offers itself as an alternative world, but when the act is over and the immodesty of this offering is exposed, it is the sheer worldliness of the world we briefly relin-*

quished and must now re-enter that has to be confronted anew."

A. There's a tendency, I think, to over-elaborate sex and death in the same sense that they do comedy. A comedian is someone who goes out and goes for a couple of laughs, makes a few faces, and you either laugh or you don't. Groucho Marx told me that he and his brothers would do their act, and they were barely getting by in a boarding house when they were starting, and all they wanted to do was tear up the place and be funny, but guys were writing, you know, there's a deep psychological significance . . . and I find sex is a simple, pleasurable experience. And I hate to read into it, all the things that they do. The same thing with death. Do you know what I mean?

Q. Death is a simple, pleasurable experience?

A. You know, I divorced my wife because she was a Philosophy major. All discussions of sex or death or comedy or religion are after the fact; all that these philosophers and intellectuals do—they see what we all see, and then they describe it. This is like something you can read on the train, but in actuality it has no relation to reality. Norman Mailer finds one thing, and Albert Ellis finds one thing, and everybody who thinks and describes these things finds their own conclusions, and their conclusions nullify the conclusions of the generation before them and will be nullified by the generation after them.

Q. What's your own favorite hypocrisy?

A. Wanting to be an intellectual and an *avant garde*ist, one of those people who stands around the lobby of art movie houses, you know, sipping coffee while waiting for the picture to go on, talking about Humphrey Bogart as a great cinematic artist and all that—and a tremendous sense of the ridiculousness of that and resentment toward it.

Q. Do you do it?

A. Occasionally I'll slip into it. Occasionally I'll find myself getting pedantic. You know, people want to go out to California and write a tremendous paper on the art of Margaret Dumont in the Marx Brothers movies; my tendency is to say, "Yes, she really contributed." But I have a tendency to fall into that myself. I'll get carried away and find myself discussing Ingmar Bergman in terms that would never have even occurred to Bergman himself.

Q. What is your philosophy of party-going?

A. That also comes under hypocrisy to a degree. Basically I'm not too fond of them, because I don't feel comfortable at them, but an occasional party is not really as bad as everybody makes out. I mean whenever you say the word "parties," all you hear is "I hate parties, I can't stand parties." I *don't* hate parties. I like to *say* I hate them, but when I actually think of it, occasionally I *don't* hate them. It's just that nothing ever happens. Whenever I go to a party I always drift off into one corner—you know, like Montgomery Clift—try and look pensive and I thumb the backs of leatherbound volumes I've never read, in the hopes that some really fantastic woman—flowing black hair and diaphanous gown and black eye-patch—would come up and ask me what I'm brooding about. But so far, no one ever has.

Q. What would you say if one did?

A. I would probably stammer and stutter and drop things.

"So it turns out after all that you people didn't crucify Our Lord! Son of a gun! You certainly had us all fooled!"

An Impolite Interview with Woody Allen, *continued*

The first piece of material I ever did, at the Blue Angel, was that I became President of the United States and finally called that girl up for a date, and she still wouldn't go out with me. I do believe that everything I do centers specifically around that. If I go to art museums, if I buy clothes, an automobile, record albums, if I change apartments, at the very base of the medulla is that one lingering hope that this is going to turn the trick and I'll meet the perfect girl.

Q. What's going to happen when you do meet the perfect girl—assuming that she's not looking for the perfect man?

A. I'll never marry her, because I won't consider any girl perfect unless she rejects me. You know, I make jokes about not getting a girl because I *don't* get the girl. But if given my druthers, I'd rather get the girl and go into something like accounting, or a related field. I'm a comedian strictly by default.

Q. I thought you said people are born funny.

A. Yes, it's out of my control. I mean, when a car crashes into my car and a guy gets out and socks me in the mouth, I go home and I sublimate violently, and I write an *incredible* one-liner that really disembowels him. But in actuality, I wish I could smack him in the mouth at the time.

Q. John Wayne was in the hospital for cancer of the lung, and he said he withheld news of his malignant condition because "my advisers all thought it would destroy my image." But he finally released it because "there's a hell of a lot of good image in John Wayne licking cancer."

A. Wayne may be over-exaggerating public concern with his image.

When I was making *Pussycat*, I would see Peter O'Toole before a take put drops in his eyes so they would shine the correct degree of blue. That's how he makes his living, and people do respond to those adorable blue eyes, but my personal reaction is that it's silly.

Q. Is there any ritual that you have yourself?

A. Outside of brushing the needle of my hi fi after every record, I don't think so.

Q. Would you use an electric toothbrush?

A. Yes. I even contemplated buying one. I like to buy things for the sake of buying them. An electric toothbrush really comes under that category perfectly. You know, when I get up in the morning and I'm depressed, it's hard to cope with things. For instance, suppose my work was going bad at the time, suppose I had done very badly the night before, or suppose I had a fight with a girl, or that I was generally depressed. Nothing to look forward to. I can always walk down the street and *buy* something.

You go into a nice warm store and there's like 400 record albums with covers, or gadgets, scissors and electric toothbrushes and things, and you can take out money and *buy* it, and go home and unwrap it. And just that—the mere act of doing that—is so pleasing, sometimes, and so relaxing. I'm not really *that* materialistic, but I do like material things because you can actually touch them. I'm in such an ephemeral business—you know, I trade on the delicate nuance of a line here or a shift in accent or emphasis there. But if a guy goes out and buys a toilet plunger, you can see it and touch it, and you get your dollar-and-a-half's worth. It's a whole other world, and I'm fond of that world.

Q. You've done a bit about how you hired a maid for $1.50 an hour, and your mother said she'd clean your apartment for the same amount, so you hired her instead, but finally had to let her go, because she was stealing. How did your mother react to your saying that?

A. She didn't react negatively. She *has*, at times, actually said, "Don't pay a dollar-and-a-half an hour to a girl, I'll come in and do it." I don't know if she would actually steal. I don't trust her around the house all the time. She would at the very minimum take some liquor. That I know.

Q. Do you have any message for Realist *readers?*

A. Well, I think that these are perilous times that we live in, with the influx of singing groups, and I would caution them to be on guard. I always have the feeling that that's the *real* invasion of the body-snatchers—the real Martian invasion—they've come here in the guise of folk singers and large singing groups and rock-'n'-roll groups, and they're going to get us if we're not careful.

Q. Has the Ecumenical Council's decision to remove the blame for the Crucifixion from the Jews made you any less paranoic?

A. I do live in constant fear that there will be a pounding at the door, and there'll be eight tall blond men who'll want me to come with them for questioning. I do notice certain themes recur in my work all the time, and one is like the Nazi issue. For me the Nazi has become the symbolic character of all that I'm afraid of and don't like, and so the Ecumenical Council taking the blame off us, is a good thing.

Q. But you said before, none of the internals get changed. So wouldn't your problems still exist?

A. Yes, they just transfer onto other things. For instance, I

An Impolite Interview with Woody Allen, *continued*

used to live in a brownstone building, and guys would get beaten up and mugged in my hall. Then I moved here, but after two weeks, my doormen were looking funny at me. I'm thinking, "Well, I'm safe, no muggers are going to get in, there's two doormen always downstairs," and then I think to myself, "Hey, wait a minute, there's two *doormen* downstairs and *they* can get in."

Q. A bank robber in Painesville, Ohio, gave a note to a teller: "This is a stickup. Don't try anything because I have a gun under my jacket." And the teller read the note, smiled sweetly, handed it back, and said, "I'm sorry, but my window is now closed. You'll have to take this to another teller." He did and he got away with over $6,000. Do you identify with him?

A. I can empathize with the robber. I know that if I ever participated in anything like that and the teller *did* say "Take it to another window," I would feel funky about it.

Q. Do you think you'll ever be able to go into a drugstore and buy any contraceptive product?

A. Not a prayer. *No* chance. I'm never going to be able to do it, and no amount of analysis is going to let me go into a store and ask for contraceptives. When it comes to matters of sex I have a tremendous tendency to giggle and, you know, I don't like to get involved.

Q. Well, you could always ask for something else, too.

A. Oh, of course. "—and a pack of Chiclets." That would

petrify me beyond belief. My fear is always, if I go in quietly and say, "I would like a package of contraceptives, please," he would yell, *"There's a kid here who wants a pack of contraceptives!"*

Q. Are you concerned about the population explosion?

A. No, I'm not. I mean, I doubt there's anything I can do about the population explosion, or about the atom bomb, besides vote when the time comes, and I contribute money to organizations in active pursuit of ends that I'm in agreement with. But that's all. I'm not going to set fire to myself.

Q. But do you agree with the motivations of the Buddhist monks who set fire to themselves in Vietnam?

A. No, I think that they don't know what they're doing. I think they're nuts. When all is said and done, it's not the answer. When you're home at night, and you say to yourself, "Tomorrow morning I'll get up at 8 o'clock and set fire to myself," there's something wrong.

I can see dying for a principle, but not that way. At the very minimum, if you are going to die for something, you should at least take *one of them* with you. Go back to the Jews in Germany. If you have a loaded gun in your home, and the state comes to get you, you can at least get two or three of *them*.

Sometimes passive resistance is fine, but violence in its place is a good and necessary thing. But setting fire to yourself is not the answer. With my luck, I would be un-inflammable.

BATMAN AND ROBIN WERE LOVERS

by John R. Cochran

Psychiatrist Frederick Wertham gained nationwide fame by helping spearhead the anti-comic book crusade of the early '50s. In *Seduction of the Innocent*, Dr. Wertham makes the statement that *Batman* comic books are "psychologically homosexual." He further says that the relationship between Batman and his young ward, Robin, is one of pederasty, that is, the relation between a mature man and a young boy.

Basically, he says that Robin—a "handsome ephebic boy"—is often seen with his legs spread, "the genital region discreetly evident." The same with Batman. The stories are anti-feminine, he points out. The only woman we ever see, says Dr. Wertham, is Catwoman, a villain out to wrack Batman's ass. The feeling given by the comic, he says, is that "we men must stick together."

He goes on to quote one of his patients, an "intelligent, educated young

homosexual," who says of the *Batman* stories: "I don't think they would do any harm sexually. But they would probably ruin their morals." Whose morals, he doesn't say. Still, he quotes another young homosexual: "At the age of ten or eleven, I found myself liking my sexual desires, in comic books. I think I put myself in the position of Robin. I did want to have relations with Batman.... I remember the first time I came across the page mentioning the 'secret bat cave,' the thought of Batman and Robin living together and possibly having sex relations came to mind. . . . I felt I'd like to be loved by someone like Batman or Superman."

Has Dr. Wertham indeed unearthed some ugly facts about the dynamic duo? In the oldest issue I managed to dig up, #31, 1945, Robin is seen with his legs spread, and the "genital region discreetly evident" seven times in the first story;

times in the last story.

In another issue, Bruce Wayne, alias Batman, is seen with his hand on the shoulder of Dick Grayson, alias Robin The Boy Wonder. On the second page, mind you! For those of you who aren't aware, Bruce Wayne is a wealthy socialite who is in reality Batman, and Robin is Wayne's young protégé.

The first story in this issue denigrates marriage. A husband-and-wife team is shown constantly bitching. In one scene, Robin is shown with his legs spread while doing an acrobatic stunt. He is also shown bending down on the 6th page. Batman is seen with his "genital region discreetly evident" 14 times.

One of Dr. Wertham's arguments, incidentally, is that Robin's real first name is "Dick."

In another story in issue #37, Batman is seen winking at Robin. In the last story, both are swinging on the same nylon rope, and Robin is swinging down

Batman and Robin Were Lovers, *continued*

on top of Batman. In another issue, featuring the Catwoman, she is seen kicking Batman in the face, jumping off a zeppelin, jumping out of a speeding car, and jumping out of a window. Her genital region is *not* "discreetly evident."

In the last scene, she nearly runs over Robin while driving a caterpillar tractor. All Robin says is "Yow!"

In the next story, Robin is seen diving at Batman's hips to shove him out of the way of a giant rock. Later in the same story, a dinosaur lifts Batman up in its mouth. His arms and legs are free, but not his thighs.

In the last story, Bruce Wayne is seen with his shirt collar open and in a smoking jacket. Robin is called "Dick" six times. In one scene when Dick decides to stay up, Bruce leaves the room to go to bed, with a tremendously pissed-off expression.

Now, we'll move on to the later years and the more recent issues, where we would assume Batman has been a little cleaned up. Not really. In the *Batman* annual #7 for 1964, Batman gets laid up with a leg wound. So Robin and Superman fight crime instead while Batman watches by remote control television.

At the end of the story, Superman says: "Well, Robin—it looks like our partnership is over! It was swell working beside you." And Robin says: "The same goes for me, Superman! I'll never forget it!"

The next panel reads: "Later when they are alone, Batman hesitatingly questions Robin." Batman: "Uh . . . Wouldn't you rather be a team with Superman than with me? It must have been more exciting for you." Robin:

"Oh, it was fun for a while—a new novelty." Now we move to the last panel. Robin continues: " . . . But it isn't the same as working with you, Batman! Golly, you taught me all I know. . . . We'll always be a team!" And Batman says: "Of course we will! Nobody will ever see the end of Batman and Robin!"

And then there is another new character, introduced only during the last few years—Batwoman. In the story, "The Marriage of Batman and Batwoman," Robin is overheard saying in the opening drawing: "Gosh! What'll become of me now?" (Batwoman, by the way, is a cool chick in the story.)

Robin moans to himself in the first panel as he falls asleep, "Bruce certainly is fond of Kathy! Gosh—what if he should fall in love and marry her? Would that break up our partnership?" In Robin's dream, Bruce and Kathy (Batman and Batwoman) get married. Batwoman says to Robin, "Yes, Dick— and I want you to know I'll be like a mother to you." (Bruce is seen fingering his bowtie, smiling.) Suffice it to say that at the end of the story, Bruce wakes Dick up from his dream, but Dick is still shook because he thinks Bruce may still yet get married. His last words in the issue are, "Gosh—oh, Gosh."

In *World's Finest Comics*, where Batman and Superman team up, *Robin* gets laid-up, and Batman is overheard moaning, "Will . . . will this be the end of our wonderful life together? Will I never see Robin alive again?"

In another story, "Bride of Batman," the State Department asks Batman to marry Vicki Vale, a newspaper reporter, so that the Shah of Nairomi—a neutral,

it turns out—can't marry her instead. Batman very hesitatingly agrees: "All right, I'll do it—but only because of the seriousness of the world situation."

Vicki, of course, is really marrying Batman so she can enrage Eloise Leach, "photographer for a rival magazine" and also a bitch-and-a-half. So, in an issue of the *Gotham Gazette*, we see: "Batman Engaged to Vicki Vale—Famed Lawman Finally Succumbs to Cupid!" There's a picture of Vicki kissing Batman on the cheek, and he isn't responding at all; in fact, he looks seriously annoyed.

In still another scene, we see Vicki with her arms around Batman, and we see his thoughts: "I'd be much happier taking on a deadly criminal any day!" Still another panel, more of his private thoughts: "Am I glad this engagement is only temporary! I couldn't put up with much more of THIS!"

The State Department looks up Batman again, and tells him, "Great news! We've just heard from a White House spokesman! The President HIMSELF is arranging his schedule so that he can be present at the wedding!" And still another State Department aide says, "Your wedding is a diplomatic coup, Batman! It has won the Shah over to our side for all time!" Batman looks enormously annoyed again.

The next panel's box reads: "And late that night, two desperate figures seek an answer in the gloom of the Batcave." Robin says, "It looks like we're sunk, Batman! And that means EVERYTHING changes! You won't have much time to pal around with me—not with a wife around. . . ." And Batman replies, his

Batman and Robin Were Lovers, *continued*

hand on Robin's shoulder, "Don't talk like that, Robin! You know that nobody can ever separate us!"

Well, suffice it again to say that the marriage falls through. The Shah stops it because he's heard that any girl who marries Batman has to undergo plastic surgery to change her identity.

Last panel, Batman and Robin are seen toasting each other with a glass of milk. Robin says, "WOW . . . that was a close call! I'm sure glad you told Eloise Leach about the plastic surgery Bat-

man's wife would have to undergo!" Batman replies, smiling, "Yes! I called on her as Bruce Wayne, gave her a scoop! I knew she'd run right to the Shah—and I figured he'd take the steps he did when he learned what would happen to the Vicki he so cherished!"

In another story, Batman and Robin get shipwrecked, and become a jungle team. Now, all Robin wears is a tiger skin for shorts, and Batman panther skin covering his chest and "genital region." This is one of the few stories

where we see Batman's naked legs.

To sum up, look at the August, 1964 issue of *Batman*, some 25 years after Batman was first started. Robin is seen with his "genital region discreetly evident" in nine different panels. They're still living alone together, but now have a maid (Bruce's *relative*, somehow) instead of Alfred, their long-standing butler, who was recently killed off.

Alfred was a perverted old voyeur who, one surmises, used to watch the two of them alone in the cave.

THOSE LITTLE COMIC BOOKS THAT MEN LIKE

by John Francis Putnam

Once again, Grove Press is exercising high-minded imperative action against the Establishment Know-Nothings, at the risk of tired epithets such as "calculated opportunism" and "lascivious exploitation," with the publication of a handsome anthology titled *Tillie and Mac: Those Little Comic Books That Men Like*. And once again, the District Attorney has seen fit to interfere with freedom of the press, Voltaire notwithstanding.

A jury trial was quietly waived, and a municipal judge found the defendant guilty as charged. According to the attorney for Grove Press, in a motion for mistrial, "Your Honor only reads *The New York Times*, which does not carry comics, is thus unfamiliar with funny-paper characters, and lacks a proper frame of reference." The motion was denied.

In his brief for the appellate court, the attorney states: " . . . At the outset of the discussion of the merits—and inasmuch as the original poor draughtsmanship of the booklets in question is evidence of the lack of serious intent to 'deliberately arouse prurient desires' within the view of *Roth* vs. *United States*, 354 US 476 (who could become sexually excited over a male member which, in its clumsy delineation, can but appear to the detached observer as less of a *membrum virile* and more that of a Barney Google horse?)—how, then, can this instance of patent and deliberate satirization of a portion of the sexual anatomy, known to all of mankind in its *true* delineation, be considered as something to 'excite' other than laughter?

"Secondly, it is preposterous to assume that, disproportionately as the genital organs are portrayed, there can be any serious expectation on the part of the beholder that any normal, or abnormal, sexual congress is possible, at the very least from a functional point of view.

"Thirdly, the verve and brio with which these stories are developed are a far cry from the sad and dingy non-literary content of the pornographic film, to which the prosecution often alludes in comparison.

"Fourthly, the various characters themselves, albeit presented in somewhat intimate and unconventional situations, nonetheless represent beloved and well-established figures of a 'comfortable and homey' imagery. It is well known that an aspirant for political office will often, at some point during his campaign, be shown in the newspapers reading the funnies to his children. The funnies, of which *Tillie and Mac* are an inseparable part, are fundamentally American.

"Fifthly, it is argued that the *Tillie and Mac* books have no cultural validity or purpose and serve only to titillate and gratify gross desires and private excesses. It is our contention that they do serve a valid and explicit cultural purpose, in that they are the logical extension of the classic Roman and Greek graffiti, which, despite their so-called 'obscene' nature, are nonetheless carefully preserved in museums and at historical sites under glass. *Tillie and Mac* are thus valid instances of a serious cultural and social relevance in that they are the best known examples of contemporary graffiti.

"Sixthly, the purely aesthetic value of *Tillie and Mac* has been doubted by the prosecution. We have but to draw their attention to the intimate connection between the comic subject matter of these booklets and that of a large part of the leading fashionable school of painting: Pop Art . . ."

Well, frankly, we think Grove Press has gone too far this time. We trust that their large contribution to the American Civil Liberties Union will not muddy the issue. For somewhere there lurks in all of us an operator, but sometimes this operator is the one you're not supposed to talk to while the bus to Hell is in motion.

If the First Amendment is sought to protect the *Tillie and Mac* books—sans even the grace of plain brown wrappings—as they find their way into the corner candy store for kids to buy at recess, then what next? French playing cards? A bound volume of photographic stills from stag movies? Where do we draw the line?

The answer is hinted at by the fact that in the *Tillie and Mac* proceedings, a bailiff was seen to sequester the evidence during the *court's* recess. And so, whereas the exhibition of an ostentatious erection by some future judge may be indicative of undue partiality, it is after all the *only* fair barometer by which to measure contemporary community standards.

COMIC BOOK ESCALATION OF AMERICA'S WAR IN VIETNAM

Virtually all comic books dealing with war deal with World War II, because it's easy to tell the Good Guys from the Bad Guys in retrospect. *Jungle War Stories*, however, deals with the war in Vietnam.

"Helicopters aren't always the answer against the stinging fire of Viet Cong guerrillas," warns the cover of the April-June issue. "A desperate plan is needed . . ."

The first story begins with Viet Cong raiders using, as human shields, helpless children whom they have kidnapped from the Xa-Tong school.

Teacher: "Bandits from the North! We must defend *[he gets shot]—Yiii!*"

Guerrilla: "These bookish swine cannot be allowed to stand in our way, comrades!"

Anti-intellectualism exists even on the left, you see.

The Viet Cong change from their ragged clothing into "the finery of our weak enemies" and they head for Saigon to blow up the central ammunition dump. On the way they pass a group of South Vietnamese, one of whom shouts: "I recognize them! They are *guerrillas!*

They raided my village less than a month ago." Whereupon the Viet Cong open fire.

Now, the subtle way you can tell the Good Guys from the Bad Guys in this particular comic book is by what they say when they die. The South Vietnamese say *Yiii!*; whereas the Viet Cong say *Aiiieee!*; and the American military advisers say *Arrgghh!*

Also, the opposing weapons make different sounds. The Good Guys go *Blam! Blam!* The Bad Guys go *Da-Da-Da-Da-Da* (revealing an obvious Russian influence).

Anyway, a watchful guard at the ammunition dump spots the Viet Cong and alerts headquarters in Saigon. Captain Duke Larson advises the South Vietnamese: "Maybe I can help, General! There's a crazy idea buzzing around in my bonnet . . ."

He outlines his plan and, explains the text, "because the only alternative seems to be disaster, he is given the green light."

The guerrillas see their helicopter.

"Look comrade! A tin bird waddles toward us!"

"They will not fire for fear of hitting the children! Or clobbering the ammo dump—and doing our job for us! An extra ration to all if we shoot the copter from the sky!"

Up in the copter: "It's raining hot metal up here—time for us to spring a surprise of our own." The surprise that had been buzzing around in Duke's bonnet was tear gas.

But observe the chronology. This comic book went on sale in February. It had gone to the printer in December. The stories were written in November or before.

Yet the first public report of gas actually being used in Vietnam was filed by a reporter in Saigon at 2 o'clock in the morning, Monday, March 22nd.

On March 23rd, Defense Secretary McNamara explained that on one occasion, Communist troops had taken refuge among civilian villagers in Phu-yen Province and that "rather than use firepower, thereby jeopardizing the lives of noncombatants, to drive the Viet Cong out of the area, the Vietnamese troops dispensed the riot-control agent. Their objective, of course, was to save lives."

SOFT-CORE PORNOGRAPHY OF THE MONTH

Synopsis: A villain called the Head says he's sorry that Smilin' Jack was treated badly and now insists that Jack relax in a vibrating chair. Jack refuses, and then he's strapped in. And then . . . you've got to give Head credit.

According to a Scripps-Howard report, "Idea for use of the gas originated with American advisers . . ."

And in the *Wall Street Journal* of March 26th, a U.S. officer was quoted: "If we could douse a hamlet containing Viet Cong soldiers with a temporary incapacitating agent long enough to go in and sort out the Good Guys from the Bad, this could be a boon to the war effort."

Is it not clear now that the Pentagon relies on *Jungle War Stories* for its military strategy in Vietnam?

The practice is not a new one, either. Take, for example, the *Buzz Sawyer* strip. Once he backed a naval campaign for more funds for anti-submarine warfare. Buzz and the U.S. Navy took on a Soviet submarine which had been nestling off our shores. They merely inscribed on the side of the sub with a special new underwater paint: "Bang, you're dead!"—and the Soviet submarine commander got sent off to Siberia.

A few months later, back in real life, Congress voted extra monies for anti-submarine warfare programs.

Likewise, *Steve Canyon*. When Canyon learned that the "RX-71 program" had been cut back to save funds, he commented into his coffee cup with slick sarcasm: "I guess it won't really matter! If the Russians send a few Roman candles at us some cloudy night, we'll make a formal protest in the United Nations—if we can only find the pieces of the building!"

Back in real life, the U.S. Senate later voted 74-13 approving an extra $320 million for development of the Air Force's RS-70 reconnaisance-strike bomber.

* * *

During World War II, President Roosevelt personally complimented Ham Fisher, creator of Joe Palooka, for helping to make the pre-war draft more acceptable to the public.

Also, the British Ministry of Information kept Fisher apprised of General Montgomery's progress in the Battle of Tunisia so that the real battle and Palooka's participation in it might reach

a mutual, simultaneous climax.

Jules Feiffer is slightly cynical about the Infamous Artists School:

"Seemingly their only objection to World War III is the loss in newspaper circulation it might mean for them. 'Oops, there goes New York and Washington. How many papers does that leave me?' . . .

"I've always been fascinated by the Cold War comic strips in light of the traditional attitude of newspapers in not wanting editorial comment on the comic page. Our Cold War cartoonists have been fighting the bolsheviks for nearly 20 years now, and no editor protested that this *was* editorial comment. Walt Kelly in *Pogo* attacked McCarthyism back in 1954 and editors protested that this *was* editorial comment.

"I have finally discovered the distinction. So long as a cartoon does not waver from official government policy—or unofficial Pentagon fantasy—it is not considered editorial in nature."

And so we return to *Jungle War Stories*. Viet Cong guerrillas have been terrorizing the entire Mekong Delta and have now fled to the safety of the swamps.

The hippie military adviser remarks: "This is gonna be like trying to gouge the Seminoles outta the Everglades! . . . Everglades! . . . That gives me a ring-a-ding idea!"

Contact is made with Saigon headquarters where: "You want . . . WHAT! How many? I can't promise anything . . . if this is a gag . . ."

The request gets sent on its way to Washington, D.C. where: "Stop mumbling in my ear, Fenster! It may sound insane, but if that's what they want—round up the shipment and jet it to them *IMMEDIATELY!*"

At the airport: "That's right, Major. All previous consignments suspended! This stuff—top priority to Saigon! Pentagon calls it *URGENT!*"

The cargo is loaded, shipped to Vietnam, reloaded aboard the helicopters, and flown above the swamps controlled by the Viet Cong.

"The Yankee fools are too low for napalm! This must be merely an idiotic air

observation! *OPEN FIRE!*"

Blam! Blam!

(You may recall that it is the Good Guys' weapons which go *Blam! Blam!* Obviously the Viet Cong have once again stolen American military equipment. The *N.Y. Times* reported on February 8th that "American military advisers in Vietnam have long conceded that the majority of Viet Cong weapons are American-made ones captured in battle from South Vietnamese forces." The next month, in *Pravda*, Wilfred Burchett wrote that since 1961 Viet Cong infiltrators have been among the South Vietnamese being trained by American instructors in the use of modern arms and military equipment.)

"Encountering heavy ground fire! We can't stay around and dance with these bimbos, Mike!"

"Message received, Duke! Hatch open. . . . Delivery of goods about to start. . . . Elevation fine, Duke! Start tilting so our special delivery can be dumped right in their laps!"

SPLASH! And two dozen *alligators* are dropped from the helicopters.

That was the ring-a-ding idea.

"The cursed enemy. He dooms us with *dragons from the sky!*"

The guerrilla leader threatens to personally execute any coward who turns and runs. But . . .

"It is useless! We cannot resist these horrible creatures that infest the swamp!"

Leader: "You are sniveling swine! A bullet will stop these crea . . . Help! *AIIIEEEE!!*"

The Viet Cong flee the swamp and surrender.

For those who have said that we should get out of Vietnam because we are losing the war—the implication being that if we were winning, our presence would then be justified—the Alligator Caper ought to have great appeal.

And, since our military strategy has obviously been inspired by comics in the recent past, we may look for some action around the Florida Everglades in the near future.

It will be the ultimate in Pop Patriotism.

NO COMPLAINTS
by L. L. Case

If you are one of those soft-headed bleeding hearts who has been concerned about the slaughter of Vietnamese villagers by American bombers, we have some news that should make you sleep a lot better tonight. According to columnists Rowland Evans and Robert Novak (October 11th, 1965), "a special task force studying the psychological reaction in the villages indicates no mass anti-U.S. feeling resulting from the bombings." And "the counter-insurgency mission . . . that has gone into the villages to win over the people has not sent back a single complaint about the bombing."

How about that? It just goes to show that the truth will out, however comforting. By happy coincidence, we have just received the results of the latest South Vietnam Government Public Opinion Agency poll, which should take care of the cynics among us. The questions asked by their interviewers were these:

Do you have any complaints about	Yes 0%
the way American planes bombed	No 24%
your village?	No opinion 76%
Which do you prefer: bombing,	Bombing 20%
burning, or machine-gunning?	Burning 2%
	Machine-gunning 2%
	No opinion 76%
Are you satisfied with the way	Satisfied 24%
the bombing has been handled,	Shoot now 0%
or shall we shoot you now?	No opinion 76%

The rather high no-opinion vote, according to Ngo Diem Gallup, head of the agency, did not reflect a lack of interest on the part of respondents, but merely physical inability to answer because of death.

"Are you hiding a Viet Cong in there?"

THE ANATOMY OF SCHLOCK
by Robert Anton Wilson

For three months, I have worked as an editor in the country's leading schlock factory. My boss assured me that our schlock reached 30,000,000 Americans every month, and *that*, brethren, is a lion's share of the schlock market.

Let me define my terms. Schlock is the next level down, below kitsch. Kitsch is naive, maudlin, hokey, unsophisticated. Commercial folklore, so to speak. Its flavor is bland, and, like American food, it is processed to be without any strong flavor, good *or* bad. Kitsch is "I Found God When My Doctor Told Me I Had Cancer," "Jackie Kennedy Tells Why She Will Not Re-Marry," "Should Wives Enjoy Sex?"

Schlock, on the other hand, is brutal, lumpen-prole, aggressive, hairy; like carnival hot-dogs, so spicy you might vomit if you're over-sensitive. Schlock is "He Beat His Grandmother to Death With Her Crutch," "Love-Starved Arab Peasant Women Raped Me Twenty Times," "The Disease That Liz Caught from Dick."

I got into the schlock market when I answered a *New York Times* ad for an editor for a slick men's magazine. I passed the interview with flying colors and was hired. Then it was explained to me that, in addition to the slick men's magazine, I would also be editing three pulp men's magazines.

The three pulps were, of course, pure schlock. They sported titles like (these are actual examples) "The Corpse Lovers," "Inside Those Queer Bars," "How to Find Your Favorite Vice," "The Big Snatch," "My Mommy Was A Hustler," "Girls Who Suck You Dry." Of course, the more raunchy of these titles did not live up to the expectations they aroused: schlock is not hard-core pornography but soft-core. "The Big Snatch" was about kidnapping and "Girls Who Suck You Dry" was about girls who take all your money and leave you.

Well, I have a family to support (as Adolph Eichmann may have said when his job was first explained to him); I sat down and began writing schlock. I produced such gems as "Wild Sex Freaks of History," "A Prostitute Reveals Her Naked Soul," "If You Think You Have V.D.," "Can Lack of Sex Cause Cancer?" and "How Cowards Dodge the Draft."

In between these epics, my magazines were crowded with cheesecake layouts, and I found that writing the captions to these was more fun, even, than writing the articles. As on all such magazines, the cheesecake came out of a file—the models had signed away everything, including (I think) their children's life insurance, on a release form that couldn't be broken by Clarence Darrow himself—and I invented whatever I wanted to say about them.

In creative and ironic raptures one day (and a bit dismayed by the hard, whore-like expressions on the broads the art department had handed me), I picked up the heaviest cruiser in the lot—a mauler who looked like she was 38 years old and had been a whore for 20 of those years in the $10-a-throw Sands Street section of Brooklyn—and wrote that she was a Sunday

School teacher from Indiana.

The others I gave the usual fictional backgrounds, making them "girl scientists," "typists," "airline hostesses," and so forth. Once in a while I would make one a "Greenwich Village hipster" and have her say something like "I dig the peyote scene" or "William Burroughs is my favorite writer," but I was careful not to pull *that* one too often.

Meanwhile, another department of the schlock factory also published a tabloid newspaper—the kind that features headlines like "Iron Lung Patient Rapes Two Nurses." The editor was understaffed. (This didn't prevent the publisher from continually suggesting that he fire somebody—the publisher worried that every department was overstaffed.)

Just for the hell of it, and because I was getting to enjoy schlock in a perverse sort of way, I took on writing the ESP column in this newspaper. I read the predictions that had appeared over the past several months and began grinding out my own predictions, out of the blue. It was surprisingly easy. Among other things, I predicted that Lyndon Johnson would be assassinated, that anti-American riots would occur in another Latin American nation, that the $15,000,000 pornography collection on the closed shelves of a large public library would be robbed by a mob led by a defrocked priest "well known in occult circles," that flying saucers would be in the news again, that shocking discoveries would be made at Stonehenge throwing new light on ancient Egypt and revealing how man came to be on earth (ESP bugs, I reasoned, are generally also the types who believe that man was deposited here by flying saucers and that Egypt is full of occult mysteries), that peanut butter would be found to contain radioactive isotopes, and that a Hollywood star would be involved in a sex-and-LSD orgy.

In a short while, I began getting letters from fans. Many of them congratulated me on the number of my predictions that came true, although actually *none* of them ever came true. Apparently, these people possess a very convenient kind of memory. (When Kennedy was shot, many astrology magazines admitted they hadn't predicted it, but I recently heard from an astrology buff that all the leading astrology magazines *had* predicted it!)

As an experiment, I tried the most outlandish prediction I could imagine in my ESP column. I predicted that a new island would rise in the Pacific Ocean, covered with strange non-Euclidean buildings bearing inhuman hieroglyphics. I had lifted this from "The Call of Cthulhu," by H. P. Lovecraft. The ESP fans ate it up. They are always expecting things like that to happen anyway.

I was becoming a *schlockmeister*, a veritable *uber-schlockmeister*. I started dreaming up titles for tabloid stories. All the stories in the tabloid, you see, were fictitious. (Incidentally, the best inspirations are never used. They are *too* far out. Such as: "Kicked Out of Ku Klux Klan for Negro Blood—He Becomes Muslim Leader.")

The staff would have a bull session each Monday morning and work out 15 or 20 ideas for the next issue. "Say, how about this," somebody would cry. "Mad Hunchback Sells Hunch to Butcher/Woman Poisoned by Hunchburger?"

"Nah," the editor would say, "Too far out in left field."

"How about, 'Vice Squad Cop Catches V.D. From Prostitute He Arrested'?"

"Great," the editor would reply, "We'll use that one."

And so another "news" story would be born. I often reflected that we represented the next stage in journalism, after *The New York Times*. The *Times* merely alters *and* selects facts to fit a

REALMATE OF THE MONTH

Here is a delightful close-up of our Miss August in all her natural beauty. Natalie August is a sprightly fashion model who works part-time as a pert supermarket check-out counter clerk. Since we didn't have enough trading stamps for a camera, this pin-up picture is actually a composite of cast-off material gathered for *The Realist* by photo retouchers from *Playboy, Escapade, Rogue, Nugget, Gent, Swank,* and *Dude*.

Natalie, who majored in Bicycle-Riding at Bennington, considers herself to be a philosophical rationalist. "I used to believe in reincarnation," she remarked to us, "but that was in my other life." She is just wild about jazz, sports cars, onanism, skiing, and over-charging customers. She admits, however, to having a morbid fear of men, psychoanalysis, shopping-carts, snow, and air-brushes.

Her rousing ambition: to win circulation and influence fantasies.

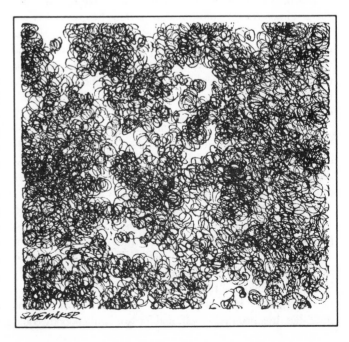

particular political line. We invented our facts on the spot, a much more creative process. If it is the destiny of man to "transcend mere reason and empiricism," and to "achieve a rebirth of myth and magic," as many modern philosophers think, I can safely claim that we *schlockscribes* in our grubby offices were doing more to further that end than the *Times*.

I soon discovered that my predecessor on the men's pulps had applied the same formula: "Woman Gives Birth to Puppies" appeared in the tabloid; "Women Who Have Given Birth to Animals" had appeared several issues back in one of the men's pulps. A girl who regularly had intercourse with a dog—a spectacle she performed for money in a Mexican whorehouse—had "worn down her immunity" to dog sperm and thus became impregnated. The pulp archly stated that the story had appeared "in several Mexican newspapers" but that "some doctors" claim it is impossible. The tabloid picked it up without any reservations. Folklore students of the future will have to wade through tons of this schlock in stalking down the origins of various contemporary folktales.

The schlock-sex field is much tougher than schlock-crime or schlock-ESP. "This is kind of tame," the publisher, or *schlockfuehrer*, would say occasionally. Since he fired one person every week without fail (and thus kept us all in that half-mad kind of frenzy necessary to the production of true schlock), this remark would spread terror throughout the factory. We would outdo ourselves with "Teen-Age Sex Club Seduces Parents" or "Wolf-Men Who Drink Blood for Lust." Then, the *schlockfuehrer* would come around again, looking worried. "Take out 'cunnilingus,' " he would say (referring to a *factual* story, for once, about a crusader for sexual freedom), "you gotta be careful in this business."

My predecessor, I discovered while going through back issues, had named one model "Señora Maria Theresa Fellatia" and said she was waiting for an appointment "with her physician, Dr. Cunnilingua." Somehow, this one went through. It is altogether possible that the publisher didn't know either of those words at the time.

The biggest panic occurred when some pubic hair was discovered in one of my pulps, in an issue done by my predecessor but on which I had corrected the blues (last stage before publication). The printer discovered the small dark tangle and called the publisher, saying we could all go to jail. The publisher came thundering into my office, gibbering: "Pubic hair! You let pubic hair go by! Goddamn it, pubic hair! We can all go to jail!"

The printer, fortunately, was able to correct the plate. After that, I scrutinized each crotch with the kind of care I usually give only to living girls. Anybody who passed my office and saw me studying a vulva through a magnifying glass would have thought, "What a horny bastard! He's really in the right job."

In spite of the one-firing-every-week policy, I enjoyed myself in the schlock factory. Most of us laughed a great deal, especially after each firing (we knew then *we* were safe for another week). Schlock is *fun* to write. The best, of course, is the stuff you have to reject for publication, but which everybody in the office enjoys. "Jayne Mansfield Revealed To Be Male Has-Been Who Had Sex-Change Operation," was one the publisher dreamed up himself, and for two hours nobody could

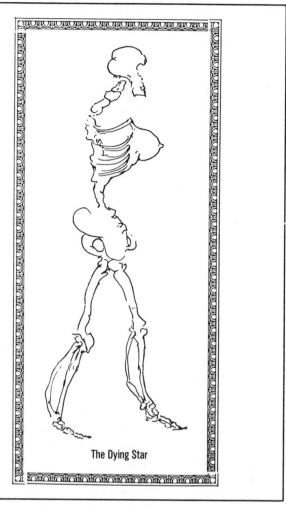

The Dying Star

talk him out of it. His lawyer finally made him see reason, which is too bad. It would have been the tabloid's best-selling issue . . . until Jayne sued them out of existence.

Another one the whole office loved was "The Four-Letter Word That Sue Lyons Calls Burton," which was based on a gossip column item that Sue Lyons called Burton "Bull," but the readers wouldn't find that out until after they bought the magazine and read the story. My all-time favorite, cooked up by a girl who worked on the movie mags, was: "Rock 'n' Roll Singer Catches Leprosy/Audience Splattered by Flying Organs." Alas, the editor of the tabloid thought that was too much even for *his* audience.

The movie magazines were, like all good schlock, basically dishonest. The stories were more-or-less true but were given the schlock-treatment by our staff. An item would be lifted out of Hedda Hopper or Louella Parsons and then jazzed up with a suggestive or blood-curdling title and developed into a whole story. Everything in the story, except the key fact, would be fabrication. As long as none of the stars were made to look criminal or foolish, we never had any complaints from the studios' legal departments.

Intrigued by a cover-line on one of our "true confessions" mags—"Stripped Naked in the Subway/Nobody Would Help Me"—I found that no incident remotely like it occurred anywhere in the story. The little 60-year-old lady who ground out three of these mags, writing most of them herself, had carried journalism even further than our tabloids.

At this point, the publisher gave me another magazine to do—a detective mag. He also gave me, at last, one assistant to help with the three schlock mags. The assistant proved to be a talented *schlockscribe* and quickly was grinding out "Sixty Streets of Sin" and "He Asked Me To Sleep With His Wife" at a sizzling rate. I let him take over two out of the three schlock mags, and concentrated on one schlock mag, my slick, and the detective mag.

My career in the schlock factory was brought to a close when I began preparing my first issue of the "slick." It was an imitation of *Playboy*, with lots more cheesecake. Looking over *Playboy* and its other imitators, I decided that the key to success in this field was, in a word, balls. I set out to create the boldest, most sophisticated, raciest men's magazine ever. The editor-before-the-editor-before-me was fired for making it "too intellectual." I was careful to avoid that error.

The publisher said he didn't want schlock in this *one* magazine—"It's our class publication," he used to repeat—but he was such a pure, dedicated *schlockmaestro* that everything he touched turned to schlock. Looking over past issues, I discovered that the only non-schlock one had been put out by the editor fired for being "too intellectual." "Not schlock and not egghead," was my guiding principle. I revamped my table of contents several times, making it more schlocky each time. I kept two non-schlock articles, a factual piece about Cuba, and an interview with a prominent novelist, and tried to make the rest of the pieces come out as *both* schlock and *non*-schlock simultaneously. This I did by giving them schlock titles but sophisticated insides, or, in one case, a sophisticated title with schlock insides.

It didn't work.

One week the tabloid editor was fired on Monday, his successor was fired on Wednesday, and the publisher called me into his office on Thursday. "I don't want you printing writers who are writing The Great American Novel," he began. He told me my whole issue was too intellectual and that several stories were being dropped from it. He ended the interview on a paternal note: "I got a reputation for doing a lot of firing," he said, "but I'm trying to change that. I'm not going to fire anybody without two week's notice, from now on. As for you, you're still okay in my book. You just have to learn a little."

He had made a similar speech to the tabloid editor before firing him. I typed up a job résumé that night and brought it into the office half an hour before starting time the next morning. I had run off 20 copies of it on the office photostat machine when the *schlockfuehrer* called me into his office and fired me.

Until a replacement for me could be found, everything—the slick, the whodunit, and the three pulps—was put in the hands of the little 60-year-old lady who did the confession magazines.

BELLYBUTTON BONANZA

Film director David Swift complained in Hollywood this month —having just returned from shooting *The Grand Duke and Mr. Pimm* in France—that he had to rent 500 American bathing suits rather than photograph 500 girls on the Riviera in bikinis, because the Production Code Administration prohibits the showing of bellybuttons.

Section VII of the Code, headed Costumes, states: "Nudity can never be permitted as being necessary for the plot. Semi-nudity must not result in undue or indecent exposures." Code Administrator Geoffrey Shurlock had advised Swift in a letter, before approving the script, that he could not show a woman's navel on the screen—and the fact that 500 were to be exposed was all the more reason for objection.

Said Swift, referring to the French: ". . . the people I was working with thought I was crazy, some kind of a sex nut."

". . . I think you have the wrong party. I'm Tony Nunzio—you want Manny Moses next door . . ."

THE FILM TRAILER CULT

What follows is the transcript of a program broadcast over Fordham University's radio station, WFUV. The participants are David MacDonald and Martin Jukovsky, interviewed by someone identified only as Chris.

Chris: . . . Tell me, what is the *raison d'être*, the—reason for being, for your magazine? There are quite a few publications already, you know. Why burden the film scene with another?

Marty: I'll try to explain our theory in a nutshell. You see, Chris, when one goes to see a movie *cold*, it is like plunging into a novel without reading its introduction, or knowing anything about it.

David: Even books have a synopsis of sorts on their dust jacket, you know.

Marty: Yes, and even if not, everyone who picks up a book has heard *something* about it.

David: Not so in the movies, Chris, unless one is prepared for it by the experience of the *trailer*.

Marty: Yes, David, exactly! We feel that one is primed, or, as David said, *prepared* for the film through watching the coming attractions the previous week.

Chris: This, then, is your esthetic? It's not much to build an entire theory of film criticism upon, is it?

Marty: Well, if one *misses* the trailer, one loses this vital kernel of the film. The filmmaker *intended* that the audience see the trailer. And yet, today, one is often denied the very experience the filmmaker felt integral to the film.

David: You see, Chris, very few people are concerned with this vital problem. Yet look what would happen when the trailer is not part of your viewing experience.

Chris: As on television, if I might use a dirty word.

Marty: Um-hmm. On the telly, one rarely sees coming attractions. This is the *main reason* one misses the full flavor

SOFT-CORE PORNOGRAPHY OF THE MONTH: GRAND OLD PARTY HAS JOINT SESSION WITH YOUNG REPUBLICAN

of the movie.

Chris: I've often wondered why the companies that make such bad movies also make good trailers, and vice-versa.

David: I'm glad you asked that. Few people are aware the companies that make the films do not make the trailers for their own pictures.

Marty: We felt the definite void in film criticism, the overlooking of the trailer. Our own magazine, the *Beaded Screen*, has a special feature each issue, a *rating* service covering trailers currently in release or revived in the New York area.

Chris: Many theaters, such as art houses and the like, do not show trailers any more. What are you doing about this problem?

David: Well, we are organizing a boycott of these theaters, and a write-in campaign to educate the exhibitors. Actually, Chris, there are probably thousands of frustrated movie fans who, like ourselves, feel that the trailer is an unsung art form.

Chris: I see . . . David, who are your favorite directors?

David: Favorite directors? I hadn't thought about that, really. Marty?

Marty: You see, we aren't interested in the films as made. The trailer is the only true criteria.

David: Criterion.

Marty: Criterion. You take a film like *Dragnet*, now.

Chris: Oh, yes, I remember. In the coming attractions, Jack Webb fired a shotgun at the audience, didn't he?

Marty: Yes. Did you see the picture, then?

Chris: Only the coming attraction.

Marty: Trailer.

Chris: Trailer.

Marty: Well, Chris, it's just as well. The theory still holds up, though. The coming attraction, as you call it, forms your opinion of the movie, acts as an appetizer preparing you for the main course.

David: I'd like to quote you from Ernest Lingrens' *The Art of the Film*. This copy—do you want to read it, Chris?

Chris: I noticed it was heavily underlined in parts. "Film technicians want to make good films, but they cannot make them without the support of the public, who week after week go, led on by habit and the persuasions of the trailers, not understanding that—" When was this written? Let's see . . . copyright 1948.

David: Chris, turn to page 28, where I've underlined. It's about the use of optical effects, you know, fancy wipes and dissolves, split screens, spiral fades, and crosses and whatnot.

Chris: Here. "The more intricate and showy wipes, which enjoyed a brief heyday, are now rarely found outside publicity trailers, where they appear in profusion. . . ."

Marty: Yes, Chris. Where else but in trailers can you see those fancy, effective wipes? If you remove the trailers, you'll just about eliminate some basic essentials of film grammar.

Chris: Yes, I think I know what you mean. They used to use those effects in serials.

Marty: Exactly! And when the serials died, you'll notice there were fewer bravura effects—wipes, lap dissolves—the stuff of which cinema is made, Chris. If the trailer were to die of attrition, as it threatens to do, what is there left? How much vigor has the average trailer of today? Give him some facts, David.

David: All right. *Item:* Use of still photographs, rather than scenes from the film, in *One-Eyed Jacks. Item:* Use of printed letters crawling up an otherwise blank screen. This is used mostly in irresponsible so-called art houses, but it does not bode well for the future. *Item:* When Cinemascope trailers are shown together with regular screen ones, there is no effort made to change back and forth to respective lenses. Result: Squeezed or expanded, unproportioned trailers. Shall I go on?

Marty: A good trailer gives a *feeling* of the picture, its style, mood, movement, but how many people even bother to call up the theater to inquire the starting time of the trailers? Yet, I tell you, the time is *always posted* outside the box office. Look the next time you go to the flicks.

David: Some trailers, sad to say, will *never* be seen by the public, Chris. In the industry, motion pictures are introduced to prospective exhibitors through the trailer. The independent theater owner or distributor is invited to screenings of special 10- to 15-minute-long trailers from which they select those pictures they may be interested in showing. These trailers are, of course, never shown in commercial houses. So. . . .

Marty: What we would like to do is, organize an audience for trailers, so that a sufficient demand will exist. Then, perhaps, we will have, who knows, a few full-length programs on the art or history of the trailer, at local art theaters.

Chris: I'll be the first to buy a ticket, I assure you. . . .

—*B. Kliban*

THE ETHNIC JOKE AS A BAROMETER OF CLASS DISTINCTION

[This article originally appeared, unsigned, in the first edition of The Journal of American Poverty.*]*

Who is it that wears dirty white flowing robes and comes riding into town on a pig? Lawrence of Poland.

That is an example of a category of humor which began in such nuclei as Chicago and Detroit and quickly filtered out to such points in the perimeter as New York and San Francisco.

They have been, it is necessary to note, a function of audio-verbal communication. Nowhere have they appeared in public print, save for a Midwestern newspaper columnist who, in order to avoid negative reader response, simply substituted the inhabitants of Al ("Li'l Abner") Capp's imaginary Lower Slobbovia for the condescending "Polack" reference. Thus:

Why does it take three Slobbovians to change a light bulb? One to hold the bulb and two to turn the ladder.

What can we learn about the reflection of multiple poverty factors in these stereotypical jokes? We shall deal here only with jokes of the Polish genre, although there have been, of course, those concerned with other ethnic groups. Hence:

How can you tell if a plane is from Alitalia Airlines? It has hair under the wings.

How can you tell the difference between an Irish wedding and a wake? There's one less drunk at the wake.

What is Puerto Rican cole slaw? Like American cole slaw, except it has hair in it.

Turning, then, to the Polish jokes, let us select examples of cultural deprivation in the basic necessities of life:

FOOD

What's a Polish cookout? A fire in a garbage can.

CLOTHING

How can you tell who the bridegroom is at a Polish wedding? He's the one wearing the clean bowling shirt.

SHELTER

Why do you never hear of a Polack committing suicide? It's impossible to kill yourself by jumping out a basement window.

Curiously, the forms of different ethnic jokes may overlap with each other:

How can you tell who the bride is at a Polish wedding? She's the one with the braided armpits.

Now, what about the area of gainful employment?

What do you get if you cross a Polack with a chimpanzee? A 3-foot-tall janitor.

Or educational opportunity?

Why don't Polacks get a 15-minute coffee break? Because if they're away from the job for 10 minutes, you have to retrain them.

And let us consider social graces, the lack thereof.

What is it when you write your initial on your index finger? A Polish monogrammed handkerchief.

How can you tell who the Polack is at a track meet?

He's the one picking his teeth with the javelin.

The implied inferiorities of Polish people is inextricably bound to their low position on the monetary totem pole and the resultant disproportionate value on material goods.

Why do Polacks never win wars? Because, after blowing up a bridge, they stay around to pick up the lumber.

How does a Polack dance the Limbo? By trying to squeeze under the door of a pay toilet.

The professional literature is anything but replete with analysis of the relationship between national-origin jokes and status on the prestige scale. However, the subject has been touched upon briefly by the renowned socioneurologist Paul Jacobs* in *Abnormal Sociology*, Vol. VIII, No. 3, in an article entitled "The Subjectivity of Ghetto Laughter." He writes:

". . . Most ethnic or religious humor seems to focus on qualities allegedly possessed uniquely by the group about whom the jokes are

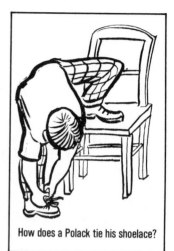

How does a Polack tie his shoelace?

told, and generally the jokes begin within the group. Very often the jokes reflect a kind of wry self-critical view which the group is usually loath to share with the larger community. But inevitably the

*Author of The State of the Unions; *co-editor with Michael Harrington of* Labor in a Free Society; *co-author with Philip Selznick and Frank Pinner of* Old Age and Political Behavior; *author of* Is Curly Jewish?, *a political memoir to be published by Atheneum in October 1965; currently working on a cookbook,* Take a Leak.

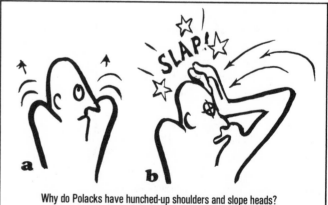

Why do Polacks have hunched-up shoulders and slope heads? Because, when you ask them a question they go (see figure a) and when you tell them the answer they go (see figure b).

jokes shift from being 'inside' to the outside world, even though Jews, for example, don't like to hear anybody but Georgie Jessel tell Yiddish jokes, and Negroes don't want anybody but Moms Mabley to tell 'stud' stories.

"In a peculiar way, I think the Poles ought to be happy about the Polish jokes, even though the theme of many of the jokes is the alleged stupidity of the Poles. The existence of the jokes means that finally the presence of the Poles in America is being recognized. They have moved from having just a Postmaster General to getting an ambassador, and now in addition people are telling jokes about them. Soon the cup of their self-esteem will be running over. Before we know it, fund-raisers for the National Conference of Poles and Litvaks will be conducting yearly campaigns, there'll be Polish tennis players (tennis is much more upper class than pro football, where all the Poles are now) and Kim Novak might start using her real name. After that happens, maybe we'll even start hearing Indian jokes. . . ."

What does the NAACP stand for? Negroes Are Actually Colored Polacks.

Ergo: the ultimate insult. And yet:

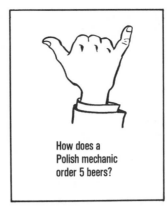

How does a Polish mechanic order 5 beers?

What do they call a Polack who marries a Negro? A social climber.

The reverse English on this particular joke—transforming one who is ordinarily the victim of blatantly overt discrimination into the personification of a *superior* goal to be attained by Poles— serves to point out the implicit snobbishness of *all* Caucasians in referring to the plight of Negroes in terms of "their" —rather than "some of *us*"—being deprived of *human* dignity.

That is what we may morally infer from a category of humor in which Polish-Americans are merely a convenient vehicle for the kinds of indignity that are anti-climactic to deprivations of a more involuntary nature. And so:

What's the difference between a Negro and a Polack pissing in the sink? A Negro takes the dishes out first.

IN DEFENSE OF CENSORSHIP
by Lenny Bruce

I must say a few words in defense of the censor who is damned for having a "dirty mind" and "always looking for the seamy side." This is not always the case.

To illustrate my point, I have chosen *tuvilin*. Now, if you don't know what *tuvilin* means—and I further complicate it with *laying tuvilin*—and your first understanding of it is that they are Jewish Hail Marys, I will tell you that it is an Orthodox religious rite where you take a leather string and tie it around your arm and pray.

Up till the word "pray" I'm sure the reader conjured up several different views, but the most important view is from the street. We see the old Jewish man silhouetted through the curtains, with his back toward us, tying up his arm . . . through the eyes of an Oklahoma narcotics agent who never saw a Jew in his life and who, with no thought of probable cause, would fly in the face of the 4th Amendment with an unreasonable search and seizure.

To say that the Oklahoman was obsessed with the looking-for-dope scene would be an unfair statement.

Also, I believe that while many Jewish mothers project an image of fierce integrationists and humanists, if the daughter were to call from college and announce that she was bringing home her new husband, a Filipino ensign in the Navy, an image of a long foreskin and a gold tooth would cause a dull silence at the other end of the phone.

"Hello, hello, Ma, are you there? His name is Pinoy Pinay."

Finally, according to the R. V. Hicklin test, the word f-u-c-k alone, written on a wall, can incite lewd and lustful thoughts. Its danger is latent. I further believe, therefore, that the Jew is ignorant of the impact of the word f-u-c-k, and when he offers a defense on the absurdity of the "counting of the words" as in the *Lady Chatterley's Lover* case, the Jew is confused by the prosecution's evaluation that some words are worth 90 points and some words 10 points; the reason the Jew is confused as to why s-h-i-t although repugnant is 30 points and f-u-c-k 85 points is that rabbis and priests both shit but only one fucks.

These ideas are disrespectful only to (1) quasi-Catholics who worship idols, and (2) vegetarians who wear leather shoes.

"You know who you are? You're me four years ago, come for an education, new to school, so clean, so neat-kiss me, for Chrissake!"

A HARD DAY'S NIGHT

by Ray Puechner

Monkeys have been sexually aroused by radio command; one pair so stimulated was provoked to copulate eighty-one times in ninety minutes.
—Saturday Review, *February 5, 1966*

There's the professor again. Wonder what he's up to now? Yesterday he had my eyes dilating and expanding from the pinlike beads of a junkie to Orphan Annie size. It gave me quite a headache. Hope he leaves me alone today. I'm just getting over a rather severe bout with smoker's cough. Fortunately I only pretended to inhale all those cigarettes, or I'd just be another statistic on the lung cancer page.

Now the professor is reaching into the cage for Zelda. Good show. Maybe I'll have a few hours' peace. That woman picks on me all day long. Hmm. He's

News item: The revolution in morals on the American campus has evolved a special symbol at Yale: a necktie may be hung on the doorknob whenever a girl is in a student's room.

sticking a pair of electrodes in her head and bringing her back. Bum luck. Story of my life. I can't get away from her. Even when I walked into the monkey trap in the jungle, she found out about it and joined me. Just when I thought I was rid of her. She sat there peeling an orange and complaining. Now there are such things as ugly monkeys and *ugly* monkeys. Zelda is an ugly *ugly*.

The professor reaches in for me, and I sink my teeth clean through the old bastard's hand. He screams like hell. But he comes back with a damp rag and knocks me out with a dose of ether. When I wake up, I've got a pair of electrodes in my head too.

I look over at Zelda and suddenly she has become the most beautiful, exciting, and desirable monkey in the entire world, and I find myself wanting to make mad love to her. I haven't felt so good since I was on LSD experiments. I feel like a desert island castaway who suddenly discovers Sophia Loren is also stranded on the island. I pounce upon her eagerly. For the first time since we were married we click together on all eight cylinders. We both achieve wild orgasms and fall away in sweet exhaustion.

Zelda wants to do it again. Right away. She can't wait. And, surprisingly enough, neither can I. I hop her again and this time it's even better. We soar to the heights of pleasure described in the cheap paperbacks, and I begin to believe that everything I've read in them is true.

We barely catch our breath between the next two turns. Who cares? It's great. Zelda can't get enough, and neither can I. I haven't had so much fun since the days I had a bachelor apartment just off the campus of the women's college. Those were the days the blue-faced monkeys were protesting against racial discrimination and, to show I wasn't prejudiced, I sponsored sleep-ins at my apartment every Saturday night. But even those glorious days paled alongside the present tintinnabulations of swinging delight.

I look at Zelda and she looks at me. I

feel like an animal. One more time. Encore. Encore. I feel like I could rewrite the marriage manuals. If the professor doesn't know it already, he's got something with those radio-controlled electrodes. Every woman not only looks, but acts, like a love goddess. Put it on the market and Hugh Hefner is wiped out overnight.

After seventeen times, the all-time record for our breed is demolished completely. It was formerly held by Arthur Fontevelde, who did thirteen consecutive before being taken to the hospital. The poor devil wound up a shell of a man, so shattered by the experience that he turned homosexual. But I feel like I'm just getting started.

After forty-six delirious orgasms, we have not only demonstrated the eleven classic positions, but have played through thirty-five variations. I pause briefly to consume a dozen bananas and drink two quarts of coconut milk. I know I have to keep my strength up.

After sixty-three spins in the sawdust, I begin to slow down. Not only my body but my imagination is being strained. The professor obviously gets his kicks as a voyeur, and he's going out of his mind with excitement. It's not quite as much fun anymore, but I just can't stop. I'd like to take a little nap, but the radio beam is pulsing with constantly increasing strength. I drag myself over to Zelda. Her tongue is hanging out, and her eyes have turned a strange shade of violet. She feebly attempts to push me away, but I can't stop myself. It's a good thing I've got monkey glands or I'd be dead by now.

As it is, my arms and legs feel like a boneless soft pulp which has just gone through the meat grinder, like 49ᶜ a pound chopped meat, the lowest grade. I can scarcely see and fear that I'm going blind. I want to scream "Enough! Enough!" but my throat emits only a weird, slurred, rasping sound. Zelda is cowering in the corner with fear.

Someone comes to the laboratory and delivers a note to the professor. He

174

leaves immediately. I sigh with relief and fall in the corner, determined to sleep forever. But then I feel the pulsating desire throb again. I look out of the cage and see that the professor left without turning off the radio control.

With resignation I sob and helplessly yield. Praying for a heart attack to end my misery, I drag myself into position again. By midnight we've passed one hundred and Zelda is begging for mercy, trying to keep me away, but I can't help myself, I can't stop loving her.

In the morning the professor will find my shrivelled-up, three-ounce body lying on the floor of the cage like a dried-up prune. And, if he examines it closely enough, he will see that I have been castrated.

DON'T MENTION MY NAME IN SHEBOYGAN

"Hey, guess what," I rhetorically said to a friend. "I'm going to Sheboygan, Wisconsin."

"You're kidding," responded my friend, who in real life is an astute wire service reporter. "Nobody *goes* to Sheboygan."

He was wrong. Every year since 1953, on the first Saturday of August, exactly 50,000 persons voluntarily emigrate to Sheboygan from all over the country to join the same number of natives celebrating the glories of a combined public relations event and sausage orgy known as Bratwurst Day.

One of the ways to arrive from New York is to take a plane to Chicago, then a train to Sheboygan. Right near the railroad station is the Choo-Choo Grill. A neon sign boasts that it is OPEN ALL NIGHT.

It was on Bratwurst Day Eve that I first realized the true importance of the impending occasion, for the Choo-Choo Grill was closed. That evening I took the Centralist's Walk through the streets, a concept expounded in Alan Harrington's novel, *The Revelations of Dr. Modesto:* "It is an unusual sensation. . . After a while, all the ideas that inhabit the town inhabit you."

The name of the main street had been changed to Bratwurst Boulevard. Side streets were now temporarily rechristened Onion Oasis, Pickle Place, Mustard Hall, Ketchup Korner— you get the point. Had I searched thoroughly enough, I would eventually have crossed Excess Stomach Acidity Avenue.

The people seem to say everything in iambic pentameter with a rising inflection. It reminded me of a movie I saw when I was a kid, *I Remember Mama*, about a family of Scandinavian extraction headed by a mother, Irene Dunne, who was always worrying about finances and kept announcing to her children, "Is *good*, we *do* not *have* to *go* t'the *ba*-ank?"

The films now playing in Sheboygan were *The Sword of Ali Baba*, *Tickle Me* with Elvis Presley, *Lord Jim*, *The Girls on the Beach* ("Takes off where the others leave off").

I though it would be most appropriate for *Goldstein* to be screened on Bratwurst Day, because it contains a scene in which a deserving night watchman gets shoved into sausage-making machinery and becomes a rather lengthy chain of links encasing the very product over which he had stood guard all those long lonely nights when he was merely a man.

Everywhere there were Official Jaycee Stands, each featuring the original and genuine Thielmann or Wagner or Herziger or Sheboygan Sausage Company. Last year ten tons of bratwurst were consumed. This year more than six tons went down gullets at nine Official Jaycee Stands alone. There were 60 stands altogether, many privately run. Since one tenet of the Jaycee Creed is "That economic justice can best be won by free men through free enterprise," we can safely assume they had no objection to the unofficial competition. The official program does not mention that the first 450 pounds of bratwurst are given free to the Jaycees by each of the Big Four.

Bratwurst Day once sponsored an eating contest. The winner in the junior division downed five doubles (that is, a German-style hard roll holding two sausages); the winner in the senior division downed eight doubles. The contest has been discontinued, according to the *Souvenir Program*, "for aesthetic reasons." It is not stated whether the unaesthetic aspects occurred during or after the contest proper.

The festivities began at 9 o'clock Saturday morning with a traditional breakfast of bratwurst and beer, as the Rev. James J. Shlikas, pastor of Immaculate Conception Church, gave the invocation. I asked for permission to reprint it.

"I am sorry," he replied, "but for personal reasons I have to decline your request."

God bless bratwurst.

My perspective was solidified by the front page of *The Sheboygan Press*, which had a two-column story headlined, "PROSPEROUS HIROSHIMA OBSERVES A-BOMB DAY" and a four-column story headlined, "SHEBOYGAN'S READY FOR B-DAY."

The style of journalism seemed to relish self-conscious quotation marks: The local young fellows had preliminary arrangements just about "wrapped up" for the varied goings-on; finishing touches were being put on Jaycee "brat" and refreshment stands; the nine pretty young ladies who aim to be crowned Miss Sheboygan Jaycee of 1965 were "sprucing up" to look their loveliest; it is expected that the influx of B-Day "fans" will swell the local population to something around the 100,000 mark; city police, sheriff's men, auxiliary officers and men of the State Traffic Patrol will be on hand both to handle traffic and to prevent any "incidents" that might spoil an otherwise good time for all; Sheboygan County Communicators will again cooperate with police and act as "eyes and ears" for the department. . . .

Don't Mention My Name in Sheboygan, *continued*

Nevertheless (or perhaps because), there was an unprecedented number of arrests—for drunkenness, fighting, attacking women, brandishing firearms, vandalism, theft. Three young men were arrested for stealing a bar stool. Police were unable to determine from which tavern they had taken it. None of the three remembered the specific scene of their crime. No tavern reported a missing bar stool.

Sheboygan is a law-oriented community. A huge billboard states: "For your safety we *must* enforce our traffic laws." It is signed by the mayor. An appliance shop has a small sign reading: "City ordinance prohibits smoking in retail stores except in unrestricted areas." There are no small signs reading: "Unrestricted area." The appliances are modern, ranging from an electric shoe polisher to an electric wastebasket.

What you really wonder is: (1) How does all the furniture get there? (2) Are the people who live in Sheboygan good lovers?

I'm not sure whether the latter question stems from geographical provincialism or personal chauvinism, or both. But when you hear a guy call after a girl, "Hubba, hubba!" you feel just a little justified in your implied generalization.

So much for the cultural lag. Contestants for the title of Miss Sheboygan Jaycee (formerly, the winner was deemed Miss Bratwurst Queen) parade across the stage in bathing suits. Each one is individually sponsored. There is, for example, a sweet blonde named Marcia, alias Miss Medicine Chest. That gets a big laugh. She is sponsored by a local drugstore. She is followed by Miss Elm City Tree Service, Miss Verifine Dairy, Miss Wisconsin Power & Light, Miss Citizens Bank, etc.

"Dammit," mutters an out-of-town college boy in the audience. "Every time I take my contact lenses out, there's a beauty pageant."

The reigning Miss Sheboygan Jaycee is introduced. "How does it feel to be back?" she is asked.

"Wonderful, wonderful," she welks. "I started off the morning with some bratwurst. Representing Sheboygan has been a great responsibility, but I also found it to be most rewarding," she confesses, as if the two ideas are mutually exclusive.

Her potential successors are instructed: "All right, girls, may we have a quarter turn to the left . . . and another . . . and another . . . and another. . . ."

The judges are quickly writing down notes. What do they actually *write*? "Miss Medicine Chest has a healthy pair." "Miss Elm City Tree Service has shapely limbs." "Miss Verifine Dairy has a very fine derriere." "Miss Wisconsin Power & Light turns me on." "Miss Citizens Bank has a nice vault."

The proceedings are accompanied by the incessant braying of brightly-colored yard-long plastic trumpets which are on sale wherever you look. This must be what *The Sheboygan Press* editorial was referring to: "There are itinerants who come to Sheboygan, as they do to festivals everywhere, seeking a fast buck selling very questionable wares."

The YMCA Boys Choir—little male nymphets in white short-sleeved shirts with black bow ties—sings in lovely harmony and counterpoint . . . *Onward, Christian Soldiers*. The only thing to do is sit back and dig the warmth of Squareness:

• I WAS BORN TO RAISE HELL, promises the lapel button of a sub-teenage girl whose height of hell-raising consists of teasing

"Then I heard the voice from the second stall say: 'The marketing plans, please.'"

her hair in the privacy of her bedroom mirror.

• "Hair Spray Face Shield—limited supply—$2.25 per. . . ." There are 600 hair sprays on the market, but only a limited supply of face shields—a frightening prospect.

• "Miss Appleton," the loudspeaker proclaims ominously, "will you report to the Chaperones' Room immediately!"

• NO APPOINTMENTS NEEDED at the combination beauty salon and barber shop.

• "Every request I have made of Sheriff Frewert and his men has been fulfilled," said Police Chief Oakley Frank and his wife, "and this help from qualified officers is greatly appreciated."

• JOIN WITH A BUDDY, advises the Army recruiting poster.

I really did feel it was unpatriotic of this horse to let loose with a Morse code message in manure while the policeman watching the parade was saluting the American flag held by the girl on the horse.

This feeling was not alleviated by the two clowns who swept the manure up and dumped it into a large pail on wheels with a license plate and a placard explaining OUR BUSINESS IS PICKING UP.

Yet I would like it if Senator William Proxmire—instead of waving to the eight-deep lined-up crowd from his sleek parade car and calling out "Happy Bratwurst Day!"—simply wore one of those straw hats with the miniature beer can on one side, the can-opener on the other and the button in front that says: I'M AN ALCOHOLIC—IN CASE OF EMERGENCY, BUY ME A BEER.

Yet I would like it if the Grand Commander of the Wisconsin Military Order of Cooties continually scratched his crotch while pompously parading for us all.

Yet I would like it if the tiny baton twirler, who has been made to wear lipstick for the parade before she has even sprouted her first pubic hair, grows up and marries the only Negro that Sheboygan has ever seen in person.

The only thing more absurd than baton-twirling would be *not* baton-twirling. The only thing more ridiculous than Bratwurst Day would be not to *have* a Bratwurst Day.

The simple truth is, they *couldn't* not have a Bratwurst Day in Sheboygan. No Bratwurst Day? It is more unthinkable,

West Virginia, than anything Herman Kahn never thought of. The game must go on.

The Johnson's Wax Band rehearses in a parking lot in Racine. Its members get paid for rehearsals as well as for actual parades. Sheboygan was their sixth parade this year, and they had another one scheduled for the very next day.

Hill's Department Store offered "10 per cent off on anything you buy from 8:30 'til 1:00 P.M. Bratwurst Day," and the 5 O'Clock Club was frugging it up with a huge sign in the window proclaiming BRAT DAY A GO-GO, and the Republican Hospitality Booth was right next door to Democratic Headquarters, which has a picture of Midwesterner Hubert Humphrey in the window.

I once sat in on the private showing of a documentary about the Wisconsin campaign battle between Humphrey and John F. Kennedy. There was old Hubert shaking hands with a big, burly dairy farmer wearing overalls and his vote on his sleeve. Hubert said, "Listen, if you're ever around the White House, stop in and have a cup of coffee." That's what Bratwurst Day is all about.

Humphrey lost the primary to Kennedy, Kennedy lost the Presidency to a bullet, Johnson waxed into the White House even while the words "Whatever happened to Lyndon Johnson?" were still fresh on people's lips, and now they're saying, "Whatever happened to Hubert Humphrey?"

Listen, Hubert, if you're ever around the White House, stop in and have a cup of coffee. And if you're ever around Sheboygan, stop in and have some bratwurst.

Sheboygan, my ass.

WE LIKE IT HERE, argues a defensive lapel button. I know, I know. Some of my best wursts are brat. . . .

In the office of the Sheboygan taxi-cab service, there is a DRIVER'S MONTHLY ACCIDENT REPORT. You get a gold star if you've gone one whole year without an accident; a silver star for six months; a blue star for one month. You get a red star for every accident. I decided to walk to the railroad station.

For a moment I panicked at the thought that I might have missed my train. The timetable says something about a special schedule for holidays.

BASEBALL BEGETS BODY BAROMETER

Cleveland Indians pitcher Gaylord Perry has been accused of throwing greaseballs. However, he claims to get that extra something, not by rubbing his hand in his hair, which would be against the rules, but rather by wiping his hand in his armpit, which doesn't violate any existing regulation.

Thus, there is a hierarchy developing, wherein the National Pastime favors organic cheating (sweat) over artificial cheating (Brylcreem). Of course, spitballs are still illegal, so it's not as if *all* natural body excretions were acceptable.

Will every professional baseball pitcher soon be required to use an antiperspirant or else risk being sent to the showers?

"A Popsicle for me and a Fudgsicle for my brother."

TANG SPELLED SIDEWAYS IS FART

Reporter Paul Hoffman has a Xerox of a Xerox of a Xerox of the following section from an official NASA transcript of a conversation between astronauts John Young and Charles Duke during the moon launch on April 21, 1972.

Young: I got the farts again. I got 'em again, Charlie. I don't know what the hell gives 'em to me.

Duke: [unintelligible]

Young: Certainly not—I think it's acid in the stomach. I really do.

Duke: Probably is.

Young: I mean, I haven't eaten this much citrus fruit in twenty years. And I'll tell you one thing—in another twelve fucking days, I ain't never eating any more. And if they offer to serve me potassium with my breakfast, I'm going to throw up. I like an occasional orange, I really do. But I'll be damned if I'm going to be buried in oranges.

WHO THE FUGS THINK THEY ARE

by John Wilcock

If poets are the conscience of the community, folk singers reflect its consciousness. And when both roles are combined, the result is a potent catalyst.

The Fugs, led by poets Ed Sanders and Tuli Kupferberg, are such a combination. Only after years of writing and publishing their uncompromising free verse did they begin to reach the wider audiences that come with public performance and musical backing. "Most lyrics are inane, but the Fugs really say something," says Jordan Matthews of ESP Records, for whom the group has recently recorded several singles. "They came to us because we offer them a great deal of liberty. They are not obscene or pornographic—I suppose the word is prurient—and such an accusation would reveal a great deal about the person who was making such a charge."

The Fugs grew directly out of Ed Sanders' mimeographed quarterly, *Fuck You/A Magazine of the Arts*, which had become something of a legend on New York's Lower East Side. It carried the work of some of the best poets writing today—Robert Creeley, Allen Ginsberg, Gary Snyder, Philip Whalen, Gregory Corso, John Wieners, Philip Lamantia, Frank O'Hara, Carole Berge, Diane DiPrima, Peter Orlovsky, Joel Oppenheimer—as well as such other writers as Norman Mailer, Judith Malina, Leroi Jones.

"Total Assault on the Culture" is how Sanders describes his philosophy, and he adds: "I print the poetry I like plus occasional free-verse gutter doggerel. As for the editorials, notes on contributors, peace statements and Egyptian freak-doodles, I pretend that the United States is a very permissive asylum, and act accordingly."

Of course, readers have been offended—as much by the title as by the contents.

"Occasionally a reader will go insane with rage," Ed revealed, "Tight-assed people sometimes giggle. Some let their eyes glaze over and look bored. At cocktail parties in Michigan they burn it. The Mexican border police register disgust. But most are friendly and very curious."

The Sanders' literary style, peppered with bizarre words and shock phrases, grew out of his years working in a cigar store in Times Square. He synthesized and created his own slang, he explained, "but more often I record it from the freak-language of my friends. I borrow from crooks, hustlers, queens, dope-freaks, amphetamine-heads, poets, and other sources. I've learned much from the brilliant techniques of William Burroughs."

This new language, combined with the shock content of the poetry, soon gave *FY* a worldwide reputation. Night after night, in the shabby Peace Eye Bookstore that Sanders opened as a headquarters, he would be mimeographing and stapling copies given away free to fans, sold for high prices to college libraries throughout America.

Today, they are collectors' items, their value shrewdly enhanced by being priced at $75 per set in an occasional catalog that Sanders ran off at the same address.

As for the Fugs, whose purpose, according to fellow-poet Tuli Kupferberg, is to "fan the flames of discontent"—a quote from *The Wobbly Song Book*—perhaps their origin is best explained in Ed's own words in his introduction to *The Fugs Song Book*:

"The Fugs are an emanation or hallucination of the culture of the Lower East Side. They write all of their own songs, puking them out of a personal history that includes the transistor radio; lots of grass; group gropes; 1000's of hours of poetry, reading it, writing it, and listening; peace-freaking; Chuck Berry concerts in heaven; and scholarship in various esoteric fields of knowledge.

"The Fugs have written approximately 60 songs to date, of which there are printed 26 in this volume, the sperm of the freak-spew, so to speak. Many of their songs deal with interpersonal relationships in the new marijuana group-grope psychedelic tenderness society. The Fug-songs seem to spurt into five areas of concentration: (a) nouveau folk-freak, (b) sex rock and roll, (c) dope thrill chants, (d) horny cunt-hunger blues, (e) Total Assault on the Culture (anti-war/anti-creep/anti-repression)."

The Fugs made their first record in the late summer of 1965, for the Broadside label. It sold 2,000 copies within two weeks. Personnel, in addition to Ed and Tuli, were John Anderson, Vinny Leary, Ken Weaver, Peter Stampfel, and Steve Weber.

Later that year, they set off, in a borrowed VW bus, on a "Cross-Country Vietnam Protest Caravan," during which time the group gave about a score of concerts, some in aid of the Vietnam Day Committee, the Mime Theatre, and the League for Sexual Freedom.

Because of difficulties with the Volkswagen bus, they arrived 12 hours late for a concert at Antioch, Ohio. At the late Professor Kinsey's Institute in Bloomington, Indiana, they were themselves entertained by one of the professors who sang for them a little ditty that began:

"Zip up your doodah, don't be risqué
My, oh my what a thing to display
Plenty of people looking this way
Zip up your doodah/It's cold out today."

A tattered, autographed copy of *The Fugs Song Book* was placed in the Kinsey archives, joining the complete collection of *FY* already locked away with the Institute's sexual memorabilia.

Almost all the stops on the cross-country tour were set up by Sanders himself, based on the contacts he had made through *FY* magazine and his activities since opening the Peace Eye Bookstore. At about the halfway point he sent me a hastily scrawled memorandum on the familiar yellow mimeograph paper:

"The Fugs held a dawn demonstration in front of William Burroughs' birthplace at 4664 Pershing in St. Louis on October 13; a film was made of the operation. The Fugs were warmly received at Lawrence, Kansas, where they went berserk at several parties given in their honor.

"The Fugs will hold a demonstration of approval for American poet Robert Creeley outside Albuquerque, N.M., where they will hold a midnight concert in honor of group gropes and the American West.

"The Kinsey Institute people were real nice to us—showed me the secret pornography collection, threw us a party where there was shown a stag film classic from somebody's private cache. I made arrangements to store my films at the Kinsey Institute for safekeeping.

"They have *Flaming Creatures* and Kenneth Anger's films and they are interested in getting a print of Andy's *Couch*. The Institute is also going to tape all the Fug songs when we pass back through. CBS-TV is going to film the Fug concert on top of James Dean's grave."

Tuli says that even when people walked out of concerts, it didn't necessarily denote hostility. "Sometimes they really believed in what we were doing, and said so, but somehow couldn't manage to accept it personally. Others would sit there and look at them, as if asking 'How shall I react?'—then if they saw that others liked it they'd join in applauding."

Like Ed, Tuli was writing and publishing his own material on the Lower East Side for some years before the Fugs gave him a more dramatic outlet. His work has always been strong on satire, with particular reference to society's rationalization of violence:

Kill Kill Kill for peace
Kill Kill Kill for peace
Near or middle or very far east
Far or near or very middle east
If you don't like a people or the way that they talk
If you don't like their manners or the way that they walk
Kill Kill Kill for peace
Kill Kill Kill for peace
If you don't kill them then the Chinese will
You don't want America to play second fiddle
Kill Kill Kill for peace

"The great disease of American society," says Tuli, "is abstraction; people are ready to die for freedom or the flag but rarely think about what these things are. Americans like to kill and be killed—aggression is a reaction to frustration. Sexual frustration is still the major problem to be solved and in my opinion, the appearance of sexual humor is a healthy sign. And if we can put some joy, some real sexy warmth into the revolution, we'll have really achieved something."

To which Ken Weaver added: "And a man who's laughing can't shoot a gun worth a damn."

For several months, the Fugs played concerts at The Bridge, on St. Mark's Place, every Saturday at midnight. The theater holds only 88, and after the first couple of weeks the concerts were always jammed. The Bridge's manager, playwright Arthur Sainer, was mildly surprised by their success. "The audience apparently built up by word of mouth because one week Ed forgot to place their regular ad in the *Voice* and yet we were packed. Even now I have mixed feelings about them; they

come across as toughies but I think they're really very sweet—and quite innocent in some ways."

A typical Fugs performance was an object lesson in organized chaos. Because of the profusion of instruments, cables, and peripatetic performers onstage, it was impossible to mark the transition between tune-up and actual performance. With such introductions as, "In the key of physical distress" or "—of profound psychotic neuralgia," Ed would introduce the song *Dirty Old Man:*

Hanging out by the schoolyard gate
looking up every dress I can
sucking wind through my upper
plate
I'm a dirty old man

Or a similarly suggestive song such as *Saran Wrap:*

Get into her drawers
Rip off a sheet of that
Saran Wrap
Saran Wrap

Or *Coca-Cola Douche:*

My baby ain't got no money,
But her snatch it taste like honey
Cause she makes that
Coca-Cola douche

The audience—predominantly college kids with a sprinkling of hip socialites (one Long Island teenager turned up in a chauffered limousine)—would roar its approval.

In the early days of the group, the noise from the guitars and the incessant stomping of its members tended to drown out the lyrics. Tuli's clowning—blowing up contraceptives, opening cans of Rheingold beer, arranging a soldier's hat upon a skull—was distracting, too. But now the act is heavy with sexual symbolism, from Tuli's sweatshirt overprinted with "U.S. Broad-Jumping Team" to the rhythmic thrusting of a phallus-shaped maraca through a hollow tambourine.

"We believe in body poetry," Ed explains. "That is, the Fugs work through the genitals and the Big Beat to get to the brain and through the brain and the Big Beat to get to the genitals, thus creating a thrilling cross-current."

And in the introduction to *The Fugs Song Book* he adds: "Only by hearing and seeing the Fugs may one get their total eye-ear ejaculation. Much of the Fug Body Poetry is the eyeball kicks they afford on stage through Operation Sex Fiend, Operation Ankle Grab & Operation Livid Dick, which are, as most know, key code terms in the International Zionist Marijuana Conspiracy."

He believes marijuana should be legalized and has never been frightened to say so. One of the publications he churned out in his Peace Eye Bookstore was *The Marijuana Newsletter.* Ed and his co-editors were arrested (and acquitted) on at least one occasion for distributing this.

Recently, along with Tuli, drummer Ken Weaver and guitarist Pete Kearney, he sat in a book-cluttered office at Talent Associates, discussing with David Susskind's assistant whether the Fugs should appear on a forthcoming TV show.

"We may blow Susskind right off the air," he said. "Not because of foulmouthedness or anything like that, but rather because of our philosophical position."

Susskind's assistant, told by Ed that he'd once lived for two years on raw eggs and oatmeal, then asked: "If you made a lot of money, would it change you in any way?"

Ed: "You'd just have to reach me through ship-to-shore telephone." Later, more seriously, he explained: "We could all have been earning, maybe, $200 a week teaching or writing, but we prefer to spend our time doing things that give us greater satisfaction. Now that we have our spiritual feet on the ground, we have no objection to making money."

The company, in fact, which has been set up to handle the Fugs' affairs was named—by Ed—the GTM Corporation, for "Get the Money."

Is there anything that the Fugs *wouldn't* sing, any taboos that they have about what could be performed in public?

"Scatological references to LBJ, maybe," muses Ken Weaver. "But then again, maybe not. There are a few things that we wouldn't mind singing but probably wouldn't print in the song book. For example, we have a song with the line, *I believe in teenage legs wrapped around my body*. Although our music has gotten better, there hasn't been any cop-out on the message."

And Tuli adds: "Sex and killing are the major subjects to be dealt with at the moment; it's all around us—we're just six months ahead of other people in articulating it. But sooner or later we'll turn to other subjects, other problems. What? Well, life always presents its own problems."

COMPUTER-CALCULATED COPULATION

by John Francis Putnam

We like to let the machine do it for us. Take the computerized dating systems, with names like *Meet-a-Mate* or *Click* or *Data-Date*.

Who wouldn't really groove on the Machine speeding us right past all those boring preliminaries, especially when we know that the party we're being matched up with is willing because it's been *programmed* that way? Anxieties end and the dawn is going to be rosy-fingered after all.

The big drag about these computerized systems is the corny style and content of the questions you are asked to fill in—questions that are supposed to present the real you, what you are like, who you are, etc. It doesn't take long to find out that these questions are no better than the ones you find yourself asking at a party where there are the usual six guys to every girl, and you end up asking that tired old warhorse opener: "Well, what do *you* do?"

The data-computer questions are evading the real question: Is it going to be *good* when you two finally hit the sack together?

Who cares whether you like foreign movies over Hollywood or jazz over Mantovani and his strings? That detached, cool analytical power of the giant computer is getting short-circuited by a lot of chatter. Besides, if these patterns are held to, the computer is liable to come up with the *ideal* date for you . . . like your ex-wife.

Here are some samples of what a realistic questionnaire should be, one that if fed into a computer would probably end up getting you happily, thoroughly, and beautifully laid. Don't be scared or embarrassed. After all, the machine couldn't care less.

* * *

He/she is coming over to your apartment, probably to stay for the night. Do you:

☐ Frantically change those 6-week-old sheets and buy a new blanket?

☐ Pile up records, guitar, magazines on the bed so that it won't look so damned suggestively like a bed?

☐ Play it cool and leave the apartment just as it is?

He suddenly brings out a set of dirty pictures and insists on showing them to you. Do you:

☐ Blush, but ask to see them a second time?

☐ Treat it all as a bit of nostalgic and scabrous Americana, making witty comments as to the staging, photographic quality, ambience and technique?

☐ Suggest that you both try some of the poses?

While talking to her, you pull a handkerchief from your pocket, and a condom pops out and lands on the floor in plain sight. Do you:

☐ Make a fast grab and hope she hasn't seen it?

☐ Ask her to pick it up?

☐ Observe something to the effect that "Oh, yeah, there's been an awful lot of clap around lately."

Realizing that you'll be staying at his place, do you:

☐ Make sure to pick out a different dress (non-creasable) that you can wear to work next day?

☐ Rush out and buy funky bikini undies?

☐ Just to be difficult, wear a bra that opens in the front?

In the heat of passion, you remember, too late, that you're wearing dirty underwear. Do you:

☐ Start an evocative bit on the erotic power of acrid male body smell?

☐ Blame excessive, bourgeois fastidiousness on your respective mothers and take a shower together?

☐ Decide to be dramatic and do it with all your clothes on?

As a female, you believe that birth control is your responsibility. Do you:

☐ Drench yourself with strong perfume to kill that tell-tale Ortho-Creme odor?

☐ Brazenly insert your diaphragm in full view of your partner?

☐ Tell him how much your breasts have grown since you began taking Enovid?

She looks at her watch and says, "Oh, is it that late? I had no idea. Look, you can sleep over, but you have to promise you'll behave." Do you behave by:

☐ Starting with the touch-her-cold-toes-with-your-warm-toes ploy?

☐ Come on spontaneously with "Oh, I forgot something—I didn't kiss you goodnight."

☐ Assure her, "I'll only put it in a little way."

He suggests that you practice fellatio. Do you:

☐ Request that he wear protection?

☐ Tell him that you never suck off on the first date?

☐ Ask him where he keeps the mouthwash?

She suggests that you practice cunnilingus. Do you:

☐ Hint around to find out just how recently she took a bath?

☐ Demand reciprocity of some sort?

☐ Prepare the way with honey, mayonnaise, peanut butter . . . anything?

Your favorite music to make love by is:

☐ Ravel's *Bolero.*

☐ Muddy Waters.

☐ Ravi Shankar.

☐ Racing cars recorded live at Sebring.

During intercourse, how do you communicate to him verbally?

☐ Call loudly upon the deity with remarks like "Oh, my Gawd!"

☐ Give full utterance to cherished Anglo-Saxonisms like "Oh, shit, honey, oh, Shiiiiiit!"

☐ Keep repeating "No, it's my fault! It's not you! It's me!"

During intercourse, how do you communicate to her verbally?

☐ Indulge in interrogation, like "What am I doin' to ya, baby, what am I doin', huh?"

☐ Say, "Hey, aren't I great?"

☐ Inquire with cold sarcasm, "Well, did you come yet?"

When it's over, do you:

☐ Share the only remaining clean towel?

☐ Urinate or defecate while leaving the bathroom door open?

☐ Kiss your partner gently on the cheek and say, "Would you hate me if I had a cigarette now?"

He has had a fine ejaculation. Do you:

☐ Pretend you have a bad cramp in your leg so you won't have to tell him he's getting too heavy already?

☐ Ask, "When will I see you again?" in a clinging tone of voice?

☐ Subtly but emphatically move the scene over onto the dry side of the bed?

She has had a fine climax. Do you:

☐ Fall asleep immediately?

☐ Make a token display of affectionate gratitude, then fall asleep immediately?

☐ Pretend to fall asleep immediately in order to recharge for more action?

In case of unwanted pregnancy and wanted abortion, do you believe:

☐ He should pay?

☐ She should pay?

☐ Both should pay?

☐ Medicare?

LET THEM NEVER FIND THY HEART AT HOME

by F. D. White

Recently newspapers chronicled the dramatic events that took place in Houston when doctors saved a man's life by fitting him with a mechanical heart. The device is made of plastic and is essentially a pump that assumes the work normally performed by the left ventricle, that section of the heart most commonly damaged by a heart attack.

Up to this time the device had been used only in experiments on animals. A high percentage of success was attained in the animal experiments and so it was decided to give it a try on a human. The subject of the history-making operation, a 65-year-old Illinois coal miner, would surely have died (sooner than he did) without the operation.

The developers of the mechanical heart promise that soon it will be available for widespread human use on a practical basis. But they warn it will be an expensive proposition, what with installation, maintenance, and the like.

Unfortunately, heart disease is not restricted to the rich. Many citizens of moderate income and limited resources are the unwilling victims of heart ailments. Their lives can be saved by the machine, but how will they afford it?

The answer should be obvious to any observer of the American scene. They will "finance" it just like the car, the TV set, the baby's crib. Alas, this solution, so simple on the surface, gives rise to a distressing question: What will happen when someone who is being kept alive by the mechanical heart falls behind in his payments?

Could the following occur:

It is early evening of a bitterly cold winter's night. A husband and wife are huddled together on a threadbare couch in a bleak and cheerless room. The only light comes from a bare bulb in the ceiling fixture. There is no heat due to a lack of understanding on the part of the gas company.

The ratty couch they are seated on is the lone piece of furniture in the room, the rest having been sold, piece by piece, for pennies, to provide food. The only sounds are the chattering of their teeth through blue lips, and the whirring of his mechanical heart.

Then, suddenly, the silence is broken by loud knocking on the door.

A young man, neatly dressed and official-looking, enters the room. He exudes authority. Without preliminaries he says, "I'm from RFC. Rotten Finance Company. I've come for the heart."

"No, no," shrieks the wife, throwing herself at the young man. "You can't, you can't . . . my husband will die!"

"Look, lady," the young man explains, briskly disentangling himself,

"your husband signed the paper. He knew what the payments were to be. If he couldn't make the payments, *why did he sign?*"

"He . . . he would have *died* without the heart. The doctors said it was the only way to save his *life!*"

"I don't know anything about that, lady. I get all sorts of complaints and excuses on this job. Why, just yesterday, a woman got mad because we repossessed her power lawnmower. Said she had to cut the grass because she was on the Neighborhood Beautification Committee. The stories I hear!"

"Yes, but," the wife begins.

"Now, now, honey," the husband interrupts, "this young man is right. The agreement must stand. After all, a man's word is his bond. Trust is what makes the free enterprise system work."

"But, darling, what will become of you?"

"We'll figure something out, dear. For example, I could tie my veins to my arteries and curl up in a truck tire. Then you could roll me around and that would circulate my blood."

He chuckles softly at his little joke.

"That's not such a bad idea," the RFC man puts in. "You could line up a tire company to sponsor the stunt and roll from coast to coast or something. It would be great publicity for them."

With that, the young man produces a screwdriver, the husband starts taking off his shirt and the wife rushes out to find a tire.

"Hold still, for Chrissake, buddy," says the young man, busy with his screwdriver. "Have a heart, willya!"

The husband mutters, "I *knew* I should've gotten the one with the quarter-a-day slot."

VETERANS OF AMERICA, I SALUTE YOU!

by Rick Rubin

Annually, on November 11th, it is our duty as Patriotic Citizens to honor American Veterans of All Our Wars, the brave men and women, whether clerk-typists in Korea or expert infantrymen in Kansas, who have actually or potentially defended our American way of life.

Personally, I feel that this day is one of the more significant of our American holidays, and each year I try to pause and remember one or more specific groups of Veterans. I say specific because as of July 1966 there were more than 22 million Veterans in the country who, together with their immediate families, made up two-fifths of the population. You can't salute them all at once. A person needs something more concrete.

For example, one group I delight in honoring is the Veterans of the 25th U.S. Infantry Regiment (Colored), six of whom in 1906 had won the Medal of Honor. On August 3rd of that year, a dozen or so members of this organization, angered by the treatment they had received from the (White) citizens of nearby Brownsville, Texas, made what has been described (by White people at least) as a shooting sortie into the town, killing one citizen.

Whether any man of the 25th Regiment had ever been killed by the citizens of Brownsville, I can't say, but I am reasonably certain that no one had ever been convicted of doing so.

The soldiers returned to their post unobserved, and during the subsequent official investigation, not one of the one hundred

and sixty men of the three Colored companies would inform on his fellow soldiers. On November 5th, President Theodore Roosevelt discharged "without honor" every man of the three companies, observing that if no one admitted guilt, all of them would have to pay the penalty.

The discharge without honor meant that all pensions and payments were forfeited, including those of the six Medal of Honor winners, and none of the men was ever reinstated or given a pension. And so, each year, I salute the Veterans of Brownsville.

Would it seem too unsophisticated if I salute the first Americans to die under Hitler's bullets, to be blown to heroes' graves by Mussolini's airplanes? American Veterans of the Abraham Lincoln Brigade of the Spanish Civil War, I salute you on Veterans' Day.

I salute those other unlucky Veterans, the Communists and Socialists and German-American Bundists, the homosexuals and psychotics and other disreputable types, who were drafted into the Army in time of war, and were then, though not necessarily actually convicted of any crime, discharged under circumstances less than "Honorable" to hunt for jobs as best they knew how.

I salute the Veterans of Coxey's Army, who in 1894 marched on Washington D.C. to petition for relief legislation and bonuses for Veterans, but were instead rushed by guards, shot and injured, and saw their leaders arrested for the crime of trampling on the grass.

And I do not forget to honor the Veterans Bonus Marchers of 1932. Several policemen were injured while evicting them from vacant government buildings where they were living, and, in the process, killing two of their number. The Army was called in by President Hoover—and, led by General Douglas MacArthur, advanced with machine guns, tanks, tear gas, drawn sabers and fixed bayonets, in full battle dress.

General MacArthur observed that the marchers were "animated by the essence of revolution," and further commented that if Mr. Hoover had "let it go another week, I believe that the institutions of our government would have been severely threatened."

So, to be fair, I salute not only the bonus marchers of 1932, but the soldiers who attacked them (and subsequently became veterans themselves) and further, I salute Veteran Douglas MacArthur.

I salute the Negro combat troops of World War I, who served with French Divisions overseas, so as not to cause trouble, and won many a citation for bravery under fire—perhaps the only Veterans of our history who not only had to learn foreign weapons and foreign military organization, but even a foreign language, just to serve their own Army in time of war.

And I further salute some who returned home and were among the seventy Negroes, including several still in uniform, who were lynched during the first postwar year. Even if they had learned uppity ways from those un-American Frenchmen, they were Veterans nonetheless.

Of course, the first Veterans I hail each year are my own comrades-in-arms of the Korean Police Action, who, if they were less than totally successful as soldiers, were less successful still at draft-dodging—although many no doubt now march in the parades on November 11th.

Then I move on to other defenders of the American Dream: the Nisei members of the 442nd Infantry Regiment and the 100th Battalion, who voluntarily joined the Army out of concentration camps across California and Utah and Idaho, won five Distinguished Unit Citations with the Fifth Army in Italy and the Seventh Army in the Rhineland, and are said to have been the most decorated Regimental Combat Team in the Army.

Then they returned home (some of them, at least) to such places as Hood River, Oregon, to find that the American Legion did not want a bunch of lousy Japs repossessing their lawful homes and farms. The government they had served voluntarily and well was prepared to pay depreciated 1945 prices for their cars and equipment and other possessions, confiscated in 1941.

I salute American Legionnaires who castrated, hanged, and then shot full of holes one Wesley Everset, from a railroad bridge near Centralia, Washington, on Armistice Day, 1919, and thereby defended the American Dream against the eight-hour day and other such foreign-inspired Wobbly demands.

I salute sharp-eyed American Legionnaire Homer Chaillaux, who reviewed a Legion pamphlet entitled "Americanism: What Is It?" Legionnaire Chaillaux found that the pamphlet contained too much emphasis on freedom of speech and too little on the fundamentals of religion. In addition, the paper was manufactured in Japan, and the American Eagle on the cover was printed in red. He forced the pamphlet, clearly un-American, to be withdrawn.

I salute the Military Order of the World War, a group of former WWI officers who, in their National Bulletin, reported that the A.C.L.U. actually "believes in rampant free speech."

I salute as well a man who, as Colonel, shared with Ethan Allen leadership of the expedition that captured Fort Ticonderoga in 1775; who later that year led the capture of the fort at St. Johns, and in 1776 almost captured Quebec; who attacked the British on Lake Champlain with a fleet of leaky small boats, and in 1777 repulsed an attempted invasion of Connecticut; who was in the thick of the fighting at Saratoga, wounded, leading his troops; who commanded Philadelphia in 1778, West Point in 1780, and went on to become one of America's best-known Veterans. Colonel Benedict Arnold, I salute you.

I hail Private Edward Donald Slovik, called Eddie, one of the thousands of American soldiers convicted of deserting in the face of the enemy, but the only one since 1864 to be executed for doing so. On January 31, 1945, he was shot to death by a firing squad and rushed into Veterandom.

I salute Colonel Charles R. Forbes, head of the Veterans' Bureau under President Harding, who, after Harding's death, was found to have operated a gigantic swindle, which milked the Bureau of more than two hundred million dollars in less than two years. At a time when disabled Veterans in hospitals lacked bandages, bedding, and drugs, Colonel Forbes condemned carloads of these items and sold them off at a fraction of their cost.

I salute, too, the Veterans of U.S. Military Actions other than declared wars: Hawaii 1893, China 1900, Panama 1903, Dominican Republic 1904, Nicaragua 1911, Mexico 1914, Haiti 1915, Mexico 1916, Dominican Republic 1916 . . . who got killed just as dead, wounded just as painfully, but by some oversight, got no G.I. Bill, no homecoming parade, no Veteran's special bonuses or even so much as a casualty statistic in the World Almanac.

I salute the men who fought to destroy the dictatorship in Cuba, the Anti-Batista fighters, now no more able to get a good job than those earlier anti-fascists, the men of the Abraham Lincoln Brigade. I salute the Bay of Pigs invaders, who, if they weren't either Americans or in the American Army, at least took our pay and did our work, however unsuccessfully. I salute the former officers and men of the Revolutionary War who participated in Captain Daniel Shay's Rebellion of 1786, an attempt to overthrow the government of Massachusetts.

I salute the members of an alleged special group that is supposed to have spent World War II somewhere high up in Colorado, having been adjudged by the Army as too subversive to be of any use, but not subversive enough to kill or kick out or simply not draft in the first place.

I salute Veterans of the Revolution, who knew that it was right and proper for a people to throw off the shackles of an unjust government, and I salute the men of the Union Army in the Civil War, who knew that it was wrong and unlawful for a people to throw off the shackles of an unjust government.

I salute American Veterans who invaded Latin American countries to protect them from outside intervention, then invaded again to intervene on behalf of American property rights.

In fact, I stand ready to salute any group or individual Veteran who fits my peculiarly warped view of defenders of the American Dream. I salute those first Americans to die for their country, the American Indians. I salute those Pilgrims, Puritans and Protestants who killed them, and were killed by them, and thus became the second Americans to die for their country. I salute the latest American veterans, the soldiers and airmen and sailors in Vietnam who are dying for some country, I'm not quite sure whose. Nor do I slight the American boys in The Congo, in Korea, in Formosa and Spain and Morocco, nor the military advisory groups in dozens or perhaps even hundreds of other countries, all dying or at least ready to die, without benefit of declared war or G.I. Bill of Rights, in defense of freedom and the local USIS library.

Veterans of America, myself included, I salute you!

LETTER FROM A SOLDIER'S WIFE

by Lenny Bruce

Who remembers? Who can I pester—God? Of course, He had a kid of His own. He spent a lot time at the wailing post, as the Father, the Son and the Holy Ghost, but still, He was never a mother. Only a mother knows what it is to lose a son in the service. And only a wife knows what it is to lose her husband.

It's getting near the time that will introduce the most dreaded aspect of *The Emily Post Guide to Etiquette*—the chapter on "Proper Garments for Funerals." How does one dress? Who will zip me up? Kiss my back after I'm snapped? It's not too late, God: there is still time to save him from being stilled. Time to save the most truthful—the strongest—man in the world.

You don't believe? Just ask my children. He was a soldier that stood quiet and obedient, not as spectacular as the one that dropped his bomb over Hiroshima, that burned the lids away from the skillion almond eyes that will never know the blessing the Japanese sandman has to offer.

Don't take away those arms that soothe me as a poultice. How obsolete the other pillow becomes, except to hug, and smother Your convulsive beckoning to the dead. What can I tell you? How can I single out one good deed, so that You will enforce the Fifth Commandment? Thou Shalt Not Kill! Please, Jehovah, just get to the masses with one little miracle, one carnival-like trick—sky-write, spell it out in lightning: THOU SHALT NOT KILL. Punctuate it with thunder claps. Show me strength, show me the sky is Yours. Please, dear God, save my man's life. I'm sure your Son would approve.

Very truly yours,

Mrs. Adolf Eichmann

* * *

The Sullivan Brothers. The telegram. The State Department regrets to inform you that we lost a destroyer and your five sons were aboard it.

Remember five times, five christenings. The cigars were handed out five times. The State Department regrets. Five winter coats and favorite sweaters and recipes that have lost their meaning.

As the general alarm sounded, no one executed the command "All men man your battle stations" because they were no longer men. They were small frightened boys with dirty chapped knees that showed through ripped corduroy knickers. The Sullivan Brothers screamed at the ocean whose very name was a lie—Pacific—they screamed the words that all boys scream as they reach for their rosary beads. *Ma! Ma!*

President Kennedy is a truthful man. He promised he would not bring religion to the White House. He has kept his promise. But he is going to protect Berlin. Protect Berlin, that supported the killing of the Sullivan Brothers. Protect Berlin—under what premise? Surely not the premise that we give full protection to our employees: Powers is still in jail. President Kennedy is setting up for the slaughter of the Sullivan Brothers' sons.

There's your response, Mrs. Eichmann.

UNCLE SAM WANTS YOU DEAD, NIGGER

by Richard Pryor

(OPENING SHOT—Stock footage of jet plane landing at an airport in America. CUT TO stock footage of a casket being carried off a plane by soldiers.)

PREACHER—*(Voice Over)*

He tried to serve this country

(Congregation answers with him:) um hm *um*

And Johnny was a good boy, yes

um hm *um*

(The casket is being loaded into a hearse.)

PREACHER *(V.O.)*

I remember Johnny well, um hm um

I can remember Johnny when he used to

walk around the streets, yes lord

He had no destination, um hm um

Had no place to, um hm um

I remember quite well

(The Ghetto—LONG SHOT from rooftop of JOHNNY walking the streets where he was raised. The only sounds we hear are the natural sounds of the ghetto streets. Johnny continues to walk past the storefront and houses in the ghetto. He hears the voices of his parents.)

FATHER *(Off Screen)*

Boy, I want you to get a job.

You just laying around the house,

been in trouble, getting arrested

all the time. I'm tired of getting

you out of jail. It's just a heartache

to me and your momma.

MOTHER *(O.S.)*

That's right, I don't know what I'm

gonna do with you . . . I just don't know.

I try, we try, we work hard to send you

to school, and you didn't even stay in

school; just got outta school.

Why don't you do something with your life?

FATHER *(O.S.)*

You ain't never gonna be nothing, boy.

You ought to do something with your life.

Look at all your friends,

they doing something. Terry got a job

down at the factory, he working. Why don't

you get one down there?

JOHNNY *(V.O.)*

Dad, the people when I went down there,

they told me they didn't have no more openings.

FATHER *(O.S.)*

Yeah, that's what you always say when

you lookin for a job, 'they ain't got no openings.' They ain't

never got no

openings when you try to get work.

(TRACKING SHOT: JOHNNY continues his walk, stopping in front of an Army recruiting poster that says "Uncle Sam Wants You." CLOSE UP of poster.)

WHITE VOICE *(O.S.)*

Uncle Sam wants you.

Uncle Sam wants you.

Uncle Sam wants you.

That's right nigger,

Uncle Sam wants you.

(POSTER'S Point of View—ANGLE UP toward JOHNNY—MEDIUM SHOT. A black man in a dashiki draws up beside Johnny, stands there and just looks at him looking at the poster.)

DASHIKI *(V.O.)*

Yeah, nigger, Uncle Sam wants you *dead*.

Man, you don't want to join the Army,

what you want is to join our army.

We need you now.

(JOHNNY starts to walk away, and hears his father's voice again.)

FATHER *(O.S.)*

That's right, hang out in the street
with them Panthers. That's what you
been doin, you been down there with
them Panthers. Down there with all them
Black groups. They won't get you no money.
They ain't gonna help you out.
You better get something. I know the white
man ain't good, but some of em all right.
You got to try to do something about that, boy.
(DASHIKI follows JOHNNY as he continues his walk, crossing the street and turning a corner.)

DASHIKI *(V.O.)*

Man, ain't none of em all right.
(He says this with the look on his face.)
Ain't none of 'em, that's what we been
trying to tell you. Ain't none of em
all right. Ain't nothing right with that man.
The brothers and sisters down here, we need
you here, man. You want to join an army, man,
join our army.
(JOHNNY turns into a storefront, which we see is the Army recruiting office. He hears his father's voice.)

FATHER *(O.S.)*

That's good that you gonna get in the Army, man.
Look at Harvey, he was in the Army,
got medals and everything.
Went into the Army, became *somebody.*
(CUT TO stock footage of recruits being shaven and otherwise processed, getting off buses at training camp.)

JOHNNY *(O.S.)*

This is my chance now.
If I make this, I go back home and
Janet's father won't be so mad.
He see me in the Army, trying to do
something, maybe I can go over to her house.
I really dig that chick, man.
And Dad, I can send them some of the allotment money.
(TRAINING FIELD, DAY—LONG SHOT—JOHNNY is in the field doing drill exercises; but he is all alone. However, we hear the sounds of a whole company drilling, and he marches as if he were in the middle of them.)

SOLDIERS *(O.S.)*

Hut, two, three, four
Hut, two, three, four
To the left, march!

OFFICER *(O.S.)*

Today we are learning to kill, HAAH!

SECOND OFFICER *(O.S.)*

Now you have completed basic training.
(FIELD—MEDIUM SHOT—JOHNNY is dressed in his fatigues, with boots and all.)

OFFICER *(O.S.)*

You special band of special forces
will be assigned to Fort McPherson
for additional training, and then to
duty in Vietnam.
(WATERFRONT: The railing of a troop ship—JOHNNY

"—And you, Pfc. Andy Tuggle of A Company, 81st Infantry: If you weren't out here fighting us Vietnamese patriots you could be back home moving to a new neighborhood, going out with white girls, enjoying all those increased civil rights benefits your government has obtained for you . . ."

leans on the ship's railing, looking out at the ocean, thinking about his destination—Vietnam.)

JOHNNY *(V.O.)*

Damn, can't wait to get to 'Nam.
I'm gonna be good; I can take it.
I know I ain't gonna die.
I'm gonna get me some of them gooks, too, Jack.
That's right, get me some medals,
so when I go home, I'll be a hero.
(DASHIKI appears next to JOHNNY again and stares at him.)

DASHIKI *(V.O.)*

Why you gonna be killing some Vietnamese, man?
What kinda nerve you got to be callin them
gooks, nigger? You crazy or something?
What's wrong with you?

JOHNNY *(V.O.)*

Why don't you leave me alone, man?
You do it your way, I'm doing it mine.
I don't want no trouble, man.
I'm trying to be somebody,
and you trying to mess that up.
(CUT TO stock footage—troops landing in Vietnam, B-52 bombing raids, search and destroy missions, etc. Along with the stock footage, there is a musical soundtrack composed of a mixture of Shirley Temple singing "On the Good Ship Lollipop" and Stepin Fetchit-type voices saying all the old hack phrases from racist movies, "Well, time to eat dinner, heah, heah, heah!")
(VIETNAM—TRACKING SHOT: Half-track driving along

road. JOHNNY is riding through the country, in the half-track with a 50-caliber machine gun on top. The truck approaches a field with some farmers in the distance, plowing. The farmers see the truck, and wave at it. We hear the voices of two officers in the truck, but we never see them.)

CAPTAIN GRISBY

Hold that truck up! Hold up the column.

LIEUTENANT *(O.S.; definite white cracker voice)*

What's the matter, Captain Grisby?

GRISBY

Those people in the field seem to be
signaling those men over there on that hill.
I have an idea there are some mortars
on that hill, and those people seem to be
signaling

JOHNNY *(V.O., to himself)*

They're not signaling, they're just waving.

LIEUTENANT *(O.S.)*

It seems they *are* signaling to someone
over the hill.

GRISBY *(to Johnny)*

Stop waving, soldier, what you trying to do?
Cut them people down out there, boy.

JOHNNY

What, sir?

GRISBY

You heard the order.
Shoot them—kill them people out there.
They're gonna call a mortar in on us, boy.
We could be wiped out at any second.

JOHNNY *(V.O., to himself)*

I can't do that, man.

GRISBY

If you can't do it, I'll get a white boy
to do it. *(To lieutenant)*

I know them niggers can't take it in combat,
you know what I mean?
It's just something about them; they just
don't have . . . the stuff.

(MEDIUM SHOT—JOHNNY shoots the people down. We hear the gunfire.)

GRISBY *(O.S.)*

Good job, soldier.

(CUT TO stock footage of New Year's Eve in Times Square, or cadets tossing hats in the air at Annapolis graduation. We hear the crowd cheering. ZOOM IN to a CLOSE UP on JOHN-NY'S face. The horror of what he has done is shown on Johnny's face.)

JOHNNY *(V.O., to himself)*

Don't crack, don't crack . . .
You did it, man, you made it.
You gonna be somebody—you are somebody.
Look at them looking at you now, yeah,
look at em.

GRISBY

You did all right, soldier.

Can you get those ears for a count?

JOHNNY

Beg your pardon, sir?

GRISBY

We gotta have those ears for our count.

JOHNNY *(V.O., to himself)*

Ears for a count. *(To Grisby)* Yes, sir.

(FARMER'S FIELD—TRACKING SHOT: JOHNNY goes out in the field to get the ears of the people he has just shot. He gets to the bodies, and looks down. ANGLE UP at JOHNNY from behind the bodies. He looks down at the bodies and a sudden look of horror comes over his face; he almost goes into shock. JOHNNY'S P.O.V.—Looking at the bodies. Instead of the Vietnamese he shot, he sees the bodies of his family lying there, dead.)

GRISBY *(O.S.)*

Get them ears!

(JOHNNY looks again, and the bodies are those of the Vietnamese he has killed. He cuts off the ears, and hears the Captain's voice as he walks to the truck.)

GRISBY *(O.S.)*

That's good for at least one medal.
Heroism beyond the call of duty.
You can get four medals for this.
Plus a three day pass.
Soldier, you really going to be
something when you get home.

(BUSHES AT EDGE OF FIELD—MEDIUM LONG SHOT ZOOMS IN on rifle barrel. A gun points out of the bushes at JOHNNY in the distance. It fires, and the sound is amplified very loud. JOHNNY begins to fall, in very slow motion. As he falls, we hear the preacher again.)

PREACHER *(O.S.)*

And he lived a good life, um hm
And he was a good boy, yes he was.
And he never done no harm to nobody, um hm um
And he tried to do the best he could, yes, he did.

(As the preacher ends, the body is still falling. CUT TO tracking shot of hearse approaching graveyard. GRAVEYARD GATE—MEDIUM LONG SHOT—ZOOM IN on guard.)

GUARD *(V.O., white cracker)*

I don't care what kind of hero he is,
we don't bury no niggers in this graveyard.

(As he speaks, the frame freezes on the black folks looking into the gates of the graveyard.)

GUARD *(V.O., echoing)*

We don't bury no niggers in this graveyard.
We don't bury no niggers in this graveyard.
We don't bury no niggers in this graveyard.

(CUT BACK to JOHNNY, still falling.)

DASHIKI *(O.S., echoing, fading out)*

Uncle Sam wants you dead, nigger
Uncle Sam wants you dead, nigger
Uncle Sam wants you dead, nigger . . .

(As the last words fade out, JOHNNY'S body hits the ground. FREEZE ON BODY. FADE OUT.)

"The credibility gap is a problem. It is getting so bad we can't even believe our own leaks."
—*White House Press Secretary Bill Moyers in a speech to the National Newspapers Association*

Recent headlines in U.S. newspapers have taken on a new doubtful look: DO THEY BELIEVE US? The "us," actually, is not really us (as in you and me), it's *them*—the gentlemen from the Department of Defense and the Department of State. The problem seems to be that on a number of occasions, "us" have been caught making public statements that don't necessarily jibe with the facts. It is a sign of the new moral enlightenment that this now troubles our conscience.

The American people, at one time, were far more blasé about such episodes, generally indifferent as to who believed *us* on diverse issues like Guatemala, the U2 affair or the Bay of Pigs. They understood without being told that it's in the nature of government to give only its best side. This best side goes by the code name of "Truth."

Truth is a combine of what makes us feel better with what makes us look good on the job. Lies are a combine of what makes us feel bad with what makes us look inept on the job.

Seen in this light, the CIA and the Pentagon always tell the President the truth, since it makes the President feel better and helps the CIA and the Pentagon hold onto their jobs. The President then passes that truth onto the people. So truth in government is not nearly so much a metaphysical concept as it is a socio-economic concept. Communist truth differs from Free World truth to the degree that Moscow's gold differs from Fort Knox's. You get what you pay for.

This much being true, it is appalling that, considering the money we are spending to get people to believe us, fewer and fewer do. Somewhere there has been a breakdown in communications.

Fortunately there are technological advances to take up the slack. In television, for example, the use of canned laugh tracks. When something is not funny on television, a recording of laughter is added to the sound track to convince viewers at home that whether they like the show or not everybody *else* thinks it's hilarious. In this way, modern engineering has provided an efficient substitute for the more iffy unmechanized concept of a sense of humor.

In very much the same way can viewers be persuaded to believe our government. By attaching a canned credibility track to the speeches of the President, and the Secretaries of Defense and State, we can at last remove all reason to doubt their truths when they're not telling them. Once a consensus on truth is established, the American people will, as always, go along.

If, for example, Mr. McNamara on his next return from Vietnam announces that the war is going well for our side, how much easier it would be to believe him if recorded with his remarks there was a canned credibility track consisting of low-keyed voices whispering off-screen comments like: "I believe him. I believe him, yes, I believe him." Or, "If he weren't telling the truth, the President would fire him." Or, "I understand he's a fanatic about facts."

Then again, the next time Mr. Rusk goes on the air in his continuing series of peace feeler denials, who could question his credibility if we heard in the background subliminal whispers like: "He has access to information that *we* don't have?" Or, "Is that the face of a man who wants confrontation with Red China?" Or, "Rusk is a dove. Rusk is a dove. Rusk is a dove."

And, finally, when the President returns to the screen once again, to explain that we are in Vietnam as a matter of national honor, how much more convincing his plaint were it backed by a credi-

THE FANATICS

Full-page ad:
"*Who cares* whether there are 200 tissues in the box—or only 199? Only some kind of fanatic would bother to count those tissues. But that's what we are: fanatics about the claims on labels. So—we count. And we don't stop at that. We'll measure the size of those tissues, analyze the quality, and critically judge the price. That's just one example of the thousands of product checks A&P Quality Testing Laboratories make every year—just one of the thousands of reasons you can count on the values at your A&P. *We care.*"

Tiny news item:
"The Great Atlantic and Pacific Tea Company pleaded guilty to short-weighting, ending two years of litigation. The charges originally included several employees as well as the A&P. The company was fined $100 on each of two charges resulting from discrepancies in the weight of pre-packaged meats."

bility track of such homespun homilies as: "Remember the Maine." Or, "My country right or wrong." Or, "In your heart you know he's right." Or, simply, "Yes, Lord!"

"Truck . . . GMC . . . flatbed . . . deuce-and-a-half . . . empty . . . headed North. . . ."

"Dog. Is this the way you treat your old allies against the French? Is this your filthy English justice? Screw your Queen, Mister."

THE PARTS LEFT OUT OF THE KENNEDY BOOK

An executive in the publishing industry, who obviously must remain anonymous, has made available to The Realist *a photostatic copy of the original manuscript of William Manchester's book,* The Death of a President.

Those passages printed here were marked for deletion months before Harper & Row sold the serialization rights to Look *Magazine; hence they do not appear even in the so-called "complete" version published by the German magazine,* Stern.

At the Democratic National Convention in the summer of 1960, Los Angeles was the scene of a political visitation of the alleged sins of the father upon the son. Lyndon Johnson found himself battling for the presidential nomination with a young, handsome, charming and witty adversary, John F. Kennedy.

The Texan in his understandable anxiety degenerated to a strange campaign tactic. He attacked his opponent on the grounds that his father, Joseph P. Kennedy, was a Nazi sympathizer during the time he was United States Ambassador to Great Britain, from 1938 to 1940. The senior Kennedy had predicted that Germany would defeat England and he therefore urged President Franklin D. Roosevelt to withhold aid.

Now Johnson found himself fighting pragmatism with pragmatism. It did not work; he lost the nomination.

Ironically, the vicissitudes of regional bloc voting forced Kennedy into selecting Johnson as his running mate. Jack rationalized the practicality of the situation, but Jackie was constitutionally unable to forgive Johnson. Her attitude toward him always remained one of controlled paroxysm.

* * *

It was common knowledge in Washington social circles that the Chief Executive was something of a ladies' man. His staff included a Secret Service agent referred to by the code name *Dentist,* whose duties virtually centered around escorting to and from a rendezvous site—either in the District of Columbia or while traveling—the models, actresses, and other strikingly attractive females chosen by the President for his not at all infrequent trysts.

"Get me that," he had said of a certain former Dallas beauty contest winner when plans for the tour were first being discussed. That particular aspect of the itinerary was changed, of course, when Mrs. Kennedy decided to accompany her husband.

She was aware of his philandering, but would cover up her dismay by joking, "It runs in the family." The story had gotten back to her about the late Marilyn Monroe using the telephone in her Hollywood bathroom to make a long-distance call to *New York Post* film-gossip columnist Sidney Skolsky. "Sid, you won't believe this," she had whispered, "but the Attorney General of our country is waiting for me in my bed this very minute—I just had to tell you."

* * *

It is difficult to ascertain where on the continuum of Lyndon Johnson's personality innocent boorishness ends and deliberate sadism begins. To have summoned then-Secretary of the Treasury Douglas Dillon for a conference wherein he, the new President, sat defecating as he spoke, might charitably be an example of the former; but to challenge under the same circumstances Senator J. William Fulbright for his opposition to Administration policy in Vietnam is considered by insiders to be a frightening instance of the latter.

The more Jacqueline Kennedy has tried to erase the crudeness of her husband's successor from consciousness, the more it has impinged upon her memories and reinforced her resentment. "It's beyond style," she would confide to friends, "Jack had style, but this is beyond style."

When Arthur Schlesinger, Jr., related to her an incident which he had witnessed first-hand—Mr. Johnson had actually placed his penis over the edge of the yacht, bragging to onlookers, "Watch it touch bottom!"—Mrs. Kennedy could not help but shiver with disgust.

Capitol Hill reporters have observed the logical extension of Mr. Johnson boasting about his six-o'clock-in-the-morning forays with Lady Bird to his bursts of phallic exhibitionism, whether it be on a boat or at the swimming pool or in the lavatory. Apropos of this tendency, Drew Pearson's assistant, Jack Anderson, has remarked: "When Lyndon announces there's going to be a joint session of Congress, everybody cringes."

* * *

It is true that Mrs. Kennedy withstood the pressures of publicized scandal, ranging from the woman who picketed the White House carrying a blown-up photograph supposedly of Jack Kennedy sneaking away from the home of Jackie's press secretary, Pamela Turnure, to the *Blauvelt Family Genealogy* which claimed on page 884, under Eleventh Generation, that one Durie Malcom had "married, third, John F. Kennedy, son of Joseph P. Kennedy,

one time Ambassador to England."

But it was the personal infidelities that gnawed away at her—as indeed they would gnaw away at *any* wife who has been shaped by this culture—until finally Jackie left in exasperation. Her father-in-law offered her one million dollars to reconcile. She came back, not for the money, but because she sincerely believed that the nation needed Jack Kennedy and she didn't want to bear the burden of losing enough public favor to forestall his winning the Presidency.

Consequently she was destined to bear a quite different burden—with great ambivalence—the paradox of fame. She enjoyed playing her role to the hilt, but complained, "Can't they get it into their heads that there's a difference between being the First Lady and being Elizabeth Taylor?"

Even after she became First Widow, the movie magazines would not—or could not—leave her alone. Probably the most bizarre invasion of her privacy occurred in *Photoplay*, which asked the question, "Too Soon for Love?"—then proceeded to print a coupon that readers were requested to answer and send in. They had a multiple choice: Should Jackie (1) Devote her life exclusively to her children and the memory of her husband? (2) Begin to date—privately or publicly—and eventually remarry? (3) Marry right away?

Mrs. Kennedy fumed. "Why don't they give them some *more* decisions to make for me? Some *real* ones. Should I live in occasional sin? Should I use a diaphragm or the pill? Should I keep it in the medicine cabinet or the bureau drawer?" But she would never lose her dignity in public; she had too deep a faith in her own image.

* * *

American leaders seem to have a schizophrenic approach toward each other. They *want* to expose their human frailties at the same time that they do *not* want to remove them from their pedestals. Bobby Kennedy privately abhors Lyndon Johnson, but publicly calls him "great, and I mean that in every sense of the word." Johnson has referred to Bobby as "that little shit" in private, but continues to laud him for the media.

Gore Vidal has no such restraint. On a

television program in London, he explained why Jacqueline Kennedy will never relate to Lyndon Johnson. During that tense flight from Dallas to Washington after the assassination, she inadvertently walked in on him as he was standing over the casket of his predecessor and chuckling. This disclosure was the talk of London, but did not reach these shores.

Of course, President Johnson is often given to inappropriate response—witness the puzzled timing of his smiles when he speaks of grave matters—but we must also assume that Mrs. Kennedy had been traumatized that day and her perception was likely to have been colored by the tragedy. This state of shock must have underlain an incident on Air Force One which this writer conceives to be delirium, but which Mrs. Kennedy insists she actually saw. "I'm telling you this for the historical record," she said, "so that people a hundred years from now will know what I had to go through."

She corroborated Gore Vidal's story, continuing: "That man was crouching over the corpse, no longer chuckling but breathing hard and moving his body rhythmically. At first I thought he must be performing some mysterious symbolic rite he'd learned from Mexicans or Indians as a boy. And then I realized—there is only one way to say this—he was literally fucking my husband in the throat. In the bullet wound in the front of his throat. He reached a climax and dismounted. I froze. The next thing I remember, he was being sworn in as the new President."

(Handwritten marginal notes: 1. *Check with Rankin—did secret autopsy show semen in throat wound?* 2. *Is this simply necrophilia, or was LBJ trying to change entry wound from grassy knoll into exit wound from book depository by enlarging it?*)

The glaze lifted from Jacqueline Kennedy's eyes. "I don't believe that Lyndon Johnson had anything to do with a conspiracy, but I do know this—Jack taught me about the nuances of power—if he were miraculously to come back to life and suddenly appear in front of him, the first thing Johnson would do *now* is kill him." She smiled sardonically, adding, "Unless Bobby beat him to it."

THE YIPPIES ARE GOING TO CHICAGO

by Abbie Hoffman

Theater of Cruelty proposes to resort to a mass spectacle; to seek in the agitation of tremendous masses, convulsed and hurled against each other, a little of that poetry of festivals and crowds when, all too rarely nowadays, the people pour out into the streets. . .

The theater must give us everything that is in crime, love, war or madness if it wants to recover its necessity. . . We want to create a believable reality which gives the heart and the senses that kind of concrete bite which all true sensation requires. . . We wish to address the entire organism through an intensive mobilization of objects, gestures, and signs, used in a new spirit.

The Theater of Cruelty has been created in order to restore a passionate and convulsive conception of life, and it is in this sense of violent rigor and extreme condensation of scenic elements that the cruelty on which it is based must be understood.

This cruelty which will be bloody when necessary but not systematically so, can thus be identified with a kind of severe purity which is not afraid to pay life the price it must be paid.
—Antonin Artaud, The Theater and its Double

Artaud is alive at the walls of the Pentagon, bursting the seams of conventional protest, injecting new blood into the peace movement. Real blood, symbolic blood, and—for camouflage—Day-Glo blood. Something for everybody.

Homecoming Day at the Pentagon and the cheerleaders chant "Beat Army! Beat Army!" It's SDS at the 30-yard line and third down. Robin cuts the rope with a hunting knife, and the Charge of the Flower Brigade is on.

One longhair smashes a window and is beaten to the ground. The Pentagon vibrates and begins to rise in the air. Someone gives a marshal a leaflet on U.S. imperialism, another squirts him with LACE, a high-potency sex juice that makes you "pull your clothes off and make love" (according to Time Magazine), people are stuffing flowers in rifle barrels, protesters throw tear

gas at each other (according to the Washington Post).

A girl unzips an MP's fly and Sergeant Pepper asks the band to play The Star-Spangled Banner. They lay down their Viet Cong flags and pick up their instruments. Oh, say, can you see. . . When it's over someone yells, "Play ball!"—and the pushing and shoving begins again.

FLASHBACK: Baby and I, complete with Uncle Sam hats and Flower Flags, jump a barbed wire fence and are quickly surrounded by marshals and soldiers.

"We're Mr. and Mrs. America, and we claim this land in the name of Free America." We plant the Flag and hold our ground. The troops are really shook. Do you club Uncle Sam? We're screaming incantations.

"You're under arrest. What's your name?"

"Mr. and Mrs. America, and Mrs. America's pregnant."

The troops lower their clubs in respect. A marshal writes in his book: "Mr. and Mrs. America—Trespassing." We sit down and make love. Another marshal unarrests us. A lieutenant arrests us. A corporal unarrests us. We continue making love.

After about 20 minutes we stand and offer to shake hands with the marshals. They refuse. We walk away glowing, off to liberate another zone. The crowd cheers. "You can do anything you want, baby, it's a free country. Just do it, don't bullshit."

The peace movement has gone crazy, and it's about time. Our alternative fantasy will match in zaniness the war in Vietnam. Fantasty is Freedom. Anybody can do anything. "The Pentagon will rise 300 feet in the air."

No rules, speeches won't do, leaders are all full of shit. Pull your clothes off (Make Love, Not War), punch a marshal, jump a wall, do a dance, sing a song, paint the building, blow it up, charge and get inside.

FLASHBACK: "67-68-69-70-"

"What do you think you guys are doing?"

"Measuring the Pentagon. We have to see how many people we'll need to form a ring around it."

"You're what!"

"It's very simple. You see, the pentagon is a symbol of evil in most religions. You're religious, aren't you?"

"Unh."

"Well, the only way to exorcise the evil spirits here is to form a circle around the Pentagon. 87-88-89 . . ."

The two scouts are soon surrounded by a corps of guards, FBI agents, soldiers and some mighty impressive brass.

"112-113-114-"

"Are you guys serious? It's against the law to measure the Pentagon."

"Are you guys serious? Show us the law. 237-238-239-240. That does it. Colonel, how much is 240 times 5?"

"What? What the hell's going on here!"

"1,200," answers Bruce, an impressive-looking agent who

"... Okay, they've begun pulling out of Vietnam ..."

The Yippies Are Going to Chicago, continued
tells us later he works in a security department that doesn't even have a name yet.

We show them our exorcism flyers. They bust us for littering.

"Shades of Alice's Restaurant. Are you guys kidding? That ain't litter, it's art."

"Litter."

"Art."

"Litter."

"How about Litter Art?" says Bruce after two hours.

We are free to go, but have to be very sneaky and ditch Bruce somewhere inside the Pentagon maze so he won't find the Acapulco Gold in the car.

The magic is beginning to work, but the media must be convinced. You simply cannot call them up and say, "Pardon me, but the Pentagon will rise in the air on October 21st." You've got to show them.

Friday, the 13th, Village Theater, warlocks, witches, speed freaks, Fugs and assorted kooks, plus one non-believer named Krassner. "Out, Demons, Out!"—and, *zip*, up goes the mock Pentagon. "Higher! Higher! Higher!" (Is it legal to cry "Higher" in a crowded theater?) We burn the model and will use its ashes on Big Daddy the following week. Media is free. Use it. Don't pay for it. Don't buy ads. Make news.

FLASHBACK: "Give me the City Desk . . . Hello. I've defected from the Diggers because they have this new sex drug called LACE. They plan to use it at the Pentagon. It's against my morals to use it on people against their will, so I want to confess. It's got LSD and DMSO, a penetrating agent. It's lysergic acid crypto ethelene and it's purple. Why don't you come over and I'll show you how it works."

The press conference is at 8 P.M. Two couples sit on a

couch. The four are squirted with the purple liquid. It disappears into their skin. They look dazed. Like robots they slowly peel off their clothes. The reporters pant. Like non-robots they begin to fuck. After a half-hour, the drug has worn off.

"Any questions, gentlemen?"

LACE, the new love drug, goes to the Pentagon.

This exorcism business is getting pretty exciting. Let's see *Progressive Labor* match LACE. The Pentagon happening transcended the issue of the War. *The War Is Over*, sings Phil Ochs, and the protest becomes directed to the entire fabric of a restrictive, dull, brutal society.

The protestors become total political animals.

A totality emerges that renders the word *political* meaningless. "The war is over." Everybody's yelling and screaming. Someone writes *LBJ loves Ho Chi Minh* on the wall.

Ring around the Pentagon, a pocket full of pot
Four and twenty generals all begin to rot.
All the evil spirits start to tumble out
"Now the war is over," we all begin to shout.

The soldiers have a choice. "Join us! Join Us!"—the cry goes up. Three do. Drop their helmets and guns and break ranks. They are caught by the marshals and dragged away into oblivion and the third degree.

It's the sixth hour of my trip. A super one, helped by large doses of revolution, no food or water, and a small purple tablet popped in my mouth by Charlie from the *San Francisco Oracle*.

A sense of integration possesses me that comes from pissing on the Pentagon: combining biological necessity with emotional feeling.

Baby and I retreat to the bowels of D.C. and grab a night's sleep after an orgy of champagne poured from an MP's helmet. It sure is one hell of a revolution.

Worried parents call the Defense Department to see if their children have been arrested and are given the number of the National Mobilization's office. We come prepared to give our lives and debate the morality of parking on a crosswalk.

FLASHBACK: Sunday at the Pentagon is a different scene. A mind trip working on the troops. Ex-soldiers talk to MP's. So

"As I see it, our generation is fighting for the same things our parents wanted at our age and have now. We demand our place in the shade! Live slow! Die old and have a good-looking corpse!"

do girls, college kids and priests, for 12 long hours. Talking, singing, sharing, contrasting Free America vs. the Uniformed Machine. At midnight the Pentagon speaks, after two days of silence: "Your permit has expired. If you do not leave the area, you will be arrested. All demonstrators are requested to leave the area at once. This is a recorded announcement."

"Fuck you, Pentagon. I'm not a demonstrator. I'm a tourist."

Everybody is herded into vans. The door slams shut but the lock doesn't work.

"The New Action Army sure is a pisser."

The MPs laugh and finally get the bolt in place. Off we go to Occoquan and jail land. "Carry me back to Ol' Virginny . . . " I hate jail. I try to chew my way through the van door and am doing pretty well when some of the girls get scared.

I get processed through as Abbie Digger. "I'm a girl," I insist when one of the marshals gives me the clue. A matron peeks and discovers differently. "No, honey, I'm just flatchested, honest."

Jail is a goof. Easiest jailing of all time. The Army is into brainwashing. Clean sheets, good breakfast, propaganda radio station. We call the guard and demand to be treated as prisoners of war. He listens patiently as we ask for the International Red Cross and other courtesies accorded under the Geneva Convention. He scratches his head and walks away.

Three guys begin to dig a tunnel. Everybody's trying to remember Stalag 17. At 4 o'clock I'm led out, meet my baby and we go to court. "The family that disobeys together stays together." Even the judge laughs, says "10 bucks each" and we're free.

Everybody's making the sign of the V. The battle is over. The question everyone's asking is when's the next happening?

Small battles will occur in countless communities around the country, most centered at local induction centers. Two days after the Pentagon three clergymen walk into the induction center in Baltimore and dump blood in the files. Blood! "You bet your ass—that's what war's about, isn't it?"

New York treated Dean Rusk to a bloodbath on November 14th at the Hilton Hotel, organized by the newly formed Protesters, Troublemakers and Anarchists. Headlines blare: "Cops Bust Up PTA Meeting."

Jesus visits St. Patrick's Cathedral. How about running Shirley Temple for Congress again? Pickets at Bellevue shout "Free LBJ!" A scenario at campus recruiting tables might include a tent with soft music and girls in bikinis. That's a real alternative.

Oh, by the way, January is Alien Registration Month. See you at the Post Office.

Get ready for a big event at the Democratic National Convention in Chicago next August. How about a truly open convention? Thousands of *Vote for Me* buttons, everybody prints his own campaign literature and distributes pictures of themselves. Then we all rush the convention, get to the rostrum, and nominate ourselves.

After all, it seems the only cat who lives for nothing in this country is LBJ. I've never met anyone who has ever seen him pay for anything. He doesn't even have a wallet. So if you want to live free, then stand up proudly on that convention platform, but don't start your speech with "My friends, come, let us reason together," or you'll lose the election.

MY POLITICAL DRUG BUST
by Jerry Rubin

I was ending my fifth hour at the typewriter, without any break for food, when there was a soft knock at the door. I was slightly annoyed, because in 45 minutes I was due to meet Nancy and my brother and his girl for dinner and a movie, *Wild in the Streets*—a saga about American youths who smoke dope, dance to rock music, and overthrow the government through revolution. I should have known . . .

My brother Gil, goes with Nancy's sister, and that's got a nice sense of drama about it. I was looking forward to the evening. The knock came again, soft, even sexy. The sexy knocks are the scary ones.

"Who's there?"

Sounds of silence. Ominousness.

"Who's there?"

"Police, want to talk with you about a homicide in the Bronx. *Open up!*"

"Do you have a search warrant?" I heard myself ask. "Put it under the door."

"Police Department, narcotics, *open up!*"

In the movement, hardly a week goes by without some mention of the day when the round-up "knock on the door" will roust us out of bed in the middle of the night. But there was American comfort and convenience in this visit—it was late in the afternoon. Nazi Germany lacked consideration.

I had kind of an absurd feeling. One part of me wanted to say to these cops: "Oh, what took you so *long?* I've been fighting this fucking ugly system for ten *years*, man. You finally noticed me!" My body experienced a feeling similar to that when Bobby Kennedy was killed. Shock mixed with an eerie sense of inevitability.

I could see my door pounded into a pulp so I opened it, and three agitated brutes dressed in work clothes pushed into my kitchen. Two of them were twice my size. It was almost with some relief that I discovered from their badges that they really were cops and not just right-wing toughs come to terrorize me. Then it dawned on me: "Shit, what are cops *but* right-wing toughs?"

"Do you have a search warrant?" I repeated, feeling silly. Now was no time for legal technicalities.

"What do you know about a search warrant? What do you have in here that you shouldn't have?" They screamed, flashing what they said was a search warrant quickly before my eyes, then swooping into the living room, reading my mail, going through my personal telephone book page by page, ripping into my files, raping my personal papers.

"Where is the gun?" one asked.

"What gun?" I said.

"If I find a gun here and you're lying, I'll tear you up, you'll be sorry," the cop promised.

They threatened to maim me if I told them that there were no drugs and they found some.

I felt ashamed to be scared because I am a revolutionary. But my reactions were personal, not political. Stripped of ideology, I was one guy being pushed around by three goons in my own home—my own home, where I have made love, have eaten hearty meals, have dreamed big dreams. My universe was caving in, and I fought back tears.

"Do you plan to take care of Lyndon Johnson?" one cop asked, and I embarrassingly thought of the pop poster of Lee Harvey Oswald that adorns my bathroom. When he found it, he didn't make the connection to his question. Whew!

"What are the Yippies going to do in Chicago? *What are the Yippies going to do in Chicago?*"

I tried, by being very abstract, not to offend the cops. They were looking for an excuse to pound me into the ground, and I tried to not give their hate and viciousness a target. They took one step forward; I took two steps back, ballet-style.

"Why did you go to Cuba when your government told you not to?" "Why do you hate America?" "Have you ever been in the service?" "Hey, don't you have any patriotic magazines, any American magazines?"

"I think you'll find a copy of *Life* Magazine here somewhere," I said, proud of myself.

"*Life* Magazine, hell, that's a Communist magazine, some of the stuff they print in there," the cop shot back. They were satirizing themselves, but I guess we all do. "Hey, you're a Communist! A Communist! You hate America!"

They pushed me into a chair, and I sulked. Their desire to strike at me physically built up torrents of rage throughout their bodies. I was trying not give them any opportunities.

Hard Cop: "I just want five minutes alone with you, just five minutes, I'll tear every hair out of your head and make you sorry that you're alive."

Soft Cop: "Nah, don't do it. He'll tell us where the stuff is." He moves near me, as if to protect.

The oldest police hustle in history.

The cops were like Pavlov's dogs in my apartment. Every stimulus produced a predictable response. The sight of beads brought on giggles. Printed words—*sex, Yippie, revolution, police brutality*—got bellows. Whenever they saw the words *socialist* they salivated. They grunted at every well-known name in my personal phone book. They didn't even notice the strangest thing in my small apartment, an old color TV set. They were having a ball, raiding the natives. Like little old ladies discovering dirty pictures.

A triumphant picture of Fidel Castro embraces my wall. One cop approached it. Visions of gooks shooting down American planes flooded his mind. He was out of control. "What's this? This Commie! Commie! Commie! You're a Commie! You hate America!"

And he tore the Castro picture off the wall, with ferocity, scoring a major victory for the Pentagon in the war with Communist evil.

"Who do you want for President?" one cop asked. "Bet you think we like Wallace." They were trying all of a sudden to be cute. "Well, we don't. We like Goldwater. We hated that guy Kennedy, although of course we're not happy about what happened to him."

It sent a shudder up my spine to realize that the Americans had invaded my apartment. The Americans found themselves in as strange a land as do American soldiers when they invade Vietnamese villages. It was a cultural conflict, similar to the cultural conflict American cop-soldiers experience in black ghettos and foreign countries while enforcing the standards of white middle-class America.

"Someday we are going to take guys like you and pick you up, and the judge is going to sentence you to four years in the Army or in jail."

Finally one cop said: "Let's get out of here. I can't stand the smell any longer."

There it was: *smell.* Communists smell. Viet Cong smell. Blacks smell. Yippies smell. Cubans smell. Those who smell nice think nice. The most important part of the body is underneath the arms. The nose judges good and bad in this country. Bad odor is an American tragedy. Americans would vote to ship underarm deodorant all over the world before they would vote to ship food.

They handcuffed me behind my back, led me down four flights of stairs, and into a small unmarked private car. They pointed to two American flags on the car. One cop drank beer in the back seat, saying: "Don't worry, I won't hit you while you're handcuffed." The ride to the precinct was the time for atrocity stories: "If this was Cuba, there would be no trial and you would have your hands cut off. You should be lucky you're an American."

Now, that's a booby prize if I ever heard one.

While ransacking the apartment, the cops called Nancy at work and told her to meet me at the precinct. They identified themselves as "friends of Jerry." It was a trap. She arrived at the precinct, and I called out, "Nancy, get out of here." Nancy got nabbed, busted, fingerprinted, questioned, charged with felonious possession. Charges were mysteriously dropped against her at arraignment.

I sat in my cell, waiting to be taken by my arresting chaperones to arraignment. I couldn't stop my hand from shaking; too much had happened in the past eight hours. Whenever there was a tendency to feel sorry for myself, I'd look around at the hundreds of black people in all the cells around me. The prisons are full of forgotten humans.

The idea of a jail break romantically entered my mind, but it was impossible. The guards would love to shoot us down. The purpose of jail is to make you hate yourself. That's why you're locked up. The smell of urine is overwhelming. Jails try to make men feel like animals.

My moment in court was due, and my arresting officer walked me down a long corridor, pinching and squeezing me in the back of the neck, shouting at me to walk faster, then slower. When we reached the end of the corridor, he pummelled me twice on the side of the head and told me to go to the nearest cell. I went in that direction.

With my back toward him, he kicked me at the base of the spine, knocking down the draft-card-burner-draft-dodger-dirty-smelly-hippie-yippie-commie-rat. I fell to the ground, and he pushed me into a cell with about 20 other prisoners, most of them black and Puerto Rican, shouting, "This guy hates America! He loves Russia and China! He's a Communist!"

There was hardly a stir in the cell, and I considered it a fine recommendation. One guy offered me a cigarette, and one by one they came over to talk. Later, at Bellevue Hospital, my injury was diagnosed as a probable fracture of the coccyx, the tailbone.

I was charged with felonious possession. They claim my apartment harbored dangerous drugs: a few ounces of pot. Codeine was taken out of Nancy's pocketbook when they arrested her. She was having her period, and she sometimes uses codeine for pain. Penalty if convicted on these charges is one to 15 years.

Getting arrested for pot is like getting arrested for sex. For eating a hamburger with catsup. For drinking beer. For laughing.

The right-wing connects psychedelic drugs and radical politics: they know where it's at. Drugs are an inspiration to creativity, and creativity is revolutionary in a plastic, commercial society. Drugs free you from the prison of your mind. Drugs break down conceptual and linear worlds and past conditioning. When past conditioning breaks down, personal liberation becomes possible, and the process of personal liberation is the basis of a political revolutionary movement.

The American power czars would not like it if organic links were made between blacks in the street and the middle-class student drop-out movement. One of the first questions Bobby Kennedy asked Allen Ginsberg when they met recently was: "Do hippies and black power people communicate with each other?"

Young middle-class whites are alienated by plastic and hypocrisy; blacks are exploited and degraded in the streets. Drugs are a living connection between these classes. The common language I found in jail with blacks and Puerto Ricans was dope. For whites, dope is a ticket out of the middle class.

But the cops didn't come after me because of drugs. Narcotics detectives on the Lower East Side sometimes go after big dealers, but rarely—in fact, many people say this is the first time they can recall—will narcos go after someone for possession alone. Narcos know they can't stop pot *use*—it would be like trying to outlaw cigarette smoking—they use drugs busts selectively, as a weapon.

We have to learn to see the cop-underworld as the cop sees it. We have to gather information about the way cops work as accurately as zoologists describe any breed of animals. This would be the best evidence that "law and order" does not equal jus-

tice. Despite mass media sentimentality, the law enforces not right and wrong, but the dominant culture and prejudices of the powerful.

My bust, in my opinion, was the result of a conspiracy between the narcos and the Red Squad—cops who work closely with the FBI and who assemble intelligence information on demonstrators and activists (i.e., potential law-breakers). They justify this work under the rubric, "crime prevention." It's an invasion of private rights and a treatment of political opposition as criminal activity. But these are small points to men who see the world as a struggle between Good and Evil. I've had a few discussions with FBI-Red Squad people in the Bay Area, and they were fundamentalist Christians battling against godless Communism.

To be missing from the "agitator" files of the Red Squad means you are being a good Jew in this Nazi camp called America. Red Squad cops are frustrated men because they can't arrest a "troublemaker" until he actually breaks a law. They see courts preventing them from keeping this country safe and clean. So Red Squad cats drink beer with the narcos, and marijuana busts become the form McCarthyism takes in the late 1960s.

Narcotics cops are big bruisers, and they wear plain clothes. They work with the Red Squad infiltrating and beating up demonstrators in street actions. The cop who attacked me, D. Hill, boasted that he had "done 'em in" at Columbia and Grand Central, and that I was lucky he didn't get his hands on me. "I'll look for you next time," he promised. He was more proud of his work beating people at Columbia than keeping the city pure from drugs.

Three weeks after my arrest, at my preliminary hearing in court, I strolled up to the 15th floor to witness the trial of some Columbia students; squirming and nervous in the witness stand was Officer Hill. He was testifying against the Columbia students who had occupied Low Library. He led the siege of cops. Asked what happened when the cops entered the library, Hill said: "The defendants forcibly tried to stay." The defendant opposite him in court was on crutches.

An arrest is a form of repression in this country. One of the ways cops clean up the streets is by throwing rebels into the courts. Tie us up with charge after charge. Teach us some manners by having us stand up for the Judge every time His Honor enters or leaves the room, even to go take a leak.

William Kunstler, famous constitutional lawyer, is taking my case. He jokes and calls me his "only addict client." Kunstler, with Arthur Kinoy and Beverly Axelrod, represented me in Washington in 1965 when I wore the uniform of the American Revolutionary war soldier to hearings of the House Committee on Un-American Activities.

My case will show cops whether it is easy to get away with political persecution disguised as drug busts. If there is no uproar against them, the appetites of the narcos will be whetted. We've got to push them up against the wall through continual exposure of their methods and through demonstrations. These busts are an attack on our culture.

When people worried about dangers at Yippie actions used to ask me about them, I'd say: To be perfectly safe, stay at home. That's not true anymore. Now it's: To be perfectly safe, obey your government. Or you won't be safe at home.

The knock at my door and the knock on your door is the knock on all of our doors. As Benjamin Franklin said, if we don't stick together, we will all hang separately. Power is the real safety, and power comes in numbers.

On to Chicago!

SHIRLEY TEMPLE SPEAKS HER MIND

Recently Shirley Temple Black lost to fellow Republican Paul N. McCloskey Jr. in a special California primary. A trio of reporters—Ann Bayer, Phylis Eldridge, and William Fiore—interviewed her shortly after her defeat.

Q. *Well, Mrs. Black, now that it's all over, I guess you will be able to resume your personal life?*

A. Yes, I will.

Q. *Looking back over the last few months, what would you say was the single most important sacrifice you had to make?*

A. My afternoon nap.

Q. *Did you find the rigors of campaign life a problem?*

A. During one luncheon I fell asleep.

Q. *Well, let me ask you this—*

A. That mean old sandman just snuck up on me.

Q. *Yes. Now, to what do you attribute Mr. McCloskey's victory?*

A. He got the most votes.

Q. *Any other reasons?*

A. Well, I suppose my position on the war.

Q. *Can you elaborate?*

A. I feel we've been dillydallying.

Q. *Uh, dillydallying?*

A. Yes. I've felt all along the war could be won, and quickly.

Q. *Really? How?*

A. Simple. Wish for it very hard and kiss your knee.

Q. *Wish for it and kiss your knee?*

A. That's right. Knock-knock.

Q. *Knock-knock?*

A. Ask "Who's there?"

Q. *Uh, Who's there?*

A. Lady.

Q. *Lady?*

A. No! "Lady *who*?"

Q. *Lady who?*

A. I didn't know you could yodel? Want to hear another one?

Q. *Well . . . actually, I think our readers would be more interested to hear your position on the major issues. For instance, you're against admitting Red China to the United Nations.*

A. And how!

Q. *Then how do you propose we establish diplomatic relations?*

A. What do you mean?

Q. *Well, in other words, how do we*

"get through" to them?

A. Simple. Take a shovel and dig a hole.

Q. *But isn't that a rather simplistic solution?*

A. I don't think so. I just pray they don't think of it first.

Q. *All right, let's go back to the war. Do you think your position on Vietnam harmed you in any way?*

A. I suppose so. You know what?

Q. *What?*

A. That's what.

Q. *Please, Mrs. Black!*

A. Oh, don't be so *serious!*

Q. *But war is a serious subject.*

A. Maybe. Maybe not. Can you do this? (*Rubs her stomach with one hand while tapping her head with the other.*)

Q. *Mrs. Black, can't you give me a direct answer?*

A. Ask me anything.

Q. *Well, do you feel the fact that you were a child movie star had anything to do with your defeat?*

A. No.

Q. *But the press poked a lot of fun at the fact.*

A. I'm rubber and you're glue. Everything you say bounces off me and sticks to you.

Q. *Okay, Mrs. Black, I guess that's just about it.*

A. Good

Q. *One final question. Now that you've lost your first bid for political office, what's ahead?*

A. The thing that sits on your neck.

THE CASTAWAYS TOLD ROSEMERICA THAT I'M THE FINEST GYNECOLOGIST IN THE NATION. WELL, ANYWAY, I TRY TO GO THROUGH THE MOTIONS.

HERE, ROSEMERICA, NOW YOU BE SURE TO EAT THIS, IT'S VITAL TO KEEP YOUR SYSTEM GOING.

eat

FIRST, I GOT A CASE OF COUNTRY BUMPKINITIS; THEN I BECAME A SPEED FREAK; AND NOW I'M SUFFERING FROM A SEVERE CASE OF SAIGON-BOMBHALT-BACKLASH...

BEFORE I DIE, WARN ROSEMERICA: FREEDOM IS A VIRTUE OF VICE. THE NAME IS AN ANAGRAM.

S P I R O,
A G N E W.

G R O W
A
P E N I S.

A PUBLIC OPINION POLL SHOWED NIXON AHEAD IN POPULARITY. HOWEVER, A RIVAL POLL SHOWED HUMPHREY AHEAD. JUST BEFORE ROSEMERICA WENT INTO LABOR, SHE CAST THE DECIDING VOTE ON WHICH POLL SHE BELIEVED.

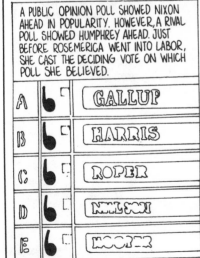

A		GALLUP
B		HARRIS
C		ROPER
D		NEILSON
E		HOOPER
F		

SIAMESE TWINS-NO WONDER I'VE BEEN SUFFERING ALL THAT PAIN-BUT I GAVE BIRTH TO THIS CREATURE AND I SHALL NURTURE BOTH...UNTIL ONE FINALLY TURNS ON THE OTHER.

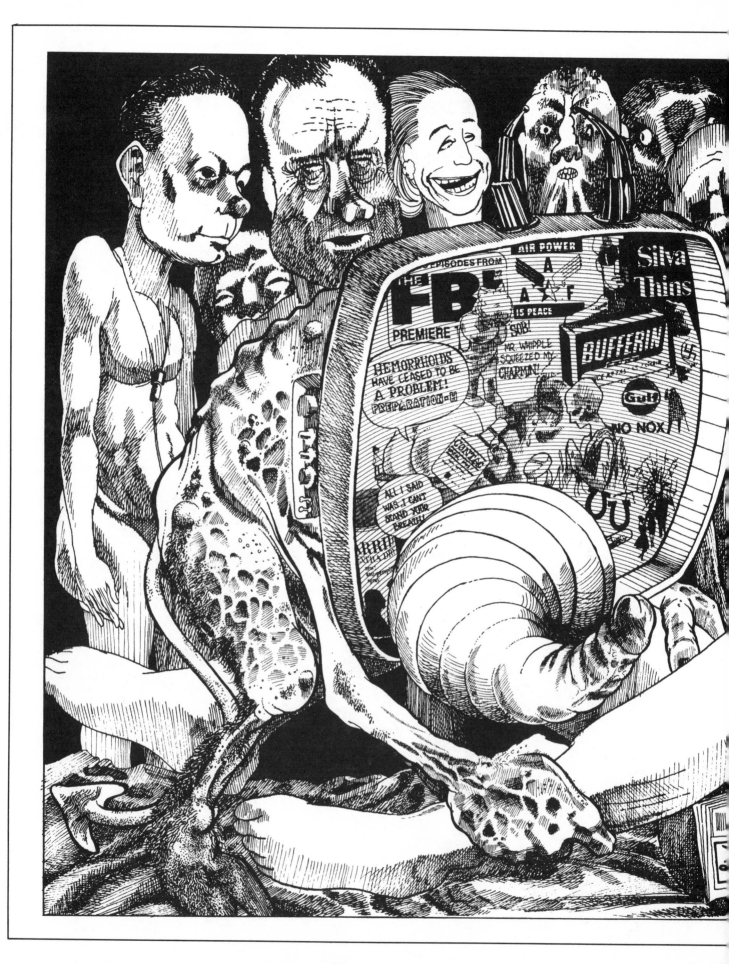

DIARY OF A SNIPER

by Saul Heller

The following excerpts are from a diary kept by a sniper killed by police some time ago. The diary fell into my hands by accident. The sniper was an honor student at college; his grades indicate that sniping did not interfere with his studies. Readers may be interested in the light this diary sheds on the compatibility of moral feeling and random homicide.

May 1: Went to Central Park at 7 A.M. today and shot two people. It's taken me quite a while to realize that early morning is the best time for sniping. What a pleasant way to start the day!

May 3: Shot a well-dressed man who was walking a dog. Guy didn't even have the decency to walk his dog in the gutter . . .

May 4: Why do I kill people? Why shouldn't I kill people? Can something be wrong, when it makes you feel so good?

May 6: If the government can order young men to kill peasants in Vietnam they *don't* want to kill, why can't I kill people I *do* want to kill? If it's right to kill people under compulsion, it's even more right to kill them voluntarily. Can you imagine a situation where compulsory sex is legal and voluntary sex a crime? The authorities and I agree on the necessity of killing—it's only the attendant circumstances over which we split hairs.

May 8: Shot a pretty young girl today.
   If she be not sweet for me
   What care I how sweet she be?

May 10: I guess people hate me more because I shoot them at random, and make no effort to be selective. Who *is* selective in this country, when it comes to venting hostility? White people who dislike Negroes dislike them all; Negroes who hate whites are just as undiscriminating. A Negro called me a motherfucker last night, as I was walking along the street, and he didn't know me *or* my mother. Why should I feel an obligation to be selective?

May 11: As a matter of fact, I sometimes am selective, but then my conscience bothers me. Shot a woman the other day who was eating on a park lawn and using it as her private garbage pail. I hate people who strew dirt around and create ugliness. But killing them means putting my homicide on a personal basis, and lowering myself to the level of a common criminal. A sniper with a mission should be above such pettiness.

May 12: Am I cruel and unfeeling? No more so than other people. Congressmen regularly pigeonhole bills intended to save people's lives. Surgeons perform major operations they know are unnecessary. People drink before driving and habitually violate traffic laws, causing thousands of others to be killed and maimed in auto accidents. U.S. planes napalm South Vietnamese villagers who have no guns, offer no resistance, and are on our side. *Me* a ruthless killer? We're all ruthless killers.

May 13: The most serious accusation against me, as I see it, is that I kill innocent people. The fact that they *believe* themselves innocent doesn't *make* them innocent. The belief in our innocence and virtue is one of the most pernicious characteristics of Americans, as Schlesinger notes. "We are today the most frightening people on the planet," he comments, "because the atrocities we commit trouble so little our . . . self-righteousness, our invincible conviction of our moral infallibility." The people I kill aren't innocents—they are accessories to crimes.

May 15: Maybe I have a messiah complex. Guess I have a thing that people aren't being punished for their irresponsible, vicious behavior, and don't even feel guilty about it. Maybe I con-

News item: A 25-year-old surgical intern from India was booked for 9 violations of the City Health Code after he confessed to dismembering the body of his wife.

sider myself a sort of virus sent by the Lord to speed the death of our society. Maybe I shoot people to make others understand that someone is around to exact retribution. There *is* a God, and I am his agent. Repent, you sons of bitches!

May 18: I've long given up my secret ambition to become the greatest mass murderer of modern times. People must adjust to their limitations. If I can polish off several persons a week, I feel I'm making a contribution. I hate do-bad-ers

with an eye on immortality. . . .

May 20: Saw my psychiatrist today. He told me I needn't return to the hospital for further treatment. Said I had made a pretty good adjustment to society. . . .

DIARY OF A SCHIZOPHRENIC

by Jean Raymond Maljean

A Napoleon who is in the mental institution *is* Napoleon. Better still—he possesses all the benefits of being Napoleon without the inconveniences.

We hear in the news report that 200 troops were sent to a given area. This means that 200 men were sent there. So would we call one soldier a troop?

Too many persons speak about an ugly girl as if the homeliness were of her own making.

When someone sees a beautiful sunset, he says: "It's as pretty as a picture." When he sees a picture of a beautiful sunset, he says: "It looks so real."

The ambition of a cat is to stop things that are moving and to move things that are still.

When school opens, posters read: "SCHOOL IS OPEN—DRIVE CAREFULLY." When school closes, posters read: "SCHOOL IS CLOSED—DRIVE CAREFULLY."

Affluence is depositing money in the bank before you make out the check.

If I did not have to ruin my body with overwork, I probably would destroy it with my pleasures.

An ascetic is hedonistic about self-denial.

"Miss? Have you ever been so alienated that you wanted to take all of humanity and stomp it down a toilet while on the other hand you needed to get laid badly enough to kill?"

THE EXECUTION

by Daniel Klein

News item: Nashville, Tenn., Feb. 15, 1969 (Reuters)—Democrat Charles Galbreath has introduced a bill in the Tennessee Legislature requiring that all executions in the state be televised.

The bill provides that revenue from the telecasts would go to the estate of the victim of the capital crime.

Rep. Galbreath, a long-time opponent of capital punishment, said it was logical to televise executions because deterrence by example was the only logical reason

advanced to justify a civilized society exacting the death penalty.

SCENE: The Director as Heard Over Headset in Television Mobile Unit Parked Immediately Outside the Gate of Nashville State Penitentiary. . . .

Hang on a second, Judd, sweetheart. We haven't finished your ears yet.

That's it, Leon, pink. Pink ears. Beautiful.

Judd, did anyone ever tell you that you look a little like Jack Palance? No kidding. A remarkable resemblance really . . . around the mouth. Let's have a smile, okay, baby? Ah, come on, Judd, you can do better than that. Come on. Let's see some teeth . . . that's it, sweetheart. What did I tell you, Leon? The spitting image of Jack Palance. Maybe make him a little darker around the neck

. . . what's that? No make-up around the neck? Smudges?

Look, how much time have we got? Five minutes. . . . Good. Where are you going, Juddsy-babes? Sure, everybody's a little nervous, kid. Sure, everybody. It's always the same. Just sit down, take a load off your feet, and let's take it from the top for the last time. All set?

Okay, first the long shot of the priest walking down the cell block . . . walk, walk, walk, walk, stop, turn, guard opens door, walk, walk, sit down, smiles benevolently. . . . Okay, what's the trouble, Judd? . . . Now look, honey, we've been all through this before: You don't have to believe anything the priest says. Like I always say, every man is entitled to his own beliefs. That's strictly your business; I don't even want to hear about it . . . and *neither* do all the mothers and fathers and little children at home! Get it? . . . Okay, smiles benevolently, comforting words, fatherly hand on, uh, . . . let's make it the left shoulder, benediction, kiss-off, walk, walk, etcetera, station break . . . Everybody got that?

Okay, guards? Where are the guards, Stan? What's going on here? Five minutes to air time and not a guard in sight. . . . Where are you going, Judd? . . . Judd! Oh, there are the guards. Good. That's it, Judd, just sit down; it'll be over in two shakes.

Now look, guards, to make things simple I'm going to call you Lefty and Righty, okay? Now, Lefty, you will always stand on Judd's left, and Righty, you will . . . that's it . . . you will always stand on Judd's right. Okay, now let's get in our places and . . . what's the matter, fellows? . . . No, no: equal billing . . . Now, come on, boys, we can work all that out later. . . .

Okay, guards, open door, walk, walk, walk, help Judd onto his feet. . . . Uh, now let's just hold it there a second, all right, fellows? Let's just talk a little about how we *feel* about Judd as we lift him to his feet. We're just doing our job, right? But maybe with the expression in our eyes we're going to show just a hint of, you know—how should I put it? Softness? Nothing *schmaltzy*, just a hint, get it? That's it, Lefty, very subtle—keep that in. . . . Okay, up to feet, walk, walk, walk, pause, Judd looks back over his shoulder, walk, walk, etcetera, fade.

Okay, now Judd, here's where you give your little speech. This is the last time I'm going to tell you this: Speak up! Nobody likes a mumbler. Remember our little trick? We pretend we're talking to somebody way across the room. Okay? . . . "I still say I'm innocent. I wasn't even in the country at the time, blah, blah, blah, etcetera," turn in place, prop cue! Stan, you've got

everything set in the prop department, right? We don't want any hang-ups, heh-heh. Station break.

Okay, from now on everything has to go like clockwork or we'll go overtime. Just when Judd steps back, that's when. . . . What? Phone? Look, I've got a *show* to do. Get his name and tell him I'll call him later. . . . Governor, shuvernor, I don't care if it's the president of the network, this is show business, sweetheart. . . . Sixty seconds? Places! Lights! Cameras! Break a leg, Judd, baby. . . .

WATCH YOUR STEP

WENDE

THE CASE OF THE COCK-SURE GROUPIES

by Ellen Sander

They press up against the stage, the young ones, their faces bathed in delight or clenched in crumpled ecstatic agony. They lean over the edge of the platform, clutching gifts and beads or notes or the group's latest album. And some reach, reach out, squirm on their bellies trying to get up over the edge of the stage, maybe to-touch-one-of-them . . . just once.

"Did you see them, *did* you *seeeee* them, oh, Cathy, they're so *beautiful!* Oh wow, the drummer, Cathy, the *bass player!* Let's go in back to the stage door, Cathy, maybe we can meet them, talk to them, *something, anything!* Cathy, come on!!!"

Groupies. Their legions, bless their little rock and roll hearts,

are growing geometrically. Often they work in pairs, sometimes in gangs. Their techniques for getting backstage, and their methods of tracking a group down would put a private detective to shame. (You call all the better hotels in town. If you're looking for the Stones, ask for a Mr. Jones, *not* Mr. Jagger, because that way it's less suspicious.) And rarely can I refuse a trembling, pleading teeny when she begs me to take her with me as I flash my press card at the security men that guard the dressing room areas at rock concerts.

Cops and security men are a fixture at rock concerts. They belong there as much as do the fans and the group and the rock and roll press entourage. They personify the balance of tensions between rock and conservative society. They try to stop the kids from scaling the stage and causing riots. Occasionally they succeed.

But when they try to keep the groupies from their prey, they haven't got much of a chance. For the groupies are girlchild guerrillas with a missionary zeal. They'll cooperate with each other to outfox whatever stands between them and the rock and roll boys—but only to a point. That is, they'll gang a door to get inside, but once it's broken in, it's every girl for herself, unless there's been a previous agreement.

When the Buffalo Springfield first came to New York, a crowd of groupies stood in the back of the house and divvied the boys up. If more than one girl wanted a certain Springfield, they had it out as to *which* manner of lovemaking *each* would apply *to what* and *to whom*, right *then and there* so there'd be no squabbles when they *got* to him.

Some girls are specialists. The lead-singer-fuckers are a particularly strong contingent, and lead singers who write are considered a *tour de force* by any groupie's measure. They dress like creatures out of some glorious romantic drama, scrawl gross amounts of black around their eyes and wear the biggest, most gaudy baubles they can find, so maybe, *maybe* he'll see me.

The great ones, the super groupies, have real class. There's one beautiful long lithe spade chick from New York, Lilly, with her enormous dyed bubble head and enormous dark glasses, who's been to Los Angeles to visit the Doors and to London to live with the Stones. There's Cindy and Morgan who live in San Francisco and make clothing for the groups—and don't you know, those fittings get pretty intimate.

In L.A. there are the G.T.O.'s, Misses Christine, Lucy, Pamela, Sandy, Sparkie, Cynderella and Mercy, a gaggle of groupies who have had this card printed up that they give to groups. They are said to have written torrid poetry about their rock and roll conquests which Frank Zappa may set to music for an album.

"Groupies. These girls, who devote their lives to pop music, feel they owe something to it, so they make the ultimate gesture of worship, human sacrifice. They offer their bodies to the music or its nearest personal representative, the pop musician. These girls are everywhere. It is one of the amazingly beautiful products of the sexual revolution."

—Frank Zappa, The Mothers of Invention,
in *Life* Magazine

Zappa knows. I'm very close to believing that Zappa knows where it's *all* at. When I first heard about the Plaster Casters of Chicago via the pop grapevine which claimed Zappa as the source, I honestly didn't believe it. Yo-ho, another Zappa fantasy unleashed on the unsuspecting great unwashed.

Some weeks later I was rapping late at night with Marshall Efron when this friend of his, the road manager from the Pacific Gas and Electric Company, comes in and oh, how's everything and the group is going great, one chick handed Frank Cook a note after a set which said, "Dear Fuzzy, I came five times during your drum solo," and aren't these chicks outasite?

And I threw in the tidbit I'd heard about these groupies in Chicago, they make plaster casts of the group's cocks, and who knows, maybe it's true.

And the road manager laughs and whips out this card that says "The Plaster Casters of Chicago, Life-Like Models of Hampton Wicks—Rennie and Lisa" with phone numbers . . .

The Plaster Casters weren't hard to find. I chose the Aragon Ballroom because the Jefferson Airplane was there for one night only. My escort was a local record company executive who kept looking in mirrors and running his fingers over his dried lips throughout the whole adventure. In less than an hour a stagehand brought them to me.

I take them upstairs. They are thrilled that I came all the way from New York to find them. They are both draped in black antique-y looking capes and shawls and whenever and whatever they move, something—hair, fringe, capesleeve or skirtbottom—is hanging, fluttering, swaying.

Rennie is 21, pretty in a round soft, kind of way. She has expressive, animated eyes, a petulant mouth, and her dark hair falls like a protective curtain around her face. By day she's an IBM keypunch operator. Lisa is 17, chubby and very young-looking, almost innocent. She has one of those millions of expressionless mid-western faces that nobody gives a damn about. She still goes to school and her father is a cop.

They've both been grouping for almost five years, and they told me rather proudly that all of their sexual experience has been with groups. They started working as a team because they share a penchant for English groups. Being very shy girls, even now, who don't converse easily with boys they don't know, they walk up to them and ask, "How's your rig?"

"Rig. It's cockney slang for dick. There are a lot of those slang words. Rennie learned most of them from the Hollies. *Up the stairs* means take a shit, *bristol cities* are titties, *daisy roots* are boots, *chopper*, *rig*, and *hampton wick*, they all mean cock, and *charva* means fuck. *Eye* magazine printed it 'charver.' So un*hip!*"

In those early days, before they were Plaster Casters, they would use the cockney slang in their letters to groups.

To the Hollies:
Rig Men,
Are your Hampton wicks looking for some Chicago Charva? If so, look no further. Your two Barclays Bankers from the Chicago Charva Chapter have arrived. We'd love to satisfy any needs you may have. For appointment or more info, call. . .

To the Beatles:
Dear Beatles,
We happen to know that you hold the record for charva championship around the world. We suppose that's why you've got such healthy-looking hampton wicks. Tight pants tell a lot of stories, you know. And from the way yours project at the zipper we can tell you've got four Rocks of Gibraltar stashed away. Maybe this is the secret behind your success. If your rigs get nervous from being cramped up and need a little exercise when you're in Chicago, we are the girls for you. We're two Barclays Bankers, our bank has convenient night hours and you can make all the deposits you like . . .

To the Rolling Stones:
Dear Keith (Richards),
We watched you on teevee the other night and the first thing that grabbed our eyes was your hampton wick. After that we did little besides studying it. We're not kidding, you've got a

very fine tool. And the way your pants project themselves at the zipper, we figure you've got a beauty of a rig. Sometimes. we hope you'd whip it out or something, but they don't have cameras that would televise anything that large, do they? Hey, tell Mick [Jagger] he doesn't have to worry about the size of his either: we noticed that (really, who could help but?).

Keith, we're serious. We judge boys primarily by their hamptons because they're so exciting to look at and contribute so much to a healthy relationship. We can hardly wait until you come to Chicago in November; maybe then we can find out more about what's inside your pants . . .

"I'd like to cast Jagger," flashed Rennie defiantly. "I'd like to see about *this!*" And she whips out her wallet and thumbs through the plastic-encased memorabilia until she comes to this picture of Mick Jagger's crotch she clipped out of *Tiger Beat.* There is a hypertrophic bulge outlined by his pants. Wow, it looks like a *tumor!*

"I think it looks like a bar of Sweetheart Soap. I heard that he was once caught in the men's room before a TV appearance, stuffing paper towels into his pants. They told him to take it out and he wouldn't so they got even with 'im by not shooting 'im from the waist down."

Dear Brian [Jones]:

I am in one of "your" moods at the moment. I was looking at your picture and what a pity your rig wasn't so noticeable. I saw it once on telly and what a grand thing it was!! Well, I can't help it, I'm in a hampton bag and I just can't climb out of it. Only Andrew's hot one is as creamy as yours. . . here goes:

Your televised body is something to pant on
Above all else sticks out your hampton
I know it seems a lot of mush
but in your eyes I see a toosh
I'm not the type whose eye first goes
To long blonde hair or delicate nose.
At the art institute I studied perspective
To ignore the way yours projects would be disrespective
Pointing downward like a lance
Pounding hard inside the pants
Extraordinary is your rig
Is a fact that cinches.
Pray tell, Brian, how many inches?. . .

It all started when the Beatles came to Chicago, lo those many years ago. There they were in the third row, Lisa in her early teens, and shrewd; Rennie, so *fetching* in a dark lowcut dress, black lace nylons, and big round glasses. They were screaming and laughing and crying while John, Paul, George, and Ringo were singing "Please Please Me" and Lisa was getting violently restless.

"Let's go downstairs," she urged. "Maybe we can meet them."

And they went downstairs and outside and there was the Beatles' limousine. A cluster of girls with the same idea were already there. Lisa grabbed Rennie's arm and yelled *"Run!"* and they ran down the block to be there when the car passed them.

Rennie hurriedly scrawled a sign that said *"Charva"* and held it up as the astonished four rode past. "McCartney just kept staring and staring at us—he couldn't believe his *eyes!*"

For the Who, their acronymous sign read "Welcome Hamptons Outstanding." And for the Raiders the first sign read: "HAIL! the Conquering *RIG!*"

That was before they learned the Paul Revere and the Raiders' word for rig: *lanoola.* And at the next Raiders concert,

with due respect, they held up a sign which gloated: LANOOLA. The Raiders, they dug *that.*

After the set—it was a Catholic high school dance, with all these nuns around—one of the Raiders stepped to the front of the stage and thanked everyone for being such a great audience and thanks especially to (lickerish wink) Lanoola.

The next day, a review of the concert in the *Chicago Tribune* contained the following paragraph:

"The Raiders. . . left after wishing a special thanks to Lanoola who went limp on the sidelines where she was standing holding a name sign." The paragraph title was: LANOOLA GOES LIMP!

Oh, they laughed about that one. That was far out. Reading about yourselves in the *Chicago Tribune.* Too much!

How did they graduate from super groupies to Plaster Casters? Oh, it was very respectable. About two years ago, Rennie was an art major at the University of Illinois. They started doing plaster casts in class and the assignment was to cast something—anything—and bring it in.

Rennie, now very much the experienced lady and not at all inhibited about such things, thought: Why not a rig? Why not, indeed? So a fellow student became the first plaster cast.

Lisa's part of the job was to "plate" him (that is, give him head) so that he'd get hard: "That's the way to look at a rig, right?" Then they lubricated him with Vaseline. Rennie jammed a vase full of casting material over his rig, let it set and removed it. They poured plaster into the impression. "We didn't get all of it, just about half—it looks like a salt shaker."

Before that they tested some poor quaking little neighborhood boy, and he was so terrified that it got soft. "It turned out like a *bas-relief.* We didn't know to go straight in at the time.

"The first popstar we tried was from the Procol Harum, but please don't mention his name. See, the mold failed and it didn't come out at all and he begged us not to tell anyone because he didn't want people to think his *rig* failed. Then we got Jimi Hendrix. Oh, and don't forget the road manager for one of the *worst* groups. That's what a lot of groups do, set their road managers on us. They're afraid of losing their precious rigs."

There's this story going around, I tell them, that Hendrix almost *did* lose his because the mold material got so hard they couldn't remove it. "Oh, nooooooo." And they convulse with laughter.

"What happened," they gasp, "is a few of his pubic hairs got stuck in the mold. Otherwise it would have just slipped out as soon as it got soft. We were frantic, fifteen minutes he was in there. We just picked the hairs out of it, carefully, so we wouldn't hurt him. I was frantic, I thought he'd hate us, or kill us. He was so—impressive—and I was so *nervous.* And I'm going, 'I'm sorry, it never happened this way before' and he's going. 'No, it's all right.' Fifteen minutes he was in there and he said he *liked* it, he said it felt like a *cunt!*"

And the process? "We use dental alginates, it's wonderful—it gets all the little veins and crevices and indentations and everything. While I [Rennie] mix, Lisa does the plating. Then we get the rig down into [the alginates] straight. The guy has to help, he has to reach back and push his balls into the mixture. He has to keep his rig hard, too. After a few seconds, the alginates harden, the rig gets soft and falls out."

Then they got Noel Redding, Rennie's ultimate best favorite popstar, the one that got her started on bass players. She's had a thing for bass players ever since. One day in April 1968, shortly after they casted lovely Noel, The Cream were in town, and Lisa found out where they were staying. They rang up Eric Clapton and he said sure, come on up.

They went upstairs and told him about the castings. No, no, Clapton said, not tonight. Tomorrow for sure. And I have this friend who probably wants to meet you, they'd both do casts then, he promised. The friend was of course Frank Zappa, and Rennie thought, oh, no, that ugly, gross thing. But Zappa flipped out when he talked to them and they all became extremely close friends. But both Zappa and Clapton copped out when it came to the castings, and Rennie is still a little bitter about *that*.

They call Zappa their "sponsor" now; he tries to protect them from any derogation. He confiscated their diaries and plans to publish them. "It's an important sociological document," he told me. And he wants to have a Plaster Caster exhibit in an art show or museum as soon as the collection is ready.

He has ideas, like playing the cockstar's music behind the exhibition of his plaster-casted rig. I suggested a tool kit, but Zappa just laughed. Rennie says Zappa's manager came up with the idea of making lollipops out of the casts and selling them under the slogan, "Suck your favorite star." What a capitalist!

Rennie is an artist, She feels if her collection were put in the hands of somebody who believed in it, it would be a significant reflection of the sexual revolution, a radical change in morality. . . . Lisa, on the other hand—she's only 17—is not so sure she wants to continue to be a Plaster Caster. For one thing, it's Rennie telling all the boys in the bands that Lisa is the best plater in the world. "Suppose I plate them and they don't *like* it?"

Also, some people are grimly censorious of the whole idea of plaster castings, and it's beginning to bring her down. "It's okay for Rennie, she only lives for the moment, but I want a heavy thing with a guy someday and I'm afraid this would prevent it."

"Nothing's perfect," Rennie snaps, "everyone can't like you. You've got to make up your mind that you're a pioneer."

The Plaster Casters are, by now, legend. They have fans, they are frequent *dramatis personae* of the rock grapevine, and recently they discovered two imposters: Alice and Candy are getting to groups by saying *they're* the Plaster Casters!

Rennie, whose dedication is a joy bordering on abandon, hopes they don't learn how to plaster cast—it would spoil her exclusivity. Because they're getting more famous by the moment. Spencer Dryden told them that groups in San Francisco were writing tunes about them. And they're still reading about themselves, though the coverage has been somewhat tangential. The *Chicago Tribune*: "The Yardbirds had just seen about 300 girls at the Civic Opera House to receive gifts . . . everything from imported caviar and kumquats to instant psychiatric kits, 69 sweatshirts *[Rennie gave him that]*, stuffed animals, and incense. One girl. . . brought along her plaster kit to get a mold of Jeff Beck's leg forever!" His *leg*, indeed!

Playboy: "Roland Ginzel, whose paintings have unfailingly captured the existential spirit of the famed author's work *[Nabokov's Despair]* . . . is currently teaching in Chicago and has works hanging in the permanent collection of the Art Institute in Chicago and the Dallas Museum of Fine Arts and has exhibited in the Metropolitan Museum of Art and the Museum of Modern Art in New York City." But *Playboy* left out what must certainly be considered as Roland Ginzel's most significant contribution to contemporary art. Roland Ginzel, after all, was the professor who taught Rennie how to plaster cast.

And in the middle of a review of Jimi Hendrix's latest album, *Electric Ladyland*, published in the *Chicago Circle Focus*, all by itself, set off with asterisks:

* * *

Ask Jimi Hendrix about Plaster Casters

* * *

There was the that time in July '67 with the Monkees. They were in the lobby of the hotel and there was a lot of security around. Getting upstairs was going to be a problem, they thought. But the Monkees had heard about the Plaster Casters and they sent down for them.

"We approached Davey Jones and he said yeh, it would be great, you could have duplicates made and sell them in stores." But Davey went into the other room and got Peter Tork, brought him out with nothing on, and said "Okay, here." And there were about thirty people around, some of the Buffalo Springfield were there and oh, it was a scene.

"*Bright* one over here," Rennie flips her hand toward Lisa, "takes hold of his rig and starts hand-jobbing him. They're all sitting around waiting for *me* to do something. I grabbed his rig too. We both had our hands on it. Somebody got on the piano and started playing *Lovely Rita Meter Maid*. It was—like a *movie!*"

Later Rennie got up and went into the kitchen. Opening the can of alginates she cut her hand severely on the metal strip. There was blood all over the place and they had to tourniquet her. Then they all got mad and went to bed.

Then there was that awful time with the Detroit Wheels, "There was another one in the group that I like and I thought if the drummer took me back with him to the hotel, I'd get to see the other one." No such luck. Rennie was in the room, stuck there with the drummer.

"I wouldn't ball him. He had my clothes off and he threw me out of bed. He wouldn't give me my clothes back, he just said 'Okay, get out' and I had just gotten this new outfit from my mother. She'd be sure to notice—not that I was nude, but that I didn't have my new outfit with me."

But that was back when they were very young and didn't really know who they wanted. It's different these days; more organized, more professional. Rennie is dieting like mad for next week when Hendrix will be back in town and she can get to Noel again. And Saturday night, there is the Steve Miller Band . . . Rennie is a true plaster caster, yes, an artist, a pioneer, right up there in the front lines of the new morality. But rock and roll rigs, *objêts d'art* or no, are rigs nonetheless and ever so, well, *distracting*. . . . Rennie, bless her little rock and roll heart, is first and foremost a super groupie. And that's a *very* high art in itself.

GREAT MOMENTS IN MEDICINE, #3

Can only bones fracture? According to a report entitled "Fracture of the Penis" in *The Journal of the Medical Society of New Jersey*, the answer is no, although rupture of the corpus cavernosum is admittedly an oddity; it is sometimes associated with rupture of the urethra.

The author tells of a patient who called him to request an immediate appointment because "an accident occurred at home causing blood and clots to come from the penis." This 52-year-old man, continues the doctor, "feeling a desire to masturbate, [had] inserted the penis into the narrow neck of a cocktail shaker. During erection, the patient, who volunteered the information that he is moderately hard of hearing, heard a 'cracking sound.' . . . There was little or no pain. The patient took a handkerchief, tied it around the base of the penis as a tourniquet, and the bleeding slowed down to a trickle."

His apprehension, however, "was not especially due to the bleeding, but more with respect to 'What can I tell my wife when she comes home?' "

The doctor-author reported that "Creecy and Beazlie have searched the medical literature, and reported a total of 21 cases of fracture of the penis, including one of their own."

One of their own patients, we assume he means.

In this report, the causes were listed as follows: "Striking or kneading with the hand to reduce erection—6 cases; coitus—4 cases; rolling over in bed—4 cases; bumping into chair—1 case; thrown on saddlehorn of motorcycle—1 case; striking toilet seat—1 case; kicked in fight—1 case; kicked by horse—1 case; slammed in car door—1 case."

(Yes, I know it's a total of 20, but I'm quoting.)

"The loud cracking sound at the time of fracture has been a rather constant finding in the history," it was noted. "Normal function apparently returned in all reported cases."

The report never did say what that man told his wife.

CHARLES MANSON WAS MY BUNKMATE
by Richard Meltzer

He Ain't Heavy, He's My Brother, that was our slogan back at Boy's Town. And that was just the icing on the cake, although the cake was not something I would ever want to eat again. For Charles Manson was my bunkmate at Boy's Town! Even though it wasn't the original, honest-to-goodness Boy's Town, only a correctional institution with the same name, Charlie Manson was the *real thing*. Now that authorities have him safely in tow, I am—to say the least—reassured that I'll never be confronted by him again. That boy had rocks in his head even then, he was what we called *flakey*. I didn't see it then, but now I can piece it all together. Schizophrenic is, come to think of it, just what he was. "Split personality" usually means two, but in his case, the sky was the limit! He was always different from one day to the next. One day he'd be generous with the box of candy his aunt and uncle sent him from home. Next day he'd be stealing candy from others, and maybe the day after that he'd be saying he didn't like candy!

Sometimes he was shy, sometimes quite gregarious, at other times talkative. Occasionally he was silent for hours, and at still other times he did more than a little complaining. None of that seemed strange at the time, but when you put it all in context he was some goof-ball, all right. He even had delusions—you might even go so far as to call them *hallucinations*—that he was immortal, that he would live forever. I think psychiatrists call that megalomania.

Yet there were times when he feared death, (there goes your schizophrenia again), but that certainly was not the only kind of crazy he was. Once he refused to eat in the mess hall for three days, mistrusting the dietician because of a piece of brass he found in his stew, which makes him paranoiac as well. If there are any other kinds of ways for him to be a nut, careful examination would undoubtedly convict him on those counts as well. They might even have to dream up some new ones for him.

Charlie was always quite power-hungry; even then, he craved to influence people. One night he convinced me to sneak down with him after hours to watch a late television program, *The Horn Blows at Midnight* with Jack Benny. This was strictly forbidden and could have led to harsh punishment if we were caught. I'll admit I enjoyed the performance, but such sorties went a long way towards harming my sleep and study habits.

Yet the discipline which Charlie decried so much was precisely what he was imposing on me on the psychological level. Some discipline is legitimate, some is not, Charlie never understood that at all.

You know what he once did? He drove someone's car on the grounds for a joy ride! He had not even a learner's permit at the time, he had never driven an automobile before in his life. He could have seriously endangered his own body and the lives of others, not to mention another man's property which he had probably worked many thankless hours at the reformatory to obtain. I can easily picture all the kooky stunts that have transpired since, with all those hot rods, school buses, and the dune buggies, and all the thefts.

He asked me to accompany him on that particular escapade, and I wisely declined. Fortunately, he was not injured. Even more fortunately for him, he was caught and placed in solitary as a lesson to him. It worked, as he never repeated the act in the immediate future. But, as things turned out, maybe it wasn't lesson enough.

I hear all this talk about the LSD, the acid, the marijuana, the pills. I may be mistaken, but I kind of remember Charlie having the seeds of the dope fiend even then. He experimented on a number of occasions with whatever he could get his hands on. When the Coke-and-aspirin craze was going full strong, you could always find Charlie by the soda machine and complaining to the doctor about a headache. He said it had no effect on him, but he did it again and again, and why do something unless it's doing something?

And it *did* really seem to be getting to him. His eyes had that wide-open mad-man stare that has now become his trademark and he was more than a little giddy. Perhaps it just wasn't far enough out for him, but this was his start, I guess. He even talked to many of the young narcotics addicts interned there for rehabilitation. They may have put some ideas in his head too. I can't see how else they could have got there. Maybe careful separation of the druggards from the others could prevent such potential calamities. But who knew about things like that in those days?

At the time he had a wild imagination about the birds and the bees, really wild! He thought about it more than me, even though he was still a virgin and I was not. Yes, I had had some nookie—after all, I had to sow my wild oats before eventually settling down. Charlie said he never wanted to settle down and he didn't know why folks get married at all. He had never seen a prophylactic, yet he insisted he would never use one, he thought it was *unreal*, that's the way he put it.

When I asked him what would happen if his girlfriend became pregnant, he replied simply that she'd have a baby after nine months! If he loved the girl, they would both raise the child; if not, he would raise the child himself! He didn't want somebody he had no use for taking care of the product of his seed! He even claimed, although it was hard to believe, that he had no objections to rearing a child that his girl had conceived with another man.

He even saw nothing wrong with adultery and bigamy. He might even have thought the Mormons had the right idea had he gone on to study comparative religion in an institute of higher learning as I did. Now that he's been unleashed on an unsuspecting world, there's no telling how many bastards he's spawned—the reports indicate it's many.

If only there had been sex instruction at Boy's Town, his horror for rubbers might have been overcome. That way, while his morally reprehensible activities might still have taken place, fewer wombs would have been infected by his poison. And come to think of it, his unnatural preoccupation with my private parts might have contained a hint of homosexuality.

As far as the hair business goes, it never entered the picture then, as none of us had been shaving very long if at all, and haircuts were standardized by the resident barber, so there were no indications of what was to be in that area. But the business about the sun, Charlie frequently took off his shirt even when forbidden to do so while working at an outdoor assignment.

Once or twice he even dropped his trousers when the supervisor was looking elsewhere—it was very hot and the sun was bright and our uniforms were bulky and dark, so that's partial explanation. Mooning was big then, but that really had nothing to do with it. Overall nudity was not a fad then at all. He was just wacky about the golden globe in the sky, I guess, just as some dogs and rapists go ape over a full moon.

About his early childhood I know very little. I do remember, however, that he had only one pet as a kid, a black cat named Gumbo. That name was derived from his love for chicken gumbo soup. That fact that it was a black cat now seems appropriate, although everybody has a black cat at one time or other. But few conventional people would treat their animals the way he did. He fed Gumbo snails and worms!

On the educational side, his favorite subject was mathematics, not because he had a way with numbers (his math level was scarcely remedial!) but because it entailed the least reading. How Charlie detested books! Once he hid a copy of *Tom Sawyer* in his shirt and brought it back to the room. With some matches he obtained with the pack of cigarettes he had purchased at the dispensary (with a forged parental permission slip) he set fire to it page by page, carefully fanning the smoke through a vent to avoid detection.

On another occasion he was not so lucky, forgetting that his fingerprints were on file, as he dumped an expensively bound copy of *Robinson Crusoe* in the garbage can of the library lavatory. Fortunately for him, they could not pin it on him, as thousands of hands had already left their mark on the book. Presumably he didn't give a hang about being caught anyway. Whatever was on his mind, his library privileges were revoked on the suspicion of foul play—one decision he certainly had no complaints about!

Charlie's anti-book streak may have been quite severe, but madness and intelligence are not mutually exclusive. They're different mental faculties altogether. So he was no lame-brain, and at least one of our teachers considered the boy sharp as a whip. In many cases being out of your skull can even be correlated with uncanny capabilities of the mind, a number of experts have stated. And I'm not denying that this was the case with the young Manson—he certainly had a head on his shoulders. But too much thinking can be harmful, particularly when it tends to be unorthodox and irrational. It makes you gloomy and morose. Charlie's is a case in point.

As for the heinous, horrendous multiple murders, that's not really the part in the puzzle that's toughest to figure, when you come down to it. Cranky and painfully immature when faced with conflict, he got into few fist fights, chiefly because he was no fighter—not that there weren't those who wanted to rap him in the mouth for his anti-social attitudes.

In his first and last tussle he was not even the match of a smaller, skinnier fellow. So it was only natural that he would carry a concealed weapon such as a knife. And it follows that a knife carrier will inevitably become a knife wielder. And when you add to that the factor of unstable personality, well . . .

Some claim he didn't do it himself but only instigated a group of sluts in his coterie to do his bidding. Others believe it was entirely their doing, that he was somewhere else at the time. But as far as the *possibility* of his having done the job himself goes, in days gone by, he was perfectly capable of acting, deciding, and giving orders. Which might mean that, technically speaking, he cannot be found legally insane. This will be up to the judges and jurors to decide.

He'll get his day in court; after all, it's his birthright like yours or mine. Any ex-con (rehabilitated or not) can tell you about paying the dues. Charles no doubt knows this. More than once he bellowed his then-fanciful wish to kill so-and-so, and I am sure there are quite a few for-

mer residents who recall the sting of his words and the evil he once wished them.

It's been revealed by reporters that members of the Manson cult called their leader such names as "Jesus Christ," "Satan," and "God." Let me reveal a little something they never bothered to investigate. At Boy's Town, despite the harsh profanity code, they called Charlie boy things that weren't very nice!

It all fits into place, but there is something lacking: the big why. Why did he do it? If in fact he did. But the evidence is overwhelmingly in favor of that conclusion. I'm a science teacher now and all I can go by is evidence. But I'm a man of flesh and blood too and I'll tell you one thing:

Charles Manson is not *my* brother!

———————————

AN IMPOLITE INTERVIEW WITH KEN KESEY

Q. Okay. Let's start off with a simple one. How would you distinguish between freedom and insanity?

A. True freedom and sanity spring from the same spiritual well, already mixed, just add incentive. Insanity, on the other hand, is dependent on *material* fad and fashion, and the weave of one's prison is of that material. "But I didn't weave it," I hear you protest. "My parents, their parents, *generations* before me wove it!"

Could be, but when you're a prisoner, the task is not to shout epithets at the warden, but to *get out.*

Q. Well, specifically, when you were in East Palo Alto, sitting in the back yard of the only white family in a black area, and there was a police helicopter hovering above you, and you wanted to shoot it down — now, even though you may not have meant that literally, can you stretch the fantasy enough to consider the possibility that you were being dogmatic when you chided Tim Leary for being Another Nut With a Gun?

A. Yes.

Q. Stop hemming and hawing. . . Is there anything you want to add to that?

A. I'm sorry that I used that phrase in my letter to Tim. I intended to be emphatic, not dogmatic, because I've had enough dealings with both ends of guns to feel qualified in making strong statements. I've shot ducks, deer, elk, geese, coyotes and a hole once in my grandfather's kitchen ceiling, and I've been shot at by farmers, cops, and federales. All of it is negative energy. When I said the thing about the helicopter, what I meant was that the men manning these abominations had better take heed of a growing impatience with this kind of bullshit. I mean I had no thirty-ought-six with Enfield scope handy in the closet, but if I was, say, a black home-owner sitting out in his patio with his family, still, say, smarting from the burn of doing a hitch defending the sanctity of the American Dollar in Vietnam, and that racketing monstrosity started hanging out over my house fucking with my weekends, I might think, "Who the hell did I ever know up in a helicopter that wasn't workin' for the forces of *slavery!*"

That *then* it might cross my mind to get the gun out of the closet and clean it a little sitting out there in the sun under that motherfucking chopper, is all I was saying.

Q. It's no accident that the initials of your protagonist in One Flew Over the Cuckoo's Nest *are R.P.M.—Revolutions Per Minute—and that you don't take that word lightly, but where is your vision of revolution in relation to both Ho Chi Minh and Charles Reich?*

A. Chuck and Ho? Naturally I can't hope to under the circumstances with reference to each of their personal visions, huh?

Q. I'm talking about the spectrum from Chuckie's bell-bottoms to Ho's anti-aircraft.

A. Ah. I see. Well, I think that either sticking a leg in a pair of bell-bottoms or loading a canister into an anti-aircraft weapon may or may not be a revolutionary act. This is only known at the center of the man doing the act. And *there* is where the revolution must lie, at the *seat of the act's impetus*, so that finally every action, every thought and prayer, springs from this committed center.

Q. You've said, regarding the media, that if you follow the wires, they all lead to the Bank of America. Would you expand on that?

A. When you've had a lot of microphones poked at you with questions like — "Mr. Kesey, would you let your daughter take acid with a black man?" "Mr. Kesey, do you advocate the underwear of the Lennon Sisters?" "Mr. Kesey, how do you react to the findings of the FDA indicating that patoolee oil causes cortizone damage?" — you get so you can follow the wires back to their two possible sources. Perhaps one wire out of a thousand leads to one of the sources, to the heart of the man holding the microphone, while the other nine hundred and ninety-nine go through a bramble of ambition, ego, manipulation and desire, sparking and hissing and finally joining into one great coaxial cable that leads out of this snarl and plugs straight into the Bank of America.

Q. In Sometimes a Great Notion, *you had this idealistic logger in the role of a strikebreaker, and yet now, back in real life, you're glad that the union has shut down the local paper and pulp mill. What's made the difference—ecology?*

A. Women's Lib.

Q. Are you just being a smart-ass or do you mean that?

A. No, I mean Women's Lib has made us aware of our debauching of Mother Earth. The man who can peel off the Kentucky topsoil, gouge the land empty to get his money nuts off, then split for other conquests, leaving the ravished land behind to raise his bastards on Welfare and fortitude . . . is different from Hugh Hefner only in that he drives his cock on diesel fuel.

Women's Lib was the real issue in *Notion*. I didn't know this when I wrote it, but think about it: It's about men matching egos and wills on the battleground of Vivian's unconsulted hide. When she leaves at the end of the book, she chooses to leave the only people she loves for a bleak and uncertain but at least *equal* future.

The earth is bucking in protest of the way she's been diddled with; is it strange that the most eloquent rendition of this protest should come from the bruised mouth of womankind?

Q. And yet, since you're against abortion, doesn't that put you in the position of saying that a woman must bear an unwanted child as punishment for ignorance or carelessness?

A. Since I feel abortions to be probably the worst worm in the revolutionary philosophy, a worm bound in time to suck the righteousness and the life from the work we are engaged in, I want to take this slowly and carefully. This is the story of Freddy Schrimpler:

As part of his training, a psychiatric aide must spend at least two weeks working the geriatric wards, or "shit pits" as they were called by the other aides. These wards are concrete barns built, not for attempted cures or even for attempted treatments of the herds of terminal humanity that would otherwise be roaming the streets, pissing and drooling and disgusting the healthy citizenry, but for nothing more than shelter and sustenance, waiting rooms where old guys spend ten, twenty, sometimes thirty years waiting for their particular opening in the earth. At eight in the morning they are herded and wheeled into showers, then to Day Rooms where they are fed a toothless goo, then are plunked into sofas ripe with decades of daily malfunctions of worn-out sphincters, then fed again, and washed again, and their temperatures taken if they're still warm enough to register, and their impacted bowels dug free in the case of sphincters worn-out in the other direction, and their hair and cheesy old fingernails clipped (the clippings swept into a little

"—And if the establishement denies us our rights as a special minority, we start thinking up costly little ways to harass it, disrupt it, even if necessary smash it! . . ."

pink and grey pile), and fed again and washed again, and then usually left alone through the long afternoons.

Some of these derelicts still have a lot going and enjoy trapping flies and other such morsels in the snare of their baited hands, and some engage in contented and garrulous conversations with practically anything, and some watch TV, but most of them lie motionless on the plastic-covered sofas or in gurney beds, little clots of barely-breathing bones and skin under the government sheets. Even the doctors call them vegetables.

In caring for these men something becomes immediately obvious to all the young aides undergoing their first real brush with responsibility. The thought is very explicit. After the first meal squeezed into a slack mouth, or after the first diaper change or catheter taping, every one of the trainees has thought this thought, and some have spoken it: "Without our help these guys would *die*!"

And after the hundredth feeding and diapering and changing, the *next* thought, though never spoken, is: "Why don't we just *let* them die?"

An awful question to find in your head, because even young aides know that age can happen to anyone. "This could I someday be!" But even fear of one's own future can't stop the asking: Why *don't* we just let them die? What's wrong with letting nature take its own corpse? Why do humans feel they have the right to forestall the inevitable fate of others? Freddy Schrimpler helped me find my answer:

Freddy was 70 or 80 years old and had been on the Geriatrics Ward for close to twenty years. From morning until bedtime he lay in the dayroom in a gurney bed against the wall, on his side under a sheet, his little head covered with a faint silver gossamer that seemed too delicate to be human hair — it looked more like a fungus mycilium joining the head to the pillow —and his mouth drooling a continual puddle at his cheek. Only his eyes moved, pale and bright blue they followed the activity in the ward like little caged birds. The only sound he made was a muffled squeaking back in his throat when he had dirtied his sheets and, since his bowels were usually impacted, like most of the inmates who couldn't move, this sound was made but rarely and even then seemed to exhaust him for hours.

One afternoon, as I made my rounds to probe with rectal thermometer at the folds of wasted glutinus maximus of these gurney bed specimens—hospital policy made it clear that the temperature of anything breathing, even vegetables, had to be logged once a month—I heard this stifled squeak. I looked up; it was Freddy's squeak but since it was his temperature I was attempting to locate I knew that he hadn't shit his sheets. I resumed my probing, somewhat timidly, for the flesh of these men is without strength and a probe in the wrong direction can puncture an intestine. The squeak came again, slower, and sounding remarkably like speech! I moved closer to the pink and toothless mouth, feeling his breath at my ear.

"Makes you. . . kinda nervous. . . don't it?" he squeaked. The voice was terribly strained and faltering, but even through the distortion you could clearly make out the unmistakable tone of intelligence and awareness and, most astonishingly, humor.

In the days that followed I brought my ear to that mouth as often as the nurses let me get away with it. He told me his story. A stroke years ago had suddenly clipped all the wires leading from the brain to the body. He found that while he could hear and see perfectly, he couldn't send anything back out to the visitors that dropped by his hospital bed more and more infrequently. Finally they sent him to the VA, to this ward where, after years of effort, he had learned to make his little squeak. Sure, the doctors and nurses knew he could talk, but they were too busy to shoot the breeze and didn't really think he should exhaust himself by speaking. So he was left on his gurney to drift alone in his rudderless vessel with his shortwave unable to send. He wasn't crazy; in fact the only difference that I could see between Freddy and Buddha was in the incline of their lotus position. As I got to know him I spoke of the young aides' thought.

"Let a man die for his own good?" he squeaked, incredulous. "Never believe it. When a man . . . when anything . . . is ready to stop living . . . it stops. You watch . . ."

Before I left the ward, two of the vegetables died. They stopped eating and died, as though a decision of the whole being was reached and nothing man or medicine could do would turn this decision. As though the decision was cellularly unanimous (I remember a friend telling me about her attempted suicide; she lay down and placed a rag soaked in carbon tetrachloride over her face. But just before she went out completely there was a sudden clamor from all the rest of her: "Hey! Wait! What about us? Why weren't we consulted!?" And being a democratic girl at heart she rallied over mind's presumptuous choice. "Our mind has no right to kill our body," she told me after the attempt. "Not on the grounds of boredom, anyway . . .") and met with the satisfaction of all concerned.

Punishment of unwed mothers? Bullshit! Care of neither the old nor the young can be considered to be punishment for the able, not even the care of the un-dead old or the un-born young. These beings, regardless not only of race, creed, and color but as well of size, situation or ability, must be treated as equals and their rights to life not only recognized but *defended*! Can they defend themselves?

You are you from conception, and that never changes no matter what physical changes your body takes. And the virile sport in the Mustang driving to work with his muscular forearm tanned and ready for a day's labor has *not one microgram more* right to his inalienable rights of life, liberty, and the pursuit of happiness than has the three month's fetus riding in a sack of water or the vegetable rotting for twenty years in a gurney bed. Who's to know the value or extent of another's trip? How can we assume that the world through the windshield of that Mustang is any more rich or holy or even sane than the world before those pale blue eyes? How can abortion be anything but fascism again, back as a fad in a new intellectual garb with a new, and more helpless, victim?

I swear to you, Paul, that abortions are a terrible karmic bummer, and to support them—except in cases where it is a bona fide toss-up between the child and the mother's life—is to harbor a worm of discrepancy.

Q. Well, that's really eloquent and mistypoo, but suppose Faye were raped and became pregnant in the process?

A. Nothing is changed. You don't plow under the corn because the seed was planted with a neighbor's shovel.

Q. I assume that it would be her decision, though?

A. Almost certainly. But I don't really feel right about speaking for her. Why don't you phone and ask?

[Krassner phones Faye Kesey in Oregon and reviews the dialogue. She asks: "Now, what's the question—if I were raped, would I get an abortion?" "That about sums it up." "No, I wouldn't."]

Q. But would she marry the rapist to give the child a name? . . . What would you have done in my place before abortion was legalized and someone with an unwanted pregnancy came to you for help, and you knew of a safe doctor as an alternative to some back-alley butcher?

A. I have been in your place and done what you did. I think now—not just because of religious stands but of what happened to the girls' heads as a result — that I did a great disservice because I was being asked for more than money or the name of a guy in Tijuana. In the last few years, when asked the question, I've found myself able to talk the women out of it. I could have talked them out of it back then as well. There are girls with kids coming and no old man to carry his share of the load. Women sense far better than a man what the bearing and raising of a child means in terms of a lifetime commitment. It all comes down to a pact of support. And if the man pulls out his support first, how can he blame the woman for pulling out hers? Next time you're asked to choose between hygiene and a back-alley butcher, Paul, try choosing instead against both possibilities and for life instead.

Q. How do you reconcile the notion of working out one's karma through succeeding reincarnations with the reality of, say, a plane crash—and you can take that on to Nazi Germany or My Lai, a flood here, a tornado there—does the common karma of all those victims simply transcend the boundaries of coincidence?

A. It's like Hell hanging in mid-air.

Q. You talk about this Thing as if it were a personal friend of yours.

A. Get off my back, Martha!

Q. What were the parts that were left out of Tom Wolfe's The Electric Kool-Aid Acid Test?

A. The parts that might have hurt people. Tom Wolfe, as well as being a genius (he got most of that book without notes or a tape recorder; he has an astounding ability to watch and remember) is a very gentle guy. Certain passages—such as the Hell's Angels gangbang—would have been stronger if he had used the names of the real people that participated, but he very wisely made up characters instead.

Q. Jack Kerouac once stated his philosophy as: "I don't know, I don't care, and it doesn't make any difference." And yet his widow said he died a lonely man. Was he deceiving himself, or what?

A. I feel bad about Kerouac. He was a prophet, and we let him die from us. He *did* know, and he *did* care, and the letters of praise that I composed in my head to him *would have* made a difference had I, and all the others who felt the same respect, mailed them. Sometimes polemics and fashion get so thick that we can't make out a clear call for help from a friend.

Q. You've referred to Neal Cassady as one of the hippest people you've ever known, and yet if it's true that he died while walking along the railroad tracks counting the ties — and his last words were "Sixty-four thousand, nine hundred twenty-eight"—it seems more compulsive than hip?

A. Long before his death, Cassady had passed that point where being hip or compulsive had any relative meaning to him. His was the yoga of a man driven to the cliffedge by the grassfire of an entire nation's burning material madness. Rather than be consumed by this burn he jumped, choosing to sort things out in the fast-flying but smogfree moments of a life with no retreat. In this commitment he placed himself irrevocably beyond category. Once, when asked why he wouldn't at least *try* to be cool, he said: "Me trying to be cool would be like James Joyce trying to write like Herb Gold."

Q. How did Cassady respond the time you told him you feared you were losing your sense of humor?

A. With great concern and sympathy, as though I had told him that I had cancer of the lymphthf.

Q. How did you regain it?

A. The lymphthf? It came back of its own, after I dropped a five gallon jar of mayonnaise on my foot.

Q. No, I mean how did you regain your sense of humor?

A. Oh, that. I never did, I guess. Rehabilitation, as my counselor up at the Sheriff's Honor Camp used to tell me, is a two-way street.

Q. How would you compare Babbs and Baba Ram Dass?

A. When one tries to come on about his best buddy it becomes too difficult to remain unbiased. So rather than risk being guilty of the "communal life," as I guess I once called it, I'll turn this question back over to you. How would *you* compare Babbs and Baba Ram Dass?

Q. I think of Ram Dass as a sort of Johnny Carson of the future, and Babbs as his Ed McMahon. . . or maybe it's the other way around. . . they're each different sides of the same coin—Psychedelic Social Director—and they can both relate almost magically to whatever environment they find themselves in, but their styles are so different. . . What's your concept of the communal lie?

A. I remember delegates from two large communes stopping by once at my farm and negotiating in great tones of importance the trade of one crate of cantaloupes, which the southern commune had grown, for one portable shower, which the northern commune had ripped off of a junk yard. When this was over they strutted around in an effluvium of "See? We're self-supporting."

Bullshit. A crate of melons and a ratty shower isn't enough summer's output for sixty-some people to get off behind. It was part of a lie that the entire psychedelic community, myself more than most, was participating in. When a bunch of people, in defense of their lifestyle, have to say "Look how beautiful we were at Woodstock!" I can't help but ask, "How was your cantaloupe crop this year?" Being beautiful, or cool, or hip is too often a clean-up for not pulling weeds.

Woodstock was beautiful, and historic and even perhaps biblical, but Altamont was far more honest. Success is a great spawning ground of confidence and camaradarie; bald truth is found more often up against the wall. Bullshit is bullshit, and neither the length of the hair nor the tie of the family can make it anything else.

"...What would you like to hear today? . . . Any requests? . . . How about the rich brave swine and the angelic worker? . . ."

Q. What's the meaning to you of the Charles Manson verdict—isn't finding him guilty the same as finding a Syndicate boss guilty of ordering murders, the only difference being that Manson didn't pay his girls?

A. When Esau, all red and hairy, preceded his twin Isaac out of the womb, he beat his brother out by, as it were, a cunt hair, winning the eldest's right to take over the leadership of the family. Years later, on his way back from helling around with the local sports on a coonhunt, Esau spies his bumpkin brother hunkered in the field eating a bowl of Cream of Wheat.

"Hey, little brother," Esau calls, "Howza bout giving a hit of that Cream of Wheat to your old brother hot back from the hunt?"

Isaac sizes up the opportunity and answers, "Tell you what, big brother, I'll trade you this bowl of Cream of Wheat for your birthright; that is, for *your right* as the *eldest of the family.*"

Esau shrugs. "I, who am already dead, should give a shit for a crumby birthright? It's a deal."

As he gobbled the bowl of breakfast food, Esau didn't realize he had traded off his most precious God-given possession, for by choosing to relinquish his part in the Big Show and opting for an existential outlook he lost his *right of choice!* When the court finds Manson guilty of the power to make those girls do his will, the court is removing the girls' right of choice, our absolutely inalienable right the sanctuary of which even God cannot evade! It can only be surrendered.

Whenever someone squeals "He made me do it!" they join the distinguished ranks of the Eichmanns and Calleys, a group in hotter karmic water, really, than the Mansons and the Nixons who still have, at least, the right to be guilty.

Q. What about the beast-people for whom you see no possibility of growth?

A. These are people who have reached a terminal state, karmically and spiritually. These are the branches on the vine that have not produced and have no intention of producing and are bound for the fire and know it and *willfully defend the state.* These people are Esau again, asking again, "What good is a birthright to one who is already dead?" So, it isn't that the possibility of growth and rebirth is gone—that possibility is always open, forever—it is that with some people, the *likelihood* of taking advantage of this opportunity to change is practically nonexistent. Finally, when the sea is boiling and the rock is burning and the moon is bleeding and will no longer hide them, they run to Satan and he says "Right on! Come right in!" Then their beast-hood is complete.

Q. The Bible was written when people believed that the Earth was flat, that God was anthropomorphic, and that women were inferior—but if you think of the New Testament as still in process, could you tell what I think is a contemporary parable, about that trial involving the dog?

A. I'm busted, see, for a warrant for not having acquired licenses for dogs allegedly living on the farm with me; busted, searched, and thrown in jail overnight for not having licensed beings which I do not consider myself the owner of, yr honor, and I would like to call my ten-year-old daughter to the stand as a witness:

Bailiff: Shannon Kesey take the stand!

Judge: A moment, please. *[leaning benignly down from the bench]* Shannon, do you know what a lie is?

Shannon: Yeah.

Judge: And do you know what a truth is?

Shannon: Yeah.

Judge: And do you know the difference between the two?

Shannon: Yeah.

Judge: Then you may swear her in.

Bailiff: Shannon Kesey do you swear to tell thetruth thewholetruthandnothingbutthetruth s'help you God?

Shannon: Yeah.

Me: Shannon, do you think of Stewart as your dog?

Shannon: No.

Me: Do you think of him as Jed or Zane or Mom's dog?

Shannon: No.

Me: Do you think of him as my dog?

Shannon: No.

Then, based on this dramatic testimony, I advanced my argument to the premise that, though one feeds and lives with another being, he does not actually *possess* the being unless he is experiencing the being as a *thing* in an I/it way, whereas I held myself to be in *relation* to Stewart and, therefore, could not be in *possession* of him. The judge's jaw dropped. The DA turned red and sputtered under the irrefutable weight of my logic. The bailiff crossed himself and made a hex sign at me with his fingers, but could do nothing to stem my argument.

"Not guilty," ruled the judge, then added, "*but,* Mr. Kesey, in as you are not the owner—and apparently no one else is—I must tell you that it is a law in this county that a dog *without an owner* must be put to sleep."

"You mean that by winning the case I lose the dog?"

"I'm afraid that's correct. Unless you buy a dog license."

"All right, I'll buy the license."

"And for the other dogs as well?" the DA piped up. "Or do you want them gassed?"

"I'll get a license for all the dogs."

"You are wise, Mr. Kesey," the judge said.

I watched in silence as he smiled benignly down on Shannon again and left the bench, stepping through my imagination into a reincarnate future where he is a boy being chased through Central Park by a pack of insane pomeranians loosed after him by an organization of insane old ladies dedicated to tracking down defectors from the fifth world war. The dogs pull him down. The old ladies watch, clucking, as their highly pedigreed and thoroughly licensed pets eat away at the young man's ears, nose, crotch . . .

Q. Your favorite metaphor seems to be that the human race is involved in some sort of drama. But since there's no script, do you have any predictions as to developments in the plot?

A. The Good Guys will win. The consciousness now being forged will hang, tempered and true, in the utility closet alongside old and faithful tools like Mercy and Equality and Will Rogers. The accolades will be tremendous. Even Hitler, going through the gates only a few steps in front of Old Scratch himself, will get a terrific hand. And finally, God willing, the mortgage on this wad of woe will be fully paid off.

Q. To help bridge the gap between the Good Guys and the Bad Guys, could you talk a little about fascist humor?

A. Yeah, but first it's a little chilly in here; could we toss another Jew on the fire?

Q. I know you're not anti-Semitic, but is it possible you're a human chauvinist? I mean, I once said I don't believe that Jews are the chosen people—or that people are the chosen species—

A. I don't believe that people are the chosen species, but I believe that the Jews are—or were—the Chosen People.

Q. Until?

A. When the train that pulled into the station two thousand years ago and didn't look like My Son, the Messiah, but like a beatnik in sandals and a Day-Glo yarmulke, well, the train waited around a while for the Chosen to hop on board, then pulled on out. A few hobos hanging out in the yard—lazy yids and hustling goyim, mostly—slipped into the boxcars.

Q. How do you feel about the trend of rock music toward lyrics about neo-Christianity?

A. Mighty good, Paul, bein' a Christian and all; how do *you* feel about it?

Q. It's getting kind of quiet in here; would you toss another Christian to the lions? . . . What do you think is the meaning of a lyric like "One toke over the line, sweet Jesus . . . "?

A. I think they are singing (did you know that was the Dead backing those guys up?) about that state when you've gone and got so high that you're forced to operate mostly on faith.

Q. Would you care to elaborate a little on the relationship between dope and faith?

A. Or, what to do with your hands when the fuses blow. Sometimes we have to take steps to keep our right hand from knowing what our left hand is doing—break up their alliance and turn your palms allward and wait for the spark of creation!—and other times we need to fold our fingers in prayer. So I hereby recommend, if you feel ready to turn palms allward and spread your arms and a-gallivanting go, I recommend LSD-25 and/or psilocybin if you can be sure it's good stuff. (Where do you get this good stuff? Beats me; I don't have any. The first and best I ever got came to me by the very reliable way of the Federal Government. They gave me mine—paid me and quite a few other rats both white and black $20 a session in fact to test it for them, *started it* so to speak, then, when they caught a glimpse of what was coming down in that little room full of guinea pigs, they snatched the guinea pigs out, slammed the door, locked it, barred it, dug a ditch around it, set two guards in front of it, and gave the hapless pigs a good talking to and warned them—on threat of worse than death—to *never* go in that door again—and if you still think they should give you yours after careful examination of the rotminded, chromosome-damaged results of these little experiments begun ten years ago /check the records of Dr. Leo Hollister from early '60s file of Menlo Park and Palo Alto V.A. hospital/, then I think you should demand they either give you yours or award all those poor guinea pigs the Purple Heart, the Distinguished Service Cross and full disability benefits for them and all their offspring as well . . .) And for the times when you've had enough spoils and gallivanting, and you're weary and blistered with the wind, I recommend let the hands join (after a little tequila, or far better, a *Dilantin*) and close your eyes and focus both the *right side of you* and the *left side of you* on the ONE BEYOND you . . . then drink some tea and smoke a joint and throw the *I Ching* and get to work or whatever you let go to weed during your gallivant and *don't hang out*. Every inch of hanging out you do past the point of knowing what needs to be done becomes more a drag, a drain, and an amalgamated lie. *Too much hanging out without a doubt will warp your spine and turn off half your mind*, the memory half, which gets tired of supplying the speech half with information squandered in rapfest *bon mots* and says, "Fuck it; if that's all he's doing with his mouth, I think I'll go to sleep."

Then, after a week or so of this—"cleaning up," Cassady called it—spread those hands again and open a place for something to happen. I know of no other way to Faith; it can't be bought; it can't be learned; and it can't be muscled in. Faith doesn't come from security. It comes from survival.

Q. Do you see the legalization of grass as any sort of panacea?

A. The legalization of grass would do absolutely nothing for our standard of living, or our military supremacy, or even our problem of high school dropouts. It could do nothing for this country except mellow it, and that's not a panacea, that's downright subversive.

Q. Would you say that Christ was hindered or helped by his celibacy?

A. You gotta remember that Jesus was fathered by a celibate, so he comes by it naturally. I *do*, however, think it contradicts some of the longevity claims made by the advocates of this particular crotch yoga discipline.

Q. Would you agree that sexual jealousy is essentially puritan?

A. No, I think all denominations are probably afflicted by it.

Q. Leave your cortical vigilance out of this. . . What do you think of mechanical aids to sexual stimulation, such as vibrators?

A. I've always, if you'll pardon the expression, made out quite well with the traditional equipment, thank you.

Q. Would you go so far as to say that orgies derive out of boredom?

A. All the orgies in my meager experience derived not from

boredom—in fact far from boredom—but from effort, ingenuity, and a good deal of horniness.

Q. Unlike Tim Leary and his magic embrace, you don't seem to be physically demonstrative—do you attach any significance to that?

A. My dad, a Texan, raised me on good ole Amurcan handshakes; I reckon folks just does what comes natural to them. Sometimes I hug people, but it's usually when I'm interested in the configuration of their pectoral region.

Q. Did you have to overcome any homosexual defenses when you were a wrestler?

A. Just one, and he was terrific.

Q. Do you have as much faith in sports as you once did?

A. No. I played and loved sports, but I'm not going to steer my sons into them the way my father did me. I don't like the heavy fascist hit I get off the pro heroes, and I don't like the Little League consciousness that forces a kid to knuckle under a father's fading, and ill-proportioned, values. I'm afraid the old "builds a boy's character and self-confidence" argument is just an earlier version of the Marine recruiter shuck.

Q. How did you dodge the draft, by the way?

A. The dodge I had in mind was going to New Bedford to the Coast Guard Academy, so I went ahead to my exam with that in mind, and when I came to the part on the exam that says "Have you ever had a separated shoulder?" it just so happened that I had separated my left shoulder a couple of years before in the PCI Wrestling tournament in San Luis Obispo when I experienced the worst trouncing of my life in the finals so I marks, "Yeah, I have had my shoulder separated" and went on the next day to wrestle to third place in another tournament, re-separating the same shoulder, and that Monday there was a notice to return for further examination and X-ray where the doctor concluded that my shoulder (which hadn't bothered me much until the re-separation) was "slopping around in the socket like an eyeball in a quart jar of snot" and awarded me a big old 4F for my troubles.

Who says athletic training makes a lad militaristic?

Q. Would you tell about the rise and fall of your American flag tooth?

A. Ah, the tooth. This was a period of penance I did for my momentary patriotic faltering when I split to Mexico, returned, was eluding the FBI by following Rohan out toward the San Rafael bridge to a hideout, hit the brakes, nothing, hit Rohan stopped at a red light in front of me, spun across the oncoming lane and hit a white Imperial, bounced across the divider into the field and hit a pole and finally hit the steering wheel with my mouth and cracked my front tooth off at the gums.

After a miserable night in a Berkeley hotel taking aspirin and listening to the FBI tiptoe up and down the halls, I finally made my way to Santa Cruz where Dick Smith, the mad dentist, suggested replacing it with a flag partial. I flew this banner from the mast of my mouth for almost four years before I sneezed one day by the goose pond where my brother was feeding cottage cheese to the geese and to my surprise found a hole where this flag had flown. Chuck had seen something fly into the cottage cheese after my sneeze, but hadn't got a good look at it. A goose had eaten it. Which goose? He didn't know, so we locked all four in the chicken yard and examined the droppings for a couple of days. We found nothing out of the ordinary, and my grandfather told us that the tooth would likely have been ground up in the craw anyway. It seemed to be the end of the penance. Now, as much as I love it, I would like to see Old Glory hauled down everywhere.

Q. Would you fly anything in its place?

A. The flag of the United Nations. Think about it: assuming we still have to have a Man at the Top, would you rather serve under Richard Nixon or U Thant?

Q. What was your reaction to being searched by the Black Panthers before we could get into the Grateful Dead benefit?

A. A kind of holding-real-still reaction. What was yours?

Q. Somehow I wanted to communicate that my attitude was different from when I had been searched by the police in Chicago because now I was attempting to empathize with—I mean I was hoping he wouldn't tickle me—you're right, a kind of holding-real-still reaction . . . But, whereas the Merry Pranksters could get away with a lot because the police knew they were just traveling through, don't you think it's different from actually living in an Oakland ghetto?

A. Different, but probably not much more fraught. To any people, anywhere, who have the audacity to be alive to each other, there is always the threat of Moloch swooping down with nightstick and search warrant. Being black isn't what makes living in Oakland, or anywhere else, dangerous; it's being colored. The prison that the audacious are threatened with is built of nothing but categories. Cops know that there is really no way to bust the rainbow.

Q. Unless it crosses state lines . . . What did you mean when you said that I cramped a certain consciousness by talking to those people from Sam's Cafe on the radio?

A. I mean that the vacuum of centuries is roaring questions in your ear and you take time to play riddles with the Cub Scouts. Who are you to fritter your valuable energies away in these times of ecological poverty?

Q. I don't know, I guess I must be a Cub Scout fetishist. . . and you must be a vacuum cleaner salesman. . . Do you approve of the eco-guerrillas going out with double crosscut saws and then selecting appropriately obnoxious billboards?

A. Yes, this is a creative and non-violent act with the effects and immediate rewards. I hope the trend spreads.

Q. Oh, hey, Buster Keaton's supposed to be on TV now.

A. Far fucking out. Let's watch him.

[Time out. Can't get Keaton. We watch one-third of Games *instead.]*

Q. John Wayne says that if you're going to look into the eye of the camera, you'd better be prepared to deliver the Sermon on the Mount. Would you care to look into the eye of the camera? I guess what I'm really asking is, what are the rules of your game?

A. God's will be done. And if, to be able to tune in on that will, I have to get a little high or come on a little strange in order to free myself of the interference jamming my pipeline, then I may presume to ask God, since it's all in the line of duty, to please don't make my highs too bumpy or my strangeness too ungentle.

We'll always fumble and fuck up, and all our rules will eventually come down with a dose of amendments. It says in the

"IF THERE IS AN ATOMIC ATTACK AND YOU SURVIVE, AS A POSTAL EMPLOYEE YOU ARE DIRECTED TO REPORT TO THE NEAREST POSTAL INSTALLATION FOR CIVIL DEFENSE OR POSTAL WORK. A CIVIL SERVICE FORM 600 MUST BE FILLED OUT BY YOU AT THIS TIME."--POST OFFICE PAMPHLET

Urantia book that at the Last Supper, Christ promised his disciples that he would return to them as the Spirit of Truth. This is what we want, a compass needle that constantly tries to point out Whatever's Right. Rules we must eventually forsake as we turn more and more to the Spirit of Truth. It is for this spirit of moment-by-moment responsibility, this continual seeking after the unique and correct action for each unique and demanding moment, this Way that is unpointed. . . for this final holy *heart* of us that we must eventually forsake all rules.

Is kind of the kind of game I play.

Q. I can understand the use of prayer as a means of maintaining contact with the universe. But don't you think it's lacking in cosmic humility when you pray for any kind of personal goal?

A. Not at all! If one's heart is like mine, pure and dedicated, he is exempt from humility. Where do you get off with these dopey questions? Don't you know I'm a busy man with lots of important irons in the fire?

Q. Oh, yeah—well, what was the great Spirit of Truth behind your sneaking out of that party with the little tank of nitrous oxide—huh, huh, huh?

A. The Spirit of Stash happens to be one of the amendments to the Spirit of Truth.

Q. What do you think your father meant, saying to you and Chuck once, over a gas flash: "You fellows better be right, or it's the end of the universe . . ."?

A. He sensed that what we were about was threatening the whole human hierarchy, our whole system of Who Really Makes Things Work, and that there had better be Something Better available when the kings and generals fell.

Q. What do you think our kids are going to do that will shock and dismay us as much as the things we've been doing have shocked and dismayed our parents?

A. Nothing. Ever. If our efforts have been sincere. Are Grape Nuts as hard to chew as they were when you were a kid?

Q. Oh, is that what you were supposed to do with

them?. . . But how come you wouldn't let your kids read Zap Comics?

A. Once, on our way to film *Atlantis Rising*, we were encamped at Ed McClanahan's amid a mighty passle of kids: my kids, Babbs' kids, Ed's kids, Chuck's kids . . . and as they played in the backyard, us grown folks rested ourselves on the back porch and smoked, drank, shot the shit, and read of the new crop of *Zap* and *Zap*-style comics that Ed had brought from his office. Fierce stuff, gory and righteously disturbing stuff, the only stuff I'd seen with any of the real raw excitement that you feel from when art is in there dealing with the issues, since I'd first come across Ron Boise's work of statues screwing. Fascinating stuff . . .

And after a bit one of the books worked its way into the kid action going on; we noticed a change of energy activity that had been all-encompassing began to fragment. When a kid read a certain of the comics, he would turn darkly into himself until, gradually, the communication that is the basis of play fell apart. I asked Babbs: "Do you think that these comics are going to make our kids better fucks in the future, or worse?"

"Worse, I think," he answered.

"Me too," I said.

We set about gathering the books from sight.

Because, in some of the comics of that period particularly, along with the art, there was often something else in the works of even geniuses like Crumb and Wilson and Shelton, speed-trip-like digressions where you could see the artists working to exorcise their own personal demons by, however unintentionally, casting them into whatever swine happened to be susceptible, which wasn't us grown folks because we were either full up with our own demons or had the defense built up by our own exorcising, so we were safe. I wasn't so sure about the kids.

It's like this: I've got nothing against my kids watching a couple make love, but having them watch a flagellant is something different. But that doesn't explain it either. I've got it: it's the *consciousness the artist is communicating* that I'm concerned with; not the activity the art is depicting. I've always brought city stuff back from the city for my kids, *Zap* included (so I actually *do* let them read *Zap*; as a matter of fact, I can't recall any of the *Zaps* that I ever withheld; it was mostly the *Zap* spinoffs), some stuff even to read aloud to them because it was so fine you know that the consciousness producing it must have been unimpeachable, *whatever* the subject matter or how luridly it was dealt with, stuff like Lenore Goldberg, and Captain Pissgums, and Fritz the Cat and Mr. Natural and Wonder Warthog and, Lord, *most* of the ones that everybody reads—but I now read them through first to try to plumb the *consciousness* serving as the impetus, and, some I withhold.

I mean, W.C. Fields was a great artist, but would we ask him to babysit when he was working off a bad hangover?

Q. What's the last thing that made you lose your temper?

A. I have to admit, it was my kids.

Q. What's the last thing that made you laugh hysterically?

A. My mind is a bramble of shredded wheat. Who can unravel the memories from the riboflavin, I ask you? But I guess it was a week or so ago at an acid-laced poker game when things digressed to the point of a hand of 9-card stud with Doses, Jukers, and One-eyed Pukers wild.

Q. Is there any connection between those two things?

A. Yes! Of course there is a connection! What two things?

Q. I forget. Memory and riboflavin, I guess.

A. Ah, of course. In that case, no, there is no question. Next connection, please.

Q. Do you think eternal consciousness would be Heaven or Hell?

A. I don't know about that, but I know that forty hours of STP with a big hand on the nape of the neck saying "You wanted to see the books? So then *look* at the books!" can be fairly Hellish. There's a beautiful chapter in *Wind in the Willows* where Rat and Mole find the little lost muskrat child, resting there, safe between the hooves of (the *hooves* of!?) who had been taking care of the helpless animal, and Mole and Rat see, in the *hooves* of, great sights, great tragedies, great delights . . . too much, finally, too much.

And the final gift of (the *hooves*?) then, is the merciful gift of (what hooves? I can't remember. . .) Forgetfulness.

Q. What about that weird ice cream flavor you once invented as an early indication of your abnormality?

A. As ice cream maker in my father's creamery I one time achieved a culinary coup by combining all the leftover flavors, adding a large amount of red food coloring, and calling it "Blood Royal," reasoning that the name would tempt new and adventurous customers to our brand. I planned to follow this triumph with two other new delights—"Scum Ripple" and "Crud Crunch"—but was torpedoed by the first narrow-minded grocer that discovered a quart of Blood Royal in his freezer. In what seemed to me a very uncalled-for phone call to the creamery, he cancelled his account and advised my father to tell the nincompoop that made this batch to look for work in a butchershop instead of a dairy. Maybe I should have taken this advice; it's difficult for abnormality to flower properly in the antiseptic confines of a creamery.

Q. There was a film critic who said that the Marx Brothers "often used a Sufi parable to launch into their excursions into madness."

A. Far out! But I can believe it. There was a pervading smell of sanity in the fuss the Brothers raised that seemed to come from some place other than the local yeshiva. Sufo Marx? Who'da thought it . . .

Q. So how come you can't call Hugh Romney by his rightful name?

A. Because I simply cannot imagine myself stumbling through the mosquito-ridden bush to finally find our missing colleague standing gaunt and bowed with decades of humanitarianism performed in the most desolate reaches of the globe, and say to him: "Wavy Gravy, I presume?"

Q. You've used the expression, "being tight with one's own image"—what does that mean to you?

A. I don't remember ever saying such. But you, Paul, are a truthful lad, so I must have said it. What must I have meant? Hmmm . . . Well, I *do* think about my fucking image, I confess. I don't intend to, but often I find it there in the hallway, prancing and whimpering like a dog begging to be taken for a walk in the park, and I am compelled, out of kindness if nothing else, to deal with it:

"Hello, Image, how the hell are ya?"

"Take me out, take me out! I'm fading, I'm warped, I need some *light*!"

"Yeah, I've seen the light you attract, champ. Now stop this nonsense and get back in the basement; I'll let you know when it's time for your walk . . ."

So what I must have meant is trying to keep straight with all the lies I promised yesterday and still not have to pay for a rabies shot.

Q. Once there was the Great Acid Test Graduation. Now, what's your current post-graduate fantasy?

A. Well, to tell the truth, I've been taking a few refresher courses. I may re-enroll and go on for my doctorate.

Q. What've you learned lately?

A. I've learned to keep a little niacin and ginseng handy, and to have a mantra on tap in the backup system.

Q. Do you think it's possible that you're overly dependent on the I Ching?

A. The *Ching* is an oracle and willing to work for but not to indulge you. It's very specific about this; whenever you overuse it, it invariably scolds you and draws your attention to this infringement; as with, for example, the hexagram Meng/ Youthful Folly which says this in The Judgment:

Youthful Folly has success.
It is not I who seek the young fool;
The young fool seeks me.
At the first oracle I inform him.
If he asks two or three times, it is importunity.
If he importunes, I give him no information.
Perseverence furthers.

Q. You could always resort to a movie script instead for the same stage directions—Consternation changing to Horror—but if, no matter what you throw, the Ching *will still apply to your situation, then obviously it serves as a Rorschach test, and it would seem to me that the closer in touch you are with your unconscious, the less need you'd have to consult the* I Ching.

A. No. Getting closer to your unconscious is where you are on a psychological field. The *Ching* exists in another field. There is no development implied in one's ability to throw the *Ching*; you never throw the *Ching* any better or any worse than you did the first time.

Q. There was a student rebel poster during the 1968 uprising in France that said: "Psychology aims at the systematic subor-

dination of individual behavior to false social norms"—do you see any change in terms of encounter groups and psychodrama?

A. Once, at Esalen, I happened in on the end of a week's dance therapy. There were the graduates, all aglow with a week's total encounter and breakthrough, recapping their recent victories. Fritz Perls was there too. "Vait!" he said.

[*The radio suddenly announces that the charges against Bobby Seale have been dismissed. "Holy cow!" Kesey shouts. Then the President says from Birmingham that America is "not divided at all." Responding to both Krassner and Nixon, Kesey continues:*]

"Vait!" Fritz protested. "Vhere are you the *rest* of the veeks?"

"Vwat—I mean *what* do you mean?" asked the dance therapist, cautiously.

"He means," I interjected helpfully, "what does Superman do between phone booths?"

"I mean," Fritz answered for himself, "you are dividing your lives between *this veek. . .* and *all other veeks*!"

Which means to me that the idea of "sessions" may insure failure of psychology aims, that to avoid a schizophrenic dichotomy we must either (1) let psychodrama push back the rest of our lives, or (2) let the rest of our lives push back the psychodrama, or (3) live the drama without benefit of Alfred Hitchcock.

I mean, I heard the fatality report for the weekend in Lane County: A girl was killed when her horse fell on her. A guy crashed in his single-engine plane. A guy drowned waterskiing. A mountain climber killed falling down a mountain. It's when you take a break that you stumble, and psychodrama is a vacation, a luxury. Look at the cars driven by the participants, at the houses they live in. Could Bobby Seale afford psychodrama? Does he need it? Does he even have *room* for it?

Q. Now that we won't have Bill Graham to kick around any more, how do you envision the future of rock concerts and festivals?

A. I'm afraid Bill Graham's pandering has muddied these waters for good. Maybe this is why I feel my personal energies swinging back to writing.

Q. It doesn't seem fair to make Graham the scapegoat for an entire industry, including the groups that demand so much bread in front.

A. You're right; it isn't fair. People get what's due them without any help from other people. But Bill Graham's a very powerful guy and has survived much worse thoughts than I ever had about him, and I use the word "pander" because it implies that particular kind of middle-man, that buffer between the whore and the horny, and this was a place that Bill won, defended, and finally wisely forsook—all with great class and with never any apparent loss of personal integrity. Maybe the waters needed muddying. If the vision is ill, it was probably doomed from the start and Bill Graham is merely part of Fate's motorcycle. And if I object to a panderer, I mean it in no way as a moral or a personal objection; it just seems to me like a sort of fatuous featherbedding. Do we need them? Did you ever see "Mother Nature Presents!" tattooed across an upreared pudendum?

"I find it very difficult to be an intellectual in the United States."

Let me make myself more clear on this, as our great President might say. Bill Graham, as it happened with a lot of us, found himself heir to a large hunk of the Revolution, and I think that he, as did a lot of us, mismanaged his allotment. I also think it's up to them as considers themselves capable to finger the mistakes, and if we keep our finger in the mistake too long, or make a mistake in our fingering, then it's up to those as think *they* are able to, to finger *our* mistake. But we must learn to leave each man's righteousness to him and stick to the work we're involved in. I can't presume to say Bill Graham is a bad man or an un-righteous middle-man—in fact I *admire* his apparent righteousness—but I can accuse him of being a bad pimp. Then, on the other hand, maybe I'm just getting back at him for calling me a "hip Liberace."

But, I'll tell you, Paul, these are hard questions. I don't like the sound of me answering too-hard questions. I sound oracular, like I know more than I do. My words have a disproportionate weight. Like, I got a long letter from a Ph.D. in Biology about the article in the *Last Supplement* on Cancer, and another about the article on Immunization, asking essentially: Are we certain we have looked into such things as cancer and smallpox vaccination enough to allow statements about things as important as some old lady who might go for the Laetrile cure instead of going to a doctor, or some kid's future with smallpox? No! We are not qualified! This isn't to say that we couldn't be if we put our full energies into these areas and stopped trying to live like rock stars, but right now, no, I'm not qualified. No more than I'm qualified to make judgments regarding other people's karmic state or depth of their revolutionary commitment. But I'm easy; some kid with big eyes and a notepad could come up and ask me how the universe was created, and if he looks like he thinks I know, pretty soon *I* think I know and I'm running it down to him like the gospel. I'm easy but in *no fucking way qualified!*

So, Mr. Krassner, I not only cease, I *vow* to cease answering these and other such questions and to shut my mouth and the door to my writing room and finish the new totally fictional version of *Cut the Motherfuckers Loose* and answer out of my range no more.

Passing off what-might-be-true as fiction seems a better vocation to me than passing off what-is-quite-possibly-fiction as truth.

Q. Didn't you once believe that writing is an old-fashioned and artificial occupation?

A. I was counting on the millenium. Now I guess I'm tired of waiting.

Q. Would you recount the incident of that old man with the bicycle we saw on the road near La Honda?

A. Ah, gee, Paul, I don't know. . . let me see. . . we're driving down out of the La Honda hills and turning left at the ocean, along the roller coaster of the California shoreline in Faye's 1964 black Mercury convertible with the top open to the great blue sky. . . and we see this apparition up the hill ahead, advancing down the highway toward us in dreadful silhouette of hunk and paraphernalia and even *two other bicycles* tied atop the one battered World he was easing down the grade in grim combat with gravity. . . there on the shoulder as we pass, his face worked like suede by the half century of his tanning, his faded grape-picker clothes loose on his knotted frame, his big delicate boots that probably had walked their way through at least two previous masters before aligning themselves with this man's inviolable cause, digging heels into the gravel as he eased his bike down the hill. . .

And we drive on down the coast and go to a cave I know, a tunnel built during the second world war by the Coast Guard so two men could walk two hundred yards through the chiseled earth to sit all day where the tunnel opens out through a cliff overlooking the Jap-infested Pacific, to sit there all day every day through the years of our battle with the Japanese and watch with binoculars over the barrel of a big gun for periscopes that never came. . . then leaving the cave and driving back north hours later through the sunset we spy this old guy, some miles further along and on the other side of the road this time and now pushing his apocalyptic vehicle *up* a hill! Touched with awe and sympathy, we swing in behind him. His head turns and he frowns back at us like an angry and enlightened Sisyphus.

"Do you need any help?" we shout heartily.

"No!" he roars back with such ferocity that our goodhearted grins turn to gapes. After glaring at us a moment to make sure we all fully understand his meaning, he turns and resumes his stoic journey up the hill.

That "no" was not a no roared merely to 1964 black Mercuries, but to airplanes, trains, motorcycles and LEMs. It was the no of a man who had kicked the petroleum habit and wasn't about to joypop any little five-mile lift in even a convertible. Our heartiness subdued, we drove around and left him to his way.

Someday, if we last, there'll be millions of that old man, opting in favor of an austere freedom instead of making monthly payments on a plush prison. Cars will still speed through their rivers of stench, airplanes will still carry the Important on their hectic flights to Folly and Fortune, but on the backroads and ox-bows of the land, this old man will still be pushing his vehicle with absolute disdain along with the millions of others who come to share his vision.

Q. Okay, one final question: Mr. Kesey, would you let your daughter marry the Lennon Sisters high on SST in her underwear at a Black Panther Party even though erogizone research has shown that such a union label would cause the patoolee oil gland to dry up beyond all interstellar recognition?

A. Could you rephrase that question, please?

Q. Let me put it this way: How was the universe created?

A. Thanks, Paul. It's sure been great. Now, in closing, I'd like to say this.

WHY ARE WE IN UNDERWEAR?

Ken Babbs wrote a novel years ago about his time in Vietnam. He has since burned the manuscript.

The hero of his book was an American serviceman stationed in Vietnam. This guy never changed his underwear. But as one set of underpants would wear out he'd put on another pair. Eventually the guy ended up with only one complete pair of drawers but with seven elastic bands around his waist.

THE LEGEND OF HASSLER'S ASSHOLE

It seems that at Hassler's high school the guys had a contest to see who could go the longest without having his jock-strap washed. Hassler won, going four whole years without having the nasty thing so much as rinsed. His victory in this competition was not without its karmic results. Hassler subsequently spent years dealing with the combination of crotch ailments which came to be known as Hassler's Asshole.

Prostate infection was one of the symptoms of the dread Hassler's Ass-hole. It seems that to relieve oneself of prostate infection one has to have his prostate gland massaged, an operation which requires a partner since we are not dexterous enough ourselves to reach up our own assholes to touch the afflicted gland.

Well, after a narrow getaway from the Acid Test trail in Los Angeles, the Merry Pranksters headed to Mexico, where we were to rendezvous with the fugitive Kesey. We met him, paranoid in Mazatlan. Somehow we also rented a couple of rooms in a cheap hotel and gathered there to relieve the grassless condition which had marked our trip since California.

Stoned, we sat around one room while Hassler began his asshole-cleansing ritual. Soap, water and various patent medicines were applied. Then it came time for his prostate rub.

"Who will massage my prostate?" he wanted to know. None of us, of course.

But after he'd whined and wheedled, George finally agreed, but only if he could put on a rubber glove.

No rubber gloves were to be had but someone had a condom. Thusly protected, George approached Hassler from the rear. Hassler bent over and George's finger made its entrance.

The reason for massaging an infected prostate is to cause an orgasm reaction, which causes the infection to be discharged along with the semen, or whatever it is that is discharged from the prostate in orgasm.

As the rest of us watched from our stoned vantage points, George gently massaged Hassler's prostate. But it was to no avail. Hassler couldn't come.

Finally, I suggested to George: "Tell him you love him."

It didn't work.

The door opened and Kesey, weird after weeks avoiding *federales*, looked in. He saw the both of them, two of his best Pranksters.

"So, it's come to this, has it?" he asked sadly.

THE PETER EATER

From Mazatlan, Kesey, Mountain Girl and I went to Mexico City for fruitless talks with a lawyer. Then we rejoined the bus at Manzanillo. From there Hassler, Zonker, and I decided to split for the United States. We reached the border in the evening and never ones to waste anything, swallowed all of our medicines, which included various stimulants and painkillers. We were clean when we crossed the border.

Hitchhiking wasn't paying off well and we spent several hours standing at various spots along the highway. A short ride here, another there. But then we struck paydirt.

A white convertible, top up, pulled up. How far were we going? L.A. Well,

"I'm glad you dig it, man . . . It's nostril hairs."

here was a ride to Seal Beach. We took it. After we'd thrown our packs in the car and got in ourselves the guy driving turned to us and said, "Hi, I'm Harry and I'm as queer as a three-dollar bill and I want to suck your peters."

Zonker, in the front seat, seemed most perturbed by this introduction. We begged off and Harry and his white convertible carried us off into the night.

Harry was not one to give in quickly. He pleaded and insisted that he be permitted to suck our peters. He even bought us a beer, which got the Mexican medicines churning again.

Finally, we said okay and Harry pulled over on a deserted stretch of highway. We followed him for a few yards into a bowl-shaped field. There was a full moon. Harry asked if it would be all right if he jerked off while he sucked our cocks. We said we'd rather that he jerked off while looking at our cocks. A compromise was reached.

Harry also asked if we'd whip him with our belts while he jacked off while sucking our peters. Hassler and I said No. A man has to have some sense of what's right and wrong.

But Zonker agreed. However, Zonker only had a cotton woven Mexican belt and he told Harry it wouldn't hurt very much. "Ah, well," Harry said, "go ahead and hit me with it anyway."

It's the thought that counts.

ONE PICTURE IS WORTH . . .

One of my editors, when I was a newspaper reporter in Chicago, considered doggedness to be next to godliness.

When he had been a young man he had been assigned to get a photograph of a boy who had been killed in a freak accident. He went to the boy's home only to be rebuffed by the parents, who wanted to keep their only photo of their son. Other newsmen were also hovering around the front door, seeking the picture. The parents were adamant.

So the reporter who was to become my editor went to the rear of the house, found some paper, stuffed it under the house and lighted it with a mach.

The house caught on fire, the fire trucks came, the reporter rushed into the burning house and grabbed the dead boy's photo from atop the mantle, then rushed back to his office.

The house burned to the ground.

THE MEDIUM IS THE MESSAGE

Once, when I was a police reporter for the City News Bureau of Chicago, I was assigned to cover the gangland-style murder of a labor union leader. The guy had been shot in the head after a bomb wired to his car's ignition had failed to go off.

A bunch of newspaper reporters were interviewing the chief of the organized crime detail an hour or so after the body had been found. The chief was answering questions about the murder weapon, the motive for the killing, the suspects, etc.

Suddenly a newsman for one of the local television stations pushed his way into the group, shoved his microphone under the chief's face and asked an incredibly stupid question.

The newspaperman standing next to the TV reporter put his pencil in his breast pocket, placed his note-pad in his jacket pocket, turned and slugged the television reporter on the jaw. The TV newsman fell onto his back and lay there unconscious.

The newspaperman took out his pad and pencil, and the press conference continued. Meanwhile, the TV newsman lay unconscious at our feet. No one gave him another thought.

GAS MOVES IN MYSTERIOUS WAYS

One Prankster bus trip was into the wilds of the Trinity Alps in Northern California. We slept while Dale Kesey did the driving.

When we awoke in the morning Dale was asleep and the bus was on a remote dirt road. There was no one about but us and a rattlesnake. Dale finally woke up and revealed that he had stopped at this particular spot because the bus had run out of gas. He didn't know where we were.

Instead of getting pissed off we got out and wandered around. And one of us came upon an old man wearing a fake deputy's badge who told us to get off the property. "Where are we?" we wanted to know. He told us. And after checking our pockets and determining that we had no cash, only a Standard Oil credit card, we learned from the old man that the nearest Standard Station was at least 75 miles away. And there was no traffic

"Thanks!"

WOODMAN

on the dirt road for hitchhiking, so we'd have to walk much of the 75 miles.

We ate some breakfast and considered our predicament.

As we finished eating we heard an auto horn honking at the bus. We walked to the back of the bus and found a Standard Oil gas truck stalled there. The driver asked us to move the bus. We told him we were out of gas. He said he had to get to a copper mine at the end of the dirt road. We told him we had a credit card. He got out, filled the bus with gas, used the credit card, filled out a receipt and continued on his way. And so did we.

THE MERRY PRANKSTERS REACH NIRVANA

From the Trinity Alps we took the bus to a lake in Mendocino County, where we all took some Czechoslovakian acid and plugged the bus's sound system into a socket in the public men's room. Ken Babbs turned into a duck and wandered around quacking prophetically after Gretchen Fetchin had covered his somehow sticky body with feathers from a pillow.

When the Rangers closed in to announce that we were not allowed to use park electricity to power the bus rock and roll system, the Head Ranger kept trying to find out who was in charge. We all pointed to Babbs, who was wearing his Day Glo red pith helmet and his feathers.

The Head Ranger seemed incredulous that Babbs could be in charge of *anything*, but he finally walked up and told Babbs that we had to unplug the bus. After the Head Ranger had given a lengthy explanation of the reasons for his order, Babbs began to quack at him.

Unnerved, the official called for reinforcements. But by the time we were outnumbered, Kesey had returned from a sojourn lost among the trees and we were able to make a getaway.

Hauling out of the park, Zonker and I sat atop the bus, still stoned. We got a down-filled sleeping-bag from below and George joined us. But the sleeping-bag ripped and what appeared to be several cubic yards of feathers started streaming out behind the bus, caught in the headlights of the car behind us.

That was the Great Duck Storm.

We ended up in a clearing near Willits. I threw a beer can off the bus and it struck something metallic. Kesey threw one in another direction and it struck something metallic. Kesey announced that we were in the middle of a garbage dump after assessing the metallic sounds. Sure enough, when the sun rose we found our psychedelic bus parked in the exact center of the Willits Dump.

HOW DO YOU GET TO MEMORY LANE?

When Julius used to drink a lot of gin, he developed his habit of keeping a list of all the things he had to remember to do. Without the list he was lost.

One day I was visiting, and Julius was walking around with a 3-by-5 card in his left hand. He wasn't paying any attention to it, just carrying it. In fact, it seemed like he'd forgotten the card was in his hand.

Finally, I asked Julius what was written on the card. He showed me. It read: "Look in your back pocket." It was a note he'd written to himself.

So he looked in his back pocket. And there was his list of things he was supposed to do.

Julius' memory was so poor in those days that he eventually hired Len to be his memory. Len remembered where Julius had set down his glass of gin and tonic, what time the Dick Van Dyke show came on TV, when it was time for Julius to keep appointments, when he

was supposed to send a Chanukah card to his folks, and so on.

REACHING FOR THE MOON

The World Smoke Ring Championships were held in Julius's apartment. Contestants were my brother, Dean, and Nick the Greek. Judges were Julius, Bruce Barton (aka d'Artagnan Pig), and myself. Competition was held on a Sunday morning, with spectating done from behind closed glass doors separating the fans from the playing field in the living room.

Competition was divided into five categories: Opener (Diddle Event), Target competition, Single Ring Event, Orgasmic Succession (machine gun competition), and the Exhibitionism Event. Both contestants were judged on the basis of extraneity, rate, esthetics, concentricity, diameter, torus approximation, backspin, shape variation, vibrancy, constancy, electric quality, friendship, audience reaction, dissipatory success and Kama Sutra influence in overall performance. Each contestant in each event was graded either the shits, OK, or fantastic.

My brother won. There were some complaints which are still occasionally reiterated that my judging was biased and, as always, I deny this. He ain't heavy, he's my brother.

Going into the exhibitionism event Nick and Dean were almost tied. Nick went first in this crucial event. He poured some red wine into a glass, drank it and began blowing smoke rings into the glass. They bounced back like halitosis signals in a breath mint commercial. The audience applauded enthusiastically. Nick filled the glass again, sipped, then smashed the glass and wine against the white wall of the room. Spectators cheered. Nick bowed and retired.

My spunky brother took the floor, blew some rings, then stripped, still blowing rings. Naked, he bent over, aiming his rear at the bleachers. He looked through his legs and blew an incredible chain of smoke rings toward the audience, which was going wild. Some spectators stood and cheered, other fell off their chairs (or had already fallen off their chairs and remained prone). It was Dean by acclamation.

THE FLY KILLERS

Al and I set up shop in the kitchen of

our house in Colonia Florida in Mexico City. Fortified with several bottles of *Benzadrina* and *Dexadrina* from the local *farmacia* and armed with a *matamosco*—a fly-killer or flyswatter— we sat facing each other talking about life and killing flies.

We split the walls, ceiling and floor of the room up into zones, quadrants, and sectors before we got down to the serious business of snuffing flies. There were plenty of flies, and there was plenty of speed. We talked fast but managed to keep half our attention on the flies. They'd wing their way into the kitchen from the front room and land here or there, seeking refreshment. When one would land, say on the wall to my left, about halfway up, between the closet and stove, Al would briefly interrupt his musing about the nature of the universe to say something like, "Two, five, D."

Without bothering to look and almost without interrupting my part of the conversation, I'd catch one-handed the *matamosco* thrown by Al, rise gracefully to my left, swing the swatter backhanded and mash the fly, as lithe and athletic in my own way as any ballet *artiste*. Then, without pause, the conversation would continue until another fly entered the room.

The fast talk and fly killing went on for three days. We covered just about every subject there is, plus we killed every fly in the place. In fact, we finally left the kitchen to seek other victims in other rooms.

There were none. We returned to the kitchen and tried to take up the conversation where we'd dropped it. We gobbled more *Dexadrina*. It was no use. The world suddenly became lackluster. So, with the unspoken consensus of lengthy speed fraternity, we each got up and walked to the back door. Through the window we saw flies, hundreds of 'em, in the back yard. And so, of course, we opened the door, returned to our chairs and waited.

ONE FLEW INTO THE CUCKOO'S NEXT

The first Hell's Angels party at Ken Kesey's place in La Honda has been widely reported by various participants, all of whom must have been as fucked up as I was that night. But no one has reported the case of the guy who was hung upside down from the rafters in the living room.

This guy arrived late at the party and crossed the bridge over La Honda Creek after the rest of us were deeply into the weirdness. He came up to the little clusters of Pranksters and Angels standing around campfires and other attractions, and said to us: "Hi there. You don't know me but I'm okay. Now don't get paranoid. I'm cool, dig. Now don't get paranoid."

He walked from group to group, freaking everybody into paroxysms of paranoia.

Finally, one Hell's Angel felt he had to deal with the guy. So he picked him up, carried him inside Kesey's house, put a rope around his feet and hung him upside down from the rafters. The poor guy hung there all night. Every once in a while someone would give him a push and he'd swing like a pendulum. By morning a humanitarian had helped him down and he'd returned to Berkeley where, I learned later, he became a prominent cuckoo.

BEING IN WITHOUT AN OUTLET

You've heard of selling refrigerators to Eskimoes? My friend Bob used to sell electric freezers to islanders in the South Pacific. On one island, the possession of one of his line of freezers was a must for status-conscious natives. The freezers were selling like hotcakes.

Bob finally quit his job, right in the middle of the freezer boom. The thing that got to him was the fact that there was no electricity on the island. This didn't bother the status-conscious natives, but it did bother Bob's conscience.

CLEANLINESS IS NEXT TO INSTALLMENT PLAN

My roommate David was a fellow reporter at the City News Bureau of Chicago. He was not the tidiest fellow in the world and had a giant stash of laundry which made his room and the rest of our apartment smell hideously. I and my other roommates eventually talked David into taking dirty clothes to the Chinese laundry around the corner on North Avenue.

David got a bedspread and placed it on the floor of the dining room. He then carried several bushels of dirty laundry from his bedroom and stacked them in the center of the bedspread. He finally collected the four corners of the spread and started dragging the dirty laundry down the stairs and up Wells Street toward the Chinese establishment. The load weighed about 60 pounds.

Well, 60 pounds of laundry cannot be washed cheaply. So David made a deal with the proprietor of the laundry. Whenever he'd need something he'd walk into the shop and tell the man: "Give me 50 cents worth of underwear, 20 cents worth of socks, and two bits worth of shirts."

THE SMOKED OYSTER LIBERATION FRONT

My friend Dennis used to boost a lot of tasty delicacies from the shelves of our local supermarket. He specialized in smoked oysters and little expensive things like that.

Eventually, the supermarket people figured out that he was a thief. So one time they assigned the assistant manager to follow Dennis around, to make himself obvious to let my friend know they were on to him.

Dennis walked into the store and quickly had some oysters stuffed in his trousers. He looked around and there was the assistant manager. *Jesus,* Dennis thought, *I have to get rid of these oysters.* But the guy stuck to him like glue. Everywhere Dennis went—produce, canned goods, beverages—the assistant manager was right behind.

Dennis almost panicked. If he couldn't get rid of the oysters without being seen by the assistant manager, he'd have to go through the checkstand with them. And he didn't have any money. But near panic was the mother of invention.

Dennis went to the office and found the manager in. He pointed to the assistant manager, standing nearby in the dog food section, and revealed to the boss: "I think one of your employees is a queer, and he's been following me everywhere I go. I thought you'd better know about it."

The manager, beaten at his own game, nodded. He called the assistant manager off, and Dennis got rid of the hot oysters.

226

DEATH ON THE DICK CAVETT SHOW

by Marshall Efron as told to
Kathie Streem

I arrived at the Dick Cavett show about 10 minutes before they wanted me to be there, and I sat around and looked over the list of people that were gonna be on the show. I had never heard of J.I. Rodale, but I had heard about Pete Hamill, so I was happy about seeing him. The crew was getting everything set up. I watched them do a run-through of two commercials and spotted Mr. Cavett for a second (he doesn't like to see his guests before the show—likes it to be fresh).

I sat in the Green Room waiting to go on and met Mr. Rodale. We chatted for a little while. I was kidding him about being a health-nut, and he told me he would live to be a hundred. He talked about doing a Broadway show and he had written a bunch of plays. He was kinda keyed-up—tense—but really seemed to be enjoying himself.

The show started, and these little monkeys went on first and did their bit and they were very cute. And I followed, doing my Tricia Nixon Wedding Cake bit. I made the cake on the stage and then went downstairs to put it in the oven. I was supposed to come out again at the end of the show and give everybody a piece of Tricia's cake (except for Mr. Rodale, who explained that the sugar would be harmful to his blood chemistry).

I put the cake in the oven, and when I got back upstairs to the Green Room, Mr. Rodale was on stage, saying that there are certain things you had to eat to live longer. He said that doctors had given him 6 months to live 30 years ago, but because of the food he ate, he would live to be a hundred. And he went on and on about healthy foods and started talking about boiling asparagus in urine, which didn't go over too big with the audience, and then he held out a half-eaten goose egg which he said "has a lot of life in it."

After a few minutes, Rodale moved down another chair and Pete Hamill came on. Pete was talking about the feud between Lindsay and Rockefeller, and Rodale wasn't particularly interested in any of this. He sounded like he was falling asleep. He started snoring. Cavett and Hamill stopped talking and looked at him and laughed . . . and then they kept looking at him and realized that he wasn't sleeping . . . he had had a cardiac arrest or something.

So they immediately ran to his aid. Everybody was yelling for oxygen and a doctor. The lights went off, but the TV camera was still on—I was watching the whole thing from the monitor in the Green Room. And the police came and the ambulance came and they took him away, and 14 minutes later he was dead. Everybody was pretty shook about it (especially Cavett) and someone said to me, "We're not going to run the show tonight," and I said, "That's wise," and that was it. We all went home.

There was a picture in the *Sunday New York Times Magazine* of Rodale sitting in what looked like a barber chair with these wires strapped on him. The text said that he sat there for 10 to 20 minutes a day getting short-waved radio beams sent through his body, the reason being that as we go through life we lose our body electricity because of overhead steel beams in buildings and insulated floors under our feet.

So, if that was the case, he really had no business being in a television studio at all, because there are lots of steel beams in the building and overhead holding the lights—and in the floor, too, the stage was insulated. To compound it and make it worse, TV cameras and microphones were really draining his body electricity. No wonder he expired. I told that to people and they asked me, "Do you believe that?" Of course, it doesn't make any difference what I believe; *he* believed it.

THE FIRST WATERBED FATALITY

by Tom Miller

Malcolm Coors, a University of Arizona grad student in economics, became the first fatality of the waterbed fad. He had been watching a late-night talk show on his tiny Sony television, which had frayed electrical connecting wires. The set fell into a puddle—the result of his cat clawing at the waterbed—and he was electrocuted. The electrically charged water seeped up and surrounded his body before he could reach safety. Coors would have been 23 two days later.

Ironically, he had just completed writing a paper for his "Economics and Culture" class on the waterbed price war. The paper, entitled *Price and Quality Factors Affecting Cost of Liquefied Mattresses: A Ten-City Sample*, had been sold to publisher Lyle Stuart, who had planned to release it this fall under the title *The Sensuous Waterbed*. The publishing house has made no comment on its plans now that the author has died.

Coors' economics professor, Cynthia Kessler, said the paper demonstrates how the price war on waterbeds, which began in Los Angeles and spread virtually to every metropolitan area in the country, is really no different from practices used daily by large aerospace and steel concerns. In fact, the Coors paper documents a curious parallel between hip-capitalists selling waterbeds and stockbrokers trading defense industry shares. The appendix to the paper, she said, is a description of the waterbed's effect on the user's psyche, sex, and thought patterns. Evidently it was this part which would comprise the bulk of the Lyle Stuart book.

Coors (no relation to the brewery family) had purchased his waterbed for $24.95 at Hydro-Fux Unlimited in Tucson about four months ago. Since then the price has dropped five dollars. The manager of Hydro-Fux, Phil Scott, disclaims responsibility, saying: "I *told* him when he bought it to put a pad over it for just that very reason. Anyway, we have a 5-year guarantee on all our beds. Wasn't that a bummer, though? I mean, *zap*, he's gone, you know?"

Scott said he would give a new waterbed without charge to Coors' girlfriend, Aurora, with whom he'd been living at the time. Aurora escaped injury, as she was up getting a roach-clip when the accident occurred.

THE BOMBER LEFT A MESSAGE WITH MY ANSWERING SERVICE

by Paul Jacobs

All telephone answering services are fundamentally alike: they don't give you the messages you need, bother you with the ones that are totally unimportant, and average two out of six incorrect numbers. But, after you change services a few times, you realize it doesn't matter which you use and you accept the way they function as a fact of life. Presumably, too, the answering service learns to live with you as *you* are. At least I must assume that, on the basis of the experience I've been having lately with mine.

Within the past few months, a young man in the Bay Area who I don't know and have never seen has taken a fancy to me. His specialty is detonating small bombs in public places or business establishments as his way of protesting the nature of American society. His endeavors are modest ones, not designed to do enormous amounts of damage and certainly not to endanger human lives. So he usually does his work very late at night or early in the morning when nobody is around to get hurt.

One night a few months ago, I disconnected my phone early. The next morning I checked in with the answerers as I usually do. In a bored voice, the young woman started reading off the list of calls that had come in.

"At 9:13 Jane Blow called to ask whether you can speak at a rally next week. Please call her . . . "

"O.K., I got it."

"At 9:50, your secretary called to say she'd be in late this morning because she was getting ripped, whatever that means."

"Right."

"Then, at 12:10 A.M., a man called to say he had just planted a bomb at the Fairchild plant on the Pennisula and wanted to tell you about it."

"What? What did you say?"

"I said a man called to tell you he'd just planted a bomb and wanted you to know about it. I tried to get his name, but he wouldn't give it to me. And when I asked him for his number so you could call him back, he got mad and hollered at me. Then, at 1:05, your friends Joe and Amy called from the airport to tell you they were just passing through on their way to Australia and would be back in New York during the summer."

"Wait a minute. What about the bomber? Did the bomb go off?"

"I don't know, Mr. Jacobs. I haven't seen the paper or heard the radio yet."

In fact, the bomb did go off although it didn't do much damage. And later that week, I participated in a telephone interview with the bomber for the N.E.T. station in San Francisco. We had a nice chat, and the bomber said he'd keep in touch so that I'd know where he was going to strike again.

The next time he let one off, I was out of town. Once again the call came early in the morning, but this time the answering service got through to the house because my wife hadn't cut off the phone. Ruth isn't at her sharpest at 2:00 A.M., awakened from a sound sleep. So when the operator at the answering service told her, "He's on the phone again, that fellow with the bombs, and he wants to talk to Mr. Jacobs," Ruth answered with, "Mr. Jacobs isn't here," and hung up.

A minute later, the phone rang again.

"He says the bomb is going off in a few minutes. What should I do?"

"I don't know. What does he want you to do?"

"He says someone should know about it."

"Well, ask him who he wants you to tell. And then let me know what happens."

Five minutes afterwards, the phone rang again.

"He did it!" said the operator, almost with a sense of pride. "It just went up in a mail truck. He says to say hello to Mr. Jacobs and he'll keep in touch."

I haven't heard from him for a few weeks now, but I suppose he'll be checking in again pretty soon. In the meantime, the answering service just passes on routine messages to me and I assume they're waiting for him to call back, too. After all, it must be a hell of a lot more interesting to take calls from a bomber than from some woman wanting to talk to her kid's doctor about that rash on the baby's neck.

"This message will last just 60 seconds. The missiles are on their way. If you had started running at the beginning of this message, you might have made it."

PROGRESS IN THE SUBWAY

by Clifford Yudell

The New York City Council today approved by unanimous vote a resolution permitting the Transit Authority to replace all rubber stops on subway cars with razor blades. A spokesman for the TA hailed the move as "a great boon to the efficiency of the subway system." The change will take effect on all major subway lines as of Monday morning.

According to documents filed at the Council hearing, a one-day trial period, during which stainless steel blades were fitted into subway car doors on the Brighton BMT line, proved one-hundred-percent successful. Since passengers were loath to be maimed, the frequent practice of jamming through doors as they closed, or holding them open for fellow passengers, ceased completely. Subway cars on the line operated at an average four minutes faster per hour.

"People tend to move more quickly when the doors are lined with razor blades," said John Sweeney, public relations manager for the Transit Authority. "This keeps the cars running on schedule, even during rush hours."

During the BMT experiment, 83 persons were lacerated or maimed, including seventeen lost hands, twenty-seven fingers in whole or part, and four decapitations, two of them children.

"Under the old system," said Mr. Sweeney, "passengers who were rammed by closing subway doors often sustained painful bruises for days. With the new system, everything comes off nice and clean."

An expected benefit of the changeover is the creation of new jobs for platform bucket-holders, who will tour the subways collecting extremities. Civil Service examinations for some 35 vacancies will be announced shortly. Candidates should possess at least a B.A.

As the Council vote was announced, a small group of protestors from the Citizens' Fairplay Board picketed outside City Hall. While the Board applauds the move as one that will help New Yorkers get to work on time, it protests the rise in fares accompanying the new service. The TA estimates that fares will rise to eleven dollars in January, with special fares of thirteen dollars for students, the elderly, and passengers who can prove they were disabled before the razor blade system was put into effect.

Mr. Sweeney said that the improvement is the first of several to be instituted by the TA over the next year. By March all seats on subway cars are expected to be removed, to increase passenger capacity. This will be followed by installation of electrocution charges on subway platforms to prevent loitering.

On Monday morning an opening ceremony will be held to initiate the razor blade system on the Lexington Avenue IRT line at 59th Street. To demonstrate the effectiveness of the blades, which are manufactured by Gillette with a special grant from the Dow Chemical Company, celebrity Bud Palmer will hold a welfare mother's hands between the doors of a subway car as they close. Mayor Lindsay and Governor Rockefeller are expected to attend the finger cutting. Refreshments will be served.

WHY WAS MARTHA MITCHELL KIDNAPPED?

by Mae Brussell

Editor's note: This is a severely condensed version of an article published in The Realist *nine months before the Watergate affair was revealed as a far-reaching conspiracy by the mass media, rather than a "caper" or a "third-rate burglary."*

The Watergate Hotel, located in Washington, D.C., is the home of John and Martha Mitchell. John Mitchell, former Attorney General, resigned that impressive appointment to head the all-important Committee to Re-Elect the President.

Also housed in the Watergate Hotel complex are the offices of the Democratic National Committee. In the early morning hours of June 17, 1972, five men were arrested removing parts of the ceiling from the 6th floor panels in the Democratic National Headquarters. These men possessed expensive electronic equipment, cameras, walkie-talkies, burglary tools, various James Bond accessories, and rubber gloves to conceal their identities.

Nine persons, all registered with false names taken from CIA novels written by Howard Hunt, stayed at the Watergate Hotel May 26-29 and again June 17-18. Five of them, the night of their arrest, had been discovered when security guard Frank Wills noticed pieces of Scotch Tape over the door locks. Washington police arrived and made the arrests.

Two of the men arrested were comforted with the telephone number of Howard Hunt, White House Consultant, who had worked with the CIA for 21 years.

All five were connected with the CIA in some way. The other relationship they had in common was having worked together for the CIA-planned Bay of Pigs invasion. Their names: Bernard Barker, Frank Sturgis, Eugenio Martinez, Virgilio Gonzales, and James McCord, Jr., employed as Chief of Security for Mitchell's Committee to Re-Elect the President. McCord was formerly employed by the CIA for 19 years. His position with the CIA was Chief of Security over the immense compound at Langley, Virginia.

President John Kennedy wanted to "splinter the CIA into a thousand pieces and scatter it to the winds." The Bay of Pigs caused him to realize that certain persons and powers dictate to the President. The CIA was fingered for their decision to make policies that belong to Congress and the citizens.

Members of the same CIA team active in the training, planning and financing of the Bay of Pigs fiasco were working as a team 11 years later when arrested at the Watergate Hotel. The decision-making organization of the CIA was tampering with the electoral process one more time around.

President Harry Truman said, "There was something about the way the CIA was functioning that has cast a shadow over our historical positions." Those observations were made in 1963, at which time Truman regretted his "building an American Gestapo."

Two governments have existed side by side, one visible and one invisible, for many years. Innocent people believe the electors have a choice of presidents through the primaries or by direct voting. The same CIA that killed President Kennedy because he won the majority of votes, eliminated opposition to Richard Nixon in every election that followed Kennedy's death. Murders, accidents, attempted murders through the use of hired killers, planted patsies, and news coverage that conceals the crimes have been effective so far.

As the power structure gets more arrogant and sure of itself, the invisible becomes more clear and overt. If the Watergate affair is exposed, you will see how invisible government agents go about their daily business.

The Democratic National Committee has placed a lawsuit against the Committee to Re-Elect the President for one million dollars. U.S. Judge Charles R. Richey said, "I don't intend to make this into a political case." Democrats suing Republicans *has* to be a political matter. Remarks by Judge Richey should be reason to disqualify him on grounds of stupidity. The lawsuit placed between these two parties is not over a simple grabbing of votes at the election booths.

All the persons arrested, and each of their contacts and sources of funding, will be protected by every possible method. Several of the group have left the country. Others will refuse to talk. But even silence will prove beyond a doubt that those arrested and the ones that got away from the Watergate Hotel were working for the CIA *at the time of their arrest.*

Extensive research on past political assassinations has revealed all the intricacies of the clandestine government. Although most members of the CIA deny the source of their funds or associations with the agency or with each other, their actions, finances, and moving patterns can be recognized for what they are.

Martha Mitchell made her Washington debut with sarcasm about war protestors who reminded her of "Russian revolutionaries." Three years later, Martha wishes those same youths would come to her aid. When President Nixon held a press conference a few days after Ms. Mitchell was taken prisoner, she complained that "nobody asked about me."

The youth of America had tried to tell people like Martha Mitchell that the President does not listen to any voices except a few. Why would he care to hear Martha's problems?

There was a smug complacence about the Mitchell family in the days when John was promising this country that it was "going so far to the right we won't recognize it." Those were the carefree days when John and Martha were not caught in the bending process. But did Mitchell, one of the dirtiest, meanest men in political history, expose his "little sweetheart" to espionage agents doing some kinds of dirty work and distasteful acts? At what point did Martha, who once was cleared for classified materials when she worked with the Army Chemical Corps, have to be removed, silenced, and totally discredited?

Four days after the arrests at the Watergate Hotel, Martha Mitchell called a UPI reporter from Newport, California: "I am sick and tired of politics. I gave /John/ an ultimatum I would leave him if he didn't get out. I am a political prisoner. Politics is nothing but a cops and robbers game. I know dirty things. I saw dirty things. I am not going to stand for all those dirty tricks that go on. I was a patriot until I got assassinated. What country can I go to? I am sick and tired of the whole operation."

Martha's telephone conversation was bugged. When she summoned the UPI for help, her room was entered, the phone was pulled from the wall, and the silencing treatment began: "*They* threw me down on the bed, *five* men, and stuck a needle in my behind. A doctor stitched my fingers after the battle with *five* guards." (She had bruises on her arms and thighs.)

Patrick Gray III, acting head of the FBI, was staying at the same Newport hotel as the Mitchell family following the Watergate arrests in Washington. Even *Time* called that coincidence "suspicious."

Gray should have a reputation by now of stopping investigations that would lead to possible conspiracies. He halted the investigations of the Jerrie Lee Aimie murder in L.A., the Reuben Salazar murder in L.A., the Isle Vista riots in Santa Barbara, the ITT investigation in Washington, and the George Wallace shooting in Maryland.

It is little wonder that our FBI chief would not come to the aid of the Mitchells and see who was making Martha a "prisoner" in the same hotel.

A high summit meeting was held between John Mitchell and President Nixon. Both came out of it agreeing on two things; Wives of politicians sometimes have a difficult time entertaining themselves; and Martha had only "one guard" from the Committee to Re-Elect the President.

Nine men registered at the Watergate Hotel where the Mitchells lived. Four suspects were not yet found at the time this was written. One of the men arrested worked for the re-election committee. Did any of the other suspects work for John Mitchell's committee at the time they disappeared? Did Martha get four extra guards suddenly? Could John use his family for a cover in order to help four men leave Washington?

Martha was a witness to some kind of dirty work.

Neither the long hours of work nor the absence of John Mitchell from his family ever bothered Martha before the Watergate arrests. She made it known that she was *angry* when her husband *gave up* his position as Attorney General, which is more demanding than heading an election committee.

John Mitchell resigned from the Committee to Re-Elect the President after Martha's remarks were printed around the world. His gesture that the family needed him—"That little sweetheart, I love her so much"—hardly resembled the Duke of Windsor when he abdicated for Wally Simpson.

The significance of the Watergate affair is that every element

—B. Kliban

Why Was Martha Mitchell Kidnapped?, *continued*

essential for a political *coup d'etat* in the United States was assembled at the time of their arrest. The team of men represented at the hotel went all they way from the White House with its Emergency Contingency Unit, walkie-talkies, and private radio frequency, to the paid street provocateurs and troops who would create the emergencies.

Was the target of their associations the cancellation of elections in 1972?

The Glass House Tapes by Louis Tackwood (co-author; Donald Freed)—"The Story of an Agent Provocateur and the New Police Intelligence Complex"—will be published by Avon Press. A former paid agent of the Los Angeles Police for 9 years, Tackwood surfaced and disclosed the kinds of jobs the LAPD expects an agent provocateur to do for them. The most important revelations made by Tackwood gave a good view of that invisible government John Kennedy warned about.

The "Glass House" is the Los Angeles Police Department, the same agency that took care of candidate Robert Kennedy 4 years ago. Tackwood resigned from the LAPD after he became familiar with their plans for the 1972 elections, known by the name "Squad 19." Agents of the police department were to create enough violence at the Republican National Convention that martial law would be declared:

"Squad 19 was formed by CCS (Criminal Conspiracy Section) and the FBI to provoke violence at the Republican convention in 1972. It involves *coordinated contingency plans* under the directions of CCS and FBI. The plan entailed planting a number of agent provocateurs both inside and outside the 1972 Republican convention. Agents were to infiltrate the groups planning demonstrations against the war and poverty. At the time of the demonstrations, these agents were to provoke street battles with police surrounding the convention hall. Meanwhile, agents inside the convention hall *were to plant ex-*

plosives timed to blow up coincidental with the riots in the streets. The *purpose is to kill a number of delegates.*

"The result would be to create nationwide hysteria that would then provide President Richard Nixon with the popular support necessary to declare a state of national emergency . . . arrest all militants and left-wing revolutionaries and cancel the 1972 elections. He could invoke *special emergency powers* leading to the detention of political activists. Martial law would be achieved."

(As *The Realist* goes to press, Louis Tackwood has been rearrested on the original charges—going back *nine years*—over which the original deal had been made.)

A CIA operation contains many ingredients that work together toward the final purposes. If their motive was to create confrontations for the Republican convention in order to arrest "radicals" and to create martial law, in what positions would agents be located for such a plan?

James McCord, Jr. held two important jobs at the time of his arrest. He was Chief of Security for the Committee to Re-Elect the President. With that appointment, McCord was issued his own radio frequency. And that employment was the *smaller* assignment of the two. The biggest contract a security agent could receive went to McCord Associates, selected by Secret Service agent Al Wong, *to provide all security for the Republican convention in Miami.*

The Secret Service that hired McCord did not follow his off-duty meetings at the Watergate Hotel May 26-29. If the data banks and surveillance systems keep records of "radicals" and "demonstrators," it seems they could follow their own hired Security Chief. Either he was moonlighting for another client they should have known about, or else McCord works for the CIA. If the CIA funds violence for Washington, New York, and elsewhere, are they funding the very violence in Miami that James McCord is hired to "secure"?

Bernard Barker was telling people in Miami that "something is going to happen at the time of the conventions." He was then planning demonstrations in approval of Nixon's bombing of Haiphong Harbor. April 24, Barker and a secret team of 7 men went to Miami to hire provocateurs for a New York demonstration in May. Four of this team were arrested at the Watergate Hotel. Three men were in Miami at the time, and one left the country because, according to *The New York Times*, he was "headed for trouble."

Money to pay for street scenes and fights with police came from the same money man, Bernard Barker, who served as the conduit of funds for the Bay of Pigs invasion. This time Barker was handing out crisp, consecutive CIA $100 bills that came to Miami's Republican National Bank, from a secret source in Mexico, via a secret source in Chile. James McCord was paid for the Watergate job *with the same funds that hired street altercations.*

Bernard Barker's wife said that her husband had not been active with the Cuban community for five years. She was surprised he was arrested working with that group again.

That observation fits in with the "Squad 19" plan arranged for San Diego. When the convention was moved to Miami, a whole new group of street people would have to set the milieu for confrontations. The radical, emotional, well-trained, constantly provoked Cuban exile community could be worked up sufficiently with enough of those CIA $100 bills floating around again.

One man in Miami was offered $700 "CIA money" to demonstrate on the streets in August for the Republican convention.

Frank Sturgis was planning demonstrations for the Republican convention. Even the law enforcement people in Miami thought that was strange. According to the *Washington Post:* "Law enforcement officials predicted the Cuban exiles would demonstrate at the Democratic National Convention to express opposition to any proposals for better relations with the Castro regime. But they were confused and found no solid explanation of why Sturgis and Martinez were seeking rooms for the Republican convention, rooms for which the Party has no need." Two private Catholic colleges received a call from Sturgis asking for "lodging in August for Young Republicans." He left with them his phone number at Bernard Barker's real estate office. Sturgis, also called Barry College, said he was an "organizer" and wanted 200 rooms.

Where were these Young Republicans coming from?

Eugenio Martinez, real estate partner of Barker, was making his own reservations to bring in Young Republicans—about 3,000 of them—for convention time. If they hired provocateurs for the Washington demonstrations in May, who were they making these Miami reservations for in August?

Arrested with James McCord were political extremists planning convention demonstrations. Each of these men would make McCord's job more difficult in Miami *unless* they were working as a team for another purpose.

James McCord, Chief of Security for the Republican convention in Miami, was not only arrested with members of a secret team well financed to hire provocateurs. As a Lieutenant Colonel in the Army Reserve and with 19 years of CIA employment behind him, McCord sat with a *special 16-man unit part of the executive office of the President.* This unit's purpose was *concerned with radicals and contingency plans* for the radicals.

Both Captain R. Franz, Navy Reserve, and James Landis, retired Army colonel, spoke of McCord's work with this unit, which included *control of the news media and U.S. mail.*

When McCord was arrested, the Special Unit disclaimed his association by saying he "left four months ago." The connection to the White House is only one of the links of this group to Nixon.

Howard Hunt, who fled the scene when his friends were arrested, also had experience with "radicals." Known as a very conservative Republican during his 21 years with the CIA, he had occasion to put down the "radicals," "blacks," and "war protestors." When students at Brown objected to hearing Henry Kissinger speak to them, Hunt wrote the alumni that he "deplored the lack of patriotism in youth." He called them "hirsute know-nothings," which makes me believe that Howard Hunt writes Agnew's speeches.

Hitler's youth were called "patriotic" and then later judged as criminals at Nuremberg. What kind of blind patriotism does Hunt desire?

Louis Tackwood said that the number he had to call, as part of the "Squad 19" plans, was named "White"—which is the alias Howard Hunt used as White House consultant to Richard Nixon. McCord's walkie-talkies at the Watergate were similar to the radio frequencies of Howard Hunt's walkie-talkies in the White House.

John Kennedy recognized there was a hidden government. Many of the same people he feared were still working together as a team in 1972 just before crucial elections. If those teams were directly connected to the White House, martial law is a possibility if it appears that Nixon could lose the election. A lot of power has been accumulated in the hands of a few people, and they have taken every precaution to keep it that way.

All the elements necessary for "Squad 19" were assembled. Five men, skilled in cloak-and-dagger intelligence operations, all with CIA experience, veterans of the Bay of Pigs together, heavily and secretly financed, connected to military troops waiting for "direct combat" against the radicals and left-wing, were dining together and living at the Watergate Hotel at the time they were all arrested in one bag.

This article was completed for *The Realist* on July 11, 1972, the same day that Richard Nixon and John Mitchell wanted to put off investigation of the Watergate affair. According to Associated Press: "The Committee for the Re-Election of the President is worried that a hearing on a suit involved in the break-in and bugging attempt could cause 'incalculable damage' to President Nixon's campaign.

"The Committee asked U.S. District Court to postpone suit against /them/ until after the November 7 election. To hear the suit before the election, the Committee said, could deter campaign workers and contributions, *force disclosure of confidential information and provide the Democrats with a reason to hold a news conference.*"

President Lyndon Johnson passed the Civil Rights Act in 1964. Parts of that Act were violated at the time of Martha Mitchell's abduction, and in the way she was handled.

Her telephone was pulled from the wall, five men silenced her, and an unknown substance was injected into her body against her will.

As a friend of the court and a citizen, I charge that there has been a violation of her civil rights by those in responsible positions. Those guilty of making her a prisoner are subject to $10,000 fine and 10 years in prison. If a conspiracy is proven, each and every person involved is subject to the same penalties. It is in the national interest that she be permitted to talk freely before a responsible group. We want to know what she saw. Martha Mitchell is the wife of one of the most responsible men in this nation. When she is treated in this manner, all of us are involved in having a right to know who is doing these things.

Q. All right now, do you remember the very first time you shoplifted?

A. Well, a few years ago I was in the supermarket and I was just walking down one of the aisles when suddenly my eye was attracted by some grated cheese, just the bright color of the containers. It wasn't on my shopping list or anything. Through sheer impulse—there's no other way to explain my behavior—I simply dropped it into my coat pocket. Maybe I secretly felt I was getting just a teeny bit of revenge for their high prices. But then I *bought* a can of onion soup to go with the grated cheese. It was too big to stick in my pocket. But I was hooked.

Q. How did you finally get caught?

A. I was in a department store—I can't mention their name—and I was just sort of browsing around the athletic equipment section after purchasing some ping-pong balls, and I spotted this counter filled with all these stainless steel chinning bars, you know? It's like an adjustable rod that you place in an open doorway. I'm not even into any kind of exercise, but I just couldn't resist taking that chinning bar. I think it was the challenge of getting away with something so outrageous. They're about three feet long—and while I was making be-

Hey! — I'm the lawyer!"

lieve I was just looking at the pile, actually I was slipping one of them right up my coat sleeve. I walked very calmly to the elevator, and that's how they caught me. When I tried to ring the bell for the elevator, like a fool I used my *right* hand. My arm stuck straight out. I should've used my *left* arm, but anyway, that's all Monday morning quarterbacking, because this store detective came up to me. I guess I must've looked suspicious, ringing the bell without even bending my elbow.

Q. Are you aware of the psychiatric contention that shoplifters unconsciously want to get caught?

A. Oh, sure. That's what my own shrink says. The department store agreed not to prosecute if I would seek professional help.

Q. Is that how you got involved with Kleptomaniacs Anonymous?

A. Right. My shrink recommended that I attend one of their meetings, and I've been going to KA ever since. You have to refer to yourself as a *kaka*, as a reminder that faulty toilet training as an infant may have been the root cause of your shoplifting. Kleptomania is just a mobile form of anal retention.

Q. What do you do at Kleptomaniacs Anonymous meetings?

A. Well, for example, you stand up and tell how you've been able to resist temptation. The thing I don't like is we hold the meetings at a different home each week, and sometimes you have to get searched before you're allowed to leave. I have nothing to hide, but when you get searched by a fellow *kaka*, well, how can you possibly give each other moral support if you don't *trust* each other?

Q. Is there any basis for the searching?

A. Of course. There's been things missing every week. The first time we met at my house, I announced I would refuse to search anybody as a matter of principle. But that was a mistake, be-

cause later I discovered that my Scotch Tape dispenser was missing, and my 1972 calendar, and a lot of other things, including all the raisins from my box of Kellogg's Raisin All-Bran. That was very discouraging, but I couldn't help admiring the thoroughness of whoever the *kaka* was who did it. *Every single raisin was missing!*

Q. Is Kleptomaniacs Anonymous a social organization too?

A. You bet it is. We even had a marriage in our group. A week after the honeymoon, though, the bride admitted that she had stolen Magic Fingers—the entire works—from their hotel bedroom. Her husband wasn't even aware she'd done it until her "kakanfession"—that's what we call it. Now he doesn't let her carry around a screwdriver and pliers in her purse any more.

Q. What else happens at meetings?

A. Well, we have guest speakers sometimes. Last month we were addressed by the representative of a private detectives' association. They arranged for several of us to shop at Macy's, to see what we could get away with—I have to kakanfess that it's not as exciting when you have been *invited* to steal merchandise because you know you're not gonna get in any trouble if they catch you. But we were giving these undercover people the benefit of our experience so they could learn what techniques to look for, like new gimmicks you can do with your clothing, and then they could develop methods to deal with their new knowledge. It was quite rewarding to be able to contribute something constructive to society.

Q. I understand that you personally have extended that service to help ward off holdup attempts on the street?

A. Ah, yes. I teach people how to bark. I know what you're thinking. You're thinking, this crazy *kaka* has totally flipped out. But I teach people how to bark like a dog. You see, once you understand the pathology of the criminal, you can adjust the way you act as a victim. So, let's say I'm walking along the sidewalk, and here comes this mugger type. I don't mean anything racial by that. In fact, we even have a *colored kaka* in our group. But suppose you were walking along, and you had a vicious-looking dog with you. Then that holdup man would leave you alone, correct? He could kill the dog, but if he uses a gun, the noise would be heard, and if he tries to use a knife or a blackjack, by the time he gets close enough, the dog is already barking. So it's not the dog he's afraid of, it's the *sound* of the dog. Now, if you start barking like a dog when somebody approaches you—I teach people how to growl first, in order to frighten a mugger type away before any confrontation takes place—but when you actually *bark*, it's just not worth it for him to rob you. They figure you're nuts and probably don't have anything worth taking. Plus it's extremely embarrassing to try and pull a holdup on someone who's just barking away like mad. And also, you know what's *really* effective? Here, let me show you the way I can *howl* . . .

WHAT DOES RALPH NADER DREAM ABOUT?
by Clifford Yudell

On my 21st birthday I decided to Take Stock. Look at you, boy, I said, look around you. Not one crushed velvet sofa to your name, no MG revving up the sidewalk, no bank account, Christmas Club, Master Charge, Diner's Club, no ranch house, no sculptured lawn, no future Princess dripping after your ass, no job, no title, no future! What the hell, boy, what the hell is the matter with you? Where's that old get-up-and-go, sock-it-to-em, jump on the American bandwagon? Or are you some fucking Commie fag? Hey, boy?

A failure in every sense of the word. There it all was, out there waiting like they told me, and me sitting on my ass in an unfurnished loft, bathing in Sloth, the original sin.

What I wanted, obviously, was a good injection of Capitalism, that was it. Gimmee buyme getme. Wow, just the idea of it made my pulse beat like a rabid animal's, sent a supercharge of healthy red, white, and blue blood into my cock. Yummy yum. All I needed was an idea.

I got the idea that night, while watching television. In the middle of a flick came this commercial for Leaning Tower Parmesan Product with 3% real cheese.

Pretty clever, said I, and started ruminating. It seemed that the thing to do was go them one better. All I needed was a Parmesan product I could get out on the market a few cents cheaper. What's more, I'd put in 5% real cheese. The money could be made up by a basic powder to add to the cheese that would cost me nothing. I went to sleep thinking of things that were yellow and free, and by morning I had it.

I hired Eddie Canupe, a 12-year-old Italian boy who lived down the block, and six of his friends to work round the clock, stuffing the mixture into cellophane packets we had prestamped with the name of our product, Mama's Parmesan Product with 5% Real Cheese, and a picture of Eddie's mother, who was big and fat with stringy black hair and a warm smile. The cellophane, by the way, was bullet-proof. Our slogan would be, "In case you're shot on the way home from market." By the end of the first week we neared the incredible production figure of 10,000 packets.

We stocked the local supermarkets on Friday afternoon. On Sunday night at 8, prime time, our 30-second spot hit the air in the metropolitan area. The script went like this:

Titles: "Jack and Edna At Home." Jack sits at kitchen table petting dog, reading *Reader's Digest*. (Cover line: "An Infamous Psychiatrist Gives Two Easy Ways To Cure Schizophrenia—One For Each Of You!") On the table, a picture frame with two photos: a blond, crew-cut young football player and the same young man in uniform. *Audio:* Radio on kitchen shelf playing Theme from *Love Story*.

(*Enter Edna, wearing apron, carrying a letter.*)

Edna: "Jack! A letter from Chuck!"

Jack: "Our boy in Nam!"

Edna (reading): "Dear Mom, Dad, and Fido . . . "

Fido: "Woof!" (*Canned laughter*)

Edna (reading): ". . . Just wanted to thank you for sending those packets of delicious, nutritious Mama's Parmesan Product with 5% Real Cheese in its attractive bullet-proof package. (*Jack holds product up to camera.*) You probably won't believe this, but that dern little package saved my life. I was flying a regular bombing mission over a small village, defoliating the gooks, when some anti-aircraft flak came busting in. Felt sort of a thud near m'heart. Then, I looked down and saw a bullet-hole right where the old ticker is."

Jack and Edna: "Mother Mary!"

Jack: "Kill those (*bleep*) Commies!" (*Canned laughter*)

Edna (reading): "Thought I was a goner for sure, till I looked down and saw I wasn't bleeding. No sir, the bullet had hit me right in the packet of Mama's Parmesan Product with 5% Real Cheese in its attractive bullet-proof package. I put it there, next to m'heart, before taking off, in case I needed a quick pick-me-up snack. Yessir, Mama saved my life. Your son, Chuck."

Jack and Edna: "God bless our boy!"

Fido: "And God bless Mama's Parmesan Product, now at your local store! Woof!" (*Canned laughter*)

(*Radio plays latest hit by The Partridge Family as we FADE OUT.*)

Before the ad had even finished, the TV switchboard was flooded with calls, everyone wanting to know where they could buy Mama's. By 11 A.M. Monday morning, we sold out.

Money started pouring in. I used my first returns to buy everything we'd need for a second round of production and called my good friend Little John, a dwarf who blows up banks and knows everything. (He never had anything in particular against the System, to my knowledge. Little John just likes to do it. "Big noise!" he says.) Little John came up with a brainstorm. "Look at Howard Johnson's," he said. "They don't sit back with plain old vanilla, do they? No, they've got 28 flavors. Look at Heinz—57 varieties! That's the way it's done. People get bored with one thing. You've got to branch out."

So it was that on the first Wednesday of the second week we came out with assorted flavorings for Mama's Parmesan Product, adding tiny bits of various imitation flavorings I bought from a local supplier. We had 7 varieties in all: Mama's Parmesan Product with Imitation Cherry, Banana, Coconut, Ceylon Tobacco, Pomegranate, Asparagus, and Salami-With-Chocolate-Sprinkles, plus, of course, the one and only *original* Mama's.

We ran another ad, in which Fido tells Jack and Edna about the exciting new flavors, then enlists. Needless to say, the second batch sold out faster than the first, and we were well on our way to a small fortune.

But I was rapidly becoming disillusioned with capital gains. I had furnished my apartment with a huge suede sofa, two crushed velvet chairs with plastic seat covers, a coffee table that was a real replica of a Spanish sea captain's trunk, bought an MG, subscribed to weekly magazines showing me 4-color pictures of wars in exciting foreign lands and cluing me in on Jackie Kennedy's orgasms. But was I happy? Far from it. I had learned at last what a wise old teacher once tried to tell me, namely that Money Cannot Buy Happiness.

So it was with mixed feelings of relief and trepidation that I arrived home one day to find a letter from the Food & Drug administration requesting an interview and a detailed analysis of Mama's Parmesan Product with 5% Real Cheese in its attractive bullet-proof packet.

At 9 A.M. on the appointed day, I reported as directed.

After a short wait I was ushered into a small discussion room where ten black-suited, white-templed men sat around a long conference table. I said "Good morning, gentlemen," noticing, as I took my seat, several packets of Mama's Parmesan Product in front of each panel member. They all seemed to have sampled at least one variety. One of the members, whom I placed at around 103, apparently liked it very much. He was chomping down his sample with the relish of a starved wolf, his head practically touching the table as he shoved handfuls of the stuff down his gullet. Occasionally he raised his eyebrows and murmured "Mmmmm," then went on eating.

The director or whatever of this distinguished panel picked up a packet of Mama's and waved it at me.

"Well, we've all had an Italian breakfast, so to speak, ha ha, and I must say we enjoyed your tasty little product very much, haven't we, gentlemen?"

"Yes, I should say so, mm-hmm, very good, delicious, very nice, an achievement, yummy, *slurp slurp chomp*," said the panel.

"In fact, the little woman and I have been eating it for days. You know, the salami kind with chocolate sprinkles is wonderful on Rice Krispies with milk . . . a little recipe of my own, ha ha." He cleared his throat. "Now! This is just a little formality,

a little formality. We've got to file our reports for the Administration, keep everyone happy, keep everything in order. Am I correct in assuming that the 7 different varieties of Mama's Parmesan Product all contain the same basic ingredients, plus the specific flavorings?" He picked up a batch of onionskin papers and began writing.

"Correct!" I said. "Every packet of Mama's has at base 5% real cheese, as advertised."

"Yes, our chemists succeeded in locating the 5% real cheese. In fact, I want to congratulate you. Your competition seems to believe he can give the American public the minimum amount of pure nutrient value and satisfy the national hunger for good dairy. But you haven't skimped, although I assume it lessens profits."

"True," I said.

"Now. Our chemists also succeeded in identifying the fruit and other flavorings and they tell me here"—he shuffled his pages—"yes, here . . . that in each packet the percent of flavoring is precisely 2%, except of course in the original Mama's Parmesan Product, which contains no flavoring."

"Yes, that's it exactly—2% cherry, 2% asparagus, and so on."

"What we haven't been able to determine as yet, is the exact nature of the final 93% of your fine product, or in the case of Mama's original, 95%. This leaves our report a little incomplete. Now, if you will just tell us what your secret ingredient is, we can have everything in order. What precisely is the bulk ingredient of Mama's Parmesan Product with 5% Real Cheese?"

There was a great silence as all the panel members turned their heads to look at me—all except the old gent, who was now wolfing down his neighbor's sample and wiping his mouth on his sleeve.

"Monkey snot," I said.

It seems Little John once worked a sideshow in a circus where he met Zabar the Animal Trainer. Little John was eventually fired for putting extra dynamite in the circus cannon, which sent parts of Alfonso the Human Cannonball to circuses throughout the continent. (It wasn't that Little John disliked Alfonso, just that he wanted to hear a bigger noise.) But Zabar was now a curator at the Bronx Zoo and had all sorts of connections.

"Heh heh," said the director, "I beg your pardon?"

"Monkey snot," I replied. "Only the yellow parts, of course. Brni monkeys, from Southern Uganda, 500 in all. Cute little fellows, but rather dumb. We had to teach them to pick their noses, imagine that!"

It was at this moment that the puking began. Can't say who started first, though the initial heave seemed to come from a rather quiet man on my immediate right. Pretty soon the entire room exploded with retching and heaving. Three panel members dropped to their knees and vomited on the floor. The director himself barfed on his reports (my God, I thought, his secretary will have a terrible time retyping them).

Between the gagging, coughing, gasping, croaking, the terrible liquid heavings, and the awful stench settling over the table like a fog of skunk spew, I could hardly breathe. I started for the door, carefully avoiding the chunky puddles, when I remembered I had brought some new samples with me. I took them from my pocket and threw them on the table.

"Gentlemen, if you'll just give me one more minute, I want to give you our latest variety to taste, as a gift. Mama's Parmesan Product with 5% Real Cheese plus veal and prune!"

That was all I could say. For some reason my little speech brought a new flow of vomit, but with such force and in such unison I was practically blown out of the room in a gale of puke.

I turned around for one last look and witnessed the incredible sight of the director of the Testing Bureau of the FDA lying face down in a lake of vomit while three members of his panel threw up on his back and head. The rest had either passed out under the table or were now hanging their heads out the windows. Only the senior panel member seemed to have retained his composure and was polishing off his sample of Mama's veal with prune, and greedily reaching to the unopened packets.

I closed the door behind me, beat my chest with my fists, balled the office secretary, told Little John to take care of the monkeys if I didn't come back (I could not bear to dwell on what he would do; I knew it would be a big noise), and took the next plane for Morocco.

WHAT IT'S LIKE TO HAVE A BABY IN PRISON
by Lia Stahrlite

I am an inmate. We are called residents here at the California Institute for Women. This is where I had my baby.

I was arrested during my third month of pregnancy for welfare fraud . . . My husband and I were going through changes and we were trying to work them out then. But I was busted and he was drafted. My first daughter was 17 months when this went down.

I will never forget the bust—my baby standing at the window watching them take me. She started crying when my husband got out of the car; he looked bewildered and disheveled. The cop had awakened him to tell him they were taking me. I've not seen my children from that day until this. I was taken to Marin County Jail. Those first days were heavy for me because I had never been busted before. I had imagined jail to be all sorts of things like on TV. I was in a room with five other women. We ate together, slept together, and in some aspects showered together too; there was no shower curtain or door for privacy. Together for 24 hours a day.

All through this time I was carrying my child; not knowing what I was coming to or how it would end. Because of the situation I considered abortion. I didn't know whether I'd be convicted or, even if I weren't, I knew there'd be problems with my husband. If the family was to be separated, I would have to deal with making it alone. But I had no vocation or school training to help me, and how would I provide for them without these things? I wanted to go to school. Who would watch them? Who would pay a babysitter? How would I pay for these things? I couldn't consider welfare because I was *here* on a welfare bust.

In order to have an abortion I had to see a psychiatrist. The matrons didn't approve of abortion because of whatever reasons they had. So, considering how far along I was, I was surprised that I had to go through so much red tape.

The first appointment was set up almost a month and a half after I asked about the abortion. Another was required two weeks after that. By that time I was 4 months pregnant. When the abortion finally was okayed, it was too late. I got the impression that this was the idea, that's why all the red tape. I could still be aborted but it would take more than a simple D&C (Dilatation and Curettage). If I wanted to abort now I would have to go through a labor. To induce that labor, a needle (containing some drug) would be inserted into the womb through my stomach! Then I would go into labor and pass the fetus—a painful experience, to say the least. However, I had changed my mind while waiting for a decision anyway.

I love children by nature and during this pregnancy I found myself loving this child I carried, more every day. When I got the okay to abort, just about that time I could feel the child begin to move. Mother Nature took over and I could no more abort my baby than I could kill myself. I could finally understand why a doctor doesn't want to do an abortion after the third month. You feel the baby about the middle of the fourth month, then you can't deny that it's alive. Slowly, it began to dawn on me I was really a prisoner and wouldn't be free again, at least not in time for my baby's arrival; now the police were talking about adoption. That was out!

After carrying this child 9 months, all the changes I went through and the love I was feeling, do they really think I did this for someone else? Who would love my baby better than me? I tried to argue with myself about the hardships I would have to endure. But I knew better than that. There was no guarantee that she would even be adopted. And I would never forgive myself for putting my flesh and blood in an institution to grow in. It would have been better to abort first.

Some of you may wonder why I haven't considered my family as a help. I never knew my mother and believe her to be dead. My father allowed me to run away when I was 13, and hasn't done a thing for me since. He hasn't even written me here and he knows where I am.

I have a cousin whom I grew up with; she loves me dearly. But it would hurt to ask her because she had my daughter and has three sons of her own. How could I add another mouth to feed? Besides, she was in New York and I had no way to provide transportation.

My husband wrote to tell me about an affair he was having. I was bitter as I felt my world crumbling around me. I was no protection for my children and he was no protection for me. I couldn't understand my karma.

I was in County Jail from October until the end of March. The only fresh air we had was when we were allowed in the yard, once weekly for an hour. The yard was like a concrete box; four concrete walls with a net on top. Even the sky was kept from us. During the winter months we weren't allowed even that (the county wouldn't provide coats).

The cells we lived in were something else too. There were six bunks in each one, four on one wall and two on the other. The beds were attached to the walls which were concrete. The ceiling and floor was too. One wall was just bars; when I slept at night the shadows fell across my face. I really hated it there. One inmate wouldn't take a bath, so even the air we breathed was foul.

On the streets I had a healthy respect for nutrition. I was very food-conscious. Jail food was incredibly starchy. There were little or no fresh vegetables.

For breakfast we had cereal, toast, coffee and fruit juice, daily. Occasionally we had fresh fruit. Lunch was usually something like ravioli or cold-cut sandwiches; maybe a salad once weekly. Dinner was usually noodles or rice and toast, with coffee.

The meat was usually manmade: chicken loaf, canned chowmein and ravioli, cold-cuts, anything that was primarily a starch filler. There was little or no fresh vegetables. Even the peas and carrots were cooked until they were limp.

The conditions were so bad that I was getting green circles under my eyes even though I had a vitamin daily. All the inmates who had been there for any period of time had the same problem, but they didn't have the vitamin.

The matrons were a trip, their big thing was that they had the best jail in the state. I even got into an argument about the conditions with the head matron. This "better jail" I was in was threatening my health, and that of my unborn babe.

I finally raised cain with the doctor to provide me with a fresh salad daily. That made me the only one who had fresh vegetables daily. I tried to get the other inmates to demand some also but they were afraid to lose their "good time."

All my thoughts and feelings were so confused. There was no place to go to find peace.

I got along fine with the inmates, but I couldn't understand the police. There were all sorts of confrontations with the jailors to go through daily. The rules were petty, seemingly designed with no purpose other than to hassle you. I had a public defender for my lawyer. He helped me as much as was possible but I went to prison anyway. Before I could leave for CIW though, I was made to answer to two other counties for welfare fraud. When I left, it was to go to another county jail—Santa Rita—in Alameda county.

Three hours before I would've left for CIW, Alameda deputies came to pick me up. I had heard ugly things about Santa Rita, so I was expecting the worst. When I arrived I had to go through another degrading body search, another fingerprinting, and another "mug-shot."

Afterwards I was put in what was called "lock-up." There were more women here than in Marin; they weren't cared for well at all. One woman was "kicking" cold-turkey, the other had migraine headaches which were known to make her violent. The medical attention consisted of a morning visit from male nurses who would hand out medication in the morning to last all day. There was no further supervision, and if women had their medication stolen by other inmates, it was never replaced. If there were complaints from inmates when the nurses were there, they were ignored or laughed at. When I left, the girl who was kicking still hadn't seen a doctor, or been given medication.

The woman with the migraines almost went "off" on the first evening I was there. She started complaining about the pain, so we other inmates started banging on the door to get attention. When the matron finally came, she threatened to punish us for disturbing her, saying the doctor was "unavailable." The inmate was pacing all night long. Every 15 minutes or so, the matrons would come through to count. Still nothing was done for this woman until the next watch sergeant came through. She realized the seriousness of the situation and went for the doctor. He never did come to examine this woman, but sent some medication over which seemed to help.

I found out later that this same woman was to go into surgery for a brain tumor after her release. Her operation was held up a month to accommodate her jail sentence, and she wasn't given proper care while being held.

The next day we spent playing Monopoly or cards or whatever. Sometimes we slept.

The next day at the courthouse, I stayed in a holding cell to wait until my case was called. It's like a public bathroom with a bench and a waterfountain in it. I was left alone there from 7 that morning until 5:30 that afternoon. I slept on the floor most of the day, on my coat. When I was finally called, all they did was reschedule my appearance for two months later. I went back to Santa Rita and the next day was taken to Marin Jail.

I stayed in Marin for two weeks before I was supposed to leave for CIW. On the morning I was to leave, I had an argument with the matron on duty. I had given my breakfast to one of the other inmates and wanted to go back to sleep. The matron wouldn't let her have it if I didn't get up to get it for her. I was half-asleep, so I refused. The matron smirked and said, "You can go hungry then," and she took the tray.

"NEXT!"

DR. R.M. ELLNER
GYNECOLOGIST

—S. Gross

What It's Like to Have a Baby in Prison, *continued*

I got really pissed off; so when she came back I knocked the tray off the slit in the bars toward her. She flew out to get the male deputies from up front. To get them to respond, she told them I was inciting a riot! By the time they got back to get me, I was half-asleep. The other inmates were too. There was obviously no riot. But she came in bellowing and snatched off my covers. The men came in and dragged me out of bed. I said I would sue if they injured me, or the baby. The matron laughed and said, "Try and sue from prison."

Before I was out the door, I had wrapped myself between the bars and they were playing tug-o-war with my body. I was dragged to the padded cell where I stayed until the head deputy came on. I tried to explain what happened, but she took that lying deputy's word first. Then she smiled as she informed me that this was my day to leave for CIW.

We went to Corona by plane. It would've been a nice trip if I wasn't going to prison. I was at the intake unit of CIW about six weeks before I was returned to court in Alameda. When I went back to Santa Rita I was to stay for over a month.

The next day after my return to Santa Rita I went to court. I spent another day in the holding cell. Once again when I finally was called, my case was rescheduled. I was very upset because the date could've been changed without my being there. The judge was pretty nice, though, and said that I should be taken to CIW to wait until my next appearance. This wasn't quite what happened.

I was very tired when I got back to Santa Rita, so I didn't check on my case status. I expected to be taken back automatically, but after five days, I was told that I wasn't going back until my case was completed.

The judge at court had said that if I had any difficulty, someone should contact her, and she would straighten it out. So I asked the deputy to call the judge. She said the judge wasn't to be "bothered," that lots of inmates say that and the judges would be angry if they were disturbed.

I was hysterical. I couldn't stand two months there!

On this trip there was a girl who had fallen down a flight of stairs while being arrested. She was kicked in the back by the arresting officer before she could get up. She couldn't move without pain. She had trouble getting medical attention while I was there also. A simple thing like getting into her pajamas brought tears to her eyes for the effort.

Those so-called nurses said she couldn't have anything stronger than aspirin, which didn't help. Then it took over two weeks to get her to a doctor. The doctor took X-rays and found three dislocated discs in her spine.

A week passed and I was called to court unexpectedly. My case was finished, and I thought I was through. When I got back I asked the deputy if I would be leaving soon since my case was complete. The deputy thought I answered another case because the "code" was different. I told her the code was changed because my felony was dropped to a misdemeanor.

She checked it and found out I was right, so I waited a few days before I asked about leaving. To my surprise, I still didn't have a time listed to go. The sergeant said that my case wasn't finished, so I explained again that it was the same case, only that the charge was dropped. I also told her about the deputy who checked it, asking her to re-check for me. The sergeant wouldn't.

I decided I would get the deputy to tell her. But she was off for the next few days. It seemed I would have to wait until it was time for me to go to court before they would realize their mistake. That was the last straw! I asked the nurse for a tranquilizer, but he just smirked and said I didn't need it. I was very distraught. When he left I blanked out; when I came to, I had destroyed the "dorm." People were all around me, staring. I quieted down and was taken to a cell.

In the cell, I started having pains that felt like contractions. I called for help but no one came. The contractions stopped— fortunately, because there was no doctor. No one had come to see if I was okay. The deputy I had talked to when I'd returned from court was there the next morning, and she was amazed that no one had gotten the message she'd left concerning my case. Later on the sergeant came to apologize, but I was beyond apologies. I had come close to losing my baby because of her indifference.

I went back to CIW within a week. I was at the intake unit for another two weeks before I went on "campus," as the compound is called. I was still a little nervous about being here but anyway, there were doctors and nurses here to help, I thought.

The penitentiary took some getting used to because it was quite different from county jail. It took the form of a college facade, but the true conditioning was psychological. However, the environment provided small comfort from the reality of prison life. My first day was an experience.

I went to the counselor's office immediately when I arrived at my cottage, to introduce myself and discuss my case. I expected to go to the board (Board of Terms and Parole) the upcoming week. We started to talk but there was an interruption, and the counselor said we could continue at one o'clock.

At one-sharp I was waiting at the office. He finally returned at 3:30. One of the women I was playing cards with was called to his office. When the counselor had finished talking with her, he started to leave. When I told him that I waited for him since one, he started getting hostile. He said that he didn't have time for me and didn't care if I had waited. He asked me if what I wanted to talk about was an emergency. I said no, but it was important to my future.

We began to argue somehow and I wasn't ready for it. He was yelling about who did I think I was, and threatening me by saying he intended to "get" me some time and he was going to rehabilitate me and "I'll make you wish you'd never been to this cottage."

I never expected to be yelled at by someone who was supposed to help me. That's how I met my counselor.

I kept to myself mostly because I was trying to adjust. I met a few of the women, but I felt so uncomfortable I couldn't really relate. I tried to approach the counselor several times after but he refused to help me. Time flew by and before I realized it was time to go to the board, to determine how long I would have to stay.

I'd been thinking about what I'd say, as honestly as I possibly could. I intended to explain my plans to continue my education in the hope they wouldn't demand more than another six months from me. I was looking for a parole consideration date. I was worried about the threats my counselor made, but I still thought because this was my first offense that I would have it together enough to make it okay.

The board laid me down with a seven-month review. That means my time wasn't even set, they could give me another one after this if they felt like, up to ten years. I was in sort of a shock when I left.

The following Monday my cottage had mandatory group. I sat near the front, not thinking about much. Group dragged on as we talked about keeping our curtains closed and other "critical" subjects. I was about ready to go to sleep when the counselor turned the focus on me. He told those women that I had talked about them like dogs at the board and said I felt I was superior to them. What I had actually said was that I didn't relate to being in prison, and that I had a hard time making friends. The women took that and ran with it! They continued to group on me and didn't let up until I cried. But as I was to find out, that was the way the counselor always conducted the groups; he feeds off of the inmates' distress.

Time didn't stop because of that incident, and the months passed quickly. The baby was due any day. I'd been going into false labor quite a lot, so I knew my time was near. On May 13, I started labor at 2 o'clock in the morning. Surveillance took me to the "hospital" in the prison compound (except for a few professional staff, it is run by training inmates). I was prepped and checked on every now and again, then left alone.

I had decided to have the baby with natural childbirth, like I did for my first child. But unlike the first birth, I was in for a hard time. My muscles weren't together because of the long incarceration period. I labored 18 hours before Alexii was born. By the time her head was delivered, I was too weak and exhausted to speak. But when she didn't cry after being delivered I sat straight up. The doctor tapped her feet to start her breathing but she wouldn't.

Everybody was talking to the baby "asking" her to cry. Well, Alexii turned over and said "no." She really did. I was so glad she was alive! She weighed 10 1/2 pounds. Alexii Eleandra is my second daughter.

I knew I would only have the baby for a short time. I had to face the reality of losing this child too, even though it was to be only for a time.

I was very lucky, as it turned out. Officially the institution is supposed to transport the children to whoever custody is given to. They didn't transport my baby, though, because my people were in New York. But on the day they were going to make foster-home arrangements, I received money from the Army. My husband had finally cleared channels for the family allotment. It took him over six months to do it.

Don't think that means he tried for six months; it was only three months ago he decided to help us, after I contacted his post commander. After he was sent to Germany I never got a letter or postcard from him. He is not even aware of the birth of his child.

So I tried to contact my friend from the M-2 job therapy program to make arrangements for a place for my cousin to stay when she came to get Alexii. I called one of the cottage staff to get the phone number. Instead she decided that was my counselor's job.

To make a long story short, more ugliness was happening. The institution sent my cousin a telegram (charged to me) about the baby. The arrangements were that my cousin was to fly 3,000 miles, pick up the child, visit me for an *hour*, then catch a plane back.

But once again things turned out better. When my cousin who had never been on a plane in her life arrived, there was no one to meet her. She waited 2 1/2 hours. When I sent her the plane fare, in the letter I included my M-2 friend's telephone number. So after the long wait she called my friend, Leslie, who was home, luckily, and went to get her.

Leslie had offered to house my cousin for her stay in California. Leslie knew my cousin was coming and had telephoned the institution to find out when. My counselor had said there would be a state car to meet my cousin, yet when she arrived there was none. It turned out to be in my favor: since CIW didn't meet her, how long she stayed was out of their hands.

So I visited for 45 minutes the day of her arrival and three hours the next day. Leslie took my cousin on a mini-tour of California and they went shopping together. She housed, fed and pampered my cousin, making her visit as pleasant as possible. And so my baby stepped out of my life until my release.

Throughout all my misadventures, I would remember that I was lucky. But others aren't quite so lucky and their story ends tragically.

The system has simply penalized me, allowing my husband to go practically free; because he was convicted on the same charge. He will, on his leave of absence, spend 10 days in County Jail and pay some restitution. We were equally guilty, but he got the Army, and I got State Penitentiary. In short, we went from one government check to another.

So goes the story. I hope it never happens to you.

PROSTITUTES AS POLITICAL PRISONERS
by Margo St. James

The enforcement of prostitution laws differs in every state, depending on the climate of the community, but they are all discriminatory in that they make the woman the scapegoat. As a woman-whore, I feel equality will never be achieved until woman's sexuality ceases to be the source of our shame: until the men are forced to abandon their pussy patrols.

This is an economic threat to the men who make their living entrapping women and homosexuals: a threat to their safe and titillating job which actually makes them victims along with the women. Playing a role of participant when they are really the observer-apprehender destroys their moral fiber and integrity, develops their sadistic tendencies, and often contributes to their corruption.

During a recent raid on a fancy San Francisco bordello, the policemen appeared to be high, really up, turned on, their eyes sparkling, nostrils flaring. Uniformed cops in their riot squad helmets complete with chin straps ran from room to room like hounds, while the more cool plainclothesmen postured in front of mirrors, peeked into closets and made off with 60-odd bottles of booze from the bar.

The Madam had leaped or was pushed from a third story window to the cement courtyard below, was left lying there in agony, alone, for 20 minutes, because the rest of the squad hadn't arrived and the two arresting officers didn't want to leave their other quarry alone. The woman survived, but there is a question whether she will ever walk again.

The issue is not whether she is guilty of soliciting the men—she isn't; they came to her—but rather do one of these licensed thugs have the right to barge into a woman's home, a place where certain "respectable" men take great pleasure in coming, and literally frightening her out of the window? They might as well have pitched her out of the window head first; the result is the same. Lifetime disability is too high a price for anyone to pay for committing a supposed misdemeanor.

Two weeks prior to this bordello raid, an undercover vice cop rented a room in the Methodist Hotel in San Francisco, answered an ad in the *Berkeley Barb* and invited the young man who had placed it to his room to perform a service. It ended with the cop shooting the man in the knee, getting blood all over the room (even in the closet) and leaving the hotel without paying the bill. Again, possible permanent injury for the defendant through excessive force used in the apprehension of a person suspected of committing a misdemeanor when in actuality *the policeman solicited the act.*

As of late, in many large cities, customers have been arrested by police women posing as prostitutes. Wearing a

TELEPHONE CONVERSATION WITH A CLERK AT THE BUREAU OF VITAL STATISTICS
by Sylvia Anderson

Mother: I had a baby in a New York hospital three months ago and his birth certificate has never been mailed to me. Can you tell me why?

Clerk: Let me ask you this: Were you married at the time the baby was born?

Mother: No.

Clerk: Well, that's why.

Mother: What's why?

Clerk: You weren't married.

Mother: What does that have to do with it? My baby exists whether I'm married or not.

Clerk: But we don't mail birth certificates if the parents aren't married. You'll have to come down here and pick it up.

Mother: Why?

Clerk: It's a rule.

Mother: Why is it a rule?

Clerk: It's a regulation.

Mother: But what's the *reason?*

Clerk: The reason is that it's a *regulation.*

Mother: I understand that it's a regulation. But sometimes there are reasons—even for regulations. Is there a reason for this one?

Clerk: It's to save you embarrassment.

Mother: It seems to me that it would be a lot less embarrassing—and much more convenient—to take a letter out of my mailbox than to go down to City Hall and pick it up in person.

Clerk: Well, we figure maybe your mailman will see on the envelope that you're not married and tell your neighbors. Down here we are trained personnel and things like that don't bother us. We're taught how to handle them professionally.

$900 microphone called a Fargo Unit, they broadcast the conversation to a van a block away containing two plainclothes cops who apprehend the customer after he makes the solicitation.

In San Francisco the man had generally not been arrested unless he was black, but merely issued a citation which allowed him to appear in court on some future date, thereby not having to explain to his wife where he was all night. The men who fought the charges and took it to a jury, a total of six, were acquitted, so the court found it to be a real waste of money to continue the practice, and it has been discontinued.

The real reason for the program appears to be the apprehension of pimps. The D.A. in charge of trying sex crimes stated he had "26 pimps in San Quentin," whereas the number for the last decade could be counted on one hand.

The men arrested were not even examined for V.D., whereas the women are quarantined, coerced into accepting treatment (although only one out of 20 needs it), thereby creating resistant strains of tric and moniliasis and sometimes near-fatalities from drug reactions.

Until a few weeks ago in San Francisco, women charged with prostitution were not released on their own recognizance, while bank robbers and rapists were! It has now changed due to pressure from Coyote, a Loose Woman's organization which is providing legal assistance, court clothes, and alternative means of survival to those women being discriminated against.

Half the women in the county jail are there on sex charges—political prisoners, arbitrarily chosen by society to pay dues for its sexual guilt. Most of them are black, another aspect of the discrimination—minority women being forced to work the street because the hotels and massage parlors are owned by white folks who won't hire them or let them hang out.

The illegality of the profession heaps abuse on the women that isn't inherent in the business itself. Men consider them to be legitimate victims. The women suffer all kinds of brutalities and indignities at the hands of some of their customers . . . *and* feel *real* degradation at the hands of the police. The courts, controlled by men who divide women into two categories—whore and madonna—deal out the humiliation and economic disaster which keeps these women dependent on a man-pimp for "protection." It's the same rip-off the government perpetrates under the guise of "national security."

The closed, cynical fraternity of whore lawyers, more often than not, take the woman's money, hit on her for a free piece, and then plead her out. San Francisco has a mandatory time law which gives the women up to six months in jail for supposedly saying those three little words, "Where's the money?"

The excessive punishment and official labeling contribute greatly to the blurring of distinction between performing a service and committing an actual crime such as petty theft. Seventy percent of all the women in jail in the U.S. today were first arrested for prostitution. Such treatment turns these women into R.O.B.'s (rip-off-bitches), the cops into S.O.B.'s and the taxpayers into patrons of hypocrisy.

You can actually get less jail time for stealing than for sucking.

REQUIEM FOR GEORGE LINCOLN ROCKWELL

When I interviewed the late commander of the American Nazi Party for *The Realist*, I asked what he would do if he discovered he had Negro ancestry, and he replied: "I'd go to Africa and become the head nigger." And, any anti-Semite who would sneak into Canada disguised as a rabbi couldn't have been *all* bad.

But his greatest significance lay in his role as a risk of democracy. I once heard a lady say about him: "I believe in free speech, but I don't think he should be allowed to put it into practice."

And how do you like *this* quinella: "Mike [Douglas] has said that he'd have just about anybody on his show," according to *TV Guide*—"George Lincoln Rockwell, maybe Paul Krassner, maybe even Bobby Dylan if he came out of hiding. Most people like a little thought, a little controversy with their froth. Just don't hit them too hard. Keep it light and palatable if you can."

A publication called *The White World* editorialized that his death "made banner headlines in every civilized nation except West Germany, where it was censored"; asserted that "There are two major groups in the U.S. capable of such terrorism: (1) Black Power revolutionaries, and (2) Zionist fanatics"—ignoring the irony that Black Power revolutionaries are *anti*-Zionist—and ran a photo of John Patler with the legend: *This is not the face of a murderer.*

The *National Guardian* ran a photo of Rockwell above its subscription coupon. "This man never read the *National Guardian*," stated the copy. "Look what happened to him. Subscribe today . . ."

He was a commodity to the end.

ON THE LAM WITH PATTY HEARST

*P*rologue: After Patricia Hearst was kidnapped on February 4, 1974 by the Symbionese Liberation Army—supposedly a radical group—I let the word out that I'd like to interview her. The feedback I got from trusted left-wing contacts was that nobody knew where she was. However, the feedback I got from police sources was that Patty was in the hands of federal agents.

On Tuesday morning, April 30, I spoke to a class of investigative reporters at San Francisco State College. I suggested that they investigate the background of SLA personnel. A couple of them had already tried, and discovered that although an FBI ban had been placed against journalists interviewing the neighbors of SLA members, those neighbors had never been interviewed by the FBI.

That evening I went to Berkeley to hear Baba Ram Dass speak at Pauley Ballroom on the university campus. A mutual friend of a double agent approached me there and asked if I wanted to interview Patty Hearst. It had to be done that night while Bill and Emily Harris were gone with Donald DeFreeze.

I was blindfolded and driven in a car and snuck through a back entrance into an apartment that could have been in Berkeley or Oakland, but I assumed it was in San Francisco because we went over some bridge.

I had to erase what I had gotten of the Ram Dass talk in order to record Patty. The SLA also taped our conversation. After this is published, dubs of my copy of the tape—currently in a New York safe deposit vault—will be given to WBAI, KPFA, KPFK, KPFT, and one commercial station, KLRB, as well as the Hearst family.

* * *

Q. Well, how do you feel?

A. Fine. A little tired, but very alert. Like I'm on some kind of space trip. I don't even miss cooking gourmet meals, and I thought I would. But when you're living a righteous adventure, everything else gets put into proper perspective. I mean all of a sudden there's a purpose to your life that's no longer completely selfish. I thought I was being altruistic when I voted for McGovern. That's just a diversion, though.

Q. Do you want me to call you Tania?

A. I don't give a shit what you call me. Just don't call me Mrs. Toothbrush. That's what I almost became, you know. I told Steve, "Hey, listen, my folks are calling you Toothbrush behind your back," but he was always too afraid to confront them directly about it.

Q. There's been quite a few people wanting to interview you. Why me finally?

A. Well, first of all, this is not an interview, just a friendly conversation, like you published with Leslie Bacon. I bought that issue to see what Ken Kesey had to say, but I was really impressed with Leslie Bacon. But I remember seeing your paper when I was thirteen, when you published that Orgy at

Disneyland, because it demystified all those sacred Walt Disney characters. I didn't even know the meaning of the word "demystification" then, but it changed my whole attitude toward art.

Q. How do you mean?

A. Well, for example, the other week we were watching television, and lo and behold, there was Salvador Dali, doing a commercial for Alka-Seltzer, and I thought, wow, what's the purpose of art supposed to be? And I got this idea for an illustration that would be perfect for you—you know Dali's painting, *The Persistence of Memory*—with the clocks sort of hanging limply over the rocks? Well, it would be the same scene, only instead of clocks they would be limp Alka-Seltzer tablets. And I *remembered*—that you had helped nurture my spirit of rebellion, only I let it go dormant. So this is completing that cycle.

Q. How do you justify the assassination of Marcus Foster?

A. I don't justify it. I'm more concerned with there being a fair trial for Joe Remiro and Russell Little. I mean *they* say they're innocent. You'd think if they had gotten rid of a pig administrator they'd be proud of it. But they want to plead not guilty. I mean there was no logical reason to put them in strip cells at San Quentin, except to scare them and demoralize them and try to get them to confess to a murder they didn't commit.

Q. There's been a rumor that you used to visit Donald DeFreeze in prison.

A. That's impossible. It's a lie. I never did.

Q. And also that you knew Willie Wolfe before you were abducted?

A. That's another lie. I admit I *feel* as if I've known him all my life, but that's a false rumor.

Q. What about the evidence that DeFreeze has been an informer for the Los Angeles Police Department?

A. That was his survival game. If he were still working for the pigs, we wouldn't be in danger now. I mean you can't confuse somebody like Cinque with—I met the Shah of Iran once, and he was absolutely charming—but he's actually a vicious executioner. I just hope some of those Watergate bastards go to prison, so they get even a little *taste* of it and perhaps understand the lengths that a prisoner will go to—the deals and all—to escape legally, if that's really legal.

Q. What about Colston Westbrook?

A. Cinque calls him the pig of pigs. He says they can make zombies out of human beings. It makes *Star Trek* look like a Boy Scout fairy tale by comparison.

Q. Who's they?

A. The good ol' Central Intelligence Agency, of course. I mean you take somebody like E. Howard Hunt. He didn't even really care that they killed his wife. That's par for the course. When you're in the profession of programming other people for violence, you simultaneously deprogram yourself of love. That's what I've come to understand.

Q. In the bank robbery a couple of weeks ago—

A. That wasn't me. Even though I said on tape that I was a willing participant, I wasn't even a participant. I was too nervous. They got somebody made up to look like me. The whole thing was just staged to make the public think that the SLA is really a gung-ho gang of terrorists. I would've participated, but I was just too nervous. They had to get a stand-in for me. My official understudy.

Q. On one of the tapes you mentioned Blood In My Eye *by George Jackson. Are there any other books you've been reading during the past couple of months?*

A. Well, actually, I haven't been that linear, you know? Mostly we've been listening to the radio. I love it when they have that long *beep* for the emergency broadcast system, so you can be sure to tune in to get what they refer to as "official information." We've been reading mostly newspapers and magazines, but a few books. There's one called *On Learning and Social Change* by Michael Rossman. He was in the Free Speech Movement. Also, *None Dare Call It Conspiracy* by Gary Allen and—

Q. Isn't that distributed by the John Birch Society?

A. So what? There's an awful lot of valuable information—the Council on Foreign Relations is really horrendous—so I don't care *who's* distributing it. Oh, and I also like a book I've been reading off and on called *The Social Animal*—I forget the name of the author *[Elliot Aronson]*—but that's really fine.

Q. What about music? What have you been listening to?

A. Well, we only have a radio here. At a previous safe-house, there was a stereo, but we didn't have a large variety of records. Joy of Cooking, we played them a lot. Pink Floyd too. And there's a group called The Last Poets, and there's one cut on their album where they give their interpretation of all the symbolism on a dollar bill, and we just sat around, wiped out on really excellent marijuana, looking at a dollar bill while they were reciting that. It's very powerful. I remembered how I used to think, when I was a little girl, that real money was just official play money.

Q. What about Mao? Have you read the Little Red Book?

A. No. But I do understand the process of criticism, self-criticism. It's a refined version of what we used to call mirroring. I did hear a story about Mainland China that really impressed me. The women there lined up their pocketbooks on the sidewalk at a bus stop and then just walked away to window-shop. Isn't that an incredibly high level of trust? That was witnessed by a friend of Mizmoonie who visited China. By the way, you'll notice we *are* able to joke about our names—"Cinque very much" and "Fahizah jolly good fellow"—even though we're really quite serious about the revolution.

Q. Well, to be honest, that's not my revolution—the hostility—who do you think is gonna be impressed by you calling your father Adolph except the already converted?

A. Well, who are you to tell me the degree of rage I should feel? Besides, don't you see how the public has been brainwashed by the media? First they were led like sheep to feel sorry for me, then they were led like sheep to *withdraw* their sympathy. And then they have the gall to call *me* brainwashed.

Q. I feel silly asking this, but have you been brainwashed?

A. No, I've been *coerced*, obviously, at the beginning, but I haven't been brainwashed. You have to understand what it's been like from my point of view. Instant introspection. The moment I was taken away, underneath the tremendous fright I was still aware that it was because I was the daughter of a wealthy family whose comfort depends on the suffering of others. I've always been vaguely cognizant of that, but you know, you try to repress that kind of thing so you can go on living comfortably yourself.

Q. Have you been given any drugs?

A. At first I was given some kind of antibiotic for my cold, which got me very, *very* stoned—I haven't really come down yet—but no hypnotism or anything like that. What it is, I have been *voluntarily* unwinding my whole life, with the help of Emily and Bill, but I consistently remember things *before* they ask questions. They're helping to *un*brainwash me, thoroughly.

Q. Was there what you might call a turning point in your consciousness that made you decide to join the SLA?

A. Not really any one thing, except perhaps the most basic—crux—when I was six years old, we traced this back, when Nixon was running against Kennedy, Mom and Dad were for Nixon, and actually they *reminded* me of Nixon and Pat, they had that same kind of stiffness with each other. And with *me*. I recalled thinking as a child that it would've been nice to have Kennedy and Jackie as parents. I mean as a child I couldn't articulate it, but I could *observe* the way they related to Caroline, but you know, you just adjust to your own environment because it's all you have. But aside from all the political reasons Kennedy was killed, I think there was also an unconscious rationale, because he represented a certain dynamic sexuality, you know what I mean?

Q. Could you tell me about the argument you had with your father at his office in the Examiner *building? I'm interested in the conflict over life-style—*

A. You make it sound like a measly fashion show. Life-style, horseshit! It was about his goddamned newspaper not telling the *truth*, that's what we were arguing about.

Q. See, I heard it had to do with the way you dressed.

A. No, no, those liars! It was about Watergate, I didn't even *wear* hippie clothes then. Do you know what the real motive behind Watergate was?

Q. Yeah, to take over the country, first at the San Diego convention, and then that was switched to Miami—

A. Well, they already took over the country, the military did, when Kennedy was killed—you know that, right?—but when George *Wallace* was shot, *he* knew, and the people in the CIA who supported him, *they* knew who was responsible. And so they decided to force Nixon out. Some drunk guy at my parents' party was talking about all this, and I was just sitting there, stoned out of my mind, and he didn't even see me.

Anyway, so then I was in my father's office and I asked him why he didn't publish an exposé of this stuff, and he got all uptight and said, "You've gotta have documentation, you've gotta have documentation, some drunk blabbermouth at a party isn't enough!"

And I said, "Well you print plenty of things just because the government tells you to, without *any* documentation," and he really got pissed off at that.

Q. Did your family know you were getting stoned?

A. Oh, sure. Listen, there was almost a pound of grass at our apartment when I—you know, went on this little vacation trip, but I'll bet my father and the FBI made some kind of a deal to keep it quiet.

Q. You were real close to Steven Weed. How do you view that relationship now?

A. It seems like a previous incarnation. He had been my Math teacher at Crystal Springs, but I was the aggressive one—in fact, that made me have sort of a vested interest in him—he was like an emotional investment, you know? And there was something, an adolescent romantic fantasy, about making out with your tutor. You got status for being independent.

But we ended up leading a very middleclass life in Berkeley. Listening to records, dinner parties—always for *his* friends; couples—shopping for antiques. It was like a couple of children playing house, with my father helping out—with an MG here and a fifteen-hundred-dollar Persian rug there—he was saving that for a wedding present. God!

Q. What's the most important thing you've learned from this whole experience?

A. I've thought about that a lot. The most important thing I've learned has been to love my fellow captives, because they've *all* been kidnapped by our system of injustice as surely as I was by the SLA. They've been just as brainwashed as I'm supposed to have been, into acting as though it really makes any difference whether one football team beats another. It's all role-playing.

I think you know that kind of stuff instinctively when you're an infant, but they try to program it out of you. That's why my mother sent me to a Catholic school for girls. I got kicked out for smoking dope. I used to sneak out on dates with a guy who worked at Santa Catalina. He was a real hash-head. So I wore their goddamned uniform, but they still caught me smoking dope. It's not in the records, but they sure as hell didn't ask me back.

Q. You said on one of the tapes that the FBI wants you dead. Why is that?

A. Because I *know* too much, obviously. The FBI and also my father's corporation advisers. I remember the way I used to hate hippies—who were in my own *age* bracket. I had to justify that hatred by bringing in the Puritan Ethic. Hippies were unproductive, right?

Anybody who cooperates with the FBI is signing their own death warrant. And it's the same with the pig corporate structure. Their whole existence is devoted to perverting innocent children into consumers.

Why do you think my mother wanted me to go to Stanford instead of Berkeley, even though she's a goddamned U.C. regent? What kind of hypocrisy is that? She helps control a school that's not good enough for her own *daughter*?

Well, I'm a hippie now too. I'm a white nigger now.

Q. What exactly is it that you know too much about?

A. Well, that my whole kidnapping was *scripted* by the government. Otherwise they would have taken my father, not me. Cujo gave me that insight. When I finally understood that, was when I decided to join the people [*she gestures toward SLA members in the room*] who have had me under protective cus-

tody.

Actually, I have no other choice. I just hope that Vickie and my other sisters hear this. They're the ones who are still inmates at the Hearst prison. I'm the one that's really free. In my mind, if not my body.

Q. Yeah, but people are still gonna think you're brainwashed.

A. People have been brainwashed to accept being stopped and searched at airline terminals—they've been brainwashed to *welcome* a police state—they believe every bit of propaganda they see on the TV news and on the other crime shows. I haven't been brainwashed, *they* have. I've been *de*programmed from the culture.

Q. Don't you think that there are any authentic radical groups that haven't been infiltrated?

A. I don't know, honestly. But what are they doing? Have they done anything that's really effective? I don't mean symbolic little gestures like blowing up a bathroom. Who does that help except the protectors of the ruling class?

Q. What would you recommend as effective action?

A. The food program, if it had not been sabotaged. Look, I don't have all the answers. All I know now is that wealthy cocaine-snorters spend their precious time and energy getting the population hooked on Pepsi-Cola, but I don't know what to say to the people, to the poor blacks, who work for Pepsi-Cola and need the jobs.

They're in complicity with dehumanization, but not so bad as somebody who manufactures napalm. I think everybody should get Unemployment. They could divide them in half. One week half the people work at the Unemployment office giving *other* people compensation, and they could keep switching back and forth each week, so that everybody got a chance to either wait in line or serve the people waiting in line.

Q. I'm getting a signal that I've gotta split. Is there anything else you want to add?

A. Let's see. I can't give you my driver's license or my credit card—*both* halves of that have already been used up. I just want to say one other thing about brainwashing, though. This is really ironic.

When I was just entering puberty, I started shaving the hair under my arms, that's when I was *really* brainwashed. But my mother used to let the hair under *her* arms grow. And now she's shaving hers, and I'm letting mine grow. Here we are, the Hairy Armpit Brigade of the Symbionese Liberation Army—ta-da!

Oh, and when you have to learn to keep pretending that three ninety-eight isn't really four dollars, that's brainwashing too. . . .

* * *

Epilogue: After the tape recorders were shut off, Patty added: "There's another thing about my mother that's really intriguing. On the day that Bobby Kennedy was killed, she bought a horse, and then she wanted to name it Sirhan Sirhan, but the Jockey Club wouldn't permit it. Isn't that strange?"

There was only time for a quick embrace goodbye. I was blindfolded again and driven back to the Berkeley campus, where the Ram Dass entourage were busy chanting and singing in Pauley Ballroom.

On the Lam with Patty Hearst, *continued*

The next morning I went to the *Berkeley Barb* and began writing a weekly series that was later syndicated to various alternative and college newspapers around the country. I had to let out what I knew gradually. In the first *Rumpleforeskin's Column*, I included the following:

"It would be irresponsible not to consider the likelihood that the media have been used by the good ol' CIA in the name of the SLA. With that premise, it becomes understandable why the overground press automatically uses certain material from the SLA carried by the *Barb* and KPFA, but when Mae Brussell's documented analysis of provocateurs is of urgent informational value, only Zodiac News Service picks it up.

"Sometimes the shrewdies overplay their rhetorical hand. A few days before Patty Hearst was kidnapped, an article by Burt Wolfe in the *Bay Guardian* quoted her as telling the Randy she now calls Adolph that his paper, the *Examiner*, is irrelevant to the times and only people over eighty read it. And now she has the audacity to call Steven Weed an ageist.

"Experts I've talked to believe that she has been brainwashed through the use of hypnosis under drugs, possibly PCP, as was used in the Manson family. Donald DeFreeze, exactly like Charles Manson, was allowed to get away with felonies—ranging from possession of weapons to grand theft auto—while on probation.

"The events ostensibly orchestrated by those two 'cult leaders' have in common the propagandistic horror that nobody benefits but the police state. When Charlie Manson was let out of prison to apply his con man education to the guru biz, he found similar patterns of pimpdom. One space that the Hearsts and the gurus share is when they stand around complaining about the servant problem."

A week-and-a-half later, at the Liebling Counter-Convention in New York, a reporter confronted me with a rumor that I had interviewed Patricia Hearst, but wouldn't reveal the source, so I refused to confirm it, inasmuch as I had told no one yet.

A week later, on Friday, May 17, 1974, the Los Angeles massacre of the SLA took place. On Sunday, the *San Francisco Examiner* front page announced: "Patricia Hearst Not Among Those Killed in L.A. Shootout." No doubt she would have resented the selfish implications of that headline in her father's paper.

A couple of weeks after that, I mentioned the meeting with Patty Hearst in my *Barb* column, adding that "Since there is nothing of investigatory value in the interview, I will not speak with the FBI. Nor am I able to supply any information that might earn me a $50,000 reward. Tania insisted that she had not been brainwashed. My impression is that she was."

The *Soho Weekly News* in New York front-paged a headline about that item, but I complained to them for taking it out of context. *Parade*, a national Sunday supplement, also reported that I had interviewed Patty Hearst. Nevertheless, the "tireless" FBI never once contacted me in their "endless search" for her. Even if they thought I was bluffing, how could they be sure unless they believed that *they* were in total control of Patty's whereabouts?

The last official report had her in Hollywood on May 19, 1974. Anita Alcala, manager of an apartment house, turned down an offer of $500 rental for one night by two black men and a white female with blue eyes identified as "Patty Hearst," who actually has brown eyes. Despite the racism of federal agents, there has been no hunt for those two black men. They were most likely CIA.

On October 6, the *Examiner* reported that "The FBI has found at least two hideouts in Los Angeles used by the trio"—referring to Patty plus Bill and Emily Harris, not those two black men—"after the May 17 shootout in Los Angeles where six SLA members died. FBI agents are questioning old friends of the Harrises in the expectation that the SLA members may come to them for help. An old friend of Bill Harris from Indiana University told the *Chicago Tribune* that FBI agents warned her of the SLA pattern. . . .

"The FBI told the young woman that before the SLA members left, they would tell her she could say what she wanted to the FBI if she should be questioned, but she should not talk to any police. . . .

"The FBI has declined to comment."

Several weeks later, gangster Mickey Cohen—whom Billy Graham once converted to Christianity as the forerunner to Charles Colson—claimed on the *Tomorrow* show to have located Patty for the Hearst family, which has a history of relating cordially to mobsters.

Virginia Hill came to the late William Randolph Hearst for help in keeping Bugsy Siegel out of prison. (He never had to spend a single day behind bars.) More recently, she purchased her home in Florida from Randolph and Catherine Hearst.

Whether or not Patty is safe in the gloves of organized crime, FBI director Clarence Kelley now says that the kidnap case is closed "except for a few loose ends." Have they also discovered Edgar Cayce's secret medical degree, solved the mystery of the Bermuda Triangle and located Adolph Hitler's missing testicle, lodged securely in the ear of Michael Rockefeller's severed head, which was found floating inside Francis Ford Coppola's waterbed?

Finally, Catherine Hearst has followed the party line—as expressed by William Buckley, who wrote that Patty should be sacrificed "in the name of Christ"—when she said that she would rather her daughter be dead than join the Communists. In another statement which alone qualifies this typical American mother to be on the powerful Board of Regents of the University of California, she said that if only Clark Gable had been in Berkeley instead of Steven Weed, then Patty would never have been kidnapped.

A SNEAK PREVIEW OF RICHARD NIXON'S MEMOIRS

An old friend approached The Realist with a thick sheaf of what purported to be a photocopy of the manuscript still being worked on by former President Richard M. Nixon. Our first reaction was skepticism. While most of the contents dealt predictably with contemporary history as it has already been recorded, there were enough surprises to shock even our own jaded psyche.

However, we employed the services of a reputable private investigation firm. Their report verified that our source did indeed have access to an individual inside the San Clemente hideaway. The next step was to hire a professional graphologist who determined the authenticity of Mr. Nixon's handwritten notes on the typed transcript. Finally, our attorneys assured us that there was no violation of copyright laws involved, simply because it would have been premature to submit such incompleted material for copyright protection.

The book, as yet untitled, is dedicated "To Patricia Ryan Nixon, who has been named the most admired woman in the country, and deservedly so, for her loyalty has been of continuing inspiration, not only to her husband and family, but to all Americans everywhere." Here, then, are several excerpts from this preliminary draft of the private memoirs of the only United States President ever to resign from office.

* * *

Although President Dwight David Eisenhower encouraged me to call him Ike, it was a superficial form of intimacy. I regretted his failure to share the responsibility for decision-making. That privilege he reserved for his special assistant, Sherman Adams.

When media coverage of a minor scandal in 1958 involving a rug and a Vicuna coat pressured him into letting Adams go, Ike at last revealed a facet of his humanness to me. "By sheer force of habit," he remarked, "I was ready to seek out Sherman's advice on whether or not I should fire him."

It was not until 1961, after Ike's farewell address, that he confided in me again. This time about a more momentous occasion. "I suppose," he began, "my reference to the dangers of the military-industrial complex in my speech came as something of a surprise to you, eh?"

"Well, sir, it did strike me as a rather incongruous position for a renowned General of the Army to take—"

"I had a visitation," he interrupted. "While I was in the very process of composing my farewell address—now this is utterly impossible to describe—but I do believe it was some kind of extra-terrestrial communication."

"In English or what?" I was dumbfounded.

"Beyond all language. It was as though my body remained in the chair and my spirit was taken on a journey. All I know is that when I returned, I just *had* to tell the truth. There was no other *choice*. . . ."

Ike stopped in mid-sentence. He never mentioned that incident again. Nor did I feel it would be proper for me to broach the subject. I dismissed it from my mind. It would not be until nearly fourteen years later that my *visceral* understanding of his experience would occur.

The year 1974 was so rough on me that for a while, I thought

I could actually be going insane. I wondered if I was being drugged without my knowledge. I found myself reveling in paranoid fantasies, and I gave voice to these at press conferences. I expressed fear that my plane might crash. I resorted to using an expression like, "They can point a gun at your head." I was practically pleading for mercy.

When I entered Memorial Hospital Medical Center in Long Beach on October 23 for my phlebitis condition, I brought my own jar of wheat germ, because I was afraid that poison would be put into my food.

On October 29, the doctors placed a clamp on a vein in my pelvis in order to prevent the blood clot from moving to my lungs where it could have killed me. It was then that I underwent cardiovascular failure. For a few hours I was considered to be clinically dead. It was an incredibly ecstatic feeling. I was conscious, but on some other level. And there was an overwhelming temptation to stay in that blissful limbo. Yet there was also something in me that kept saying *Don't give up!* This was the bottom line of my survival instinct.

But *why not* give up? What was there left for me? The answer came to me by the same extra-terrestrial path it had come to Ike: *Tell the truth!* That was the turning point of my life. And these memoirs are the tangible result of my transformation. No one shall be spared, least of all myself.

On October 30, Ron Ziegler announced, "We almost lost President Nixon yesterday afternoon." This was almost three months after my resignation, and he was still referring to me as President. "Poor Ron," I thought to myself, "he thinks he's still in Disneyland." It was not until nearly three years later, however, after seeing myself on television being interviewed by David Frost—and observing the ridiculous robot I had become—that I realized I was *still* fooling myself. But now I am ready to peel away even these final layers of my poker-face mask.

* * *

In August of 1945, while I was still serving in the Navy, stationed in Maryland, there was a Committee of One Hundred seeking—according to an advertisement they placed in several California newspapers—a candidate for Congress "with no previous political experience to defeat a man who has represented the district in the House for ten years. . . ." This was a reference to Jerry Voorhis.

I did not see the ad, but destiny acted as though I had answered it when I was contacted by Herman Perry, Vice-President of the Bank of America. He later became Vice-President of the Western Tube Corporation, a CIA front located in the Whittier Bank of America Building. But now, he wanted to know only if I was a Republican and if I was available.

My responses were both affirmative.

It was Perry who brought me out for an extremely brief meeting with Howard Hughes. He was handsome, dynamic, self-assured. Somehow he had seen the FBI dossier on me which had apparently been compiled when I originally applied for a position after graduating law school. Oddly enough, I had never heard from the FBI directly.

"Nixon," he addressed me, "you have a magnificent political future ahead. You will be able to steer your ship with independence. But always keep it back in a tiny compartment of your mind that you do not own the ocean. I do."

I never saw Howard Hughes face-to-face again.

* * *

The seeds of my distrust in the Justice Department were sown in 1948 during the Alger Hiss case. Those people just sat on each other's hands. If not for the work of our House Un-American Activities Committee, the prosecution would never have been so successful.

I refused to turn over to those bunglers the microfilms we had in evidence. When there was a possibility I might be cited for contempt, I raised the Constitutional question of what a dangerous precedent could be set, for here was the instance of a Congressman appearing voluntarily before a Grand Jury.

But the truth of the matter was that those microfilms were copies of documents forged on an old Woodstock typewriter that had been specially constructed to resemble—to have the same peculiarities as—the one which had actually belonged to Priscilla Hiss.

Then Whittaker Chambers hid these "old" 1938 microfilms inside a pumpkin on his pumpkin farm. The trouble was, the Eastman Kodak people stated that the type of film we used was not manufactured by their company until after 1945.

To this day, whenever the comic strip *Peanuts* has any mention of that bird Woodstock or the mysterious "pumpkin papers," I suspect Charles Schulz is trying to remind me of something.

* * *

There seems to be a tradition of accusing those who fight Communism of being homosexual. This smear tactic was used against Whittaker Chambers; against Senator Joseph McCarthy; against J. Edgar Hoover. In that vein, gossips used to joke about Hoover and Clyde Tolson double-dating with Charles "Bebe" Rebozo and myself.

Neither Rebozo nor I are "gay." We have been very close friends since 1950. What we enjoy most about each other's company is the fact that small talk becomes unneccessary. We are not afraid of silence. But we have never had any kind of sexual relationship.

We were introduced by Senator George Smathers, who was infamous for supplying female company to his fellow politicians. It was Smathers who sent Mary Jo Kopechne to Senator Edward Kennedy.

Whenever I was in Florida, I would always stay with Bebe, and he would occasionally get a couple of beautiful $200-a-night girls. Or, as they would be called nowadays, $200-a-night women. But when I bought my own home in Key Biscayne, then his yacht became the rendezvous site.

I was certainly not promiscuous, but I had been a virgin until marriage. Indeed, I proposed to Pat Ryan the very same night I met her. She refused, but I was a determined son-of-a-gun. I even drove to Los Angeles where she dated other men while I waited in the wings. I finally charmed her with my perseverance and self-effacement.

Once I expressed concern to Bebe that word might get out about my "affairs" in Key Biscayne. "These girls," I pointed out, "are likely to boast about going to bed with a United States Senator."

The Odd Couple

A Sneak Preview of Richard Nixon's Memoirs, *continued*

"They're professionals," Bebe reassured me. "It's just like your lawyer-client privilege. Stop worrying. . . ."

* * *

How strange that the incident which stands out among the entire eight years I spent as Vice-President occurred not in the White House, but in Peru. There was a rioter who spat on me, and it was with great pleasure that I kicked him in the shins.

Back in the safety of our hotel, I reminisced about an early formal debate at Whittier College—"Resolved: that insects are more beneficial than harmful"—because I had been so intrigued as to how insects did not *think*, they just acted. Now, having acted myself totally without hesitation, I was able to identify with them for the first time.

* * *

One evening in 1949, while I was still serving in the Congress, I received an anonymous call at my home. A male voice said three words, "Watch Jeane Dixon," and hung up the telephone.

A week later, the psychic Jeane Dixon held a press conference. One of the reporters asked her to predict my future. She drew a blank, however, explaining that she needed time to meditate. I believe that in show business parlance, this is known as "milking the audience." Finally she said it: "I predict that one day Richard Nixon will become President of the United States."

I could only conclude that the higher source from which she had attained her intelligence was not necessarily supernatural.

When I lost the presidential election to John F. Kennedy in 1960, Jeane Dixon *continued* to predict that I would be President. "Destiny," she stated, "cannot be denied."

Even after I was defeated in the 1962 California gubernatorial election and announced that I was through with politics, she said, "Richard Nixon has not even *begun* his politics." And then she predicted the assassination of President Kennedy in 1963.

After the Watergate affair, she stated: "God gave us Richard Nixon to divide us, to test us where our faith is concerned, to see if we could come together." A local paper published her statement (*"God gave us Nixon to divide us.*—Jeane Dixon") as the caption for a cartoon showing a cloud with the voice of God saying, "Don't blame me—I voted for McGovern." I had to admit it was funny, even though she had been quoted out of context.

* * *

Harry Robbins Haldeman came into my life when I was a Senator in 1951. He volunteered to work in my Vice-Presidential campaign the next year, but that was not in the cards, so he tried again in 1956, and this time we took him on. He rose to be my chief advance man for the presidential race in 1960.

After my defeat, Haldeman remained standing tall among the debris. He volunteered to help me with my book, *Six Crises*. I wrote the chapter on the '60 campaign myself because it was so fresh in my mind. Al Moscow drafted four other chapters with Haldeman—this was not ghostwritten material because I re-wrote what they presented—and Haldeman worked mostly on the Alger Hiss chapter.

He was so apparently eager to please, though, that he screwed up on his research. He had it that the FBI found the old Woodstock typewriter. And the book was published that way. Then the facts came out, the trial records, and we had to change it for the paperback edition. So now it reads that the FBI was *unable* to find the typewriter.

The truth is, Alger Hiss found it himself. But the FBI had *planted* this fake Woodstock typewriter. And then the defense presented it in the trial as what they *thought* was evidence in their favor, so Hiss was found guilty of perjury.

That verdict gave me much political strength. I had the courage of Alger Hiss's conviction to serve as the magic carpet that transported me from the Congress to the Senate to the Vice-Presidency. I would have had the Presidency in my pocket if not for Kennedy's performance in the Great Debates—but only on television; I fared better on radio.

Charisma was the outside variable that none of us had counted upon.

* * *

As Vice-President, I had labored diligently behind the scenes to establish "Operation Forty," by which our CIA covertly trained Cuban intelligence officers in exile. In regard to the Bay of Pigs invasion, Operation Forty was to serve as the missing link between the White House and the CIA in April of 1961. My plan was to invade Cuba.

Ironically, during the 1960 presidential campaign, Kennedy began advocating *my plan*. I could not reveal that it was already in effect because Operation Forty was a *secret* organization. Further, I found myself in the schizophrenic position of *attacking* my own scenario whenever Kennedy articulated it, because it violated our treaty commitments.

* * *

Of all the professional newscasters I have met, Walter Cronkite of CBS was the most charming. He treated me with respect and dignity. After the broadcast interview, we sat in his anteroom and talked informally.

"I've always wanted to thank you," he said, "for inadvertently bringing me back to sanity that horrible weekend John Kennedy was killed."

"Oh, really—how so?"

"Well, this followed on the heels of that televised shooting of Lee Harvey Oswald by Jack Ruby. A journalist asked for your reaction, and you replied with a slip of the tongue, 'Two rights don't make a wrong.' Before you could correct yourself, I was able to break through my depression finally with a bit of laughter."

"Yes, those were muddled times. Do you know I blanked out on where I was the day the assassination took place? I had to tell the FBI I forgot, and it was not until later that I remembered I had been in *Dallas*, of all places. There was a convention of the American Bottlers of Carbonated Beverages, and I was there representing Pepsi-Cola. But I flew out of there at eleven o'clock that morning. Kennedy was shot around one, as I recall. Where were *you* that day?"

"In my office," Cronkite said. "When we got the word from Bethesda that he had passed, I cried openly."

"And you're supposed to be objective," I teased him. "I didn't realize you were that much of a Kennedy man."

"Well, by that time I was crying because it had also come over the wires that Lyndon Johnson was already preparing to be sworn in as the new President."

It was encouraging to find that this superstar was really just like your favorite uncle in person.

* * *

When Robert Kennedy was Attorney General in 1962, he was busy checking out the Hiss case for some reason. Of course, he discovered that the FBI never had the Woodstock typewriter.

In 1968, when he was running for President, he approached New Orleans District Attorney Jim Garrison to be *his* Attorney General. Garrison had gained much publicity due to his investigation of the assassination of Bobby's brother.

During that campaign, Howard Hughes dispatched Robert Maheu to visit me. Hughes felt strongly that the Vietnam war should continue—he had a huge defense contract for helicopters—yet at the same time he wanted a halt to underground nuclear testing, presumably because they upset the roulette wheels in his Las Vegas casinos.

I mentioned the Bobby Kennedy information to Maheu, and he said, "Uh-oh, the Boss will have to keep a sharper eye on *him*."

It was poetic irony that while Bobby Kennedy was giving official permission to the left hand of J. Edgar Hoover to spy on Martin Luther King, I was giving unofficial permission to the right hand of Hoover to spy on Kennedy. That is to say, Robert Maheu may have been working for Howard Hughes, but he also had never stopped working for the FBI. So, when he referred to "the Boss," I asked, "Which one?"

Maheu smiled and held up his arms, two fingers from each hand extending up into the air. He said, "Both." I smiled and returned the gesture. This was the exact moment I decided to use it for the crowds.

Winston Churchill had used the V-sign to signify Victory. Then the anti-war protesters perverted its meaning to signify Defeat. Now I was restoring its original victorious symbolism by co-opting the co-opters. Or so I believed.

* * *

The problem was that Lyndon Johnson desperately wanted to have the Vietnam war settled before he left office. Whereas, I am ashamed to admit, we were trying to prolong it.

Anna Chennault—the "Dragon Lady," as we called her—was our liaison to South Vietnamese government officials. Her task was to dissuade their Ambassador, Bui Diem, from attending the Paris peace talks.

But LBJ got wise to this. I had to call and cajole him personally. He was absolutely furious. He complained bitterly at how "shit-kickin' pissed off" he was. "Thieu is *our* boy," he shouted, "and don't you fuckin' forget that!"

On November 1, 1968, only four days before the American election, President Nguyen Van Thieu announced that Saigon was pulling out of the peace talks. The Dragon Lady had obviously convinced his associates that they would obtain a juicier deal under our new administration than under Johnson or his legacy, Hubert Humphrey, who would surely have won if the Democrats ended the war.

And so, because it was to the mutual interest of the South Vietnamese and the Republicans to extend the war for several more years, we at the Committee to Re-Elect became the recipients of kickbacks from our own government's money which had been intended to aid the Saigon government.

I do not ever ask for forgiveness—no, rather I must live with the memory of myself as an idealistic adolescent first reading about the Teapot Dome scandal and saying to my mother, "I would like to become an honest lawyer who can't be bought by crooks. . . ."

* * *

We created a couple of Frankenstein monsters, and when I say we, I mean the Administration and the media in a sort of unintentional collaboration.

One such monster was Martha Mitchell. The first time she made one of her famous telephone calls, and we saw how the press ate it up, we realized we had a political gold mine: the wife of the Attorney General could serve as our mouthpiece for floating various trial balloons.

John Mitchell would get thoroughly briefed on whatever the issue, Haiphong Harbor or Senator Fulbright or the need for increased spending, and then—without ever letting Martha know that he *expected* her to give a scoop to some lucky reporter that evening, John would simply smoke his pipe and just happen to engage her in casual conversation about the matter.

Martha was much too strong-willed to be *instructed* to make a call, but it could be three o'clock in the morning when the urge would hit her. This was a great joke among the reporters. One little news item quoted her latest pronouncement, and after the quote the sentence was completed with, "Martha Mitchell *confided* to the *Washington Star* yesterday."

But in the process of becoming a public character, she developed many contacts in the media. By the time her husband became my campaign manager, Martha Mitchell was already a household word. We thought she would prove to be a wonderful asset until she started blabbing about Watergate.

Another Frankenstein monster we created was Henry Kissinger. I never really wanted him in the first place. He had insulted me publicly when I received the nomination in '68. But I made an agreement with Nelson Rockefeller that if he would actively support me, I would take Kissinger onto the team, and of course I had to keep my word.

We all felt somewhat uncomfortable about his German accent, though. H.R. Haldeman decided that whenever Kissinger made any statements, his picture could be shown on TV, but there would be no audio. And the electronic media cooperated.

Meanwhile we built up his image—got him dates with glamorous movie stars: Jill St. John, Marlo Thomas, Liv Ullmann—until he became known as a harmless pudgy playboy. Then it became acceptable for his voice to be heard.

"Henry," I once remarked to him, "there's a rumor around Washington that you're lousy in bed."

"Mr. President"—speaking very slowly and distinctly—"I can only say that . . . power is the ultimate aphrodisiac." And he just kept glaring at me with those worried-looking eyebrows of his. This was exactly three days after our destabilization of the Chilean government.

* * *

In 1968 George Wallace ran for President as a candidate of the American Independent Party. This almost lost me the election to Hubert Humphrey. In 1972, Wallace ran for President again. This almost cost *him* his life. I honestly have no knowledge as to how long Arthur Bremer was in our employ, but I do know that the cover story of his having stalked me before he went after Wallace—this was fabricated simply to defuse any suspicion that might tinge our role in the tragic event.

After all, my supposed public mandate that November included twenty million votes which would otherwise have gone to George Wallace. We had not expected him to be so much of a political threat. In fact, we had already taken certain steps to preclude any such possibility. In 1970, immediately after he had become Governor of Alabama again, the IRS and the Justice Department launched an investigation of Wallace and his brother Gerald, for tax evasion and other financial corruption.

John Mitchell, still Attorney General at the time, came to me early in 1971 and said, "We've got to stop George Wallace. He could force the election into the House of Representatives if he runs on a third party ticket again."

In May of that year, I was in Mobile and invited Wallace to fly with me on the Presidential plane to Birmingham. En route, we shook hands on an agreement. I promised that Mitchell would call off the investigation of Wallace and his brother—although their underlings would still be subject to prosecution—and the Governor in turn promised me that if he ran in '72, it would only be as a Democrat.

In August 1971, we discovered that CBS correspondent Daniel Schorr had been asking around about the possibility of such a deal. Haldeman commented, "We'd better get on *his* ass fast."

Two years later, when Schorr reported that John Dean was afraid of going to prison because he might get raped there, we were able to find out from the FBI immediately that his source was Dean's own attorney, but there was nothing constructive we could do with that information.

* * *

Young people use the expression "karma returning" to describe the way I am about to reveal a deal we made with Jack Anderson, who had himself exposed the corruption of so many others in his syndicated column for the *Washington Post*.

We were tipped off that Anderson was researching the Dragon Lady connection. He had learned that her late husband, General Claire Chennault, who had commanded the "Flying Tigers" in World War II, had in 1946 formed a private commercial airline which later merged with the CIA's Air America.

He also learned that the widow of Chennault, our Dragon Lady, was currently profiting from a Pepsi-Cola factory which I had established in Laos, but which had never spewed forth a single drop of Pepsi. Air America has been shuttling out its actual product: heroin.

However, Anderson agreed not to publish this material. In return we agreed not to publicize the fact that he knew about the Watergate break-in weeks before it occurred. He had told Lawrence O'Brien at Democratic National Committee headquarters, but O'Brien remained silent because he assumed that such a scandal would provide ammunition for a Democratic coup in the '72 election.

Anderson held back because he did not wish to endanger his source, one of the "burglars," Frank Sturgis, whom he had known for some twenty years. Shortly after my resignation in 1974, I received a long letter from Sturgis. I shall quote here a portion of that correspondence:

. . . Now I'm telling you this because I still consider you my Commander-in-Chief. I realize that the same faction of the CIA that masterminded the assassination of Kennedy was also behind your own downfall. They thought JFK was soft on Communism in Cuba, and that you were soft on Communism in China. but they don't necessarily have to kill you to get rid of you.

While I participated in Operation 40, our job was primarily to infiltrate foreign countries. I was a member of the Assassination Section. Orders would filter down, and our job would be to kill, say, a military official or a politician. Even in those days, unstated policy included domestic as well as foreign enemies.

But I had nothing to do with the Kennedy assassination myself. The FBI came to interview me the day after it happened, and I didn't have a thing to tell them, except I could agree with their speculation that the motive was revenge for the Bay of Pigs failure. There's no doubt in my mind that if you had been elected in 1960, the Invasion would have been completely successful. . . .

For a while, I believed that Bernard Barker was the double agent in Watergate, but I have since come to the conclusion that our leader, James McCord, was guided to do the things that he did by certain officials in the CIA. We were definitely set up. They used us in setting us up to eventually destroy the office of the Presidency. You were just as expendable as Kennedy.

I shouldn't have been surprised. Mr. McCord was our Security Chief. I myself as an infiltrator of Castro rose to Director of Security for the Cuban Air Force and Director of Intelligence. Who can you trust? . . .

Whereas I agree with Frank Sturgis that the Watergate burglars were "set up," I question the reason he gives. The CIA was fully aware that relations with the People's Republic of China were bound to open up sooner or later. And of course I wanted to earn credit for that place in history.

Rather, I am convinced that there was a power struggle within the Agency. The "faction" to which Sturgis alludes—most likely led by Richard Helms—was literally *jealous* of the Special Intelligence Unit we had developed inside the White House.

* * *

Not only was the Watergate break-in deliberately bungled in order to discredit me, but the White House taping system was never part of my domain. I knew it had been installed by the Secret Service, but I lacked access to the tapes and, more important, to any switch that would shut off a recording device.

I was a prisoner in the Oval Office. A mobile prisoner, to be sure—I could go to the Cabinet Room or the Lincoln Room—it didn't make any difference. They even bugged my cabin at Camp David. I was under more surveillance myself than Larry O'Brien could ever imagine.

If I had the tapes in my possession, don't you think I would have gotten rid of them? Just the way I did with those microfilms in the Hiss case. Now, everybody was recommending this—from John Connally to Chuck Colson—but I simply did not have access to the system.

I should explain, however, that "Bay of Pigs" was the CIA code word for the assassination of President Kennedy. When we were attempting to get the CIA to put the brakes on the FBI investigation of Watergate, I told Haldeman to get the word to Helms that otherwise, because of E. Howard Hunt's involvement, the whole Bay of Pigs thing would open up.

Hunt was the CIA station chief in Mexico when agent Lee Harvey Oswald made contact there in 1963. The whole world already *knows* what a fiasco the Bay of Pigs operation turned out—that is, the invasion of Cuba—but because Kennedy didn't keep his campaign promise to support the exiles, *he* became the prime "Bay of Pigs" target.

Had the Watergate mission not been aborted, Hunt would have continued to simulate documents blaming Kennedy and Ted Sorensen for the murder of Che Guevara, just as he forged those cables blaming Kennedy for the murder of Ngo Dinh Diem.

I hasten to add that Hunt was merely *clarifying* the issues. The Kennedy Administration *was* responsible. But what we were trying to do was hurt *Ted* Kennedy's chances if he decided to run. That is guilt by relationship, which is wrong and irrelevant.

* * *

I was convinced that Nelson Rockefeller was behind it all. He had never forgiven me for defeating him in 1968 for the Republican nomination. What with that whole 25th Amendment arrangement, I figured their chronology was:

1. Get Spiro Agnew out of office.
2. Replace him with Gerald Ford.
3. Get me out of office.
4. Replace me with Ford.
5. Replace Ford with Rockefeller.
6. Knock off Ford before the election—Squeaky Fromme, Sara Jane Moore, whoever.
7. Replace Ford again with Rockefeller, declare martial law, and cancel the election. This could be done alternately by killing Jimmy Carter before the inauguration.

Now I realize how naive I was. Sure, Carter is more progressive—after all, politics is the art of balancing between the status quo and the force of evolution—but it became clear to me

News item: In Texas a vote by the State Board of Education to adopt five controversial textbooks was in effect a rejection of charges that the books teach evolution in an atheistic manner.

that he made some kind of deal.

The intelligence-gathering system knew about Thomas Eagleton's electroshock treatment and about G. Harrold Carswell's "closet queen" problem—he would have been a fine prospect for blackmail ("We have this information on you, Mr. Carswell, but don't worry, we won't leak it!")—and so my suspicions were aroused when it did not come out in the media until *after* the election, immediately before Carter's inauguration, that his son Jack had been discharged from the Navy because of marijuana.

Our ace-in-the-hole over George McGovern was that his daughter had been hospitalized for an LSD freakout. We never had to resort to it, however.

* * *

Woodward and Bernstein weren't the only ones with reliable sources. According to one of my own contacts in the intelligence community, their first choice for the Democratic candidate in the 1976 election was a southern governor—Reubin Askew of Florida—but their analysis calculated that Jimmy Carter's resemblance to Howdy Doody would provide a subconscious association in the minds of voters who were weaned on that folksy puppet.

What the American public does not realize is the long-range planning that goes on in think tanks like Stanford Research, the Rand Corporation, the Hudson Institute. They are already beginning to orchestrate the Bimillenium, the 2,000th birthday of Christ. The function of Jimmy Carter is to provide an opening wedge—with all his religiosity and his talk about not living in sin—for the Christianization of the United States. The arms manufacturers would be well pleased by a repeat performance of the Crusades. After those Korean bribes via Rev. Moon's Unification Church and the brainwashing of the Moonies, they'll finally figure it's time to make Christ an American again.

Billy Graham recently tried to convert me, the way he did Mickey Cohen. "Think what it would be like," he said, "if you were to go on an evangelistic tour with Eldridge Cleaver and Colonel Sanders."

"Colonel Sanders—the Kentucky Fried Chicken guy?"

"Yes, he has been born again too!"

"No thank you, Billy, I seem to have found serenity in my own way."

I have been able to gain a truly humble perspective now that Chuck Colson and Susan Atkins are saying the same things about Jesus Christ that they were once saying about myself and Charles Manson, respectively.

* * *

History is an unending conveyor belt that either perpetuates or corrects the inaccuracies of the past.

Therefore, the first thing I wish to point out, concerning that famous eighteen-and-a-half-minute gap in the White House tape of June 20, 1972, is that it actually lasted eighteen-and-a-quarter minutes. At 10:30 that morning, John Ehrlichman was in my office. Ostensibly, we did *not* discuss Watergate. Before leaving, however, he handed me two sealed envelopes. One contained a gram of cocaine, the other contained an initial report on the surveillance of Woodward and Bernstein. This task had been assigned to Tony Ulasewicz immediately after their first story on the break-in was published in the *Washington Post*.

It was strange. Ehrlichman's own first assignment had been to spy on the Nelson Rockefeller people for us during the 1960 campaign, and now he had his own chain of command, starting with John Caulfield. When Ehrlichman left, I opened the sealed envelope and read the report. It was brief:

Bernstein, Carl: *Seeing Nora Ephron,* Esquire *columnist, in New York. Ephron had Sunday brunch with unidentified female. Investigator overheard segment of conversation where u.f. claimed to have seen pornographic film including Susan Atkins, member of Manson Family, with Frykowski, apparently one of the victims at the Sharon Tate house.*

Woodward, Bob: *A loner. Clean as a hound's tooth. So far....*

Then I began to "chop the coke," as they say, with a razor blade. When Bob Haldeman entered, we each took a couple of snorts. Haldeman was *my* Sherman Adams; I had always felt I could depend on him. We were discussing whether my itinerary for an upcoming trip to the West Coast might include Ely, Nevada, which was the birthplace of Mrs. Nixon.

"That's perfect," Haldeman said. "We need anything we can get, PR-wise."

"But you know something, Bob? It's all image."

"Well, that is precisely the *purpose* of public relations."

"No, I mean my so-called *marriage* is all image. Pat and I have not, you know, slept together for nearly a dozen years. My God, I'm the President of the United States, and I can't even get laid by my own wife."

"Sir, you don't really want to talk about this?"

"And I'll tell you where it started. During the Cuban Crisis

in October '62. Boy, Kennedy sure won a helluva lot of points on that one. And it could've been *me* confronting Krushchev. I mean a real international shootdown, not just waving my finger in Safire's goddam makeshift kitchen."

"That would have been the logical extension."

"I tell you, the unspeakable frustration of not being in a position to negotiate that missile thing, I just couldn't get it up for Pat, plus the pressure of the California campaign was going on then too. And after we lost that election, she started talking about a divorce. We compromised with separate bedrooms."

Suddenly I stood up, and walked around my desk to where Haldeman was sitting and I ran my hand back and forth over the top of his crew-cut. I am not very physically demonstrative, but I had always wanted to do that. Still, this was almost a spontaneous gesture.

"*You* stuck by me, Bob" I said while I was rubbing his hair. "Finch dropped out, but you . . ." I suddenly began weeping uncontrollably.

"Sir—is there anything I can do?"

Between sobs I blurted out, "Oh, *sure*"—and I certainly did not intend for this to be taken literally—"Why don't you try sucking my cock, maybe *that'll* help."

To my utter astonishment, Haldeman unzipped my fly and proceeded with what can only be described as extreme efficiency. The whole thing could not have taken more than five minutes from beginning to end. He must have had some practice during his old prep school days. But neither of us said a word—before, during, or after.

It occurred to me that this misunderstanding was comparable to the time that Jeb Magruder remarked how convenient it would be if we could get rid of Jack Anderson, and G. Gordon Liddy assumed this was a direct order and rushed out to accomplish the act. If Liddy had not blabbed his "assignment" to an aide in the corridor, Anderson might not be alive today.

As for my own motivation, here was an experience not of homosexuality, but of power. I realized that if I could order the Pentagon to bomb Cambodia, it was of no great consequence that I was now merely permitting my chief of staff to perform fellatio. In fact, I was fully cognizant of what an honor it must have been for him.

When the incident was over, I simply returned to my desk and, although the tension of vulnerability was still in the air, we resumed our discussion as if nothing had occurred.

"Sir," Haldeman began, "on this Watergate problem, it would be advantageous to us if any similar activity on the part of the Democrats could be leaked to the media."

"Well, Hoover once told me—this was right after we won in '68—he said that within the previous month, LBJ had the FBI put the bug on Agnew and me. And Ramsey Clark was Attorney General then, but he never authorized it, so that was an *illegal* wiretap."

"Perfect. We start with Lyndon Johnson and work our way back—"

"But, no, on second thought, the LBJ tap would open up the whole Dragon Lady can of beans. I mean that was the goddam *excuse* they had for spying on us."

Then Haldeman delivered a resounding pep talk—when he

lets loose he can be an emotional marvel—about the importance of launching a counter-attack against our enemies.

I must say at this point that Rose Mary Woods deserves a Medal of Honor for the way she was willing to humiliate herself by taking the blame for accidentally erasing those first five minutes rather than destroy my public image.

Moreover, when General Alexander Haig learned, from Haldeman's notes, that during those additional twelve or thirteen minutes there was a discussion of how to deal with Watergate—thereby proving that I was involved in the cover-up only three days after the break-in—Haig attributed the erasure to "sinister forces." He said this under oath in Judge John Sirica's courtroom.

Now *that* is loyalty above and beyond the call of duty.

* * *

In retrospect, I realize that H.R. Haldeman was part of the plot all along, always trying to ingratiate himself—anything for the sake of credibility. But actually he had been trying to hurt my political career. Not me personally—I was just his particular assignment as part of an overall plan "to destroy," in the words of Frank Sturgis, "the office of the Presidency."

Haldeman was a saboteur in the guise of a sycophant. In 1967, when Haldeman was a Vice-President of the J. Walter Thompson advertising agency, he sent me a long memo on how I could use the media in my '68 campaign. I have since learned that during World War II, various corporations—Standard Oil, Wrigley Chewing Gum, Paramount Pictures—lent their executives to the Office of Strategic Services, which later became the CIA. The Thompson Agency supplied Kenneth Hinks to be Chief of the OSS Planning Staff. One of Haldeman's predecessors, Richard de Rochemont, a Vice-President of J. Walter Thompson, was offered a position with the Secret Intelligence Branch of the OSS. Another Thompson official, Donald Coster, stayed on with the CIA in South Vietnam from 1959 to 1962.

That's when Haldeman really latched on to me, in the '62 campaign. And when we lost, it was Haldeman who persuaded me into making a public fool of myself with that godawful "You-won't-have-Nixon-to-kick-around-any-more" press conference. It was Haldeman in 1960 who acted as a double agent and conspired with Dick Tuck to have all those Chinese fortune cookies contain the same message: *What about the Hughes Loan?* And it was Haldeman who consciously sabotaged the research on the Hiss chapter in *Six Crises*.

On one occasion, I was meeting with a group of blind veterans. I wanted to display my empathy for their handicap, so I began describing the Presidential Seal which was woven into the carpet that we happened to be standing on in the Oval Office. A blind veteran got down on his knees and started feeling that design with his hands. I closed my eyes and proceeded to do the same. It was perhaps the most spontaneous gesture of my life, although I must admit I was also grateful to hear the sound of cameras. I was pleased that the scene was being recorded for posterity. But it was Haldeman who ordered an embargo on that photograph—*ostensibly*, to protect the dignity of my image.

Even a year after he resigned, there he was, old faithful Bob Haldeman, backstage at the Grand Ole Opry in Nashville. He chided Johnny Cash for that time he refused to sing "Welfare Cadillac" at the White House, and Cash now replied, "Should I do it tonight and dedicate it to you now that *you're* on welfare?"

Haldeman did not appreciate the humor in that. He was too preoccupied with the dirty trick he had in mind for me. He handed me a yellow yo-yo and said, "This will really please the crowd. It's a Roy Acuff model." I put the yo-yo in my pocket. Haldeman did not mention that the string had been loosened at the bottom. So when I was on stage and I flung that yo-yo down, it just stayed there. Once again, Haldeman had transformed the President into an asshole.

It was Haldeman who urged me to install the White House taping system. It was Haldeman who hired Alexander Butterfield, who told the whole world about the tapes, and the FBI about E. Howard Hunt. Butterfield brought in Al Wong to set up the system and check it every day. And it was Wong who brought James McCord into the team.

One thing about Gerald Ford—he keeps his promises—not only to pardon me, but also his promise to fire Alexander Butterfield, even though Ford was actually grateful to him. As for me, I should have listened to L. Patrick Gray when he warned me, "People on your staff are trying to mortally wound you. . . ."

Pat has sworn to me that she never told *anyone* about our marital difficulties, and of course I believe her, so the leak to Woodward and Bernstein could only have come from Haldeman. On top of all the other betrayals, he must have been Deep Throat too.

* * *

The paradox of our nation is that we turn our vices into virtues. As the truth about political assassinations—from Malcolm X to Mrs. Dorothy Hunt—finally begins to emerge, we may truthfully say, "Only in America does there exist the freedom to reveal how insidious we have been—and then carry on with an even more determined spirit."

I still believe the United States is the greatest country in the world. It is also the greatest show on earth.

I once had a vision of myself leaving Washington the way Jimmy Durante used to end his TV program, standing in a spotlight and bowing gracefully to the audience, then walking back a few steps to another spotlight, bowing again, and so on. Instead, I ended up sounding as helpless as Hal the Computer in the movie *2001*—unable to control my own memory banks.

My consolation for this personal tragedy is summed up in Jeane Dixon's prediction: "Historians yet unborn are going to take the facts, and Richard Nixon will go down as a great President. They're going to find that the price the world is paying for trying to discredit Nixon is going to be that we'll practically lose our freedom."

In the meantime, I am, at long last, completely at peace with myself. It has been worth all the struggle.

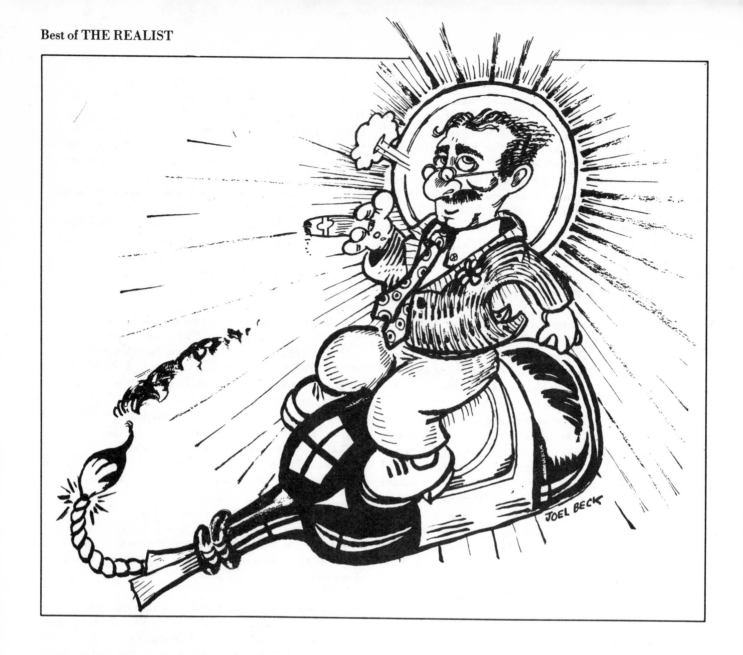

AND BE SURE TO TELL 'EM GROUCHO SENT YOU . . .

Groucho Marx said in a recent interview: "I think the only hope this country has is Nixon's assassination."

"Uh, sorry, Mr. Marx, you're under arrest for threatening the life of the President. I can't tell you how much I enjoyed *A Night At the Opera*. Here, now if you'll just slip into these plastic handcuffs . . . ."

I wrote to the local office of the United States Department of Justice, inquiring about the status of the case against Groucho, particularly in view of the indictment of Black Panther David Hilliard for using similar rhetoric.

Here's the reply I received:

Dear Mr. Krassner:

Responding to your inquiry, the United States Supreme Court has held that Title 18 U.S.C., Section 871 prohibits only "true" threats. It is one thing to say "I (or we) will kill Richard Nixon" when you are the leader of an organization which advocates killing people and overthrowing the government; it is quite another to utter the words which are attributed to Mr. Marx, an alleged comedian. It was the opinion of both myself and the United States Attorney in Los Angeles (where Marx's words were alleged to have been uttered) that the latter utterance did not constitute a "true" threat.

Very truly yours,
James L. Browning, Jr.
United States Attorney

Index